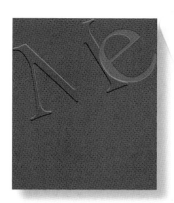

INSURANCE PLANNING

Your unique textbook registration number is below. Please register your new textbook at www.money-education.com for access to our Student Practice Portal, updated errata, Money Tips, and other valuable resources.

AZBA0712420

INSURANCE PLANNING

James F. Dalton
Michael A. Dalton
Thomas P. Langdon
Joseph M. Gillice

7th Edition

Money Education
3116 5th Street
Metairie, LA 70002
888-295-6023

Printed in the U.S.A.

ISBN: 978-1-946711-31-1

ABOUT THE AUTHORS

James F. Dalton, MBA, MS, CPA/PFS, CFA®, CFP®

- CEO, Money Education
- Adjunct professor at George Mason University (2014 - 2017)
- Adjunct professor at Georgetown University (2002 - 2014)
- Former Executive Vice President, Assessment Technologies Institute LLC
- Former Senior Vice President, Kaplan Professional
- Former President, Dalton Publications LLC
- Former Senior Manager of KPMG, LLP, concentrating in personal financial planning, investment planning, and litigation consulting
- MBA from Loyola University New Orleans
- Master of Accounting in Taxation from the University of New Orleans
- BS in accounting from Florida State University in Tallahassee, Florida
- Member of the CFP Board of Standards July 1996, Comprehensive CFP® Exam Pass Score Committee
- Member of the AICPA and the Louisiana Society of CPAs
- Member of the Financial Planning Association
- Member of the *Journal of Financial Planning* Editorial Review Board
- Author of *Money Education's Quick Sheets*
- Co-author of *Cases in Financial Planning: Analysis and Presentation* (1st - 4th Editions)
- Co-author of *Retirement Planning and Employee Benefits* (1st - 16th Editions)
- Co-Author of *Fundamentals of Financial Planning* (1st - 6th Editions)
- Contributing Author of *Insurance Planning* (1st - 7th Editions)
- Contributing Author of *Estate Planning* (1st - 12th Editions)
- Author of Kaplan Schweser's Personal Financial Planning Understanding Your Financial Calculator
- Author of Kaplan Schweser's Understanding Your Financial Calculator for the CFA® Exam
- Co-author of BISYS CFA® Study Notes Volumes I and II
- Co-author of Kaplan Schweser's Personal Financial Planning Cases and Applications
- Co-author of the Kaplan Schweser Review for the CFP® Certification Examination, Volumes I–VIII and Kaplan Schweser's Financial Planning Flashcards

Michael A. Dalton, Ph.D., JD, CPA, CLU, ChFC, CFP®

- Former Chair of the Board of Dalton Publications, L.L.C.
- Professor Emeritus, Accounting and Taxation, Loyola University in New Orleans, Louisiana
- Adjunct professor at George Mason University (2014 - 2017)
- Adjunct professor at Georgetown University (2002 - 2014)
- Former Senior Vice President, Education at BISYS Group
- Ph.D. in Accounting from Georgia State University
- J.D. from Louisiana State University in Baton Rouge, Louisiana
- MBA and BBA in Management and Accounting from Georgia State University
- Former board member of the CFP Board's Board of Examiners, Board of Standards, and Board of Governors
- Former member (and chair) of the CFP Board's Board of Examiners
- Member of the Financial Planning Association
- Member of the *Journal of Financial Planning* Editorial Advisory Board
- Member of the *Journal of Financial Planning* Editorial Review Board
- Member of the LSU Law School Board of Trustees (2000 - 2006)
- Author of *Dalton Review for the CFP® Certification Examination: Volume I – Outlines and Study Guides, Volume II – Problems and Solutions, Volume III - Case Exam Book, Mock Exams A-1 and A-2* (1st - 8th Editions)
- Author of *Retirement Planning and Employee Benefits* (1st - 16th Editions)
- Author of *Estate Planning* (1st - 12th Editions)
- Author of *Fundamentals of Financial Planning* (1st - 6th Editions)
- Author of *Insurance Planning* (1st - 7th Editions)
- Co-author of *Income Tax Planning* (1st - 13th Editions)
- Co-author of *Cases in Financial Planning: Analysis and Presentation* (1st - 4th Editions)
- Co-author of *Dalton CFA® Study Notes Volumes I and II* (1st - 2nd Editions)
- Co-author of *Dalton's Personal Financial Planning Series – Personal Financial Planning Theory and Practice* (1st - 3rd Editions)
- Co-author of *Dalton's Personal Financial Planning Series – Personal Financial Planning Cases and Applications* (1st - 4th Editions)
- Co-author of *Cost Accounting: Traditions and Innovations* published by West Publishing Company
- Co-author of the *ABCs of Managing Your Money* published by National Endowment for Financial Education (NEFE)

Thomas P. Langdon, JD, LL.M.
- Professor of Business Law, Gabelli School of Business, Roger Williams University, Bristol, RI
- Principal, Langdon & Langdon Financial Services, LLC (Connecticut-based tax planning & preparation firm)
- Former Professor of Taxation at The American College, Bryn Mawr, PA.
- Former Adjunct Professor of Insurance and Economics at The University of Connecticut Center for Professional Development
- Former Member (and Chair) of the CFP Board's Board of Examiners
- Master of Laws (LL.M.) in Taxation from Villanova University School of Law
- Juris Doctor, from Western New England College School of Law
- Master of Science in Financial Services from The American College
- Master of Business Administration from The University of Connecticut
- Bachelor of Science in Finance from The University of Connecticut, Storrs, CT.
- Chartered Financial Analyst (CFA), Certified Financial Planner (CFP), Chartered Life Underwriter (CLU), Chartered Financial Consultant (ChFC), Accredited Estate Planner (AEP), Chartered Advisor in Philanthropy (CAP), Certified Employee Benefits Specialist (CEBS), Chartered Advisor in Senior Living (CASL), Registered Employee Benefits Consultant (REBC), Registered Health Underwriter (RHU), Associate in Life & Health Claims (ALHC), and Fellow of the Life Management Institute (FLMI)
- Associate Editor of the *Journal of Financial Services Professionals*
- Co-author of *Estate Planning* (1st - 12th Editions)
- Co-author of *Income Tax Planning* (1st - 13th Editions)
- Contributing author of *Insurance Planning* (1st - 7th Editions)
- Faculty member for National Tax Institute

Joseph M. Gillice, MBA, CPA, CFP®
- President, Dalton Education, L.L.C.
- Former Director of University Programs for BISYS Education Services
- Former adjunct instructor in financial planning at Georgetown University in Washington, D.C.
- Former adjunct instructor in financial planning at Duke University in Durham, NC
- Instructor in live online financial planning programs for Rice University, New York University, and Northwestern University
- Author of *Financial Calculator Essentials*
- Co-author of *Fundamentals of Financial Planning* (1st - 6th Editions)
- Co-author of *Insurance Planning* (1st - 7th Editions)
- Co-author of *The Dalton Review® Pre-Study Materials in Fundamentals of Financial Planning and Insurance*
- Co-author of *The Dalton Review® Pre-Study Materials in Investment Planning*
- Developed the Online Executive Certificate in Financial Planning program for New York University and Northwestern University
- MBA from Georgia State University
- BS in finance from Florida State University

ABOUT THE CONTRIBUTING AUTHORS

Sherri Donaldson, CFP®, ChFC®, MSFS, CASL®, CAP®, EA

- Editing Princess for Money Education
- Former Author/Editor/Lead instructor, Keir Educational Resources
- Former Assistant Vice President, Senior Training Specialist, M&T Securities
- Former Associate Financial Consultant, M&T Securities
- Former Financial Sales Specialist, Nationwide Financial
- Former Financial Services Representative, Nationwide Retirement Solutions
- MSFS from The American College Bryn Mawr, PA
- BS in business, concentration in financial services, Pennsylvania State University
- Member of the Financial Planning Association
- Contributing Author of *Cases in Financial Planning: Analysis and Presentation* (4th Edition)
- Contributing Author of *Retirement Planning and Employee Benefits* (16th Edition)
- Contributing Author of *Fundamentals of Financial Planning* (6th Edition)
- Contributing Author of *Insurance Planning* (6th - 7th Editions)
- Contributing Author of *Estate Planning* (11th - 12th Editions)
- Contributing author of *Investment Planning* (2nd Edition)
- Co-Author/Editor of Keir *General Financial Planning Principles* textbook
- Co-Author/Editor of Keir *Risk Management and Insurance Planning* textbook
- Co-Author/Editor of Keir *Introduction to Financial Planning* textbook
- Co-Author/Editor of Keir *Retirement Savings and Income Planning* textbook
- Co-Author/Editor of Keir *Tax Planning* textbook
- Co-Author/Editor of Keir *Estate Planning* textbook
- Co-Author/Editor Keir *Investments Planning* textbook
- Editor Keir *Financial Plan Development* and *Practical Applications for Your Financial Calculator* textbook
- Co-Author/Editor Keir CFP® exam review books (*Core Knowledge Book 1* and *2*, *Essential Keys* book, *Case Studies* book), practice exams, flashcards, MP3 scripts, Key Concept Infograhics, and Quick Concept videos

Randal R. Cangelosi, JD, MBA

- Practicing litigator throughout Louisiana, in business/commercial law and litigation, products liability litigation, wills and trust litigation, environmental law and litigation, medical malpractice defense, and insurance law and litigation
- Has successfully defended numerous corporations, businesses, and doctors in jury and judge trials
- Juris Doctorate from Loyola University New Orleans
- Masters of Business Administration from Loyola University New Orleans
- BS in Finance from Louisiana State University
- Member of the American & Federal Bar Associations
- Member of the Bar of the State of Louisiana
- Member of the New Orleans and Baton Rouge Bar Associations
- Board Member of La Lupus Foundation
- Board Member of Baton Rouge Chamber of Commerce
- Former Board Member of the Baton Rouge Area Chapter of the American Red Cross
- Admitted to practice before US District Courts, Western, Eastern & Middle Districts of Louisiana
- Admitted to practice before the Federal 5th Circuit Court of Appeals
- Admitted to practice in USDC, Southern District of Iowa (Pro Hac Vice)
- Admitted to practice in Circuit Court of Wayne County, Mississippi (Pro Hac Vice)
- Admitted to practice in Circuit Court of Barbour County, Alabama (Pro Hac Vice)
- Admitted to practice in Court of Common Pleas, Darlington County, South Carolina (Pro Hac Vice)
- Admitted to practice in Los Angeles County Superior Court, California (Pro Hac Vice)
- Admitted to practice in Superior Court of New Jersey: Morris County (Pro Hac Vice)
- Admitted to practice in 17th Judicial Court, Broward County, Florida (Pro Hac Vice)
- Former Chairman of New Orleans Bar Association, Community Service Committee
- Former Chairman of New Orleans Bar Association, Food and Clothing Drives
- Co-author of *Personal Financial Planning: Theory and Practice* (1st - 3rd Editions)
- Co-author of *Professional Ethics for Financial Planners*

Acknowledgments & Special Thanks

We are most appreciative for the tremendous support and encouragement we have received throughout this project. We are extremely grateful to the instructors and program directors of CFP Board-Registered programs who provided valuable comments on all the previous editions of this textbook. We are fortunate to have dedicated, careful readers at several institutions who were willing to share their needs, expectations, and time with us.

We also owe a special thanks to all of our reviewers for their constructive feedback. Their thorough editing, detailed calculation reviews, helpful suggestions for additional content, and other valuable comments, improved this text. To each of these individuals we extend our deepest gratitude and appreciation. We extend a special thanks to the following professionals for their thorough reviews.

Dr. James Coleman has over 15 years teaching experience, including undergraduate, graduate, and Executive MBA programs at Troy University, Mercer University, and Dalton State College. In addition, as Vice President of Market Results, a financial planning training and consulting firm, he has helped hundreds of candidates pass the Certified Financial Planner™ exam over the last decade. Prior to his academic career, Jim spent over a decade in public accounting and corporate management, concluding with the position of Managing Director of Public Relations at Federal Express, where he was responsible for the company's global public and investor relations activities. His degrees include a MS and Ph.D. from University of Alabama as well as BBA in accountancy from University of Mississippi.

Donna D. Dalton made a significant contribution to this textbook by her thoughtful and meticulous editing throughout the book. She performed numerous reviews, and provided invaluable feedback throughout the entire project. We are extremely grateful for her contributions. This book would not have been possible without her extraordinary dedication, skill, and knowledge.

Dr. David W. Durr has over 25 years teaching experience primarily in the areas of investments, financial planning, portfolio management, corporate finance and risk management. Durr holds the Arthur J. Bauernfeind Endowed Chair in Investment Management at Murray State University. Dr. Durr earned a Ph.D. in finance from the University of North Texas, a Master of Business Administration degree from Stephen F. Austin State University and a Bachelor of Business Administration from the University of Texas at Austin. Dr. Durr holds the Certified Financial Planner (CFP®) designation and the Chartered Financial Analyst (CFA) designation. Each year he teaches financial planning classes and review courses throughout the United States.

Barbara Gavitt is currently the Vice President of Product Development for A.D. Banker & Company ITP. Barb has worked in the insurance and financial services industry and as educator and trainer since 1991. She has developed curriculum and facilitated training for insurance and securities licensing programs, continuing education, insurance designation programs, and professional development. Barb completed the Certificate in Distance Education program from Indiana University in 2011 and holds a BS in Education from Eastern Michigan University. She is also a Certified Distance Education Instructor, CDEI™, through the International Distance Education Certification Center (IDECC®).

Andrew J. Head, MA, CFP® brings 14 years of financial services experience to his position as the Director of the Western Kentucky University CFP® Board Registered Financial Planning Programs as well as the WKU Center for Financial Success. He joined the faculty at WKU in 2010 and teaches courses on Estate Planning, Tax Planning, Risk Management & Insurance Planning among others. He is the faculty advisor to the WKU Financial Planning Association (FPA) Student Chapter as well as serving on the Board of Directors for FPA of Kentuckiana. Outside of his duties with WKU, Andrew operates a multi-state fee-based RIA.

Gary J. Knoepfler, Jr., CPCU, FIC has been involved in the insurance industry in Louisiana since 1977. His experience includes Marketing, Underwriting and Management with Southern Insurance Service and several divisions of the American International Group (AIG). From 1990 until February 2011 he was the Branch Supervisor of Reimbursement Consultants, Inc, a company that handles a specialized area of workers' compensation claims, and he is now an independent consultant and a Field Agent with the Knights of Columbus. Gary attended LA Tech University and earned his Chartered Property Casualty Underwriter (CPCU) professional designation in 1993.

Robin D. Meyer is a valuable member of our Money Education team. She worked diligently with the authors and reviewers to manage the project, performed numerous reviews, and provided invaluable feedback throughout the entire project. This book would not have been possible without her extraordinary dedication, skill, and knowledge. Robin is the joy in our office as she always works tirelessly with a great work ethic and an enormous sense of humor. We are always grateful for her contributions to our products as well as our office happiness.

Katheleen F. Oakley is the Academic Program Director for classroom and web-based CFP Certification Education programs in the Susanne M. Glasscock, School of Continuing Studies at Rice University. She is co-author of Money Education's Cases in Financial Planning, Analysis and Presentation, 1st edition textbook and instructor manual. Kathy is also former vice president and chief financial planning officer with Kanaly Trust Company (Houston, Texas), the former director of financial planning for the Houston office of Lincoln Financial Advisors, and a former board member of the Pearland Economic Development Corporation. She is a member of the Financial Planning Association. Kathy received her BS in Finance and an MBA from the University of New Orleans.

Dr. Moshe Shmuklarsky has a keen personal interest in the conceptual underpinning and practical knowledge related to business and personal finance as reflected by his Master of Business Administration from the John Hopkins School of Professional Studies and a Certificate in Personal Financial Planning from the Georgetown University. Dr. Shmuklarsky has more than 25 years experience in research and development of drugs and vaccines. Through the application of the Balanced Score Card, Dr. Shmuklarsky has transformed the Department of Clinical Trials at the Walter Reed Army Institute of Research in Washington DC to a center of excellence in clinical research.

Ken Stephenson has over 30 years of healthcare experience with organizations on all sides of the healthcare spectrum. He received his Bachelor of Science in Business from the University of Houston, and his Master's in Business Administration from the University of St. Thomas in Houston. He holds a Fellow in Health Insurance Advanced Studies from the American Health Insurance Plans organization.

Kristi Tafalla is an attorney and personal financial planner specializing in income tax and estate planning. She teaches estate planning, income tax planning and comprehensive case courses through various CFP® Board-Registered Programs as well as comprehensive reviews for the CFP® certification. She is a contributor to Money Education's *Estate Planning for Financial Planners* and *Retirement Planning and Employee Benefits for Financial Planners*.

PREFACE

Insurance Planning is written for undergraduate and graduate level students interested in acquiring an understanding of financial planning from a professional financial planning viewpoint. The text is intended to be used in an overall curriculum in financial planning in an Insurance course or in a course that combines Fundamentals of Financial Planning and Insurance.

This text was designed to meet the educational requirements for a Insurance Course in a CFP® Board-Registered Program. Therefore, one of our goals is to assure CFP® Board-Registered Program Directors, instructors, students, and financial planners that we have addressed every relevant topic covered by the CFP® Board Exam Topic List and the most recent model curriculum syllabus for this course. The book will be updated, as needed, to keep current with any changes in the law, exam topic list, or model curriculum.

Special Features

A variety of tools and presentation methods are used throughout this text to assist the reader in the learning process. Some of the features in this text that are designed to enhance your understanding and learning process include:

- **Learning Objectives** – At the beginning of each chapter is a list of learning objectives to help you focus your studying of the material. These learning objectives will provide a preview of the important topics covered in the chapter.

- **Key Concepts** – At the beginning of each subsection are key concepts, or study objectives, each stated as a question. To be successful in this course, you should be able to answer these questions. So as you read, guide your learning by looking for the answers. When you find the answers, highlight or underline them. It is important that you actually highlight/underline and not just make a mental note, as the action of stopping and writing reinforces your learning. Watch for this symbol:

⠿ *Key Concepts*

- **Quick Quizzes** – Following each subsection you will find a Quick Quiz, which checks and reinforces what you read. Circle the answer to each question and then check your answers against the correct answers supplied at the bottom of the quiz. If you missed any questions, flip back to the relevant section and review the material. Watch for this symbol:

✏ *Quick Quiz 0.1*

- **Examples** – Examples are used frequently to illustrate the concepts being discussed and to help the reader understand and apply the concepts presented.

- **Exhibits** – The written text is enhanced and simplified by using exhibits where appropriate to promote learning and application. Exhibits are identified with the following symbol:

- **Cases** – Several chapters contain real world case summaries to help the reader appreciate the application of particular topics being discussed in the chapter.

- **Key Terms** – Key terms appear in **boldfaced type** throughout the text to assist in the identification of important concepts and terminology. A list of key terms with definitions appears at the end of each chapter.

- **End of Chapter Questions** – Each chapter contains a series of discussion questions and a sample of multiple-choice problems that highlight major topics covered in the chapter. The questions test retention and understanding of important chapter material and can be used for review and classroom discussion. Additional problems are available at money-education.com by accessing the Student Practice Portal.

- **Quick Quiz Explanations** – Each chapter concludes with the answers to the Quick Quizzes contained in that chapter, as well as explanation to the "false" statements in each Quick Quiz.

- **Glossary** – A compilation of the key terms identified throughout the text is located at the end of the book.

Student Practice Portal
available by registering your textbook at money-education.com

TABLE OF CONTENTS

Chapter 3 | Health Insurance

Chapter 6 | Disability Insurance

Chapter 7 | Long-Term Care Insurance

Chapter 8 | Annuities

Chapter 9 | Property and Liability Insurance

Chapter 10 | Credit Protection

Chapter 11 | Social Security

Appendix

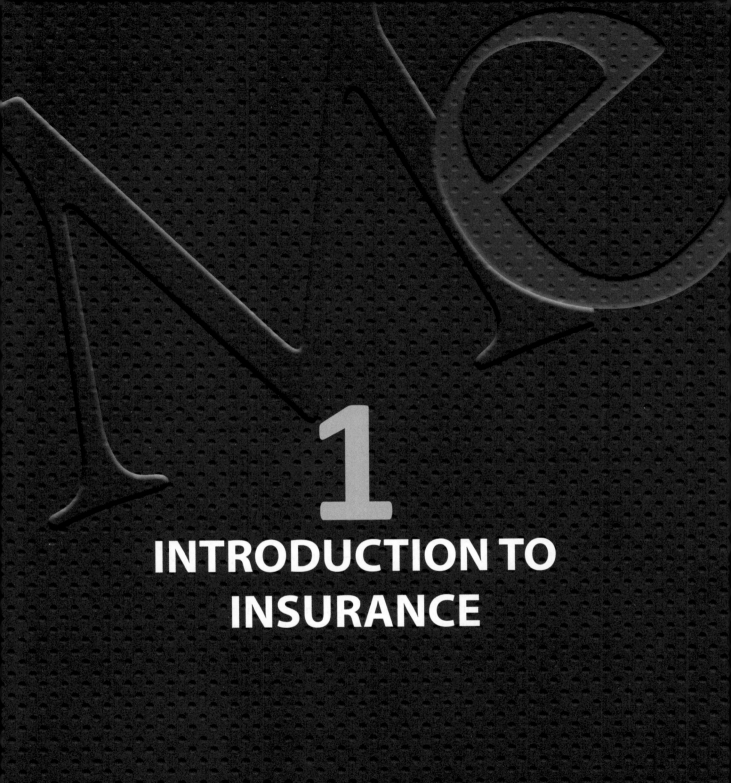

1

INTRODUCTION TO INSURANCE

INTRODUCTION

"Nothing in life and nothing that we do is risk-free."[1] Our everyday life is full of risks and uncertainties. Many of these risks can have overwhelming impacts on our lives. For example, in 2018, a total of 33,654 people died in U.S. motor vehicle crashes[2]. In addition,

- There were 1,318,500 fires reported in the United States in 2018. These fires caused 3,655 civilian deaths, 15,200 civilian injuries, and $25.6 billion in property damage (including $12.4 billion in losses from major California wildfires).[3]
- There were 3,400 triplet births in 2018.[4]
- There were 282,161 robberies in the United States in 2018.[5]
- There were 21 lightning fatalities in the United States in 2018.[6]
- There were a total of 20 authenticated, unprovoked shark attacks across the United States in 2018.[7]

Having your home burned to the ground from a fire is devastating, mentally as well as potentially financially. Having triplets? That may also be devastating, mentally, as well as financially. While extremely unlikely, being struck by lightning is certainly devastating in that it is likely to cause death, which in turn may be financially disastrous to family members.

Some risks are unavoidable. Some are easily avoidable. For example, it is easy to avoid shark attacks by staying out of the ocean. It is also easy to minimize shark attacks by staying in the very shallow waters or swimming in waters that have minimal or no reported shark activity. There are other methods that one might use to minimize shark attacks, such as shark spray.

Most shark attacks do not result in death. However, most are extremely painful, may result in the loss of limbs, and will generally require time in the hospital. Therefore, most shark attacks have a financial cost. This potential cost is not something that most people think about when they step off the sandy beach into the murky waters of the ocean.

For those who are willing to accept the risk of entering the ocean, where sharks reside, they could attempt to jointly lower the severity of any financial cost of a shark attack. They could do this by each voluntarily contributing a small sum of money into a shared pot. With as many people who enter the ocean, contributing even a single dollar could create a massive pot of money to help the victims of shark bites. There may be some ocean goers who choose to not join the group and thus, not be covered by the pool of funds. Some might even argue that surfers and those who frequent the ocean are at greater risk compared to the casual beach vacationer and should therefore contribute two dollars. This concept of pooling risk and pooling resources is the basis of insurance today. The concept that those who are at greater risk, such as the surfers, should be required to pay more in premiums to be covered is also a key part of insurance today.

---

1. Quote from Ken Salazar, former United States Secretary of the Interior
2. National Highway Traffic Safety Administration.
3. www.nfpa.org/research/reports-and-statistics/fires-in-the-us
4. www.cdc.gov/nchs/fastats/multiple.htm
5. https://ucr.fbi.gov/crime-in-the-u.s/2018/crime-in-the-u.s.-2018/topic-pages/robbery
6. https://www.weather.gov/safety/lightning-fatalities18
7. Shark Research Institute

Insurance, as described in our shark example, is equivalent to paying money into a pot that will pay in the event that someone is hurt, injured, or in need based on the risk that is being insured. However, there are other ways to minimize loss from risks.

Two ways to minimize losses are to avoid the risk and to minimize the risk. For example, it turns out that more than 80 percent of the victims of lightning are male and most strikes occur during the summer months. It also turns out that a significant percentage of lightning strikes occurred while victims were fishing. While the data is clear that males are more likely to be struck by lightning, it is unlikely that lightning picks out the males from the females. It is more likely that it is the activities that males are engaged in that result in being struck by lightning. Given this limited information, it should be easy to reduce the likelihood of being hit by lightning by avoiding fishing, for example. Just by avoiding fishing or avoiding the summer months while fishing will reduce the likelihood of being stuck by lightning.

How would someone avoid risk? In the case of sharks, staying out of the ocean will avoid the risk. In the case of lightning, staying indoors will likely accomplish this avoidance of risk. However, it is often not possible or practical to completely avoid risk. Ocean activities are enjoyable and most people are rightly unconcerned about shark attacks. Likewise, most people are conscious of the risks of lightning strikes and mitigate these risks in various ways, including not holding a 1 iron to the sky in a thunderstorm in the middle of a fairway.[8]

HISTORY OF INSURANCE

Insurance is very common today. We are required to have liability insurance to obtain a drivers license. We are asked if we want insurance when we purchase a vacation or buy electronics that cost more than about $100. However, insurance is not a new financial concept or product. Interestingly enough, the use of "insurance" dates back to thousands of years BC where traders used the principles of insurance to minimize the risk of loss. In addition, the Greeks and the Romans set up guilds or organizations designed to care for the families of members who died. If a member died, the guild provided for the needs of the families that were left behind.

In 1666, the Great Fire of London consumed over 13,000 homes. Out of this devastation was born the need for fire insurance. Many of the early companies that began after the fire had their own fire department to minimize the damage of fire for the members whose property was insured with them. Over time, the idea of a municipal fire department replaced the flawed concept of each company maintaining its own fire department.

The oldest documented insurance company to come out of this tragic event was started back in 1710 and was originally know as Sun Fire Office. Today, it is part of, through various acquisitions, the company known as RSA Insurance Group, which is based in London, England and generates approximately $7 billion in annual income.[9]

Although the Greeks and Romans set up guilds to care for surviving family members, the first life insurance policy taken out is credited to Richard Martin in 1583. The policy was a one-year term policy on the life of William Gybbon, who was a citizen of London. Initially, the insurer refused to pay when

---

8. Lee Trevino, a very successful professional golfer who competed with Jack Nicklaus, was actually hit by lightning in 1975. His famous quote is that "not even God can hit a 1 iron."
9. www.rsagroup.com

Gybbon died within that year. However, after the case was adjudicated, Martin was awarded the proceeds.[10] Today, life insurance is sold in many forms, from inexpensive term insurance to more expensive permanent policies that are designed to provide coverage for life.

Disability insurance has its beginnings in England with the Railway Passengers Insurance Company of London in 1849. This insurance was to provide protection for the dangerous journeys on the relatively new train system.[11] Disability insurance has expanded significantly from those early days. Today, disability policies insure against sickness and accidents and have numerous definitions of what it means to be disabled. This flexibility in terms of how a disability is defined allows for consumers to acquire the proper type of coverage based on their particular needs.

Germany became the first nation in the world to adopt an old-age social insurance program in 1889, designed by Germany's Chancellor, Otto von Bismarck. The idea was first put forward, at Bismarck's behest, in 1881 by Germany's Emperor, William the First, in a ground-breaking letter to the German Parliament. William wrote: "*. . . those who are disabled from work by age and invalidity have a well-grounded claim to care from the state.*"[12]

By the time America moved to social insurance in 1935 the German system was using age 65 as its retirement age. But this was not the major influence on the Committee on Economic Security (CES) when it proposed age 65 as the retirement age under Social Security. This decision was not based on any philosophical principle or European precedent. It was, in fact, primarily pragmatic, and stemmed from two sources. One was a general observation about prevailing retirement ages in the few private pension systems in existence at the time and, more importantly, the 30 state old-age pension systems then in operation. Roughly half of the state pension systems used age 65 as the retirement age and half used age 70. The new federal Railroad Retirement System passed by Congress in 1934, also used age 65 as its retirement age. Taking all this into account, the CES planners made a rough judgment that age 65 was probably more reasonable than age 70. This judgment was then confirmed by the actuarial studies.[13]

In 1935, there were 7.8 million Americans who were age 65 or older. The average life expectancy for a 65 year old in 1940 was 12.7 years for males and 14.7 years for females. As President Franklin D. Roosevelt said on August 14, 1935, at the signing of the law authorizing Social Security, the intent of the Social Security program is to "give some measure of protection to the average citizen and to his family against the loss of a job and against poverty-ridden old age." At its inception, Social Security was intended to provide retirement benefits only. In 2019, over 64 million Americans received more than $1 trillion in benefits from The Social Security Administration. The program provides many more benefits than were initially contemplated, including benefits to retired workers, spouses, family members, and disabled workers. In addition, Medicare, which was passed into law in 1954, provides health benefits for those who are age 65 or older.

---

10. *The Life Insurance Game*, by Ronald Kessler, Holt, Rinehart and Winston, New York, 1985.
11. A. P. Woodward. "The Disability Insurance Policy"
12. SSA.gov/history
13. SSA.gov/history

Exhibit 1.1 | Social Security Costs 1940 to 2023

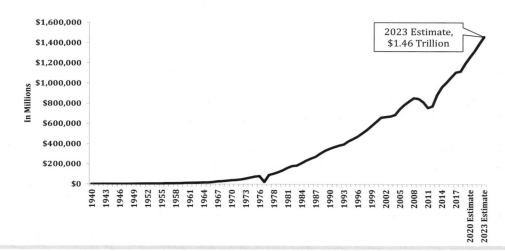

Source: White House Budget Historical Files

In addition to the more common forms of insurance, there are more esoteric types of insurance. Lloyds of London is the most famous insurance company in the world providing unusual types of insurance. Lloyds is an insurance market of members that was founded in a coffee shop in 1688. The company began in marine insurance, but is more famous for the unusual policies it writes. For example, it has written the following unusual insurance policies:

- Ben Turpin, silent film comedian of the 1920s, bought a $25,000 insurance policy with Lloyd's, payable if his trademark crossed eyes ever uncrossed.
- In the 1930s, "Jimmy 'the Schnozzle' Durante's infamously large nose was insured by Lloyd's for $140,000."
- Marlene Dietrich insured her voice for $1,000,000.
- Bruce Springsteen insured his voice for £3.5m.
- Bette Davis insured her tiny waist against weight gain for $28,000.
- Betty Grable insured her legs for $1,000,000.
- In 2006, David Beckham, famous soccer player, insured his legs for £100m.
- Dolly Parton has insured her breasts for £3.8m.
- Rolling Stones' guitarist Keith Richards' hands are insured for $1.6m.
- James Dean took out a policy on his life for $100,000 just a week before his tragic death at the age of 25.[14]

These are but a few of the famous and unusual policies underwritten by Lloyds, which is known as the world's leading market for specialized insurance. Lloyds is also well known for Kidnap and Ransom (K&R) insurance, which is becoming more important for celebrities and corporate executives around the world.

There are other types of unusual insurance. Athlete's have special needs in terms of insurance in the event of an injury disabling them from playing their sport. In terms of extremely unusual insurance, a London based company sold more than 30,000 alien abduction insurance policies throughout Europe, according to Geico's website.

---

14. www.lloyds.com/lloyds/about-us/history/innovation-and-unusual-risks/going-out-on-a-limb

INSURANCE INDUSTRY

Today, the insurance industry is a significant part of the United States economy with U.S. insurance net premiums written totaling over $1.22 trillion in 2018.[15] The insurance industry employed over 2.8 million people in 2019, and accounted for over two percent of the U.S. economy.[16]

Insurers in the United States rank among the largest purchasers of corporate, sovereign, state, and local bonds. Insurer investment portfolios also include short-term commercial paper, asset-backed securities, and other financial instruments. Some U.S. insurers are significant participants in other institutional markets, such as the derivatives and securities lending markets.

Insurers have also been diversifying by expanding into new geographic markets and developing a greater array of insurance product offerings and services. Some insurers and non-insurance affiliates have become more involved with the broader U.S. financial markets, not only as customers or counterparties, but also by engaging in activities such as banking and asset management services. Evidence of this interconnectedness of insurers with the broader financial system was apparent in the 2008 financial crisis. Although firms such as American International Group (AIG) represent the most prominent examples, other insurers were also affected by the 2008 financial crisis.

In Title V of the Dodd-Frank Wall Street Reform and Consumer Protection Act (the Dodd-Frank Act), Congress established the Federal Insurance Office (FIO) within the U.S. Department of the Treasury. In addition to advising the Secretary of the Treasury (Secretary) on major domestic and prudential international insurance policy issues and serving as a non-voting member on the Financial Stability Oversight Council (Council), FIO is authorized, pursuant to the Dodd-Frank Act, to:
- monitor all aspects of the insurance industry, including identifying issues or gaps in the regulation of insurers that could contribute to a systemic crisis in the insurance industry or the U.S. financial system;
- monitor the extent to which traditionally under-served communities and consumers, minorities, and low- and moderate-income persons have access to affordable insurance products;
- recommend to the Council that it designate an insurer as an entity subject to regulation as a non-bank financial company supervised by the Board of Governors of the Federal Reserve System (Federal Reserve);
- coordinate federal efforts and develop federal policy on prudential aspects of international insurance matters, including representing the United States, as appropriate, in the International Association of Insurance Supervisors and assisting the Secretary in negotiating covered agreements; and
- consult with States regarding insurance matters of national importance and prudential insurance matters of international importance.

---

15. http://www.iii.org/fact-statistic/industry-overview
16. Bureau of Labor Statistics (BLS)

PERSPECTIVE OF THE TEXT

The perspective of this text is that of a professional advisor who is providing professional services to clients in the area of risk management and insurance. In order to provide the highest level of service to the client, the advisor must have a thorough knowledge of important areas of risk and the best methods for mitigating those risks.

The advisor must have a working knowledge of risks that can wreak financial havoc on a person's or family's financial situation. Some of these risks are:

- premature death
- disability
- health issues
- liability issues
- property damage
- long-term care needs
- running out of money during retirement

The advisor must also have a thorough understanding of products that can minimize the financial impact of such events. Many of the products are complex and have numerous tradeoffs that the consumer must navigate.

Advisors need a deep understanding of retirement, disability, and survivorship benefits provided by Social Security and the benefits provided by Medicare to properly advise clients of the government sponsored safety net programs and to determine any gaps that need to be filled to meet client goals or needs.

By performing a thorough analysis of the client's loss exposures (losses that might occur), the advisor and client are able to work together proactively to employ the best and most efficient methods for dealing with each of the risks to which the client is exposed.

Exhibit 1.2 | Overview of the Text

Chapter(s)	Topic
2	Characteristics of Insurance
3	Health Insurance
4	Life Insurance
5	Life Insurance: Advanced Concepts
6	Disability Insurance
7	Long-Term Care Insurance
8	Annuities
9	Property & Liability
10	Credit Protection
11	Social Security

2

THE RISK MANAGEMENT PROCESS AND CHARACTERISTICS OF INSURANCE

LEARNING OBJECTIVES

1. Identify and explain the four categories of risk.
2. Describe and explain the personal risk management process and its seven steps.*
3. Identify and measure liability, automobile, homeowners, flood, earthquake, health, disability, long-term care, and life risks.*
4. Describe how insurers use risk pooling to pay for losses incurred by policyholders.*
5. Determine and select the best risk management alternatives using the risk management decision chart for individuals.
6. Provide examples of the four primary risk management techniques available to individuals.*
7. Explain the causes and contributors to losses including perils and hazards.
8. Identify the requisites for an insurable risk.
9. Describe insurance as a legal contract including the elements of a valid contract and the unique characteristics of an insurance contract.
10. Describe law of agency.
11. Differentiate the types of insurance companies.
12. Define and communicate key insurance policy terms, coverage, conditions, & exclusions.*
13. Describe the underwriting process and adverse selection.
14. Calculate co-insurance costs for property.
15. Identify the various valuation methods used in insurance.
16. Explain the factors that affect policyholder premiums and recommend appropriate methods for reducing household insurance costs.*
17. Describe how the insurance industry is regulated and rated.

* CFP Board Resource Document - Student-Centered Learning Objectives based upon CFP Board Principal Topics.

INTRODUCTION

As discussed in Chapter 1, insurance is a product used by individuals and companies to transfer risks and the financial uncertainty regarding those risks to third party insurers. These individuals and companies pay a premium to a third party insurance company, which determines the premiums based upon the expected claims to be paid out during a given time period. The theory behind insurance is that individuals and companies are pooling their premium dollars, so that anyone in the pool of similar risks that suffers a financial loss, will be able to recoup most (if not all) of those financial losses. The third party insurer is providing a convenient way to pool and manage those risks that it insures.

Insurance coverage is usually a critical component of a personal comprehensive financial plan. As a financial advisor, it is important to have an in-depth understanding of various types of risk exposures, appropriate types of insurance, and dollar amounts of appropriate coverage for an individual or family. Most individuals require some or all of the following:

- Life insurance to protect against financial losses due to premature death
- Health insurance to protect against the financial impact of injury or sickness for all family members
- Disability insurance to protect against the loss of income from the inability to work due to sickness or accident
- Property insurance to protect a home, personal property, the personal auto, or other assets
- Long-term care insurance to provide benefits for custodial care and/or skilled nursing care
- Personal liability insurance to protect personal assets and future earnings from potential liability judgments

One of the financial advisor's most important responsibilities is to assist individuals and families in avoiding catastrophic financial losses. This chapter explores types of insurable risks, elements of an insurance contract, legal characteristics of an insurance contract, the risk management process, and risk management techniques.

CATEGORIES OF RISK

Insurance is simply a legal contract between the insured and the insurance company (insurer), by which the insured transfers risks to the insurer and the insured pays a premium to the insurer. In return for the premiums, the insured receives a promise from the insurer to pay in the event the insured experiences a covered financial loss. There are certain types of risks that can be transferred to an insurance company, while other risks are not transferable because they are not insurable. These uninsurable risks are discussed later in this chapter. **Risk** is defined as the chance of loss, uncertainty associated with loss, or the possibility of a loss. Risk can be divided into four categories:

- Pure and Speculative Risk
- Subjective and Objective Risk
- Fundamental and Particular Risk
- Non-financial and Financial Risk

> ## Key Concepts
>
> 1. Distinguish between pure risk and speculative risk.
>
> 2. Identify the differences between subjective and objective risks.
>
> 3. Determine why the law of large numbers is useful for insurance companies.

Pure and Speculative Risk

Pure risk is the chance of a loss or no loss occurring. With pure risks, there is no chance of experiencing a gain. An example of a pure risk is, either your car is in an accident and damaged or it is not. Pure risks are insurable, since an insurance company is only going to pay when the insured actually suffers a financial loss. Pure risks include many of the same risks all individuals are exposed to and the types of risk a planner must evaluate and plan for each client. Examples of pure risks include:

- Premature death of a primary wage earner
- A prolonged illness or injury of a client or family member
- The inability of the client to work because of sickness or accident
- Wind damage to the personal residence
- The inability of the client to take care of himself in old age
- A legal judgment against the client

Speculative risk is the chance of loss, no loss, or a profit. Speculative risk is the risk that an investor takes when buying a stock or an entrepreneur takes when starting a business. The investor or entrepreneur makes an investment and takes the risk in the hopes of experiencing a profit. Insurance is not available for speculative risks because most speculative risks are willingly entered into for the purpose of making a profit.

Subjective and Objective Risk

Subjective risk is the risk that an individual perceives based on their prior experiences and the severity of those experiences. Individuals perceive risks differently and their behavior in addressing those risks depends upon that perception. If an individual perceives the subjective risk to be high, then the individual will take appropriate steps to reduce the subjective risk.

Example 2.1

Every Friday night, Kendrick and Ivan go to their local bar to celebrate the start of a new weekend. They typically have multiple shots of whiskey and wash them down with a few mojitos. One Friday night, while driving home, Kendrick is pulled over and arrested for DUI. Kendrick serves six months in jail, pays a $10,000 fine, and serves 200 hours of community service. Ivan on the other hand, manages to drive home each Friday night without being stopped. The next time Kendrick and Ivan go out, Kendrick has one drink and calls a cab to drive him home. Ivan on the other hand, has multiple drinks, gets in his car and drives home. Kendrick currently has higher subjective risk than Ivan, because Kendrick perceives severe negative consequences of another DUI. Objective risk in this case is measured by blood alcohol level.

For an insurer, **objective risk** is the difference between the expected and actual losses. As the number of loss exposures (or the pool of insureds) increases, objective risk is reduced because the actual results are more likely to approximate expected claims. Objective risk varies indirectly with the number of loss exposures in an insured pool. The better an insurer is able to manage its objective risk, the more efficiently they can price premiums.

Example 2.2

An insurance company has 50,000 auto policies and expects to pay claims on 10% or 5,000 policies during the year. The actual claims for the year are 4,900 which is 100 fewer claims than the insurance company expected. The variation between expected claims of 5,000 and actual claims of 4,900 is objective risk. Objective risk is generally measurable while subjective risk is a feeling.

Fundamental and Particular Risk

Fundamental risk is a risk that can impact a large number of individuals at one time, such as war or an earthquake. Fundamental risks are difficult for insurers to insure, because they can lead to severe financial consequences for the insurance company. Some fundamental risks, such as war or a nuclear hazard, are uninsurable. Other fundamental risks, such as an earthquake or flood, are insurable but require a separate earthquake or flood insurance policy. Some fundamental risks, such as flood insurance or unemployment insurance, require government support or social insurance programs.

A **particular risk** is a risk that can impact a particular individual, such as death or the inability to work because of a sickness or accident. An important difference between fundamental risk and particular risk is that fundamental risk will impact a large group of individuals simultaneously, whereas a particular risk only impacts one individual.

Non-financial and Financial Risk

Non-financial risk is a risk that would result in a loss, other than a monetary loss. An example of non-financial risk is the emotional distress a family experiences when a loved one dies. **Financial risk** is a loss of financial value, such as the premature death of a family's primary wage earner. Life insurance can protect against this financial risk, help the family achieve financial goals and provide a lump-sum amount to pay expenses for the family during the grieving process.

Exhibit 2.1 | Understanding Risk

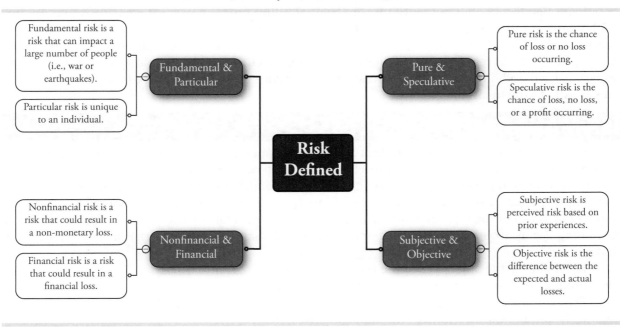

Probability of Loss

The probability of loss is the chance that a loss will occur. For example, suppose historical data establishes that one in 10 males (10%) age 50 are going to become disabled in a year. It is possible with a sample size of 10 that all 10 could become disabled or that none of the sample become disabled. As the pool of insureds increases to 100,000, it is more likely that the actual number of disability claims for the pool will be 10 percent as expected. The larger the sample size, the more likely the actual losses will approach the expected losses.

Law of Large Numbers

The **law of large numbers** is a principle that states that actual outcomes will approach the mean probability as the sample size increases. So, if a coin is flipped 10 times, we would expect five heads and five tails. However, with only ten flips, it is more likely that the actual results will be different than a 50/50 distribution between heads and tails. Here is a computer simulation of a coin being flipped 10 times. This exercise was conducted five times, with the following results for each.

Round	Heads vs. Tails	Result
Round 1	2 vs. 8	20/80
Round 2	3 vs. 7	30/70
Round 3	6 vs. 4	60/40
Round 4	4 vs. 6	40/60
Round 5	7 vs. 3	70/30
Total	22 vs. 28	44/56

With a small sample size, the average result was 44 percent heads and 56 percent tails. When the computer simulation determines the outcome of 100 coin flips, the percentage of heads versus tails is 48.5 percent heads and 51.5 percent tails; however at 1,000 flips the percentage is 49.4 percent heads and 50.6 percent tails. As sample size increases, the actual results of the coin flips approach the expected probability of 50/50. The law of large numbers is useful for insurance companies because the larger the insured pool, the more likely actual losses will approach the expected losses, thereby reducing forecasting error and objective risk. This results in insurance premiums that are more efficient and thus are less costly to the insured.

RISK MANAGEMENT PROCESS

The financial planning process requires that a planner obtain information to assess the client's personal and financial circumstances, analyze the client's current course of action and potential alternative courses of action, and develop financial planning recommendations designed to meet the client's goals. To accomplish these tasks, the advisor must incorporate the risk management process. The risk management process includes the financial planner reviewing all of the client's risk exposures and determining the appropriate risk management technique for each risk. The risk management process includes:

- Determining the objectives of the risk management program
- Identifying the risks to which the individual is exposed
- Evaluating the identified risks for the probability and severity of the loss
- Determining the alternatives for managing the risks
- Selecting the most appropriate alternative for each risk
- Implementing the risk management plan selected
- Periodically evaluating and reviewing the risk management program

Determining the Objectives of the Risk Management Program

The first step in the risk management process is to determine the objectives of the risk management program. Risk management objectives are typically to protect assets, earning capacity, human life value, and health. Objectives may also include less tangible aspirations such as providing peace of mind or protecting family relationships. For example, a parent who plans to leave the family business to a child who works in the business might choose to purchase life insurance of equal value for the benefit of the child who does not work in the business in order to reduce the risk of sibling jealousy or rivalry because one child inherited more than another child.

The objective for each area of risk can range from obtaining only the amount of protection required by law (e.g., auto insurance) to obtaining the most cost-effective protection against risk to providing the most comprehensive protection with little regard to cost. A client may also state a broad objective such as to insure only those risks that have the potential for causing catastrophic financial loss and to do so at the minimum premium.

Identifying the Risks to Which the Individual is Exposed

The next step is to identify all possible pure risk exposures of the client. *Identifying the potential risk* is primarily a function of the client's lifecycle position. The risk exposures for an individual may be subdivided into the following categories.

1. Personal risks that may cause the loss of income (untimely death, disability, health issues), or cause an increase in the cost of living (disability, health issues).
2. Property risks that may cause the loss of property (automobile, home, or other asset).
3. Liability risks that may cause financial loss (injury to another or to property for which the client is determined to be financially responsible).

≔ *Key Concepts*

1. Explain the risk management process.

2. Describe the four responses to pure risks.

3. Identify the most appropriate risks to insure based on loss severity and loss frequency.

The client's lifecycle position will help to determine if the client needs to protect against premature death, disability, and long-term care. The charts in the following examples identify the likely potential risks for a specific client based on the client's lifecycle position.

Example 2.3

Frank (age 33) and Shyla (age 31) are married with one child, Frankie (age 10). Frank and Shyla both work, each earning $60,000 per year. They have a 30 year mortgage, with 25 years remaining, and two car loans. They want to retire at age 62 and they plan to pay for Frankie's college education.

Potential Risks	Relevant	Reason
Life (Premature Death)	✓	They will need a lump-sum amount to retire their debt, and fund their retirement and education goals.
Health	✓	They need health insurance to cover major medical expenses.
Disability	✓	During their working years, disability coverage provides protection if one of them is unable to work because of sickness or accident.
Property	✓	The residence and personal autos should be insured because any loss could have catastrophic financial consequences.
Long-Term Care		They are too young to need long-term care which is more relevant in their 50's.
Personal Liability	✓	The risk of a lawsuit due to their negligence should be insured.

Example 2.4

Chandler (age 66) and Monica (age 65) are married with four adult children and ten grandchildren. Chandler and Monica are both retired, on Social Security and Medicare, and have significant retirement savings. They own their primary residence and their two autos are debt free. They do not believe they will be subject to estate taxes. Their risks are identified below:

Potential Risks	Relevant	Reason
Life (Premature Death)		They have already reached retirement, have zero debt, and do not need insurance to pay estate taxes.
Health	✓	Health insurance is important, although they qualify for Medicare at age 65. They may consider supplemental insurance to pay for gaps in Medicare (discussed later in the Social Security chapter).
Disability		They are already collecting retirement benefits, so they are not concerned about not being able to work for income.
Property	✓	The residence and personal autos should be insured because any loss could have catastrophic financial consequences.
Long-Term Care	✓	The risk of needing long-term care based on their age is relevant.
Personal Liability	✓	The risk of a lawsuit due to their negligence should be insured.

Identification of loss exposures for individuals and families can also be approached through the use of checklists, survey forms, questionnaires, or financial statement analysis. These types of systematic approaches help to ensure that the advisor and client avoid overlooking potential risk exposures.

Identification of loss exposures through financial statement analysis involves a review of the Statement of Financial Position to identify property loss exposures and a review of the Income Statement to identify income loss exposures. Each line item on the statement is examined to determine potential loss exposures for that item.

Example 2.5

Alphie Gainer is reviewing the Statement of Financial Position for her client Bibi Montana, as provided below, to assist with development of a plan to manage the risks to which Bibi is exposed.

Assets			Liabilities and Net Worth		
CURRENT ASSETS			**CURRENT LIABILITIES**		
Cash (on hand)	$10,000		Chase Credit Card Balance	$3,000	
Checking Account	$45,000		HSBC Credit Card Balance	$5,300	
Total Current Assets		$55,000	**Total Current Liabilities**		$8,300
Investment Assets			**Long-Term Liabilities**		
401(k) Plan Account Balance	$440,000		Boat Loan	$18,000	
Roth IRA	$210,000		SUV Loan	$20,000	
Total Investment Assets		$650,000	Student Loan	$28,000	
			Mortgage on Residence	$198,000	
			Total Long-Term Liabilities		$264,000
Personal Use Assets					
Residence	$350,000				
Boat	$47,000				
SUV	$28,000				
Jewelry	$25,000		**Total Liabilities**		$272,300
Household Items	$175,000		**Total Net Worth**		$1,057,700
Total Personal Use Assets		$625,000			
Total Assets		$1,330,000	**Total Liabilities & Net Worth**		$1,330,000

Alphie has identified risk exposures as follows:

Loss Exposures Related to the Statement of Financial Position		
Account	**Perils Exposed To**	**Consequences**
Cash (on hand)	Fire Burglary	Loss of cash Loss of cash
Retirement Assets	Superannuation (outliving assets in retirement) Diminishing health	Insufficient income to support needs Need/cost of long-term care
Primary Residence	Fire Vandalism Water damage Trees in close proximity Injury of others on premises	Loss of use/cost of repair Reduction in value/cost of repair Cost to repair or replace Cost to repair dwelling due to damage from falling trees Medical costs to be paid
Boat	Damage to boat	Loss of use/cost of repair
SUV	Damage to vehicle Damage to property of others Injury of others or self	Loss of use/cost of repair Cost to repair or replace Medical costs to be paid
Jewelry	Fire Burglary Misplacement	Loss of value/cost to replace Loss of value/cost to replace Loss of value/cost to replace

Alphie will employ a similar technique in reviewing Bibi's Income Statement so as to ensure that potential loss exposures related to income are also revealed. By employing this systematic approach in combination with life cycle analysis, Alphie is confident that she has not overlooked risks to which Bibi's is exposed.

Evaluating the Identified Risks for the Probability and the Severity of the Loss

Once the potential risks are identified, the planner must analyze each of the risks based on expected loss frequency and loss severity. When evaluating risks based on their expected loss frequency, the objective is to determine how often the event is likely to occur. Loss severity measures the dollar magnitude or the absolute dollar amount of the expected financial loss were it to occur. Based on the relationship between expected loss frequency and loss severity, an appropriate risk management response to the risk can be identified and implemented. Only those risks that have severe financial consequences but occur infrequently are appropriate to transfer or insure. Examples include the inability to work because of sickness or accident, premature death, an auto accident, or a house fire.

Determining and Selecting the Best Risk Management Alternative

Selecting the appropriate risk management technique is the most critical component of the risk management process. A risk that is not properly managed may have severe financial consequences for the client. Determining the appropriate response to a pure risk requires an understanding of the techniques for risk management, which include:
- Risk Reduction
- Risk Transfer
- Risk Avoidance
- Risk Retention

Risk reduction and avoidance are primarily used to control or reduce the frequency or severity losses, while risk retention and transfer are used to finance losses that actually occur.

A planner may use a matrix to analyze each risk, such as:

Severity / Frequency	Low Frequency of Occurrence	High Frequency of Occurrence
High Severity (catastrophic financial loss) (e.g., long-term disability)	Transfer and/or Share Risk Using Insurance	Avoid Risk
Low Severity (non-catastrophic financial loss) (e.g., car gets dented in parking lot)	Retain Risk	Retain/Reduce Risk

Risk Reduction

Risk reduction is the process of reducing the likelihood of a pure risk that is high in frequency and low in severity. Examples of risks that are high in frequency and low in severity are: car door dings, the common cold, and damage to inexpensive personal property. Risks that are high in frequency and low in severity are risks that should be reduced by taking steps to reduce the likelihood of a loss occurring.

Risk	Risk Reduction Implementation
Car Door Dings	Do not park a car next to other cars.
The Common Cold	Exercise, take vitamins, eat healthy foods, and wash hands frequently.
Damage to Household Property	Do not let children play with a ball in the house.

Example 2.6

Ashton and Demi are married with two children, ages eight and four. They have a two-car garage where Demi parks her SUV next to Ashton's car. Every time Demi parks her SUV next to Ashton's car in the garage, the four year old opens the door of the SUV and a new ding is put in the side of Ashton's car. After six months, there are multiple door dings in the side of Ashton's car. The frequency of the door dings is high, but the severity of having the door dings fixed is relatively low. The cost of repair is only a couple hundred dollars.

The appropriate steps for Ashton and Demi to reduce their risk would be to help the four year old open the door of the SUV or for Ashton to park his car in the driveway.

Risk reduction can also be used in conjunction with risk transfer (to an insurance company) for low frequency high severity perils to reduce the likelihood of a loss occurring or the severity of a loss as a result of certain perils, which helps to reduce insurance premiums. For example, a discount may be provided on a homeowners policy if burglar alarms or a sprinkler system are installed.

Risk Transfer

Risk transfer involves transferring a low frequency and high severity risk to a third party, such as an insurance company. Examples of risks that are low in frequency but high in severity include disability (or the inability to work), premature death, or damage to a personal residence. These risks do not occur very often, but when they do, there are severe financial consequences that should be transferred and insured. Non-insurance transfers of risk are also available for certain risk exposures and can be accomplished through means such as warranties or hold harmless agreements.

Example 2.7

Erica (age 33) and Daniel (age 35) are married with two children, ages two and four. Erica works as a vice-president of marketing earning $125,000 per year and Daniel works in the home, taking care of the children. Erica and Daniel own a house with an outstanding mortgage of $400,000. They have saved $75,000 for retirement and anticipate needing $1.25 million. They have not started saving for their children's college education but they anticipate needing $80,000. Erica and Daniel are concerned about Erica becoming disabled or dying prematurely. If this were to occur, the family would not have the financial resources to payoff the mortgage or fund their retirement and education goals. Disability and premature death are risks that are low in frequency but high in financial severity. Both disability and premature death are risks that should be transferred using insurance.

Risk Retention or Accepting the Risk

Risk retention is accepting some or all of the potential loss exposure for risks that are low in frequency and low in severity. Examples of risks that are low in frequency and severity include minor property damage to a personal residence or personal auto. Deductibles and copayments are forms of risk retention where the insured is sharing in the first dollar of a financial loss. Risk retention is an appropriate risk management strategy for risks that are low in frequency and low in severity. Failure to select an alternative risk management strategy necessarily results in retention of the risk which may or may not be the best course of action.

Example 2.8

Latoya just purchased a 1977 VW Bug for her 16-year old daughter, Ashley, for $500. Latoya decided not to purchase collision insurance on the car, since the severity of a loss would be $500. Latoya is retaining the risk of the car being totaled and suffering a financial loss of 100% or $500. However, Latoya does need liability insurance in the event Ashley was in an accident and sued. A judgment against Ashley (and Latoya) could potentially have severe financial consequences and the liability portion of the risk should be transferred/insured.

Risk Avoidance

Risk avoidance is a risk management technique used for any risks that are high in frequency and high in severity. Activities that will very frequently result in severe financial consequences should be avoided.

Example 2.9

Levon smokes about three packs of cigarettes per day. As a matter of fact, just before he falls asleep at night, he smokes one last cigarette in bed.

Example 2.10

Brandon likes to drink heavily while tailgating before a football game. During the football game, Brandon drinks heavily and, after the football game, has a few more drinks before driving home.

Both examples, smoking in bed and drunk driving, are risks that will frequently lead to a loss (house fire or DUI accident) and result in high severity or a large financial loss. High frequency and high severity risks should be avoided. Avoidance can be applied to many pure risks, such as:

- The risk of being injured on a construction site – avoid the construction site.
- The risk of dying in a private plane crash – avoid flying in private planes.
- The risk of getting a DUI – avoid drunk driving.
- The risk of getting into an accident while talking or texting on a cell phone – avoid cell phone use while driving.

The techniques for managing risk can be applied independently or can be combined in various ways. For example, a homeowners insurance policy is often purchased as a means of dealing with the risk of a fire destroying the home. That homeowner policy will contain a deductible, which is a partial retention of loss (and helps to reduce the premium for the insurance policy by eliminating the administrative burden of small claims). The homeowner may also have a sprinkler system or fire extinguishers in the house to help reduce the size of the loss should a fire occur. The combination of risk management techniques helps to create a more efficient plan for dealing with risk.

✓ *Quick Quiz 2.2*

1. Selecting the appropriate risk management technique is the most critical component of the risk management process.
   a. True
   b. False

2. Risk reduction is the process of avoiding pure risk that is high in frequency and low in severity.
   a. True
   b. False

3. Risk transfer involves transferring a high frequency and high severity risk to a third party, such as an insurance company.
   a. True
   b. False

True, False, False.

Example 2.11

Using the information from **Example 2.5** for Bibi Montana, Alphie reviews Bibi's existing risk management plan and insurance policies and makes the following recommendations:

Risk Management Audit Recommendations For Bibi Montana June 15, 20XX		
Risk Problem Area	**Recommendation**	**Action Plan**
Excess cash on hand (homeowner insurance limits coverage of cash to $200)	Limit cash kept in home to $200 (or secure in fireproof safe bolted to floor)	Bibi will move all cash except $200 to checking account
Insufficient liquid assets to cover the cost of long-term care in retirement	Purchase long-term care insurance	Planner will set up joint meeting with LTC insurance specialist
Primary residence is underinsured for dwelling replacement	Increase coverage in homeowner policy to cover full replacement cost of dwelling	Bibi will contact her property-casualty agent
Inconsistent deductibles in home and auto coverage (homeowner policy with $250 deductible and auto policy with $1,000 deductible)	Increase deductible on homeowner policy to $1,000	Bibi will contact her property-casualty agent
Lack of umbrella liability coverage (current liability coverage in home, auto, and boat policies of $100,000 is insufficient for an individual with over $1 million of net worth)	Purchase $2 million umbrella liability insurance policy and ensure that the underlying coverages in home, auto, and boat policies meet the requirements of the umbrella policy	Bibi will contact her property-casualty agent
Swimming pool is not enclosed inside a fence (liability)	Install a fence to surround swimming pool	Bibi will contact company to install fence

Implementing the Risk Management Plan Selected

The planner should work closely with the client to insure implementation of appropriate risk management techniques. Simply identifying and selecting the risk management technique are insufficient without implementation. The risk management plan should reflect the chosen response to a risk scenario. If risk reduction is the appropriate response to a given risk, the proper risk reduction program must be designed and implemented. If a decision is made to retain a risk, the individual must determine whether an emergency fund will be used (e.g., pet needs medical care). If the response to a given risk is to transfer the risk through insurance, an assessment and selection of an insurer usually follows. Implementation may require collaboration with other professionals such as insurance agents, brokers, or specialists.

Periodically Evaluating and Reviewing the Risk Management Program

The purpose for periodic evaluation and review is twofold. First, the risk management process does not take place independently from external influences. Circumstances change over time, and risk exposures can change as well. The risk management response that was suitable last year may not be the most appropriate this year, and adjustments may need to be made.

Example 2.12

The first time Kathy met with her financial planner was three years ago. At that time, Kathy was single, age 30, earning $80,000 per year and renting a home. Today, Kathy is married, age 33, and has two young children, John age 1.5 years old and Bob three months old. Kathy's salary is now $125,000 per year and her husband works from home and takes care of the children. Three years ago, her financial planner would have recommended disability insurance, renter's insurance, and possibly a small life insurance policy. Now that Kathy is married, with children and a home, the planner would continue to recommend disability insurance, but also homeowners insurance and significant life insurance. Without periodic monitoring of a client's risks, it is possible to have new risks that are not covered or inappropriately managed. Kathy needed a small amount of life insurance while single; but after getting married, having children, and purchasing a home, she needs significantly more life insurance.

Second, errors in judgment regarding the selected alternatives may occur, and periodic reviews allow the planner and client to discover such errors and revise the risk management plan as appropriate.

CAUSES OF FINANCIAL LOSS

Perils

Perils are the immediate cause and reason for a loss occurring. Perils can be the result of an accident or sickness. Common perils include:
- Accidental death
- Disability caused by sickness or accident
- Property losses caused by fire, windstorm, tornado, earthquake, burglary, and, collision of an automobile

Perils can be specifically insured (named) in an insurance policy on a "named peril" basis where only the specific perils listed in the policy are covered. Alternatively, a policy can cover perils on an "open perils" basis, which covers all perils unless specifically identified and excluded.

Exhibit 2.2 | Typical Covered Perils for Auto and Home

Personal Auto Policy (PAP)	Homeowners Insurance Policy (HO)
Fire	Fire
Storm	Lightning
Theft	Windstorm
Collision	Hail
Hail	Riot
Flood	Falling Objects
Contact with a Bird or Animal	Weight of Ice, Snow, and Sleet
Falling Objects	Smoke
Earthquake	Explosion
Windstorm	Theft

The above list is not complete, but is an example of some of the perils covered by each policy.

Hazards

Hazards are specific conditions that increases the likelihood of a loss occurring. A hazard does not cause the actual loss, but simply increases the probability of a loss. There are three types of hazards:

- Moral
- Morale
- Physical

The underwriter of the insurer must be aware of and be able to identify and manage these hazards.

Key Concepts

1. Identify typical perils covered under a personal auto policy.

2. Identify typical perils covered under a homeowners insurance policy.

3. Differentiate between moral, morale, and physical hazards.

Moral Hazard

Moral hazard is the potential for loss caused by the moral character of the insured such as the filing of a false claim with the insurance company. Burning down your own house or claiming a theft occurred when it did not are types of moral hazard. Insurance companies cannot afford to insure false claims because insurance is only meant to provide coverage in the event of an actual financial loss, ones that are not intentionally caused or fraudulently claimed by the insured.

Example 2.13

Maurice, a famous college football player for State University, filed a false police report that he had $10,000 worth of clothing, cash, and jewelry stolen from a borrowed car. There actually was no theft. The football player was hoping to collect a $10,000 check from the insurance company for the alleged stolen items. However, he found himself in jail charged with filing a false police report.

The filing of a false insurance claim is an example of a moral hazard and cannot be insured. If false claims were paid by insurers, it would result in increased premiums and people that actually need insurance would be unable to afford the insurance products.

Morale Hazard

Morale hazard is defined as indifference to risk due to the fact that the insured has insurance. Consider the person that drives to a convenience store to purchase a gallon of milk. They pull into the parking spot, leaving the car running and doors unlocked while they enter the convenience store. This person is not concerned about their car being stolen perhaps because they have auto insurance.

Insurers want to incentivize an insured to prevent morale hazard. The way an insurer accomplishes this is through the use of deductibles. With a deductible, the insured pays the first dollars of loss until the deductible is satisfied. Thus, when an insured is considering leaving the keys in the ignition and the car running while they are in a convenience store, the insured may stop and think "do I want to risk paying a $500 or $1,000 deductible if my car is stolen?" Deductibles help to align the best interest of the insurer and the insured to reduce the risk of morale hazard.

> ## ☑ *Quick Quiz 2.3*
>
> 1. Perils can be specifically covered in an insurance policy on a "named peril" basis where only specific perils listed in the policy are covered.
>   a. True
>   b. False
>
> 2. Physical hazard is indifference to a loss created because the insured has insurance.
>   a. True
>   b. False
>
> ⟶ True, False.

Physical Hazard

Physical hazard is a physical condition that increases the likelihood of a loss occurring. Examples of physical hazards include wet floors, icy roads or roads with poor lighting. A physical hazard does not actually cause the accident or the loss, it is simply just a condition that increases the probability of a loss occurring.

Example 2.14

Peter is walking down the sidewalk to the local hardware store. While looking across the street he doesn't notice the banana peel on the sidewalk, steps on it, slips and falls breaking his arm. The banana peel was a physical hazard that increased the likelihood of someone falling.

REQUISITES FOR AN INSURABLE RISK

Not all risks are created equal, and not all risks are insurable. A risk that is ideally situated to be an insured risk meets the following requirements:

1. It has a large number of homogeneous exposures.
2. The insured losses must be accidental.
3. The insured losses must be measurable and determinable.
4. The loss must not be financially catastrophic to the insurer.
5. The loss probability must be determinable.
6. The premium for risk coverage must be reasonable and affordable.

Items 1 – 5 are required from the insurer's perspective for the insurer to be willing to provide insurance for a particular risk. Item 6 is a requirement of consumers and represents the likely willingness to purchase an insurance product to cover a pure risk.

Large Number of Homogeneous Exposures

There are two important requirements for a risk to be insurable. The first requirement is that there are a large number of exposures. The second requirement is that the large number of exposures is homogeneous. Both of these requirements are important for a risk to be insurable meaning an insurance company can accurately predict future losses and charge affordable premiums based on forecasted claims.

> ### ☰ *Key Concepts*
>
> 1. Identify the requisites for an insurable risk.
>
> 2. Identify why the law of large numbers is important to insurance companies.

Law of Large Numbers

The **law of large numbers** tells us that the more similar the events or exposures, the more likely the actual losses will equal the expected losses. This is important for an insurance company so that the actual claims they pay are very close to the probability of total losses. If the pool of insureds is small, the actual losses could vary significantly from the expected losses, which could lead to financial insolvency of the insurer.

Example 2.15

Assume the probability of males, ages 55-64, dying this year is one out of 1,000, and each insured owns a $1 million death benefit policy. For every pool of 1,000 males, the insurance company is going to charge premiums based upon paying one death benefit (or $1 million) claim this year. If the insurance company experienced two, three or four deaths this year from this pool, their actual death benefit claims would be $2, $3 or $4 million, which is significantly greater than the expected total losses of $1 million per 1,000 male pool. The premiums charged for a probability of one out of 1,000 may not offset two or more deaths if such variance continued for many years.

Example 2.16

Now, assume the probability of males dying this year, between the ages of 55 - 64 is 890 out of 100,000. Now the insurance company is able to base premiums on 890 claims out of 100,000 insureds. If 900 - 910 of the age 55 - 64 group insureds die this year, the deviation from the expected results is much smaller, since the population of insureds is 100,000 rather than 1,000.

Large Number of Homogeneous Exposure Units

An insurance company needs the pool of loss exposures to be homogeneous (alike). This allows the insurance company to more accurately predict the loss probability and charge an appropriate premium. For example, when determining the premium for an auto policy, the type of car driven is a risk factor. The insurance company pools all male drivers of sports cars with turbo V-8 engines into one group of homogeneous risks and charges a risk premium. Other drivers who drive a four-door, four-cylinder Honda Accord are classified into a different homogenous risk pool and charged a lower premium because the risk exposure is greater for a sports car than for a four-door sedan. Also, consider an Alaska King Crab fisherman working on the Bering Sea with 60-foot waves in the freezing cold versus a stand up comedian. The probability of the insurance company paying a disability or life insurance claim on an Alaska crab fisherman is much greater than paying a disability or life insurance claim on a stand-up comedian that gets hit by a tomato for a bad joke.

Insured Losses Must be Accidental

Actual losses must be accidental because premiums are based on the probability of a loss occurring based on historical information and claims. A tree falling on a house during a bad storm is an accidental loss and covered because the insurer can estimate the probability of losses based on historical information and claims of trees falling on a house. However, intentionally burning down a house that you own and insure to collect the insurance proceeds is an intentional act and is not a covered loss. If insurance companies covered intentional acts of insureds, premiums would increase and may become unaffordable for most individuals.

Example 2.17

Troy and Ben live in the same neighborhood. Unfortunately, a tornado hits their neighborhood and destroys Ben's house. The damage from the tornado is accidental and unexpected. It is the type of loss that can be insured.

Example 2.18

Next week, Troy's house burns down. After the fire department investigates, it turns out that the cause was arson by an unknown person. Even though arson is an intentional act, it was random from the perspective of Troy being insured. This type of loss is also insurable.

Loss Must be Measurable and Determinable

Since most losses covered by an insurance contract result in a financial payment to the insured, the actual timing of the loss and amount of the loss must be known. A typical insurance contract is going to offer the promise to pay in the event of a loss, but that promise to pay is only good for a period of time. Consider insurance on a primary residence. The premium is paid for the year, so the insurance company agrees to pay in the event of a loss, if the loss occurs during that one-year period. Once that time expires, the insured must pay a new premium to receive the promise from the insurer to pay for a loss over the next one year.

Losses must also be measurable in terms of the amount of loss. If the probability of a loss is too uncertain, the risk will be considered uninsurable. Back in the mid 1950s, it was determined that the loss caused by a nuclear power plant melt down was too uncertain and potentially so severe that the insurance industry excluded the cost of nuclear power plant failures from insurance policies.

When considering insurance on a primary residence, it is fairly easy to determine the amount to rebuild the house in the event it burns to the ground. However, it is more difficult to determine the amount of cash or jewelry kept in the house, in the event of theft and/or fire. For hard to value items and those that have moral hazard associated, the insurer may place specific limits on such items.

Typical limits placed on items in a homeowners policy include:
- Money / Cash = $200
- Jewelry, Furs, and Watches = $1,500
- Firearms = $2,500
- Silverware and Goldware = $2,500

If an insured owns items that exceed these limits, it will be necessary to provide the insurance company with documentation regarding the value and then increase the underlying limits of the policy. Riders and endorsements enable an insured to increase these underlying limits for an increased premium and are discussed later in this text.

Loss Must Not be Financially Catastrophic to the Insurer

Some loss exposures are so financially devastating because the loss would impact too big an area or segment of the population, that an insurance company cannot afford to pay all the claims if the event occurs. The amount that an insurance company receives for any loss is relatively small in comparison to the total possible. For example, a war or nuclear hazard could affect such a large area, such as multiple cities and states, and the financial loss would be so severe, that an insurance company could not afford to pay all of the claims. A loss exposure that would be financially catastrophic to the insurer is an uninsurable risk, which is why an insurer excludes perils such as flood, earthquake, nuclear hazard and acts of war.

Example 2.19

Hurricane Katrina hit Louisiana and Mississippi in September of 2005 causing over $81 billion in property damage. Much of the damage shown on the news was the result of massive flooding when the levees surrounding New Orleans and the local parishes were breached. Approximately ½ of all residents affected by the flooding did not have flood insurance. Flood is excluded from homeowners' insurance policies; it must be purchased from the National Flood Insurance Program administered by the Federal Emergency Management Agency.[1] One of the issues raised in the aftermath of Hurricane Katrina was whether the property damage and losses were the result of windstorm or flood. Homeowners who did not have flood insurance argued that the damage from a hurricane is due to windstorm, which is a covered peril under a homeowners policy. However, the insurance industry argued that the damage was caused by flooding when the levees were breached.

The terrorist acts on September 11, 2001 which, in addition to the loss of over 3,000 lives, caused almost $10 billion in losses for the insurance industry. The insurance companies did not call the events of 9/11 an "Act of War," which is an exclusion on property insurance policies. However, shortly after 9/11, insurance companies began to exclude "Acts of Terrorism" from insurance policies. As a result, The Terrorism Risk Insurance Act of 2002 was passed to provide a federal government "backstop" for losses arising out of acts of terrorism. Private insurers are now able to offer coverage for acts of terrorism, with the federal government paying 90 percent of losses above a threshold.[2] The Act has been extended through 2027 via various Terrorism Risk Insurance Program Reauthorization Acts.[3]

Premium Must be Reasonable

Premiums must be reasonable and affordable for the insured. Before an individual transfers a risk to an insurer, the individual will conduct a cost benefit analysis of the premium relative to the risk and severity being covered.

Example 2.20

Sydney, age 17, drives a 15-year-old Honda Accord with 175,000 miles on the car. The fair market value of the car is $800. To insure the car in the event of a collision, the premium is $900. The benefit Sydney would receive if she totals her car would be $800, less any deductible. Sydney would be better off self-insuring against the risk of property damage to her car.

---

1. FEMA http://www.fema.gov
2. http://www.thefreelibrary.com/Understanding+the+benefits+of+the+Terrorism+Risk+Insurance+Act.+...-a096554237
3. https://home.treasury.gov/policy-issues/financial-markets-financial-institutions-and-fiscal-service/federal-insurance-office/terrorism-risk-insurance-program

---

Example 2.21

DeAndre, age 33, drives a new Mercedes Benz, with a fair market value of $50,000. To insure the car for collision, the premium is $900 per year. The benefit DeAndre would receive if he totals his new Mercedes would be $50,000 less his deductible. DeAndre is better off transferring the risk of property damage to his $50,000 Mercedes for the $900 premium rather than self-insuring.

The insurance company must also conduct their own cost-benefit analysis. The costs of filing and settling small claims, such as minor fender benders, causes auto policy premiums to increase. As a result, insurers use deductibles that require the insured to cover the first dollar in losses. These deductibles are typically $250 to $500, but may be $1,000 to a few thousand dollars, and effectively dissuade small claims. Deductibles prevent the filing of small severity claims, which helps to keep the premiums of auto policies down. Deductibles also reduce morale hazard.

LAW OF INSURANCE CONTRACTS

A contract is a legal agreement that binds two parties to each other to perform certain obligations. The following elements must be present for a contract to be valid:

- Mutual Consent
- Offer and Acceptance
- Performance or Delivery
- Lawful Purpose
- Legal Competency of all Parties

> ### ≡ *Key Concepts*
>
> 1. Identify the elements of a valid contract.
> 2. Define conditional acceptance.
> 3. Identify the two categories of legal competence.
> 4. Define the parol evidence rule.

Mutual Consent

Mutual consent implies that both parties to the contract have a mutual understanding regarding the scope of the contract and they are in agreement as to the terms of the contract. Typically contracts may be terminated by mutual consent of both parties.

Offer and Acceptance

Offer and acceptance consists of one party making an offer to purchase a good or service and the acceptance is when consideration is received. Consideration can be in the form of a cash payment or providing a service.

Example 2.22

Mike is selling his Mercedes and is asking $50,000. Joe offers Mike $45,000 for the car. Mike agrees to accept $45,000 and Joe hands Mike a check for $45,000. The original offer was $50,000, Joe made a counter-offer of $45,000 and the acceptance was when Mike agreed to the price of $45,000.

Example 2.23

Joe went to his insurance agent to apply for auto insurance for his new Mercedes. Joe completes the auto insurance application, and attaches a check for the full amount of the premium, $1,000, to bind the policy. The agent then sends the application and the binder to the insurance company which then can accept the offer.

With insurance there is also a temporary binder or a "conditional acceptance." For property insurance, the agent can issue a binder providing immediate temporary coverage until a permanent policy is issued by the insurance company and premium paid by the insured. Alternatively, the insurance company may determine that their underwriting standards have not been met and they will not issue a permanent policy. Conditional acceptance is used to provide temporary coverage for life insurance between the time of application and the time the policy is issued, but the coverage is conditional on the applicant paying the first premium payment and meeting the underwriting standards for the policy.

Example 2.24

At the same time he applied for his auto insurance, Joe completed a life insurance application and paid the first premium payment of $1,000 based on standard underwriting criteria and rates. The insurance agent gave Joe a conditional receipt stating that Joe is covered immediately so long as the policy would have been issued upon final review by the underwriter. If Joe leaves the insurance agent's office and gets hit by a bus and dies, and the insurance company would typically have accepted his application, Joe would be covered and his beneficiary would receive the death benefit. As long as Joe met the typical underwriting standards of the insurance company, he will have coverage. Coverage would not exist if the premium was returned and Joe was notified that the policy was not accepted at the rating applied for.

Performance or Delivery

In order for a contract to be enforceable, the party to a contract must perform a duty under the contract. Using the previous example, if Joe is buying a car from Mike and gives Mike a check for $45,000, Joe has performed under the contract. He would expect Mike to hand him the keys and title to the car. If Joe asked Mike to deliver the car to his front door before Joe pays, then Mike cannot enforce payment from Joe until the car is delivered to Joe's front door.

Lawful Purpose

Another element of a valid contract is that the subject of the contract cannot be contrary to public policy or be in violation of any laws. If the subject matter of the contract is illegal, then the contract is not enforceable. If Joe enters into a contract to pay Mike $10,000, to steal Mike's neighbor's Mercedes, neither Joe nor Mike will be able to enforce the contract, as the contract is not valid. To steal the neighbor's Mercedes is a violation of the law.

Legal Competence of All Parties

When entering into a contract, both parties must be legally competent. Otherwise, the contract is unenforceable. Legal competence includes the following situations:

- **Minors** - In most states, a minor is under the age of 18. If a minor enters into a contract, the minor can void the contract at any time. If one party can void a contract at any time, there really is not an enforceable contract.
- **Lacking Sound Mind** - A person lacking a sound mind does not have the capacity to understand the purpose and terms of the contract. Therefore, the contract lacks a meeting of the minds or mutual consent. Examples of persons lacking sound mind include a person who is drunk, mentally handicapped, or under the influence of drugs.

Other important considerations of a contract include the **parol evidence rule**, which provides that "what is written prevails." Any oral agreements prior to writing the contract have been incorporated into the written contract. Oral agreements that are not reflected in the written contract are not valid.

LEGAL PRINCIPLES OF INSURANCE CONTRACTS

Principle of Indemnity

The **principle of indemnity** asserts that an insurer will only compensate the insured to the extent the insured has suffered an actual financial loss. In other words, the insured cannot make a profit from insurance. However, the principle of indemnity does not assert that an insured will recoup 100 percent of any loss, as most policies have deductibles and limits on the amount of losses covered. An exception to the principle of indemnity applies for life insurance. Life insurance policies are "valued policies" in which the insurer agrees to pay the face amount of the policy, regardless of the value of the life insured.

A **subrogation clause** in an insurance policy requires that the insured relinquish a claim against a negligent third party if the insurer has already indemnified the insured. A subrogation clause entitles the insurer to seek a claim against a negligent third party for any claims paid to the insured. The principle of indemnity and the subrogation clause are closely aligned to accomplish the goal of preventing an insured from profiting from insurance.

✸≣ Key Concepts

1. Distinguish between the principle of indemnity and subrogation.

2. Identify the difference in insurable interest as between property and liability insurance versus life insurance.

3. Identify the difference between a representation, warranty, and concealment.

Example 2.25

Alice's car was severely damaged as a result of an accident caused by Mel. Fortunately, Alice's insurance company settled her claim within two days and she was able to replace the car. Under the subrogation clause in Alice's auto insurance policy her insurance company can seek reimbursement from Mel's insurance company, or from Mel himself, if necessary.

Principle of Insurable Interest

The **principle of insurable interest** asserts that an insured must suffer a financial loss if a covered peril occurs, otherwise no insurance can be offered. The principle of insurable interest is closely aligned with the principle of indemnity, which both limit the insured from experiencing a gain using insurance.

Property and Liability Insurance

An insurable interest for property and liability insurance must exist both at the inception of the policy and at the time of loss. If no insurable interest exists at the inception of the policy, then there is an incentive on the insured's behalf to damage the property. If there is no insurable interest at the time of loss, then the insured who received a monetary settlement would experience a profit from the insurance claim, which would violate the principle of indemnity.

Example 2.26

Rodney purchases a property insurance policy on a wine warehouse, in the amount of one million dollars. Rodney does not have any financial interest in the wine warehouse. Mysteriously, the wine warehouse burns to the ground and Rodney collects the face value of the policy. This scenario would be a violation of the principles of insurable interest and indemnity as Rodney would have experienced a profit from this insurance policy when he had no insurable interest.

Example 2.27

For the past ten years, Teresa has owned a wine warehouse and has property insurance on the warehouse in the amount of one million dollars. Teresa decided to sell the wine warehouse, but keep the property insurance policy. Shortly after selling the warehouse, it mysteriously burned to the ground. If Teresa collected under the property policy, it would be a violation of the principles of insurable interest and of indemnity.

Life Insurance

An insurable interest for life insurance need only exist at the inception of the policy. A life insurance policy is not an indemnity policy. It instead pays the face value of the policy based on the "value" of the amount of insurance purchased. Some people refer to this as a "modified" indemnity policy or an "agreed to value" policy.

Example 2.28

When Daphne and Nial were married, Daphne purchased a life insurance policy on Nial and named herself as the beneficiary. After being married for two years, they divorced but Daphne continued to pay the premiums on the life insurance policy. Ten years after their divorce, Nial died. Daphne will be able to collect the death benefit from the life insurance policy because Daphne only needed to have an insurable interest at the inception of the life insurance policy.

To purchase life insurance, the owner of the policy must have an insurable interest in that person's life. An insurable interest exists for a person to purchase life insurance on their own life and name either themselves or someone else as the beneficiary. An insurable interest also typically exists for close family relationships and may also exist for business relationships.

Example 2.29

Norm and Clifford started a pilot training school together and they each own 50% of the business. Norm and Clifford decide to take out life insurance policies on each other's life, so that in the event one business partner dies, the proceeds from the life insurance policy can be used to buy the deceased partner's share of the business from the decedent's heirs. Since Norm and Clifford are business partners, they each have an insurable interest in the life of the other.

Principle of Utmost Good Faith

The principle of utmost good faith requires that the insurer and insured act in a manner that is forthcoming with all information about the risks being considered during the underwriting process. The insured and the insurer follow three legal doctrines during the application and throughout the life of the policy:

- Representation
- Warranty
- Concealment

Representation

A **representation** is a statement made by the applicant during the insurance application process. A representation can be an oral statement or information disclosed on an insurance application such as age, gender, occupation, marital status, and family medical history. A misrepresentation during the application process can lead to the insurer voiding the insurance contract. In order for the contract to be voidable, the misrepresentations must be material and the insurer must have relied on the misrepresentation to issue the policy. A misrepresentation is considered "material," if during the application process the insured knew the statement was false, and the insurer would not have issued the insurance contract but for the false misrepresentation. Misrepresentations about age and gender for a life insurance policy are not considered material. The insurance company will simply determine the benefit based upon the actual age or gender of the insured and the amount of premium actually paid.

☑ Quick Quiz 2.6

1. The subrogation clause asserts that an insurer will only compensate the insured to the extent the insured has suffered an actual financial loss.
   a. True
   b. False

2. An insurable interest for life insurance must exist both at the inception of the policy and at the time of loss.
   a. True
   b. False

3. A representation is a statement made by the applicant during the insurance application process.
   a. True
   b. False

False, False, True.

Example 2.30

Raquel, age 40, has always been told that she has looks ten years younger than her actual age. Raquel recently completed a life insurance application and stated her age as 30, rather than 40. Based on a female age 30, the premium for a one million dollar policy was $400. A few months later, Raquel was hit by a bus and died. Upon reviewing the death certificate, the insurer realized that Raquel was 40 and not 30. The insurer calculated a death benefit of $600,000 based on the amount of coverage a $400 premium would have purchased for a 40-year-old female.

Warranty

A **warranty** is a promise made by the insured that is part of the insurance contract. The warranty can be a promise to perform or take a certain action. Alternatively, a warranty can be a promise by the insured to not do something. A breach in warranty may allow the insurer to void the insurance contract and not pay any claims.

Example 2.31

Chuck and Cindy own a baseball hitting facility and are constructing a new addition to their building. In an effort to reduce their insurance premiums and as a requirement of the policy, they agree to install a fire sprinkler system throughout the building. They then warrant in the application that they have installed the sprinkler system. During construction, they decide to not have the sprinkler system installed, as it would cost more than they anticipated. If a fire causes a loss, the insurer will likely avoid paying the claim, as Chuck and Cindy breached the warranty.

Concealment

Concealment occurs when the insured is intentionally silent regarding a material fact during the application process. The insurer has the right to void an insurance contract based on material concealments by the insured. In order for the insurer to void a contract or avoid paying a claim because of concealment, the insurer must prove that the insured knew the concealed fact was material.

Example 2.32

Rey is completing a life insurance application and answers questions such as:
- What is your age, marital status, height, and weight?
- Are you a smoker?
- Do you pilot small planes?
- Do you scuba dive?
- Do you have any other dangerous hobbies?

Rey answers "no" to all of the questions on the insurance application. Rey does not disclose that he likes to "base jump," which is jumping off tall buildings and bridges with a parachute in his hand and releasing the parachute at the last possible moment. Rey's insurance company could void paying a claim if Rey dies as a result of a base jumping accident.

UNIQUE LEGAL CHARACTERISTICS OF INSURANCE CONTRACTS

Adhesion

Insurance contracts are contracts of **adhesion**, which is a "take it or leave it" contract. The insured has no opportunity to negotiate the terms of the contract. Before an insurance product can be sold in a state, the state insurance commissioner must approve the product. The product is then sold "as is" and the insured must accept the policy as written. Since the insured has no ability to negotiate the terms of the insurance policy, the courts will rule in favor of the insured if there are ambiguities found in the contract. The insurer had the opportunity to draft the contract clearly and therefore will be charged for any ambiguities.

Key Concepts

1. Identify the distinguishing characteristics of insurance contracts.
2. Determine if property and life insurance policies are assignable.

Aleatory

Insurance contracts are **aleatory** in nature, which means the dollar amounts exchanged between the insured and the insurer are unequal. The insured may pay a lifetime of premiums for a disability insurance policy and never collect a benefit under the policy. Alternatively, an insured may pay a small premium for a life insurance policy, and his heirs may collect a large face value after only one premium payment if the insured dies while covered by the policy.

Unilateral

Insurance contracts are **unilateral** in that there is only one promise made, and it is made by the insurer to pay the beneficiary in the event of a covered loss. The insured in not legally obligated to make premium payments. As long as the insured makes the required premium payments, the insurer is legally obligated to provide coverage under the terms of the policy.

Quick Quiz 2.7

1. Insurance contracts are aleatory in nature, which means the dollar amounts exchanged are even.
   a. True
   b. False

2. The insured is not legally obligated to make a premium payment.
   a. True
   b. False

3. Property insurance policies cannot be assigned to a third party without the consent of the insurer.
   a. True
   b. False

False, True, True.

Conditional

Insurance contracts are **conditional** in that the insured must abide by all the terms and conditions of the contract if the insured intends to collect under the policy. If the insured has violated any of the terms or conditions under the policy, the insurer may not pay a claim. One of the conditions of a policy is that the insured take steps to mitigate and reduce any additional damage to property after a covered loss. Another condition is that the insured timely pay the premiums.

Example 2.33

During a severe storm, a tree falls on the roof of Jill's home causing a large hole. Jill discovers the hole immediately but does nothing. The storm continues to rain on Jill's house for the next three days and the rain causes additional damage to the interior of Jill's house. Jill did not take any steps to cover the hole in her roof and the rain causes extensive damage to her walls and floors. The insurance company will pay for the damage to Jill's roof but will not pay for the interior rain damage because Jill did not take the appropriate precautions to prevent (mitigate) further damage after the tree fell on Jill's roof.

Personal

Property insurance polices are personal contracts between the insurer and the insured. Therefore, the policy cannot be assigned to a third party without the consent of the insurer. When applying for property insurance, the insurer evaluates the riskiness of the applicant based on their credit score, work history, and other personal factors. When the property is sold, the new buyer needs to apply for their own property insurance to give the insurance company an opportunity to evaluate the riskiness of the new owner.

Life insurance contracts, unlike property insurance contracts, can be assigned without the consent of the insurer because the contract continues to cover the insured regardless of who owns the policy. Assigning ownership rights to someone else even one who has no insurable interest under the life insurance contract does not change the underlying insurer's risk associated with the insurance contract.

LAW OF AGENCY

The law of agency describes the relationship and authority an agent possesses when acting on behalf of a principal. A principal, such as an insurance company, hires an agent (insurance agent) to act on the principal's behalf and enter into agreements on behalf of the principal. The authority that an agent possesses is the result of express, implied, and/or apparent authority. In the case of an insurance agent, the statements or actions of the agent that are in the course and scope of the agency agreement will bind the insurance company to the insured.

⋮≡ *Key Concepts*

1. Differentiate between express, implied, and apparent authority.

2. Identify how a waiver may impact the insurer's ability to deny a claim.

3. Identify how estoppel pertains to insurance contracts.

Express Authority

Express authority is given to an agent through a formal written document. In the case of an insurer and insurance agent, the express authority is an agency agreement. The agency agreement specifically outlines the duties, responsibilities, and scope of authority that the agent can act upon and thus bind the principal. The agency agreement stipulates the terms, conditions, and length of period the agent is allowed to sell insurance policies and bind the insurer to the insured.

Implied Authority

Implied authority is the authority an agent relies on to do their job when the expressed authority is insufficiently precise. It is also the authority that a third party relies upon when dealing with an agent, based upon the position held by the agent. When a customer walks into an insurance agent's office, the customer will see the company logo on the front door, signs on the wall of the agent's office with the company's logo, and business cards on the agent's desk. All of these signs would lead the customer to believe that the agent sitting behind the desk has the implied authority to bind the insurance company if the customer purchases an insurance policy.

Apparent Authority

Apparent authority is when the third party believes implied or express authority exists, but no authority actually exists. If an insurance company and agent had an agency agreement which expired, it is the responsibility of the insurance company to lock the door to the office, take down any signs, and remove the business cards and company letterhead. The insurance company must take the necessary steps to remove any indications of implied authority. If a customer reasonably relies on apparent authority and is issued an insurance policy by an agent who no longer has either express or implied authority, the insurance company is bound by the policy.

Example 2.34

Paulie walks into his insurance agent's office to purchase an auto policy for his new convertible sports car. Paulie notices the business cards on the desk with both the insurance company's logo and his agent's name. There is company letterhead on the agent's desk along with policy applications. Paulie completes the auto policy application and pays the first year premium. Upon leaving his agent's office, he gets into an accident and totals his new sports car. Little does Paulie realize that his agent's agency agreement expired last week, and the agent was not really licensed. However, Paulie will still have coverage from the insurer due to the principle of apparent authority.

Waiver

A **waiver** is relinquishing a known legal right. If an insurer waives a legal right, it may not deny paying a claim based on the insured violating or breaching that right.

Example 2.35

Esai is applying for a health insurance policy. Before the policy can be issued, Esai must complete an application and take a physical exam. Esai completes the application but never takes the physical exam. The insurer issues Esai the health insurance policy. The insurer cannot later deny paying claims on the policy because Esai did not take a physical exam because by issuing the policy, the insurer waived the physical exam requirement.

Estoppel

Through the legal doctrine of "**estoppel**," the principal will not be able to deny the insured an insurance contract. Estoppel is where a person is denied a right he might otherwise be entitled to under the law. Estoppel applies when one party relies on information from another party and that information causes harm to the party who relied on the information. The party who made the statements can be estopped from denying the statements.

Example 2.36

Walter and his wife walk into an insurance agent's office and take out a $10 million life insurance policy on Walter's life, with his wife as the beneficiary. Walter's wife asks the insurance agent if the policy will pay a death benefit if Walter commits suicide and the agent responds "yes." Two days later, Walter is found dead from an apparent suicide. Walter's wife then attempts to collect the $10 million death benefit under the policy. However, the policy has a "Suicide Clause" that stipulates that if the insured commits suicide within two years of the policy being issued, then the premiums will be returned and no death benefit will be paid. Although the insurer will attempt to produce the policy and suicide provision, the insurer may be estopped from denying the claim based on information the agent expressed to Walter's wife, presuming she can prove the agent's statements.

CHARACTERISTICS OF INSURANCE COMPANIES

Types of Insurance Companies

Stock Insurers

A stock insurer is an insurance company that issues stock, and is owned by shareholders with the intent of earning a profit. A stock insurer collects premiums, pays operating expenses, and may return dividends to shareholders based on the performance of the company. The Board of Directors for a stock insurer is responsible for making decisions to pay dividends to the shareholders. These dividends are taxable to the shareholders. Also, shareholders elect the Board of Directors.

Mutual Company Insurers

A mutual company is an insurance company that is owned by the policyholders, not shareholders. The policyholders elect the Board of Directors for a mutual company. Profits earned by a mutual company are returned to policyholders in the form of a dividend. The dividend is not treated as taxable income but it is a return of premiums paid.

Key Concepts

1. Identify the difference between stock insurers and mutual company insurers.

2. Identify the differences between agents and brokers.

3. Determine the underwriting process.

4. Understand the term adverse selection.

5. Explain why insurance companies are reinsured.

Agents and Brokers

Agents

Agents are legal representatives of an insurer and act on behalf of an insurer. Agents are only permitted to sell the policies written by their company. Agents have the authority to bind the insurer to an individual. There is typically a difference between the authority an agent has when selling a property and casualty policy versus a life insurance policy. An agent may immediately issue a temporary binder on an auto policy over the telephone. A temporary binder is temporary insurance coverage until the insurance company issues the permanent policy. However, an insurance agent may not immediately bind an insurer when selling a life insurance policy. The insurer must approve the life insurance application before coverage is issued.

Brokers

Brokers are legal representatives of the insured and act in the best interest of the insured. A broker may sell insurance polices from any one of a number of different insurance companies. Since the broker does not represent the insurer, they may not bind an insurer.

Insurance brokers typically help individuals obtain property and casualty, life, and health insurance. Some brokers assist in surplus lines market, which are markets where there is a need for a particular type of insurance but no insurance product exists in that state. A broker may use an insurer that is licensed in another state to provide the insurance product.

Reinsurance

Reinsurance is a means by which an insurance company transfers some or all of its risks to another insurance company. The company that transfers the risk is the ceding company, while the company accepting the risk transfer is the reinsurer. The primary reason an insurance company may want to transfer risk is to reduce the exposure in their portfolio of insured risks. A company may decide to transfer some of their risks to create additional portfolio capacity so as to underwrite new policies.

Example 2.37

Hurricane Katrina made landfall over Louisiana and Mississippi on August 29, 2005. Hurricane Katrina caused $81 billion in property damage, with approximately $40 billion in losses covered by reinsurance companies. Some of the largest reinsurance companies in the world shared in the losses as a result of hurricane Katrina.

Reinsurance Company	Dollar Amount of Loss from Katrina
Berkshire Hathaway	$3.0 billion
Munich Re	$1.5 billion
Swiss Re	$1.0 billion

Market Info Briefing October 21, 2005, Guy Carpenter

IMPORTANT PROVISIONS AND FEATURES OF INSURANCE CONTRACTS

Policy Provisions

Most insurance contracts are generally designed with similar provisions, including:

- Definitions of terms used in the contract
- Declarations
- Description of what is insured
- Perils covered
- Exclusions
- Conditions

> ### ≔ *Key Concepts*
>
> 1. Identify the typical sections of an insurance contract.
>
> 2. Identify examples included in each section of an insurance contract.

Definitions

The **definition section** of an insurance policy defines key words or phrases used throughout the insurance contract. The purpose of these definitions is to define the meaning of the words, phrases, or terms as used in the contract. A policy may include the following definitions, among others:

- Insured: Upon the insured's death a death benefit is payable to the beneficiary.
- You, Your: Refers to the owner of the policy.
- We, Us, Our: Refers to the insurance company (insurer).

Declarations

The **declarations section** describes exactly which property or person is being covered. For property insurance, the declarations page will describe the property, address, owner of the property, name of the insured, amount of coverage, deductible, and premium. For life insurance, the declarations page will contain the insured's name, face value of the policy, term or length of the policy, and the issue date.

- End of Initial Term Period: This identifies the last date the policy is effective.
- Amount of Insurance: This is the amount of the death benefit or policy limit that is payable to the beneficiary of the policy.
- Premiums: Depending on the type of the policy, this section may identify the amount of the current premium and perhaps any renewable premium.

Exhibit 2.3 | Homeowners Declarations Page

(1) Insurance Company

POLICY NUMBER: 123-45-678
POLICY EFFECTIVE DATE: JAN 1 2019

Summary

NAMED INSURED AND ADDRESS

(2) JANE DOE
1234 HAPPY LANE
CITY, TX 00000

YOUR AGENT IS

A. GENT
(123)-456-7890

POLICY NUMBER (3)

123-45-678

(4) POLICY PERIOD

EFFECTIVE JAN 1 2019 TO JUN 1 2019

(5) LOCATION OF PROPERTY

1234 HAPPY LANE
CITY, TX 00000

Coverage

(6) COVERAGE	(7) LIMITS	(8) DEDUCTIBLES (SECTION I)
SECTION I		We cover only that part of the loss over the deductible stated.
DWELLING	$200,000	WIND AND HAIL - $2,000 (1%)
OTHER STRUCTURES	$25,000	ALL OTHER PERILS - $2,000 (1%)
PERSONAL PROPERTY	$150,000	
LOSS OF USE	$50,000	
SECTION II		
PERSONAL LIABILITY (EACH OCCURRENCE)	$300,000	
MED PAY TO OTHERS	$5,000	

(9) TOTAL PREMIUM $1,205.95

Your Policy Documents

HOMEOWNERS POLICY

HO100-01

(10) ENDORSEMENTS

AB1234
CD5678
EF0000

1. Insurance Company
2. Policyholder Name
3. Policy Number
4. Policy Period - the period of time your policy provides coverage
5. Location of Property
6. Coverage - The damage on injuries an insurance company agrees to pay for under the policy
7. Coverage Limits - The maximum amount your insurance company will pay for each covered accident, for each type of coverage
8. Deductible - The amount you owe in a loss before the company pays its part
9. Premium - The amount you pay an insurance company for your policy
10. Endorsements - Policy changes that give you more or less coverage and may change your premium

https://www.opic.texas.gov/news/dec-page/

Description of What is Being Insured

The **description section** describes exactly what is being insured. For a life or health insurance policy, the name of the insured is included in this section. For a property and casualty policy, the address of the property is in the description.

- Insured: Name of the insured
- Effective Date: The start date of when the policy is effective
- Age and Sex of the Insured: Used to determine the insured class and premium due for life, health, and disability policies

Perils Covered

The perils covered section may cover perils on a named peril basis where specific perils are listed as covered in the policy. Alternatively, the policy may cover perils on an open peril basis, which covers all risks of loss that are not specifically identified and excluded in the exclusions section of the policy. For term life insurance, the peril covered is death of the insured within the term period.

Exclusions

The **exclusions section** of an insurance policy will exclude certain perils, losses, and property. Perils are excluded because they may be uninsurable, there is a moral hazard, or the coverage is potentially financially catastrophic to the insurer. Examples of excluded perils for a property insurance policy include:

- War or nuclear hazard
- Flood
- Power failure
- Intentional acts
- Neglect
- Movement of ground

Losses excluded from a policy may be due to the insured not taking steps to mitigate after a covered loss has occurred. Also, some property is not covered such as damaged or stolen business property in the home.

Example 2.38

Business interruption insurance is commonly used to replace a business's lost income or pay for extra expenses incurred when the business is forced to close or relocate temporarily due to a covered peril. For example, if Ourtown Animal Hospital's building is damaged in a fire and the business must remain closed for a short period of time and then spend a few months in a temporary location until repairs are completed, business interruption insurance would replace the lost income and cover the cost of the temporary location. Due to the COVID-19 pandemic of 2020, state governors required a large number of businesses to close temporarily in an effort to contain the spread of the disease. Unfortunately for many of those businesses who held business interruption insurance, the policies either contained an exclusion for business interruptions due to epidemics and pandemics, or the policy, as is common in this type of insurance, specified that recoverable losses are those due to "physical damage from a covered peril to an insured location." If there was no physical damage and no endorsement to the policy to cover infectious or communicable diseases, there was no valid claim under which businesses could recover lost income due to the forced closure.

Conditions

Conditions are provisions in an insurance policy that require an insured to perform certain duties. If the policy conditions are violated, the insurer may refuse to pay the full amount of the claim. Examples of conditions include:

- Notifying the insurer in the event of a loss
- Filing of a police report in the event of a theft
- Cooperating with the insurer after a loss
- Taking appropriate steps to reduce further damage after a loss

Miscellaneous Provisions

Miscellaneous provisions in an insurance policy cover topics not addressed within other areas of the policy. Examples of miscellaneous provisions include:

- **Errors in Age or Sex:** In the event of a misstatement of age or sex, the death benefit payable under a life insurance policy will be based upon the actual age or sex at death.
- **Suicide Exclusion:** A typical exclusion under a life insurance policy is if the insured commits suicide within the first two years of the policy. Premiums will be returned in the event of the insured committing suicide.
- **Payment of Benefits:** This section will outline where and how the death benefit will be payable to the beneficiary.
- **Grace Period:** The grace period identifies the amount of time after the due date of the premium that the policy will stay in force. If the premium is not paid within the grace period, the policy will lapse. The typical grace period is 31-60 days.

Riders and Endorsements

An **endorsement** is a modification or change to the existing property insurance policy. A **rider** is a modification or change to a life or health insurance policy. Riders and endorsements are a way for an insured to customize a policy, since insurance policies are contracts of adhesion and the insured has no opportunity to negotiate the terms of the contract. If there are conflicting terms between the policy and a rider or endorsement, then the rider or endorsement language prevails.

> ## ⋮≣ *Key Concepts*
>
> 1. Differentiate between a rider and an endorsement.
>
> 2. Identify the purpose of a deductible.
>
> 3. Identify the purpose of coinsurance.

A property insurance policy is typically endorsed when the insured owns property in excess of the coverage limits within the policy. If a policy only provides coverage of up to $1,500 in jewelry, an endorsement can be used to increase the jewelry limit to an amount appropriate for the value of the client's jewelry.

A rider can be added to a disability policy that waives the premium if the insured becomes disabled for a short period of time.

UNDERWRITING AND MANAGING ADVERSE SELECTION

Underwriting is the process of classifying applicants into risk pools, selecting insureds, and determining a premium. An underwriter is responsible for evaluating risks and determining whether the risk is insurable or non-insurable. The underwriter is also responsible for managing adverse selection. **Adverse selection** is the tendency of those that most need insurance to seek it while those with the least perceived risk avoid paying the premiums by not buying insurance. In an ideal world the insurer would only insure those persons least likely to have a claim. However, that would not lead the insurer to profitability as those who are least likely to have a claim are also most likely to self insure. An underwriter wants to maintain an appropriate mix of those that need insurance and are likely to file a claim versus those that are unlikely to file a claim. The underwriter follows underwriting principles that are established by the company. These principles outline acceptable risks, borderline risks, and risks that are unacceptable.

Information used in the underwriting process is typically obtained from the following sources:
- the application and any pertinent appended documents,
- affidavits submitted by the agent or broker,
- routine and detailed investigations when warranted,
- insurance bureaus and associations (for example, life insurance companies have access to the Medical Information Bureau (MIB), an association of approximately 430 insurance companies that accumulates and provides medical information relative to life insurance applicants),
- actual medical examinations for life insurance applicants and on-premises inspections for property insurance applicants, and
- outside agency reports such as driving records from the DMV or the insured's credit score.

An underwriter groups risks into similar classes and assigns a premium or class rate to all members of the class, such that the premium is expected to cover all claims, operating expenses, and produce a profit.

The underwriter attempts to manage adverse selections with the use of deductibles, copayments, and coinsurance.

Deductibles and Copayments

Deductibles are the first dollars in a loss, which the insured is responsible to pay. Deductibles may be a flat dollar amount such as $250, $500, or $1,000. A deductible may also be a percentage of the covered loss, which is typical for flood insurance or homeowners insurance in states like Florida. The purpose of such a deductible is to reduce the filing of small claims, reduce premiums, and eliminate moral and morale hazard. Without deductibles, the paperwork, time, and resources needed to process claims of $50 or $100 would make insurance premiums unaffordable. Deductibles also serve as motivation for an insured to take precautions to avoid losses or to prevent the filing of false claims since an insured with a deductible will not receive 100 percent of the value of loss. An example of a deductible is when a person must pay the first $1,000 of medical expenses each year, and then 20 percent of all expenses over that amount. The insurer pays 80 percent of covered medical expenses that exceed the $1,000 deductible.

Example 2.39

Blanche has a two-year-old car she purchased for $40,000 which is now worth $30,000. Her car recently caught on fire and was a complete loss. Her insurance company paid her $29,500, which is the actual value of her car, less her $500 deductible.

Copayments are paid in addition to deductibles or as a substitute for deductibles and are commonly used in health insurance policies. **Copayments** are loss-sharing arrangements whereby the insured pays a flat dollar amount or percentage of the loss in excess of the deductible. An example of a copayment is when a person is covered for health insurance by a HMO, PPO, or POS and pays $25 each time he or she goes to the doctor.

Example 2.40

Donna goes to her physical therapist twice weekly to help relieve the pain and stiffness in her shoulders. As part of her insurance policy, she pays $35 per visit. The remainder of the charges are covered by her health insurance policy.

Coinsurance

For property insurance, **coinsurance** defines the percentage of financial responsibility the insured and the insurer must uphold in order to achieve equity in rating. Coinsurance in property insurance encourages insureds to cover their property to at least a stated percentage of the property's value, or else suffer a financial penalty. Because the vast majority of property losses are partial, without coinsurance clauses many insureds would attempt to save money on insurance by purchasing less insurance than the full value of their property. While underinsuring is not illegal, it presents a problem for the underwriter and actuary who base expected loss estimates, and thus premiums, on the full value of the properties in the insured pool.

The amount paid for a property insurance claim with a policy with a coinsurance clause is determined by comparing several values. If the insured purchases coverage that meets or exceeds the coinsurance requirement (usually 80 percent of replacement value for homeowners insurance), then payment on a claim for a loss will be the lesser of the face value of the policy, replacement cost, or actual expenditures. However, if the insured purchases coverage that is less than the coinsurance requirement (say, 60 percent of the replacement value), then payment on a claim for such a loss will be the greater of the actual cash value (ACV) or the result of the following formula subject to the limit of the face value of the policy.

The coinsurance formula is:

$$\frac{\text{Amount of Insurance Carried}}{\text{Amount of Insurance Required}} \times \text{Covered Loss - Deductible} = \text{Amount Insurer Pays}$$

The purpose of coinsurance in a property insurance policy is to encourage the insured to maintain a stated percentage of minimum coverage. Otherwise the insured will become a coinsurer and proportionately share in any loss.

Example 2.41

Jerry owns a home with a replacement cost of $500,000. A tree falls on Jerry's house, causing $100,000 in damage. Jerry has a policy with an 80% coinsurance amount and a $500 deductible.

How much will the insurer pay if Jerry carries $300,000 of coverage?

$$\frac{\$300,000}{0.80 \times \$500,000} \times \$100,000$$

= $75,000 - $500 = $74,500 (paid by insurer)

Example 2.42

How much would the insurer pay if Jerry had $400,000 of coverage?

$$\frac{\$400,000}{0.80 \times \$500,000} \times \$100,000$$

= $100,000 - $500 = $99,500 (paid by insurer)

Example 2.43

How much would the insurer pay if Jerry had $600,000 of coverage?

$$\frac{\$600,000}{0.80 \times \$500,000} \times \$100,000$$

= $150,000* ($99,500 paid by insurer)

* The insurer payment is limited to the loss of $100,000 less the deductible of $500, therefore $99,500. The insured has over insured but is subject to the principle of indemnity.

The maximum amount the insurer will pay is up to the covered loss or the face value of the policy or policy limits, less any deductible, even though the coinsurance formula may result in a percentage greater than 100 percent.

Coinsurance is also a term used in medical insurance indemnity policies. In these policies, coinsurance refers to the percentages paid by the insurer and the insured for claims after a deductible has been met and before the out-of-pocket maximum (OPM) is reached. The **out-of-pocket maximum** represents the maximum dollar amount that the insured will pay under the policy in a given year and includes the deductible, the insured's portion of the coinsurance, and generally any copayments. For example, in a plan with an 80/20 coinsurance formula, a $1,000 deductible, and an out-of-pocket-maximum of $4,000, the insured will pay 100 percent of all covered costs until the $1,000 deductible is reached. After the first $1,000 in claims, the insured pays 20 percent of covered costs until the $4,000 OPM is reached. The insurance company is responsible for 80 percent of covered costs after the deductible is met and 100 percent of claims once the insured reaches the OPM.

Example 2.44

Captain Jack has a medical insurance policy with a $4,000 deductible and 90/10 coinsurance with an out-of-pocket maximum of $5,000. He had several medical procedures during the current year. In January, he had a small procedure to remove skin cancer costing $5,000. In April, he had his knee scoped, which cost $18,000. In November, he found out he had a hernia and decided to get it repaired before the end of the year. His hernia repair cost $12,000. For the year, Jack's out-of-pocket-expenses total $5,000.

	Skin Cancer	Knee	Hernia	Total
Jack's Deductible	$4,000	$0	$0	$4,000
Jack's Coinsurance	$100	$900	$0	$1,000
Insurance Co's Coinsurance	$900	$8,100	$0	$9,000
Insurance above OPM		$9,000	$12,000	$21,000
Total	**$5,000**	**$18,000**	**$12,000**	**$35,000**

Note that Jack's coinsurance for the knee scope would be calculated as 10% x $18,000 = $1,800; however, Jack has a maximum out-of-pocket limit of $5,000. Since he previously paid $4,100 out-of-pocket during the year, his coinsurance for the knee scope is reduced to the remaining $900 ($5,000 - $4,100 = $900).

Example 2.45

Gina has surgery to repair her labrum costing $20,000. Her deductible is $3,000 and she has an 80/20 coinsurance clause with an out-of-pocket maximum of $5,000. How much will Gina pay for her procedure?

Loss	$20,000
- Deductible	$3,000
Covered Loss	$17,000
Gina's coinsurance (up to the OPM)	$2,000
Insurance Co.'s coinsurance (up to the OPM)	$8,000
Insurance Co.'s coinsurance (above the OPM)	$7,000
Gina's out-of-pocket-maximum	$5,000
Loss paid by insurance Co.	$15,000

VALUING PROPERTY FOR LOSSES

Insurance policies must not only specify what perils are covered and what is excluded, but must also explain how losses are to be valued. Without valuation provisions in the policy, the insured and the insurer would not have clarity over how much a particular claim is worth.

Insurance policies generally value and pay losses based on one of three valuation methods:
- Actual cash value
- Replacement cost
- Appraised or agreed upon value

> **☰ Key Concepts**
>
> 1. Differentiate between actual cash value, replacement cost, and appraised value.

Actual Cash Value

Actual cash value represents the replacement cost less the depreciated value of the property. Actual cash value is used to value the amount of coverage for a personal auto or personal property in a homeowners policy or business property policy.

Example 2.46

Three years ago Mayiah purchased a new car for $30,000. Yesterday, she was in an accident and her car was totaled. Her car had depreciated by $12,000 over the three years she owned the car. The actual cash value of the car was $18,000 ($30,000 - $12,000), which is how much the insurer will pay Mayiah for her loss, less any deductible.

For personal property in a homeowners policy actual cash value (ACV) means replacement cost less depreciation.

Replacement Cost

Replacement cost represents the amount to repair or replace property, without any deduction for depreciation. Replacement cost is the method used to value damage to a personal residence (dwelling) under a property insurance policy.

Example 2.47

A windstorm blows off a portion of the roof on Sylvia's house. The cost to replace the damaged roof is $75,000. Under the replacement cost method of valuing a loss, the insurer will pay the full $75,000 less any deductible to repair the damaged roof.

Personal property can be valued using actual cash value (ACV) or replacement cost (RC). Replacement cost is preferable to the insured because the insured will receive the full dollar amount to replace the damaged property rather than the depreciated value under actual cash value.

Example 2.48

A tree falls on Jesse's house damaging his room and crushing his refrigerator. The roof damage is valued at $15,000. He purchased the refrigerator 10 years ago for $2,000. A similar new refrigerator costs $1,900 today. The actual cash value of the refrigerator is now $200. If Jesse has replacement cost for the roof but actual cash value for the refrigerator, his insurance company will pay $15,000 for the roof and $200 for the refrigerator less any applicable deductible. However, if Jesse has replacement cost for both the roof and refrigerator, Jesse will receive $15,000 to repair the roof and $1,900 to purchase a new refrigerator, less any deductible.

Appraised or Agreed Upon Value

Appraised or agreed upon value is when items are hard to value or when the insured owns property that exceeds standard limits of a property insurance policy. Typically jewelry, art, furs, and collectibles are covered using appraised or agreed upon value; such that any underlying limits in the property insurance policy are increased.

REGULATING THE INSURANCE INDUSTRY

The insurance industry is regulated primarily at the state level, but federal law also overlaps state insurance regulation. At the federal level, the Gramm-Leach-Bliley Act of 1999 repealed the Glass-Steagal Act, which prevented banks, investment firms, and insurers from competing outside of their core business. As a result of the Gramm-Leach-Bliley Act, banks and investment firms can sell insurance, and insurance companies can provide banking and investment services. Now that firms in financial services provide insurance, banking, and investment services, the regulatory environment has become more complex with firms now subject to regulation by the Federal Reserve for banking, the Securities and Exchange Commission on investments, and state regulation for insurance products.

The insurance industry is highly regulated by three levels of state government, which are:
- legislative
- judicial
- executive or State Insurance Commissioners

Legislative

The legislative branch of state government passes laws and regulations that regulate how insurance companies conduct business in their state. The legislature defines how insurance products are sold, controls how insurance agents are licensed, and protects consumer rights by passing consumer protection laws.

Judicial

The judicial branch of state government rules on the constitutionality of laws passed by the legislative branch. The judicial branch also rules on decisions and actions taken by the executive branch. The judicial branch provides oversight of the legislative and executive branch, along with the insurance industry.

Executive or State Insurance Commissioner

All states have a state insurance commissioner, which is an elected or appointed position. The state insurance commissioner is responsible for enforcing the legislature's laws and regulations, licensing of insurance agents, reviewing rate increases, and auditing insurance companies.

☷ *Key Concepts*

1. Identify the three levels of state regulation of the insurance industry.

2. Determine if the NAIC has regulatory power.

3. Identify the goals of the NAIC.

4. Differentiate between various methods to regulate insurance rates.

National Association of Insurance Commissioners (NAIC)

The National Association of Insurance Commissioners (NAIC) is a voluntary organization of insurance regulators from the 50 states, the District of Columbia and the five U.S. territories (Guam, Puerto Rico, Virgin Islands, American Samoa, and Commonwealth of the Northern Mariana Islands).[4] The mission of the NAIC is to "assist state insurance regulators" in serving the public. The goals of the NAIC are to:
- Protect the public
- Promote competition
- Promote fair treatment of insurance consumers
- Promote the solvency of insurance companies
- Support and improve state regulation of insurance

The NAIC does not have regulatory power, but it does issue model legislation to address problems within the insurance industry. Although states may or may not adopt the model legislation, the NAIC recommendations have been influential and the NAIC has helped to achieve greater uniformity in state insurance laws and regulations.

The NAIC also provides a watch list of insurance companies based upon financial ratio analysis. The ratio analysis measures the financial health of an insurance company. To promote solvency and avoid insurers from being unable to pay claims, life and health insurance companies are subject to a Risk-Based Capital test (RBC) that was developed by the NAIC. Risk-based capital measures how much capital is invested and the riskiness of the investments. The more risky the investments, the more capital the insurer is required to maintain. If the insurer does not maintain adequate capital, then regulatory action may be required. Regulatory action may include the state seizing, rehabilitating, or liquidating the company.

---

4. http://www.naic.org/index_about.htm

Insurance Rate Regulation

The rates that insurance companies use when determining premiums are regulated at the state level. The regulation varies by state and rate laws may also differ based upon the insurance product. Some of the insurance rate regulation laws include:

- Prior Approval Law
- File and Use Law
- Use and File Law
- Open Competition

Prior Approval Law

Under prior approval law, an insurance company must file the rate increase request with the State's Insurance Commissioner's office. The rate increase will either be approved, disapproved, or modified. During 2009 and 2010, many states denied health insurance rate increases due to the increasing unemployment rate and potential political fallout arising from 10 to 20 percent health insurance rate increases.

File and Use Law

States that allow a "file and use" law permit an insurance company to file the rate increase with the State Insurance Commissioner's office and immediately implement the rate increase. The state insurance commissioner may later deny the rate increase in which case the insurance company must rebate the premiums paid under the denied rate.

Use and File Law

A "use and file" state permits an insurer to increase rates, but they must file the rate increase within a specific time period, as determined by state law. Both the "file and use" and "use and file" laws avoid any delays associated with the rate increases being approved, as they allow the insurer to implement rate increases quickly.

Open Competition

Open competition laws allow insurers to set their own rates, and the State presumes that supply and demand will determine the appropriate rates for various insurance products. The open competition approach assumes that fair competition among insurers will result in efficient premium prices.

SELECTING AN INSURANCE COMPANY

The financial stability of an insurance company is a primary determinant for selecting an insurer. Rating agencies analyze and evaluate the financial health and ability of an insurer to pay claims. The better the insurer's rating, the more likely they are to sell policies, as consumers will have confidence in the insurer's ability to pay claims, should the insurer experience a loss.

Rating Agency	Highest Ratings		Lowest Ratings	
A.M. Best	A++	A/A-	C/C -	D
Fitch	AAA	AA	B	CCC
Moody's	Aaa	Aa2	B1	Caa
Standard and Poor's	AAA	AA-	B+	CCC
Weiss	A+	B -	D	E

A consumer should compare insurer ratings across several rating agencies. An insurer with consistently high ratings across multiple rating agencies is a low risk and acceptable provider. However, an insurer with consistently low ratings from multiple rating agencies is a high risk and should be avoided.

Most state insurance commission websites provide information regarding insurance companies authorized to do business in their state, including information regarding complaints against the insurer (including the number of complaints and reason for the complaint), asset and balance sheet information, reserve information, and financial strength. The NAIC website provides similar information on its Consumer Information Source (CIS) page.[5]

For some applicants, the selection of an insurance company may be also be based on the insurance company's philosophy and standards. Some insurers specialize in insuring identified groups and may offer more favorable classifications or pricing for those groups, and some insurers are willing to insure risks at favorable rates that are viewed as substandard by others. For example, when applying for life insurance, some insurers require medical examinations and some do not. When a life insurance applicant has a medical condition that may be of concern in the underwriting process, an insurance broker (as opposed to an insurance agent who is limited to the policies from one company) may search among many insurance companies to find the best underwriting for the condition. Similarly, when property insurance is needed for property with specialized use or hazards, an insurance broker may search among many companies to find the best underwriting for the property.

5. https://eapps/naic.org/cis

General Guidelines for Insurance Policy Selection

The following general guidelines may be recommended by advisors to clients for use in selecting insurance policies. Many of these guidelines will be expanded upon throughout the remaining chapters of this text.

- Recognize that cost is a constraint for most clients. The amount of money available in the budget to spend on insurance is finite; therefore, priorities must be established for which types of policies will be purchased and decisions must be made regarding what is considered a fair trade-off between adequate coverage and cost of premiums.
- A client's subjective risk assessment (risk tolerance) will be a factor in determining which types of loss exposures he or she is willing to assume in their entirety or retain partially via deductibles and waiting periods. Determining which risks are essential to transfer to an insurance company will be largely based on frequency and severity; however, the client's psychological assessment of the risk will vary from person to person and situation to situation and will impact insurance decisions. For example, a client who has provided care for an aging parent may feel that long-term care insurance is essential because she does not want her children to endure the physical and emotional strain that she experienced caring for her own parent. A client who has not had such an experience may deem long-term care insurance an unnecessary expense.
- Insure first and to high limits against risks that could be catastrophic to the client. Examples include loss of income to family due to death or disability of a "breadwinner;" loss of income or accumulated assets due to medical expenses associated with illness, accident, or long-term care; loss of accumulated assets and perhaps future income due to legal liability associated with ownership of land or premises, driving a car, boat or RV, and the carrying on of business or professional activities; and the possible serious reduction in standard of living due to outliving the assets accumulated to provide a retirement income.
- Obtain an adequate amount of replacement cost property insurance on principal assets (e.g., the home, auto, or jewelry).
- Use group coverages (such as those offered by an employer) and social insurance (such as Social Security) as a foundation and individual policies to fill in gaps in types and amounts of coverage.
- Ensure that retained risks via deductibles, coinsurance, waiting periods, or the decision to self-insure align with assets (e.g., emergency funds) or disposable income available to cover the losses.
- Avoid limited policies and highly restrictive policy provisions.
- Shop for the best pricing among reputable and financially strong insurers.
- Purchase home and auto insurance from the same insurer to receive discounts on premiums for both policies.
- Insurance premiums can be reduced through actions such as installation of fire extinguishers and smoke and burglar alarms, maintenance of a good driving record, cessation of smoking, and increasing the insured's credit score.

KEY TERMS

Actual Cash Value - Represents the depreciated value of the property.

Adhesion - A take it or leave it contract.

Adverse Selection - The tendency of those that most need insurance to seek it out.

Agents - Legal representatives of an insurer and act on behalf of an insurer.

Aleatory - A type of insurance contract in which the dollar amounts exchanged are uneven.

Apparent Authority - When the third party believes implied or express authority exists, but no authority actually exists.

Appraised or Agreed Upon Value - Used for hard to value items and where the insured may own property that exceeds standard limits of property insurance policy.

Brokers - Legal representatives of an insured and act in the best interest of the insured.

Coinsurance - The percentage of financial responsibility that the insured and the insurer must uphold in order to achieve equity in rating.

Concealment - When the insured is intentionally silent regarding a material fact during the application process.

Conditional - The insured must abide by all the terms and conditions of the contract, if the insured intends to collect under the policy.

Copayment - A loss-sharing arrangement whereby the insured pays a flat dollar amount or percentage of the loss in excess of the deductible.

Declarations Section - The section of an insurance policy that describes exactly what property is being covered.

Deductible - A specified amount of money the insured is required to pay on a loss before the insurer will make any payments under the policy.

Definition Section - The section of an insurance policy that defines key words, phrases, or terms used throughout the insurance contract.

Description Section - The section of an insurance policy that describes exactly what is being insured.

Endorsement - A modification or change to the existing property insurance policy.

Estoppel - The legal process of denying a right you might otherwise be entitled to under the law.

Exclusion Section - The section of an insurance policy that will exclude certain perils, losses and property.

Express Authority - Authority given to an agent through a formal written document.

Financial Risk - A loss of financial value, such as the premature death of a family's primary wage earner.

Fundamental Risk - A risk that can impact a large number of individuals at one time (earthquake or flood).

Hazards - A specific condition that increases the potential or likelihood of a loss occurring.

Implied Authority - The authority that a third party relies upon when dealing with an agent based upon the position held by the agent.

Lacking Sound Mind - The state of not having the capacity to understand the purpose and terms of the contract, therefore the contract lacks a meeting of the minds or mutual consent.

Law of Large Numbers - A principle that states the more similar events or exposures, the more likely the actual results will equal the probability expected.

Minors - In most states, a minor is under the age of 18. If a minor enters into a contract, the minor can void the contract at any time.

Moral Hazard - The potential loss occurring because of the moral character of the insured, and the filing of a false claim with their insurance company.

Morale Hazard - The indifference to a loss created because the insured has insurance.

Mutual Consent - Common understanding and agreement between parties to a contract regarding what the contract covers and the terms of the contract.

Non-Financial Risk - A risk that would result in a loss, other than a monetary loss.

Objective Risk - The variation of actual amount of losses that occur over a period of time compared to the expected amount of losses.

Offer and Acceptance - Consists of one party making an offer to purchase a good or service, and the acceptance is when consideration is received.

Out-of-Pocket-Maximum - The sum of the deductible, the insured's portion of the coinsurance, and generally any copayments by the insured.

Parol Evidence Rule - States that "what is written prevails." Oral agreements that are not reflected in the written contract are not valid.

Particular Risk - A risk that can impact a particular individual, such as death or the inability to work because of a sickness or accident.

Perils - The immediate cause and reason for a loss occurring.

Physical Hazard - A physical condition that increases the likelihood of a loss occurring.

Principle of Indemnity - Asserts that an insurer will only compensate the insured to the extent the insured has suffered an actual financial loss.

Principle of Insurable Interest - Asserts that an insured must suffer a financial loss if a covered peril occurs, otherwise no insurance can be offered.

Pure Risk - The chance of loss or no loss occurring.

Reinsurance - A means by which an insurance company transfers some or all of its risk to another insurance company.

Replacement Cost - Represents the amount to repair or replace property, without any deduction for depreciation.

Representation - A statement made by the applicant during the insurance application process.

Rider - A modification or change to a life or health insurance policy.

Risk - The chance of loss, uncertainty associated with loss, or the possibility of a loss.

Risk Avoidance - A risk management technique used for any risks that are high in frequency and high in severity.

Risk Reduction - The process of reducing the likelihood of a pure risk that is high in frequency and low in severity or of reducing the severity of losses from certain perils.

Risk Retention - Accepting some or all of the potential loss exposure for risks that are low in frequency and low in severity.

Risk Transfer - The process of transferring a low frequency and high severity risk to a third party, such as an insurance company.

Speculative Risk - The chance of loss, no loss, or a profit.

Subjective Risk - The risk an individual perceives based on their prior experiences and the severity of those experiences.

Subrogation Clause - A clause in an insurance policy that requires that the insured relinquish a claim against a negligent third party, if the insurer has already indemnified the insured.

Underwriting - The process of classifying applicants into a risk pools, selecting insureds, and assigning a premium.

Unilateral - There is only one promise made; and in the case of an insurance contract, it's made by the insurer to pay in the event of a loss.

Waiver - The relinquishment a known legal right.

Warranty - A promise made by the insured that is part of the insurance contract.

DISCUSSION QUESTIONS

SOLUTIONS to the discussion questions can be found exclusively within the chapter. Once you have completed an initial reading of the chapter, go back and highlight the answers to these questions.

1. Describe the personal risk management process.

2. List the four responses to managing risk.

3. Define a peril.

4. Define the three main types of hazard.

5. List some unique characteristics of an insurance contract.

6. Explain the differences between pure risk and speculative risk.

7. Explain the four differences between subjective and objective risks.

8. Describe the law of large numbers and why it is useful for insurance companies.

9. List typical perils covered under a personal auto policy.

10. List typical perils covered under a homeowners insurance policy.

11. What are the requisites for an insurable risk?

12. Describe the elements of a valid contract.

13. Define conditional acceptance.

14. Define the parol evidence rule.

15. Explain the differences between the principle of indemnity and a subrogation clause.

16. When must an insurable interest exist for property, liability, and life insurance?

17. Define representation, warranty, and concealment.

18. List unique characteristics of insurance contracts.

19. Describe the differences between express, implied, and apparent authority.

20. Identify the differences between agents and brokers.

21. List the responsibilities of an underwriter.

22. Identify why insurance companies are reinsured.

23. List and define typical sections of an insurance contract.

24. Differentiate between a rider and an endorsement.

25. Describe the purpose of a deductible.

26. Describe the purpose of coinsurance in a property insurance policy.

27. Describe the differences between actual cash value, replacement cost, and appraised value.

28. Identify the three levels of state regulation of the insurance industry.

29. Identify the goals of the NAIC.

30. Describe the differences between various methods to regulate insurance rates.

31. List some general guidelines for insurance policy selection.

MULTIPLE-CHOICE PROBLEMS

A sample of multiple choice problems is provided below. Additional multiple choice problems are available at money-education.com by accessing the Student Practice Portal.

1. The risk that individuals of higher than average risk will seek out or purchase insurance policies is called?
    a. Peril.
    b. Hazard.
    c. Law of Large Numbers.
    d. Adverse Selection.

2. The principle of indemnity requires that:
    a. A person is entitled to compensation only to the extent that financial loss has been suffered.
    b. Insured cannot indemnify himself from both the insurance company and a negligent third party for the same claim.
    c. The insured must be subject to financial hardship resulting from the loss.
    d. The insured and insurer must both be forthcoming with all relevant facts about the insured risk and coverage provided for that risk.

3. When must an insurable interest exist for a life insurance claim?
    a. At the policy inception and time of loss.
    b. At the policy inception only.
    c. At the time of the loss only.
    d. Either at the policy inception or at the time of the loss.

4. Joe walks into his insurance agent's office and notices his agent's name on a business card and the insurer's name on letterhead. If an agency agreement exists, what type of authority does Joe believe his agent has to enter into an insurance contract?
    a. Express Authority.
    b. Implied Authority.
    c. Apparent Authority.
    d. None of the Above.

5. Which of the following statements regarding loss severity is true?
    1. Loss severity is the expected number of losses that will occur within a given period.
    2. Loss severity is the potential size or damage of a loss.

    a. 1 only.
    b. 2 only.
    c. Both 1 and 2.
    d. Neither 1 nor 2.

QUICK QUIZ EXPLANATIONS

Quick Quiz 2.1
1. True.
2. False. Objective risk is the variation of actual amount of losses that occur over a period of time compared to the expected amount of losses.
3. True.

Quick Quiz 2.2
1. True.
2. False. Risk reduction is the process of reducing the likelihood of a pure risk that is high in frequency and low in severity.
3. False. Risk transfer involves transferring a low frequency and high severity risk to a third party, such as an insurance company.

Quick Quiz 2.3
1. True.
2. False. Morale hazard is indifference to a loss created because the insured has insurance. A physical hazard is a physical condition that increases the likelihood of a loss occurring.

Quick Quiz 2.4
1. True.
2. True.
3. False. A loss exposure that would be financially catastrophic to the insurer (not the insured) is an uninsurable risk.

Quick Quiz 2.5
1. False. Typically contracts may be terminated by mutual consent of both parties.
2. True.
3. False. If a minor enters into a contract, the minor can void the contract at any time.

Quick Quiz 2.6
1. False. The principle of indemnity asserts that an insurer will only compensate the insured to the extent the insured has suffered an actual financial loss. A subrogation clause in an insurance policy requires that the insured relinquish a claim against a negligent third party, if the insurer has already indemnified the insured.
2. False. An insurable interest for property and liability insurance must exist both at the inception of the policy and at the time of loss. Insurable interest for life insurance must exist only at the inception of the policy.
3. True.

QUICK QUIZ EXPLANATIONS

Quick Quiz 2.7
1. False. Insurance contracts are aleatory in nature, which means the dollar amounts exchanged are uneven.
2. True.
3. True.

Quick Quiz 2.8
1. True.
2. True.
3. False. A waiver is relinquishing a known legal right. Estoppel is where through a legal process, you are denied a right you might otherwise be entitled to under the law.

Quick Quiz 2.9
1. False. Agents are legal representatives of an insurer and act on behalf of an insurer. Brokers are legal representatives of an insured and act in the best interest of the insured.
2. False. Brokers do not represent the insurer so they may not bind an insurer.

Quick Quiz 2.10
1. True.
2. True.

Quick Quiz 2.11
1. False. Replacement cost is the method used to value damage to a personal residence under a property insurance policy. Actual cash value is used to value the amount of coverage for a personal auto or personal property.
2. True.
3. False. A PAP uses actual cash value when providing coverage for a personal auto.

Quick Quiz 2.12
1. True.
2. True.
3. True.

**Additional multiple choice problems
are available at
money-education.com
by accessing the
Student Practice Portal.
Access requires registration of the title using
the unique code at the front of the book.**

3
HEALTH INSURANCE

1. Understand the need for health insurance.
2. Describe the fundamental changes imposed by the Affordable Care Act.
3. Discuss group health insurance and its features and types.
4. Discuss the need for individual health insurance and the different types of policies.
5. Describe the common provisions in a health insurance policy.
6. Differentiate the types of group and individual health insurance plans.
7. Describe the taxation of health insurance policies.
8. Compare and contrast group and individual health insurance alternatives, including fee for service and managed care health plans.*
9. Describe the Consolidated Omnibus Budget Reconciliation Act of 1985 (COBRA).
10. Explain alternatives for acquiring health coverage including COBRA and Medicaid.*
11. Describe health savings accounts and flexible spending accounts.
12. Incorporate expected retiree health costs in a client's retirement plan in consideration of household financial resources, existing or future coverage under group insurance plans, and Medicare*.

* CFP Board Resource Document - Student-Centered Learning Objectives based upon CFP Board Principal Topics.

INTRODUCTION

Effective financial plans help individuals make appropriate financial choices that improve their financial health. However, without physical health, an individual will not have a good quality of life. Unlike the risks associated with death and disability, most people tend to understand health risks and know that having adequate protection against those risks, in the form of health insurance, is a desirable financial goal. Poor health presents a substantial risk of catastrophic losses. When an individual chooses to self-insure against health risks and a major health problem emerges, all of the individual's assets are at risk. Health care treatments can be expensive, and may deplete a person's accumulated savings (for retirement, children's education, and major purchases), leaving the individual financially insecure. Transferring the risk of incurring major health care costs to an insurer is prudent, especially when there is a possibility that other financial goals will be jeopardized if proper risk management plans are not in place.

Key Concepts

1. Highlight the reasons that explain why group health insurance is the most popular type of health insurance.

2. Highlight the reason that explains why group health insurance can be provided cost effectively.

3. Define the two primary types of group health insurance.

4. Describe how a copay, a deductible, a coinsurance, and a maximum out-of-pocket amount work in conjunction with each other.

While transferring the risk of extensive medical expenses to an insurance company will rest at the core of the risk management plan for health care, other risk management techniques will likely be employed along with it. Regular exercise and a healthy diet are risk reduction techniques the client may participate in, and controlled risk retention in the form of deductibles and coinsurance payments will be necessary.

The annual and lifetime cost of health care, including insurance premiums, deductibles, copays, coinsurance amounts and items not covered by insurance can take a significant portion of the family's budget, especially in the retirement years. When a person who is fully insured under the Social Security system reaches age 65, that person can obtain government-provided health insurance from the Medicare system.[1] Medicare Part A, which is paid for by payroll tax deductions during the participant's working career, covers hospital costs. Medicare Part B, which is paid for by payroll tax deductions plus a monthly premium amount deducted from the participant's Social Security benefits, covers medical costs (doctors bills, lab tests, and the like). The traditional Medicare system leaves numerous gaps in coverage that must either be covered out-of-pocket or covered via a Medicare Supplement policy. The details of Medicare health insurance are covered in Chapter 10. This chapter focuses primarily on private individual health insurance, including Medicare Supplement insurance, as well as group health insurance.

The Kaiser Family Foundation's 2016 Consumer Expenditure Survey reports that non-Medicare households (below age 65) spend an average of six percent of household income on health care while Medicare (age 65 and older) households spend an average of 14 percent of household income on health care (see **Exhibit 3.1 Definition of Disability**).[2] Proper analysis and evaluation of available health insurance options will allow the planner and client to identify any gaps in coverage and devise a plan that will most effectively meet the client's needs at an affordable cost.

Exhibit 3.1 | Percent of Household Income Spent on Health Care

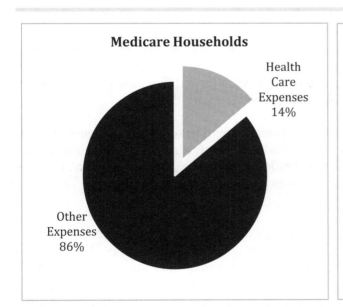

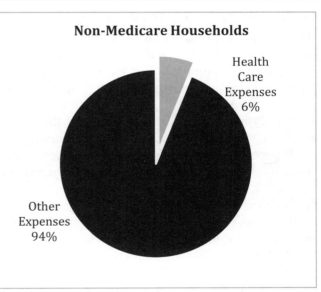

---

1. Those who are not covered under Social Security can also obtain Medicare at age 65 for an additional fee. See Chapter 10 for details regarding Social Security and Medicare.
2. https://www.kff.org/medicare/issue-brief/the-financial-burden-of-health-care-spending-larger-for-medicare-households-than-for-non-medicare-households. Note that the survey does not include those receiving care in an institution (such as a nursing home), therefore it likely underestimates the average cost of care for Medicare households (a larger percentage of whom receive care in an institution).

While the Affordable Care Act (ACA) is the current law of the land, healthcare has been a contentious topic since the ACA's enactment in 2010. Many in Washington, D.C. have vowed to repeal the ACA or repeal and replace the ACA since its enactment. In his first executive order, President Trump gave authority to various government departments to roll back certain aspects of the ACA. During President Trump's first half of his first year (2017) in office, the House of Representatives passed a "repeal and replace" healthcare bill. However, the Senate was unable to pass a similar bill. President Trump did eliminate the penalty for those who do not maintain minimum essential health care coverage as part of the TCJA (Tax Cuts and Jobs Act) of 2017. In March 2020, the Supreme Court accepted an appeal on the ACA. Its decision should be reached by the end of 2020 or 2021. Given the extreme feelings surrounding the topic, it is unlikely that the healthcare law will be fully settled anytime soon.

DEDUCTIBLES, COINSURANCE, AND MAXIMUM-OUT-OF-POCKET

In addition to premiums paid to purchase a health insurance policy, clients are likely to incur other costs in the form of deductibles, copays, and coinsurance payments. Fortunately, qualified health insurance plans include a maximum-out-of-pocket limit to cap the annual out-of-pocket amounts paid by the insured (although some costs do not count toward the maximum-out-of pocket limit, as discussed below). Details regarding how these costs apply to various types of health insurance plans are discussed along with each type of plan later in this chapter, but a preliminary understanding of these terms will provide a better understanding of the general nature of health insurance.

Deductibles and Coinsurance

Most medical insurance policies will have an initial deductible, perhaps $500, $1,000, or even $5,000 per person or per family. This deductible requires the insured to bear the first set of covered charges before the insurance company is liable for any benefit payments. The reason for a deductible is to hold down premium costs by eliminating small claims and the expenses associated with them.

Another type of cost-sharing provision is the coinsurance provision found in some medical policies. This provision specifies that the insurance company will be responsible for only a specified percentage, such as 80 percent, of covered medical expenses in excess of the deductible. The other 20 percent must be borne by the insured but only up to the maximum out-of-pocket limit.

Embedded Deductible

Family plans with an embedded deductible actually have two deductible types: an individual deductible and a family deductible. The individual component allows each covered individual in the family to satisfy the deductible for their own medical expenses and move to the coinsurance phase from the policy before the family has collectively met their deductible. The family component relates to the family as a whole, and is the amount of covered expenses that the family must meet before moving beyond the deductible.

Example 3.1

The Jones family has a health care plan with an embedded deductible. The individual annual deductible amount is $2,300, and the family deductible amount is $4,600. After the deductible has been satisfied, the coinsurance is 80/20. The only medical expenses for the year were for Dad, who had a skiing accident resulting in $6,500 of covered medical expenses.

The family's combined expenses total $6,500. Here's how they paid the deductible:

	Expenses	Deductible (paid by family)	Amount Subject to Coinsurance
Dad	$6,500	$2,300	$4,200
Mom	$0	$0	$0
Daughter	$0	$0	$0
Son	$0	$0	$0
Total	**$6,500**	**$2,300**	**$4,200**

The total paid by the Jones family is $2,300 + ($4,200 x 20%) = $3,140

Example 3.2

The Johnson family has a health care plan with an embedded deductible. The individual annual deductible amount is $2,300, and the family deductible amount is $4,600. After the deductible has been satisfied, the coinsurance is 80/20. The family was in a boating accident where all four family members required varying amounts of medical intervention. The family incurred the following expenses:

	Expenses
Dad	$3,200
Mom	$1,850
Daughter	$800
Son	$650

Because their plan has an embedded deductible, there are two components. First, once the entire family's deductibles total $4,600, they collectively move into the next level of coverage. Second, until they meet the collective family deductible, individual family members can move to the next coverage level after meeting the individual deductible amount of $2,300.

In this example, only Dad has met the individual deductible amount of $2,300, so the final $900 of his expenses moves into the coinsurance level. At this point, the family still has to meet an additional $2,300 deductible amount to satisfy the aggregate family deductible. The family's combined expenses total $6,500. Here's how they paid the deductible:

	Expenses	Deductible (paid by family)	Amount Subject to Coinsurance
Dad	$3,200	$2,300	$900
Mom	$1,850	$1,850	$0
Daughter	$800	$450*	$350
Son	$650	$0	$650
Total	**$6,500**	**$4,600**	**$1,900**

At this point, the family deductible has been met.

Non-Embedded Deductible

Plans having a non-embedded family deductible do not embed or insert the individual deductible option into the family deductible amount. As a result, the insureds must satisfy the entire family deductible amount before the policy will help pay for any individual's medical expenses. One family member can meet the entire deductible or it may require several family members to do so. Either way, the family must meet its entire deductible before any expenses move to the coinsurance level.

Example 3.3

Assume the same facts for the Jones family as **Example 3.1**, however, the plan has a non-embedded deductible. The change will require that the family pay the total $4,600 before the insurer will make any payment.

The deductible amount for the family is $4,600, and there is no individual amount. After the deductible has been satisfied, the coinsurance is 80/20. The only medical expenses for the year were for Dad, who had a skiing accident resulting in $6,500 of covered medical expenses.

The family's combined expenses total $6,500. Here's how they paid the deductible:

	Expenses	Deductible (paid by family)	Amount Subject to Coinsurance
Dad	$6,500	$4,600	$1,900
Mom	$0	$0	$0
Daughter	$0	$0	$0
Son	$0	$0	$0
Total	**$6,500**	**$4,600**	**$1,900**

The total paid by the Jones family is $4,600 + ($1,900 x 20%) = $4,980.

Note that with the embedded deductible, the total paid by the Jones family was $1,840 less.

Example 3.4

Assume the same facts for the Johnson family as **Example 3.2**, however, the plan has a non-embedded deductible. The change will make the family pay the total $4,600 before the insurer will make any payment.

Because their plan has a non-embedded deductible, it only has the aggregate family deductible component. After the entire family's expenses total $4,600, they collectively move into the next level of coverage. Until that point, the insurer will make no payments.

The family's combined expenses total $6,500. Here's how they paid the deductible:

	Expenses	Deductible (paid by family)	Amount Subject to Coinsurance
Dad	$3,200	$3,200	$0
Mom	$1,850	$1,400*	$450
Daughter	$800	$0	$800
Son	$650	$0	$650
Total	**$6,500**	**$4,600**	**$1,900**

At this point, the family deductible has been met

The total paid by the Johnson family is $4,600 + ($1,900 x 20%) = $4,980. In this case, there is no difference from the embedded deductible.

A planner will need to understand how to evaluate the policy in order to recommend an appropriate emergency fund for the client to ensure any annual out-of-pocket costs can be covered or to assist the client with decisions regarding which type of policy to select or what features to look for.[3] In some cases, there may be a single family member who is likely to have higher medical expenses than others during the year, potentially making the embedded deductible more attractive for that family.

Maximum-Out-Of-Pocket (MOOP) Limits

Qualified health plans include a provision that places a cap on the amount that the insured will be called upon to pay during any one calendar year. The cap on an insured's payments may be called a stop-loss or an out-of-pocket maximum. Each policy must be examined carefully to understand precisely how the maximum is computed.

Embedded and Non-Embedded Maximum-Out-Of-Pocket (MOOP)

Embedded and non-embedded MOOPs function in the same way as their deductible counterparts. This means, among other things, that the determination of whether a MOOP is embedded or non-embedded only applies to policies covering the primary insured and at least one other family member.

---

3. Licensing or certification may be required for planners to provide certain types of advice.

Beginning January 1, 2016, a provision of the Affordable Care Act (ACA) limits maximum out-of-pocket (MOOP) expenses on all non-grandfathered plans. In 2020, the MOOP limit must be no higher than $8,150 for an individual and $16,300 for a family. These amounts are indexed annually, and represent the most a policyholder will have to pay during the policy period (e.g., one year) for covered expenses. The MOOP typically includes the deductible, along with any other cost sharing, such as copays and coinsurance. However, the MOOP does not include premium payments and plans are permitted to exclude amounts charged by non-network providers from counting toward the MOOP (in-network and out-of-network providers are discussed in conjunction with managed care plans later in this chapter). Unlike in previous years, plans must now include a provision for an embedded MOOP such that, once any individual has expenses exceeding the individual MOOP amount (e.g., $8,150), the plan must pay the excess of covered expenses for that individual regardless of whether the family MOOP has been met. This is quite similar to how embedded deductibles function. With these regulations, it should be relatively easy to determine annual expense maximums, but that is often not the case, and is a good reason for the financial planner and client to review coverage, likely expenses, and whether the services of out-of-network providers will be utilized.

Example 3.5

Family members Jeff, Lizzy, Gregory, and Tamara have the following medical expenses during the year (Jeff and Gregory were also injured in a biking accident later in the year).

For simplicity, assume the expenses listed below include the deductible, copays, coinsurance and all other covered costs. Also assume an embedded individual MOOP of $8,150 and a family MOOP of $16,300.

	Expenses	Out-of-Pocket (paid by family)	Remainder (paid by insurer)
Jeff	$2,000	$2,000	$0
Lizzy	$3,500	$3,500	$0
Gregory	$10,000	$8,150*	$1,850
Tamara	$9,000	$2,650**	$6,350
Jeff	$8,000	$0	$8,000
Gregory	$6,000	$0	$6,000
Total	$38,500	$16,300	$22,200

*At this point, Gregory has met his embedded individual MOOP.
**The family has met the total MOOP.

Example 3.6

The Anderson family has a policy with an individual MOOP of $8,150 and a non-embedded family MOOP of $16,300. For simplicity, assume the expenses listed below include the deductible, coinsurance, and all other covered costs. They had the following medical expenses during the year:

	Expenses	Out-of-Pocket (paid by family)	Remainder (paid by insurer)
Dad	$20,000	$16,300*	$3,700
Mom	$10,000	$0	$10,000
Daughter	$500	$0	$500
Son	$1,200	$0	$1,200
Total	**$31,700**	**$16,300**	**$15,400**

At this point, Dad has single-handedly met the family MOOP, and no further out-of-pocket payment is required.

Example 3.7

Assume the same facts as in **Example 3.6** for the Anderson family, however, they had different covered medical expenses during the year as follows:

	Expenses	Out-of-Pocket (paid by family)	Remainder (paid by insurer)
Dad	$10,500	$10,500	$0
Mom	$4,000	$4,000	$0
Daughter	$3,000	$1,800*	$1,200
Son	$1,750	$0	$1,750
Total	**$19,250**	**$16,300**	**$2,950**

At this point, the family has met their MOOP, and no further out-of-pocket payment is required.

Beginning in 2016, the vast majority of policies are required to include an embedded MOOP. As a result, the maximum deductible for an individual will be equal to the maximum MOOP for an individual, $8,150 in 2020.

Regardless of the plan or MOOP provisions, without special endorsements or exemptions, ACA plans do not reimburse expenses incurred outside the U.S. This means any plan holder traveling outside this country should explore reasonable options, such as international travel insurance or travel medical insurance, in the event medical expenses may be incurred in a foreign location.

THE AFFORDABLE CARE ACT

The Patient Protection and Affordable Care Act of 2010 and the Health Care and Education Reconciliation Act of 2010 are collectively referred to as The Affordable Care Act (ACA). **Exhibit 3.2** outlines some of the key provisions of the Affordable Care Act.

Exhibit 3.2 | Key Provisions of the Affordable Care Act (ACA)

Year Effective	Key Provisions
2010	• Elimination of discrimination against children with pre-existing conditions. • Elimination of lifetime coverage limits. • Children allowed to remain covered under their parents' insurance until age 26.
2011	• Flexible Spending Accounts (FSAs), Health Savings Accounts (HRAs), and Health Reimbursement Arrangements (HRAs) may no longer reimburse for over-the-counter medications unless prescribed by a physician.*
2013	• Individual taxpayers with more than $200,000 of earned income and families with more than $250,000 of earned income will pay an additional 0.9% in Medicare tax. • Individual taxpayers with AGI above $200,000 and joint filers with AGI above $250,000 will pay a 3.8% Medicare tax on investment income. • Health care FSA contributions limited to $2,500 per year (to be indexed for inflation). • AGI threshold for deducting medical expenses as an itemized deduction increased to 10%.**
2014	• Qualified health plans can no longer deny coverage based on pre-existing conditions. • All individuals must have minimum essential coverage or they will pay a per person penalty of up to 1% of income (minimum amount of $95) in 2014. The penalty increases to 2% of income in 2015 (minimum amount of $325) and 2.5% of income in 2016 and 2017 (minimum amount of $695 indexed for inflation). The penalty for children under age 18 or in college is 50% of the above amounts. The combined family penalty will be limited to 300% of the individual penalty for the year.*** • Employers with 50 or more employees will be required to provide minimum essential coverage for employees or have to pay an additional tax of $2,100 per employee per year (to be indexed for inflation).
2017	• Reduced the tax penalty for the individual mandate to $0 for tax years after 2018. The mandate continues to exist, but without penalty for not following it.

In response to the COVID-19 epidemic of 2020, the Coronavirus Aid, Relief, and Economic Security Act (CARES Act) eliminated the rule requiring a prescription to purchase over-the-counter medicine with HSA, FSA, or HRA funds.

**Through various subsequent Acts Congress reduced this threshold to 7.5% for 2017 - 2020.*

***The tax penalty for the individual mandate was repealed for tax years after 2018.*

The Affordable Care Act (ACA) mandates that individuals obtain health insurance that meets the law's definition of minimum essential coverage. Individuals who do not receive employer-sponsored coverage, and who do not purchase a qualified health insurance contract from a government-sponsored health insurance marketplace or from the private insurance market, were initially subject to a tax penalty. The penalty has been reduced to $0 for tax years after 2018, although the mandate still exists essentially without penalty for not following it.

Essential Benefits as a Result of the Affordable Care Act

To meet the definition of a Qualified Health Plan (QHP), all health insurance plans sold on or off the exchange (exchanges are discussed below) must meet ACA guidelines for cost sharing (deductibles, coinsurances, and maximum out-of-pocket limits) and must cover the following 10 essential health benefits:[4]

1. Outpatient services, such as doctor visits or tests done outside a hospital
2. Emergency services
3. Hospital stays
4. Pregnancy and baby care
5. Mental health and substance abuse services, including behavioral health treatment
6. Prescription drugs, including generic and certain brand-name drugs
7. Rehab and habilitative services (those that help people recover from an accident or injury and those that help people with developmental issues)
8. Lab tests
9. Preventive and wellness services (along with those that help people manage chronic conditions, including chiropractic care)
10. For children only, dental and vision services

The mandate to obtain a health insurance policy with minimum essential coverage began in 2014. Some individuals are, however, exempt from the mandate.[5] Exempt individuals include:

1. Those who are conscientiously opposed to purchasing insurance based on religious grounds
2. Individuals who are members of a health-care sharing ministry (a tax-exempt organization whose members share both religious beliefs and medical expenses that are incurred in accordance with those beliefs)
3. Individuals who are not citizens or nationals of the United States who are either non-resident aliens or are unlawfully present in the United States
4. Incarcerated individuals
5. Individuals with no affordable coverage
6. Members of Indian tribes
7. Household income below filing threshold
8. Individuals with hardship exemption certification

Individuals who are not covered by an employer plan may obtain a qualified health plan (QHP) offered by a health insurer in the individual market, or may purchase a policy from a government-sponsored health insurance marketplace. The ACA refers to policies acquired in either of these two ways as insurance offered in the individual market.

---

4. Some health plans were grandfathered when the ACA rules came into effect and may not cover these 10 essential health benefits, so each policy should be examined carefully.
5. Treas. Reg. §1.5000A-3.

Health Insurance Marketplace

In order to increase health care coverage and affordability, the Affordable Care Act contained a provision for the establishment of Health Insurance Exchanges (also known as Health Insurance Marketplaces or Federal Facilitated Marketplaces (FFMs)). The exchanges are meant to create an organized and competitive market in which individuals may purchase health insurance. The exchanges offer a variety of qualified health insurance plans to choose from and provide information about each plan to help consumers understand and compare their options. Some Marketplaces are operated by states (such as California and Maryland), while others are run for states by the federal government (www.healthcare.gov).[6]

To be eligible to shop for insurance in an exchange, the person must be a resident of the state where that Marketplace is located, must be a U.S. citizen or lawfully present in the U.S., and may not be incarcerated. While anyone meeting these requirements can purchase coverage in the Marketplace, not everyone will qualify for premium tax credits.

Premium Tax Credits

Taxpayers with moderate incomes who purchase health insurance coverage through the Health Insurance Marketplace may be eligible for a Premium Tax Credit. In addition to meeting income guidelines, qualifying health insurance must be purchased through the Health Insurance Marketplace, the insured must be ineligible for coverage through an employer or government plan (including Medicare and Medicaid), the taxpayer must file a joint tax return with their spouse if they are married, and the taxpayer cannot be claimed as a dependent by another taxpayer.

The premium subsidies were designed to assist millions of Americans who could not otherwise afford health insurance. In order to be eligible, the taxpayer's household income for the year must be at least 100 percent but less than 400 percent of the Federal Poverty Level (FPL) for the taxpayer's family size. For example, to determine eligibility for premium tax credits in 2020, the 2019 federal poverty level guidelines are used. A family of two with income between $16,910 and $67,640 was between 100 percent and 400 percent of the FPL, and that family would qualify for a premium tax credit (the lower the income within the range, the higher the credit amount). For a family of four, the range is $25,750 to $103,000. If income is below 100 percent of the FPL the individual or family may qualify for Medicaid, a federal and state program that assists with medical expense coverage for those with limited income and resources.

Those who are eligible to receive the premium credit can choose to have some or all of it paid directly to the insurance company in 2020 in order to reduce current premiums, or to receive the credit when filing their 2020 income tax return in 2021.

Open Enrollment

In general, enrollment in non-group health plan coverage on or off the Marketplace can only be done during the Open Enrollment period. The Open Enrollment period for 2020 was scheduled for November 1, 2019 to December 15, 2019, with an effective date of January 1, 2020.[7] Limiting enrollment to certain periods of time helps to at least minimally mitigate the risk of adverse selection (people enrolling in

---

6. https://www.healthcare.gov/marketplace-in-your-state/
7. Some states may offer extended open enrollment periods.

health insurance after they already know they are in need of expensive care), which is likely to occur since insurers are no longer permitted to deny coverage based on medical underwriting.

Generally, once the open enrollment period has ended, individuals and families will not be able to enroll in on or off Marketplace health plans until the next open enrollment period. An exception is available, however, if certain changes in circumstances occur during the year. In that case, there will be a special 60-day opportunity, called a special enrollment period (SEP), to enroll in health plans on or off the Marketplace outside of the open enrollment period. Events that may trigger the special enrollment opportunity include:

- Loss of eligibility for other coverage such as loss of employer provided coverage due to termination of employment or a student's loss of student health coverage due to graduation. There is, however, no special enrollment period granted if health insurance is lost due to the insured not paying his premiums.
- Addition of a dependent, such as a spouse upon marriage or the birth of a child. No special enrollment period will be granted due to pregnancy, however.
- Divorce or legal separation.
- Loss of dependent status, such as a child covered under a parent's plan reaching age 26.
- Moving to another state or outside of the health plan's service area.
- Exhaustion of COBRA coverage (discussed later in this chapter). Note, however, that simply choosing not to pay COBRA premiums any longer does not trigger a special enrollment period. If a client decides that COBRA premiums are too expensive, he or she will need to stay on COBRA until the next Marketplace open enrollment period begins. Only exhaustion of COBRA benefits triggers the special enrollment period.
- For those enrolled in a Marketplace plan, income increases or decreases large enough to change the individual's or family's eligibility for subsidies. Beginning in 2020, those who purchased a policy outside of the exchange at least 60 days prior to a decrease in income making them eligible for the premium tax credit or subsidies will also have a SEP available to change to a plan purchased through the Marketplace allowing them to receive the premium tax credit or subsidy.[8]

Comparing Policies

One of the goals of the ACA and the health insurance marketplace is to make it easy to compare various health plans. One item of comparison will, of course, be costs. Plans offered on or off the exchange may be managed care plans (discussed later in this chapter), so a comparison of doctors, hospitals, care facilities, and pharmacies who are participating providers should also be considered, along with how any medications that are taken regularly are treated under each plan. Every plan sold in the Marketplace is required to provide a link on the Marketplace web site so that consumers are able to search the plan's health provider directory to find out whether their health providers are included.

Each qualified health plan will also provide information regarding deductibles, copays, co-insurance, and maximum out-of-pocket costs. Preventive health services must be covered entirely with no cost to the insured.

---

8. This new SEP is optional for state-run exchanges. CFR 155.420 (d)(6)(v).

Summary of Benefits and Coverage (SBC)

The ACA requires that all QHPs provide a copy (in print or electronic form) of a Summary of Benefits and Coverage (SBC) by the first day of any open enrollment period (see **Exhibit 3.3 | Summary of Benefits and Coverage Completed Example**). This Summary is intended to make it easier for those shopping for health insurance to understand and compare health plan choices. The SBC is required to contain the following elements:

- A description of the coverage, including the cost-sharing, for each category of benefits
- The exceptions, reductions, or limitations on coverage
- The cost-sharing provisions of the coverage, including deductible, coinsurance, and copayment obligations
- Renewability and continuation of coverage provisions
- A coverage facts label or coverage examples (common benefits) showing scenarios for having a baby (normal delivery) or for managing Type 2 diabetes (routine maintenance, well-controlled)
- A statement that the SBC is only a summary and that the plan document, policy, or certificate of insurance should be consulted to determine the governing contractual provisions of the coverage
- A contact number to call with questions and an Internet web address where a copy of the actual individual coverage policy or group certificate of coverage can be reviewed
- An Internet address (or other contact information) for obtaining a list of the network providers, an Internet address where an individual may find more information about the prescription drug coverage under the plan or coverage, and an Internet address where an individual may review the Uniform Glossary, and a disclosure that paper copies of the Uniform Glossary are available
- A uniform format (four double-sided pages in length, and 12-point font)

Exhibit 3.3 | Summary of Benefits and Coverage Completed Example

Summary of Benefits and Coverage: What this Plan Covers & What You Pay for Covered Services

Insurance Company 1: Plan Option 1

Coverage Period: 01/01/2022-12/31/2022

Coverage for: Family | Plan Type: PPO

> ⚠ The Summary of Benefits and Coverage (SBC) document will help you choose a health <u>plan</u>. The SBC shows you how you and the <u>plan</u> would share the cost for covered health care services. NOTE: Information about the cost of this <u>plan</u> (called the <u>premium</u>) will be provided **separately. This is only a summary.** For more information about your coverage, or to get a copy of the complete terms of coverage, [insert contact information]. For general definitions of common terms, such as <u>allowed amount</u>, <u>balance billing</u>, <u>coinsurance</u>, <u>copayment</u>, <u>deductible</u>, <u>provider</u>, or other <u>underlined</u> terms, see the Glossary. You can view the Glossary at www.[insert].com or call 1-800-[insert] to request a copy.

Important Questions	Answers	Why This Matters:
What is the overall <u>deductible</u>?	$500 / individual or $1,000 / family	Generally, you must pay all of the costs from <u>providers</u> up to the <u>deductible</u> amount before this <u>plan</u> begins to pay. If you have other family members on the <u>plan</u>, each family member must meet their own individual <u>deductible</u> until the total amount of <u>deductible</u> expenses paid by all family members meets the overall family <u>deductible</u>.
Are there services covered before you meet your <u>deductible</u>?	Yes. <u>Preventive care</u> and primary care services are covered before you meet your <u>deductible</u>.	This <u>plan</u> covers some items and services even if you haven't yet met the <u>deductible</u> amount. But a <u>copayment</u> or <u>coinsurance</u> may apply. For example, this <u>plan</u> covers certain <u>preventive services</u> without <u>cost sharing</u> and before you meet your <u>deductible</u>. See a list of covered preventive services at https://www.healthcare.gov/coverage/preventive-care-benefits/.
Are there other <u>deductibles</u> for specific services?	Yes. $300 for <u>prescription drug coverage</u> and $300 for occupational therapy services. There are no other specific deductibles.	You must pay all of the costs for these services up to the specific <u>deductible</u> amount before this <u>plan</u> begins to pay for these services.
What is the <u>out-of-pocket limit</u> for this <u>plan</u>?	For <u>network providers</u> $2,500 individual / $5,000 family; for <u>out-of-network</u> providers $4,000 individual / $8,000 family	The <u>out-of-pocket limit</u> is the most you could pay in a year for covered services. If you have other family members in this <u>plan</u>, they have to meet their own <u>out-of-pocket limits</u> until the overall family <u>out-of-pocket limit</u> has been met.
What is not included in the <u>out-of-pocket limit</u>?	<u>Copayments</u> for certain services, <u>premiums</u>, <u>balance-billing</u> charges, and health care this <u>plan</u> doesn't cover.	Even though you pay these expenses, they don't count toward the <u>out-of-pocket limit</u>.
Will you pay less if you use a <u>network provider</u>?	Yes. See www.[insert].com or call 1-800-[insert] for a list of <u>network providers</u>.	This <u>plan</u> uses a <u>provider</u> <u>network</u>. You will pay less if you use a <u>provider</u> in the <u>plan's</u> <u>network</u>. You will pay the most if you use an <u>out-of-network provider</u>, and you might receive a bill from a <u>provider</u> for the difference between the <u>provider's</u> charge and what your <u>plan</u> pays (<u>balance billing</u>). Be aware, your <u>network provider</u> might use an <u>out-of-network provider</u> for some services (such as lab work). Check with your <u>provider</u> before you get services.

(DT - OMB control number: 1545-0047/Expiration Date: 12/31/2019)(DOL - OMB control number: 1210-0147/Expiration date: 5/31/2022)
(HHS - OMB control number: 0938-1146/Expiration date: 10/31/2022)

Page 1 of 5

Summary of Benefits and Coverage Completed Example (Continued)

Important Questions	Answers	Why This Matters:
Do you need a referral to see a specialist?	Yes.	This plan will pay some or all of the costs to see a specialist for covered services but only if you have a referral before you see the specialist.

⚠️ All **copayment** and **coinsurance** costs shown in this chart are after your **deductible** has been met, if a **deductible** applies.

Common Medical Event	Services You May Need	What You Will Pay		Limitations, Exceptions, & Other Important Information
		Network Provider (You will pay the least)	Out-of-Network Provider (You will pay the most)	
If you visit a health care provider's office or clinic	Primary care visit to treat an injury or illness	$35 copay/office visit and 20% coinsurance for other outpatient services; deductible does not apply	40% coinsurance	None
	Specialist visit	$50 copay/visit	40% coinsurance	Preauthorization is required. If you don't get preauthorization, benefits could be reduced by 50% of the total cost of the service.
	Preventive care/screening/ immunization	No charge	40% coinsurance	You may have to pay for services that aren't preventive. Ask your provider if the services needed are preventive. Then check what your plan will pay for.
If you have a test	Diagnostic test (x-ray, blood work)	$10 copay/test	40% coinsurance	None
	Imaging (CT/PET scans, MRIs)	$50 copay/test	40% coinsurance	
If you need drugs to treat your illness or condition More information about prescription drug coverage is available at www.[insert].com	Generic drugs (Tier 1)	$10 copay/prescription (retail & mail order)	40% coinsurance	Covers up to a 30-day supply (retail subscription); 31-90 day supply (mail order prescription).
	Preferred brand drugs (Tier 2)	$30 copay/prescription (retail & mail order)	40% coinsurance	
	Non-preferred brand drugs (Tier 3)	40% coinsurance	60% coinsurance	
	Specialty drugs (Tier 4)	50% coinsurance	70% coinsurance	
If you have outpatient surgery	Facility fee (e.g., ambulatory surgery center)	$100/day copay	40% coinsurance	Preauthorization is required. If you don't get preauthorization, benefits could be reduced by 50% of the total cost of the service.
	Physician/surgeon fees	20% coinsurance	40% coinsurance	50% coinsurance for anesthesia.

[* For more information about limitations and exceptions, see the plan or policy document at [www.insert.com].]

Summary of Benefits and Coverage Completed Example Continued

Common Medical Event	Services You May Need	What You Will Pay		Limitations, Exceptions, & Other Important Information
		Network Provider (You will pay the least)	Out-of-Network Provider (You will pay the most)	
If you need immediate medical attention	Emergency room care	20% coinsurance	20% coinsurance	None
	Emergency medical transportation	20% coinsurance	20% coinsurance	
	Urgent care	$30 copay/visit	40% coinsurance	
If you have a hospital stay	Facility fee (e.g., hospital room)	20% coinsurance	40% coinsurance	Preauthorization is required. If you don't get preauthorization, benefits could be reduced by 50% of the total cost of the service.
	Physician/surgeon fees	20% coinsurance	40% coinsurance	50% coinsurance for anesthesia.
If you need mental health, behavioral health, or substance abuse services	Outpatient services	$35 copay/office visit and 20% coinsurance for other outpatient services	40% coinsurance	None
	Inpatient services	20% coinsurance	40% coinsurance	
If you are pregnant	Office visits	20% coinsurance	40% coinsurance	Cost sharing does not apply for preventive services. Depending on the type of services, a coinsurance may apply. Maternity care may include tests and services described elsewhere in the SBC (i.e., ultrasound).
	Childbirth/delivery professional services	20% coinsurance	40% coinsurance	
	Childbirth/delivery facility services	20% coinsurance	40% coinsurance	
If you need help recovering or have other special health needs	Home health care	20% coinsurance	40% coinsurance	60 visits/year
	Rehabilitation services	20% coinsurance	40% coinsurance	60 visits/year. Includes physical therapy, speech therapy, and occupational therapy.
	Habilitation services	20% coinsurance	40% coinsurance	
	Skilled nursing care	20% coinsurance	40% coinsurance	60 visits/calendar year
	Durable medical equipment	20% coinsurance	40% coinsurance	Excludes vehicle modifications, home modifications, exercise, and bathroom equipment.
	Hospice services	20% coinsurance	40% coinsurance	Preauthorization is required. If you don't get preauthorization, benefits could be reduced by 50% of the total cost of the service.
If your child needs dental or eye care	Children's eye exam	$35 copay/visit	Not covered	Coverage limited to one exam/year.
	Children's glasses	20% coinsurance	Not covered	Coverage limited to one pair of glasses/year.
	Children's dental check-up	No charge	Not covered	None

[* For more information about limitations and exceptions, see the plan or policy document at [www.insert.com].]

Page 3 of 5

Summary of Benefits and Coverage Completed Example Continued

Excluded Services & Other Covered Services:

Services Your <u>Plan</u> Generally Does NOT Cover (Check your policy or <u>plan</u> document for more information and a list of any other <u>excluded services</u>.)		
• Cosmetic surgery • Dental care (Adult) • Infertility treatment	• Long-term care • Non-emergency care when traveling outside the U.S. • Private-duty nursing	• Routine eye care (Adult) • Routine foot care

Other Covered Services (Limitations may apply to these services. This isn't a complete list. Please see your <u>plan</u> document.)		
• Acupuncture (if prescribed for rehabilitation purposes) • Bariatric surgery	• Chiropractic care • Hearing aids	• Weight loss programs

Your Rights to Continue Coverage: There are agencies that can help if you want to continue your coverage after it ends. The contact information for those agencies is: [insert State, HHS, DOL, and/or other applicable agency contact information]. Other coverage options may be available to you, too, including buying individual insurance coverage through the <u>Health Insurance</u> <u>Marketplace</u>. For more information about the <u>Marketplace</u>, visit <u>www.HealthCare.gov</u> or call 1-800-318-2596.

Your Grievance and Appeals Rights: There are agencies that can help if you have a complaint against your <u>plan</u> for a denial of a <u>claim</u>. This complaint is called a <u>grievance</u> or <u>appeal</u>. For more information about your rights, look at the explanation of benefits you will receive for that medical <u>claim</u>. Your <u>plan</u> documents also provide complete information on how to submit a <u>claim</u>, <u>appeal</u>, or a <u>grievance</u> for any reason to your <u>plan</u>. For more information about your rights, this notice, or assistance, contact: [insert applicable contact information from instructions].

Does this plan provide Minimum Essential Coverage? Yes.
<u>Minimum Essential Coverage</u> generally includes <u>plans</u>, <u>health insurance</u> available through the <u>Marketplace</u> or other individual market policies, Medicare, Medicaid, CHIP, TRICARE, and certain other coverage. If you are eligible for certain types of <u>Minimum Essential Coverage</u>, you may not be eligible for the <u>premium tax credit</u>.

Does this plan meet the Minimum Value Standards? Yes.
If your <u>plan</u> doesn't meet the <u>Minimum Value Standards</u>, you may be eligible for a <u>premium tax credit</u> to help you pay for a <u>plan</u> through the <u>Marketplace</u>.

Language Access Services:

[Spanish (Español): Para obtener asistencia en Español, llame al [insert telephone number].]

[Tagalog (Tagalog): Kung kailangan ninyo ang tulong sa Tagalog tumawag sa [insert telephone number].]

[Chinese (中文): 如果需要中文的帮助，请拨打这个号码[insert telephone number].]

[Navajo (Dine): Dinek'ehgo shika at'ohwol ninisingo, kwiijigo holne' [insert telephone number].]

> *To see examples of how this **plan** might cover costs for a sample medical situation, see the next section.*

PRA Disclosure Statement: According to the Paperwork Reduction Act of 1995, no persons are required to respond to a collection of information unless it displays a valid OMB control number. The valid OMB control number for this information collection is **0938-1146**. The time required to complete this information collection is estimated to average **0.08** hours per response, including the time to review instructions, search existing data resources, gather the data needed, and complete and review the information collection. If you have comments concerning the accuracy of the time estimate(s) or suggestions for improving this form, please write to: CMS, 7500 Security Boulevard, Attn: PRA Reports Clearance Officer, Mail Stop C4-26-05, Baltimore, Maryland 21244-1850.

[* For more information about limitations and exceptions, see the <u>plan</u> or policy document at [www.insert.com].]   Page 4 of 5

Summary of Benefits and Coverage Completed Example Continued

About these Coverage Examples:

 This is not a cost estimator. Treatments shown are just examples of how this plan might cover medical care. Your actual costs will be different depending on the actual care you receive, the prices your providers charge, and many other factors. Focus on the cost-sharing amounts (deductibles, copayments and coinsurance) and excluded services under the plan. Use this information to compare the portion of costs you might pay under different health plans. Please note these coverage examples are based on self-only coverage.

Peg is Having a Baby (9 months of in-network pre-natal care and a hospital delivery)		**Managing Joe's Type 2 Diabetes** (a year of routine in-network care of a well-controlled condition)		**Mia's Simple Fracture** (in-network emergency room visit and follow up care)	
■ The plan's overall deductible	$500	■ The plan's overall deductible	$500	■ The plan's overall deductible	$500
■ Specialist copayment	$50	■ Specialist copayment	$50	■ Specialist copayment	$50
■ Hospital (facility) coinsurance	20%	■ Hospital (facility) coinsurance	20%	■ Hospital (facility) coinsurance	20%
■ Other coinsurance	20%	■ Other coinsurance	20%	■ Other coinsurance	20%

This EXAMPLE event includes services like:	**This EXAMPLE event includes services like:**	**This EXAMPLE event includes services like:**
Specialist office visits *(prenatal care)*	Primary care physician office visits *(including disease education)*	Emergency room care *(including medical supplies)*
Childbirth/Delivery Professional Services	Diagnostic tests *(blood work)*	Diagnostic test *(x-ray)*
Childbirth/Delivery Facility Services	Prescription drugs	Durable medical equipment *(crutches)*
Diagnostic tests *(ultrasounds and blood work)*	Durable medical equipment *(glucose meter)*	Rehabilitation services *(physical therapy)*
Specialist visit *(anesthesia)*		

Total Example Cost	**$12,700**	**Total Example Cost**	**$5,600**	**Total Example Cost**	**$2,800**
In this example, Peg would pay:		**In this example, Joe would pay:**		**In this example, Mia would pay:**	
Cost Sharing		*Cost Sharing*		*Cost Sharing*	
Deductibles	$500	Deductibles*	$800	Deductibles*	$500
Copayments	$200	Copayments	$900	Copayments	$200
Coinsurance	$1,800	Coinsurance	$100	Coinsurance	$400
What isn't covered		*What isn't covered*		*What isn't covered*	
Limits or exclusions	$60	Limits or exclusions	$20	Limits or exclusions	$0
The total Peg would pay is	**$2,560**	**The total Joe would pay is**	**$1,820**	**The total Mia would pay is**	**$1,100**

Note: These numbers assume the patient does not participate in the plan's wellness program. If you participate in the plan's wellness program, you may be able to reduce your costs. For more information about the wellness program, please contact: [insert].
*Note: This plan has other deductibles for specific services included in this coverage example. See "Are there other deductibles for specific services?" row above.

The plan would be responsible for the other costs of these EXAMPLE covered services.

https://www.dol.gov/agencies/ebsa/laws-and-regulations/laws/affordable-care-act/for-employers-and-advisers/summary-of-benefits

Metal Tiers

To simplify comparisons of qualified health plans (QHPs), plans are categorized by "metal" tiers, Bronze, Silver, Gold, or Platinum, as follows:

1. Bronze Plan - a plan that pays the actuarial equivalent of 60% of the estimated costs of health services.
2. Silver Plan - a plan that pays the actuarial equivalent of 70% of the estimated costs of health services.
3. Gold Plan - a plan that pays the actuarial equivalent of 80% of the estimated costs of health services.
4. Platinum Plan - a plan that pays the actuarial equivalent of 90% of the estimated costs of health services.

Exhibit 3.4 | Insurer and Insured Cost Sharing by Metal Category

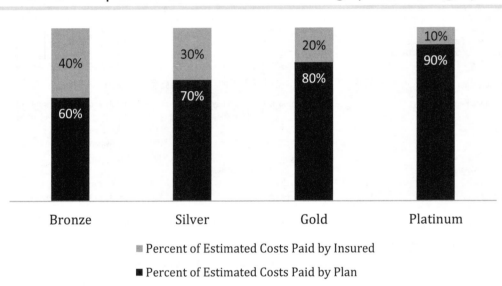

As plans move from Bronze to Platinum, the premiums increase due to the incremental risks that are transferred to the insurance company offering the package. Bronze plans have the highest cost sharing, which means the insured will pay a higher portion of any health care bills. The cost sharing amount in Silver plans will be a bit lower for the insured than Bronze plans. Gold plans tend to have even lower cost sharing, and Platinum plans have the lowest deductibles, copays, and other costs to the insured. Low-income taxpayers may qualify for a reduction in the cost of obtaining required health insurance through the premium assistance tax credit discussed previously, and, if they purchase a Silver plan, they may qualify for reduced cost-sharing expenses. Premium tax credits and reduced cost sharing are only available for policies purchased directly from the health care marketplace.

A good place to start in selecting a plan is to have the client request records of past treatment from her doctors (some doctors make this information available to patients online under a secure patient account) to determine frequency and level of use. While the past does not guarantee similar results for the future, clients with ongoing health issues will be better able to assess which plan will provide the necessary benefits with a cost-sharing structure that fits the client's budget.

Catastrophic Plans

Catastrophic plans may also be offered to individuals under the age of 30 and individuals who are exempt from the individual mandate. This includes individuals qualifying for hardship exemptions, including those whose plans have been canceled and who are unable to find another plan that is affordable. A catastrophic plan must be designed so that it provides the essential health benefits listed above, but provides no benefits for any plan year until the individual's share of the cost has matched the out-of-pocket limits for HSAs (excluding coverage for preventive health services; HSAs are discussed later in this chapter). In addition, coverage must be provided for at least three primary care visits.

Marketplace vs Non-Marketplace

The ACA created the Marketplace and gave consumers the option to purchase coverage in a manner similar to the group plans discussed later in this chapter. Some of the basic features of plans within the Marketplace are outlined in **Exhibit 3.5**.

Exhibit 3.5 | Basic Features of Marketplace Plans

- Plans must provide comprehensive essential benefits
- Coverage cannot be denied because of pre-existing conditions
- Rates cannot be increased on an individual basis
- Preventive services are automatically covered with no additional out-of-pocket cost to the insured beyond the premium

Consumers still have the option to buy coverage outside of the Health Insurance Marketplace, but in doing so, may face a different cost and benefit environment. One of the major differences is that non-Marketplace coverage does not provide premium tax credits or cost-sharing assistance. This can be a significant factor for people who meet the income limits (income between 100 percent and 400 percent of the federal poverty level for tax credits; income between 100 percent and 250 percent for cost-sharing assistance).

The four metal plan tiers (bronze, silver, gold, and platinum) are available within or outside the Marketplace Exchanges. Regardless of the tier, consumers may have greater choice of provider networks when they get coverage using non-Marketplace options, which may provide a strong reason to look outside the Marketplace. That said, each of the tiers must meet the ACA essential health benefit requirements. Policies purchased through private insurers (i.e., non-Marketplace) may have at least slightly higher premiums, but may also provide additional provider options. The decision to look inside or outside the Marketplace can impact consumer satisfaction and potential expense. However, knowing the options will help the planner guide clients as they make those decisions.

Attempting to predict future health care needs for a client who has always enjoyed good health may be a bit daunting, but knowing and understanding the health care plan's maximum out-of-pocket expenses enables a planner to evaluate a best-case scenario, a worst-case scenario (maximum possible loss), and a most-likely (maximum probable) scenario. This analysis will then provide guidelines for emergency fund accumulation and/or contributions to Health Savings Accounts (HSAs, discussed later in this chapter).

GROUP HEALTH INSURANCE

Group health insurance is the most common method of obtaining health insurance today for working adults. Most working individuals obtain their health insurance coverage by participating in their employer's group health insurance plans. Self-employed individuals with employees may offer a group health insurance plan as well to attract and retain qualified employees.

The ACA requires large employers (an employer that, at any time during the year, employs at least 50 people) to provide a minimum level of health insurance coverage to employees or face significant tax penalties. Small employers (those employing fewer than 50 workers at all times during the year) are encouraged by means of tax credits to provide health insurance to their employees.

Medical expense insurance as an employee benefit is usually highly valued by employees and their families. The high cost of medical treatment makes a health plan an important benefit for an employer to offer to attract and retain employees. The tax advantages to employers and employees make the employer-paid plan a cost-effective way to provide the coverage.

The most attractive feature of group health insurance is the ability to obtain coverage at a reasonable **premium**. Underwriting a large group of individuals permits the insurer to spread the claims risk among the pool of participants. Having a large group of participants also spreads the administrative costs of the plan across many people. Both of these factors contribute to lower premiums for group insurance when compared to individual health insurance policies.

Eligibility

To be eligible to purchase group health insurance, an individual has to be affiliated with a group that is covered by a group health insurance policy. Typically, all individuals who are employed on a full-time basis (or are members of a qualifying group) at a company that provides group health coverage are eligible to participate in the group plan. Sometimes non-employer groups provide coverage for their members as well. Common examples are local Chambers of Commerce (which may offer a group plan that can cover the employees of all member companies), labor unions, and professional associations (such as the American Bar Association or the American Institute of Certified Public Accountants). Individuals who obtain health insurance through the government insurance marketplace are also purchasing a form of group insurance, although insurance sold through the health insurance marketplaces is referred to as insurance offered in the individual market.

Features of Group Health Insurance

Group policies are underwritten based on the average age of the group, but a higher premium may be charged for those insured who use tobacco products. Group contracts typically cover most full-time employees. This coverage helps prevent adverse selection risk for the insurer, which is the risk that healthy members of the group will opt out of coverage, leaving only those with greater expected health care needs covered in the plan. Unlike the situation with employer group insurance plans, which can minimize adverse selection by requiring all employees to be eligible for the plan, the government marketplace health plans, which allow individuals to "opt in," may pose greater adverse selection risk.

The employer typically enrolls all eligible employees in the plan, and pays some or all of the premiums for coverage. Many insurance carriers require at least some contribution from the employer. When the employee must pay part of the health insurance costs, those costs are typically paid through payroll deduction. Since the employer shoulders a large part of the administrative burden by enrolling employees and paying premiums, part of the administrative cost savings realized by the insurer can be passed on to the employer in the form of lower group-health insurance premiums.

Types of Group Health Insurance

There are two primary types of group health insurance:

1. Group basic medical insurance
2. Group major medical insurance

When the features of these plans are combined into one policy, the policy is a group comprehensive major medical insurance plan.

Group Basic Medical Insurance

Historically, group basic medical insurance covered hospital, physician, and surgical bills, but typically had low policy limits. Due to the low policy limits, group basic medical coverage was often used in conjunction with group major medical insurance. However, today, the Affordable Care Act prohibits health plans from putting annual or lifetime dollar limits on most benefits so group basic medical insurance on a stand alone basis will not meet the requirements of minimum essential coverage under The Affordable Care Act.

Group Major Medical Insurance

Group major medical insurance coverage typically supplemented basic medical coverage by paying for a wider array of services and, traditionally, by increasing policy maximums. As as result of the Affordable Care Act, lifetime maximums are no longer permitted. Sometimes these policies are referred to as group supplemental insurance plans.

Group Comprehensive Major Medical Insurance

The vast majority of group plans are comprehensive major medical insurance plans which combine the benefits of basic medical coverage and major medical coverage and are simply referred to as health insurance plans. Typically, plan deductibles are relatively low, and the employee may be required to make a copayment when receiving services. After the plan deductible has been met for the year, the insurance company usually pays 80 percent of the cost of health care and the participant pays the remaining 20 percent until a maximum annual out-of-pocket limit is reached. Once the annual out-of-pocket maximum is reached, the insurance company pays 100 percent of the costs of care for the remainder of that year. There are various ranges of coinsurance between the insurer and the insured, including 60/40, 70/30, 80/20 and 90/10.

Example 3.8

Dylan is a participant in his employer's group comprehensive major medical insurance plan. The plan has a $200 deductible and a $1,500 out-of-pocket maximum. If Dylan is injured in an accident and his medical costs total $2,000, Dylan will have to pay the first $200 to cover the deductible and will pay $360 (20% of the remaining $1,800 in medical costs) for a total of $560. The plan will pay the remaining portion of the cost or a total of $1,440. The next time Dylan needs medical attention within the same year, he will not have to pay another deductible since the deductible has to be satisfied only once per year, but he will pay 20% of the costs until his total out-of-pocket costs for the year (including the deductible) are $1,500. In other words, Dylan will have to pay a maximum of $940 more for the year before the insurer pays 100% of future costs for the year.

Traditionally, comprehensive major medical plans were not favored by employees, since they resulted in the employee paying up to the out-of-pocket maximum each year. Many employees and unions favored first-dollar-pay type plans, in which the employee would make a small copayment (of, perhaps $5 or $10) each time they visited a physician, and the insurance company would pay for the balance of the bill. First-dollar-pay type plans have higher premiums than comprehensive plans due to the increase in benefit payments made by the insurance company, and the increased administrative costs incurred. More recently, however, with the creation of Health Savings Accounts (HSAs) and the new federal requirements concerning health insurance coverage for employees, high deductible plans have enjoyed a renaissance as a means to provide adequate healthcare coverage while cutting premium costs for employers. Additional details regarding the various types of policies in the major medical insurance category are discussed later in this chapter.

The Mechanics of Group Health Insurance

When offering group medical insurance to employees, the employer does have some flexibility regarding which employees are eligible for coverage. For example, coverage might only be offered to full-time employees (excluding part-time) who have worked for the company for at least 30 days (the probationary period whereby the company has the opportunity to ensure that the employment relationship is likely to last long-term before any employee benefits are offered).

Most large employers will allow the employee to choose from multiple types of policies with various choices of deductibles and coinsurance amounts. Employees may also be permitted to choose coverage for self-only, self plus spouse, or family (covering the employee, spouse, and all dependents). These selections typically must be made during the group's open enrollment period; for example, employees may have to choose their benefits for the upcoming year during October of the current year. When new dependents are added during the year (for example a child is born), there will be a limited time period, usually 30 days, following the event to add that dependent, and coverage will commence as of the date the dependent becomes eligible.

Dependent coverage is typically the same as the coverage for the employee, and eligible dependents are the spouse and any children under the age of 26 (including step-children, adopted children, and those born out of wedlock). A child under age 26 can remain on their parent's plan even if the child is married, does not live with the parents, is not financially dependent on the parents, or is eligible to enroll in his or her own employer's plan.

While group plans are not required to offer health benefits to an employee's domestic partner (unmarried same-sex or heterosexual partners), many plans do make the benefits available. Clients involved in domestic partnerships should be advised to check with their human resources department or health plan administrator for benefit availability. Some companies may set requirements such as a minimum time frame (e.g., 12 months) that the couple has been together, or may require proof of financial interdependence (e.g., a copy of a joint lease or joint mortgage).

When a domestic partner (as opposed to a same sex spouse) becomes covered under a plan, there are some federal tax implications that the client should be aware of. If the employer pays any part of the health insurance premium for the domestic partner, the employee will be taxed on that amount. An employee who will be taxed for additional premiums may wish to have increased taxes withheld from their paycheck to avoid a larger tax bill at the end of the year. When a domestic partner does not have health insurance coverage available through their own employer, paying the additional taxes for dependent coverage through the employee's group plan is still likely to be more cost efficient than obtaining an individual policy. If the domestic partner does have coverage available through their own employer, then the planner will need to help evaluate the coverage offered under each group plan versus the dependent coverage of a domestic partner.

Since the overturn of Section 3 of the Defense of Marriage Act (DOMA) in 2013, same-sex married couples are treated the same as heterosexual married couples under federal tax rules. When a same-sex spouse is covered under an employer-provided health insurance plan, the additional premiums paid for that coverage may be paid on a pre-tax basis, the same as for a heterosexual spouse.

Coordination of Benefits
When an individual is covered under more than one group plan, the coordination of benefits (COB) provisions apply to determine which policy is the primary payer of any claims, and which policy is the secondary payer. These provisions are designed to ensure that the total benefits paid from all policies do not exceed 100 percent of the allowable expenses incurred.

While coordination of benefits provisions may vary, the approach proposed in the model legislation drafted by the National Association of Insurance Commissioners (NAIC) is frequently used. States typically adopt some or all of the model legislation. Some of the more common coordination provisions are described below. Note that in each case, the plan designated as the primary plan will pay benefits without regard to other insurance.
- A plan that covers the person as an employee is primary to a plan that covers the person as a dependent. For example, husband and wife both have health insurance coverage through their employers that covers both husband and wife. The plan through the husband's employer is primary for him and secondary for the wife. The plan through the wife's employer is primary for her and secondary for her husband.
- The plan covering a person as an active employee, or as a dependent of, an active employee is primary to a plan covering the person as a retired or laid-off employee.
- A plan covering a person as an employee, retiree, or dependent of an employee or retiree is primary to COBRA coverage. (COBRA coverage is a continuation of group insurance following termination of employment and is discussed later in this chapter).
- A person covered as a dependent of an active employee, who also has retiree coverage from their previous employer, and is covered under Medicare will have primary coverage as a dependent of an active employee (if the employer has 20 or more employees; if fewer than 20 employees,

Medicare pays first and the employer coverage pays second), Medicare pays second, and then the retiree coverage last (because retiree coverage is meant to supplement Medicare).

- Coverage for dependent children of divorced or separated parents may be determined by court decree. In the absence of a court decree stating otherwise, coverage for dependent children is treated as follows:
  - For a dependent child whose parents are married, or unmarried but living together, the plan of the parent whose birthday (month and day only, not year) is earlier in the calendar year is primary. For example, if the father's birthday is June 6th and mother's birthday is September 2nd, then the father's plan is primary and the mother's plan is secondary.
  - If the dependent child's parents are divorced, separated, or are not living together, and there is no court decree allocating responsibility for the child's health care coverage, then the order of benefits is as follows: the plan covering the custodial parent is primary, followed by the plan covering the custodial parent's spouse, then the plan covering the non-custodial parent, and lastly the plan covering the non-custodial parent's spouse. The custodial parent is the parent awarded custody of the child by a court decree, or in the absence of a court decree, the parent with whom the child resides more than one half of the calendar year.

Example 3.9

Trevon Taylor's employer provides group medical expense insurance covering the family, including his wife, Deja, and their son, Jalen. Deja's employer also provides a group plan covering the family. The plans both have typical coordination of benefits clauses. If Deja and Jalen are injured in an accident and have eligible medical expenses, under typical coordination of benefits clauses, Deja's group plan will pay all of her medical expenses because her policy will be primary. Although she is covered under Trevon's group policy, that dependent coverage for Deja will be secondary. Jalen is covered as a dependent under both policies, so the policy for the employee with the earlier birth date on the calendar will be primary.

Regulation of Employer-Provided Health Insurance

In many cases, the employer offering health insurance coverage will contract with, and pay premiums to, a health insurance company that provides the benefits and administration and also assumes all claims risk. This type of structure is called a fully insured group plan.

Group health insurance is regulated at both the federal and state level. States are primarily responsible for regulating insured group plans, but the Affordable Care Act (ACA) gives the federal government some control over various provisions, such as waiting periods for coverage to begin and certain preventive services the plan is required to cover.

Self-Funded Plans

Some large employers, usually those with at least several hundred or several thousand employees, may choose to self-fund their group health plan by setting aside a pool of money to be used to pay claims of employees as they arise. Since this shifts the risk for paying claims to the employer, many of these plans will choose to partially insure by purchasing a policy, called a stop-loss policy, to cover claims above a certain threshold. Self-insured plans often have a contract with a third-party administrator to handle the administrative functions and claims. For this reason, the employee may not even realize that the plan is self-funded. Self-funded plans are not regulated at the state level, so they do not have to meet requirements imposed by state law when a state mandates coverage for certain medical services or treatments.

Self-funded plans have to meet nondiscrimination rules (under Section 105(h) of the IRC) that are not currently imposed on fully insured plans. Self-funded plans must ensure that the plan does not discriminate in favor of highly compensated individuals (HCIs) in regard to eligibility or benefits. If discrimination does occur, the HCI will be taxed on the excess benefits he or she received from the plan above those received by non-HCIs. For purposes of Section 105(h), a highly compensated individual is one of the top five highest paid officers, a greater than 10 percent shareholder, or in the top 25 percent highest paid employees.

While fully insured health plans do not currently have to meet the same nondiscrimination rules as self-insured plans, fully insured health insurance offered through cafeteria plans must meet the nondiscrimination provisions of cafeteria plans under Section 125 of the tax code. A cafeteria plan is a written plan under which the employee may choose to receive cash as compensation or select from a menu of tax-free fringe benefits. Also worth noting is that the tests for nondiscrimination and definition of highly compensated individual for cafeteria plans are different from those used for self-funded plans.[9]

Summary Plan Descriptions and Summary of Benefits and Coverage

All employer-provided health plans, including both fully insured and self-funded plans, are also federally regulated by the Department of Labor under the Employee Retirement Income Security Act of 1974 (ERISA). ERISA grants employee-participants certain rights, such as the disclosure of important plan information (provided via a Summary Plan Description), timely and fair processing of benefit claims, the right to elect temporary continuance of group health coverage after losing coverage (see COBRA later in this chapter), the right to a certificate evidencing health coverage under the plan, and the right to recover benefits due under the plan.

The Summary Plan Description (SPD) is one of the most important documents for the planner and client to review. The plan administrator is legally required to provide the SPD to participants free of charge. This SPD is the document that tells participants how the plan operates and what benefits are provided, including information about when an employee becomes eligible to participate in the plan, how services and benefits are calculated, and how to file a claim. If, for some reason, the client is unable to obtain a copy of the SPD from the plan's administrator, they can request a copy from the DOL's EBSA (Employee Benefits Security Administration).

Final regulations issued jointly by the Departments of Health and Human Services, Labor, and Treasury (the Agencies) on Feb. 9, 2012, require that, effective September 23, 2012, participants receive a Summary of Benefits and Coverage (SBC) that is presented in clear language and in a uniform format to help consumers to better understand the coverage they have and allow them to compare their coverage options across different types of plans. An example of an SBC is provided in **Exhibit 3.3 | Summary of Benefits and Coverage Completed Example**. In addition employees must also receive a copy of the Uniform Glossary, which provides standard definitions of terms commonly used in health insurance coverage. The SBC does not replace the SPD, but may reference the SPD in its footnotes.

---

9. A detailed description of cafeteria plans and rules is beyond the scope of this textbook, but can be found in Money Education's *Retirement Planning and Employee Benefits* textbook.

Mental Health Parity

The Mental Health Parity and Addiction Equity Act prohibits large group employer-funded plans (covering over 50 employees) from imposing financial requirements (such as copays or deductibles) or treatment limitations on mental health and substance use disorder benefits in a way that is more restrictive than those imposed on other medical benefits.

Family Medical Leave Act (FMLA)

The Family Medical Leave Act allows eligible employees to take unpaid, job-protected leave for certain family and medical reasons. While on leave, the employee can continue group health insurance coverage as if he or she were not on leave.

Eligible employees are entitled to 12 weeks of unpaid leave for the birth of a child, adoption of a child, to care for a family member (spouse, child, or parent) who has a serious health condition, or for a serious health condition that makes the employee unable to perform his or her essential job functions. Twenty-six weeks of leave is available during any 12 month period for the employee to provide care for a covered military service member who is a member of the employee's family (spouse, child, parent).

Tax Advantages of Employer-Provided Health Insurance

As an employee benefit, none offers more tax advantages than health insurance paid for by the employer. When the employer pays all or a portion of the premium, the employer is permitted a tax deduction for the premiums paid (as long as total compensation is reasonable). Although this is an economic benefit to the employee, which typically requires that the employee be taxed on that amount, tax law provides that for health insurance premiums, this economic benefit is not taxable income to the employee.

When the health insurance plan is contributory, meaning employees share in the cost of premiums, the share of premiums paid by employees is typically withheld from their paychecks on a pretax basis. In addition, any benefits received from the plan are also tax-free to the employees. If employees pay their share of the premiums after-tax, then the premiums can be added together with their other qualified medical expenses that were not reimbursed by insurance, and can be deducted as itemized deductions on Schedule A of their income tax returns; however, only the total expenses above 10 percent (reduced to 7.5 percent for 2020 by the SECURE Act) of adjusted gross income will be deductible.

For self-employed individuals (sole proprietors, partners in a partnership, LLC members, and greater-than-2% S-corporation owners) who do not have an employer-provided health plan available through another employer or spouse's employer, premiums paid by the business on behalf of the owner will first be taxable income to the owner, and will then be deductible as an above-the-line tax deduction on the owner's federal income tax return (Form 1040). The deduction for health insurance premiums, however, cannot exceed the earnings from the business (for example, if the business produced a loss for the year, no premium deduction will be permitted). For greater-than-2% S-corp. owner-employees, the premiums will be included as taxable income on the owner-employee's W-2, and are then deducted above-the-line on the Form 1040.

Example 3.10

Raven's employer has set up a health insurance plan, and her employer takes $100 contributions per month from each employee's pay check for the cost of the plan. The total cost of coverage is $5,500 annually for Raven's family. Raven had surgery this year, and the insurer paid $4,000 of the expenses. What are the income tax consequences of the health care expenditures for Raven?

The cost of a health plan paid by the employer is not taxable income to the employee, so Raven does not report income for the employer's payment. The employer can deduct the cost of the health plan, and an employee does not report income for this benefit. The benefits paid by the plan are also not income to Raven. Raven cannot deduct her share of the contributions because they are taken out of her pay on a pre-tax basis. In other words, Raven is not taxed on this income taken out of her pay, so she cannot take a deduction for it.

Health Care Reform and Employer-Provided Coverage

A number of provisions from the Affordable Care Act that apply to group health plans have been implemented. When discussing the rules of the ACA, however, it should also be noted that some plans are considered "grandfathered plans," and portions of the ACA are not applicable to these plans.

Provisions of the Affordable Care Act have benefited insureds by eliminating annual or lifetime limits on essential benefits, by prohibiting preexisting condition exclusions, and by permitting children to remain covered under a parent's policy up to age 26, regardless of whether the child is a dependent of the parent or is a student. Non-grandfathered fully-insured and self-insured plans must also provide coverage for certain preventive services with no coinsurance and no deductible.

In addition, the ACA prescribes maximum out-of-pocket expense limitations. In 2020, the annual limit on out-of-pocket costs is $8,150 for self-only coverage or $16,300 for family coverage. These dollar amounts are increased annually.

The ACA also permits the use of "rewards" under health-contingent wellness programs offered in connection with group health plans. Rewards can come in many forms, but are generally limited to 30 percent of the cost of employee-only coverage, although the maximum permissible reward for wellness programs designed to prevent or reduce tobacco use is 50 percent (in essence, this creates a tobacco premium surcharge of up to 50 percent; the "reward" for not smoking is that you avoid the penalty of a higher premium). If these incentive plans are used, reasonable alternatives must be provided in order to avoid prohibited discrimination. **Example 3.11** illustrates two versions of rewards within health-contingent wellness programs.

Example 3.11

Camila participates in her employer's health-contingent wellness program, which is activity-based. At the beginning of the program, she completed a self-reported Personal Health Assessment (PHA) and a biometric health screening. Based on this information Camila was provided individualized information about her current health and how to improve it, and was able to participate in activities designed to assist her in improving her health behaviors. As a reward for completing the activities in the behavior change campaign, Camila's group health insurance copay for doctor visits was reduced by $20 and her deductible was reduced from $700 to $350.

Camila's brother, Mateo, participates in his employer's health-contingent wellness program, which is outcome-based. Mateo can receive a 30% discount on his health insurance premiums by maintaining a Body Mass Index (BMI) within a certain range, plus an additional 20% discount for not smoking (the total maximum discount permitted when smoking cessation is included is 50%).

Limits on Coverage Delay

For group health plans (including both insured and self-insured plans), the maximum time an otherwise eligible employee can be required to wait before coverage becomes effective is 90 calendar days, following a maximum 30 day orientation period. For example, if the employee begins work on September 15th, the 30 day orientation period ends on October 14th (as measured by adding one month and subtracting one day) and group health insurance coverage must begin no later than January 13th (the 91st day from the end of the orientation period).[10]

Employer Shared Responsibility

On Feb. 10, 2014, the IRS and Treasury issued final regulations on the Employer Shared Responsibility provisions under section 4980H of the Internal Revenue Code. The shared responsibility rules began in 2015 and apply only to employers who employ at least 50 full-time employees or a combination of full-time and part-time employees that is the equivalent of 50 full-time employees. A full-time employee is defined as one who works an average of at least 30 hours per week.

The Employer Shared Responsibility rules require these employers to offer affordable health coverage providing at least a minimum level of coverage to 95 percent or more of full-time employees and their dependents, or the employer will be subject to a shared responsibility payment of $2,570 (for 2020) per full-time employee (minus up to 30); but only if at least one full-time employee receives a premium tax credit for purchasing individual coverage in the Health Insurance Marketplace. Many insurance companies offering employer-provided insurance provide a calculator on their website that can be used to estimate the amount of shared responsibility payments. The majority of businesses will fall below the 50 full-time equivalent employees and will, therefore, not be subject to the Employer Shared Responsibility provisions.

Beginning in 2016, large employers (with 50 or more full-time equivalent employees as defined under the Shared Responsibility provision) are also required to report prior year information regarding coverage offered to full-time employees, including whether the coverage met the minimum value

---

10.https://www.federalregister.gov/documents/2014/06/25/2014-14795/ninety-day-waiting-period-limitation

requirements. These reports must be submitted to the IRS and a statement provided to all full-time employees. Form 1095-B and Form 1095-C must be provided to individual taxpayers no later than January 31st of the following year. Form 1095-B is sent by the insurer and Form 1095-C is sent by the employer; employers with self-insured plans send both forms.

In order to meet the minimum value requirements, the plan must cover at least 60 percent of the total allowed cost of benefits under the plan. In other words, the plan must be designed in such a way that it would be expected to pay at least 60 percent of the total cost of medical services for a standard population, leaving 40 percent or less of the costs to be paid by the employees (the equivalent of a Bronze plan). Thus, if the deductibles, copays, and other out-of-pocket costs for employees were more than 40 percent of the total costs of medical services, the plan would not meet the minimum value requirements. The IRS and Department of Health and Human Services (HHS) have produced a minimum value calculator that employers, insurance companies, third-party administrators, or other entities can use to input plan information such as deductibles and copays and receive a determination as to whether the plan provides minimum value.

Exhibit 3.6 | Employer Shared Responsibility Summary

What is it?	An ACA rule requiring large employers to offer affordable health coverage to at least 95 percent of full-time employees and their dependents.
Who does it apply to?	Employers who employ at least 50 full-time employees (or the equivalent thereof).
Penalty for non-compliance	A shared responsibility payment of $2,570 (for 2020) per full-time employee (minus up to 30); but only if at least one full-time employee receives a premium tax credit for purchasing individual coverage in the Health Insurance Marketplace.
Reporting	Form 1095-B and Form 1095-C.
Minimum value requirements	The plan must be designed in such a way that it would be expected to pay at least 60 percent of the total cost of medical services for a standard population, leaving 40 percent or less of the costs to be paid by the employees (the equivalent of a Bronze plan).

Small Employers

Small employers (those with 50 or fewer full-time employee equivalents) may be eligible to purchase insurance plans through the Small Business Health Options Program (SHOP) Marketplace operating in each state. An FTE Calculator is available to help small employers identify whether they qualify to purchase coverage through SHOP.

The SHOP marketplace was designed to help these small businesses provide health coverage to their employees, with the employer required to cover all full-time employees who work over 30 hours per week on average in order to purchase coverage through SHOP. Due to a large number of cumbersome requirements, SHOP exchanges have not been well-utilized (as of January 1, 2017, only 7,554 employers utilized the SHOP program, covering just 38,749 lives), causing many states to discontinue their SHOP exchanges.[11]

INDIVIDUAL HEALTH INSURANCE

Need for Coverage

When a client does not have health insurance coverage under a government-sponsored program, such as Medicare or the government health insurance marketplace, and does not have access to employer-provided or other group health insurance, the client should consider purchasing an individual health insurance policy.

Premiums on individual health insurance are typically higher than premiums on group health insurance, which may encourage some individuals to self-insure instead of purchasing coverage. Everyone should have, at a minimum, coverage for catastrophic medical expense needs, such as unforeseen major surgery or hospitalization, even if they choose to self-insure for routine medical expenses, such as annual physical exams, tests, and office visits.

≔ *Key Concepts*

1. Describe some of the common exclusions in major medical policies.

2. Describe the inverse relationship between deductibles and premiums.

3. Define out-of-pocket maximum.

4. Describe what medical expense insurance covers, and name the subcategories of it.

Example 3.12

Dermot is a healthy, unemployed individual who does not qualify for participation in any group health insurance plans. The cost of a health insurance plan that pays everything except a small copayment per office visit is prohibitive. Therefore, Dermot decides to self-insure for small recurring costs, and purchase insurance to cover only major, unexpected medical expenses. By choosing a policy that has a high deductible, Dermot can minimize the premium cost of obtaining the insurance protection, while also protecting his other assets should he get sick and need extensive medical treatment.

Subsequent to the passage of the Patient Protection and Affordable Care Act of 2010 and the Health Care and Education Reconciliation Act of 2010, all U.S. citizens and residents are mandated to obtain health insurance, although the tax penalties for failing to comply have been eliminated. As mentioned earlier in this chapter, catastrophic plans may also be offered to individuals under the age of 30 and individuals who are exempt from the individual mandate.

Cost of Individual Policies

Unlike group coverage, which is often subsidized by the employer, a person purchasing an individual health insurance policy will typically be responsible for paying the full premium. He or she will not receive the benefits of the administrative efficiencies that reduce premium costs within a group. The individual health insurance plan is underwritten by taking the applicant's age, geographic location, and tobacco use into consideration. Individual policies sold both in and out of the Marketplace are categorized by the metal tiers and generally must provide the minimum essential coverages discussed previously.

---

11. https://www.federalregister.gov/documents/2018/04/17/2018-07355/patient-protection-and-affordable-care-act-hhs-notice-of-benefit-and-payment-parameters-for-2019.

Eligibility

As with other forms of insurance, in the past individual health insurance could only be obtained if the person seeking coverage was relatively healthy at the time the policy was issued. Those with existing conditions requiring extensive medical treatment traditionally had to pay large premiums to offset the risk that the insurer was undertaking, or the existing condition may have been excluded from the policy. The 2010 health care legislation prohibits exclusions for preexisting conditions on any health insurance policies issued after 2013.

Types of Individual Policies

Major Medical Insurance

Similar to group major medical insurance plans, **individual major medical plans** provide coverage for hospital, physician, and surgeon fees, medications, and durable medical equipment (such as wheelchairs and hospital beds). Routine eye and dental exams are usually not covered under a major medical insurance policy, and the policy often has exclusions for self-inflicted injuries and medical procedures that are purely cosmetic in nature. The coverage provided by major medical policies often differs from carrier to carrier, so it is important to pay attention to the policy terms, coverages, and exclusions when making policy comparisons and selecting coverage. Many carriers, for example, impose maximum charges for various medical procedures or hospital stays, such as a limit of $800 per day for inpatient non-ICU hospital stays, and may also impose additional limits on treatments such as mental health visits.

Exhibit 3.7 | Common Exclusions in Comprehensive Major Medical Policies

• Intentionally self-inflicted injury	• Expenses covered by a government agency
• Expenses incurred outside the U.S. or Canada	• Participating in a riot or rebellion
• Expenses covered by workers' compensation	• Rest cures
• War or any act of war	• Active duty military
• Eyeglasses	• Experimental procedures
• Eye refractions	• Hearing aids
• Dental expenses (unless due to injury)	• Cosmetic surgery (except when necessitated by injuries)
• Routine physical examinations	
• Custodial care	• Alcoholism or drug addiction (limited benefits are sometimes provided)

Historically, the lifetime policy limits per covered person on major medical insurance were often high, such as $1 million. The Affordable Care Act has removed the lifetime cap for all policies issued after September 2010.

The annual **deductible** for a major medical policy can vary from hundreds of dollars to several thousand dollars. If the major medical insurance policy covers a family, the deductible typically applies on a per person, per year basis. There is an inverse relationship between the amount of the deductible and the size of the premium: as the deductible grows, the premium gets lower since many of the first health care expenses encountered during the year will be paid for by the insured, reducing claims-flow and administrative burdens for the insurer.

For comprehensive individual major medical coverage policies, after the deductible amount has been met, the insurance company pays a percentage of the medical costs, and the insured pays the remainder as a **coinsurance** amount. Typical structures for such a policy are 80%/20% or 60%/40%, up to an annual out-of-pocket maximum. The **out-of-pocket-maximum** is the sum of the deductible and the insured's portion of the coinsurance.[12] Family policies will often have an individual deductible and out-of-pocket maximum, as well as a family deductible and out-of-pocket maximum (embedded deductibles and MOOPs).

Once the insured's out-of-pocket expenses, including the deductible and coinsurance amounts, equals the out-of-pocket maximum, the insurance company pays 100 percent of any additional health care costs for that year.

Example 3.13

Randy and Kelly are married and have three children. They are covered by a comprehensive major medical insurance policy with a $250 deductible per person, 80% / 20% coinsurance provision, and an annual out-of-pocket maximum of $2,500. In a softball game this year, Randy slid into second base and dislocated his knee to the point that he needed knee replacement surgery. The surgery cost $25,000. There were no other health care costs incurred this year.

Randy's knee replacement surgery will result in him paying a $250 deductible. Randy must also pay 20% of the cost of the knee surgery in excess of the deductible amount, up to his out-of-pocket maximum of $2,500. Twenty percent of $24,750 equals $4,950, but Randy will only have to pay $2,250 in addition to the $250 deductible, which is the amount that is necessary to bring his total out-of-pocket expenses up to the annual out-of-pocket maximum.

---

12. Out-of-pocket-maximum is the term most insurance policies use to describe the maximum amount an insured will have to pay for a given year. However, some texts use the term, stop-loss, to describe this amount.

Example 3.14

Preston has shoulder surgery in January to repair the tear in his labrum, which he got while working out at cross-fit. His health insurance policy has a $1,000 deductible, an 80/20 coinsurance provision, and an out-of-pocket maximum of $6,250. Assume that his shoulder surgery cost $26,000, including hospital charges and doctor charges. Also assume that he goes to physical therapy (PT) eight times per month for six months. The copayment for PT is $35 per visit. How much does Preston pay for his medical expenses associated with the shoulder surgery?

Preston will pay his total out-of-pocket maximum of $6,250, as follows:
- Deductible $1,000
- 20% of $25,000 = $5,000 ($26,000 - $1,000 deductible)
- PT of $250 / Total PT charges are $1,680 (48 visits x $35) but the out-of-pocket maximum has been reached after Preston pays $250.

The insurance company will cover the remaining costs for the year.

Insurance Company Covers 100% of Costs Above Out-Of-Pocket-Maximum		
Out-Of-Pocket-Maximum = $6,250		
Copayments 1. Primary Care Dr. – $35 per visit 2. Specialists – $50 per visit 3. Urgent Care - $50 per visit 4. Ambulance Service $50 per day	20% Coinsurance Deductible = $1,000	Insurance Company Pays 1. 100% Wellness Visits 2. 80% Coinsurance 3. Other costs, such as certain labs or X-rays

Basic Medical Expense Insurance

Unlike major medical insurance policies, basic medical expense insurance policies only cover specified types of medical expenses and as such, do not meet the requirements for minimal essential coverage under the Affordable Care Act. Basic medical expense insurance may pay for actual expenses incurred when receiving health care, or may pay a lump sum upon the occurrence of some event affecting one's health. In either case, the policy limits are likely to be very low compared with major medical policies. While obtaining basic medical expense insurance is better than having no health insurance at all, planners should recognize that the policy limits may not be sufficient to cover the expenses incurred.

The most common types of basic medical expense insurance include hospital expense insurance, physicians expense insurance, and surgical expense insurance.

Hospital expense coverage, as the name implies, pays for costs of medical care while the insured (or family members, if a family policy) is in the hospital. Amounts billed directly by the hospital are covered, subject to policy limitations, but separately billed items, such as doctor, surgeon, and x-ray fees for services performed outside of a hospital are not covered by a hospital expense policy. Many policies limit coverage to a specified number of days, such as 60, 90, or 180 days.

Physicians expense insurance provides coverage for fees charged by physicians for office visits and tests that are not performed in the hospital (such as blood work, x-rays, and non-surgical procedures).

Surgical expense insurance pays for surgeon's fees when a surgical procedure is not conducted in a hospital. If the surgical procedure was conducted in the hospital, these expenses would be covered by the hospital expense coverage policy.

TYPES OF GROUP AND INDIVIDUAL PLANS

Both group and individual health insurance plans can be written on an indemnity basis (reimbursement) or on a managed care basis.

Indemnity Health Insurance

Indemnity health insurance is also referred to as a traditional health insurance plan or a fee-for-service plan. Indemnity health insurance plans allow participants the benefit of having a wide range of health care practitioners at their disposal. Indemnity plan participants are not limited to a service network system for medical care. Indemnity health insurance is the most flexible type of insurance policy, but participants also pay some of the highest premiums in order to have the flexibility of choosing their own health care providers. Typically, indemnity plans have deductibles and coinsurance for major medical.

> ### ⦂≣ *Key Concepts*
>
> 1. Describe the differences and similarities between an HMO and a PPO.
>
> 2. Explain the reasoning behind the criticism of managed care insurance plans.

Managed Care Insurance

Managed care insurance emerged from a desire to reduce the costs of health care while increasing competition among service providers. When compared to indemnity medical plans, managed care approaches to health care restrict participant choice of health care providers and often require participants to obtain pre-approval from insurance company representatives as a condition of obtaining covered treatment that is not considered emergency care. Companies offering managed care have also been criticized for prohibiting physicians from discussing alternative options of care with the patients, creating an ethical dilemma for the health care provider who is determined to act in the best interest of the patient. Despite their shortcomings, managed care approaches to health insurance have assisted in somewhat containing the cost of medical services over time.

There are four main types of managed care approaches to health insurance coverage:
- Health Maintenance Organization (HMO)
- Preferred Provider Organization (PPO)
- Point-of-Service Plans (POS)
- Exclusive Provider Organization (EPO)

Health Maintenance Organizations (HMOs)

Health Maintenance Organizations (HMOs) were authorized by the HMO Act of 1973. HMOs consist of a group of physicians who provide comprehensive care for their patients and are organized in an effort to control the rising cost of healthcare. HMOs can be for-profit or not-for-profit and can be sponsored by insurance companies, Blue Cross Blue Shield, physicians, hospitals, labor unions, or even consumer groups. HMOs emphasize both cost control and preventive care.

The typical services provided under HMO plans are physician services, outpatient services at a hospital, inpatient health services in a hospital, diagnostic laboratory services, home health services, mental health care, and perhaps even services for such items as vision care and dental care. HMOs emphasize preventive medical care so that illnesses and diseases may be detected and treated early, avoiding higher costs later on. The insured pays a flat monthly premium to the HMO for all covered services from participating physicians and perhaps also a small copayment, such as $25 per visit.

HMOs operate under three basic types of plans: staff practice plan, group practice approach, and the independent physicians contract.

- **Staff practice plan:** Salaried doctors and other medical care professionals are employees located in a common facility owned by the HMO. Insureds under the HMO plan thus go to this facility for their medical care.
- **Group practice type of HMO:** There is usually one site where all of the medical care providers are located, but this site is owned by the medical care providers, rather than by the HMO. Also, the medical care providers usually are not salaried employees of the HMO. Under the individual practice association type of HMO, individual medical care practitioners are members of the plan and work out of their own offices.
- **Independent Physicians Contract:** The independent physicians contract with the HMO to serve HMO plan participants, receiving a flat annual fee, called a capitation fee, for agreeing to provide medical service for each HMO member, whether or not the member uses them as a **primary care physician** or receives services from them. The flat capitation fee is paid, regardless of the extent or complexity of the service provided to a patient, thus serving to discourage physicians from providing unnecessary medical treatment. Some HMOs combine the features of more than one of these basic types of plans.

One of the most important disadvantages of an HMO is the limited range of choices that the plan participant has as to where he or she may receive medical care. In most circumstances, the hospital or the physician must be a member of the HMO in order for the plan participant to be eligible for medical care from that provider (except for cases of true emergencies). Those insured under an HMO will typically have a primary care physician (PCP) who serves as gatekeeper, making referrals for specialist care when the PCP deems it necessary. The advantage of having a primary care physician, however, is coordination of care. The PCP serves as the quarterback calling the plays on the field and all of the team members (physicians and specialists) work as one unit to provide efficient care and share information about care needs.

Some HMOs permit their members to obtain service outside of the insurance company's provider network, but payments for services performed by an out-of-network provider will typically be smaller than claims allowed for similar services provided within the network, which effectively increases the cost to the participant. Typically, however, the HMO does not cover care received out-of-network as a result of patient choice. However, the HMO is responsible for providing medically necessary services as needed, so if the network lacks a specific type of provider, the insured can petition, with the support of the PCP, to have the HMO cover an out-of-network provider. Some states have "any willing provider" laws requiring the HMO to allow subscribers to use other providers who, while not under contract with the HMO, are willing to comply with the HMO's standards and to accept its contractual prices for services provided to subscribers.

Along with coordination of care, other advantages of HMOs are that the service provided is broad and deep, minimal use is made of deductibles and coinsurance provisions, an when the insured stays in the network she will not receive any unexpected bills.

Exhibit 3.8 | Advantages and Disadvantages of HMOs

Advantages
• Coordination of care
• Pre-set fees for health care/no unexpected bills (surprise bills)
• Low copayments; little use of deductibles and coinsurance provisions
• Total health care costs are generally lower and more predictable than with PPO or POS
Disadvantages
• Gatekeeper for specialists services so it is sometimes difficult and complicated to get specialized care
• Potentially longer waits for non-emergency doctor appointments
• Any health care costs from out-of-network providers, except in emergencies, are generally not covered

Preferred Provider Organizations (PPOs)

A **Preferred Provider Organization** is an arrangement between insurance companies and health care providers that permits members of the PPO to obtain discounted health care services from the preferred providers within the network. Unlike an HMO, which limits choice of physicians and other health care providers, a PPO typically has a larger provider pool for participants to choose from. Participants are not required to receive services from preferred providers, but higher deductibles and coinsurance payments may apply when services are obtained from providers outside of the network. The members of the PPO are willing to offer care at a reduced cost to the employer or insurance company, in return for the large volume of business that the sponsoring employer or insurance company will direct to the PPO practitioners.

☑ *Quick Quiz 3.3*

1. PPOs typically have a wider network of health care providers from which to choose than HMOs.
   a. True
   b. False

2. The emergence of managed care plans was born from a desire to decrease competition among health care providers.
   a. True
   b. False

True, False.

Exhibit 3.9 | HMO vs. PPO

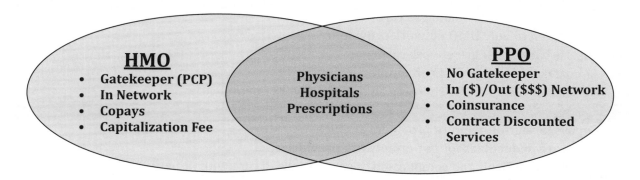

HMO
- Gatekeeper (PCP)
- In Network
- Copays
- Capitalization Fee

Physicians
Hospitals
Prescriptions

PPO
- No Gatekeeper
- In ($)/Out ($$$) Network
- Coinsurance
- Contract Discounted Services

Exhibit 3.10 | Advantages and Disadvantages of PPOs

Advantages
• Health care costs are relatively low when using in-network providers
• No gatekeeper required for specialist consultations, including out-of-network providers
• Primary care physician is not required
• Yearly out-of-pocket costs are limited
Disadvantages
• Out-of-network treatment is more expensive
• Copayments are generally larger than with HMOs
• May need to satisfy a deductible, especially with out-of-network providers
• Coinsurance may apply, and be higher when out of network

Point of Service Plans (POS)

A **point of service plan (POS)** is considered a managed care/indemnity plan hybrid, as it mixes aspects of in-network and fee-for-service, for greater patient choice. Members choose which option they will use each time they seek health care.

Like an HMO and a PPO, a POS plan has a contracted provider network. POS plans encourage members to choose a primary care physician from within the health care network. This physician becomes the patient's "point of service." If the patient prefers an out-of-network provider, the in-network primary care physician may make referrals outside of the network, but higher deductibles and coinsurance payments may apply if the insured is receiving services on the indemnity side.

POS plans are becoming more popular because they offer more flexibility, lower costs, and freedom of choice than standard HMOs, PPOs, or indemnity plans.

Exhibit 3.11 | Advantages and Disadvantages of POS Plans

Advantages
• Freedom of choice for managed care
• Not limited to only HMO network providers
• Costs are lower for in-network care
• Annual out-of-pocket costs are limited
• No referral is needed for choosing an out-of-network doctor
Disadvantages
• Copays for out-of-network providers are high
• There are deductibles for out-of-network providers
• Sometimes difficult and complicated to get specialized care with in-network providers

Example 3.15

Kindra recently lost her job and her group health insurance along with it. Since she is temporarily out of work, she cannot afford the high premiums for a qualified health plan or COBRA (extension of group coverage). Fortunately, Kindra is in good health and can purchase a short-term policy (at a fraction of the price of a QHP) to cover any large medical bills she may incur over the next three months while she seeks employment.

Since these plans are not QHPs, they sometimes do not cover routine doctor visits, maternity care, or prescriptions, and they may have dollar limits on the total amount of coverage provided. Short-term plans will usually have deductibles and coinsurance, and are not required to offer a maximum out-of-pocket limit. Planners and clients considering the purchase of a short-term policy must be sure to fully understand what is and is not covered under the plan, and any coverage limitations that may apply.

Exclusive Provider Organizations (EPOs)

An **Exclusive Provider Organization** is a managed care plan under which services are covered only when received from in-network doctors, specialists, or hospitals. No coverage is provided outside the network unless due to an emergency. An EPO is similar to an HMO but typically does not require a primary care physician to serve as the gatekeeper to specialist care (no referrals are needed to see a specialist), although a PCP may be selected if coordination of care is desirable. With an EPO, hospital stays often must be approved in advance (unless an emergency). Premiums tend to be higher than an HMO due to the flexibility of seeing a specialist without a referral, but tend to be lower than a PPO since only in-network care is covered.

Exhibit 3.12 | Advantages and Disadvantages of EPO Plans

Advantages
• Ability to select a PCP for coordination of care if desired
• Typically have a low copay for in-network care
• Premiums are typically lower than PPO or POS (but higher than HMO)
• No referral is needed to see a specialist
Disadvantages
• No out-of-network coverage (unless an emergency)
• Limited to in-network providers

Short-Term Health Plans

As an alternative to an ACA qualified health plan, some healthy individuals may choose to use short term health plans to help bridge gaps in coverage at an affordable price. These plans do not provide minimum essential coverage, they usually exclude any pre-existing conditions, and, in addition to meeting underwriting standards on initial application, the plans must be renewed periodically by again going through a medical underwriting process. Prior to October 2, 2018, the maximum term permitted was three months, however, the maximum term is now 364 days and renewals are permitted up to a maximum total duration of 36 months. A few states (such as New York and California, among others), however, prohibit the sale of short-term health policies within their states. The biggest advantage to short-term health policies is the low premium, which can be as low as 1/2 or 1/3 the cost of a qualified health plan.

Consumer-Directed Health Plans

Consumer-directed health plans (CDHPs) are a combination of a high deductible medical insurance policy and a Health Savings Account (HSA) which is used to accumulate funds on a tax-advantaged basis to pay health care expenses subject to the deductible and other cost sharing. CDHPs are becoming a very popular way for employers to reduce the cost of providing health care benefits to employees. The use of a CDHP provides for significant premium savings for the employer, who will frequently use part of that premium savings to contribute to the employee's HSA account in order to assist the employee with the high deductible. Another nice advantage to the employee is that if the employee remains healthy for a number of years and does not spend the money in the HSA account, it accumulates earnings, and none of the contributions or earnings are forfeited upon termination of employment.

HEALTH SAVINGS ACCOUNTS (HSA)

One of the newer concepts in health care coverage is creating a consumer directed health plan called a health savings account or HSA. This plan combines a high deductible medical expense insurance policy with a savings account. Insureds decide how much of their savings will be spent on health care and, therefore, are given an incentive to minimize the initial health care costs each year.

Insureds with consumer-directed health care plans may be more likely to participate in wellness programs and to do more research on alternatives for receiving care. For example, insureds may research the quality and cost of going to an urgent care center versus the emergency room for non-life-threatening ailments.

⋮≡ *Key Concepts*

1. Understand how HSAs are designed to facilitate tax-deferred savings for health care needs.

2. Describe how HSAs work.

3. Explain how FSAs can assist employees with health care costs.

4. Contrast HDHPs with HSAs and FSAs.

Health Savings Accounts (HSA) may be set up by individuals or employers, but are always owned and controlled by the individual. They allow eligible individuals to save for health care costs on a tax-advantaged basis. Contributions made to the HSA by the plan participant are tax-deductible as an adjustment to gross income (above-the-line), and distributions from the HSA to pay for qualified medical expenses are excluded from income. If an employer makes contributions to an HSA on behalf of an employee, and the contribution limits are not exceeded, the employer contribution is not included in the taxable income of the employee.

From a financial planning standpoint, HSAs are effectively emergency funds for medical care costs. Younger individuals, who are less likely to incur large medical expenses, may choose to use a high deductible health insurance plan and establish an HSA to begin to accumulate a pool of money that can be used for future medical expenses. As the individual ages, and more medical services are needed, he or she can safely continue to use a high deductible health insurance plan (which will have a substantially lower premium compared to plans that pay the first dollar of medical-care costs) because of the presence of the health care emergency fund - the HSA. An individual can minimize insurance (risk-transfer) costs by accumulating HSA funds starting in early years and using high-deductible health insurance plans (HDHP, discussed below) throughout their work life expectancy.

Eligibility

To be eligible to make HSA contributions, an individual must be covered by a high deductible health insurance plan (HDHP). Individuals who are covered by Medicare, another health insurance policy, or individuals who are dependents of another person for income tax purposes are not eligible to make contributions to HSAs. One major exception to the dependent eligibility rule is that spouses who independently meet the requirements to establish an HSA may open up their own HSA even though they are listed with the spouse on a jointly filed income tax return.

Financial planning clients who are married should also be aware that they will be ineligible for an HSA if they are covered under any other health plan. Ineligibility applies even to a spouse's non-HDHP or a spouse's FSA (flexible spending account, discussed later in this chapter) if it is permitted to be used for the client's medical expenses. However, if the FSA is limited to paying only the client's dental and vision expenses and the client is not covered under the spouse's health insurance policy, then the client may still be eligible for an HSA as long as the other HSA rules are met.

High Deductible Health Insurance Plans

High deductible health insurance plans (HDHP) include plans with a deductible of at least $1,400 for individual coverage and $2,800 for family coverage in 2020, with a maximum out-of-pocket amount of $6,900 for single coverage and $13,800 for family coverage in 2020.

Exhibit 3.13 | HDHP Deductibles and Out-of-Pocket Expenses (2020 and 2019)

	Individual Coverage		Family Coverage	
	2020	2019	2020	2019
Minimum annual deductible	$1,400	$1,350	$2,800	$2,700
Maximum annual deductible and other out-of-pocket expenses*	$6,900	$6,750	$13,800	$13,500

This limit does not apply to deductibles and expenses for out-of-network services if the plan uses a network of providers. Instead, only deductibles and out-of-pocket expenses for services within the network should be used to figure whether the limit applies.

Plans that allow office visits with only a copay amount paid by the insured prior to meeting the full deductible do not qualify. An HDHP may, however, provide preventive care benefits as prescribed by the ACA, along with care for a range of chronic conditions (e.g., beta blockers to treat congestive heart failure or insulin to treat diabetes), without a deductible or with a deductible less than the minimum annual deductible.[13] In response to the COVID-19 pandemic in 2020, otherwise high deductible health plans are also permitted to provide coverage for medical care services and testing for COVID-19 prior to satisfaction of the minimum deductible without loss of status as an HDHP.[14]

Before establishing an HSA account the client and planner should verify with the insurer that the plan qualifies as an HSA-compatible plan, or should check the declarations page of the policy for the words "qualified high-deductible health plan" or a reference to IRC Section 223. There are some family plans that have deductibles for both the family as a whole and for individual family members. Under these plans, if you meet the individual deductible for one family member, you do not have to meet the higher annual deductible amount for the family. If either the deductible for the family as a whole or the deductible for an individual family member is below the minimum annual deductible for family coverage, the plan does not qualify as an HDHP.

Example 3.16

For 2020, Maurice's annual deductible for the family plan is $3,500. This plan also has an individual deductible of $1,500 per family member. If one family member meets the individual deductible amount, the family deductible is treated as having been met. For example, if Maurice, his spouse, and each of their two children each incur $1,000 of expenses no one family member has met the individual deductible, but together they have met the family deductible (4 x $1000 = $4,000) so any additional expenses will be subject only to coinsurance. Alternatively, if Maurice incurs $2,000 of expenses, at that time the family deductible is treated as having been met since Maurice's expenses exceeded the individual deductible amount. Additional expenses incurred by Maurice or any other family member will be subject only to coinsurance.The plan does not qualify as an HDHP because the deductible for an individual family member is below the minimum annual deductible ($2,800) for family coverage.

Contribution Limitations

The maximum amount that can be contributed to an HSA for the calendar year is $3,550 for individual coverage, and $7,100 for family coverage in 2020. Amounts contributed by both the employee and the employer count in this total. For those who are age 55 or older, the annual limit is increased by $1,000 in 2020. The full amount may be contributed and deducted regardless of the actual amount of the deductible or maximum out-of-pocket expenses.

Those who enroll in a HDHP and become eligible to make HSA contributions part way through the year are permitted to make the full annual contribution so long as they were eligible for an HSA as of the first day of the last month of the tax year (December 1 for most taxpayers), however, the insured must continue to be covered under a HDHP for a full year afterward (the "testing period," through December 31 of the following year for most taxpayers) or taxes and a 10 percent penalty will apply to contributions

---

13. A list of specific services that qualify can be found in IRS Notice 2019-45.
14. IRS Notice 2020-15.

allocated to months prior to becoming HSA-eligible. Alternatively, the annual maximum contribution can be prorated to a monthly amount and only the amount allowable for the number of months the insured is actually covered by the HDHP can be contributed. The insured must be covered by the HDHP on the first day of each month to be eligible for that month.

Example 3.17

Sinbad, who is single, recently started a new job and will begin coverage under the employer's HDHP on August 15, 2020. Sinbad's HSA eligibility begins September 1, 2020 (the first month in which he is covered by a HDHP on the first of the month). He can elect to limit his contribution for the year to the pro-rated monthly maximum for September - December: 4 months x (1/12 x $3,550) = $1,183. Alternatively, under the "last month of the year rule," as long as he is still HSA-eligible on December 1, 2020, he can contribute the full $3,550 for the year, but must continue to be HSA-eligible though December 31, 2021 to avoid paying taxes and penalties on the excess contribution for the months prior to his becoming HSA-eligible in 2020 ($3,550 - (8/12 x $3,550) = $2,367 subject to tax and penalty if he does maintain the HDHP for the full testing period year).

Contributions may be made pre-tax through payroll deduction or may be made by the insured to the HSA account, in which case the insured is entitled to an above-the-line tax deduction (a deduction which reduces adjusted gross income (AGI)). Contributions can be made until the due date of the tax return for the year (not including extensions), which will be April 15th of the following year for most taxpayers.

Individuals enrolled in Medicare are not allowed to contribute to an HSA since Medicare is not a high deductible plan. However, funds accumulated in an HSA prior to Medicare enrollment may continue to be used to pay for health care expenses beyond age 65 and enrollment in Medicare.

HSAs are individually owned and are not required to be sponsored by an employer, although employers may contribute to them through a cafeteria plan. An HSA can be opened through banks, insurance companies, or other approved IRA (individual retirement account) trustees or custodians. Being individually owned means that, even if the employer contributed to the HSA on an employee's behalf, upon termination of employment, the HSA still belongs to and is controlled by the employee.

When an individual or family changes health plans part way through the year and no longer qualifies for an HSA, a portion of the contribution that was previously made may be subject to taxation, plus a 10 percent penalty based on the prorated formula described previously.

Another advantage of HSAs is that earnings on the contributions to an HSA are not taxed currently, and distributions used to pay for qualifying medical expenses are tax-free and penalty-free.

A taxpayer has the ability once during his or her lifetime to roll over funds from an IRA into the HSA, up to the yearly HSA contribution limit. The taxpayer will not be allowed to deduct these rolled over amounts but will be allowed to access these funds for health care expenses. In the event that the taxpayer becomes ineligible for an HSA account within 12 months of these rollovers, the rolled over amount will be subject to income taxes and penalty.

Exhibit 3.14 | Contribution Limits (2020 and 2019)

Year	Individual Contribution Limit	Family Contribution Limit	Additional Catch-Up Contribution (55 or older / Single and Family)
2020	$3,550	$7,100	$1,000
2019	$3,500	$7,000	$1,000

Distributions

Distributions from an HSA that are used to cover qualified medical expenses are exempt from income tax. All other distributions before age 65 are subject to both income tax and a 20 percent penalty tax. Once the account owner reaches age 65, and is therefore eligible for Medicare health insurance coverage, distributions from the HSA that are not used to pay for medical expenses will be subject to income tax, but no penalty tax will apply.

Qualified medical expenses include:
- Medical expenses for the account owner/insured and any dependents that are not reimbursed by a health insurance policy
- COBRA health insurance premiums (COBRA is discussed later in this chapter)
- Long-term care insurance premiums
- Health insurance premiums if the account owner is receiving unemployment compensation

The elimination of the 20 percent penalty on nonqualified distributions after attaining age 65 creates a significant advantage for account owners who remain healthy through their lives and into their retirement years since they will be able to access the dollars in the HSA account for other retirement goals by paying the income tax on the earnings, but avoiding a penalty. It is possible for healthy individuals to accumulate significant amounts inside the HSA through both annual tax deductible contributions and earnings in the account. HSAs, similar to IRAs, can be invested in many different types of investment vehicles such as savings accounts, money market funds, bank CDs, stocks, bonds, or mutual funds. The choice of investment vehicle must, of course, be made with caution as to the level of risk associated with it. It would be wise to keep at least enough for one or two years of maximum out-of-pocket expenses in a safe and non-fluctuating investment.

HSA owners are permitted to roll the funds from one HSA into another HSA once per year without triggering adverse income tax consequences (i.e., the imposition of an income tax on the amount distributed plus, if applicable, the 20 percent penalty). If the rollover is not completed as a trustee-to-trustee transfer, the participant has 60 days from the date of distribution to roll over the distribution to a new HSA to avoid the imposition of income tax on distributed amounts that were not used to pay for medical costs.

The 20 percent penalty on nonqualified distributions is waived if the account owner becomes disabled or deceased. HSA accounts allow a beneficiary to be named to receive the HSA funds in the event of death of the account holder. When the owner of an HSA dies prior to distributing all of the assets in the account, the remaining balance can be transferred to the named beneficiary. If the beneficiary is the spouse, the spouse is treated as the owner of the HSA and the normal HSA distribution rules apply. If the account is left to anyone other than the spouse, the death of the participant terminates the HSA, and the remaining balance will be subject to income tax (but not penalty) in the hands of the beneficiary. In the event there is no beneficiary named, the account will be distributed and taxed to the account owner's estate.

Flexible Spending Accounts

Some employers offers a **Flexible Spending Account (FSA)**, which permits employees to defer income to the FSA to pay for out-of-pocket health care costs with pre-tax dollars. The FSA approach minimizes employee outlay since the FSA converts what would have been after-tax employee expenditures for the benefits selected to pre-tax expenditures. The plan provides employees a degree of choice to receive either cash as compensation or the cash to pay for the costs of certain benefits. The FSA is funded entirely through employee salary reductions, only requiring the employer to bear the administrative costs. Salary reductions elected by employees to fund the nontaxable benefits available under the plan are not subject to income taxes or payroll taxes (Social Security and Medicare FICA Taxes).

Contribution Limits
The maximum salary deferral for a health care FSA in 2020 is $2,750 Salary reductions must be elected before the compensation is earned. The elections to reduce salary for a flexible spending account are made annually before the beginning of the year for which the reduction will be effective.

Distributions - Use It or Lose It
Funds contributed to the FSA may be used for payment of medical expenses not covered under a health insurance plan, such as copays and coinsurance payments, eyeglasses, and dental care expenses. However, any funds not used during the year may be forfeited back to the employer.

FSAs must comply with the use-or-lose rule since they are not permitted to defer compensation. However, a "run-out period" allows extra time during the following year for submission of invoices for reimbursement of expenses incurred during the plan year (a plan year is not always a calendar year). During this time, the employee can still be reimbursed from the FSA for expenses incurred during the prior year (the year for which funds were contributed). The period of time permitted for these claims (the run-out period) will vary from employer-to-employer and can be found in the Summary Plan Description provided by the employer.

Exhibit 3.15 | Run-Out Period vs. Grace Period

Run-Out Period	Allows extra time to be reimbursed for expenses incurred in the prior year.
Grace Period	Allows funds from the prior year to be used for expenses incurred during the first 2½ months of the current year.

In 2005, the IRS modified the "use it or lose it" rules to extend the time period through which employees can use FSA funds.[15] This extension of time, referred to as a grace period, must apply to all participants in the FSA cafeteria plan. Expenses for qualified benefits incurred during the grace period may be paid or reimbursed from benefits or contributions remaining unused at the end of the immediately preceding plan year. The grace period must not extend beyond the fifteenth day of the third calendar month after the end of the immediately preceding plan year to which it relates (i.e., "the 2½ month rule"). The effect of the grace period is that the participant may have as long as 14 months and 15 days (the 12 months in the current cafeteria plan year plus the grace period) to use the benefits or contributions for a plan year before those amounts are "forfeited" under the "use-it-or-lose-it" rule.[16]

Example 3.18

Employee A plans to have eye surgery in 2020. For the 2020 plan year (a calendar plan year), Employee A timely elects salary reduction of $2,750 for a health FSA. During the 2020 plan year, Employee A learns that she cannot have the eye surgery performed, but incurs other medical expenses totaling $1,400. As of December 31, 2020, she has $1,350 of unused benefits and contributions in the health FSA. Consistent with the use-it-or-lose-it rules she would forfeit the $1,350 if it is not used by March 15, 2021.

The Affordable Care Act, enacted in March 2010, established a uniform standard that applied to FSAs. Under the standard, the cost of an over-the-counter medicine or drug could not be reimbursed from the FSA account unless a prescription was obtained. The change did not affect insulin, even if purchased without a prescription, or other health care expenses such as medical devices, eye glasses, contact lenses, copays and deductibles. As a result of the COVID-19 pandemic in 2020, the CARES Act (Coronavirus Aid, Relief, and Economic Security Act of 2020) repealed this rule, once again allowing over-the-counter drugs to be purchased from an HSA or FSA without the need for a prescription after December 31, 2019.

Over the last decade, the IRS has considered various methods of relief for taxpayers using FSAs. In October 2013, the IRS made modifications to the "use-or-lose" rule for FSAs, and made further modifications to the same rule in 2020.[17] These modifications allows §125 cafeteria plans to be amended to allow up to $550 of unused amounts remaining at the end of a plan year in a health FSA to be paid or reimbursed to plan participants for qualified medical expenses incurred during the following plan year, provided that the plan does not also incorporate the grace period rule discussed above. This carryover of up to $550 does not affect the maximum amount of salary reduction contributions that the participant is permitted to make to the FSA for the year. This carryover option provides an alternative to the grace period rule.

---

15. IRS Notice 2005-42.
16. For FSA plan years for which the grace period expires in 2020 (e.g., a 2019 calendar-year plan with a grace period through March 15, 2020), the IRS has temporarily permitted plan amendments to extend the grace period though December 31, 2020 to assist with expenses related to the COVID-19 pandemic. IRS Notice 2020-29.
17. IRS Notice 2013-71 an IRS Notice 2020-33.

Example 3.19

Employer sponsors a §125 cafeteria plan and health FSA with a calendar plan year, an annual run-out period from January 1 through March 31 in which participants can submit claims for expenses incurred during the preceding plan year, and an annual open enrollment season in November in which participants elect a salary reduction amount (not to exceed $2,750) for the following plan year. The plan is timely amended to provide for a carryover that allows all participants to apply up to $550 of unused health FSA amounts remaining at the end of the run-out period to the health FSA for expenses incurred at any time during that plan year. The plan does not provide for a grace period with respect to the health FSA.

In November 2020, Participant A elects a salary reduction amount of $2,750 for 2021. By December 31, 2020, A's unused amount from the 2020 plan year is $800. On February 1, 2021, A submits claims and is reimbursed with respect to $350 of expenses incurred during the 2020 plan year, leaving a carryover on March 31, 2021 (the end of the run-out period) of $450 of unused health FSA amounts from 2020. The $450 amount is not forfeited; instead, it is carried over to 2021 and available to pay claims incurred in that year so that $3,200 (that is, $2,750 + $450) is available to pay claims incurred in 2021. A incurs and submits claims for expenses of $2,700 during the month of July 2021, and does not submit any other claims during 2021. A is reimbursed with respect to the $2,700 claim, leaving $500 as a potential unused amount from 2021 (depending upon whether A submits claims during the 2021 run-out period in early 2022).

Uniform Coverage Rules Applicable to Health FSAs

The maximum amount of reimbursement from a health FSA must be available at all times during the year (properly reduced as of any particular time for prior reimbursements for the same period of coverage). Thus, the maximum amount of reimbursement at any particular time during the year cannot relate to the amount that has been contributed to the FSA at any particular time prior to the end of the plan year. Similarly, the payment schedule for the required amount for coverage under a health FSA may not be based on the rate or amount of covered claims incurred during the coverage period. Employees' salary reduction payments must not be accelerated based on employees' incurred claims and reimbursements. The uniform coverage rule applies only to health FSAs and does not apply to FSAs for dependent care assistance or adoption assistance.

Example 3.20

Employer C maintains a calendar year cafeteria plan, offering an election between cash and a health FSA. The cafeteria plan prohibits accelerating employees' salary reduction payments based on employees' incurred claims and reimbursements.

For 2020, Employee N timely elects salary reduction of $2,750 for a health FSA. N pays the $2,750 salary reduction amount through salary reduction of $229 per month throughout the year. Employee N is eligible to receive the maximum amount of reimbursement of $2,750 at all times throughout the year (reduced by prior reimbursements).

N incurs $2,750 of medical expenses in January of the current year. The full $2,750 is reimbursed although N has made only one salary reduction payment of $229. After N submits a claim for reimbursement and substantiates the medical expenses, the cafeteria plan reimburses N for the $2,750 of medical expenses. Employer C's cafeteria plan satisfies the uniform coverage rule.

The employer is at risk for the total annual amount an employee elects to allocate to health benefits under his FSA even if the employee terminates employment before funding the amount used from the plan. In addition, if the employee fails to use all contributed amounts within a certain time period, contributions are forfeited back to the employer (use-it-or-lose-it).

While the use-it-or-lose-it feature on a health FSA may seem unfavorable, the significant tax savings makes them very attractive for payment of recurring medical expenses such as prescription drugs taken on a regular basis, annual eye exams and eyeglasses or contact lenses, routine dental visits, etc.

Exhibit 3.16 | Advantages and Disadvantages of HSAs and FSAs

	Advantages	Disadvantages
HSA	• Pre-tax contributions • Funds carry over from year to year • Funds can be invested • Permits reimbursement of over-the-counter medication purchases • Can be used to pay long-term care insurance premiums	• Must have a high deductible health plan to qualify • Some HSAs have annual fees • Some participants may not fully appreciate the tax benefits of the HSA
FSA	• Pre-tax contributions • Participants have total control over how to spend the money within the related health care or dependent care options* • Can be used for "optional" medical procedures (LASIK eye surgery, braces, etc.) • Can be used for child care or dependent care* • Permits reimbursement of over-the-counter medication purchases	• Money must be used by 2½ months after end of plan year or lose it • Cannot receive distribution amounts that are covered under another health plan • Limited to $2,750 (2020)

The dependent care option under and FSA is a separate election from the health care FSA and is limited to $5,000 per year.

HEALTH INSURANCE POLICY PROVISIONS

Policy Provisions of Group and Individual Plans

Health insurance policy provisions for groups are very similar to the provisions typically found in individual policies and in disability insurance policies. A summary of some of the more important policy provisions that are relevant to health and disability (discussed in Chapter 5) insurance are provided below.

Preexisting Conditions

Insurance works by spreading unknown risks (such as the risk of contracting health conditions that require medical treatment) across a pool of individuals. If it were possible for consumers to purchase insurance when they had a known condition or disease requiring medical treatment for a fraction of the cost of the treatment itself, a rational consumer would wait until he or she had a need for insurance (a pending medical expense) to obtain it. Under these circumstances, it would be impossible for the insurance company to spread those risks across the pool of insureds and generate a profit for performing that service.

The purpose of the preexisting condition clause is to prevent adverse selection against the insurance company, and to permit the risk-spreading function to work. If healthy individuals who will not require medical services for the current year are not part of the premium paying pool, there is no way to spread the risk across the pool, and the purchase of a policy by a sick person would be little more than a disguised attempt to transfer a known cost to the insurance company. Despite the potential for adverse selection, the Affordable Care Act does not permit exclusions for preexisting conditions after 2013. As a consequence, applicants cannot be denied insurance due to a preexisting condition. The Act attempted to mitigate this risk of adverse selection via a penalty for not having insurance, however, the penalty has since been eliminated. Another way that the Act attempted to mitigate the risk of adverse selection is to limit enrollment to specified time-frames (open enrollment and special enrollment periods, as discussed previously), which serves to discourage individuals from waiting until discovery of an ailment requiring high-cost treatment to seek insurance since they may have to cover costs in their entirety until the next open enrollment period. While the majority of health insurance plans sold today do not contain limits for pre-existing conditions, some health insurance plans with grandfathered status under The Affordable Care Act, are still permitted to contain pre-existing condition clauses and provisions.

> ### ≔ *Key Concepts*
>
> 1. Describe some health insurance policy provisions that are particularly relevant to financial planners.
>
> 2. Briefly describe the taxation of an individual's health care benefits.
>
> 3. Explain the different coverage periods for different individuals, under the COBRA plan.
>
> 4. Describe how Medicare and HSAs work in conjunction with one another.
>
> 5. Describe the benefit of standardization of Medigap plans.

Incontestability Clause

When a health insurance policy is issued on a non-cancelable or guaranteed renewable basis (described below), the policy often includes an **incontestability clause**. The incontestability clause protects the insured by preventing the insurer from challenging the validity of the health insurance contract after it has been in force for a specified period of time unless the insured initially obtained coverage fraudulently.

Grace Period

As is the case with all insurance policies, an insurance company will only undertake the risk the insured is trying to transfer when the insured compensates the company for undertaking the risk. If policy premiums are not paid by the due date, the health insurance policy will lapse. However, when the policy includes a **grace period**, the policy will remain in force and will not lapse as long as the premium is paid within a specified number of days after the due date. A one-month grace period (which usually translates to a period of 31 days) is very common in health insurance policies. However, most plans sold on the Marketplace have a 90 day grace period.

Reinstatement Clause

Health insurance policies, such as disability and long-term care insurance, include a procedure for policy reinstatement should coverage lapse due to nonpayment of premium. Certain policies specify a time limit within which the insured may reinstate the policy without proof of insurability. Other policies require the insured to again submit to the underwriting process before coverage is reinstated. Reinstated policies usually exclude coverage for illnesses incurred during the first ten days after reinstatement (again to control adverse selection problems). Upon appeal from the policyholder, medical insurance policies purchased in the health insurance marketplace may allow for reinstatement of the policy for a period of time, provided that all missed premiums are repaid. If reinstatement is denied, the policyholder will need to wait until the next open enrollment period to obtain a new policy.[18]

Time Limit Clause

The time limit clause is attached to the policy so that an insurer may void a policy on the grounds of misrepresentation made by the insured on the application for coverage. The insurer must usually discover and contest the misstatement during the first two years the contract is in force. After that time, the policy is incontestable and misstatements may not be used against the insured to void a policy or deny a claim. This is similar to the incontestability clause in a life insurance contract.

Renewability Clause

Health insurance that is underwritten on an annual basis may prevent insureds from obtaining access to needed health care if they get sick.[19] If, for example, the health insurance company does not reissue the policy when the renewal date is reached simply because the insured had contracted some form of disease or health condition in the prior policy period, access to treatment may be jeopardized. This is the opposite of adverse selection risk. In this instance, once a person becomes sick, the insurance company

---

18. https://www.healthcare.gov/apply-and-enroll/health-insurance-grace-period/
19. In health care, underwriting on an annual basis refers to the need to answer health-related questions at the start of each renewal period. Since the enactment of the ACA, underwriting at the time of renewal typically applies only to short-term medical insurance plans.

could decide to drop that person from coverage so that it does not have to pay health care providers for the care given to the participant.

To prevent this from happening, and to give policy holders some protection against policy cancellation, different renewability rights are provided in health insurance contracts (note: some of the following renewability provisions no longer apply to ACA-qualified medical insurance plans since proof of insurability is no longer required, but may still be utilized in other types of health insurance such as disability or long-term care insurance), including:
- Non-cancelable
- Guaranteed renewable
- Conditionally renewable
- Optionally renewable

Non-Cancelable
Non-cancelable policies prevent the insurance company from canceling the policy for any reason provided that the policy premium is paid. Usually, the policy will specify that it is non-cancelable for a specific period of time, or until the insured reaches a stated age. Some policies also specify that, during the non-cancelable period, no changes to the policy may be made, including changes to the premium. Non-cancelable policies provide the greatest degree of protection to the insured, since the insured can force the insurance company to provide continued coverage simply by paying the premium on the policy. A non-cancelable renewal provision is more common with disability insurance than medical or long-term care insurance.

Guaranteed Renewable
Guaranteed renewable health insurance policies require the insurance company to renew the policy for a specified period of time or until the insured attains a certain age (such as age 65, when eligibility for Medicare is established). Provided the insured pays the premium, the insurance company must renew the policy during the stated period. Unlike the case with non-cancelable policies, which do not permit increases in premiums, the premium on a guaranteed renewable policy may be increased on a class basis (i.e., increased across the board for all similarly situated insureds). The premium may not be increased for one participant simply because he or she has contracted a disease or health condition requiring treatment. ACA qualified health plans are guaranteed to be renewable so long as premiums are paid, but premiums may increase with each renewal period.

Conditionally Renewable
When a policy is conditionally renewable, the insurance company may not cancel it during the policy term (which is typically one year). However, the insurance company reserves the right to cancel the policy when it is up for renewal. The conditions that will cause the policy to be canceled on the renewal date are often specified in the contract itself. Planners should be attentive to these provisions when placing conditionally renewable insurance with clients. Short-term health insurance plans, which are not ACA qualified health plans, may be conditionally or optionally renewable.

Optionally Renewable
An optionally renewable policy permits the insurance company to cancel the policy at any time, except during the term of the existing contract. Unlike a conditionally renewable policy, which specifies the conditions that will result in loss of coverage, under an optionally renewable policy the insurance

company can cancel coverage for any reason. Optionally renewable health insurance contracts give the client little peace of mind, and should be carefully considered prior to purchase.

TAXATION AND HEALTH INSURANCE

An individual who is not self-employed and who purchases health insurance in the individual market may deduct the premiums for medical expense insurance on Schedule A of IRS Form 1040; however, the deduction will be allowed in 2019 and 2020 only to the extent that the premiums and non-reimbursed medical expenses exceed 7.5 percent of the insured's adjusted gross income. After 2020, the deduction will be allowed only when medical expenses exceed 10 percent of adjusted gross income.

For a self-employed person, a deduction for medical expense insurance premiums may be taken above-the-line on IRS Form 1040 in determining the adjusted gross income. The amount of this deduction is 100 percent of the premiums.

When group health insurance benefits are provided by and paid for by an employer, there is no taxable event for the employee. Furthermore, when the policy pays the actual cost of medical care, the insured will not have to report the benefits received as income. Normally, when an employee receives property (such as a health insurance policy) from an employer in return for his or her labor, the fair market value of that policy is subject to income tax the year it is received, under a tax rule known as the economic benefit doctrine. Congress has enacted a specific exception to this rule that allows employees to receive health benefits on an income-tax-free basis in an attempt to encourage employers to provide health insurance coverage to their employees. The employer can deduct the cost of providing group health insurance to its employees as an ordinary and necessary business expense.

When an individual receives benefits under a health insurance policy, and those benefit payments are used to pay for health care, no taxable event occurs. In this instance, the benefits are received tax-free. Some health insurance policies, such as critical illness policies (for example, a policy that pays a specified amount if the insured is diagnosed with cancer), pay a lump sum to the insured regardless of the actual expenses incurred in treating the condition or disease. When lump-sum payments such as these are received, there are no federal income tax consequences as long as the proceeds are used to pay for medical care. Amounts received in excess of the actual cost of care are subject to income tax. Benefits are also taxable if the insured deducted the medical expenses and then in the following year received payment of benefits for the same expenses. For example, if the insurance company denied a claim, the insured deducted those expenses, and then the following year the insurance company paid the claim on appeal, the payment would be taxable income for the insured.

✓ Quick Quiz 3.5

1. Adverse selection occurs when health insurance plans refuse to renew health insurance for people if they become ill.
   a. True
   b. False

2. Employers may deduct the costs of providing health insurance only if the employee includes the monetary benefit derived from that insurance as income.
   a. True
   b. False

False, False.

CONSOLIDATED OMNIBUS BUDGET RECONCILIATION ACT OF 1985 (COBRA)

Under the **Consolidated Omnibus Budget Reconciliation Act of 1985 (COBRA)**,[20] an employer that maintains a group health plan and employs 20 or more people on more than 50 percent of the calendar days in a year is required to continue to offer coverage under the plan to covered employees and qualified beneficiaries following the occurrence of a statutorily defined qualifying event as depicted in **Exhibit 3.17 | Summary of COBRA Provisions**.[21] The employer, however, is not required to pay for any portion of the cost of COBRA coverage.

Exhibit 3.17 | Summary of COBRA Provisions

Event	Beneficiary (Qualifying)			Period of Coverage
	Worker	Spouse	Dependant	
Normal termination (resigned, laid off, or fired; except gross misconduct) *(29 USCA 1163(2))*	✓	✓	✓	18 months
Full time to part time *(29 USCA 1163(2))*	✓	✓	✓	18 months
Disabled employee or dependent (must meet Social Security definition of disabled) *(29 USCA 1162(2)(A))*	✓	✓	✓	29 months
Qualified dependent (child reaches age no longer eligible for plan) *(29 USCA 1163(5))*			✓	36 months
Death of employee *(29 USCA 1163(1))*		✓	✓	36 months
Employee reached Medicare age *(29 USCA 1163(4))*		✓	✓	36 months
Divorce *(29 USCA 1163(3))*		✓	✓	36 months
Plan terminates *(29 USCA 1163(6))*	✓	✓	✓	36 months

Example 3.21

Jada, the Senior Vice President of The Amazing Company, died last week. Her widow, Jasmine, does not work and is 56 years old. Jasmine can obtain group health insurance coverage under Jada's plan for 36 months after her death.

Example 3.22

Lee, an employee of Electrical Engineering Contractors, Inc., was recently divorced from his wife, Yara. Yara is unemployed, but may obtain group health insurance coverage under Lee's plan for 36 months after the divorce.

Example 3.23

Danielle has recently finished medical school at the age of 27 and is no longer eligible to receive health insurance coverage as a dependent under her parent's group health insurance plan. During her residency, Danielle will not have access to employer-provided

---

20. Public Law 99-272 (April 7, 1986).
21. 29 USCA §1161.

group health insurance, so she may receive COBRA continuation benefits under her parent's group plan for 36 months.

Example 3.24

Rahil recently retired at the age of 65 and is currently covered by Medicare. His wife, Diya, is 63 and does not yet qualify for Medicare coverage. Diya can obtain health insurance under Rahil's group plan for up to 36 months under COBRA.

COBRA covers virtually all types of group plans that fall into the "health" plan category (for example, medical, vision, and dental plans), except long-term care plans.

COBRA Premiums

While the employer may pay for the COBRA coverage, generally the employer shifts the burden of paying the premium for the benefit to the beneficiaries. If the employer pays for the medical coverage, then the exclusion from the employee's income for accident and health benefits applies to amounts the employer pays to maintain medical coverage under COBRA. The exclusion applies regardless of the length of employment, whether the employer pays the premiums directly or reimburses the former employee for premiums paid, and whether the employee's separation is permanent or temporary.

During the statutory COBRA period, the premium charged to the employee cannot exceed 102 percent of the cost to the plan for similarly situated individuals who have not incurred a qualifying event.[22] The 102 percent includes both the portion paid by beneficiary employees and any portion paid by the employer before the qualifying event plus two percent for administrative costs. If a qualified beneficiary receives the 11 month disability extension of coverage, the premium for the additional 11 months may be increased to 150 percent of the plan's total cost of coverage. COBRA premiums may be increased if the costs to the plan increase, but generally must be fixed in advance of each 12-month premium cycle.

The election period for COBRA begins on the date of the qualifying event and must last at least 60 days from the time the beneficiary receives notification from the administrator.[23] Each of the qualified beneficiaries can choose COBRA continuation independently. When the election for coverage is made, coverage is retroactive to the date of the qualifying event. If coverage is initially waived and medical expenses are incurred during the 60-day election period, the waiver can be revoked and coverage will begin retroactively to the day of the qualifying event, so that those recently incurred medical expenses will be paid by the plan. Of course, this also means premiums must be paid retroactively, but if the medical expenses are significantly higher than the total premiums, it can be a large savings to the insured.

Individuals whose coverage terminates due to a job change will often have a probationary period before becoming eligible for coverage under the health plan of the new employer. If the employee and family members are healthy and will be eligible for the new coverage before the 60-day COBRA election period ends, a strategy some employees take is to wait and see if any medical expenses are incurred before electing COBRA. If no or low costs are incurred before the new coverage begins, the family will have saved the cost of the premiums. If the family incurs significant medical costs during that 60-day time-frame, the election for COBRA can be made retroactively. Care must be used when employing this strategy, however, because if the family has any pre-existing conditions and there is a period of more than 63 days between the old health plan coverage and the new health plan coverage, the new plan may be permitted to exclude coverage for pre-existing conditions for up to six months.

22.29 USCA 1162(3).
23.29 USC §1165 and 1166.

When the maximum period for continuation coverage under COBRA terminates, an employee must be able to exercise the conversion rights that are otherwise available under the plan, or, as an alternative, will be eligible for the special 60-day enrollment period in the Healthcare Marketplace (policies purchased though the Marketplace have no exclusions for pre-existing conditions).

Example 3.25

Brandy recently terminated her employment. Her major medical insurance ended on her last day of employment. Brandy started a new job one week after leaving her previous job. Coverage under her new employer's plan will begin after 30 days of employment. Since Brandy has 60 days to elect COBRA coverage, which will then be retroactive to the date she terminated employment, and she is healthy, she decides to wait to see if she has any significant medical expenses during the 37 days until her new group coverage begins. If she incurs costs higher than the COBRA premiums, she will elect COBRA, pay the premiums retroactive to the date her group coverage terminated, and receive benefit payments for the retroactive coverage period. If her medical costs during that time are lower than the COBRA premiums, she will not need to elect COBRA and will save the cost of the premiums.

Example 3.26

Assume the same facts as above except Brandy is going to take 18 months off to find herself. Is COBRA an appropriate election in this case? The answer is maybe. She needs medical insurance coverage of some type, but COBRA may or may not be the best option. Brandy should compare the coverage and costs of the group policy under COBRA with the cost of purchasing an individual policy, either through the marketplace or outside the marketplace, where she can purchase an individual policy without evidence of insurability during the 60-day election period for COBRA (which is also the time-frame for the special enrollment period for purchase of an individual policy). She may find that an individual policy is less costly than COBRA while still providing adequate coverage. Purchases of insurance on the Health Care Exchange are generally only permitted during the open enrollment period (November 1 - December 15 of the prior year, for coverage to begin January 1st); however, loss of group coverage due to termination of employment creates a 60-day special enrollment period.

Employees age 65 and older who have chosen not to enroll in Medicare Part B due to the employer-provided coverage should generally not elect COBRA coverage at termination of employment and should instead enroll in Medicare Part B. This enrollment is recommended because failure to enroll in Medicare Part B within eight months of termination of employment will cause the Part B premium to be permanently increased, and because COBRA premiums are typically more expensive than Medicare Part B premiums. The eight-month period is always measured from the earlier of:

1. the month after termination of employment, or
2. the month after termination of group health insurance based on the current employment, regardless of whether COBRA is elected.

PLANNING FOR HEALTH CARE COSTS IN RETIREMENT

Planning for health care in retirement is a challenging task. The cost of health care is one of the major unknown expenses that retirees face. The retiree may be fortunate enough to maintain good health throughout the retirement years. On the other hand, for many retirees, health care costs represent a significant portion of retirement spending. As mentioned previously, a recent study from the Kaiser Family Foundation reports that Medicare (age 65 and older) households spend an average of 14 percent of household income on health care.

Financial planners will be called upon to assist clients with decisions regarding Medicare and Medigap policies and continuation of employer insurance. The planner will need to estimate the costs of health care and incorporate them into the retirement plan. These costs include premiums, deductibles, copays, coinsurance payments, and costs not covered by Medicare and Medigap insurance.

Retirees who have contributed to an HSA and been healthy enough to avoid utilizing it for medical expenses over a significant time period will have a nice-sized pool of tax-free money to be used to cover qualified health care costs during the retirement years. If the employee is lucky enough to remain healthy throughout retirement, the money remaining in the HSA can be used for other expenses. Remember that there is no 20 percent penalty if money is withdrawn from the HSA after age 65 (although income taxes will be due on the funds that are withdrawn from the account if they are not used for qualified medical expenses).

As clients age, additional health care-related capital expenditures may also be necessary to enable them to remain in their home. Examples include replacing steps with ramps, replacing tubs with walk-in showers, installing handles in bathrooms, and moving washers and dryers, bathrooms, and bedrooms to the first floor of the home. These additional costs may be significant and should be estimated and included in the retirement plan.

Medicare and Medicare Supplement Insurance

Medicare is the primary insurance for those age 65 and older, but few rely on Medicare as their only source of health care coverage. Medicare is actually made up of four separate programs:
- **Part A** coverage is for inpatient hospital care, skilled nursing care, home health care services, and hospice care.
- **Part B** is for doctors' services, medical supplies provided by a doctor in his or her office, drugs administered by a physician, outpatient hospital services, the costs of home health care visits, and many other services.
- **Part C** is a Medicare Advantage plan offered by private companies but approved by Medicare. These plans cover all Medicare services, but may also offer additional coverage.
- **Part D** provides prescription drug coverage.

Traditional Medicare is comprised of Parts A and B (and D for prescription drugs at the insured's option), while Part C is an alternative to traditional Medicare (details of all Parts of Medicare are discussed in Chapter 10). One of the major issues facing retirees under the traditional Medicare program is that it leaves large gaps in coverage and does not have an out-of-pocket maximum, resulting in potentially large uncovered health care costs. For planning purposes, it is important to understand what costs are not covered so they can be planned for.

Part A does not cover hospital stays beyond 90 days (if all lifetime reserve days have been used). Part A also excludes services provided outside the U.S., its territories, and its possessions. It also covers only up to 100 days of skilled nursing care, and only following at least three days of hospitalization.

Medicare Part B excludes prescription drugs not administered by a doctor. It does not cover services provided outside the U.S., its territories, and its possessions. Part B does not cover routine physical exams (except a one-time "Welcome to Medicare" wellness visit and a yearly wellness visit, as required by the Affordable Care Act), routine eye exams, dental care, hearing aids, or eyeglasses. It also excludes luxury elective services, custodial care, elective cosmetic surgery, services covered by workers' compensation, and services provided free in a federal facility.

Part A and Part B both exclude coverage for the first three pints of blood for a blood transfusion.

Out-of-Pocket Costs for Medicare Part A
Medicare has deductibles and coinsurance amounts for both Part A and B. In 2020, individuals covered by Medicare Part A will pay out-of-pocket:
- $1,408 deductible for a hospital stay of 1-60 days (paid separately for each benefit period)[24]
- $352 per day for days 61-90 of a hospital stay
- $704 per day for days 91-150 of a hospital stay (lifetime reserve days)
- All costs of the stay after it exceeds 150 days
- Nothing for the first 20 days at a skilled nursing facility
- $176 per day for days 21-100 at a skilled nursing facility
- All costs for days over 100 at a skilled nursing facility (Medicare does not cover any of the costs of care that is primarily custodial)
- Nothing for home health care prescribed by a doctor if the insured is confined to his or her house
- Nothing for hospice care for terminal illness
- 20% of the cost of durable medical equipment
- 100% of the cost of care received in a foreign country. Since Medicare does not cover care in a foreign country, clients planning to travel abroad during retirement should be advised to purchase international travel insurance or a Medigap policy that covers emergency care received outside the U.S.

Out-of-Pocket Costs for Medicare Part B
Part B has a $198 (2020) per year deductible and a 20 percent copayment after the deductible is reached for covered physician services, including surgeon fees and physical therapy. The copay is 20 percent for outpatient mental health, and limits apply to most physical and occupational therapies. Laboratory tests are covered without a copayment. The copayments above may be higher if the physician used has not agreed to accept the amount approved by Medicare for a particular service as payment in full. There is no maximum out-of-pocket limit associated with these costs.

Medicare Supplement Insurance (Medigap Policies)
For those Medicare beneficiaries who want to fill in the gaps created by many of the limitations or exclusions specified in the Medicare program, additional coverage, so-called Medigap (also called Medicare Supplement) insurance, is available from many carriers at additional cost. There are strict federal guidelines that outline only 10 different plans that can be offered. Each plan covers different

---

24. Benefit periods are discussed in detail in Chapter 10.

amounts of the gaps in Medicare coverage. The plans are named using the letters A through N (plans E, H, I, and J are no longer offered), and plan coverages are standardized. Comparing the costs of various insurance company coverages is simplified because all carriers offering Plan D, for example, will provide the same benefits. Medigap policies only work with traditional Medicare (Parts A and B), and not with Part C (Medicare Advantage).

Medicare supplemental insurance (Medigap) must provide the following basic benefits:

1. Hospitalization - pays the coinsurance for days 61-90 under Part A, the 60-day lifetime reserve, and an additional 365 days after Medicare benefits end.
2. Medical expenses - pays the coinsurance for physician and medical service charges under Part B.
3. Blood - pays for the first three pints of blood each year.

In addition to basic benefits, Medigap plans can offer any of the following benefits not covered by Medicare:

- Coinsurance for days 21-100 at a skilled nursing facility
- Hospital inpatient deductible under Part A
- Deductible under Part B (no longer available after 2019)
- Physician and medical service charges exceeding the amount approved by Medicare
- 80% of emergency care charges in a foreign country
- At-home assistance with daily living
- Preventive care

An individual who is at least 65 years of age can buy any Medigap policy during the six-month period after enrolling for Medicare Part B. Enrolling during this period is highly recommended since, during the time of open enrollment, a person cannot be turned down for health reasons, and insurers cannot charge higher premiums based on medical conditions. Affordable Care Act rules prohibiting medical underwriting and exclusion of pre-existing conditions do not apply to Medigap policies, therefore, if enrollment occurs outside of the initial six-month open enrollment period, the insurer may require a six-month waiting period for coverage of pre-existing conditions and in some cases may deny coverage.

The Plan A Medigap policy will only pay for basic benefits. The other plans cover basic benefits and the additional benefits as shown in the following chart:

Exhibit 3.18 | Medigap Plans

Benefits	B	C	D	F	G	K	L	M	N
Deductible - Part A	✓	✓	✓	✓	✓	50%	75%	50%	✓
Skilled nursing care coinsurance		✓	✓	✓	✓	50%	75%	✓	✓
Part B coinsurance or copayment	✓	✓	✓	✓	✓	50%	75%		
Deductible - Part B		✓		✓					
Excess physician and medical service charges				✓	✓				
Emergency care in a foreign country		80%	80%	80%	80%			80%	80%
**After you meet your out-of-pocket yearly limit and your yearly Part B deductible ($198 in 2020), the Medigap plan pays 100% of covered services for the rest of the calendar year.						Out-of-Pocket Limit**			
						$5,880	$2,940		

Plan N pays 100% of the Part B coinsurance, except for a copayment of up to $20 for some office visits and up to a $50 copayment for emergency room visits that don't result in inpatient admission.

Note: Plans E, H, I, and J are no longer offered. Beginning in 2020, plans C and F are no longer available to new enrollees; however, those who had previously purchased them may continue those plans. Plan F also offered a high-deductible plan.

The government mandates that all Medigap policies of the same letter (A, B, C, D, F, G, K, L M or N) offer the same coverage to make it easier for seniors to determine which policy they need.[25]

Exhibit 3.19 | Percent of Total Medigap Enrollments

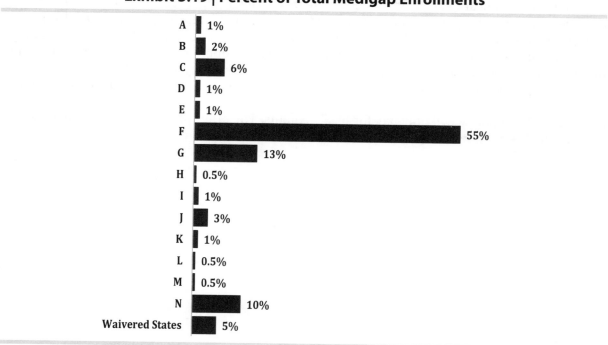

- A: 1%
- B: 2%
- C: 6%
- D: 1%
- E: 1%
- F: 55%
- G: 13%
- H: 0.5%
- I: 1%
- J: 3%
- K: 1%
- L: 0.5%
- M: 0.5%
- N: 10%
- Waivered States: 5%

https://www.ahip.org/wp-content/uploads/IB_StateofMedigap2019.pdf

25. Plans sold in Massachusetts, Minnesota, and Wisconsin (waivered states) may vary from the federal standardized coverages.

The government rules for standardization among plans do not require all premiums to be structured in the same way, so selecting a policy letter does not mean that shopping is simplified to just looking for the lowest premium.

Policies that are "community rated" charge the same monthly premium to everyone, regardless of age, but premiums may increase due to other factors (e.g., inflation, underwriting, etc). These policies tend to be the least expensive over the course of a lifetime.

Issue-age-rated policies base the premium on age at issue. The premiums will not increase based on age but may go up based on other factors.

Attained-age-rated policies base the premium on current age each year. These will be less expensive when clients are younger, but premiums will go up each year. Generally, premiums will begin to be higher than other types of policies around age 70 - 75.

Medigap policies are not subject to the ACA rules requiring coverage for pre-existing conditions. Therefore, the best time to purchase Medigap insurance is during open enrollment, which is the six-month period beginning on the first day of the month in which you are both 65 or older and enrolled in Medicare Part B. For policies purchased during this time, there is no medical underwriting based on health, although there can be up to a six-month waiting period for coverage for pre-existing conditions. This waiting period can be reduced or eliminated if you had prior creditable coverage. Many types of health care coverage will qualify as prior creditable coverage. Each month of prior coverage reduces the waiting period for coverage of preexisting conditions by one month, so if prior coverage lasted at least six months, there will be no wait. However, there cannot be a break in coverage for more than 63 days. A pre-existing condition is one that was diagnosed or was being treated within the six-month period before the date that coverage starts. Policies purchased during the open enrollment period will not have a higher premium based on health.

If an employee has group health coverage through an employer or union, he or she may want to wait to take the action of enrolling in Part B of Medicare and purchasing a Medigap policy. This delay makes sense when the employer plan provides similar coverage. When the employer coverage ends, the employee will get a chance to enroll in Part B without a late enrollment penalty, and a Medigap open enrollment period will start at that time as well. Medicare enrollment periods and decisions are discussed in detail in Chapter 10.

Medicare and HSAs
Individuals enrolled in Medicare are no longer eligible to contribute to an HSA because Medicare is not a high deductible plan; however, tax-free distributions from an existing HSA may be made during retirement to pay for qualified medical expenses.

Additional Qualified HSA expenses include:[26]
- Medicare premiums (but not Medigap premiums)
- Medical expenses for the account owner and any dependents that are not reimbursed by a health insurance policy, such as the deductible and coinsurance under Medicare
- Expenses not covered by Medicare such as eyeglasses and dental expenses
- Long-term care insurance premiums

26. Also see list of qualified expenses under the HSA section of this chapter.

Retirees age 65 or older will be able to access the dollars in the HSA account for uses other than qualified medical expenses, but they must pay income tax on the earnings (but no penalty will apply). Healthy individuals can accumulate significant amounts inside the HSA through both annual tax-deductible contributions and earnings in the account. HSAs, like IRAs, can be invested in many different types of investment vehicles, such as savings accounts, money market funds, bank CDs, stocks, bonds, or mutual funds. As previously advised, it is wise to keep enough invested in liquid assets (those that can be turned to cash quickly without loss of principal) to cover the MOOP for several years, and additional amounts above that can be invested to provide some additional growth.

CONCLUSION

Health insurance permits clients to purchase a hedge against the risk of incurring large medical care expenses. All U.S. citizens are required, under current law, to maintain a qualified health plan, although the penalty tax for not doing so has been eliminated. Planners and clients should carefully consider the most appropriate forms of insurance to purchase so that the appropriate amount of client risk exposure is transferred to insurance companies while protecting the client's asset base to achieve the client's other financial goals.

KEY TERMS

Coinsurance - The amount a patient must pay for major medical care after meeting the deductible.

Consumer-Directed Health Plan - A combination of a high deductible medical insurance policy and Health Savings Account which is used to accumulate funds on a tax-advantaged basis to pay health care expenses as a result of deductibles and other cost sharing.

Deductible - The amount a patient must pay each year before the health insurance plan begins paying.

Exclusive Provider Organization - A form of managed care in which participants receive all of their care from in-network providers. Unlike an HMO, a referral is not necessary to see a specialist.

Flexible Spending Account (FSA) - Employer-sponsored plan that permits employees to defer pre-tax income into an account to pay for health care expenses. FSAs require the employee to either use the contributed amounts for medical expenses by the end of the year, or forfeit the unused amounts to the employer.

Grace Period - A provision in most insurance policies which allows payment to be received for a certain period of time after the actual due date without a default or cancellation of the policy.

Group Health Insurance - Health plans offered to a group of individuals by an employer, association, union, or other entity.

Health Maintenance Organizations (HMOs) - A form of managed care in which participants receive all of their care from participating providers. Physicians may be employed by the HMO directly, or may be physicians in private practice who have chosen to participate in the HMO network. The independent physicians contract with the HMO to serve HMO participants, receiving a flat annual fee (capitation fee) for each HMO member, whether the member receives medical services from the provider or not.

Health Savings Accounts (HSA) - A plan that permits employees or individuals to save for health care costs on a tax-advantaged basis. Contributions made to the HSA by the plan participant are tax-deductible as an adjustment to gross income (above-the-line), and distributions from the HSA to pay for qualified medical expenses are excluded from income.

High Deductible Health Insurance Plans (HDHP) - Plans with a deductible of at least $1,400 for individual coverage and $2,800 for family coverage in 2020, with a maximum out-of-pocket amount of $6,900 for single coverage and $13,800 for family coverage in 2020.

Incontestability Clause - Clause in a health insurance policy that prevents the insurer from challenging the validity of the health insurance contract after it has been in force for a specified period of time unless the insured fraudulently obtained coverage in the beginning of the policy.

Indemnity Health Insurance - Traditional, fee-for-service health insurance that does not limit where a covered individual can get care.

Individual Major Medical Plans - Major medical insurance coverage purchased independently from an insurance company (not as part of a group).

Managed Care Insurance - Health-care delivery systems that integrate the financing and delivery of health care. Managed care plans feature a network of physicians, hospitals, and other providers who participate in the plan. Managed care includes HMOs, PPOs, EPOs, and POS plans.

Medicare Supplement Insurance (Medigap) - A health insurance policy designed to cover some of the gaps in coverage associated with traditional Medicare.

Out-of-Pocket-Maximum - The sum of the deductible plus the insured's portion of the coinsurance. Generally, it also includes any copayments.

Point of Service Plan (POS) - A form of managed care that is considered a managed care/indemnity plan hybrid, as it mixes aspects of HMOs, PPOs, and indemnity plans for greater patient choice. A primary care physician coordinates patient care, but there is more flexibility in choosing doctors and hospitals than in an HMO.

Preferred Provider Organization (PPO) - A form of managed care in which participants have more flexibility in choosing physicians and other providers than in an HMO. The arrangement between insurance companies and health care providers permits participants to obtain discounted health care services from the preferred providers within the network.

Premium - The amount participants pay to belong to a health plan.

Primary Care Physician - A physician that is designated as a participant's first point of contact with the health care system, particularly in managed care plans.

DISCUSSION QUESTIONS

SOLUTIONS to the discussion questions can be found exclusively within the chapter. Once you have completed an initial reading of the chapter, go back and highlight the answers to these questions.

1. Describe the benefits associated with group health insurance plans.

2. What is the difference between basic and major medical health insurance?

3. What is the difference between an indemnity type of plan and a managed care plan?

4. Describe the purpose of, and differences between, the "metal" tiers.

5. List some of the items required to be provided in the Summary of Benefits and Coverage (SBC) for qualified health plans.

6. What is the purpose of coordination of benefit provisions in group health insurance policies?

7. Describe the different types of renewal provisions.

8. Explain what a preexisting condition clause does.

9. Which employers are required to offer COBRA continuation coverage to their employees?

10. Who, besides the employee, qualifies for COBRA coverage?

11. Explain the tax benefits of HSAs.

12. Describe the greatest disadvantage associated with FSAs.

13. Describe how out-of-pocket maximum works.

14. What are the major types (components) of individual basic health coverages?

15. What is the tax treatment of premiums for employer-provided health insurance?

16. What is the tax treatment of benefits received from a health insurance policy?

17. What is the purpose of Medigap insurance?

A sample of multiple choice problems is provided below. Additional multiple choice problems are available at money-education.com by accessing the Student Practice Portal.

1. Non-cancelable health insurance contracts are different from guaranteed renewable contracts because:
   a. Non-cancelable policies are not guaranteed renewable.
   b. Non-cancelable policies cannot be canceled in mid-term.
   c. Non-cancelable policies cannot have a premium change.
   d. Non-cancelable policies have more liberal health benefits.

2. Mr. Johns has a major medical insurance policy with a $1,000 deductible, an 80% coinsurance clause, and an out-of-pocket maximum of $4,000. He becomes ill and is admitted to the hospital for several days. When he is discharged, his hospital bill is $5,000, and his doctor bills are $2,500. What is the amount that his insurance company will pay?
   a. $5,200.
   b. $6,000.
   c. $6,500.
   d. $7,500.

3. COBRA coverage is available for which of the following persons?
   1. A retiring employee.
   2. An employee who is terminated.
   3. Spouses and dependents of a deceased employee.
   4. An employee no longer able to work due to disability.
   a. 3 only.
   b. 3 and 4.
   c. 1, 2, and 3.
   d. 1, 2, 3, and 4.

4. The Watson family has a family medical policy that provides the following coverage for all four family members:
   - $1,000 per person embedded deductible; $4,000 family deductible.
   - $4,000 out-of-pocket limit per person.
   - 80/20 coinsurance provision.

   On a family trip, the Watson's were involved in a bizarre accident when Mr. Watson, in the lead of the group, lost footing on a steep hiking trail and plowed into the rest of the family members, causing them all to tumble down the slope. All four family members were hurt. Each person incurred medical expenses of $21,000. How much will the insurance company pay?
   a. $64,000.
   b. $67,200.
   c. $68,000.
   d. $84,000.

5. Which of the following is a characteristic of guaranteed renewability?
    1. The insurer guarantees to renew the policy to a stated age.
    2. The policy is non-cancelable and the premium may not be increased.
    3. Renewal is solely at insurer's discretion.
    4. The insurer has the right to increase the premium rates for the underlying class in which the insured is placed. Note: not for a single individual.
        a. 1 only.
        b. 1 and 4.
        c. 1, 2, and 4.
        d. 1, 2, 3, and 4.

QUICK QUIZ EXPLANATIONS

Quick Quiz 3.1
1. True.
2. False. When underwriting a large number of people under a group policy, some of the administrative costs are transferred to the plan sponsor.
3. True.

Quick Quiz 3.2
1. True.
2. True.
3. True.
4. False. The most common types of medical expense insurance are: hospital, physician, and surgical expense insurances.

Quick Quiz 3.3
1. True.
2. False. Managed care plans emerged from a desire to decrease health care costs and increase competition amongst health care providers.

Quick Quiz 3.4
1. False. Upon voluntary termination, one may stay on the employer's policy for no longer than 18 months.
2. True.

Quick Quiz 3.5
1. False. This is actually the opposite of adverse selection, which refers to ill people - or those who would derive the most benefit from insurance - being more likely to seek insurance, thereby denying the company the ability to spread risk amongst both sick and healthy participants.
2. False. The monetary benefit derived from an employer-funded health insurance plan is specifically excluded as income.

Additional multiple choice problems
are available at
money-education.com
by accessing the
Student Practice Portal.
Access requires registration of the title using
the unique code at the front of the book.

4

LIFE INSURANCE

LEARNING OBJECTIVES

1. Describe the purpose of life insurance.
2. Explain the factors commonly used in the life insurance underwriting process.*
3. Identify the parties to a life insurance policy.
4. Identify the various life-cycle stages and their impact on mortality rate.
5. Differentiate between term, whole life, variable, universal, and VUL policies and select the most appropriate type of coverage to match a client's specific circumstances.*
6. Recommend whether a policy should be replaced based upon quantitative and qualitative factors.*
7. Recommend life insurance purchase and benefits distribution options based upon needs, financial resources, and cost.*
8. Calculate a client's insurance needs using alternative approaches, including the needs approach, human life value approach, and capitalized earnings approach.*
9. Identify the types and uses of life insurance in financial planning.
10. Describe a modified endowment contract.
11. List settlement options for life insurance policies.
12. Describe common life insurance termination options.*
13. Describe the common contractual provisions in a life insurance policy.

* CFP Board Resource Document - Student-Centered Learning Objectives based upon CFP Board Principal Topics.

INTRODUCTION

When managing the personal risk exposures of individuals, life insurance, disability insurance, health insurance, and long-term care insurance are frequently purchased to ensure that a person can meet his or her financial goals by protecting accumulated wealth from the potential catastrophic losses associated with loss of life, prolonged disability, poor health, or long-term care needs. This chapter covers life insurance basic concepts and types of policies, and the planning associated with it. Chapter 5 covers tax treatment of life insurance and advanced planning concepts with life insurance. Chapter 3 covers health risks and the use of health insurance. Disability insurance is covered in Chapter 6, and long-term care is covered in Chapter 7.

It is often said that two things in life are certain: death and taxes. Many individuals tend to ignore these eventualities, particularly those who do their own financial planning without the benefit of a professional advisor. The prospect of paying taxes and contemplating one's own death are not thoughts that people prefer to harbor. The inevitability of death, however, is a very real issue when addressing financial goals. Younger people tend to ignore this risk as something too remote. While they will eventually have to face the inevitability of death, young people tend to believe that they won't have to worry about that for a long time. From a financial planning perspective, however, the younger the person, the more important the management of mortality risk (the risk of dying within the year).

The death of a family member, friend, or business associate typically results in emotional distress for survivors. Psychologists tell us that those suffering the loss of a loved one, and those diagnosed with terminal illnesses, will go through 5 stages of grief: (1) denial and isolation, (2) anger, (3) bargaining, (4) depression, and (5) acceptance. The order of the stages and the length of time each person spends in each stage will vary from individual to individual, and may be expressed with different levels of intensity.

Imagine a young surviving widow with school-age children who is not only dealing with the grief of losing a husband, but also trying to help her children to adjust to the loss of a father. If this young widow is your planning client, the last thing you want to do is deliver even more bad news: "I'm sorry but you cannot afford to continue living in your current house without your husband's income." While life insurance death benefits do not ease the emotional and physical loss, they can ease the financial burdens for surviving family members, allow them time to go through the stages of grief, and give them options. Without the death benefit from life insurance proceeds, survivors often face limited choices where additional, more favorable, options may have been available had a life insurance death benefit been provided.

There are a million similarly heart-wrenching situations that could apply to clients of any age. Life insurance helps in some of these situations and is designed to provide financial protection for survivors (family, friends, charity, business associates, and even pets) when an insured dies. Most often, life insurance will be used to replace a portion of the insured's future earning power that would be used to support dependents if the insured had lived.

In addition to providing for loved ones and paying end-of-life expenses (such as funeral and final illness expenses), there are many other personal risk exposures that can be eliminated by appropriate use of life insurance. Moreover, life insurance can be purchased to accomplish a variety of goals, including the following:

- To provide for orderly disposition of a business interest by means of a buy-sell agreement.
- To make gifts to charities (church, school, or other charitable organizations).
- To create a memorial or endowment in honor of the deceased.
- To fund special goals, such as college education for children or grandchildren.
- To build cash value that can be spent for retirement.
- To cover the life of a debtor who owes the client money. (For example, the client sold a business and is receiving installment payments. If the debtor dies prematurely, life insurance will assure that the client receives full payment.)
- To pay estate taxes and estate settlement expenses for the decedent.

PARTIES TO A LIFE INSURANCE CONTRACT

Three parties have an interest in any life insurance contract issued:
1. the owner,
2. the insured, and
3. the beneficiary.

Sometimes, the same person holds all three interests in the policy (if the proceeds are payable to his or her estate). In other cases, different individuals, groups, or legal structures may be the owners and/or beneficiaries of a life insurance policy.

The **insured** is the individual whose life is covered by the life insurance policy. When the insured dies, the life insurance company will pay the death benefit to the named beneficiary.

The **owner** of the policy is the person who can exercise the economic rights of the policy and typically, but not necessarily, pays the premiums. For example, if permanent life insurance is purchased, the owner can borrow from the cash value, pledge the cash value as collateral for a loan, and receive policy dividends (all of these situations will be discussed later). When a client wishes to access the savings element of permanent life insurance policies, he or she must be the owner of those policies. The owner and insured are often the same person. In some cases it makes sense to have the life insurance policy owned by someone other than the insured (such as the insured's spouse, a beneficiary, or a trust created to hold the policy). Typically, when a person other than the insured is the owner of the policy, the insured is attempting to reduce estate taxes, or is attempting to achieve greater asset protection of policy values than might otherwise occur. Often times, irrevocable life insurance trusts (know as ILITs) are used to purchase life insurance so that the proceeds are not included in the gross estate of the insured in order to avoid estate taxes on the proceeds.[1] ILITs and other life insurance arrangements are beyond the scope of this textbook, but are covered in the Income Tax and Estate Planning courses.

If the owner and insured are different parties, the owner will have to have an insurable interest in the life of the insured at the inception of the policy to obtain life insurance coverage, or the insured must consent to the owner purchasing coverage on his or her life. An insurable interest is an interest based upon a reasonable expectation of pecuniary advantage through the continued life, health, or bodily safety of another person and consequent loss by reason of that person's death or disability or a substantial interest engendered by love and affection in the case of individuals closely related by blood or law.[2] In other words, an insurable interest exists when there is a financial or other benefit to the continued life of another person. A person always has an insurable interest in himself and his spouse. A person will likely have an insurable interest in other family members and in his business partners. The insurable interest requirement serves the goal of preventing speculation on human life. Without such a requirement, it creates the possibility of betting on the deaths of others.

If the insured was the original owner and transfers the policy to a third party, the insured is deemed to have given consent to that third party to hold insurance on the insured's life. Insurable interest rules are designed to limit exposure to moral hazards (i.e., creating an incentive for the insured to die early as a means of collecting the death benefit).

The **beneficiary** is the person entitled to receive the death benefit. With life insurance, as well as other financial accounts that transfer ownership at the death of the owner, there is generally a primary beneficiary and a contingent beneficiary. A primary beneficiary is the person who will receive the proceeds from the life insurance policy upon the death of the insured. The contingent beneficiary is the person or persons who will receive the proceeds in the event of the insured's death and in the event that the primary beneficiary is already deceased or chooses to disclaim the proceeds.[3] Also, in the rare circumstance where the primary beneficiary murders the insured, most states have enacted slayer statutes that prohibit the primary beneficiary from receiving the death benefit, in which case the contingent beneficiary would then receive the policy proceeds. The owner of the policy can name

---

1. Less of an issue as the lifetime limit has increased to over $10 million.
2. CA Insurance Code Section 10110.
3. Disclaiming life insurance proceeds means that the beneficiary chooses to not accept the funds. A disclaimer may be used as a postmortem estate planning technique. This topic is discussed more in Money Education's Estate Planning textbook.

anyone including himself as the beneficiary. If there is no named beneficiary, the policy death benefit is typically paid to the owner, or if the owner is also the insured, to the owner/insured's estate.

Example 4.1

Randy purchased a $1 million life insurance policy on his life to protect his family in the event of his early death. Randy decided to retain ownership of the policy so that he could access the cash value of the policy. Randy did not name a beneficiary, therefore if he dies, the life insurance death benefit will be paid to his estate. The situation would be the same as if Randy had named his estate as the beneficiary of the policy. Ultimately, the proceeds will be distributed as stipulated in Randy's will, or, in the absence of a will, according to state intestacy laws. If Randy wishes for the death benefits to instead be paid directly to his family, he must name them as the beneficiaries under the policy.

As the example above illustrates, the insured, owner, and beneficiary may be the same person. Typically, when the insured is different from the owner, the owner is also named as the beneficiary on the policy.

Example 4.2

George is the insured on a $1 million life insurance policy. His wife, Weezy, is the owner of the policy. She has named herself as the primary beneficiary, and her son, Lionel, as the secondary or contingent beneficiary. If George dies, the policy will pay the death benefit to Weezy (who is also the owner), or if Weezy predeceases George, the proceeds will be paid to Lionel.

Example 4.3

Bertie is independently wealthy and expects to pay estate taxes at his death. Bertie created a trust and made cash gifts to the trust over time. The trustee used the funds to purchase a life insurance policy on Bertie's life. The trust owns the policy, pays the premiums, and is listed as the beneficiary of the policy. When Bertie dies, the trustee will use the death benefit in accordance with the instructions set forth in the trust document.

It is also possible for the owner, insured, and beneficiary to all be different parties. This is commonly referred to as the "unholy trinity." The unholy trinity is also referred to as the Goodman Triangle since it is a result of the outcome of the court case, Goodman v. Commissioner, 156 F.2d 218 (2nd Cir. 1946). When this occurs, the owner of the policy is deemed to have made a taxable transfer or gift to the beneficiary. Planners need to be very careful about potential gift and estate tax consequences of this type of arrangement (these issues are discussed more fully in the Estate Planning course).

Exhibit 4.1 | Unholy Trinity

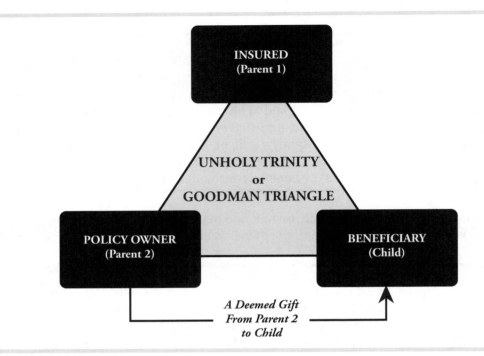

Example 4.4

Wally is the insured on a life insurance policy owned by his wife, Hilda. Hilda does not need the money, so she named Wally, Jr., their son, as the beneficiary of the policy. Wally is the insured, Hilda is the owner, and Wally Jr. is the beneficiary. During Wally's life, Hilda can access the cash value of the policy and receive policy dividends. When Wally dies, the death benefit is paid to Wally, Jr., and is considered a taxable gift from Hilda to Wally, Jr., which may cause a gift tax liability for Hilda.

When clients purchase life insurance, planners should know the identity of the insured, the owner, and the beneficiary. Without this knowledge, the planner will not be able to make appropriate recommendations for managing the client's risk and tax-planning needs. In addition, beneficiary designations should be reviewed on a regular basis and adjustments made as necessary. If a client's family situation changes (e.g., divorce, marriage, birth of a child, or death of a family member) there is often a need to change beneficiary designations accordingly.

LIFE INSURANCE UNDERWRITING

Underwriting is the process by which insurance companies decide whether to provide insurance to a customer and under what terms. Underwriters evaluate insurance applications and determine coverage amounts and premiums. They must evaluate the risk exposure and determine the premium that must be charged to insure that risk. When a company "underwrites" a policy, it accepts the risk inherent in the contract. In the case of life insurance, it accepts the risk of the insured dying prematurely and thus, having to pay the face value of the policy sooner than expected based on normal life expectancy. Many factors impact the probability of someone dying within a specific period of time. The underwriter attempts to quantify the impact of these factors on the likelihood of death and then determine an appropriate premium for that level of risk.

There are many factors that affect whether a company will issue an insurance policy on the life of a specific person. These factors will generally include the person's age, height and weight, gender, general state of health, lifestyle, medical history, profession (frequently called avocation by underwriters), financial status, hobbies, driving record, and whether they use tobacco products.

Depending on the amount of coverage requested, underwriters may request information beyond what is included in the application to evaluate the applicant's medical condition. Some of the common underwriting requirements include one or more of the following:

1. Copies of the applicant's medical records from their doctor(s)
2. An oral swab to check for tobacco or drug use, or the presence of HIV
3. A "mini" medical exam – called a paramedical exam
4. An IBP – an insurance blood profile
5. A HOS, or home office urine specimen
6. An EKG or electrocardiogram to check basic heart health
7. A full medical examination by a physician

⁞≣ *Key Concepts*

1. Understand the process of life insurance underwriting.

2. Identify the three stages in the life-cycle model.

3. Highlight/identify the reasons for life insurance.

4. Identify the three methods used to determine life insurance needs.

A person's health and lifestyle impact the mortality risk. Those with better health will generally have lower premiums. Individuals working in professions with less inherent risk will generally have lower premiums. For example it is more dangerous to work as a deep-sea fisherman or as a logger than as an insurance underwriter. Hobbies can certainly have an impact on the risk evaluation. Hobbies, such as skydiving, rock climbing, and scuba diving subject the person to more risk than other hobbies, such as collecting baseball cards. The exhibit below provides some detail in terms of the impact a specific factor may have on the underwriting process and the resulting policy premium.

Exhibit 4.2 | Impact of Select Underwriting Factors on Insurance Premiums

Factor	Risk Level & Premium Effect
Height & Weight	Those with a higher BMI (body mass index) are more risky, resulting in a higher premium.
Gender	Women tend to outlive men, resulting in lower premiums for women versus men of the same age.
Health	Chronic conditions, diseases, and high cholesterol levels are all higher risk and will result in higher premiums.
Family Medical History	Having a family history of poor health, diabetes, heart attacks or strokes, cancer, or early deaths will result in higher premiums.
Hobbies	People who engage in high risk activities (rock climbing, car racing, scuba diving, non-commercial aviation) will have higher premiums.
Driving	A history of speeding tickets or DWI/DUI arrests will likely result in higher premiums or, possibly, declination.
Financial Stability Status	Those who are more financially stable and well-off tend to be less risky and have lower premiums.

It should be noted that an underwriter will take into consideration the totality of all of the factors in determining whether or not to issue a policy and the amount of the premium. If the underwriter approves an application, the policy may be offered at "standard" rates, or at "preferred" rates if the applicant is deemed to be in better than average physical condition. For applicants who have a higher risk but who are still acceptable at higher premium rates, the underwriter may offer a "rated" policy. Life Insurance Companies frequently have numerous "Table" rating categories, such as Table A: 25% surcharge, Table B: 50% surcharge, Table C: 100% surcharge, etc. Table rates may go up to several multiples of the standard premium rate.

LIFE INSURANCE AND MORTALITY RISK

Risk Exposures from Dying Early

To understand the risk exposure of early death, it is important to have a general understanding of the life-cycle model of financial planning. Individuals typically progress through three stages from the beginning of their careers to their deaths. These stages include:

1. Asset accumulation phase
2. Conservation/risk management phase
3. Distribution/gifting phase

Exhibit 4.3 | Life-Cycle Stages

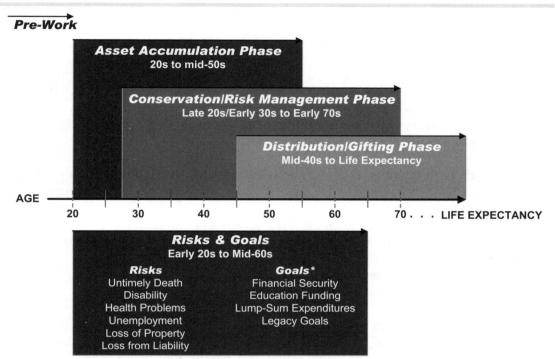

The **asset accumulation phase** of the life cycle begins after a person completes his or her schooling and enters the workforce and typically lasts until ages 45-55. The early period of this phase is characterized by relatively high debt and low savings. In the early years of the accumulation phase, individuals often marry, have children, purchase houses and cars, and make further investments in their human capital by pursuing professional or graduate education. In the later years of the accumulation phase, debt is declining, savings and investments are increasing, and earnings from work or self-employment are increasing.

During the **conservation/risk management phase** of the life-cycle model, which typically lasts from ages 45-50 until retirement (around age 65), earnings from employment have reached their peak, children enter and exit college, the outstanding balance on the client's mortgage shrinks substantially, and savings increase to support retirement. It is common for individuals in this phase of the life cycle to take a more conservative approach to investing, since retirement is on the horizon. During the early part of this phase, clients become acutely aware of their insurance needs.

The **distribution/gifting phase** of the life cycle begins near retirement and ends at death. During this phase, a person generally begins to spend down his or her accumulated assets and may begin to transfer excess assets to family members and loved ones as gifts. After the person dies, any remaining assets will be transferred to intended beneficiaries by bequest, either through a validly executed will, the probate process, or a non-probate transfer vehicle.

As individuals age, their **mortality risk** (the risk that they will die within the year) increases. While it is unlikely that a healthy 25-year-old person will die this year, some 25-year-olds will pass away. Actuaries measure the likelihood of death at each age by observing the actual incidence of death by age for the population as a whole and then publish these probabilities in mortality tables. Not surprisingly, the risk of dying (mortality risk) increases as a person ages.

If a person dies prior to accumulating sufficient financial assets to meet his or her financial planning goals, the person's family (not the deceased individual) will feel the financial impact. Life insurance can be used as a hedge against the risk of early death so that if the person dies before accumulating the wealth necessary to satisfy his financial objectives, the life insurance death benefit received by the family will cover the cost of unfunded financial goals.

As a person moves through the life cycle from the asset accumulation phase to the distribution/gifting phase, his needs for life insurance as a hedge against early death change. In the accumulation phase of the life cycle, life insurance is often used to:
- Provide an income stream for the family if the breadwinner dies.
- Pay off existing debts (such as outstanding mortgages, car loans, personal loans, and consumer credit accounts).
- Fund financial objectives (such as education for the children).
- Provide a retirement income for the surviving spouse.

Moving from the asset accumulation phase of the life cycle to the conservation/risk management phase, the need for life insurance to fund financial goals and income streams declines, but very slowly (a reverse exponential curve). Everything being equal, if a person dies at an older age compared to a younger age, the need for income replacement declines (assuming that the surviving spouse is roughly the same age). Many financial objectives will already have been partially met, such as paying down the mortgage on the principal residence and helping children to obtain a college education. Once the mortgage is paid and the children have finished school, those objectives may be fully satisfied, and life insurance to fund these objectives may no longer be needed. If the surviving spouse needs supplemental income during retirement, however, life insurance may still be needed to fund this objective.

The conservation/risk management phase may result in increased needs for life insurance as well. If the person started a business, additional life insurance may be needed to:
- Fund buy-sell agreements between the owners of the business when one of the owners dies.
- Provide liquidity for the estate of the business owner so that taxes and administration expenses can be paid without reducing the family's inheritance.

High-income individuals, or those who have accumulated significant assets during the accumulation phase, may also be interested in acquiring life insurance as a way of maintaining and enhancing family wealth. The tax benefits of life insurance make it an attractive tool to help to achieve these objectives.

As the person enters the distribution/gifting phase of the life cycle, income needs are generally not an issue and the retirement income needs should be fully funded. Ideally, when a person retires, most-if not all-of his or her financial goals are met:
- No outstanding mortgage on the house
- Children have completed school and are independent
- Other client objectives have been fully funded

The need for life insurance in the distribution phase of the life cycle often focuses on estate liquidity needs, a desire to create and sustain family wealth, or a desire to generate a large charitable gift upon death. Death benefits paid on a life insurance policy can be used to cover medical expenses prior to death (to the extent that those expenses were not covered by health insurance), funeral expenses, probate and estate administration costs, and estate and inheritance taxes, which allows the full value of the decedent's assets to be transferred to the surviving family. Properly constructed planning arrangements combined with life insurance coverage can also create a pool of capital for the family, allowing someone to achieve financial goals that extend beyond his or her death.

Measuring the Life Insurance Need

The insurance conversation can be uncomfortable for many clients because they are forced to think about and acknowledge the possibility of unfortunate events, such as disability, poor health, long-term care, or loss of property, and the certainty of death. While these events are unpleasant to think about, planning in advance for them is certain to have better outcomes than failing to plan. The insurance needs analysis is an important part of the planning for these events in the risk management process. It can be utilized to identify the appropriate types and amounts of coverage, enabling limited resources to be applied most efficiently and effectively.

The planner often begins the discussion of insurance needs by asking the client to consider what would happen if he or she died (became disabled, lost a home in a fire, etc.) today. This begins an uncomfortable, but necessary, conversation that enables the client and planner to work together to determine what goals are most important to the client, so that they may be funded through the purchase of insurance.

Single individuals are often told that they do not need life insurance or that the small policy that comes with their work benefits is enough. In many cases, that is correct. However, there are certain instances where a person who is single may need life insurance, such as to pay off a mortgage, to protect insurability for future dependents, or to provide for parents, a significant other, relative, friend, pet, or charity.

Blended families (those with children from a previous marriage) and sandwiched families (those who have to provide for minor children, as well as their own parents) tend to have even greater life insurance needs.

Once the need for life insurance is determined, a person must then decide the amount of death benefit to purchase. Over time, different approaches to calculating life insurance needs have been developed. Most practitioners use one or more of the following three models to determine life insurance needs:
1. The human-life value approach
2. The needs approach
3. The capitalized-earnings approach

Exhibit 4.4 | Methods to Determine Life Insurance Needs

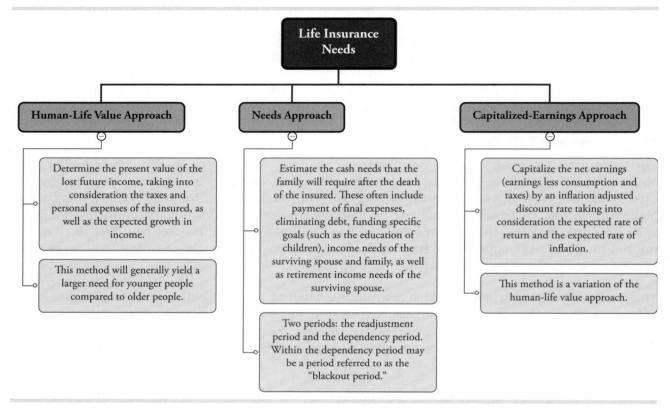

Some advisors routinely use only one of these approaches. However, a better approach is to fit the projection model to the client's circumstances instead of using only one approach. Some advisors use all three models and then consider other issues such as cash flows and rate bands to determine how much life insurance to purchase.[4]

Human-Life Value Approach

The **human-life value approach** suggests that the death benefit of a client's life insurance should equal the economic value of his future earnings stream discounted to its present value while considering his tax and consumption patterns. While religious scholars and philosophers teach us that we cannot place a monetary value on human life itself, it is possible to calculate the economic value of a person's expected future earnings. When an individual dies before reaching retirement, the loss of that person's earnings could create a hardship on the family, but with appropriate planning, that income stream can be replaced with the life insurance death benefit. Assuming that a person's income stream will be sufficient to achieve all of his or her financial goals, replacing the lost income stream for the family should permit the family to meet their financial objectives. The human-life value approach was one of the earliest techniques used to estimate life insurance needs. It was espoused by Dr. Solomon Heubner, a professor

---

4. A rate band is a death benefit amount range (such a $100,000 - $249,000, or $250,000 - $499,000) within which the insurance company uses a set premium rate per $1,000 of coverage purchased. Each higher rate band typically has a lower cost per $1,000, such that a client considering the purchase of $240,000 of death benefit may pay a lower premium to purchase $250,000 due to the change in rate band.

at The Wharton School of The University of Pennsylvania and founder of the American College of Life Underwriters, who is widely regarded as the "father of insurance education."

The steps in calculating a human-life value include:

1. Determine the family's share of earnings by identifying the person's annual earnings and subtracting personal expenses and taxes that would have been incurred (consumption and taxes).
2. Determine work-life expectancy (WLE), or the number of years he or she would have continued to earn income (alternatively stated, the number of years before retirement).
3. Calculate the present value of the family's share of earnings using an inflation-adjusted rate of return to determine the human-life value. The inflation adjusted rate of return (real return) is used to reflect both the expected rate of return on the invested death benefit proceeds and the expected growth in salary. The formula to calculate the real return is: [(1+investment return)/ (1+inflation rate of salary)]-1 x 100.

Example 4.5

Chelsea is a 30-year-old marketing executive who earns $100,000 per year. She is married to Louis and has two children. She expects her salary to increase at an annual rate of 4% until her retirement at age 65 and anticipates that the family can invest the death benefit proceeds at a rate of 5%. Chelsea and Louis' income places them in the 25% average tax bracket (including both state and federal taxes), and she uses 15% of her after-tax income for personal consumption. Based on the human-life value approach, how much life insurance should Chelsea purchase?

Using the approach outlined above, we begin by taking Chelsea's income of $100,000 and subtracting the personal expenses that she will incur. The first 25% of her income goes to the payment of taxes, making her after-tax income $75,000. Of this amount, Chelsea uses $11,250 (15% x $75,000) for her own personal consumption and contributes $63,750 (85% x $75,000) of her income toward the achievement of family goals and objectives.

Step 1: Calculate the Family's Share of Earnings (FSE)	
Annual Earnings $65,000	= Annual Taxes = $100,000 x 0.25 = $25,000
Personal Consumption	= (After-tax income x consumption %)
	= [(($100,000 - $25,000) x 0.15)]
	= $11,250
FSE	= Annual Earnings - (annual income taxes + annual personal consumption)
(Family's Share of Earnings)	= $100,000 - ($25,000 + $11,250)
	= $63,750

Since Chelsea is 30 years old and will retire at age 65, her work-life expectancy (WLE) is 35 years.

Step 2: Calculate Work Life Expectancy (WLE)	
WLE	= The expected age at retirement less the current age
	= 65 - 30
WLE	= 35 years

To determine Chelsea's human-life value and the amount of life insurance she should have on her life, we need to calculate the present value of her lifetime FSE at the inflation rate over her work-life expectancy, assuming the death benefit proceeds can be invested at a rate or return of 5%.

Step 3: Determine Human Life Value (HLV)*		
Future Value (FV)	=	0
Annual PMT$_{OA}$	=	$63,750
Interest Rate (i)	=	0.96154 [[(1.05 ÷ 1.04 inflation rate) - 1] x 100]
Term of Years (n)	=	35
Human Life Value (PV)	=	$1,886,980 (Present Value)

*Some advisers use an annuity due (begin mode) for this calculation, assuming that the family will need the income at the start of each year. The result in that case would be $1,905,124. This is within close range of the result using an ordinary annuity, and after rate bands are considered, will likely result in the client purchasing the same amount of insurance under either method.

Note: This is about 19 times her gross pay!

Using the human-life value approach to calculate life insurance needs, Chelsea should purchase a life insurance policy with a death benefit of approximately $1,900,000. If she had a life insurance policy with this death benefit and she died today, that amount, growing at the assumed annual increase in salary, will provide Chelsea's family with a full replacement of the portion of her income that she contributed toward the attainment of the family's financial goals.

When considering the use of the human-life value approach, a few relationships are worth considering. First, younger individuals have a higher human-life value (all else equal) than older persons because they will earn income for a longer period of time. As a person ages, the human-life value and the need for life insurance protection will decline. Second, as the individual's income rises (all else equal) so will their human-life value. As income increases, a greater amount will have to be replaced in the event that the person dies prior to the planned retirement date. Third, higher investment return expectations will lead to a lower human-life value, since the lifetime FSE is discounted at a higher rate. If a planner would like to make a conservative projection of human-life value, therefore, lower expected investment rates should be used.

For many people, use of the human-life value approach to determining life insurance needs may be appropriate. If the person will have funded all of his or her financial objectives for the family by retirement, will not have liquidity needs at death, does not have a need to use life insurance for business succession planning purposes, and does not wish to use life insurance to fund family legacies, the human-life value approach to determining life insurance needs will provide an insurance amount that closely approximates the family's actual financial needs.

The human life value method has some disadvantages that make it less attractive than the needs approach (discussed below) as a means of determining the death benefit amount. With the human life value approach, there is no capital retention, meaning that the life insurance is completely liquidated at the end of the family's needs. In addition there is little emotional attachment to the value of the death benefit. The insured does not have a clear picture of exactly what the death benefit amount is providing. Without a clear understanding of what this death benefit is purchasing, there is little attachment to the policy and the likelihood of the policy eventually lapsing is higher than for a policy where the insured has a clear understanding and emotional connection to the purpose.

The Needs Approach

The second approach to estimating life insurance requirements is the **needs approach**. Instead of determining the present value of a future income stream, the planner and client work together to estimate the cash needs that the family will require at and after the death of the insured. Some of the financial needs that are typically considered when calculating a life insurance amount under the needs approach include:

1. Payment of final expenses, medical care, and adjustment period expenses
2. Eliminating debt
3. Funding specific goals, such as education for children
4. Income needs of the surviving spouse and the family
5. Retirement needs of the surviving spouse

Final expenses typically include funeral costs, administration expenses, taxes (income, estate, inheritance, and generation-skipping taxes), and medical care provided shortly before death. The cash to cover these expenses will be needed within a few days to a few months after death. According to the American Council of Life Insurers, insurance companies delivered $218 million every day in 2018 to beneficiaries of life insurance policies, typically within 30 days of receiving a claim.[5]

Depending upon the level of service selected, funeral costs can be significant and must typically be paid prior to services being provided. According to the National Funeral Directors Association, the median cost of a funeral with viewing, burial, and vault was $9,135 in 2019, and the median cost of a funeral with viewing and cremation was $5,150.[6]

Many people incur most of their lifetime medical expenses within the last few months before their deaths. These expenses usually have to be paid before beneficiaries can receive inheritances from the estate of the decedent. For individuals with tight cash-flow and few liquid assets, including any estimated funeral and medical expenses in the life insurance need calculation is appropriate since the death benefit will provide additional cash resources within a relatively short period of time. Individuals with higher net worth and sufficient liquid assets may not have to include funeral expenses and medical costs when calculating insurance needs since other resources are available to pay these expenses. However, high net-worth individuals are likely to have higher costs of estate administration, and possibly higher transfer taxes that will be due within nine months of death. As an alternative to self-funding or using life insurance to fund these costs, the person can prepay funeral expenses and maintain adequate health insurance during lifetime to ensure that medical expenses are paid.

One way to ease the burden on survivors is to be able to pay off all outstanding debt at death. For example, if a person leaves a mortgaged residence to the surviving spouse, the surviving spouse will have cash flow needs to continue to service the mortgage. Paying off the mortgage simplifies matters for the survivor by eliminating the required monthly payments and thereby reducing the survivor's need for cash flow. Individuals may also wish to pay off other forms of debt, such as car loans, personal loans, student loans, and revolving charge accounts. These amounts should be included in the life insurance needs estimate.

---

5. https://www.acli.com/Consumer-Info/Life-Insurance/What-is-208-Million-Dollars.
6. The median cost is the cost at which half of the figures fall above and half of the figures below.

Aside from retirement, perhaps the largest funding objective that many families face is the (partial or full) payment of their children's higher education costs. Education is expensive. The cost of tuition and other related costs have consistently increased at a rate greater than inflation. The early death of the family's breadwinner could result in limited funding to cover college education expenses. If education funding is a goal, the planner should calculate the lump sum (present value) needed to pay for the tuition and other related costs at the target college, and include that in the life insurance needs analysis.

An emergency fund should be established to cover unexpected major expenses, and possibly the loss of employment. If a young person dies prior to establishing an adequate emergency fund, however, it may be wise to include a lump sum in the death benefit need calculation that can be set aside by the survivors to pay for emergencies so that the other portion of the policy death benefit can be used for its intended purpose.

Additional lump sums may be needed to fulfill special goals such as setting up a trust for children with disabilities or special needs, or for making charitable gifts.

Finally, when calculating life insurance requirements under the needs approach, the income needs of the surviving spouse and dependents must be considered. Income needs will vary depending upon the family circumstances, the age of the family members, and the availability of public and private benefit payments. These changes to the income needs of the survivors are often broken down into the readjustment period and the dependency period.

The Readjustment Period

After the death of a family's breadwinner, the family will need time to adjust to their new reality – a life without an important member of the family. For a period of six months to two years, the family should have access to the same amount of income that was available when the breadwinner was alive. Often, non-recurring expenses will be incurred as a result of the breadwinner's death. Having the cash flow to cover these expenses without affecting the family's lifestyle may be important. In the event of the death of a stay-at-home parent, additional funds may also be needed to allow the surviving parent to temporarily reduce working hours to assist the children through the grieving process and allow them time to adjust to their new situation, as well to locate an appropriate caregiver for the children while the surviving parent is at work.

The Dependency Period

The length of the dependency period is determined by the number of dependents and their ages. Traditionally this period lasts from the end of the readjustment period to the time when all children reach the age of majority. As members of the sandwich generation will suggest, another factor that can extend the dependency period occurs when the decedent's parents are dependents.[7] If parents rely on income to make

---

Quick Quiz 4.1

1. Generally, people accumulate wealth throughout their lives.
   a. True
   b. False

2. Life insurance can be an effective tool for enhancing a family's wealth.
   a. True
   b. False

3. Death benefits paid from life insurance cannot be used to pay the decedent's hospital bills.
   a. True
   b. False

4. Generally, as clients age, the human-life value and the need for life insurance protection will increase.
   a. True
   b. False

False, True, False, False.

ends meet, the present value of the anticipated support over the parents' lifetime should also be included in the life insurance needs calculation.

If the surviving spouse has an independent source of income sufficient to meet the needs of him/herself and the family, additional life insurance funding may be unnecessary. In some cases, however, the dependency period may have to be extended to provide supplemental income for the decedent's spouse in the event the spouse cannot work or cannot replace the income lost when the decedent died.

If the surviving spouse is caring for minor children at the time of the decedent's death, and the deceased spouse was fully or currently insured under Social Security, both the surviving spouse and the children will qualify for Social Security survivors benefits.[8] When the youngest child reaches the age of 16, survivor benefit payments to the surviving spouse will cease until the surviving spouse reaches the age of 60 (the blackout period), and the surviving spouse will typically need additional income to act as a substitute for those lost payments. When Social Security payments resume in the form of widow(er) or retirement benefits (as early as age 60 for a surviving spouse), those supplemental income payments can be replaced by the additional Social Security income. While the widow(er) benefit under Social Security is available as early as age 60, the benefits will be reduced, and the impact of the surviving spouse having earned income could cause the benefit to be further reduced or eliminated before the surviving spouse's full retirement age (66 or 67). Once the surviving spouse reaches full retirement age under Social Security, however, there will be no additional reduction due to earned income. The impact of timing on the amount of Social Security widow(er) or retirement benefits may result in the desire to provide life insurance funding until the surviving spouse reaches full retirement age under Social Security, rather than the earliest permissible age of 60. The period between the cessation of survivor benefits and the receipt of widow(er) or retirement benefits is sometimes referred to as the "blackout period" by planners. When forecasting the amount of income the surviving spouse will need, be sure to consider the impact of the blackout period on the income needs of the surviving spouse.

After calculating the amount of each of the family's financial needs, these amounts can be added together to determine the appropriate life insurance death benefit for the individual. If the person already has some life insurance coverage, or has existing assets that could be used to fund these needs in the event of an early death, those amounts can be subtracted from the total to determine the net amount of life insurance protection that should be obtained on their life.

Example 4.6 provides an analysis of a needs approach to life insurance needs and a graphical presentation of the component parts.

---

7. The sandwich generation is a term that describes people who must take care of and raise their children as well as provide care and support for their aged parents.
8. To be fully insured under Social Security, the decedent must have accumulated 40 credits under the Social Security System, and to be currently insured must have accumulated six credits in the last 13 calendar quarters. Details regarding Social Security survivor benefits and how credits are earned can be found in Chapter 11.

Example 4.6

Assume the following information:

Husband	Age 30	$100,000 income
Wife	Age 30	
Child A	Age 4	
Child B	Age 2	

- Social Security Old Age, Survivor, and Disability benefit (OASDI) until Child B becomes age 16, $2,500 per month. The spouse is no longer entitled to benefits after the youngest child turns 16.
- Social Security OASDI benefit from the time Child B becomes age 16 until Child B becomes age 18, $1,250 per month. The children stop receiving benefits upon turning 18.
- Social Security OASDI widow's benefit from age 60 to life expectancy age 90, $2,500 per month.
- College education costs $20,000 per year per child in today's dollars, at age 18 for four years.
- Total income needs of spouse for dependency period until Child B is age 22, $5,000 per month in today's dollars.
- Inflation is expected to be 3%.
- Investment rate of return is expected to be 5%.
- Funeral, last medical, and adjustment period expense equal a lump sum of $30,000.
- Mortgage and debt repayment lump sum of $200,000.
- Education inflation rate is 5%.

Calculation 1			Calculation 2		
N	=	14 x 12	N	=	2 x 12
i	=	[(1.05÷1.03-1)x100]÷12	i	=	[(1.05÷1.03-1)x100]÷12
PMT	=	$2,500	PMT	=	$3,750
PV	=	$367,494	PV$_{@44}$	=	$88,205
			PV$_{@30}$	=	$67,385*
Calculation 3			**Calculation 4**		
N	=	14 x 12	N	=	30 x 12
i	=	[(1.05÷1.03-1)x100]÷12	i	=	[(1.05÷1.03-1)x100]÷12
PMT	=	$5,000	PMT	=	$2,500
PV$_{@46}$	=	$734,987	PV$_{@60}$	=	$681,732
PV$_{@30}$		$540,315*	PV$_{@30}$	=	$382,870*

> * Note: The second present value calculation in Calculations 2, 3, and 4 use whole years instead of months (e.g., 14 in Calculation 2, 16 in Calculation 3, and 30 in Calculation 4) and use an i of (1.05/1.03 - 1) x 100 and are rounded to whole dollars. The change from months to years for the second calculation was done for simplicity and the keystrokes are not shown.

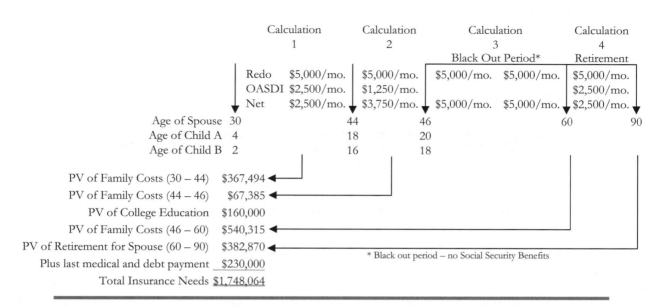

		Calculation 1	Calculation 2	Calculation 3 Black Out Period*		Calculation 4 Retirement
Redo		$5,000/mo.	$5,000/mo.	$5,000/mo.	$5,000/mo.	$5,000/mo.
OASDI		$2,500/mo.	$1,250/mo.			$2,500/mo.
Net		$2,500/mo.	$3,750/mo.	$5,000/mo.	$5,000/mo.	$2,500/mo.

	Age			
Age of Spouse	30	44	46	60	90
Age of Child A	4	18	20		
Age of Child B	2	16	18		

PV of Family Costs (30 – 44)	$367,494
PV of Family Costs (44 – 46)	$67,385
PV of College Education	$160,000
PV of Family Costs (46 – 60)	$540,315
PV of Retirement for Spouse (60 – 90)	$382,870
Plus last medical and debt payment	$230,000
Total Insurance Needs	$1,748,064

* Black out period – no Social Security Benefits

The Capitalized-Earnings Approach

The **capitalized-earnings approach** is a modification of the human-life value approach. The difference is that there is no need to determine the work-life expectancy because, assuming the investment returns are realized, the lump sum death benefit will yield enough earnings each year to provide the desired income for a perpetual period of time. This is a very efficient method for determining the approximate amount of life insurance needed for one who has dependents and life insurance needs.

This method divides the family's share of earnings (earnings less taxes and consumption) by an inflation-adjusted discount rate, which takes into consideration the expected rate of return and the expected rate of inflation (the desired increase in income to the family each year).

Example 4.7

Assume the following:

Earnings	$100,000
Raise Rate	4%
Inflation Rate	3%
Investment Rate	5%
Consumption by Insured	15%
Federal and State Taxes	25%

The numerator: Earnings - Consumption - Taxes

The denominator: $\dfrac{1 + \text{Investment Rate}}{1 + \text{Inflation Rate}} - 1$

Calculation: $\dfrac{\$100,000 - \$25,000 - \$11,250}{(1.05 \div 1.03) - 1} = \dfrac{\$63,750}{0.0194175} = \$3,283,125$

The amount of life insurance needed using the capitalized-earnings approach in this example is $3,283,125. This amount is significantly higher than the amount determined using the human life value approach. However, the human life value approach leaves less room for error since it assumes the funds will be entirely depleted at the assumed life expectancy age, while the capitalization of earnings approach provides funds in perpetuity. On the other hand, the capitalization of earnings approach likely overstates the need unless the client has legacy goals which include several generations.

Summary of the Three Methods		
Human-Life Value Approach	=	$1,886,980
Needs Approach	=	$1,748,064
Capitalized-Earnings Approach	=	$3,283,125

As illustrated in the examples, the three methods of calculating the death benefit need may vary significantly depending on individual circumstances and assumptions used. From numerous applications of the three methods, we have developed a benchmark metric of 12-18 times gross pay (a multiple-of-income approach) as the general guide for life insurance needed. While any rule of thumb, such as this benchmark metric, is a helpful planning tool, it should not be used as a substitute for a complete analysis. In addition, as stated previously, it is important that the client fully understand and appreciate the value that the death benefit brings. Otherwise the life insurance premiums may feel like an expense that is bringing little tangible value and there is a danger that the client will discontinue premium payments, allowing the policy to lapse.

After the need is determined, under one or a combination of the three methods, it must then be reduced by existing life insurance death benefits and any accumulated assets that can be utilized to fund the needs. The end result will determine the amount of additional death benefit required, if any. The next step will be to review the needs being funded to determine whether they are temporary (such as education funding for children; once the children have completed schooling the need no longer exists) or permanent needs (such as funeral expenses). This will determine the mix of term insurance, which is temporary in nature and lower cost, and permanent insurance, which is permanent in nature and higher cost.

Exhibit 4.5 | Sample Life Insurance Needs Analysis Form

Life Insurance Needs Analysis

Completed for: _____

Expenses to be Covered Upon Death	IF _____ Died Today:	IF _____ Died Today:
Funeral costs		
Estate taxes and administration		
Final medical expenses		
Mortgage pay-off		
Other debts		
Readjustment period income		
Income replacement during child dependency period		
Income replacement for surviving spouse after dependency period and before retirement		
Retirement period income for surviving spouse		
Extra expense fund		
Special Goals:		
Education funding		
Support of dependents with special needs		
Charitable contributions		
Care of pets		
Other		
Total Need	$ -	$ -
Less available assets		
Total Need to be Funded with Life Insurance	$ -	$ -
Amount to be funded with term insurance		
Less existing term insurance		
Additional term insurance needed	$ -	$ -
Amount to be funded with permanent insurance		
Less existing permanent insurance		
Additional permanent insurance needed	$ -	$ -

Date completed: _____

Completed by: _____

TYPES AND USES OF LIFE INSURANCE IN FINANCIAL PLANNING

Life insurance transfers the risk of losses associated with early death to an insurance company in return for a fee (the premium on the policy). If the insured party dies, the insurance company pays the specified death benefit to a designated beneficiary. Several types of life insurance policies exist in the market today. The type of policy that is appropriate for one person may not be appropriate for another. Planners need to understand the individual's purpose for buying and holding life insurance and select the policy that most closely matches his or her needs.

The two most common types of life insurance are term and permanent. Permanent life insurance includes universal, whole, variable, and modified endowment contracts, all of which are discussed in this section.

Term Insurance

A **term-insurance** policy, like all other life insurance policies, provides death benefit protection. If the insured dies during the term of the policy, the insurance company will pay the specified death benefit. The term of the policy may be one year, five years, 10 years, 20 years, or longer, although many term policies are designed to permit the insured to renew the policy for one or more additional terms when the initial term expires.

When a term-insurance policy is purchased, the owner pays a premium equal to the risk the insurance company is undertaking. Term-insurance policies do not have cash accumulation features and do not provide for continuing insurance after premium payments cease. Quite literally, the owner of a term policy is shifting the financial risk of death for the current year to the insurance company in return for the annual premium. If the owner wishes to shift the financial risk of death to the insurance company in future years, additional premiums must be paid.

As individuals advance in age, the actuarial risk that they will die within the year increases. This means that every year the **mortality cost**, which equals the probability of dying within the year times the face value of the policy, of the term-insurance policy increases to reflect the increased risk of death. The term-insurance premium for a young person tends to be very low due to the decreased risk of death, but term-insurance policies can get very expensive for older individuals. In fact, at age 99, the premium for a term-insurance policy approximates the death benefit of the policy (discounted for a few months of time value) since the risk of death within the year is substantial. For this reason, term-insurance policies tend to be used by younger individuals and for those who need life insurance protection for shorter periods of time to ensure that, in the event of their early death, their financial goals can be met. When the need

> ## ✸≣ *Key Concepts*
>
> 1. Describe the differences between annual renewable term (ART) life insurance, level-term life insurance, decreasing term life insurance, convertible annual renewable term life insurance, and group term insurance.
>
> 2. Describe some of the benefits and negatives of universal life insurance.
>
> 3. Describe the differences between straight (ordinary) whole life insurance, limited pay whole life insurance, modified whole life insurance, and variable whole life insurance.
>
> 4. Describe the income tax benefits that can be arranged with life insurance planning.

for life insurance is permanent, some form of cash-value policy will generally be used since the premiums on term insurance at advanced ages become prohibitive.

Example 4.8

Aside from funding her retirement, Edith's primary financial goal is to pay for the college education costs of her son, Archie. She is currently 32 years old. Edith has met with a financial planner and has developed a savings plan that will, over time, meet both her retirement and educational funding needs. If Edith dies before she can earn the money to fund these objectives, Archie's education may not be fully funded. To hedge against this risk, Edith purchases a term-insurance policy with a death benefit of $500,000 so Archie will be able to attend the college of his choice. If Edith lives, she will meet the educational funding goal through savings and investments and will no longer need to pay for the insurance. Since Edith's life insurance need is temporary and she is relatively young, term insurance is a good option.

Example 4.9

Sherman (grantor) recently created a Grantor Retained Annuity Trust. He funded the trust with stock of Wooster Enterprises, Ltd. The trust states Sherman will receive an income stream equal to 20% of the value of the stock he transferred to the trust each year for five years (thus the retained annuity). After the five-year period expires, the trust terminates, and whatever is left in the trust will be transferred to his cousin, Morgan. If Sherman dies while receiving the income stream from the trust, the value of the trust assets will be taxable in his gross estate.[9] If Sherman purchases a term-insurance policy for the five-year duration of the trust and dies during that term, the policy will provide sufficient money to pay any estate taxes. Since Sherman's need for life insurance is temporary (in this case, five years), term insurance is an appropriate product.

Example 4.10

Clarence is the president and CEO of Empress of Blandings Holdings Company, Inc. He owns a 30% interest in the company, and the remaining ownership interest is held by members of his extended family. Since Empress of Blandings is a family-owned company and the owners wish to keep it that way, they have entered into a buy-sell agreement so that if any of the current owners dies, the surviving owners must purchase the deceased owner's interest from his or her estate. The company is a large one, and neither Clarence nor the other owners expect to have sufficient cash on hand to purchase the stock as required by the buy-sell agreement. Instead, they fund the buy-sell agreement using life insurance policies purchased on all of the owners' lives. Since the need for life insurance is permanent in this case, term insurance is <u>not</u> the appropriate type of insurance to purchase.

---

9. IRC Section 2036.

There are several variations of term insurance in the market today. Perhaps the most common type of term insurance is **Annual Renewable Term (ART)**. An Annual Renewable Term policy permits the policyholder to renew the purchase for the same amount of term insurance in subsequent years without evidence of insurability, but premiums on the policy increase each year to reflect the increasing mortality risk being undertaken by the insurer. Many insurance companies will limit the renewal period to a specified number of years (or to a specific age), at which time the insured would have to then provide further evidence of insurability in order to obtain a new policy. The limitation on renewal protects the insurer against possible adverse selection risk (the risk that only unhealthy insureds will renew their term life insurance coverage).

Exhibit 4.6 | Renewable Term Premium and Yearly Renewable Term Premium (Issued as Early as Age 25)

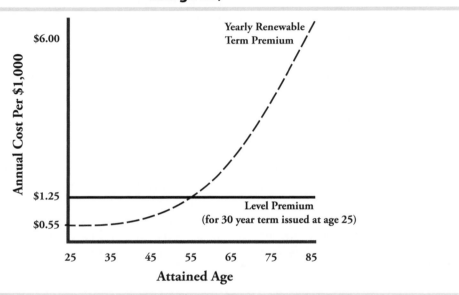

For some individuals, the increasing premium on annual renewable term insurance may be unattractive, and they would prefer to commit to a specific premium amount that will not change over a specific period of time (the term). **Level-premium term insurance** charges a fixed premium each year over a specified period of years (often 5, 10, 15, 20, 25, or 30 years), so the premium does not increase during that period. When a level-term insurance policy is purchased, the premiums paid by the owner will be larger than the premiums on an annual renewable term policy in the earlier years, but will be less than the premiums on an annual renewable term policy in later years. All else being equal, the total premium outlay on an annual renewable term policy will be less than that on a level-term policy since time value of money principles are used to discount the premiums over the leveling period. However, level-premium term may be appropriate for people who prefer simplicity in budgeting, since their insurance costs will be "fixed" over the level premium.

For individuals who do not anticipate having a permanent need for insurance, the life-cycle theory of financial planning suggests that their need for life insurance protection will decrease as they get older. As each year passes and income is earned, that income can be employed to meet their financial goals, thereby allowing them to rely less on life insurance to satisfy those goals in the event of an untimely death. **Decreasing-term insurance** allows the owner to pay the same premium for the insurance protection each year. The death benefit on the policy will, however, decrease each year to offset the increasing mortality cost due to the passage of time.

Example 4.11

Will is married to Grace, and they have three children. Five years ago, Will and Grace purchased a house subject to a 30-year mortgage. Since the children have arrived, Grace stopped working, and Will is the sole breadwinner for the family. He has expressed a concern to his financial planner that if he died before the mortgage was paid off, Grace and the children would not be able to afford to live in the house. Will purchases a decreasing-term insurance policy that he plans to keep in force for the remaining term of the mortgage. As each year passes, the death benefit will decline, but so will the outstanding balance on the mortgage. The decreasing-term policy allows Will to budget a fixed dollar amount for insurance protection while ensuring that the balance of the mortgage can be paid off in the event of his untimely death.

A common problem faced by young individuals who have a permanent need for life insurance protection is that they often cannot afford to purchase permanent life insurance. In this situation, term insurance can be used as an interim step to obtaining permanent life insurance protection. Many term-insurance policies permit the insured to convert the term policy into a permanent policy during a period of time specified in the policy, called the conversion period, without the need to provide evidence of insurability. For example, a 10-year term policy might be convertible during years two through eight, or a policy might be convertible up to a certain age. In order to reduce the amount of the premium, some companies allow the new permanent policy to be issued using the age of the insured at the time the term policy was purchased (called a retroactive or original age conversion). These conversions will, however, require a large lump-sum initial deposit in order to bring the policy's cash value (and reserves) up to the level of a permanent policy purchased at that younger age.[10]

Example 4.12

Roderick is the 22-year-old heir to Spode Enterprises, Inc. He anticipates receiving large inheritances when his grandparents and parents pass away, and would like to use permanent life insurance policies to pay for estate taxes and administration expenses when he dies. Since he just graduated from college and his salary is relatively modest, he does not currently have the funds to purchase a large amount of permanent life insurance protection. Instead, Roderick can purchase a convertible annual renewable term life insurance policy. Given his young age, the term insurance premiums will be manageable now, and he can convert the policy to a permanent policy when his income increases.

---

10. For an insurer, reserves are amounts of money held to pay future claims for death benefits. Accumulation and investment of reserves are governed by state law because reserves provide safety that the insurer will able to pay death benefits.

Term insurance provides low-cost life insurance protection that can be particularly valuable for younger individuals and for those who have temporary insurance needs. As the person's age increases, so will the premium on the term-insurance policy. Individuals with a permanent need for death benefit protection should consider the use of permanent life insurance policies (such as whole life or universal life policies, discussed later in this chapter).

The premiums for term-life insurance are very inexpensive at younger ages and the term of death benefit coverage can often be extended well into one's 80s, although the premiums at later ages may be prohibitive. Below is a an example table of level premiums for various term policies and for universal insurance, based on the age of the insured (note, however, that each insurance company sets their own rate per $1,000 of coverage based on their projections for mortality, expenses, and interest earned).

Exhibit 4.7 | Life Insurance Premium Costs Comparison for Term and Universal (per $1,000 of coverage)

Age	Term* (10-year)	Term* (25-year)	Term* (30-year)	Universal Life
25	$0.25	$0.52	$0.60	$2.31
30	$0.25	$0.56	$0.64	$2.92
35	$0.26	$0.65	$0.72	$3.77
40	$0.31	$0.96	$1.04	$4.74
45	$0.51	$1.52	$1.68	$5.99
50	$0.83	N/A	N/A	$7.45
55	$1.40	N/A	N/A	$9.05
60	$2.39	N/A	N/A	$11.74
65	$4.08	N/A	N/A	$15.40

Price is per $1,000 of coverage ($ per 000).
For very healthy non-tobacco using male insured.
* Usually available to terminate at or before age 75.

Example 4.13

As can be seen in **Exhibit 4.7**, a 25 year-old who purchases term insurance will pay only $0.25 per $1,000 of coverage. If he wishes to continue to have insurance at age 35 the cost will increase to a still reasonable $0.26 per $1,000, an no evidence of insurability will be required. The cost will continue to increase every ten years, and at greater increments beginning around age 55 as mortality risk increases significantly around that time. The final renewal period begins at age 65 and has a price tag of $4.08 per $1,000. On the other hand, the universal life premium purchased at age 25 will be a consistent $2.31 throughout the remainder of life, if the assumptions regarding earnings in the universal life policy are correct (there is a possibility that additional premiums will be required, as discussed below). This is much higher in the younger years, but much lower in the years from age 60 and up. The universal life policy can be retained through death at any age, while the term policy will no longer be available beyond age 75. These are the trade-offs that must be considered when selecting life insurance, but clearly support the use of term insurance as the most economical way to fund temporary needs.

Exhibit 4.8 | Level-Term Insurance Annual Premium Sample for Male, Age 67, Excellent Health, No Tobacco Use

Amount	10-Year Term*	15-Year Term*
$1,000,000	$6,564	$8,724
$2,000,000	$13,044	$17,364

* Prudential Insurance, quote via policygenius.com, May 2020

Exhibit 4.9 | Advantages and Disadvantages of Term Life Insurance

Advantages	Disadvantages
• Low cost per unit of coverage • Various term lengths are available and can be matched with client temporary needs • The convertibility feature protects insurability and allows for the ability to acquire a permanent policy if temporary needs transition to, or are replaced by, permanent needs	• Coverage is temporary unless renewed or converted • Renewals require a higher premium at higher ages • Renewals are not available beyond a specified age (usually age 75-80) • There is no cash value to accumulate saving or from which to borrow

Universal Life Insurance

Universal life insurance (UL) is similar to term life insurance with several additional features or options, including a cash-value accumulation account. Universal life insurance allows individuals to make premium contributions in excess of the term-insurance premium or not make them at all. For example, owners might pay in extra premiums prior to their children reaching college age, then stop all premiums during years the kids are in college, then start paying premiums again after the children have graduated and are no longer dependents.

If premiums are not paid, ultimately the policy will lapse. Any excess premiums made are deposited into a cash accumulation account that earns interest based on current market rates of interest, although there is typically a very low guaranteed minimum interest rate. The owner of the policy can make contributions to the policy at any time, and each year the insurance company will take enough out of the cash-value accumulation account to pay the mortality and expense fees (essentially, the equivalent of the term-life mortality premium).[11] As long as there is sufficient money in the policy to pay these expenses, the policy will remain in force. If there is not enough money in the policy to cover the current expense withdrawal, and the owner does not make additional premium contributions to pay for the mortality costs, the policy will lapse.

Universal life "unbundles" the life insurance product, meaning that the cash value and death benefit are treated separately. This unbundling makes the universal life policy more transparent than the whole life policy (discussed below) because a policy owner is shown the cost for mortality charges and expenses, as well as the rate at which cash value accumulates. These elements are not shown in "bundled" contracts such as whole life policies. With a whole life policy, the policy owner pays a fixed premium, and the cash values increase at a guaranteed schedule, so the insurer does not show the mortality

---

11. Mortality fees are paid to the insurance company based on the level of risk of mortality at the client's current age. Expense fees are paid to cover the administrative costs of the insurance company carrying the policy.

charges, expenses, or interest rate credited on cash value. Variable life and variable universal contracts (discussed below) are similarly "unbundled." Unbundling also allows the policy owner to access the cash value by way of withdrawals, rather than just through loans (policy loans and withdrawals are discussed later in this chapter). Because of variations in the interest credited to the cash accumulation account in a universal life policy, it is not possible to predict actual future cash values.

One of the advantages of universal life insurance is that the owner of the policy can make contributions to the policy when he or she has the cash flow to do so, and the policy will remain in force as long as the mortality and expense fees can be paid from the cash value. The cash value is invested by the insurance company, and interest is credited to the accumulation. To the extent that the earnings on the cash accumulation are used to pay for life insurance protection, the growth in investment value is not subject to tax. Over time, this creates the potential for the owner of the policy to pay for the insurance protection with pre-tax dollars (from earnings on the cash invested in the policy) as opposed to after-tax dollars (premium payments paid directly by the policy owner).

Death Benefit Options

The unbundling feature of a universal life policy also allows for flexibility regarding the death benefit. Universal life policies typically offer two death benefit options, referred to as Option A and Option B. A policy with the Option A death benefit provides a level death benefit. This means that as the cash value accumulation in the policy increases, the amount of death benefit protection decreases since the cash value self-funds a portion of the death benefit. The decrease in the net amount the insurance company is at risk of covering results in lower total mortality expenses for the insured since a lower amount of death benefit must be paid for. Clients seeking to grow cash value as quickly as possible would choose this form of death benefit since it results in lower mortality fees, thus allowing more cash to remain in the accumulation account.

The death benefit in an Option A UL policy will generally remain constant, however, once the cash accumulation reaches a specified level, the death benefit will have to increase to ensure that the policy continues to meet the definition of life insurance. A life insurance policy must have an amount "at risk" (the net amount at risk is the amount the insurance company is at risk for paying that is in excess of the cash value). If the cash value equals the death benefit, there is no longer an actuarial amount at risk.

Example 4.14

Edward purchased a universal life insurance policy several years ago and has been making contributions in excess of the current mortality and expense fees. The death benefit for the policy is $100,000, and the death benefit option selected was Option A. The cash value in the policy is $20,000 after the current year's mortality and expense fees are paid. If Edward dies this year, his beneficiary will receive a $100,000 death benefit from the insurance company. Since $20,000 of the death benefit is covered by the cash value of the policy, the amount at risk under the policy is only $80,000 ($100,000 - $20,000). Edward's mortality expense fee for the year will be based on an $80,000 death benefit, which will reduce the annual cost he will incur compared to the mortality expense fee on a $100,000 death benefit.

A policy with the Option B death benefit provides an increasing death benefit. If the insured dies, the policy death benefit will equal the specified death benefit in the policy plus the cash value of the policy. Since the insurance company is always at risk for the full death initial death benefit amount, the mortality costs to the insured will be higher throughout the life of the policy, resulting in the potential need to pay higher premiums versus a policy with an Option A death benefit. Given the same premium payment, the cash value will grow more slowly than in the Option A policy because the mortality costs are not declining. An Option B policy, then, is a better choice for someone who is less concerned about building cash value, and more concerned about increasing the death benefit amount.

Example 4.15

Refer to the facts in the prior example. If Edward chose Option B coverage instead of Option A, and he died this year, his beneficiary would receive a death benefit of $120,000 (equal to the policy death benefit of $100,000 plus the policy cash value of $20,000). The mortality expense fee that Edward will pay is based on $100,000 of insurance protection, which is the amount that the insurance company must pay upon Edward's death. Compared with an Option A death benefit, the annual costs of the Option B policy will be greater because there is a greater amount at risk, and the death benefit received by the beneficiary will be greater as well.

Exhibit 4.10 | Universal Life: Option A and Option B

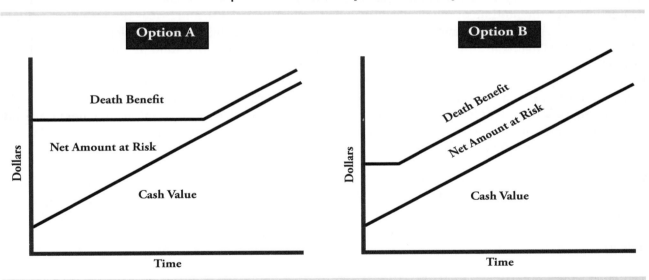

Universal life insurance is not the most cost-effective alternative for permanent life insurance because the mortality and expense fees increase each year and must be paid to keep the policy in force. A standard universal policy does not guarantee a death benefit unless there is sufficient cash value in the policy to pay the annual mortality cost. However, flexibility in premium payments is one of the attractions of universal life insurance, but that same flexibility may cause the death benefit to be reduced or, in the extreme case, cause the policy to lapse.

Exhibit 4.11 | Advantages and Disadvantages of Universal Life Insurance

Advantages	Disadvantages
• Flexibility of premium payments • Cash value earns interest based on current market rates • Tax-deferred growth in the accumulation account • Cash value can be accessed through loans or withdrawals	• UL is neither the most competitive insurance coverage nor the most competitive savings vehicle • The future yield potential of the cash value is uncertain • Due to the flexible premiums, the semi-compulsory form of savings that traditional whole life policies generate is lost • If projected returns on the cash value account are not realized, additional funds must be paid in to keep the policy in force

Whole Life Insurance

Whole life insurance provides guarantees from the insurer that are not found in term insurance and universal life insurance policies. As long as the premium specified in the insurance contract is paid, whole life insurance will remain in force during the life of the insured even if there is no longer cash in the cash value accumulation account to pay mortality and expense fees (as is the case with universal life insurance). In arriving at the premium payment amount, the insurer considers the cost of insurance protection over the lifetime of the insured (usually to age 100 or 120), and prices the premium amount accordingly.[12] As a consequence, the premiums on whole life insurance policies are larger than premiums on term life or universal life policies because the insured is pre-funding the cost of insurance protection. The premium payments over the term-insurance cost of protection are invested by the life insurance company, which typically guarantees a minimum investment return. Unlike the situation with a universal life insurance policy, which transfers investment risk to the insured, the insurer retains the investment risk on a whole life policy, and even if the invested excess premium payments are not sufficient to pay the future pure cost of insurance protection (mortality costs) each year, the insurer promises to keep the policy in force.

Whole life policies are useful when the person wants to ensure that life insurance protection will be available on a permanent basis. Whole life policies are also useful for middle-aged and older people who need death benefit protection but do not wish to retain the risk that projected rates will not be realized, requiring additional funds to be added to the policy (as would be the case in a universal life insurance policy).

The most common form of whole life policy is often referred to as an **ordinary (or straight) life** policy. It requires the owner to pay a specified level premium every year until death (or age 100 or 120). The premium can be paid on a monthly, quarterly, semi-annual, or annual basis, and the policy will remain in force as long as the premium is paid. Older straight-life policies provided that if the insured lived to age 100, the face amount (the death benefit) on the policy would be paid to the policy owner as a living benefit. If this occurs, the amount received in excess of the owner's basis in the policy would be subject to income tax, so many policies now provide for the insurance policy to remain in force until death, even if the insured lives to or past age 100, to lock in the income-tax-free character of the death benefit.

---

12. Historically, whole life policies have matured at age 100. However, most newly issued policies mature at age 120.

Exhibit 4.12 | The Savings Element of a Level-Premium, Whole Life Insurance Policy

One of the problems with an ordinary (straight) life policy is that premium payments must be made throughout the lifetime of the insured. Many individuals would prefer to make premium payments over a shorter period of time (perhaps their work life expectancy) that will be sufficient to keep the policy in force for their lifetimes. Insurance companies will often provide quotes for whole life policies on a 10 or 20-year payment schedule. At the end of the payment period, the policy is considered to be paid-up, at which time no additional premium payments are due. These policies are referred to as **limited-pay policies**. Of course, the premium on a limited-pay policy will be greater than the premium on an ordinary (straight) life policy since the lifetime premium payments are being front-loaded over the payment period.

While a person may have a need for permanent life insurance protection, the normal premiums on a whole life policy may not be affordable based on the person's current income. However, as income rises in the future, the person may be able to afford the premiums for permanent insurance. For someone in this situation who would like to lock in the insurance protection (to ensure insurability), a **modified whole life policy** should be considered. Modified whole life policies have lower premiums than regular policies for the initial policy period (often three to five years), and increase to a higher premium at the end of the initial period. This type of policy gives a person the opportunity to purchase a whole life policy with initial lower premiums which increase as the insured's income increases. A modified whole life policy is an alternative to convertible term insurance.

Whole life insurance policies can also be purchased on a single-premium basis. A **single-premium policy** requires the owner to pay a lump sum in return for insurance protection that will extend throughout the insured's lifetime. These policies require a substantial initial cash outlay, and are typically used by wealthy individuals for estate and generation-skipping transfer tax purposes. One downside to using a single-premium policy is that if the owner receives lifetime benefits from the life insurance policy by borrowing money from the cash value, income tax must be paid on the cash received to the extent of the growth on policy cash value. A single-premium policy is a form of **Modified**

Endowment Contract (MEC), which has different tax attributes than regular life insurance policies and is discussed in detail later in this chapter.

Exhibit 4.13 | Advantages and Disadvantages of Whole Life Insurance

Advantages	Disadvantages
• Guaranteed premium payments • Guaranteed growth of cash value • Guaranteed death benefit • Permanent protection • Cash value can be accessed through loans • Compulsory savings (since premium payments are required to keep the policy in force and a portion of each payment is allocated to the cash value)	• High premiums in the early years when budgets may be most strained • Low guaranteed returns on the cash value • No hedge against inflation since the death benefit remains constant throughout lifetime (e.g., Insured purchases $15,000 death benefit for funeral expenses today, but when he dies 30 years from now the actual cost of a funeral may be twice that amount while the death benefit remains the same.)

Variable Whole Life

Premiums paid to the insurance company for whole life (and universal life) policies are invested in the life insurance company's general account. This general account provides the money to pay the guaranteed death benefit and guaranteed cash values. Some people object to whole life policies on the grounds that the rates credited (earned) to the cash value accumulation within the policy are often low, increasing the premium that must be paid for insurance protection. **Variable whole life policies** provide for a fixed premium payment and permit the cash value of the policy to be professionally managed by the insurance company or an outside investment manager.

Variable life products are hybrids in that they are part insurance and part security. Variable life insurance policies require that the insurance company invest the policy owner's cash value in a separate account, rather than in the company's general investment account. The funds in this separate account are then invested into various subaccounts similar to mutual funds, each separately managed, and each with a specific investment objective. This separate account requirement is the primary characteristic that differentiates variable products from traditional fixed insurance products. Since variable products invest in separate accounts similar to mutual funds, the variable products are regulated by the SEC as securities. Variable products must be registered like other securities, and representatives who sell them must be registered with FINRA (along with being licensed to sell life insurance in their state).

This type of policy transfers investment risk to the owner, and the amount of the death benefit available on the policy will fluctuate with the performance of the underlying investments. Additional expenses will also result from the need to pay the investment advisors managing the separate accounts, increasing the premium cost. Younger individuals who have long-term investment horizons and those with moderate-to-high risk tolerance may find variable whole life policies appealing since they hope to capture some of the upside benefits of allocating their cash values to equities instead of fixed-income investments. Unlike universal life insurance policies, variable whole life policies have a minimum death benefit that will be paid regardless of the investment performance of the underlying investments as long as the scheduled premiums specified in the contract are paid.

Second-to-Die and First-to Die Policies

Whole life policies can also be tailored to meet specific financial needs. **Second-to-die** policies are often used in estate planning to provide liquidity at the death of the second spouse since this is typically when estate taxes for the couple will be due. A second-to-die policy names two insureds and pays the death benefit only when the second insured dies. Since two lives are covered by the policy, a second-to-die policy is a type of joint life insurance policy. One advantage of a second-to-die policy is that the underwriting of a second-to-die policy looks at the health of both insureds, but more weight is given to the mortality outlook on the healthiest of the two insureds since the policy does not pay until the second death. A spouse who is borderline as to insurability may be able to acquire second-to-die insurance when other coverage would not be available. Of course, if the healthier spouse is still alive when the unhealthy spouse dies, no death benefit will be paid, so it does not provide income for the surviving spouse. It can, however, provide for children or grandchildren after both spouses have died, or provide funding for special interests, such as creating an endowment in the name of both spouses

Another type of joint life policy is a **first-to-die** policy. Like the second-to-die policy, the first-to-die policy covers two individuals, but the death benefit is paid upon the death of the first individual. First-to-die policies are sometimes used to provide funding to pay off a mortgage at the death of the first spouse, to establish a fund for children's educational costs when one spouse dies early, or to provide a supplemental pool of capital for the surviving spouse to receive additional retirement income.

Policy Dividends

If the life insurance contract is a "participating policy," the policy owner may be entitled to receive dividends. Policy dividends are a non-guaranteed "return of premium" calculated annually based on favorable loss experience, investment performance (in the insurance company's general account), and/ or expenses.

Whole life insurance policies are permanent policies that are priced using current actuarial mortality assumptions. Over the past century, life expectancies have been increasing, a trend that is expected to continue into the future. Life insurance policies priced using previous mortality tables resulted in higher premiums as compared to premiums calculated using current mortality tables. In addition to favorable mortality experience which occurs when the group of insureds lives longer than they were anticipated to live based on mortality assumptions, the insurance company may realize expense savings, or greater than anticipated returns on investments than it assumed when it originally priced a life insurance policy. Insurance companies return these excess premium payments to policyholders by issuing dividends on participating whole life insurance policies. Unlike a dividend on a stock investment, which is a distribution of corporate earnings and profits and is therefore subject to income tax in the hands of the stockholder, dividends on life insurance policies are treated as a nontaxable return of part of the owner's premium payment. When dividends are paid, the policy owner can choose among five options regarding how the dividends will be received or utilized.

Policy owners can choose to receive the dividend payments in cash, which could result in taxable income to the extent that dividends exceed the premiums paid, or they may choose one of several other options provided by the insurance company. Insurance companies commonly offer options to use dividends to purchase paid-up additional life insurance protection, purchase one-year term insurance, accumulate interest, or reduce premium payments. The cash option would be an advantage over the other options when the family anticipates that it will have need of the funds and does not need additional life insurance.

Exhibit 4.14 | Life Insurance Dividend Options

1. Cash
2. Reduce Premium
3. Accumulate at Interest
4. Paid-Up Additional Death Benefit
5. One-Year Term Insurance

If the policy owner chooses the paid-up additions option, an additional amount of paid up life insurance protection is purchased, which increases the death benefit on the policy. The paid-up additions option is often attractive to individuals who have become uninsurable and would like to receive additional death benefit protection or who would like additional protection to cover inflation associated certain permanent needs such as funeral costs.

Instead of purchasing a paid-up addition to the death benefit, the policy owner could also enhance the death benefit by using the dividend to purchase one-year term insurance (sometimes called the "fifth dividend option"). This option would provide a greater death benefit if the insured dies during the year when compared to the paid-up additions option, but like all other term-insurance contracts, the coverage will expire at the end of the year unless another dividend distribution is received and is again used to purchase term insurance. Recall that if the dividend stays the same, the amount of one-year term insurance that can be purchased each year will decline due to the increasing mortality risk (and premium cost) as a result of the insured's increasing age.

If the insured does not need additional death benefit protection, the dividends can be left on deposit with the life insurance company, which will pay interest on the dividends. The owner of the policy can access these amounts at any time, and if the dividends and the accumulated interest payments are left with the insurer until the insured's death, they are added to and paid out with the death benefit of the policy. While the policy dividends themselves are not taxable, any interest earned on policy dividends is subject to income tax. Each year that interest is credited to dividends deposited with the insurance company, the insurance company will send the policy owner a Form 1099-INT that will specify the interest payments that are subject to tax.

One use of policy dividends is to use them to offset (decrease) the premium payments due on the policy for the current year. This permits the life insurance premium payments to decline over time if dividends are regularly declared.The premium payment option is an advantage when the family wishes to have its life insurance at the lowest possible cash outlay and believes that it helps the family's budgetary process to have part of the premium paid through the use of policy dividends.

Taxation of Whole Life Insurance Policies

Both the growth in the cash value of the policy and the policy death benefit are exempt from Federal income tax as long as the policy is not surrendered during the insured's lifetime.

A policy owner wanting to receive lifetime benefits from a whole life insurance policy without triggering an income tax consequence can achieve this by taking loans against the cash value of the policy. Any outstanding loans against the policy's cash value will be exempt from federal income tax, provided that the policy is in force at the date of the insured's death. However, the death benefit on the policy will be reduced by the amount of the outstanding loan.

IRC Section 101(a) exempts the death benefit on any life insurance policy from income tax provided that the policy has not been exchanged for valuable consideration. A detailed discussion of the Transfer-for-Value Rule is covered in Chapter 5.

Surrender Charges

The insurer incurs several costs when issuing a whole life insurance policy. These costs often exceed the first several premium payments. To avoid incurring losses when policy owners purchase and then quickly cancel their insurance contracts, insurance companies typically enforce a **surrender charge** that is designed to compensate them for up-front costs incurred when issuing the policy. The amount of the surrender charge and the length of the surrender-charge period are regulated by state law. Typically, surrender charges decrease over time. After a period of seven to ten years, cancellation of a life insurance policy does not result in the imposition of a surrender charge. In most cases in which careful planning is conducted, surrender charges are not a major concern, since most people who choose permanent life insurance typically want that coverage to stay in force until the death of the insured.

State insurance regulations may provide for a brief "free-look" period (typically 10 or 20 days) during which the policy may be declined by the insured for a full refund.

Nonforfeiture Options for Life Insurance

Nonforfeiture options protect the cash values of a policy owner who chooses to discontinue coverage under a whole life policy. This provision states that the insured, by lapsing or surrendering the policy, does not automatically forfeit the cash value accumulation. The nonforfeiture options give the policy owner some choice in how to receive the cash value of the policy.

The most common nonforfeiture options include:
- Cash Surrender Value
- Reduced Paid-Up Insurance
- Extended-Term Insurance

Cash Surrender Value

This option gives the owner immediate access to a certain amount of cash specified in the policy in exchange for terminating the policy. This option should be exercised with care because the same amount of cash value may be utilized to provide for a continuing amount of coverage through one of the other options. The need for life insurance declines as people retire, become older, or no longer have dependents. In any other situation in which the need for death protection has ceased or in which alternative death protection has been purchased, cash surrender is a viable option. Consumers who surrender policies may incur an income tax liability on part of the cash value accumulation to the extent

---

☑ Quick Quiz 4.2

1. All else being equal, the total premium outlay on an annual renewable term (ART) policy will be less than a level-term policy.
   a. True
   b. False

2. Universal life insurance is a form of permanent life insurance.
   a. True
   b. False

3. Universal life insurance Option A provides for increasing death benefits.
   a. True
   b. False

4. A way to receive tax-free benefits from a whole life policy during one's life is by taking a loan against the death benefit amount.
   a. True
   b. False

True, True, False, True.

---

that it exceeds the cost basis of the policy (generally premiums paid less dividends received), so a complete policy surrender should be thoroughly evaluated from a tax perspective. Note that surrender value is usually less than cash value for the first 10 to 15 years of the policy (due to surrender charges), and is reduced by any outstanding loans at the time or surrender.

Reduced Paid-Up Insurance

This option allows the policy owner to purchase a fully paid-up whole life insurance policy using the cash value of the policy. The face amount of the new policy will be dependent upon the amount of cash value accumulation, less surrender charges if applicable. Reduced paid-up insurance is essentially an option to purchase a single-premium whole life insurance policy. It is suitable for someone who wants to maintain some level of permanent death protection but does not want to pay any future premiums.

Extended-Term Insurance

Extended-term insurance uses cash surrender value as a single premium to purchase a paid-up term insurance policy equal to the original face amount for a limited period of time, usually a certain number of years and days. The length of the term protection is dependent upon the insured's age at the time he or she chooses to exercise the option. The length of coverage will also be determined by the company's current premium rates and the amount of cash available to fund the premiums. This option is most suitable for someone who wants to preserve, for only a limited time, death protection equal to the forfeited policy's face value.

Exhibit 4.15 | Whole Life Nonforfeiture Options

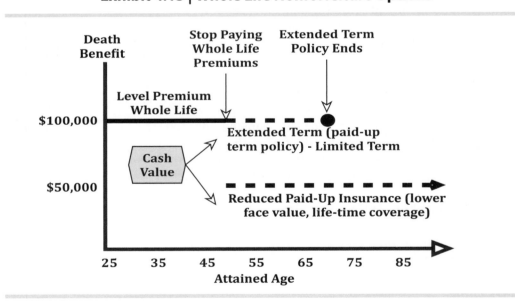

Variable Life Insurance

A **variable life insurance** policy permits the owner of the life insurance policy to direct the investment of the policy's cash value. In the case of whole life or regular universal life insurance policies, the insurance company invests the cash value in its general account and credits a rate of interest to the accumulation. Variable policies typically offer a series of investment options that include investment funds (called separate accounts or subaccounts) managed by the insurer and outside investment managers. This additional layer of complexity results in higher fees for variable policies since fees are paid at the contract level (mortality and expense fees) and at the portfolio level (investment advisory fees paid to the investment managers).

The cash value of a variable life insurance policy is held in a separate account from the insurance company's general funds and the policy owner bears all of the investment risk associated with his or her investment choices. If the cash value of a variable universal life insurance policy is invested in subaccounts that increase in value at a rate greater than the crediting rate that the insurance company offers on universal life insurance, the policy owner can benefit from either a decrease in insurance costs (if an Option A level death benefit with a decreasing amount at risk is chosen), or increased death benefits (if an Option B increasing death benefit is chosen), or, in some cases, both.

If the policy owner experiences losses from the investments he or she chooses in a variable universal policy, this can result in either:
1. increased premium costs for the owner, or
2. a lapse of the policy.

Variable whole life insurance guarantees a death benefit as long as the required premiums are continued, but the cash accumulation value has no guarantees and can even fall to zero. If the investments in the subaccounts perform better than the interest the insurer would have credited in a non-variable policy, the policy owner benefits from a larger cash value, and if the cash value grows substantially more, the death benefit will increase to ensure that the insurer has sufficient net amount at risk to maintain the policy's tax status as life insurance. If the investments perform poorly, the resulting cash value could be substantially less than with a conventional whole life policy.

Variable Universal Life Insurance Policies (VULs) are often used by young individuals who have the risk tolerance and time frame necessary to weather equity market downturns. Since VULs have a flexible premium payment option like universal life insurance policies, the policy owner can make large premium payments in early years to fund the cash value accumulation account, and, if the investments do well over a period of time, have sufficient resources in the cash value account to continue to pay the mortality and expense fees without further premium payments. From a planning perspective, early funding of VULs usually produces the best results, but owners should be aware of the Modified Endowment Contract (MEC) rules. If the policy is funded faster than seven equal payments, lifetime loan or withdrawal benefits that the owner receives from the policy are subject to income tax and possibly a penalty (as discussed below).

The ability to control the investments in a VUL policy causes the policy to be considered a registered investment security. Life insurance agents and financial planners who sell VULs must be licensed to sell both life insurance and securities (FINRA Series 6 or 7 license). Agents selling VUL policies are required to either deliver a summary prospectus (a disclosure document outlining key information relating to the contract's terms, benefits, and risks; including web addresses to obtain more detailed information) to the policy owner or make the statutory prospectus available online. The initial summary prospectus must be delivered "no later than the time of the carrying or delivery of the contract security."[13]

Exhibit 4.16 | Advantages and Disadvantages of Variable Life Insurance

Advantages	Disadvantages
• Potential for higher growth in the cash value versus conventional whole or universal life • Death benefit may increase with substantial growth in the cash value, providing an inflation hedge	• Higher fees (insurance contract fees plus portfolio management fees) • Cash value could fall as low as $0 • Additional premiums may be required to maintain death benefit (in VUL policies) if cash value falls too low • Policy terms are more complex • Policy loans may be more restricted versus conventional whole or universal life

Exhibit 4.17 | Feature Comparison of Common Life Insurance Policies

	Term Life	Whole (Ordinary) Life	Universal Life	Variable Life	Variable Universal Life
Premium $	Fixed	Fixed	Variable, subject to a required minimum	Fixed	Variable, subject to a required minimum
Death Benefit	Fixed	Fixed	May increase above initial face amount, depending on cash value accumulation	Has a guaranteed minimum, but can increase if investment experience on cash value is good	Has a guaranteed minimum, but can increase if investment experience on cash value is good
Policy Owner's Control Over Investments	None	None	None	Complete	Complete
Rate of Return on Investment	None	Fixed rate	May have a minimum guaranteed rate, but can be higher depending on interest rates	No minimum guarantee, but positive investment experience can yield very high returns	No minimum guarantee, but positive investment experience can yield very high returns
Application	Large need, limited resources	Want guarantees	Flexibility without investment responsibility	Investment responsibility, fixed premiums	Flexibility, with investment responsibility, variable premiums

---

13. https://www.sec.gov/rules/final/2020/33-10765.pdf; effective July 1, 2020.

Exhibit 4.18 | Comparison of Life Insurance Policy Costs

Policy Type	Universal Life (UL)	Whole Life (WL)	Variable Universal (VUL)	Term (30 Years)
Subject: 36-year-old female, preferred health, non-smoker **Face Amount: $1,000,000 (death benefit)** **Premium paid to age 65 or 66**				
Annual Premium	$4,703	$14,140	$8,403.28	$905*
(Pay to 65)	Yes	Yes	Yes	Yes (66)
Surrender Value (illustrated using guaranteed interest crediting)	Guaranteed 2%	Guaranteed	Guaranteed	N/A
at 15 years	$70,545	Guaranteed	Guaranteed	0
at 20 years	$94,060	Guaranteed	Guaranteed	0
at 25 years	$117,575	Guaranteed	Guaranteed	0
at 30 years	$136,387	(65) / $480,000	(65)/$210,213	Lapsed
Surrender Value (illustrated using assumed rate below)	Non Guaranteed (Projected)	CV not guaranteed	CV not guaranteed	N/A
at 15 years	$70,545	CV not guaranteed	CV not guaranteed	
at 20 years	$94,060	CV not guaranteed	CV not guaranteed	
at 25 years	$117,575	CV not guaranteed	CV not guaranteed	
at 30 years	$136,387	65 / $493,980	65 / $377,781	Lapsed
Guaranteed (i)	i = 0.2350	i = 1.2969	i = 2.9626	
Non Guaranteed Return (i) Policy (premium less term premium)	i = 1.2066	i = 1.7429	i = 3.6869	N/A

* The $905 was the median premium among 15 carriers ($835 - $1,035)

CV = Cash Value

Policy Illustrations

A **policy illustration** is a projection of the financial results that might be achieved with a life insurance policy. The projection is often based on assumptions about premium payments, investment earnings, and dividends. Generally, illustrations help to educate applicants on how a life insurance policy will work, and these illustrations are typically the primary source of financial information provided to applicants concerning a new policy.

Multiple-year policy illustration sheets are almost always used in the sale of large amounts of permanent life insurance. When properly used, policy illustrations can help a prospective purchaser understand how complex life insurance policies work. Illustrations can also help to demonstrate how sensitive a policy is to changes in such cost factors as mortality, expenses, and interest.

There are many kinds of policy illustrations. Illustrations often have several columns showing the policy year, annual premium, cash values, and death benefit. Usually, each policy year is shown on a separate line for 10 or 20 years and at key ages, such as ages 60, 65, and 70. Illustrations may show dividends and may make projections using dividends to buy paid-up additions or to reduce future premium payments. Some illustrations compare different policies, but illustrations are not an adequate way to compare costs. Since illustrations can make use of different assumptions, the projections are not always accurate for purposes of comparisons among policies.

Policy illustrations can be misused in the life insurance sales process to mislead prospective purchasers. One such misuse is to compare, without adjusting for the time value of money, amounts to be paid by the policy owner in one or more time periods, with amounts to be received by the policy owner in one or more other time periods. Another misuse is to base the illustration on overly optimistic (or undisclosed) assumptions concerning future mortality and expense charges and interest credits or the future marginal federal income tax bracket of the policy owner. A third misuse of policy illustrations arises when policy values that are not guaranteed by the insurer are not clearly differentiated from those that are guaranteed.

If an illustration assumes a tax rate, it should use a marginal tax rate that is the same as the applicant's. Illustrations based on tax rates differing greatly from the applicant's rates are misleading and could be deceptive sales practices.

The NAIC has adopted model regulations for life insurance illustrations that have been enacted in many states. These regulations do not apply to variable life or to annuities. The regulations require illustrations to include identifying information, and they require certain disclosures. In addition, the regulations prohibit insurers and agents from describing nonguaranteed items (such as dividends) in a way that implies that the items are guaranteed. They prohibit use of the term "vanishing premium" or a similar term that implies the policy will become paid up when a portion of future premiums are projected to be paid from nonguaranteed items. An illustration must also be accompanied by a summary describing the features and columns used. The summary must state that actual results may be more or less favorable than what is shown.

A planner reviewing existing life insurance policies owned by a client can (and should) have the client request an **in-force policy illustration** from the issuing insurance company. This illustration will allow the planner and client to monitor the performance of the policy versus what was expected, enabling them to correct any potential problems before they occur. For example, in a UL policy the interest rates actually earned may be less than originally expected, requiring additional premium payments to be made or the policy to be in danger of lapsing.

Modified Endowment Contracts (MECs)

A modified endowment contract (MEC) is not really another type of life insurance policy, but rather a cash value life insurance policy that has been funded too quickly.

In the 1980s, life insurance was a popular tool for taxpayers who wished to defer income from income tax. Income tax rates in the early 1980s were as high as 50 percent, and it made sense for taxpayers in high brackets to purchase universal, whole life, or variable universal life insurance policies as investments with which to defer the tax on the growth of the policy's cash value until they retired or cashed in the policy. Insureds would then expect to pay income tax on the growth of the cash value at a lower income tax rate. Since life insurance policy cash values grow on a tax-deferred basis (if the policy is cashed-in during the insured's lifetime) or a tax-free basis (if a death benefit is paid when the insured dies), life policies became popular tools to defer investment income. In theory, life insurance is a product designed to hedge against mortality risk faced by the insured, but for high income taxpayers in the 1980s, life insurance became a tool to lower tax rates on investment income. Needless to say, Congress was not amused with this use of life insurance.

In the Tax Reform Act of 1986, Congress enacted the modified endowment contract (MEC) rules.[14] These rules state that if a single-premium life insurance contract is purchased, or if a regular life insurance policy is purchased and is funded too quickly, lifetime benefits received under the policy (in particular, the ability to obtain a loan or withdrawal against the policy's cash value) would trigger income tax liability.

Congress imposed two tests to determine whether a life insurance contract meets the definition of a MEC:
1. Guideline Premium and Corridor test
2. 7-pay test

The **guideline premium and corridor test** calls for the policy to be tested using actuarial principles and specifies that the premiums can represent no more than a limited portion of the death benefit. The calculation of the corridor test is beyond the scope of this text.

The **7-pay test** states that if the cumulative premium payments made on the policy are in excess of the net level premium for the policy during the first seven years (or following a material change to the policy), the life insurance contract will be deemed a MEC.

Each form of insurance has a 7-pay premium for each age and sex combination, based on the premium that would pay up the policy with seven level payments. If at any time during the first seven years of a life insurance policy's existence, the cumulative premiums exceed the 7-pay premium times the number of years since the issue of the contract, the policy irretrievably becomes a MEC. Fortunately, there is a provision that permits removing the excess premium if done during the year in which it was paid.

A policy may also become a MEC if there are "material" changes made to the contract after June 21, 1988. Unfortunately, this term has not been clearly defined, but as a general rule, a change will be treated as material if it increases benefits under the policy. An increase to the death benefit that requires proof of insurability is a material change. Since increases in death benefit by exercising the options under a

---

14. IRC Section 7702A.

guaranteed insurability option (discussed later in this chapter) do not require evidence of insurability, that change is not a material change. When a Type B UL policy death benefit increases due to the growth of the cash value, those death benefit increases are also not material changes. Some riders that increase benefits are material changes, but adding a long-term care rider is typically not a material change (life insurance with long-term care riders are discussed in Chapter 7).

A reduction in benefits in the first seven years could also cause a previously non-MEC policy to become a MEC. This rule makes sense because otherwise an applicant could evade the MEC rules by originally applying for a policy with a very large death benefit, paying premiums for four or five years, and then simply reducing the death benefit, and, voilà, the client has funded a large cash value as a tax shelter. To avoid this backdoor access to tax shelter, when a reduction in benefits occurs during the first seven policy years, a new 7-pay test will be required. The new 7-pay test is calculated as if the policy had originally been issued with the reduced death benefit. The same reapplication of the 7-pay test applies to survivorship life (second-to-die) policies even after the first seven years.

When a premium payment that is made will cause a policy to become a MEC, the insurance company is permitted to return the premium (plus interest) within 60 days of the end of the contract year in order to prevent the policy from becoming a MEC. Many insurance companies prefer to return the premiums within 60 days of the time it is received by them, rather than holding excess premiums to the end of the year. The company will also often contact the policy owner and explain the tax implications of the excess premium before returning it to the policy owner, just in case the policy owner actually does want the premium dollars to stay in the policy and is willing to accept the MEC treatment.

When the insured dies and a MEC pays a death benefit, the death benefit is exempt from income tax. If the insured wishes to access policy values during his or her lifetime, however, distributions in the form of loans or withdrawals are taxed on a last-in first-out (LIFO), or interest-first, basis. The LIFO treatment of a MEC means that, to the extent that the value of the policy exceeds the owner's cost basis in the policy (generally, premiums less dividends received; see Chapter 5 for additional details regarding cost basis) and the owner takes some form of pre-death benefit, such distributions are subject to income tax. If the owner is under the age of 59½, the earnings portion of the distribution may also be subject to a 10 percent IRS penalty tax. The 10 percent penalty does not apply to annuitized payments (equal payments received over the life expectancy of the insured) or to payments received as a result of disability, even if the owner is under age 59½.

Example 4.16

Steady Eddy purchases a whole life policy at age 30 and pays premiums annually. When he turns 50, he borrows some of the cash value from the policy to build a swimming pool. The funds he borrowed do not exceed his taxable basis in the policy and are therefore, not taxable.

Exhibit 4.19 | MEC versus Non-MEC

	MEC Policy	Non-MEC Policy
Test	Premiums exceed 7-pay test anytime in first seven years or following a material change	Premiums less than 7-pay test during first seven years
Loans **(cash value >cost basis*)**	LIFO - Ordinary income; plus if owner under age 59½, 10% penalty tax	Not taxable income
Living proceeds **(withdrawal or surrender)** **(cash value > cost basis*)**	LIFO - Ordinary income; plus if owner under age 59½, 10% penalty tax	FIFO - No income tax until cost basis* recovered tax-free
Death benefit	Not taxable income	Not taxable income

Cost basis refers to the after-tax amount invested in the policy, which can be recovered tax-free, and is discussed in detail in Chapter 5.

Example 4.17

Sneaky Pete purchased a single-premium whole life policy ten years ago. Pete decides he needs a pool after seeing his buddy Eddy build one. He also decides to borrow the funds from his whole life policy. However, Pete's policy is a MEC because it is a single-premium policy. As a result, it fails the 7-payment premium test. Because the policy is a MEC, the loans are fully taxable to Pete, to the extent of any gain in the policy.

Group-Term Insurance

As part of their employee benefit packages, many employers offer group term insurance to their employees. **Group-term insurance** covers all eligible employees under a master contract that is obtained by the employer. Employers may offer the group-term insurance as a flat amount (for example, $50,000 or $100,000 of death benefit protection for all employees) or as a percentage of income (one, two, or three times the employee's annual compensation).

When offering group term life insurance to its employees, an employer is able to deduct the premium costs that it pays as an ordinary and necessary business expense. An income tax doctrine called the economic benefit doctrine states that when a person receives property in return for services, the value of the property received must be included in his or her income for income tax purposes. The first $50,000 of death benefit protection received by the employees, however, has been excluded from tax by Congress, which means that the employee is not taxed on the value of up to $50,000 of group-term life insurance paid for by the employer.[15] The exclusion for the cost of $50,000 of group term life insurance, however, is not available where the employee is a sole proprietor, partner, or more than two percent shareholder of an S corporation.

To the extent that the employer pays the premium for term death benefits in excess of $50,000, the value of the excess death benefit protection must be included in the employee's income and is subject to income tax. The amount subject to tax equals the amount of death benefit protection in excess of $50,000 multiplied by the applicable premium rate found in Table 1: Uniform Premiums for $1,000 of Group-Term Life Insurance Protection (Table 1).[16] If the employee contributes to the cost of the group

---

15. IRC Section 79.

term insurance through payroll deduction, that portion of the insurance received is not subject to tax under the economic benefit doctrine.

Exhibit 4.20 | Table 1: Uniform Premiums for $1,000 Group-Term Life Insurance

5-Year Age Bracket	Cost per $1,000 of Protection for One Month
Under 25	$0.05
25 to 29	$0.06
30 to 34	$0.08
35 to 39	$0.09
40 to 44	$0.10
45 to 49	$0.15
50 to 54	$0.23
55 to 59	$0.43
60 to 64	$0.66
65 to 69	$1.27
70 and above	$2.06

Example 4.18

Cindy Lou, age 48, works for WHO Inc. and, as an employee benefit, receives $200,000 of group term life insurance for which she pays $140 per year and her employer pays the remainder. Cindy Lou's taxable income as a result of the coverage is calculated as follows:

$200,000 - $50,000 = $150,000 excess coverage.

$150,000/$1,000 = 150 units of excess coverage (notice that the Table 1 cost is per $1,000 of coverage, per month).

150 units x $0.15 = $22.50 per month x 12 months = $270.

$270 - $140 paid by Cindy Lou = $130 taxable income reported on Cindy's W-2.

Protection

Group-term insurance is a very cost effective way of obtaining life insurance protection, even when the employee has to include in his or her income the imputed premium on insurance provided in excess of the $50,000 group term limit. In this case, the employee receives the life insurance protection at a fraction of the cost for which he or she could have purchased the insurance in the private market. In essence, the employee only pays tax on the imputed premium; the employee does not pay the premium itself. Depending on the employee's marginal income tax rate, this results in a significant reduction in the cost of insurance protection.

---

16. This table is found in Treas. Reg. Section 1.79-3(d)(2).

Example 4.19

Al, who is 50 years old, works for Pennant Enterprises, Inc. As part of Pennant's employee benefit program, Al receives $150,000 of group-term insurance paid for by the company. Based on the Table 1 Rates and Al's attained age, the imputed premium on the $100,000 of insurance in excess of the tax-free group term limit of $50,000 is 276 ($0.23 x 12 months x 100 units). At the end of the year, Pennant Enterprises will include an additional $276 in Al's W-2, which will be reported on his annual tax return. Assuming Al's marginal income tax rate is 25%, the tax he will incur on the inclusion of the imputed premium is $69. For an out of pocket annual cost of $69, Al receives $150,000 of term life insurance protection.

If an employee terminates from service, he or she typically has the option of converting the group term policy into a permanent, cash-value policy at a rate specified in the group contract (and based on the employee's age at the time). This conversion feature may be valuable for individuals who are not insurable since evidence of insurability is not required, and the conversion will preserve the employee's ability to purchase death benefit protection. Adverse selection is the risk that an insured facing an almost certain risk of loss will seek to transfer that risk to an insurance company. Individuals more likely to seek to convert their group-term life insurance contracts to permanent insurance when they separate from service are those who need life insurance, are sick, or expect to have a shorter-than-average life expectancy. If a terminating employee is insurable, it may be wise to first consider the cost of commercially available life insurance since the insurance companies underwriting the group plan often assume that those wishing to convert their group-term insurance to permanent insurance upon termination of employment are uninsurable and may therefore charge a higher premium, such as the rate for a male tobacco user even if the insured is a female non-tobacco user.

Although group term insurance can be very cost effective, the amount of coverage provided rarely covers an employee's needs. Individually owned insurance should be used to make-up the difference between the amount of coverage needed and the amount provided by the group policy. Individuals who may otherwise have trouble being underwritten for life insurance due to health issues should be advised to take maximum advantage of any group life insurance available without evidence of insurability.

Other Types of Group Life Insurance

Employers can also provide group whole life insurance, group universal-life insurance, and group variable-universal life insurance to their employees. Often making these types of insurance contracts available on a group basis results in cost savings for the insurer that are passed on to the employees participating in the plan in the form of lower premiums. Sometimes employers pay the premiums on these policies as an employee benefit, while others make the plans available and permit the employees to pay the premiums with after-tax dollars at the lower group rates.

Planners should be aware, however, that the income tax exclusion for the first $50,000 of death benefit protection only applies to group term insurance plans. Employer-provided group whole life, group universal life, or group variable universal life insurance benefits will subject the employee to tax on the economic benefit the employee receives, which is measured by the imputed cost of the permanent benefits. In many cases the employer will pay only for the term cost of insurance while the employee pays the cost of the permanent protection, reducing the tax implication for the employee but shifting a substantial portion of the cost to the employee.

THE LIFE INSURANCE CONTRACT AND COMMON POLICY PROVISIONS

The Declarations Page

The declarations page of the policy is a good place to look for an outline of the most pertinent information regarding a life insurance policy. The declarations page will typically include all of the following information:

- The name of the insurance company
- The name of the owner of the policy
- The name of the insured
- The policy number
- The date of issue
- The face amount of the policy
- The name of the beneficiary
- The type of insurance (for example, term or whole life)
- A statement about the free-look provision (the owner typically has 10 or 20 days to review the policy and return it for a full refund of premium if she does not wish to keep the policy).

Some policy provisions are required by state law, while other provisions are considered optional.

Along with the common policy provisions discussed in detail below, most life insurance policies include the following provisions:

- **Insuring agreement -** Payment of the face amount of the policy will be made upon receipt of proof of the insured's death.
- **Entire contract -** This provision states that the policy and the application attached to the policy and any riders constitute the entire contract between the parties. In other words, parol evidence (extrinsic evidence) may not be introduced to show that the terms of the policy are other than as written.
- **Effective date -** Life insurance policies can be backdated to take advantage of lower rates at a younger age. Backdating usually does not exceed six months and requires payment of premiums back to that date.
- **Ownership -** The ownership clause in a life insurance policy states that the person designated as the owner has the right to assign or transfer the policy, receive the policy's cash value and dividends, and borrow against the policy's cash value. The purpose of the ownership clause in a life insurance policy is to make it clear who owns the policy. The clause becomes important when someone other than the insured is the policy owner. The policy owner may be the beneficiary, or the owner may be the insured's business partner or anyone to whom the former policy owner elects to transfer the policy and its valuable rights.
- **Premium payment -** More frequent premium payments during the year result in a higher total premium. The insurer incurs expenses and loss of interest when premium payments are spread over the full year.

Exhibit 4.21 | Examples of Modal Factors

For premium modes other than annual, multiply the annual premiums by the appropriate modal factor given here:		
	Direct Bill	**Pre-Authorized Check**
Annually	1.0	1.0
Semi-Annually	0.53	0.51
Quarterly	0.285	0.257
Monthly	Not Available	0.0875

Example 4.20

Anjali is purchasing a term life insurance policy with a death benefit of $250,000. Her agent advises her that the annual premium is $630. If Anjali prefers to instead pay the premium via direct bill on a semi-annual basis, using the modal factor from **Exhibit 4.21**, each payment will be $630 x 0.53 = $333.90; which is $667.80 per year. The additional $37.80 is to compensate the insurer for the increased administrative expenses and lost interest for payments made more frequently than annually.

Additional common provisions found in life insurance policies are described in detail below.

Grace Period

Life insurance policy premiums are typically structured to be payable on a monthly, quarterly, or annual basis. To keep the life insurance policy in force, the premium must be paid on time. This requirement is particularly true for term insurance policies, which do not have cash value to keep the policy in force (permanent policies are often structured to borrow from the cash value to pay the premium on the due date unless the insured has already paid the premium: see Automatic Premium Loan Provision below). Most life insurance policies provide a **grace period**, typically spanning one month (31 days), after the premium due date for the policy owner to pay an overdue premium. Generally, the insured would not have to provide further evidence of insurability if the premium is paid within the grace period, but once the grace period expires and the policy lapses, the insured may be required to undergo additional underwriting for the policy to be reinstated.

> **:≡ Key Concepts**
>
> 1. Highlight the typical provisions found in life insurance contracts.
>
> 2. Describe the difference between a survivorship clause and a simultaneous death clause.
>
> 3. Describe the settlement options: lump-sum, interest only, and the various annuity options.
>
> 4. Describe common life insurance riders and how they benefit the insured or policy owner.

During the grace period the policy remains in force. If the insured dies during the grace period, the insurance company will pay the death benefit to the named insured and deduct from that death benefit the premium that is due. Some policies may also charge interest on the overdue premium since the insurance company loses the ability to invest the premium proceeds on the due date.

Incontestability

In the early days of life insurance, some companies would issue policies to insureds and collect premiums over several years, yet contest the validity of the contract when the death benefit was due based on an alleged misrepresentation, omission of information, or concealment of information on the application by the insured that would have been relevant in making a proper underwriting decision when issuing the policy. The incontestability clause found in life insurance policies today combats this abuse and states that once the policy has been in force for a period of time (typically two years), the insurer may not cancel the policy if it later discovers a material misrepresentation, omission, or concealment. However, the insurer may modify the benefits under the contract.

There are certain situations in which the incontestable clause will not apply because the policy is treated as being void from the time of its inception. For example, an insurer can contest a policy in the circumstances that the policy was purchased with the intent to murder the insured, the policy was lacking insurable interest at the inception of the policy, or the policy was obtained by fraudulent impersonation, for example if the insured's healthy twin sister took the medical exam in place of the unhealthy insured.

Example 4.21

Tami and Alan were married but living apart. One month after purchasing a $100,000 life insurance policy on Alan, Tami asked him over to dinner. She called 911 the next morning reporting him dead on the back porch. Turns out he had a blood alcohol level of 0.436 and more than 82 times the therapeutic level of morphine in his blood. Tami had poisoned his dessert pudding with the morphine and muscle relaxants. She was a nurse and her boyfriend happened to be the life insurance agent who had sold her the policy. Tami did not collect the $100,000 and went straight to jail serving a 60-year sentence.

Misstatement of Age or Gender

The cost of life insurance protection is based on the age and gender of the insured. As individuals get older, the likelihood that they will die within the year (as expressed in mortality tables) increases, thereby increasing the risk for the insurer. Furthermore, females tend to live longer and therefore have lower mortality risk when compared to males at the same age. To compensate for this increased risk, the insurance company charges a higher premium for the life insurance protection. If the insured misstates his or her age or gender on a life insurance application, the insurance company can, at any time (even after the death of the insured), adjust the face amount of the policy to the amount that the specified premium would have purchased at the correct age or using the correct gender of the insured. Since the date of the insured's birth will be listed on the insured's death certificate and in the Social Security Death Master File, when processing death claims insurance companies routinely check to make sure that the insured's age, as disclosed in the policy, was correct prior to paying the claim.

Example 4.22

Gloria is trim, fit, and gorgeous at age 48. People think she is close to 30-years old, and she has been lying about her age for years. Gloria purchases a 30-year term policy with a death benefit of $3,000,000 paying the level premium for a 30-year-old, which is $0.60 per $1,000 of coverage. Her total annual premium is $1,800. Unfortunately, three years later she is killed in an automobile accident. The executor of her estate sends the certified

---

death certificate to the insurer who then discovers how old she really was at the inception of the policy. The level premium for a 48-year-old female at the time of issuance was $2.00 per $1,000 of coverage. The insurer will pay the beneficiary $900,000 ($1,800 ÷ $2 x $1,000).

Suicide

The **suicide clause** in a life insurance policy is designed to hedge against the risk that individuals with suicidal thoughts will purchase life insurance and, shortly thereafter, commit suicide. Since a person who commits suicide has an actual mortality risk of one (or 100%), the normal pricing of a life insurance policy that takes into consideration the actuarial life expectancy of the individual will not result in a premium sufficient to hedge the risk of death for the insurance company. The suicide clause states that, if an insured commits suicide within a specified time (in most states, this time period is two years), the insurance policy will not pay the death benefit to the beneficiary, but will refund the premiums paid (plus possibly interest) on the policy to the named beneficiary. Since it is unlikely that a person would plan to purchase life insurance several years before planning to commit suicide, a two-year exclusion is usually considered sufficient to balance the adverse selection risk of the insurer against the potential loss of the life insurance death benefit for the beneficiaries in the event a suicide does occur.

It should be noted that if a person dies within the two year period, the life insurance company will often scrutinize the claim. The beneficiaries may have to fight to have the proceeds paid.

Example 4.23

Heath Ledger, who is famous for playing the Joker in the movie The Dark Knight, died in early 2008. His death came seven months after he took out a $10 million life insurance policy with his daughter as the beneficiary. The New York Medical Examiner's office ruled that the death was an "accident, resulting from the abuse of prescribed medications." The insurer, ReliaStar Life Insurance Co., investigated the death instead of paying the claim. After a lawsuit was filed, the insurer settled with Ledger's daughter for a sum less than the $10 million.

Reinstatement

If a life insurance policy lapses due to non-payment of premium and expiration of the grace period, the policy may permit reinstatement if the requirements specified in the policy are satisfied. Typically, the policy will specify that reinstatement without evidence of insurability is available for a short time after the expiration of the grace period (usually 31 days). Provided that past premiums plus interest on those premiums are paid to the insurer, and satisfactory evidence of insurability is provided, the insurer may reinstate a life insurance policy up to five years after the policy lapse.

Policy Loan Provisions

One of the benefits of using a permanent life insurance policy is the cash value accumulation that is attached to the insurance. The purpose of the cash value is to accumulate funds to permit the policy owner to spread the cost of the risk of protection over a long period of time, preferably until the death of the insured. The cash value can also be accessed by the policyholder in the form of a policy loan. When a policy loan is issued, there is no credit check required, there are no income tax consequences for the policy owner provided that the life insurance policy was not classified as a modified endowment contract (MEC), and the interest rate charged on the loan is typically a low rate that is specified in the contract. There is no repayment schedule or requirement, and any unpaid interest is added to the loan balance. Policy loans are generally limited to a percentage of the cash value (for example, 90 percent). Any loan outstanding at the death of the insured, plus accrued interest on the loan, is deducted from the death benefit paid to the policy beneficiary.

Example 4.24

Tiffany buys a whole life policy and pays premiums for her entire life. The death benefit of the policy is $100,000. During her life, she borrowed a total of $14,000 from the policy. When she dies, her beneficiary receives $86,000, the death benefit less the outstanding loan balance.

In financial planning, the cash value of life insurance policies can be considered part of an emergency fund since the loan provides easy access to cash at a reasonable rate of interest and can be repaid at any time. Variable policies, however, are not suitable for emergency funds since the cash value can fluctuate substantially based on the underlying investments.

Automatic Premium Loan Provision

With some whole life policies, the insurer gives a policy owner an automatic loan to pay the premium when it is delinquent. This provision will keep the policy in force as long as the cash value can continue to pay premiums. The automatic premium loan provision may be particularly beneficial for a policy owner who is developing dementia and forgets to make the premium payment, for a policy owner experiencing significant health issues and is hospitalized or disabled for a period of time and forgets or is unable to make the premium payment, or when cash values have accumulated substantially and the policy owner no longer wishes to pay the premium.

Beneficiary Designations

At the insured's death, the policy death benefit is paid to the beneficiaries named by the contract owner, or if no beneficiary has been named, to the estate of the insured individual.

Most beneficiary designations on life insurance policies are revocable, which means that the policy owner can change the beneficiary at any time. In some cases, an irrevocable beneficiary will be named on a policy. For example, a former spouse may be required to maintain life insurance for the benefit of an ex-spouse and/or children, in which case the beneficiary designation is typically irrevocable. In order to change the beneficiary on a policy that has an irrevocable beneficiary designation, the original beneficiary must consent to the change.

The individual or organization that will receive the death benefit upon the death of the insured is referred to as the **primary beneficiary**. More than one primary beneficiary may be named on a life insurance policy, which allows the primary beneficiaries to share the death benefit in the manner specified by either the policy owner or the policy itself.

Contingent beneficiaries will receive the death benefit if the primary beneficiary is not available to receive the policy proceeds. If individuals are named as the primary beneficiaries on a life insurance policy, it is important to consider the possibility that the primary beneficiary may die before the insured, causing the death benefit to be transferred to someone else. If no contingent beneficiary is named, the death benefit is generally paid to the policy owner or to the policy owner's estate (if the policy owner was also the insured). Naming a contingent beneficiary is not as important when the policy death benefit will be paid to either a trust or a corporation, since these entities do not have a natural life and are likely to be in existence when the insured dies.

The naming of beneficiaries on life insurance policies is important and it requires careful consideration to avoid delays in the distribution of benefits. Beneficiaries may be named individually or by class. Named beneficiaries are identified by their names; class beneficiaries are not identified by name. The "grandchildren of the named insured" is an example of a class designation for the beneficiaries. The advantage of a class beneficiary designation is that does not need to be adjusted if a member of the class dies or a new member is born. The biggest disadvantage of a class beneficiary designation is that it is sometimes difficult to ascertain whom the policy owner intended for beneficiaries, especially where the composition of the group has changed since the designation was made. Questions may arise as to how far-reaching the class is. For example, a class designated as "my children" may include or exclude step-children or children given up for adoption. Because of the potential ambiguity, it is usually advisable to name beneficiaries and to review them frequently rather than to name class beneficiaries. It is a good practice for a planner to include a review of beneficiaries during each annual review meeting with the client and upon any major changes within the family or family dynamics.

Minors or legally incompetent individuals should not be named as beneficiaries since a guardian or conservator may need to be appointed to manage the funds and/or, depending on state law, the funds may be restricted until the minor reaches the age of majority. In addition, an individual who is legally incompetent may be at risk of losing access to needs-based government benefits as a result of the receipt of even a small death benefit. The use of a trust is a prudent alternative in such situations.

Survivorship Clauses

A **survivorship clause** specifies that the death benefit will only be paid to the beneficiary if the beneficiary survives the insured by a specific number of days (usually 30-60 days). If the beneficiary does not survive by the specified number of days, the death benefit is paid to the contingent beneficiary. If there is no contingent beneficiary, the death benefit is paid to the policy owner or the policy owner's estate. A survivorship clause protects the testamentary intent of the policy owner by ensuring that the appropriate party receives the policy proceeds, and can minimize estate and probate complexities that might be encountered if the policy proceeds are subject to administration in two estates in quick succession.

Simultaneous Death Provisions

A **simultaneous death provision** is similar to a survivorship clause, and is effective whenever the insured and the beneficiary die within a short time of one another and it is impossible to determine who died first. Under the Uniform Simultaneous Death Act, if the insured and the beneficiary die in a common accident and the order of deaths is uncertain, the policy death benefit is distributed as if the beneficiary had predeceased the insured. When the policy owner has named a contingent beneficiary, that beneficiary will receive the death proceeds. If no contingent beneficiary is named, the policy proceeds will be distributed to the policy owner or the policy owner's estate.

Assignment

Assignment is the process of transferring all or part of the policy's ownership rights. A policyholder might wish to assign his or her interest in a life insurance contract to a bank as collateral for a loan, with or without the insurance company's consent. Two main types of assignments exist in today's insurance industry: absolute and collateral. An absolute assignment gives the entity that has received the assignment all policy ownership rights subject to any limitations set forth in the assignment. A collateral assignment is used to serve as security for debt and gives the lender or "assignee" limited ownership rights under the policy. The assignment automatically terminates when the debt is paid, and policy ownership rights are usually exercisable only if the borrower defaults on the loan.

Aviation Exclusion

Though no longer a common exclusion in policies issued today, the aviation exclusion denies coverage for those who die in noncommercial flights, such as private pilots, their passengers, and military pilots. Premiums are usually returned to the beneficiary, but the death benefit is not paid. Life insurance may refuse to cover recreational pilots.

War Exclusion

This exclusion allows the insurer to deny the death claim if the insured dies while in the military or as the result of a military action. Premiums are usually returned to the beneficiary with interest and the death benefit is not paid.

Policy Riders

Riders are provisions or endorsements that are added to a life insurance policy in order to amend the policy. Riders may be used to increase or decrease benefits, waive a condition, or amend the original contract in some specific manner. The terms "rider" and "endorsement" are synonymous. Riders that add benefits will typically have an additional premium cost associated with them. Presented below is a summary of common riders that may be added to life insurance policies.

Waiver of Premium Rider

The waiver-of-premium rider stipulates that in the event the policyholder becomes totally and permanently disabled before a specified age, such as age 60 or age 70, premiums on the contract will be waived during the continuance of any disability that lasts beyond a specified period of time, usually six months. During the disability, the policy's death benefit will remain unchanged, and cash value can continue to grow.

Double Indemnity Rider

The double indemnity rider pays twice the policy's face amount if death is due to accident. It is favored by some because of its low premium and because of the perception of a high probability of death from accidental causes in the younger years, as compared to natural causes. Those who oppose the provision argue that double indemnity is not a wise purchase because one is gambling on the cause of death. The probability of death from an accident is very low, even at the younger ages. It is unlikely that the family is really going to need twice as much in death benefit if the insured dies as a result of an accident rather than from illness, so the amount of death benefit actually needed is the amount that should be purchased and covered for both illness and accident.

Guaranteed Insurability Rider

The guaranteed insurability option or guaranteed purchase option gives the policy owner the right to buy additional specified amounts of insurance at specified dates or events, without the insured having to prove insurability. A typical option permits the insured to purchase additional life insurance at three-year intervals, beginning with the policy anniversary nearest his or her age 25 and terminating with the anniversary nearest his or her age 40. The amount obtainable at each specified anniversary may be limited to the face of the original policy or a smaller set dollar amount, such as $10,000. The inclusion of this option makes sense for a young family likely to have additional children, or for a family whose future income can be expected to rise considerably. Where the needs and the premium-paying capacity of the family are expected to increase, the use of the guaranteed purchase option makes sense.

Long-Term Care Rider

A long-term care (LTC) rider may be added to some life insurance policies for an additional premium. This rider commits the insurer to a daily, weekly, or monthly dollar benefit for long-term care if the insured is unable to perform a specified number (two or three) of activities of daily living (ADLs; eating, bathing, dressing, transferring, toileting, and continence). Additional information on life insurance with long-term care riders can be found in Chapter 7.

SETTLEMENT OPTIONS FOR LIFE INSURANCE

When an insured individual dies and the insurance company is notified of the death, the life insurance benefit becomes payable. The beneficiary can receive the proceeds in a lump-sum payment, but most insurance policies provide several alternative options for the beneficiary to receive the death benefit.

Lump-Sum Payment

Receiving a lump-sum benefit is perhaps the simplest way to complete the life insurance transaction. Sometimes the insurance company will pay the lump sum directly in the form of a check to the beneficiary. More recently, some life insurance companies have been creating an account for the beneficiary at the life insurance company in which the policy proceeds are deposited. The beneficiary receives a check book and can draw any or all of the death benefit out of the account by simply writing a check. Amounts left in the account will earn interest until withdrawn. This approach may be valuable for beneficiaries who would like to receive a lump-sum distribution but who have not yet decided how to invest or otherwise deploy the life insurance death benefit.

Interest Only

The interest-only option allows the beneficiary to keep the death benefit on deposit with the insurance company and receive periodic payments of interest on the policy proceeds. If the owner/insured is concerned about the ability of the beneficiary to manage the insurance proceeds, the interest-only option should be considered. In some cases, the beneficiary is given the opportunity to access some of the principal amount (the death benefit) in addition to receiving payments of income. The primary beneficiary is permitted to name a contingent beneficiary to receive any amounts remaining when the primary beneficiary dies.

☷ Key Concepts

1. Understand the various settlement options available with life insurance policies.

2. Consider the various options available with an annuity settlement option and the impact on the size of the annuity stream.

Annuity Payments from Life Insurance

Life insurance companies provide a variety of **annuity** options for beneficiaries. Annuities are periodic payments to an individual that continue for a fixed period or for the duration of a designated life or lives (joint and survivor annuity). Several of these annuity options are discussed below.

Fixed Amount

When the fixed amount annuity method of distributing the death benefit is chosen, the policy death benefit will be deposited with the insurance company, and the beneficiary will receive fixed payments until the proceeds are depleted. The balance on deposit with the insurance company will be credited with interest each year. As the beneficiary receives payments, the portion of each payment that represents interest earnings will be taxable to the beneficiary. The remaining portion of the payment, which represents part of the death benefit, will not be subject to income tax.

The beneficiary should choose a contingent beneficiary in case the primary beneficiary dies prior to receiving all of the payments from the insurance company. If no contingent beneficiary is named, the remaining amount in the account is typically paid to the estate of the deceased beneficiary.

Life Income

The life income option converts the death benefit into an annuity contract for the life of the beneficiary. When the life income approach is chosen, the amount of the annuity payment will depend on the size of the death benefit paid, and the age and sex of the beneficiary. Each year as payments are received, the beneficiary will pay income tax on a portion of each payment representing the growth in the annuity contract, and the remaining portion will be exempt from income tax. This result relies on the calculation of the exclusion ratio for the policy.[17] The portion of the payments representing the return of the death benefit paid under the life insurance policy will be received by the beneficiary income-tax free. Since the payments will stop when the beneficiary dies, there is no need to name a contingent beneficiary if a life income option is chosen.

Fixed Period

Instead of receiving an annuity payment over the lifetime of the beneficiary, the death benefit proceeds may be used to purchase an annuity certain, which is an annuity that will make payments for a specified number of periods (usually years). When the fixed-period option is chosen, the beneficiary's age and health are not considered in the pricing of the annuity. The only factors that matter are:
- The size of the death benefit
- The crediting rate of interest on the annuity contract

---

17. The exclusion ratio equals the investment in the contract divided by the expected return, which is the total amount of dollar distributions expected under the contract.

If the beneficiary dies prior to receiving all of the fixed payments, a contingent beneficiary can be named to receive the present value of the remaining payments. If a contingent beneficiary is not named, the payments are made to the primary beneficiary's estate.

A fixed-period annuity with a term less than the life expectancy of the beneficiary will generally result in a higher payment than a life income annuity. In financial planning engagements, using a fixed-period annuity payout may be preferential to the life income method when the beneficiary:

- Needs additional cash flow for a fixed period of time, such as until retirement age (when distributions from retirement accounts will begin).
- Suspects that he or she will have a shorter-than-average life expectancy and would like to preserve some of the death benefit value for a successor beneficiary if the primary beneficiary dies before the term expires.

Life Income with Period Certain

The life income with period certain payout method combines the benefits of the life income method with the benefits of the fixed-period method. This approach transforms the death benefit into a life annuity contract based on the age and health of the beneficiary so that payments will continue throughout the beneficiary's lifetime, yet promises to make a specified number of payments under the contract. If the beneficiary dies early, a contingent beneficiary will receive the remaining payments promised under the period certain portion of the contract, or the commuted value in a lump sum.

All else being equal, a life income with period certain payout will provide a lower periodic payment than a straight life payout would, because the insurance company is promising to make payments for a minimum period of time. A guaranteed period payment is appropriate when the beneficiary would like to have the security of annuity payments but suspects that he or she might have shorter-than-average life expectancy.

Example 4.25

Floyd was named as the beneficiary of his Aunt Josephine's life insurance policy. In his earlier years, Floyd was a free spirit and engaged in several activities that could have shortened his lifespan. Since Floyd has not had a good track record with managing money, he would like to choose a payout method that will give him income for life, but would like to make sure that his son, Garrett, gets something if he dies too soon. Floyd elects to take a life income with a 15-year period certain. If Floyd lives beyond 15 years, he will continue to receive payments for the rest of his life, and the payments will stop at Floyd's death. If Floyd dies 10 years after the payments begin, however, the insurance company will continue to make payments for an additional five years to Garrett, whom Floyd named as contingent beneficiary of the proceeds.

Joint and Last Survivor Income

With a Joint and Last Survivor Income settlement option, annuity payments are made over the joint lives of two individuals. When one of the joint annuitants dies, the survivor will receive a reduced payment for the rest of his or her life. Sometimes, a period certain is also incorporated into this option. If the beneficiary of a life insurance policy would like to ensure that another person, such as a spouse, will continue to receive benefits from the policy after the primary beneficiary's death, this type of settlement option should be considered.

Exhibit 4.22 | Life Insurance Policy Options

Nonforfeiture Options	Settlement Options	Dividend Options
• Cash surrender • Paid-up permanent policy (reduced death benefit) • Extended term policy	• Lump-sum cash • Fixed-amount installments • Fixed-period installments • Interest only • Annuity options (straight life, life with period certain, joint and survivor)	• Cash • Reduced premium • Accumulate at interest • Paid-up additions • One-year term insurance

LIFE INSURANCE POLICY REPLACEMENTS

There may be circumstances under which a policy owner considers replacing an existing life insurance policy with a new policy, perhaps due to a change in the policy owner's needs or financial situation, or due to the emergence of newer policies with enhanced features. Replacement of one life insurance policy with another, whether with the same or a different insurer, often works to the disadvantage of the policy owner. The disadvantages of replacement include the fact that the policy owner again has to pay the high first-year expenses of the new policy through a policy fee, reduced or no dividends for a period of time, and reduced or no nonforfeiture values for a time. Other disadvantages include the start of a new incontestability clause and suicide clause. A further disadvantage is that the premium for the new policy, which is based on the insured's attained age, may be higher than that for the old policy, whose premium is probably based on an earlier attained age.

A major advantage of policy replacement inures to the replacing agent, inasmuch as he or she is eligible for a high first-year commission. Policy replacements have some times been based on deception on the part of the replacing agent. When this is the case, replacement is called "twisting," a practice that is illegal in every state.

In recent years, however, policy replacements sold honestly have sometimes proven to be in the best interests of the policy owner. Due to higher interest rates and improved mortality experience, as well as sometimes more liberal policy wording, a policy owner may be in a better position under a new policy than under the one it replaces.

Most states regulate policy replacements in order to protect consumers against unfair treatment by insurers and agents. The regulations usually require the following:
- Disclosure by the agent to his or her insurer as to whether the policy being applied for will replace another policy.
- Notification by the agent to the applicant of the importance of comparing carefully the benefits and costs of the new and old policy, perhaps by consulting with the original selling agent or insurer.
- Notification to the original insurer stating that a policy replacement is being considered by its policy owner and providing information about the proposed new policy.
- Notice by the replacing insurer to the policy owner of a 10- or 20-day "free-look" period to examine the new policy without penalty.
- Delivery by the original insurer or agent to the policy owner, within 20 days, of specified information about the old policy, prepared in accordance with the disclosure regulation.

CONCLUSION

Life insurance is an effective tool that can be used to hedge against mortality risk that everyone faces. Having a basic understanding of how each policy works, when it is appropriate to use them, and how much coverage should be obtained is important for anyone wishing to provide comprehensive financial planning advice. The following chapter addresses taxation and business uses of life insurance.

Annual Renewable Term (ART) - Type of term insurance that permits the policyholder to purchase term insurance in subsequent years without evidence of insurability, but premiums on the policy increase each year to reflect the increasing mortality risk being undertaken by the insurer.

Annuity - Periodic payment to an individual that continues for a fixed period or for the duration of a designated life or lives.

Asset Accumulation Phase - This phase is usually from the early 20s to late 50s when additional cash flow for investing is low and debt-to-net worth is high.

Assignment - The process of transferring all or part of the policy's ownership rights.

Beneficiary - A person or institution legally entitled to receive benefits through a legal device, such as a will, trust or life insurance policy.

Capitalized-Earnings Approach - Method to determine life insurance needs that suggests the death benefits of a client's life insurance should equal an income stream sufficient to meet the family's needs without depleting the capital base.

Conservation (Risk Management) Phase - This phase is from late 20s to early 70s, when cash flow assets and net worth have increased and debt has decreased somewhat. In addition, risk management of events like employment, disability due to illness or accident, and untimely death become a priority.

Contingent Beneficiaries - Person(s) or organization named to receive the death benefit if the primary beneficiary is not available to receive the policy proceeds.

Decreasing-Term Insurance - Type of term insurance that allows the owner to pay the same premium for the insurance protection each year. The death benefit on the policy will, however, decrease each year to offset the increasing mortality cost due to the passage of time.

Distribution (Gifting) Phase - This phase is from the late 40s to end of life and occurs when the individual has high additional cash flow, low debt, and high net worth.

First-to-Die - Type of joint life insurance policy that covers two individuals, but the death benefit is paid upon the death of the first individual.

Grace Period - A provision in most insurance policies that allows payment to be received for a certain period of time after the actual due date without a default or cancellation of the policy.

Group Term Insurance - A type of life insurance coverage offered to a group of people (often a component of an employee benefit package) that provides benefits to the beneficiaries if the covered individual dies during the defined covered period.

Guideline Premium and Corridor Test - One of two Congress-imposed tests to determine whether a life insurance contract meets the definition of a MEC. This test calls for the policy to be tested using actuarial principles and requires the premiums to represent no more than a specified portion of the death benefit.

Human-Life Value Approach - Method to determine life insurance needs that suggests the death benefit of a client's life insurance should be equal to the economic value of the client's future earnings stream.

Illustration - A projection of the financial results that can be achieved with a life insurance policy, based on assumptions about premium payments, investment earnings, and dividends.

In-Force Policy Illustration - Allows the planner and client to monitor the performance of the policy versus what was expected, enabling them to correct any potential problems before they occur.

Insured - The person whose life is insured by the policy.

Joint and Survivor Annuity - An annuity based on the lives of two or more annuitants, usually spouses. Annuity payments are made until the last annuitant dies.

Level Premium Term Insurance - Type of term insurance that charges a fixed premium each year over a specified period of years, so the premium does not increase over that period.

Limited-Pay Policies - Type of whole life policy with a payment schedule (typically 10 or 20 years). At the end of the payment period, the policy is considered to be paid-up, at which time no additional premium payments are due.

Modified Endowment Contract (MEC) - A cash value life insurance policy that has been funded too quickly. Under a MEC, the death benefit payable to the beneficiary is not subject to income tax, but policy loans or cash value withdrawals are taxable.

Modified Whole Life Policies - Type of whole life policy with lower premiums than a regular policy for an initial policy period (often 3 to 5 years), which increase to a higher-level premium at the end of the initial period.

Mortality Cost - Equals the probability of dying within the year times the face value of the policy.

Mortality Risk - The risk that an individual will die within the year.

Needs Approach - Method to determine life insurance needs that suggests the death benefits of a client's life insurance should equal the cash needs that the family will require at death plus income replacement needs.

Ordinary (or Straight) Life - Type of whole life policy that requires the owner to pay a specified level premium every year until death (or age 100).

Owner - Person or institution who owns the policy and can exercise the economic rights in a policy, including assignment, sale, etc. Also the person who is generally obligated for the payment of premiums.

Primary Beneficiary - Person(s) (may be a group designation) or organization to receive the death benefit upon the death of the insured.

Riders - Provisions or endorsements that are added to the life insurance policy in order to increase or decrease benefits, waive a condition, or amend the original contract in some specific manner.

Second-to-Die - Type of joint life insurance policy that is often used in estate planning to provide liquidity at the death of the second spouse. A second-to-die policy names two insureds and pays the death benefit only when the second insured dies.

7-Pay Test - One of two Congress-imposed tests to determine whether a life insurance contract meets the definition of a MEC. This test states that if the cumulative premium payments made on the policy are in excess of the net level premium for the policy during the first seven years (or following a material change to the policy), the life insurance contract will be deemed a MEC.

Simultaneous Death Provision - Provision in a life insurance policy for situations in which the insured and the beneficiary die within a short time of one another and it is not possible to determine who died first, Generally the policy death benefit is distributed as if the beneficiary had predeceased the insured.

Single-Premium Policy - Type of whole or universal life policy that requires the owner to pay a lump sum in return for insurance protection that will extend throughout the insured's lifetime. These policies will always be MECs.

Suicide Clause - Provision in a life insurance policy specifying that the insurance company will not pay the benefit if the insured attempts or commits suicide within a specified period from the beginning of the coverage. The clause is designed to hedge against the risk that individuals with suicidal thoughts will purchase life insurance and commit suicide shortly thereafter.

Surrender Charge - A fee levied on a life insurance policyholder upon cancellation of the policy to cover the up-front costs of issuing the policy.

Survivorship Clause - Provision in a life insurance policy specifying that the death benefit will only be paid to the beneficiary if the beneficiary survives the insured by a specific number of days.

Term Insurance - A life insurance policy that states that if the premium has been paid and the insured dies during the term of the policy, the insurance company will pay the specified death benefit.

Underwriting - The process by which insurance companies decide whether to provide insurance to an applicant and under what terms.

Universal Life Insurance - Type of term insurance with a cash-value accumulation feature allowing individuals to make premium contributions in excess of the term-insurance premium. The excess premiums are deposited into an account with various investment options.

Variable Life Insurance - Type of life insurance policy that permits the owner of the life insurance policy to direct the investment of the policy's cash value. Variable policies typically offer a series of investment options that often include investment funds managed by the insurer and outside investment managers.

Variable Universal Life Insurance Policies (VULs) - Type of life insurance policy that combines variable and universal life insurance and gives the policyholders the option to invest as well as alter insurance coverage.

Variable Whole Life Policies - Type of life insurance that provides for a fixed premium payment and permits the cash value of the policy to be professionally managed by the insurance company or an outside investment manager.

Whole Life Insurance - Type of life insurance that provides guarantees from the insurer that are not found in term insurance and universal life insurance policies.

DISCUSSION QUESTIONS

SOLUTIONS to the discussion questions can be found exclusively within the chapter. Once you have completed an initial reading of the chapter, go back and highlight the answers to these questions.

1. List and explain the three life-cycle stages.

2. List and explain the three methods used to determine clients' life insurance needs.

3. List the benefits of term life insurance.

4. List the options available with term life insurance.

5. List the benefits of whole life insurance.

6. List the options available with whole life insurance.

7. Describe the income tax consequences associated with whole life insurance plans.

8. Describe the usefulness of a life insurance policy illustration.

9. Define a modified endowment contract (MEC).

10. Describe the benefits associated with group life insurance plans.

11. List and describe provisions commonly found in life insurance policies.

12. List and describe some common life insurance riders.

13. List the settlement options that are available to life insurance beneficiaries.

14. What are the various needs for insurance on the person in general, and life insurance in particular?

15. What are component needs that make up the needs approach to the amount of life insurance needed?

16. How do term and whole life insurance differ, and what are the advantages/disadvantages of each?

17. What are the various types of permanent life insurance?

18. What differentiates variable life insurance from variable universal life insurance?

19. At what threshold is an employee taxed on group term life insurance provided by an employer?

20. What are the various types of annuities that are settlement options from life insurance?

21. What are the various contractual provisions and options that pertain to life insurance contracts?

MULTIPLE-CHOICE PROBLEMS

A sample of multiple choice problems is provided below. Additional multiple choice problems are available at money-education.com by accessing the Student Practice Portal.

1. Which of the following life insurance policies provides the highest benefit for the lowest premium and is simply a pure death benefit policy?
   a. Term.
   b. Whole life.
   c. Universal life.
   d. All of the above.

2. Ryan and Jody are age 68 and 72, respectively, and are married. They have significant assets that will be subject to estate taxes upon the second spouse's death. Which of the following life insurance policies would you recommend?
   a. Annually renewable term.
   b. Second-to-die whole life policy.
   c. First-to-die whole life policy.
   d. Ordinary whole life.

3. Which of the following is needed to calculate the client's human-life value?
   1. Average annual earnings to the age of retirement.
   2. Estimated annual Social Security benefits after retirement.
   3. Costs of self-maintenance.
   4. Number of years from the client's present age to the contemplated age of retirement.
   a. 3 and 4.
   b. 1, 2, and 4.
   c. 1, 3, and 4.
   d. 1, 2, 3, and 4.

4. Terry has been advised by his insurance agent to purchase a variable universal life insurance policy. He has sought your advice regarding this purchase. All of the following are characteristics of a variable universal policy, *except*:
   a. The policy features increasing or decreasing death benefits and flexibility of variable premium payments.
   b. The policy owner has exclusive investment control over the cash value of the policy.
   c. The death benefit is guaranteed to be equal to the face value.
   d. The cash value of a variable universal life policy is dependent on premiums and investment returns.

5. Which one of the following statements concerning whole life insurance is false?
    a. Level-premium whole life insurance accumulates a cash value that eventually reaches the face value of the policy at age 100 - 120.
    b. Whole life insurance offers permanent protection throughout the insured's lifetime.
    c. Whole life insurance can be participating, which means the insured must participate in self-directed investments for the cash value.
    d. Whole life insurance premiums paid throughout the insured's lifetime are ordinary life policies.

QUICK QUIZ EXPLANATIONS

Quick Quiz 4.1

1. False. The asset accumulation phase generally lasts from the time one enters the workforce until retirement.
2. True.
3. False. In the event that the decedent's health insurance policy did not cover all of his or her medical expenses, life insurance proceeds are appropriately used to pay these expenses.
4. False. As clients age, the human-life value and the need for life insurance protection decreases.

Quick Quiz 4.2

1. True.
2. True.
3. False. Option B provides for increasing death benefits - the stated policy amount plus the cash value. Option A provides a level death benefit or the cash value, whichever is greater.
4. True.

Quick Quiz 4.3

1. False. The owner could be under a legal obligation (for example, divorce) to keep a specific beneficiary if the beneficiary designation is an irrevocable election.
2. False. The suicide clause is generally only in effect for a specific amount of time (usually two years). During that time, there is no payout, regardless of the reason for death or the cash value.
3. True.
4. True.

> **Additional multiple choice problems
> are available at
> money-education.com
> by accessing the
> Student Practice Portal.
> Access requires registration of the title using
> the unique code at the front of the book.**

5

LIFE INSURANCE: ADVANCED CONCEPTS

LEARNING OBJECTIVES

1. Identify the types and uses of life insurance in financial planning.
2. Understand the taxation of life insurance policies.
3. Understand tax-free policy exchanges under Section 1035.
4. Discuss viatical settlements and accelerated benefits provisions and their tax consequences.
5. Recognize the complications for a closely held business upon the death of an owner and the need for buy-sell agreements.*
6. Understand the use of life insurance and buy-sell agreements.
7. Distinguish between the three most common types of buy-sell agreements: cross-purchase agreements, entity agreements, and wait and see agreements.*
8. Explain the potential financial risk to the company due to the loss of a key employee.*
9. Identify the opportunity to provide nonqualified benefits for business owners and key executives, including Sec. 162 executive bonus plans and nonqualified deferred compensation.*

*CFP Board Resource Document - Student-Centered Learning Objectives based upon CFP Board Principal Topics.

INTRODUCTION

Chapter 4 covered life insurance needs analysis for individuals, types of policies, and policy provisions. In this chapter the focus is on the tax treatment of life insurance and business uses of life insurance.

TAXATION OF LIFE INSURANCE BENEFITS

Life insurance is generally thought to be tax free. However, the taxation of life insurance is not that simple. There are a variety of tax issues associated with life insurance. Among these are:

- Premium payments
- Death benefits
- Lifetime benefits
- Policy exchanges
- Transfer for value
- Viatical settlements
- Accelerated benefits

Premium Payments

Premium payments on life insurance policies are not tax deductible, with a few rare exceptions. For example, group term insurance premiums on insurance protection of up to $50,000 are deductible by the employer and not included in the income of the employee. Furthermore, certain types of employee benefit plans, such as VEBAs and 415 plans, can be created by an employer and funded with life insurance policies allowing the employer to deduct the premium. Another exception to the rule applies when a divorce occurs and one spouse is paying the premium on a policy owned by the other spouse under the terms of a divorce decree executed prior to 2019.[1]

---

1. The Tax Cuts and Jobs Act of 2017 eliminated tax treatment of alimony as income to the recipient and as a deduction for the payer for divorce or separation agreements executed after December 31, 2018.

Example 5.1

Loni is paying alimony to her ex-husband, Burt. Because Burt is dependent on this income, he is named as the policyowner and beneficiary of a life insurance policy on which Loni is the insured. Loni, however, is required to pay the premiums under the terms of the divorce decree executed prior to 2019. The premiums are treated as additional alimony income to Burt (as though Loni had paid cash to Burt, and Burt used it to pay the premium), and the premiums are deductible by Loni as additional alimony payments. Note that if Loni had maintained ownership of the policy but was required to name Burt as irrevocable beneficiary, the premium payments would not be treated as alimony, and therefore would not be deductible by Loni.

A final exception to the rule that premiums are not income tax deductible applies to the payment of premiums on a policy for which a charity is the owner and beneficiary. In this case, the premiums are treated as a cash contribution to the charity. The deductibility of charitable contributions is limited based on the donor's adjusted gross income.[2] Merely naming a charity as an irrevocable beneficiary is not enough to allow the premiums to qualify as a deductible contribution; the charity must actually own the policy and have the policyowner rights, including access to cash values.

Since the premiums usually cannot be deducted for income tax purposes, under most circumstances the owner of the policy will have a tax basis in the policy (representing after-tax investments in the vehicle) equal to the cumulative premiums paid for the policy. The owner's basis may be reduced when the insurance company issues dividends or when the owner makes a withdrawal from the cash value of the policy, both of which are discussed below.

> ### ✷≣ *Key Concepts*
>
> 1. Highlight some of the income tax benefits to be derived from life insurance planning, both to the policy beneficiary(ies) and the owner.
>
> 2. Determine the cost basis of a life insurance policy.
>
> 3. Describe FIFO and LIFO treatment.
>
> 4. Describe the possible tax consequences for policy exchanges.
>
> 5. Identify the exceptions to transfer for value.

Death Benefit Taxation

IRC Section 101(a) states that the death benefit received by a beneficiary of a life insurance policy due to the death of the insured is exempt from federal income tax. The income tax-free character of the death benefit is an important planning consideration. While Congress could subject life insurance death benefits to income tax, it chooses not to as a means of encouraging individuals to purchase life insurance (so that beneficiaries will not have to rely on public assistance). This favorable tax treatment also extends to death benefits paid by accident and health insurance, and death benefits paid under workers' compensation insurance plans. It does not, however, apply to "death benefits" paid by annuities (discussed in Chapter 8).

---

2. A detailed explanation of these limitations is beyond the scope of this textbook, but planners should be aware that the advice of a tax professional is advisable.

If an individual owns a life insurance policy on his or her own life, or if the proceeds of the policy are made available to the executor of his or her estate, the death benefit will be included in the owner/insured's gross estate and may be subject to estate tax. Many individuals confuse the income tax and estate tax rules concerning life insurance – believing that the death benefit is tax-free under both tax systems. If the insured does not own the policy covering his or her life, and the proceeds of that policy are not made payable to the executor of his or her estate, this understanding is correct. Many individuals, however, own the life insurance policies that cover their own lives. When this situation occurs, the death benefit is free from income taxation but is subject to estate taxation if the decedent has a large taxable estate. Most individuals will not be subject the federal estate, however, since each individual is permitted an $11,580,000 exemption in 2020.

Taxation of Lifetime Benefits

One of the benefits of owning a permanent life insurance policy during one's lifetime (even on one's own life) is that the owner can obtain several tax-free benefits from the policy prior to the payment of the death benefit. The tax treatment of lifetime benefits is largely dependent on the cost basis of the policy. The total premiums paid for a policy, less the cost of certain riders (e.g., waiver of premium riders and accidental death riders), are the starting point for determining cost basis.

As discussed in Chapter 4, dividends may be issued on life insurance policies when the pool of insured individuals experience better than anticipated life expectancies, the company's expenses are lower than expected, or the company's investment returns are higher than expected. Dividends are treated as a return of premium (a rebate of previously taxed income) and are therefore not subject to income tax. A dividend distribution does, however, reduce the owner's basis in his or her life insurance policy. If dividend distributions exceed the owner's basis, the owner would be subject to tax on those excess dividends, since he or she has already recouped the capital investment in the life insurance policy.

Owners may also withdraw cash value from permanent life insurance policies without being subject to income tax. Withdrawals are treated first as a distribution of basis (which are not subject to income tax) using the first-in, first-out, or FIFO, method of accounting. The exception to this FIFO treatment for withdrawals or loans is an MEC, which follows last-in, first-out (LIFO) rules. For MECs, earnings come out first and are taxable as ordinary income, which is taxed at the taxpayer's highest marginal income tax bracket. In addition, taxable earnings distributions from a MEC are subject to a 10 percent penalty tax if the owner is under age 59½.

When a policy loan from a MEC is taxable, the taxable amount of the loan increases the cost basis in the policy for calculating taxes on future withdrawals.

Exhibit 5.1 | Cost Basis of a Life Insurance Policy

Non-MEC	
	Premiums paid (less premium for certain riders)
-	Previous withdrawals (up to total premiums; FIFO)
-	Dividends
=	Cost basis
MEC	
	Premiums paid (less premium for certain riders)
+	Taxable loans
-	Previous withdrawals in excess of earnings (LIFO)
-	Dividends
=	Cost basis

Example 5.2

Yoon owns a MEC policy with a $100,000 cash value. She has paid $30,000 in premiums, and no dividends have been paid on the policy. If Yoon takes out a $50,000 loan, the full amount will be taxable because earnings come out first from a MEC (and she has $70,000 of earnings in the policy). If Yoon is under age 59½, she will pay a 10% penalty in addition to the ordinary income taxes. Since Yoon received a taxable loan of $50,000, her basis in the policy increases to $80,000 (the $30,000 paid in premiums plus the $50,000 taxable loan).

Example 5.3

Nia owns a MEC policy with a $100,000 cash value. She has paid $70,000 in premiums, and no dividends have been paid on the policy. If Nia takes out a $50,000 loan, she will pay tax on the $30,000 of earnings. If Nia is under age 59½ she will also pay a 10% penalty on the $30,000 of earnings that were distributed. The $20,000 that is nontaxable does not affect her basis in the contract because it is a loan rather than a withdrawal. In other words, it is not treated as a return of her investment that would reduce the basis in the contract; it is not withdrawn, just borrowed. Her new basis in the policy is $100,000 (the original $70,000 basis plus the $30,000 loan she paid tax on).

Once the owner of a non-MEC policy withdraws all of his or her basis, any further withdrawals are subject to income tax because they represent policy earnings, which are not paid out as a result of the death of the insured.

When the owner of a policy has reduced his or her basis in the policy down to zero (through receipt of dividend distributions or withdrawals) and would like to access additional policy values without triggering a taxable event, the owner can borrow from the cash value of the policy (unless it is a MEC).

Example 5.4

Pam owns a non-MEC policy with a $100,000 cash value. She has paid $30,000 in premiums and no dividends have been paid on the policy. If Pam takes out a $50,000 loan, no tax will paid because loans from non-MEC policies are not taxable. If Pam instead takes a $50,000 withdrawal from the cash value, she will first receive her $30,000 basis tax-free, and only the additional $20,000 will be subject to tax at her ordinary income rate. There will be no 10% early withdrawal penalty even if Pam is under age 59½. Alternatively, Pam could withdraw her $30,000 cost basis tax-free and borrow the remaining $20,000 as a loan, which is also tax-free in a non-MEC policy. Since Pam has withdrawn her entire cost basis in the policy, her cost basis immediately following the withdrawal is $0, but will slowly increase again as she continues to pay premiums.

Policy loans generally carry a favorable rate of interest specified in the life insurance contract and does not have to be paid back, provided that the life insurance policy remains in force during the life of the insured. When the insured dies, the loan plus accumulated interest will be subtracted from the death benefit received by the beneficiary. Provided that the policy remains in force until the death of the insured, the owner of the policy can access cash values on an income tax-free basis (unless it is a MEC).

Example 5.5

Tara bought a whole life policy and paid premiums her entire life. The death benefit of the policy is $150,000. During her life, she borrowed from the policy for various reasons. At her death, the outstanding loan, including accumulated interest, equals $32,000. Her beneficiary receives $118,000, the death benefit less the outstanding loan balance.

When a permanent life insurance policy is terminated during the life of the insured (i.e., the policy is surrendered), a taxable event may result. The difference between the amount received by the owner on the surrender of the policy (including the value of any outstanding loans) and the basis of the policy in the hands of the owner will be subject to income tax. If the owner of a policy receives less than his or her basis, the payment is considered a return of capital and is not subject to tax or treated as a deductible loss.

Example 5.6

Smitty purchased a whole life insurance policy, which permitted him to borrow against the policy in an amount not in excess of its cash value. In that regard the policy provided that policy debt consisted of all outstanding loans and accrued interest and that unpaid interest would be added to loan principal. The policy also provided that Smitty could surrender the policy and receive as a distribution the cash value of the policy minus any outstanding policy debt. Finally, the policy provided that it would terminate if the policy debt were equal to (or exceed) the cash value.

Over time, Smitty borrowed $103,548 against the policy. In addition, interest due on each loan accrued at a specified annual percentage rate pursuant to the terms of the policy. Smitty did not repay the loans.

Ultimately, the policy was terminated. Upon termination, the outstanding loans were satisfied by policy proceeds and extinguished. At that time the combined balance of the loans, including principal and interest, was $196,230, and Smitty's investment in the contract (in the form of aggregate premiums paid) was $86,663.

The insurance company issued to Smitty a Form 1099-R (Distributions From Pensions, Annuities, Retirement or Profit-Sharing Plans, IRAs, Insurance Contracts, Etc.) reflecting a gross distribution of $196,230 and a taxable amount of $109,567 ($196,230 - $86,663 = $109,567). The latter amount represented the difference between the combined balance of the loans at the time that the policy was terminated, i.e., $196,230, and Smitty's investment in the contract, i.e., $86,663.[3]

When a policy is surrendered, the owner may receive the proceeds in a lump sum, may leave the proceeds with the insurer and receive interest payments on the proceeds, or may choose an installment payment method specified in the life insurance contract. When the installment payment method is chosen within 60 days of surrender of the policy, it is possible to spread the taxable gain on surrender of the policy over several tax years using the exclusion ratio approach to calculate the taxable portion of each payment.[4] The installment method may be valuable to a high-bracket income taxpayer who realized a large gain upon surrender of a life insurance policy. If the policyowner dies before the end of the installment period, the contingent payee will continue receiving the payments with the same tax treatment.

Section 1035 Policy Exchanges

Many people wish to change life insurance policies or transform them into other types of insurance products as their needs change. Fortunately, the Internal Revenue Code specifies that when certain exchanges take place, there is a deferral of gain from one product to the next. Under IRC Section 1035, deferral applies to certain exchanges made between life insurance policies, modified endowment contracts (MECs), and annuity contracts. To qualify, the exchange must occur directly from insurance company to insurance company, and the policies must be of like-kind. Like-kind does not necessitate that a whole life policy be exchanged for another whole life policy, but rather that the old and new policies must both have the same insured and that the old policy has a similar or better tax treatment versus the new policy.

Quick Quiz 5.1

1. Premiums paid on life insurance policies are rarely tax deductible.
   a. True
   b. False

2. If the insured dies while owning the life insurance policy, the value of the policy is not includible in his or her estate for estate tax purposes.
   a. True
   b. False

3. Dividend distributions from life insurance policies are taxable to the policy owner.
   a. True
   b. False

4. A way to receive tax-free benefits from a whole life policy during one's life is by taking a loan against the death benefit amount.
   a. True
   b. False

True, False, False, True.

---

3. See Black v. Commissioner of Internal Revenue, T.C. Memo 2014-27, which is the basis for this example.
4. For a fixed number of installment payments, a calculation of the excludible amount can be substituted for the exclusion ratio. The excludible amount (the amount not subject to tax) of each payment is determined by dividing the cost basis by the number of installment payments.

As our discussion above highlights, life insurance policies are uniquely tax-favored products due to the income tax exclusion of the death benefit and the ability to access lifetime benefits on a tax-free basis. Modified endowment contracts (MECs) also provide income tax-free death benefits, but if the owner of a MEC attempts to receive lifetime benefits from the policy, those benefits may be subject to income tax since MECs use LIFO, not FIFO treatment when considering the tax consequences of withdrawals and loans. Annuity contracts (discussed in Chapter 8) provide tax deferral, but ultimately, all gains in the contract will be subject to income tax. Purely from a tax perspective, therefore, life insurance contracts are the best of the three, MECs come in second, and annuities are the least attractive, since they always result in taxable income (except a Roth IRA annuity).

Section 1035 of the Code states that if a policy is exchanged for another similar policy (for example, life insurance for life insurance, MEC for MEC, or annuity for annuity), or for an insurance product that increases the potential for assessment of income tax, the exchange of the policies is a tax-deferred exchange. No income tax will be due at the time of the exchange. If a tax-deferred exchange is desired, therefore, life insurance policies can be exchanged for other life insurance policies, MECs, or annuity contracts. MECs can be exchanged for other MECs or annuity contracts, and annuity contracts can be exchanged only for annuity contracts.

Policies that are MECs can still be exchanged tax-free under Section 1035 of the tax code; however, the policy will remain a MEC, even if exchanged for a new policy that would have passed the 7-pay test. The easy way to recall this rule is "once a MEC, always a MEC." The exchange essentially forces the otherwise non-MEC policy to become a MEC.

Exhibit 5.2 | Tax Treatment of Exchange for Life Insurance, MECs, and Annuities

	Can Be Exchanged For:
Life Insurance	• Life Insurance • Endowment • Annuity
Endowment	• Endowment • Annuity
Annuity	• Annuity (new annuity must mature at same date or earlier)

In the case of a tax-free exchange, the basis of the original contract will carry over to the new contract and will increase if additional premium payments are made to the insurance company.

Exhibit 5.3 | Nontaxable 1035 Exchanges

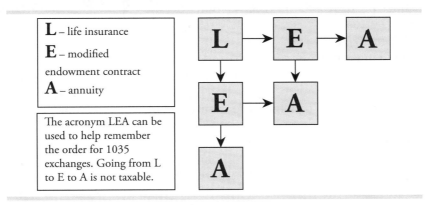

L – life insurance
E – modified endowment contract
A – annuity

The acronym LEA can be used to help remember the order for 1035 exchanges. Going from L to E to A is not taxable.

Example 5.7

Kylar purchased a permanent life insurance policy a number of years ago. Her tax basis was $15,000 at the time. She recently executed a 1035 tax-free exchange for a new policy. She has paid $2,000 in premiums since the exchange, which makes her tax basis in the new policy $17,000.

Transfer for Value

As stated above, IRC Sec. 101(a) provides that the death benefit of life insurance is income-tax-free. The major exception to this provision is the transfer for value rule. If an existing life policy is transferred for valuable consideration (transfer for value), the insurance proceeds are includible in the gross income of the transferee to the extent the proceeds exceed the basis, and are taxed to the transferee at ordinary income tax rates. Thus, the usual income tax exclusion for life insurance proceeds is lost.

Example 5.8

Rashad sells his $100,000 life insurance policy to Company L, a viatical company, for $60,000. Company L pays the $1,000 annual premium for four years before Rashad dies. The profit to Company L is calculated as follows:

$100,000 – $60,000 – $4,000 = $36,000.

The profit of $36,000 is received as ordinary income and is, therefore, fully taxable to Company L.

If the policy owner is a business and the policy was issued as a key person policy (discussed in detail later in this chapter) purchased with business assets, the transfer for value rule would not apply when the policy is subsequently sold to the insured, usually upon retirement of the employee.

Obviously, a violation of the transfer for value rule, causing the death benefit to be taxed as ordinary income to the extent it exceeds basis, is not a situation that is likely to make clients happy. The good news is that it can be reversed by a later transfer that falls under one of the exceptions listed above. For example, if the policy were later transferred back to the insured, it would no longer be considered a transfer for value.

There are five instances in which the transfer of a policy will not result in inclusion of proceeds in the income of the transferee. They are:

1. A transfer to the insured
2. A transfer to a business partner of the insured
3. A transfer to a partnership of which the insured is a partner
4. A transfer to a corporation of which the insured is an officer or shareholder
5. A transfer that results in the transferee's basis being determined by reference to the transferor's basis, such as a gift or a property settlement in a divorce

---

Example 5.9

Marlo transfers a policy to the NICE partnership of which Marlo has a 25 percent interest. The transfer of such a policy is an exception to the transfer for value rule. Upon Marlo's death, NICE partnership will receive the policy death benefits tax-free.

Life Settlements

A **life settlement** occurs when a policy owner sells the life insurance policy to a third party for more than the cash surrender value, but less than the death benefit value. In most cases, the insured is neither terminally nor chronically ill (in which case accelerated benefits or a sale to a qualified viatical settlement provider would be more advantageous, as described below). The owner simply does not want the policy any longer and determines that he or she may be able to sell it for a larger amount than could be obtained through surrendering the policy.

The purchaser of the life insurance policy is making the purchase as an investment, and will be subject to the transfer for value rule. Since a reasonable estimate of life expectancy will be needed (after all they have to keep the policy in force and will not collect on their "investment" until the insured actually dies), the policies are typically on an insured who is age 65 or older. The Tax Cuts and Jobs Act (TCJA) of 2017 imposes reporting requirements in the case of the purchase of an existing life insurance contract in a reportable policy sale and imposes reporting requirements on the payor in the case of the payment of reportable death benefits. In addition, the new law sets forth rules for determining the basis of a life insurance or annuity contract. The reporting requirement applies to any buyer who acquires a life insurance contract or an interest in a life insurance requirement after December 31, 2017 if that acquirer has no substantial family, business, or financial relationship with the insured. The buyer must report basic information about the buyer and the transaction to the IRS, the insurance company that issued the policy, and to the seller. The new law also explicitly states that the exceptions to the transfer for value rules do not apply in the case of a reportable policy sale. The new rules intend to track sales of life insurance policies, but are not intended to eliminate the exceptions to the transfer for value rules.

The tax consequences to the seller can vary depending on the facts of the situation, so the planner and client will need to collaborate with a knowledgeable tax professional to determine the tax consequences of such a sale before the client enters into a sale agreement. From the seller's viewpoint, the sale is part insurance and part investment, so the seller will have some return of basis, some ordinary income (to the extent there would have been ordinary income had the policy been surrendered rather than sold), and potentially also some capital gain (if the sale price exceeds the surrender value).[5]

Prior to the TCJA, the basis of a policy that was sold had to be reduced by the mortality, expense, or other reasonable charges incurred under the contract (known as "cost of insurance"). The new law in Revenue Ruling 2020-05 reverses the position of the IRS in Revenue Ruling 2009-13 that on the sale of a cash value life insurance contract, the insured's (seller's) basis is reduced by the cost of insurance. This change is very favorable to sellers of life insurance policies.[6]

Example 5.10

Oliver, who is not terminally ill or chronically ill, sells his whole life policy to Darth Co. for $50,000. Oliver will have income to the extent the $50,000 exceeds his basis. In addition, Darth Co. must report information about the purchase to the IRS, the insurance company that issued the policy to Oliver, and to Oliver.

Example 5.11

Assume the same facts as in the previous example, and that Oliver had made total premium payments of $20,000 and the cash surrender value at the time of sale was $42,000. His basis under the new rules is $20,000 and his taxable gain is $30,000 ($50,000 sale proceeds less $20,000 basis). $22,000 of the gain (the cash surrender value of $42,000 less the basis of $20,000) will be taxed as ordinary income, and the remaining $8,000 of gain ($30,000 total gain less $22,000 taxed as ordinary income) will be taxed as a capital gain.

Terminally or Chronically Ill Insureds

Special tax treatment is available when the insured under the life insurance policy is either terminally or chronically ill. **Terminal illness** is defined under tax law as having a life expectancy of 24 months or less, which must be certified by a physician.

---

5. Revenue Ruling 2009-13.
6. Ordinary income is taxed at the taxpayer's highest marginal tax bracket while long-term (held longer than one year) capital gains are taxed at lower rates (0%, 15%, or 20%, depending on the taxpayer's taxable income).

Accelerated Benefits Provision or Rider

An **accelerated benefits provision** or rider entitles a qualified insured to receive a pre-death benefit deemed nontaxable because they are treated as an advance payment of death benefit. Accelerated death benefits may be provided by riders to life insurance policies, or they may be included in the policy without additional premium charge. The benefit allows the insured to access a portion of the death benefit while still living if she is diagnosed with a terminal illness. The policy remains in force until the death of the insured, at which time the remaining death benefit is paid to the named beneficiary.

It is important to read the policy provisions since the insurance company is permitted to define terminally ill differently from the IRS. Some insurance companies only offer accelerated death benefits if the insured is given less than 12 or 18 months to live. This does not change the tax treatment since is less than 24 months, however it does make access to the funds more restrictive. In these cases, a sale of the life insurance policy may be necessary to fund added expenses during the final months of life.

In many cases, when an insured sells a life insurance policy shortly before death, the proceeds are used to pay for his or her medical care. To encourage use of private (as opposed to public) funds to cover these medical expenses, Congress exempts from income tax any gain on the policy realized by the terminally ill insured when sold to a viatical settlement provider. Note that the actual use of the proceeds does not change the result. As long as the insured was terminally ill when the policy was sold, there is no income tax on the gain.

Viatical Settlements

A **viatical settlement** is the sale of a life insurance policy to a third party viatical settlement provider when the insured is terminally or chronically ill. If the insured does not meet the requirements for an accelerated death benefit but still needs money for medical or other costs, a viatical agreement may be appropriate and valuable. In a viatical settlement, a policyowner who is terminally ill or chronically ill transfers a life insurance policy to a licensed viatical settlement provider in exchange for a lump-sum payment. The payment is determined by discounting the value of the death benefit to be paid when the insured dies, and the discounts can be substantial due to the uncertainty of projecting an insured's life expectancy. In most cases the offer is for only 50 percent to 85 percent of the face value.

A viatical settlement is typically provided by a company of investors who are referred to as the viatical settlement provider or the viatical company. The policyowner is the viator. The policyowner will assign the policy to the viatical company, and the viatical company will collect the death benefit at the insured's death. Since there is no requirement of an insurable interest at the time of the assignment or at the insured's death, the viatical company is able to collect the policy proceeds.

When the purchaser of a policy (the viatical settlement company) receives the death benefit, the death benefit is subject to income tax to the extent that the policy death benefit received exceeds the purchaser's tax basis in the policy. Under the transfer for value rule, when a life insurance policy is sold for valuable consideration (as in the case of a viatical settlement), the death benefit is subject to income taxation.

Typically, a viatical settlement is sought by a policyowner who cannot obtain accelerated benefits from the insurance company. For example, a policyowner/insured with AIDS or similar disease may have need of the money during his or her lifetime to pay for medical expenses or special treatment. Many insurance policies offer accelerated benefits when an insured is diagnosed with a terminal illness, and such accelerated benefits will generally be more advantageous for the policyowner than a viatical settlement. An insured who is chronically, but not terminally, ill may not be eligible to receive benefits under an accelerated benefit rider, however, making the viatical settlement a suitable option.

Under Section 101(g) of the IRC, accelerated benefits and payments from a viatical settlement are treated as though the benefits were paid by reason of the death of the insured. Since death benefits from life insurance are generally received free of income tax, the accelerated benefits and viatical settlement will also be received income-tax-free. Generally, there are no restrictions on the use that a policyowner may make of accelerated benefits or of the proceeds of a viatical settlement if the insured is terminally ill. If the owner-insured is chronically ill, as opposed to terminally ill, and the proceeds of the life insurance policy sale are used to pay for long-term care costs for the insured, any gain on the sale of the policy is exempt from income tax. Proceeds not used for medical or long-term care expenses will be subject to tax. A person is **chronically ill** if, within the past 12 months, a health care practitioner has certified that the individual has been unable to perform, without substantial assistance, at least two activities of daily living (eating, bathing, dressing, transferring, toileting, and continence) for at least 90 days. A person is also chronically ill if substantial supervision is required to protect that person from threats to health and safety due to cognitive disability (such as advanced stages of Alzheimer's disease or senile dementia).

It should be noted, however, that for a viatical settlement to be tax-free, the purchase of the policy must be made by a qualified viatical settlement provider. To be a qualified viatical settlement provider, the company must meet several rules including being licensed in the state in which the insured resides and following certain provisions of the NAIC's Viatical Settlement Model Act. Section 5 of the Model Act sets forth standards of evaluation for reasonable payments under the viatical settlement as shown in **Exhibit 5.4 | Viatical Settlement - Reasonable Payments**.

Exhibit 5.4 | Viatical Settlement - Reasonable Payments

Insured's Life Expectancy	Minimum Percentage of Face Value (less outstanding loans) Received by the Viator
Less than 6 months	80%
6 - 12 months	70%
12 - 18 months	65%
18 - 25 months	60%
25 months or longer	Greater of cash surrender value or accelerated death benefit available in the policy

Companies that are not qualified viatical settlement providers may offer substantially less than these amounts. Qualified companies will use these as minimum guidelines, but the actual offer may vary among companies. Before making a decision, a policy owner considering a viatical settlement should obtain quotes from several companies.

The accelerated benefits and viatical settlement are income-tax-free, not only to an insured, but also to a policy owner who is not an insured, such as where a spouse or family member owns the policy.

If an insured receives accelerated benefits and then lives beyond the 24 months, the insured does not then become subject to income tax liability on the benefits. The terminal illness or chronic illness condition need only be satisfied at the time of payment to the policy owner.

Planning with Accelerated Benefits and Viatical Settlements

Most insurance policies offer accelerated benefits when death is expected within 12 months, although some may be shorter, such as six months, and others may be longer, such as 24 months. The income tax laws provide the exclusion of benefits from income for payments where life expectancy is 24 months or less. Viatical settlement providers may be willing to enter into a viatical settlement where life expectancy is longer than 24 months. A viatical settlement, therefore, may be appropriate for an insured who has a terminal illness, but who is expected to live longer than 24 months and who will need the money for medical or other expenses, or for an insured who is chronically, rather than terminally, ill.

In cases where the accelerated death benefit is limited, such as to 50 percent of the death benefit amount, and the proceeds will not provide the full amount needed, a combination of the accelerated benefit and sale to a qualified viatical company may yield additional income. For example, a client with a life expectancy of 12 months who has a policy with a $100,000 death benefit that is limited to 50 percent payout for accelerated benefits could take the full $50,000 of accelerated benefits (they may actually receive slightly less than this amount due to administrative fees), leaving a remaining death benefit of $50,000. With a life expectancy of 12 months, the viatical company may offer to pay the insured 70 percent of the remaining $50,000 death benefit.

Before deciding on a viatical settlement, the policy owner should also keep in mind that the policy death benefits will no longer be available to fund the goal for which the policy was originally purchased. The

1. If your terminally ill client sells his life insurance policy and uses the proceeds to pay for a vacation rather than medical expenses, those proceeds, to the extent they exceed the client's basis in the policy, will be subject to income tax.
   a. True
   b. False

2. If your chronically ill client sells his life insurance policy and uses the proceeds to pay for a vacation rather than medical expenses, those proceeds, to the extent they exceed the client's basis in the policy, will be subject to income tax.
   a. True
   b. False

3. If a terminally ill insured with a $100,000 life insurance policy receives accelerated death benefits of $70,000, the remaining $30,000 of death benefit will be paid to his or her named beneficiary at the death of the insured.
   a. True
   b. False

4. If a terminally ill insured with a $100,000 life insurance policy sells the policy to a licensed viatical settlement provider for $70,000, a death benefit of $30,000 will be paid to his or her named beneficiary at the death of the insured.
   a. True
   b. False

False, True, True, False.

viatical settlement is usually the choice of last resort when all other sources of income have been exhausted.

Exhibit 5.5 | Comparison of Viatical Settlements and Accelerated Benefits

	Viatical Settlements	Accelerated Benefits
Who pays the policy owner?	Third-party purchaser	Insurance company
What is paid to the policy owner?	Portion of death benefit	Portion of death benefit
Who receives the death benefit?	Third-party purchaser	Beneficiary
What is the tax treatment?	Benefits are tax-free if insured is terminally (for any expenses) or chronically ill (qualified expenses only); transfer- for-value rule applies to viatical company	Benefits are tax-free if insured is terminally or chronically ill
What are the limiting factors?	Payment received may be low in comparison to the death benefit amount; death benefit is no longer available to support dependents after death of the insured	Only for insured expected to die in 6 to 24 months; death benefit reduction is no longer available to support dependents after death of the insured

LIFE INSURANCE AND BUY-SELL AGREEMENTS

In the absence of a pre-arranged plan for transfer of the business interest, a great amount of strain can be placed on the business, the remaining owners, and the family members of a deceased, disabled, or retired owner.

A buy-sell agreement funded with life insurance and disability income insurance guarantees a buyer for a retiring, disabled, or deceased owner's interest and assures a fair sale price. The agreement also fosters the continuation of the business by not allowing the departing owner's interest to fall into the hands of outsiders, persons who may not be qualified to run the business, or persons who may be incompatible with the remaining owners. While a complete discussion of buy-sell agreements and their tax consequences is beyond the scope of this chapter, an overview of this common financial planning technique, with a focus on the use of life insurance as the funding vehicle for sale of the business upon the death of an owner, is warranted.

Buy-sell agreements are legal arrangements that require the sale of a business interest owned by one individual to another individual or entity upon a specified triggering event. Buy-sell agreements are commonly used by business owners to plan for the orderly transfer and control of a business interest, to create a market for stock that is not traded on securities exchanges, and to plan for liquidity in the estate of a deceased business owner.

Additional benefits of having a properly funded buy-sell agreement in place include:

- The agreement defines the events that will trigger a sale of the business.
- The sale of the business provides liquidity for the estate of a deceased owner.
- The agreement avoids conflicts between heirs and surviving owners (e.g., the remaining owners are not stuck with the surviving spouse of a deceased owner as their new business partner).
- The orderly transfer of the business helps to maintain stability of business operations.
- Having an agreement in place assures suppliers that the business will continue to operate smoothly when an owner leaves the business.
- Having an agreement can improve the creditworthiness of the business.
- The agreement ensures a fair price, and proper funding ensures that resources will be available to pay the agreed-upon price.
- The agreement can ensure that existing owners maintain control and prevent outsiders from becoming owners.
- Having a succession plan and funded buy-sell agreement in place gives employees peace of mind regarding the stability of the company and their jobs. Without such a plan, employees may "jump ship," for example, when an owner dies, because of the fear that the business will not survive.

The most common triggering event that invokes obligations under a buy-sell agreement is the death of the business owner. A properly structured buy-sell agreement requires the estate of the business owner to sell the decedent's business interest to another entity or person, who is often a family member or close business associate of the decedent. Since an obligation to purchase a business interest is triggered at the death of the owner, life insurance is an ideal funding vehicle for buy-sell agreements triggered at death. Typically, either the business itself, or the individual or entity who is obligated to purchase the decedent's business interest will hold a life insurance policy on the decedent's life that has a death benefit sufficient to cover the purchase price of the decedent's business interest.

> ### ≔ *Key Concepts*
>
> 1. Highlight the parties to an entity agreement versus a cross-purchase agreement
>
> 2. Distinguish between an entity agreement, a cross-purchase agreement, and wait-and-see buy-sell agreement.
>
> 3. Explain why life insurance is a perfect hedge for buy-sell agreements that are triggered on the death of the owner.

Other triggering events for buy-sell agreements include disability, divorce, retirement, and withdrawal from the business, but a full discussion of these is beyond the scope of this chapter.

When working with business owners to establish the buy-sell agreement, the financial planner will need to assemble a team of professionals to ensure that all of the important elements are addressed. An attorney will be needed to draft the document to ensure that the agreement will be enforceable. In addition, in some cases the corporate bylaws, partnership agreement, or LLC operating agreement may contain some form of buy-sell agreement within them. When that is the case, either a new agreement will need to be drafted in such a way as to avoid violating any terms of that existing agreement, or the consent of everyone affected may be required to change the agreement. The attorney will be able to provide guidance on these issues. In addition, a CPA or other tax advisor will likely be needed to advise regarding the income and estate tax implications of transfers under the agreement. Also, an insurance professional will be necessary to provide guidance on the best types of life and disability policies to be used for funding the agreement.

Buy-sell agreements generally are of one of three types:
1. entity purchase (sometimes referred to as redemption agreements)
2. cross-purchase agreements
3. wait-and-see agreements

Entity (Redemption) Agreements

The simplest form of buy-sell agreement is the **entity purchase**, or redemption, agreement. This type of buy-sell agreement obligates the business entity to purchase an owner's interest in the entity upon that owner's death. This type of buy-sell agreement works well for organizations that have a separate legal existence from their owners but would not be appropriate for a sole proprietorship. Sole proprietorships are wholly owned by one person, and when that person dies, so does the proprietorship. The business of a sole proprietor may be transferred to another person or entity at the death of the sole proprietorship through a one-way agreement (discussed below), but the proprietorship cannot purchase itself.

Example 5.12

Cecil is part owner of a luxury resort hotel, Fawlty Towers. Fawlty Towers is organized as a C corporation, and the corporation is wholly owned by members of Cecil's family. To ensure that the ownership of the hotel stays within the family and to make sure that Cecil's estate has sufficient liquidity to cover its expenses at his death, Cecil enters into a buy-sell agreement with Fawlty Towers, Inc. whereby Cecil (through his estate) agrees to sell, and Fawlty Towers agrees to purchase his stock when he dies. The agreement between Cecil and Fawlty Towers is an entity purchase buy-sell agreement.

To fund the purchase obligation under an entity-purchase buy-sell agreement, the business can acquire a life insurance policy on the owner's life with a death benefit sufficient to cover the purchase amount. Life insurance is an ideal vehicle to use for this purpose, since it provides funds at the exact time they are needed (the death of the insured). Furthermore, using the death benefit to meet the purchase obligation under the buy-sell agreement does not affect cash holdings or other assets that the company may need for continued business operations.

Sometimes employees of closely-held business interests receive ownership in the business as part of their compensation packages but are not members of the control group or family that want to retain control of the business. Typically, these employee-owners are subject to buy-sell agreements that require them to sell their interest back to the company when they retire, or, if they die before they retire, when they die. Since most people survive until retirement, the most common funding vehicle for this type of buy-sell agreement is a **sinking fund** established and funded by the company so that when the employee retires, the sinking-fund has enough money to purchase the interest. There is mortality risk in these situations, however, that should be addressed. It is possible that an employee-owner will die before retirement and the sinking fund will not have sufficient money to pay for the purchase of the deceased-employee's business interest. As a hedge against this possibility, a life insurance policy could be purchased to cover any shortfall in the sinking fund. Since the life insurance need in this example is not permanent (it expires if the employee lives to retirement), use of term, universal, or variable universal life insurance policies may be appropriate.

Disadvantages

While entity buy-sell agreements have the advantage of simplicity, there is at least one disadvantage to using this structure.

If an entity buy-sell agreement is used, and the surviving owners plan to sell their business interests after the death of the first owner but prior to their own deaths, the entity buy-sell agreement will increase their taxable gain upon sale of their interests. Of course, this would not be an issue for family businesses that are not sold during the lifetimes of the family members. This disadvantage of entity buy-sell agreements is easily remedied by using a cross-purchase buy-sell agreement.

Cross-Purchase Agreements

A **cross-purchase buy-sell agreement** is an arrangement between individuals who agree to purchase the business interest of a deceased owner. Unlike an entity-type agreement, which involves the business itself, a cross-purchase agreement only involves the owners of the business.

Example 5.13

Cecil and his sister, Sybil, are equal owners of a luxury resort hotel, Fawlty Towers. Fawlty Towers is organized as a C corporation, and the corporation has been wholly owned by members of Cecil & Sybil's family since it began. Neither Cecil nor Sybil are married, and neither has any children. To ensure that the ownership of the hotel stays within the family, and to make sure that their estates have sufficient liquidity to cover expenses at death, Cecil and Sybil enter into a buy-sell agreement whereby the first sibling to die agrees to sell (through her estate), and the surviving sibling agrees to purchase the decedent's interest when she dies. The agreement between Cecil and Sybil is a cross-purchase buy-sell agreement.

To fund a cross-purchase buy-sell agreement with life insurance, each party to the agreement purchases a life insurance policy on the life of all of the other parties to the agreement so that the death benefit is sufficient to purchase the interest of any deceased owner. If there are only two parties, this approach is relatively straightforward – each party purchases one policy on the life of the other. When more than two owners are involved, however, things can get complicated, and as the number of owners grows, so does the complexity of the arrangement and the number of life insurance policies that must be purchased.

Example 5.14

Bertie, Claude, and Eustice are equal owners of Wooster Enterprises, Ltd. They have entered into a cross-purchase buy-sell agreement triggered upon death. If Bertie dies first, his 1/3 interest would have to be purchased by Claude and Eustis in equal shares. To fund the agreement, both Claude and Eustice should purchase a life insurance policy on Bertie's life that will pay a death benefit equal to 1/6 (1/3 x 1/2) of the value of the company. Bertie and Claude should each purchase a life insurance policy on Eustice's life for the same amount (in case Eustice dies first), and Eustice and Bertie should purchase a life insurance policy on Claude's life in case Claude dies first. As this example illustrates, for a three-owner agreement, six life insurance policies would have to be purchased to fund this buy-sell agreement.

The number of cross purchase policies needed to fully fund the buy-sell agreement can be calculated by using the formula:

$$\text{Number of policies} = N(N-1)$$

Where N = the number of owners subject to the agreement. The greater the number of owners, the greater the number of life insurance policies that should be purchased. For example, four owners would require twelve policies or 4(4-1).

While applying for a large number of life insurance policies does somewhat complicate the administration of a cross-purchase agreement, the real issues emerge in the annual maintenance of the agreement. Each year, each of the owners will pay the premiums on policies they own covering the lives of other owners in order to keep those policies in force. If just one owner fails to pay the premium and another owner dies, the benefits of entering into the buy-sell agreement may be in jeopardy. For this reason, the agreement may contain a clause making it a legal obligation for each owner to keep the policies in force by paying the premiums as required by the policy.

An entity agreement is a simple arrangement in which only one policy is purchased on the life of each owner and the premiums are paid by the entity. A cross-purchase agreement is much more complex than an entity agreement.

One of the advantages to a cross-purchase agreement is the ability to increase the surviving owner's basis in his or her shares of the business entity. When life insurance death benefits are received (on a tax-free basis), and are used to purchase the business interest of a deceased owner, each surviving owner's share of the business increases, but so does his or her basis in the business entity. Basis is that portion of the sale proceeds not subject to income tax, so a higher basis results in a higher after-tax benefit to the taxpayer. This benefit is unavailable with entity buy-sell agreements and is often the reason that financial advisors prefer cross-purchase arrangements.

Example 5.15

Bertie, Claude, and Eustice are equal owners of Wooster Enterprises, Ltd. The adjusted basis for each 1/3 interest is $100,000. They have entered into a cross-purchase buy-sell agreement triggered upon death. Bertie passed away, and his 1/3 interest in Wooster enterprises was valued at $334,000. The entire business was worth $1 million, leaving $333,000 each for Claude and Eustice. As specified in the buy-sell agreement, Claude and Eustice each purchase half of Bertie's 1/3 interest in Wooster Enterprise, Ltd. for $167,000. After the purchase, Claude's and Eustice's ownership percentages increased from 33% to 50%. Their basis in the ownership interests increased from $100,000 to $267,000 each ($100,000 original adjusted basis + $167,000 paid for acquisition of the interest from Bertie's estate). If Claude and Eustice immediately sold Wooster Enterprises, Ltd. for $1 million, each of them would receive $500,000 (½ the proceeds) and would have to pay income tax on a capital gain of $233,000 ($500,000 amount realized - $267,000 adjusted basis).

How would this result differ if the buy-sell agreement was structured as an entity buy-sell, and Claude and Eustice sold the business after Bertie died? As described above, Claude and Eustice would each receive $500,000 (½ the proceeds from the sale of the business) but would have to pay income tax on a capital gain of $400,000 ($500,000 amount realized - $100,000 adjusted basis). In this instance, the basis of the surviving shareholders is not affected because the corporation, not the individual shareholders, purchased the shares from Bertie's estate.

Cross-purchase agreements are typically preferred from a tax planning standpoint because:
1. they permit the surviving shareholders to increase their basis in the business interest;
2. life insurance owned by business owners outside of a corporation does not trigger any potential accumulated earnings tax.[7]

For cross-purchase agreements, consideration should be also given to what is to be done with the life insurance policies owned by the decedent after the first owner dies. For example, the agreement may provide that policies insuring the lives of the surviving partners will be retained by the decedent's estate or the decedent's spouse or that policies may be sold to a life settlement company. It is usually more advantageous for the agreement to contain a clause providing that policies must first be offered to the insured, to the business, to or other remaining owners. Such a clause should be drafted with input from a CPA regarding the effect of transfer for value rules on the taxation of the death benefit. The transfer for value rule becomes a problem when the business is a corporation and the policies are sold to other owners to facilitate a continuation of the cross-purchase agreement. If the business is a partnership, there is no transfer for value issue if the policies are sold to the surviving partners because an exception to the transfer for value rule applies when the policy is sold to a partner in a partnership.

Example 5.16

Huey, Dewey, and Louie each own 100 shares of McDuck Corporation. There are a total of 300 shares outstanding, and each share is valued at $1,000 (giving each owner a total value of $100,000). They enter into a cross purchase agreement. Huey is the owner, premium payer, and beneficiary of a $50,000 policy on Dewey and a $50,000 policy on Louie. Likewise, each of the other owners purchases a $50,000 policy the other owners. If Huey dies, his estate agrees to sell 50 shares to Dewey for $50,000 and 50 shares to Louie for $50,000. Dewey and Louie collect the death benefit of $50,000 from the life insurance policies on Huey, and use the proceeds to make the required purchase.

Dewey and Louie are now the only shareholders, each owning 150 shares at a value of $150,000. However, they only have $50,000 of life insurance on each other to fund the continuing agreement that if one of them dies, the other will buy their shares. If they are both healthy it is possible that they could purchase additional policies to fund the additional purchase. If they are uninsurable, they may need to seek funding from somewhere else. As it turns out, when Huey died, his estate became the owner of the life insurance policies that he owned on Dewey and Louie. Fortunately, under a clause in the cross-purchase agreement, Huey's estate is required to sell the policies to McDuck Corporation for their fair market value, and the buy-sell agreement will transform to a

---

7. The accumulated earnings tax is assessed to C corporations that retain more than $250,000 ($150,000 for personal service corporations, such as those in the fields of health, law, engineering, or accounting) of corporate earnings without the ability to demonstrate a legitimate business need for the accumulation of the funds. Cash value build-up inside corporate-owned life insurance, such as those used to fund an entity purchase agreement, could cause the corporation to be subject to accumulated earnings tax.

partial entity purchase (since the entity can buy the policies under an exception to transfer for value this arrangement makes sense from a tax standpoint) and a partial cross-purchase for the remainder.

One-Way Buy-Sell Agreements

When the business is a sole proprietorship (one owner), an LLC with only one member, or a corporation with one shareholder, it is possible to have a one-way buy-sell agreement. A one-way agreement is similar to a cross-purchase agreement, but with only one buyer and one seller and no reciprocity because the buyer does not expect to sell a business interest to the sole owner. The owner will agree only to sell, and the buyer will agree only to buy. Often either a family member or a key employee will have a desire to purchase the business when the owner dies. If that is the case, the buyer will purchase a life insurance policy on the current owner.

Wait-and-See Buy-Sell Agreements

Wait-and-see buy-sell agreements are a cross between entity and cross purchase buy-sell agreements. Using this approach, the business has the first option to purchase the interest of a deceased owner. If the business entity chooses not to purchase the interest, the surviving owners of the company are given the opportunity to purchase the deceased owner's interest in proportion to his or her ownership interest. If the surviving owners do not exercise their right to purchase the interest, any interest remaining is purchased by the business.

By giving both the company and the owners the right to purchase an interest, the wait-and-see buy-sell maintains flexibility between the simplicity of the entity agreement and the tax advantages of the cross-purchase agreement. Both the company and the surviving owners can assess their respective situations when the death of an owner occurs and act in a way that maximizes their combined benefits.

Wait-and-see buy-sell agreements are very useful for C corporations with large amounts of retained earnings. When retained earnings are distributed to shareholders, they are usually treated as dividend distributions and are subject to income tax. If a corporation redeems shares from the estate of a deceased owner, and the redemption does not exceed the estate and inheritance taxes plus funeral expenses incurred by the deceased owner's estate, the redemption is typically exempt from income tax. This approach results in a reduction in retained earnings at the corporate level (IRC Sec. 303). The reduction in retained earnings reduces the amount of future corporate distributions that are subject to taxes as dividends, which is a significant benefit for C corporations and their surviving shareholders. Under a wait-and-see buy-sell agreement, the corporation will typically exercise its first option to purchase the number of shares necessary to effectuate a Sec. 303 redemption (thereby reducing its retained earnings) and give the surviving shareholders the option to purchase the

> ### ✍ Quick Quiz 5.4
>
> 1. A cross purchase agreement will increase the income tax basis of survivors/owners.
>   a. True
>   b. False
>
> 2. The number of policies for five equal partners in an entity approach to buy-sell is 20.
>   a. True
>   b. False
>
> 3. The number of policies for five equal partners in cross-purchase arrangement to buy-sell is 20.
>   a. True
>   b. False
>
> 4. The premiums paid for a life insurance policy to fund a cross-purchase agreement are tax deductible to the payer.
>   a. True
>   b. False
>
> True, False, True, False.

remaining interest. If the surviving shareholders exercise this option, they will receive an increase in their basis in the business interest, which will reduce their taxable gain in the business entity should they decide to sell their interests before their deaths.

While wait-and-see buy-sell agreements are often used for C corporations, they are not frequently used for S corporations, partnerships, limited liability companies, or limited liability partnerships. Only C corporations issue taxable dividends, so the tax features of the wait-and-see buy-sell agreements are applicable only to C corporations. Wait-and-see buy-sell agreements could still be used with other types of business entities if the primary objective is to maintain flexibility in the repurchase of interests.

Life Insurance is the Perfect Hedge for a Buy-Sell Agreement Triggered at Death

As illustrated in the discussion above, life insurance is a perfect hedge for buy-sell agreements that are triggered on the death of the owner. If life insurance is purchased on the owner's life, the proceeds can be used to purchase the business interest from the decedent owner's estate. This facilitates effective transfer of ownership and control of the business entity and provides liquidity for the deceased owner's estate so that estate and inheritance taxes, funeral expenses, and end-of-life medical care costs can be paid.

What type of life insurance policy should be purchased to fund the buy-sell agreement? The answer, of course, depends on the facts. If the business is family owned, and the owner of the interest is a family member, or if there has been a long-term relationship between the owner and the business with no definitive date when that relationship will end (such as a retirement date), a permanent life insurance policy should be considered. Whole life insurance costs more up front but provides protection for longer periods of time with guarantees from the insurance company. Using term life, universal life, or variable universal life may be risky, since those policies will only remain in force as long as there is money to pay premiums or in the policy cash value to pay the annual mortality and expense charges. Whole life insurance guarantees that the money needed to buy the business interest will be there no matter how long the owner lives or continues to be involved in the operation of the business activity.

Tax-Related Issues for Buy-Sell Agreements

With an entity purchase agreement, the business entity will be the owner and beneficiary of a life insurance policy on each owner. The business entity will pay the premiums for this life insurance and the payments are not deductible by the entity. The life insurance death benefit proceeds are received income tax-free so long as the rules under IRC §101(j) are met. Section 101(j) of the IRC sets forth rules regarding employee notice and consent when a business entity wishes to purchase a life insurance policy in which the employee will be the insured and the business will be the owner and beneficiary. These rules apply not only to life insurance purchased to fund entity purchase buy-sell agreements, but also to business-owned life insurance used for key person protection or to fund nonqualified deferred compensation (discussed later in this chapter). In order to retain the income tax-free nature of the death benefit, the business is required, before the contract is issued, to:

1. Notify the employee in writing that the business (policyholder) intends to insure the employee's life, and the notice should include the maximum face amount for which the employee could be insured at the time the contract is issued, and
2. Obtain from the employee written consent to be insured under the contract and to allow continued coverage after the insured terminates employment, and

3. Inform the employee, in writing, that the business (policyholder) will be a beneficiary of any proceeds payable upon the death of the employee.

In addition to the notice and consent requirements, one of the following must also apply:

1. At the time the policy is issued, the employee is a highly compensated employee (defined under the law as: a director, a five percent or greater owner, one of the five highest paid officers, among the 35 percent highest paid employees under Section 105(h)(5), or an employee with compensation of at least $130,000 per year as indexed for inflation under Section 414(q) in 2020), or
2. At the time of death, the employee was still employed with the business at any time during the 12 months prior to death, or
3. The death benefit is paid to the insured's heirs, or
4. The death benefit is used to purchase the insured's ownership interest in the business from the insured's heirs or estate (e.g., under a buy-sell agreement).

Failure to comply with these requirements will result in the death benefit being taxed as ordinary income to the extent that it exceeds the employer's cost basis in the policy. Each year that the business continues to own the policy, it will be required to file Form 8925 with its income tax return to report information regarding the policy.

When an existing policy is transferred from the employee to the employer, the transfer itself is sufficient to meet the Notice and Consent requirement of §101(j) regarding written consent, maximum face amount, and notice that the employer will be the beneficiary of the policy.[8]

With a cross-purchase agreement, the premiums paid by each owner to purchase insurance on the lives of the other owners are not tax deductible, but the death benefits received will be income tax-free, provided a transfer-for-value problem does not exist.

Recall that the transfer of an insurance policy is exempt from the transfer for value rules and will not cause the loss of the death proceeds' tax-free nature if the transfer is one of the statutorily defined exceptions. Examples of exceptions to the transfer for value rule are:

*   A transfer of the policy to the insured.
*   A transfer to a partner of the insured or to a partnership of which the insured is a partner.
*   A transfer to a corporation of which the insured is a shareholder or officer.
*   A transfer in which the transferee's basis is determined, in whole or in part, by reference to the transferor's basis (e.g., a substituted or carryover basis).

Several of these exceptions to the transfer for value rule are useful in planning for buy-sell agreements for business owners, particularly if an owner is currently uninsurable but owns a policy that is no longer necessary in fulfilling his personal financial plan. For example, the ability of business partners to transfer existing policies either to each other or to the partnership is a valuable exception that allows the buy-sell agreement to be funded with an existing policy without adverse tax consequences. It should be noted, however, that the same flexibility is not available when the business is a corporation. There is no exception to the transfer for value rule when shareholders transfer policies to each other. The only exception for a corporation is for the insured (who is an officer or shareholder) to transfer an existing policy to the corporate entity.

---

8. Notice 2009-48.

Trusteed Agreements

To avoid the transfer for value problem with a corporate cross-purchase agreement funded with existing policies, or if the owners simply want to avoid purchasing separate life insurance policies on one another due to the large number of policies required for multi-owner cross-purchase agreement, they can use a trusteed cross-purchase agreement. Under such an agreement, a trustee owns the life insurance policy on each owner, and the owners contribute their individual share of the insurance premiums.

Trusteed agreements are a way to avoid a large number of policies while still achieving the increase in basis associated with a cross-purchase agreement. For tax purposes, the trustee is treated as a straw man (one with no substance) and the surviving owners are treated as having received the death benefit and purchased the shares of the deceased owner upon death, thus providing them with an increased cost basis.

NONQUALIFIED DEFERRED COMPENSATION

A nonqualified deferred compensation plan (NQDC) may be used as a means to provide retirement, disability, and/or death benefits to a select group of key employees to whom the employer deliberately wishes to confer preferred treatment. Unlike qualified retirement plans, such as profit sharing plans and defined benefit pension plans, which must follow stringent rules under the Employee Retirement Income Security Act of 1974 (ERISA), establishment of a nonqualified deferred compensation plan allows an employer to avoid the ERISA rules and provide benefits to a select group of key executives without having to provide benefits to rank and file employees. Nonqualified deferred compensation (NQDC) plans are often used as a supplement to a qualified retirement plan in order to offer key executives additional benefits beyond those permitted in the qualified retirement plan, or may be established by an employer that does not have a qualified plan because the employer does not desire to cover a broad group of employees, as is required for qualified plans.

It is important to understand that employers also use deferred compensation arrangements as a method of retaining key employees. This can be done either by vesting schedules or through increased benefits with additional years of service.

Key Concepts

1. Describe the advantages to the employer of nonqualified deferred compensation versus a qualified retirement plan.

2. Identify the three funding methods that may be used to provide the promised benefits under a deferred compensation agreement.

3. Identify the advantages, disadvantages, and tax treatment when a rabbi trust is used to informally fund the NQDC agreement.

4. Identify the advantages, disadvantages, and tax treatment when a secular trust is used to fund the NQDC agreement.

Some different arrangements include:
1. Golden Handshakes - severance package, often designed to encourage early retirement
2. Golden Parachutes - substantial payments made to executives being terminated due to changes in corporate ownership
3. Golden Handcuffs - designed to keep the executive with the company

Deferred Executive Compensation

Deferred compensation arrangements may be established simply to defer an executive's compensation to a future year. When an executive agrees to defer his compensation, the executive is agreeing to defer receipt of current income for a promise from the employer to pay that compensation at some later date. A high-earning, high-tax bracket executive might find this desirable as a means to supplement her retirement savings since employee contributions to 401(k) plans are limited while nonqualified deferred compensation has no maximum contribution limit. In addition, if the plan is properly structured to defer taxation of the income, the executive can avoid being taxed at the current high tax bracket by deferring income to retirement years when she is likely to be in lower tax bracket. It is important to note that an agreement to defer compensation into the future must be made prior to the compensation being earned in order for the executive to avoid being taxed on the compensation in the year in which it is earned.

Salary reduction plans are common with professional athletes. A large signing bonus, or a part thereof, is frequently transferred to an escrow agent, subject to general creditors of team or owner, to defer the receipt of taxable income until such time as the athlete is beyond his peak earning period, thereby helping to assure the athlete's future financial security.

Salary Continuation

An alternative to the salary deferral plan is a **salary continuation plan** (**supplemental executive retirement plan**, or SERP). With a SERP, none of the employee's current salary is reduced or used to provide the future benefit. The employer's promise of the salary continuation is a benefit in addition to the employee's current salary. These employer promises are often made as an inducement for a valued employee to remain or as an incentive for a new recruit to accept employment.

Note that under a salary continuation plan, the employee promises nothing. The employee may be eager to remain with the employer because of the attractive continuing salary the employer has promised, but he or she has no obligation to stay with the employer.

Funding Arrangements

The nonqualified plan may be:
1. Unfunded – the employer's promise is only secured by the company's general assets.
2. Informally funded – the employer acquires specific assets which it intends to liquidate in the future to pay the employee benefits, but the specific assets are commingled with the general assets of the company and thus are available to general creditors or the employer. Under an informally funded plan, the only security or guarantee the employee has of receiving the benefits is the unsecured promise of the employer.
3. Funded – the employer sets aside specific segregated assets unavailable to creditors.

Unfunded Promise to Pay

Deferred compensation may take any form due to the flexibility and lack of requirements under ERISA and the IRC. An unfunded promise to pay falls within the spectrum of deferred compensation. This type of arrangement will meet the standards of a substantial risk of forfeiture (discussed below) and will, therefore, meet the objective of tax deferral.[9] However, the employee is at some risk of not being paid. The employer may choose not to pay, or claim that the employee did not meet the conditions of the contract, or the employer may not have sufficient funds to pay the obligation. Obviously, the employee has the right to claim that the employer is in violation of the agreement, which may or may not yield any tangible benefit. To mitigate against such risk, employees would prefer that the employer set funds aside for the purpose of providing for the payment of the deferred obligation.

Rabbi Trusts (Informally Funded)

Deferred-compensation plans can provide for assets to be placed in revocable or irrevocable trusts to pay future benefits. **Rabbi trusts** are designed to hold funds and assets for the purpose of paying benefits under a nonqualified deferred compensation arrangement. With rabbi trusts, assets to provide benefits are placed in a trust and are kept separate from the company's other assets, but the trust assets are considered general assets of the company and are still available to the company's general creditors.

There is no guarantee that trust assets will be available to pay the promised benefits to the employee. A rabbi trust can, however, provide for springing irrevocability. Under such a provision, the rabbi trust becomes irrevocable in the event of a change of control or ownership of the employer company. The employer may also be required to make a contribution of the remaining deferred compensation needed to pay benefits if springing irrevocability is triggered.

Although the assets in a rabbi trust are for the sole purpose of providing benefits to employees and may not be accessed by the employer, they may be seized and used for the purpose of paying general creditors in the event of the liquidation of the company. Insolvency triggers, which would require payments to employees or irrevocability of the trust in the event that the employer company's net worth falls below a certain level or when the employing company is liquidated in a bankruptcy, are not permitted with rabbi trusts. Such a provision would give the employees an advantage over general creditors, which is contrary to the requirements for a rabbi trust. In this regard, rabbi trusts do not protect the executive employee from bankruptcy of the employer. Because of this possibility, the IRS has ruled that rabbi trusts that are established and follow specific guidelines will create a substantial risk of forfeiture (discussed below), as needed to obtain deferral of taxation to the executive. When these guidelines are followed, any assets within a rabbi trust are not currently taxable to the employee yet provide significantly more protection to the employee than a simple unfunded promise to pay.

Employees interested in rabbi trusts are usually concerned about their deferred assets being in jeopardy from mergers, acquisitions, or takeovers, so they are interested in the springing irrevocability, even though an insolvency trigger is not permitted.

---

9. A substantial risk of forfeiture exists when rights in property that are transferred are conditioned, directly or indirectly, upon the future performance (or refraining from performance) of substantial services by any person, or the occurrence of a condition related to a purpose of the transfer, and the possibility of forfeiture is substantial if the condition is not satisfied.

The income generated from the assets within the trust is taxed to the employer. However, the employer will receive an income tax deduction upon distribution from the trust under the terms of the deferred compensation agreement. Many deferred compensation plans will use life insurance products to avoid taxation of income to the employer.

The IRS provided clear and specific rules defining a model rabbi trust in Revenue Procedure 92-64 that must be followed to make certain that the plan will result in the desired outcome. The Revenue Procedure provides for many rules, some of which are listed below:

- the model language must be adopted almost verbatim
- the trust must be valid under state law
- the trust must state that the assets are subject to the claims of creditors in the case of insolvency
- the trustee must be an independent third party, such as a bank
- the trustee must be given some level of discretion over investment of plan assets

Secular Trusts (Funded)

Secular trusts are irrevocable trusts designed to hold funds and assets for the purpose of paying benefits under a nonqualified deferred compensation arrangement. This type of plan provides protection for the assets in the trust. The funds are set aside for the benefit of employees and are not available to the employer or subject to the claims of the employer's creditors. Since a secular trust does not create a substantial risk of forfeiture (discussed below) for the employee, assets set aside in a secular trust result in immediate taxation to the employee.[10] This tax consequence is the cost of eliminating the risk that the funds will not be paid in the future.

In order to defer taxation to the executive for a period of time, secular trusts may use a graduated vesting schedule, and only upon vesting will the recognition of income for purposes of income tax be triggered. Once the funds are vested, the employee is required to include the value of the vested benefit in income and the employer will have an income tax deduction of an equal amount.

Treasury Regulation §1.402(b)-1 provides that any employer contribution made to a trust that is not exempt from taxation shall be included as compensation in the gross income of the employee for his taxable year during which the contribution is made, but only to the extent that the employee's interest in such contribution is substantially vested at the time the contribution is made.[11] Thus, the secular trust can be effectively used in combination with a vesting schedule to defer tax for the executive.

Quick Quiz 5.5

1. Nonqualified deferred compensation plans allow the employer to take a current tax deduction for compensation expense while the employee can defer the income tax on the compensation.
   a. True
   b. False

2. An employer receives a current income tax deduction for contributions to a qualified retirement plan.
   a. True
   b. False

3. A rabbi trust can provide the employee with protection against employer insolvency.
   a. True
   b. False

4. A secular trust can provide the employee with protection against employer insolvency as well as against a change in ownership or management.
   a. True
   b. False

False, True, False, True.

10. IRC §402(b) and the Economic Benefit Doctrine.

To compensate for the increased taxable income without necessarily having an increase in cash distributions, secular trusts may provide for distributions to the participants for the purpose of paying the income tax attributable to the taxability of the benefits in the trust.

Example 5.17

Ashanti, age 45, a key executive at NBP, Inc. is covered under the company's nonqualified deferred compensation plan. Funds are placed into a secular trust for her benefit in the current year, but the plan contains a five year vesting schedule. Retirement distributions will be made to Ashanti beginning at her age 65. Ashanti will be taxed on the contributions to the trust at the time of vesting (over the next five years, at her ages 46-50), but she will not receive distributions under the plan until she reaches age 65.

The funds contributed to the trust will be invested and will generate income. The income will usually be taxable to the employee as it is earned if it is not subject to a substantial risk of forfeiture.

Example 5.18

Oxford Corporation has created a deferred compensation plan (Plan) for 50 key executives (participants), all of whom are highly compensated employees. Oxford contributes each year on behalf of each participant to a trust, T. The trust is not and never has been a qualified trust under §401(a) and is not exempt from taxation under §501(a).

T's assets are not subject to the claims of Oxford's creditors. Separate accounts that reflect the participant's share of the net trust assets and income are maintained for each participant.

A participant's entire interest in T becomes vested upon completion of three years of service with Oxford beginning on the date the individual first becomes a participant in the Plan. Participants or their beneficiaries are entitled to receive their vested interest in the net assets of T, net of applicable withholding and other taxes, on death, disability, or termination of employment. In addition, T is required to distribute to each participant each year an amount that the trustee reasonably estimates will be equal to the amount of Federal, state, and local income and employment taxes payable by the participant with respect to the increase in the participant's vested accrued benefit in T during such year. T is permitted to make the distribution in part as a distribution of cash to the participant, and in part in the form of applicable employment tax withholding under Federal, state, or local law.

This arrangement is an example of a secular trust, in which assets cannot be seized by creditors, but tax is only deferred until the participant is vested.

---

11. Such as a trust under IRC §501(a).

Tax Treatment of Nonqualified Deferred Compensation

When an employer contributes to a qualified retirement plan, the employer can take a current tax deduction for contributions made for the benefit of the employee while the tax on the benefit to the employee is deferred until the employee receives a distribution from the retirement plan. In order to achieve this beneficial tax treatment, the employer must abide by numerous rules imposed by ERISA regarding nondiscrimination, coverage, eligibility and other aspects of the qualified retirement plan.

While a nonqualified deferred compensation plan provides the employer with the benefit of flexibility and the ability to discriminate in favor of key executives, the trade-off is the tax treatment. When NQDC is offered, it is typically designed to defer taxes to the executive and the employer receives no federal income tax deduction until benefits are actually paid to the employee. All benefits are taxable as ordinary income when paid to the employee and are subject to payroll taxes (Social Security and Medicare taxes, discussed in Chapter 11) at the time when there is no longer a substantial risk of forfeiture to the employee.

For deferral of income tax to be realized, the deferred compensation plan must comply with certain income tax provisions.

IRC Sec. 409A

The American Jobs Creation Act of 2004 was signed into law on October 22, 2004 and created IRC §409A, which deals with nonqualified deferred compensation plans. The purpose of this section is to provide clear structure and guidance for these types of plans. These rules also enact harsh penalties for those plans that do not comply with §409A. Plans failing to meet the requirements of this section are subject to acceleration of prior deferrals, interest, penalties, and a 20 percent additional tax on the amount of the deferrals. These are serious ramifications for plans that fail to comply with the new rules.

If deferred compensation plans meet the requirements of §409A, then IRC §409A has no effect on the employee's gross income and taxes. If the arrangement does not meet the requirements of §409A, however, §409A generally provides that all amounts deferred under a nonqualified deferred compensation plan are currently includible in gross income to the extent that the amounts are not subject to a substantial risk of forfeiture and to the extent that the amounts have not been previously includible in gross income.[12] Compensation is subject to a substantial risk of forfeiture if entitlement to the amount is conditioned on the performance of substantial future services by any person or the occurrence of an event related to a purpose of the compensation, such as the attainment of certain earnings or equity value.[13]

> ### ☷ Key Concepts
>
> 1. Explain the difference in tax treatment for the employer for contributions to a qualified retirement plan versus contributions to a nonqualified deferred compensation plan.
>
> 2. Describe how constructive receipt, economic benefit doctrine, and substantial risk of forfeiture impact NQDC plans.
>
> 3. What is the significance of Section 409A to nonqualified deferred compensation plans?

---

12. Internal Revenue Bulletin 2006-29.
13. IRC §409A(d)(4).

In order to comply with §409A, the regulations require that the plan be established and maintained in accordance with the requirements of §409A. As part of these requirements, the material terms of the plan must be set forth in writing.[14] In addition, §409A generally provides that payments may only be made at certain times or upon certain events, including:

- separation from service
- disability
- death
- at a specified time or pursuant to a fixed schedule
- upon a change in control[15]
- upon an unforeseeable emergency

IRC §409A greatly restricts the conditions under which a plan may permit the acceleration of the time or schedule of payments under the plan. The exceptions that the law provides are minimal but include domestic relations orders, distributions for paying income tax for 457(f) plans, and the payment of employment taxes.

Substantial Risk of Forfeiture

Substantial risk of forfeiture is an income tax concept that relates to when income is subject to income tax. The rules for substantial risk of forfeiture are found in Treasury Regulation §1.83-3(c).

A substantial risk of forfeiture exists when rights in property that are transferred are conditioned, directly or indirectly, upon the future performance (or refraining from performance) of substantial services by any person, or the occurrence of a condition related to a purpose of the transfer, and the possibility of forfeiture is substantial if the condition is not satisfied. The issue of whether a risk of forfeiture is substantial remains a matter of facts and circumstances. When there is a substantial risk of forfeiture, the taxpayer is not required to include the income as taxable income. When there is not a substantial risk of forfeiture, the taxpayer is required to recognize the income currently as taxable income.

Often, a deferred compensation agreement is structured as a simple contractual promise from the employer to a key employee. Generally, this puts the employee at risk that the employer might default or breach the contract and not pay. The obligation of a deferred compensation agreement is reflected on the balance sheet of the organization as a liability. However, in terms of the ranking of creditors in the case of liquidation, all secured and priority unsecured creditors would be fully paid prior to paying the deferred compensation obligation.[16] In liquidation, a participant in a deferred compensation plan is paid before both preferred and common shareholders. Thus, it can be said that for an unfunded deferred compensation arrangement based on a simple contractual promise to pay, the employee is at a "substantial risk of forfeiture." Most deferred compensation arrangements are unfunded and, therefore, subject to the risk of nonpayment. Deferred compensation arrangements can, however, be funded, as described above in the Secular Trust section.

---

14. Although nonqualified deferred compensation plans are not required to follow all of the ERISA rules, the sponsoring employer must file information about the plan with the Department of Labor.
15. Treas. Reg. §1.409A-3(i)(5)(vi).
16. NQDC plan participants are general unsecured creditors. In the event of liquidation, claims are paid in the following order: (1) secured creditors, (2) administrative expenses and priority unsecured creditor claims, (3) general unsecured creditors, and (4) equity security holders.

Example 5.19

On November 25, 2020, Carb Corporation gives Martin, an employee, a bonus of 100 shares of Carb Corporation stock. The terms of the bonus arrangement obligate Martin to return the stock to Carb Corporation if he terminates his employment for any reason. However, for each year occurring after November 25, 2020, during which Martin remains employed with Carb Corporation, Martin ceases to be obligated to return 10 shares of the Carb Corporation stock. Therefore, each year occurring after November 25, 2020 that Martin remains employed, his rights in 10 shares of stock cease to be subject to a substantial risk of forfeiture. Thus, the value of 10 shares of stock will be included in Martin's income each year when the substantial risk of forfeiture expires. The value of this income is equal to the value of the stock on each November 25th, when the substantial risk of forfeiture expires.

Since one of the primary purposes of deferred compensation arrangements is to avoid current taxation for the key executive, these plans will almost always include a substantial risk of forfeiture so that the executive can defer payment of income tax. Employers may simply promise to pay the employee or may use some form of vesting schedule in an attempt to meet the substantial risk of forfeiture standard.

Avoiding Constructive Receipt and Economic Benefit

Constructive receipt is an income tax concept that establishes the point at which income is includible by a taxpayer and therefore subject to income tax. The rules for constructive receipt are found in Treasury Regulation §1.451-2.

Income, although not actually in a taxpayer's possession, is nonetheless constructively received by the taxpayer in the taxable year during which it is credited to his account, set apart for him, or otherwise made available so that he may draw upon it at any time, or so that he could have drawn upon it during the taxable year if notice of intention to withdraw had been given. Generally, an individual will be deemed to have constructive receipt of income if he can choose to receive the income today or in the future. For example, when interest is credited to a bank savings account, the account owner may choose not to immediately withdraw the funds, but because she has full access to the funds at any time, she is in constructive receipt and will be taxed on the interest immediately. However, income is not constructively received if the taxpayer's control of its receipt is subject to substantial limitations or restrictions. Thus, if a corporation credits its employees with stock as a bonus but the stock is not available to the employees until some future date, the mere crediting of the stock on the books of the corporation does not constitute constructive receipt of the stock.

Deferred compensation plans are structured so that employees benefiting under the plan will avoid constructive receipt and will therefore be allowed the deferral of income taxation.

As mentioned, an employee who elects to defer compensation, such as a bonus, into the future under a deferred compensation arrangement must do so prior to the compensation being earned. Otherwise, the employee would effectively have the choice of receiving current income or deferring. This choice would result in the income being considered constructively received whether or not there was a subsequent substantial risk of forfeiture.

The following are some examples of what is not considered constructive receipt:
- an unsecured promise to pay
- the benefits are subject to substantial limitations or restrictions
- the triggering event is beyond the recipient's control (i.e., company is acquired)

The **economic benefit doctrine** provides that an employee will be taxed on funds or property set aside for the employee if the funds or property are unrestricted and nonforfeitable, even if the employee was not given a choice to receive the income currently. In other words, if an employer sets aside funds for an employee and there is no risk that the employee will not receive the funds, then the funds are taxable under this doctrine at the point in time at which there are no longer any restrictions attached to the property.

Deferred compensation plans may provide for a trust to hold the funds for the employee prior to retirement or termination. Contributions to an employee's trust made by an employer will generally be included in the gross income of the employee. This means that contributions to a trust are taxable to the employee even if there is not a distribution from the trust. To be subject to income tax, the funds simply have to be unrestricted and nonforfeitable, which could occur once the employee becomes partially or fully vested.[17] An exception to this rule can be achieved through use of a rabbi trust, discussed previously in this chapter.

Under no circumstances would a simple promise to pay be subject to current income tax since there are substantial risks as to whether the payments will be made. To be taxable under the economic benefit doctrine, there must be no restrictions or risks that the funds would not be paid to the employee.

Exhibit 5.6 | Characteristics of Alternative Deferred Compensation Arrangements

	Unfunded Promise to Pay	Rabbi Trust	Secular Trust
Funded with assets	No	Yes	Yes
Funded (for purposes of ERISA)	No	No	Yes
Risk of forfeiture without employer financial instability	Yes	No	No
Risk of forfeiture if employer is insolvent	Yes Claim is below priority general creditors	Yes Claim is below priority general creditors	No
When is there taxable income to the executive?	When actually or constructively received	When actually or constructively received	Immediately upon funding by employer or vesting
When is the payment deductible to employer?	Deferred until payment is made to executive	Deferred until payment is made to executive	When constructively received and taxable to executive
Accomplishes the objective of deferral	Yes	Yes	If vesting is required

---

17. IRC §402(b).

Funding with Insurance

An unfunded plan is essentially a mere promise by the employer to pay a retirement benefit. No reserve is set aside, and the employer does not segregate any assets from its general assets to pay the benefits. The employer's promise is unsecured, and no employer assets guarantee the employee's benefit.

The "funded plan" is not frequently used because the IRS may rule that the employee is in constructive receipt of the assets; therefore, the value of the assets acquired each year must be included in the employee's gross income for the current year. The employee may avoid constructive receipt of the funding assets under a funded plan if there is a substantial risk of forfeiture.

A plan is informally funded when a reserve is established for paying benefits, but the assets in the reserve remain general assets of the employer and can be obtained by creditors in the event of the employer's bankruptcy.

Nonqualified plans are often informally funded by the purchase of:
1. A life insurance policy
2. An annuity
3. Mutual funds

A life insurance policy has the advantage that the internal buildup of cash value will not be taxable to the employer. An annuity has the disadvantage that the employer must pay income tax each year on the income. The annual income on the annuity is subject to current income tax because it is held by the employer corporation (which is a non-natural owner). While individuals do not report the annual income in an annuity, the tax rules require an entity, such as a corporation, to recognize the annual income on their tax return. Annuities are discussed in detail in Chapter 8.

The NQDC arrangement is frequently structured to pay retirement benefits to the executive or to pay a death benefit to the executive's beneficiary if the executive dies before receiving the retirement benefits. Following the rules under Sec. 101(j), as previously discussed, the employer can own a permanent life insurance policy on the executive, and be the beneficiary of the death benefit, using the policy proceeds to pay the promised death benefit as a salary continuation payment to the employee's family in the event of the employee's death prior to retirement. If the executive lives to retirement, the employer can pay supplemental retirement income to the retiree out of current company revenue and keep the policy in force after the executive's retirement. Later, at the executive's death, the employer will receive the tax-free insurance proceeds which will offset the deductible supplemental retirement benefits paid. This strategy is

---

✍ Quick Quiz 5.6

1. Deferred compensation plans are generally structured so that employees benefiting under the plan will avoid constructive receipt.
   a. True
   b. False

2. A substantial risk of forfeiture is the risk that the employee will leave the company prematurely and take the plan assets with them.
   a. True
   b. False

3. For contributions to a deferred compensation plan to be taxed because of the economic benefit doctrine, there must be no restrictions or risks that the funds would not be paid to the employee.
   a. True
   b. False

4. Life insurance is commonly used to informally fund NQDC plans that include a preretirement death benefit due to the proceeds being available to pay the promised benefits and the tax deferral of the cash build-up within the policy.
   a. True
   b. False

True, False, True, True.

sometimes referred to as a "cost recovery plan" since the cost of the supplemental benefits paid is recovered via the death benefit received by the business upon the death of the executive.

The deferred compensation agreement should not make reference to the life insurance policy in order to avoid having the plan treated as "funded." Since the employer owns the policy, the cash value of the policy will be recorded as an asset reserve account on the employer's balance sheet, while the obligation to pay the benefits appears as a deferred liability account. Earnings on assets earmarked to pay the promised benefits are taxable income to the employer each year; however, the use of life insurance has the advantage that the growth of the cash value is tax-deferred.

OTHER BUSINESS USES OF LIFE INSURANCE

Split-Dollar Life Insurance Arrangement

A **split-dollar arrangement** is a discriminatory benefit plan using life insurance. The employer and employee share the cost of a life insurance policy on the employee (usually permanent insurance such as whole life insurance or variable universal life insurance). Such arrangements are typically used by businesses to provide low cost insurance to key employees. A split-dollar life insurance arrangement is generally structured in one of either of the two following ways:

1. The endorsement method, or
2. The collateral assignment method.

The Endorsement Method
Under a split-dollar life insurance plan using the endorsement method, the employer owns the life insurance policy on the employee and the employer pays the policy premium. The employer withholds the right in the plan to be repaid for all of its premium either at the employee's death or the surrender of the life insurance policy. Usually any death benefit or cash surrender value in excess of the employer's refund is paid to the policy beneficiaries.

The Collateral Assignment Method
Under a split-dollar life insurance plan using the collateral assignment method, the employee owns the life insurance policy and the employer makes a loan to the employee to pay the policy premiums. In this case, at the employee's death or at the surrender of the policy, the employer loan will be repaid and any excess will be paid to the policy beneficiaries.

Exhibit 5.7 | Endorsement versus Collateral Assignment Method of Split-Dollar Plan

	Endorsement Method	Collateral Assignment Method
Owner	Employer	Employee
Premium Payer	Employer	Employer loan to employee
Beneficiary	Named by employee	Named by employee
Employer Repaid for Premiums	At death of employee or surrender of policy	Loan repaid at death of employee or surrender of policy
Employee Taxed	On value of death benefit + increase in equity currently accessible to employee	On difference between the market rate of interest and the actual interest charged on the loan

Uses of Split-Dollar Life Insurance

A split-dollar life insurance policy is appropriate when an employer wishes to provide an executive with life insurance benefits at a low cost and low cash outlay to the executive (the premiums are essentially paid for by the employer). Split-dollar life insurance plans are best suited for executives in their 30s, 40s, and early 50s since the plan requires a reasonable duration to build adequate policy cash value and the cost to the executive at later ages is usually prohibitive. Split-dollar life insurance can be used as an alternative to an insurance-financed nonqualified deferred compensation plan or in conjunction with a nonqualified, unfunded, deferred compensation plan. A split-dollar policy is also effective when an employer is seeking a totally selective executive fringe benefit as the nondiscrimination rules do not apply.

A split-dollar plan allows an executive to receive the benefit of current value using employer funds with minimal or no tax cost to the executive. In most types of split-dollar plans, the employer's outlay is at all times fully secured. Upon the employee's death or termination of employment, the employer is reimbursed from policy proceeds for its premium outlays. The net cost to the employer for the plan is merely the loss of the net after-tax income the funds could have earned while the plan was in effect.

Income Taxation Issues

The income tax treatment of split-dollar life insurance arrangements will be determined under one of two sets of rules depending on who owns the policy. If the executive, or someone designated by the executive, owns the life insurance policy, then the loan taxation rules apply. If the employer owns the policy, the economic benefit rules apply.

If the executive owns the policy, the employer's premium payments are treated as below-market loans from the employer to the executive. Consequently, unless the executive is required to pay the employer market-rate interest on the loan, the executive will be taxed on the difference between market-rate interest and the actual interest charged.

If the employer is the owner of the policy, the employer's premium payments are treated as providing taxable economic benefits to the executive. The executive recognizes as taxable income the value of life insurance coverage, as well as any increase in equity currently accessible to the executive. By taxing the executive on the increase in equity each year, this arrangement is discouraged.

Death Benefit - Transfer for Value

Death benefits payable from a split-dollar life insurance plan including both the employer's share and the employee/beneficiary's share are generally received income tax-free. However, the tax-free nature of the death proceeds is lost if the policy has been transferred for value (as discussed previously in this chapter).

Estate Consequences of Split-Dollar Life Insurance

Incidents of ownership will cause inclusion in the gross estate if the decedent retained the ownership or had the right to name or change the beneficiary. Inclusion in the gross estate could result from a policy transferred or assigned within the three year period prior to the insured/owner's death.

Key Person Life and Disability Insurance

Key person life insurance is designed to protect a business upon the loss of a key employee. Usually, one or two key people represent the technical genius or creative talent in a small to mid-size business. The sudden death of such a person can have a disastrous financial effect on the company. It could take years to replace the key employee with someone with the same level of talent or with the right synergy for the team. It can weaken the company's credit rating or require the sale of a portion or all of the business if there is no way to cover costs while a replacement person is found.

The tax-free proceeds from a key person life insurance policy can be used to find, hire, and train a replacement; compensate for lost business during the transition; or finance any number of timely business transactions. In addition, the cash value from a permanent life policy will appear as an asset on the company's financial statements.

The business will own, pay for, and be the beneficiary of the policy. Premiums for key person life insurance are not a deductible business expense, and the death proceeds are received tax-free.

C-corporations should adopt a corporate resolution authorizing the purchase of key employee life insurance to prove cash value build-up is for a reasonable business purpose to avoid the accumulated earnings tax becoming an issue. This precaution is not needed for sole proprietors or partnerships because they are not subject to the accumulated earnings tax. Because the business entity will be the owner and beneficiary of the policy, the rules under Section 101(j), discussed previously in this chapter, must be followed. In some cases, however, the employee may be reluctant to allow purchase of the policy for fear that the medical underwriting may reveal health issues they do not want disclosed to the employer.

Key person disability insurance can protect the business by providing funds to sustain operations and replace lost revenue while disabled key employees recover. As with key person life insurance, the business will own, pay for, and be the beneficiary of the policy.

Determining the Amount of Death Benefit to be Purchased

Valuing the key employee is largely arbitrary, but it can be based on tangible, profit-producing factors. How much financial loss would the business suffer if a key person died last night? Would the death of the key person affect the credit standing of the firm? Would the death of the key person result in a loss of customers?

One way to value the key person is to use a multiple of compensation. This method assumes that the value of the employee is reflected in their compensation package. The appropriate multiple depends on how long it might take to replace that employee.

Another method to value the key employee is calculating a replacement cost. This method factors in the amount of profit that would be lost or need to be replaced, the cost to hire a replacement, and the amount of time it will take to return to the profitability level enjoyed before the death of the key employee.

When the key employee is in a sales position, the value could also be measured by contribution to earnings. There are numerous other ways to value the key employee as well, and life insurance companies are usually willing to assist the planner and client in determining the best and most appropriate method.

Upon the retirement of the key employee, the policy can be sold to the insured key employee, or the cash value can be used to provide a supplemental retirement income to the key employee. If the policy is given, rather than sold, to the key employee, the cash value will be taxable income to the employee, and the business will take a deduction for that amount. If the policy is to be transferred to the insured and the business is a corporation, the corporate board of directors should authorize the transfer. Alternatively, the business can:

1. surrender the policy,
2. take a paid-up policy, or
3. continue to pay premiums and collect the death benefit upon the death of the key employee (assuming 101(j) rules have been met).

Section 162 Bonus Plans (Group Carve-Out Life Insurance)

The compensation package offered to executives or key employees can be broken down into two parts: cash and fringe benefits. Cash compensation includes salaries and bonuses while fringe benefits include items like medical expense insurance, disability insurance, life insurance, and other benefits. The goal of the compensation package is to meet the needs of both the business and key employees. For example, the business may be looking for tax efficiency and the ability to attract, reward, and retain key employees. The fringe benefits are often based on the specific needs of the key employees (who are often the owners). The **Section 162 bonus plan** (group carve out plan) may be attractive to key employees who are in need of additional personal insurance and to a business seeking to provide some additional benefits for key employees at a low net cost to the business and with easy administration.

With a group carve-out plan, the employer selects a group of employees for coverage on a discriminatory basis. The employer can offer executives better benefits by removing them from the group term life insurance plan. The group term life plan may also avoid being discriminatory by not including the executives. The employer can use a bonus plan (under Sec. 162 of the tax code) to pay for the coverage in a carve-out plan. The employer's cost for the plan is deductible.

Many employers adopt, for insurable highly-paid executives, some form of permanent insurance which the employer helps the executive buy. The business is able to deduct the individual policy premium as an ordinary and necessary business expense under Revenue Code Section 162 which treats the employer-paid premium as part of executive compensation. However, if the key executive is also a stockholder or a key executive whose total compensation may be questioned as being excessive, the premium payment by the employer may not be deductible.

The employee typically owns the policy and names his or her own personal beneficiary. For estate planning purposes, the policy may instead be owned by an irrevocable trust. In most cases the policy will be under complete control of the executive and will be portable if employment is terminated. In some cases, however, to encourage the executive to stay with the company for at least a certain period of time (a form of golden handcuffs), a restrictive endorsement may be attached to the policy.

Insurability is typically required for a small group of selected executives, but many insurance companies look upon these risks as very favorable and will consider "bundle" underwriting so that moderately special risk insureds may be given standard premium policies. This is balanced by the executives who may be preferred risks.

Distinction Between Owner and Employee

For income tax purposes, there is a distinction between "owners" and "employees." Owners are not eligible for many of the tax-advantaged fringe benefits that employees are afforded under the tax law. For fringe benefits (such as Section 162 bonus plans), sole proprietors, owners of partnership interests, LLC members (taxed as a partnership), and greater-than-2% S-corporation owners are treated as owners, rather than employees, even if they actively work for the business. C-corporation owners who also work for the business, however, will be treated as employees. This distinction means that for some types of entities, the goals of a Section 162 bonus plan may not be met when the owners are included in the group of employees receiving the benefits.

Quick Quiz 5.7

1. Under a split-dollar plan using the endorsement method, the employer owns the policy on the life of the employee and the employer pays the premium.
   a. True
   b. False

2. Key person insurance premiums are not deductible by the employer until the death benefit is paid.
   a. True
   b. False

3. Key person life insurance is designed to protect the business, not the key employee or the key employee's family.
   a. True
   b. False

4. A Sec. 162 bonus plan provides a method for the business to provide additional benefits to a key employee at a low net cost to the employer.
   a. True
   b. False

True, False, True, True.

Operation of a Section 162 Bonus Plan

Before a Section 162 bonus plan is implemented for a corporation, the board of directors should adopt a corporate resolution to establish reasonableness of compensation because total compensation must be "reasonable" to be tax deductible. The corporation's minutes should specify various factors justifying reasonableness, such as the services of the executive are essential to the corporation or the bonus plan is common for the industry and needed to retain key employees, or the skills of the executive are unique and contribute to the profitability of the business.

The bonus paid to the executive under a Section 162 life insurance plan will be based on the premiums for the life insurance policy, but it is common for a "double bonus" to be established because the premium amount is taxable income to the executive even if paid directly from the employer to the insurance company. The double bonus provides the executive with enough cash to pay the premiums and the additional tax on the bonus. The executive will have a net tax liability of zero.

Example 5.20

Hasan is a key executive at Birch, Inc., where he is provided with whole life insurance under a Sec. 162 double bonus plan. Hasan owns the policy and his spouse is the beneficiary. Birch Inc. pays the $10,000 premium by providing an annual salary bonus to Hasan, who is in the 35% tax bracket. Birch, Inc. uses a double bonus plan to ensure that there is no net tax outlay for Hasan. The total salary bonus will be $15,384 [$10,000/(1-0.35)], providing Hasan with $5,384 of additional compensation to pay the taxes and $10,000 to pay the annual premium. Birch, Inc. will deduct the entire bonus as compensation expense (provided that total compensation to Hasan is reasonable).

Each executive covered under the plan will apply for and own the life insurance policy covering the executive's life, so the executive will have flexibility and control over the policy, including the right to name a beneficiary. The premium amount can be provided as a cash bonus which the executive then pays to the insurance company, or the premium can be sent directly from the employer to the insurance company. If estate taxation is a concern, the policy can have third-party ownership, for example, an irrevocable life insurance trust (ILIT). When the policy is owned by an ILIT, the premiums are still taxed to the executive and are then treated as a gift to the trust under gift tax rules. Estate and gift tax treatment of life insurance is beyond the scope of this textbook, and advice from a knowledgeable estate attorney and CPA is advisable when using trusts in these circumstances.

Exhibit 5.8 | Business Insurance Summary

Strategy	Goal	Structure of Policy	Income Taxation	Transfer Taxes	Useful for which types of business entities
Stock Redemption Buy-Sell Agreement	To allow for orderly transfer of stock of a deceased, disabled, or retiring shareholder by sale to the corporation at a previously agreed upon price.	Owner: Corp. Premiums: Corp. Beneficiary: Corp.	Premiums are not tax deductible. Death benefit is income tax free.	Value of the decedent's shares included in decedent-shareholder's gross estate.	C-corp and S-corp
Entity Purchase Buy-Sell Agreement	To allow for orderly transfer of partnership or LLC owner's interest from a deceased, disabled, or retiring owner by sale to the entity at a previously agreed upon price.	Owner: Business Premiums: Business Beneficiary: Business	Premiums are not tax deductible. Death benefit is income tax free.	Value of the decedent's interest in the business included in decedent-owner's gross estate.	Entities other than corporations (corporate entity purchase agreements are called stock redemption agreements, above)
Cross Purchase Buy-Sell Agreement	To allow for orderly transfer of stock, LLC, or partnership interest of a deceased, disabled, or retiring owner by sale to the other owners at a previously agreed upon price.	Each owner purchases a policy on the lives of the other owners, is responsible for paying the premium on those policies, and is the beneficiary of the policies they own.	Premiums are not tax deductible. Death benefit is income tax free. Purchasing surviving owners get increase in basis of the business equal to purchase price.	Value of the decedent's interest in the business included in decedent-owner's gross estate. Value of policies the decedent owned on the lives of the other owners is included in the gross estate (based on replacement cost).	All entities except sole proprietor Note that a sole proprietor can enter into a one-way buy-sell to transfer the business upon death to a successor owner.
Wait-and-See Buy-Sell Agreement	Combination of entity and cross-purchase. Offer first made to the business, and any shares or ownership interests not purchased by the business are then offered to the surviving owners. Often used in combination with section 303 stock redemption.*	Entity purchases, owns, pays premiums on, and is beneficiary of a policy on the owner. Each owner also owns, pays premiums, and is beneficiary of a policy on the other owners.	Premiums are not tax deductible. Death benefit is income tax free.	Value of the decedent's interest in the business included in decedent-owner's gross estate. Value of policies the decedent owned on the lives of the other owners is included in the gross estate (based on replacement cost).	All entities except sole proprietor

*Sec. 303 allows shares to be redeemed to the corporate entity up to the amount of the estate and inheritance taxes and funeral expenses incurred by the estate, and the redemption is typically free of income tax.

BUSINESS INSURANCE SUMMARY CONTINUED

Strategy	Goal	Structure of Policy	Income Taxation	Transfer Taxes	Useful for which types of business entities
Trusteed Buy-Sell Agreement	A form of cross-purchase arrangement designed to overcome the administrative burden associated with the number of policies required to fund a cross-purchase for more than 3 owners but allowing for the income tax advantages of cross-purchase for the surviving owners.	Trustee holds one policy on each owner and keeps the stock certificates subject to the agreement . Premiums can be paid by owners or contributed to the trust by the owners. Trustee is beneficiary.	Premiums are not tax deductible. Death benefits are tax free. Surviving owners who purchase get increase in basis of the business equal to purchase price.	Value of the decedent's shares included in decedent-owner's gross estate. If the trust is irrevocable (no incidents of ownership), the policy proceeds are not in the gross estate.	Entities with three or more owners
Buy-Sell Disability	To allow for orderly transfer of a business interest upon the long-term disability of an owner by structuring the disability income policy to coincide with the terms of the buy-sell agreement (e.g., Lump sum and installment payments annually over 5 years).	Entity Purchase: The business owns, pays premium, and is beneficiary of the policy. Cross Purchase: Each owner owns, pays premium, and is beneficiary of the policy.	Premiums are not tax deductible. Benefits are tax free.	Not applicable	All entity types (sole proprietor can enter into a one-way agreement for disability as well as death)
Key Person Life or Disability Income Insurance	To protect the business from the economic loss and costs of replacing a key employee upon death or disability	Owner: Business Premiums: Business Death Benefit/ Disability Income: Business is beneficiary	Premiums are not tax deductible. Death or disability benefits are income tax free.	Proceeds not included in gross estate, but value of business is increased by the proceeds and is included in the estate if the covered key employee is the decedent-owner	All entity types with key employees

CONCLUSION

Life insurance provides valuable protection for both personal and business needs. Whether used to provide additional fringe benefits to key executives, fund nonqualified deferred compensation, fund a buy-sell agreement, or protect the business from the loss of a key employee, the tax-free nature of the death benefits available from a relatively small premium outlay is an important feature that makes life insurance attractive for funding a multitude of business needs.

KEY TERMS

Accelerated Benefits Provision - Entitles a qualified insured to receive a pre-death benefit deemed nontaxable.

Buy-Sell Agreements - Arrangements that require the sale and purchase of securities owned by one individual to another following a specified triggering event, such as the death of a business owner.

Chronically Ill - A person is chronically ill if within the past 12 months, a health care practitioner has certified that the individual has been unable to perform, without substantial assistance, at least two activities of daily living (eating, bathing, dressing, transferring, toileting, and continence) for at least 90 days. A person is also chronically ill if substantial supervision is required to protect that person from threats to health and safety due to cognitive disability (such as advanced stages of Alzheimer's disease or senile dementia).

Constructive Receipt - An income tax concept that establishes when income is includible by a taxpayer and therefore subject to income tax. Income is constructively received in the taxable year during which it is credited to the employee's account, set apart for him, or otherwise made available so that he may draw upon it at any time or so that he could have drawn upon it during the taxable year if notice of intention to withdraw had been given.

Cross-Purchase Buy-Sell Agreement - An arrangement between individuals who agree to purchase the business interest of a deceased owner.

Deferred Compensation Arrangements - An arrangement to pay an executive compensation in a future year.

Economic Benefit Doctrine - An employee will be taxed on funds or property set aside for the employee if the funds or property are unrestricted and nonforfeitable even if the employee was not given a choice to receive the income currently.

Entity Purchase (Redemption) Agreement - Type of buy-sell agreement that obligates the business entity to purchase an owner's interest in the entity upon that owner's death.

Key Person Insurance - A life or disability insurance policy on a key person whose death or disability would cause a substantial hardship to the business. The business is the owner, payer, and beneficiary of the death benefit (or disability income benefit), so that the business is protected against the unexpected loss of the employee due to death or disability.

Life Settlement - A policy owner sells a life insurance policy to a third party for more than the cash surrender value, but less than the death benefit value. In most cases, the insured is neither terminally nor chronically ill (in which case accelerated benefits or a sale to a qualified viatical settlement provider would be more advantageous). The owner simply does not want the policy any longer and determines that he or she may be able to sell it for a larger amount than could be obtained through surrendering the policy.

Rabbi Trust - A revocable or irrevocable trust that is designed to hold funds and assets for the purpose of paying benefits under a nonqualified deferred compensation arrangement. The assets in a rabbi trust are for the sole purpose of providing benefits to employees and may not be accessed by the employer, but they may be seized and used for the purpose of paying general creditors in the event of a liquidation of the company. Assets within a rabbi trust are not currently taxable to the employee.

Salary Reduction Plans - A nonqualified plan designed to receive deferral contributions from executives to reduce their current taxable income.

Sec. 162 Bonus Plan (Group Carve Out) - A fringe benefit offered to a select group of executives where the employer pays a salary bonus to the executive for the purpose of paying premiums on a permanent life insurance policy owned by the executive. A double bonus may be paid so that it covers the taxes due on the premium bonus, resulting in a net cost of $0 to the employee.

Secular Trusts - Irrevocable trusts designed to hold funds and assets for the purpose of paying benefits under a nonqualified deferred compensation arrangement. A secular trust does not create a substantial fist of forfeiture to the employee. Assets set aside in a secular trust results in immediate inclusion of income to the employee.

Sinking Fund - A sinking fund is a fund established by a company to pay for future expenses or to retire debt or fulfill another obligation such as the obligation to repurchase stock from a retiring owner/employee. It is created by setting aside income over a period of time (generally years).

Split-Dollar Arrangement - A discriminatory employee benefit plan using life insurance. The employer and employee share the cost of a life insurance policy on the employee (usually permanent insurance such as whole life insurance or variable universal life insurance). Typically used by businesses to provide low cost insurance to key employees.

Substantial Risk of Forfeiture - An income tax concept that relates to when income is subject to income tax. A substantial risk of forfeiture exists when rights in property that are transferred are conditioned, directly or indirectly, upon the future performance (or refraining from performance) of substantial services by any person, or the occurrence of a condition related to a purpose of the transfer and the possibility of forfeiture is substantial if the condition is not satisfied.

Supplemental Executive Retirement Plans (Salary Continuation Plan, SERP) - Nonqualified deferred compensation arrangements designed to provide additional benefits to an executive during retirement.

Terminally Ill - Under tax law, a person is terminally ill if a physician has certified that death expected within 24 months.

Viatical Settlement - The sale of a life insurance policy to a third party viatical settlement provider when the insured is terminally or chronically ill.

DISCUSSION QUESTIONS

SOLUTIONS to the discussion questions can be found exclusively within the chapter. Once you have completed an initial reading of the chapter, go back and highlight the answers to these questions.

1. What are the general tax implications of life insurance?

2. List three exceptions to the general rule that life insurance premiums are not tax deductible.

3. Describe why a client might want to take a loan out from a non-MEC whole life insurance policy and what the consequences of that loan would be.

4. Describe the tax treatment of a loan from a MEC policy.

5. Describe the tax treatment when a life insurance policy is surrendered during the insured's lifetime.

6. What are the requirements for an exchange of one policy for another policy to qualify for tax deferral under Section 1035 of the tax code?

7. How does the transfer for value rule impact the tax treatment of life insurance death benefits?

8. What is a life settlement, and what is the tax treatment?

9. What is the tax code definition of terminally ill and chronically ill for purposes of accelerated death benefits and viatical settlements?

10. Define a viatical settlement.

11. What is the advantage of accelerated death benefits over a viatical settlement?

12. What is the structure and purpose of an entity purchase, or redemption, buy-sell agreement?

13. What is the structure and purpose of a cross-purchase buy-sell agreement?

14. What are the tax differences between entity and cross-purchase buy-sell agreements?

15. What is a nonqualified deferred compensation plan and what is it used to accomplish?

16. List three ways a nonqualified deferred compensation plan can be funded.

17. Describe a rabbi trust used to informally fund a nonqualified deferred compensation plan.

18. Describe a secular trust used to fund a nonqualified deferred compensation plan.

19. Why is substantial risk of forfeiture necessary in nonqualified deferred compensation plans?

20. What is split-dollar life insurance?

21. What is key person insurance, and who does it protect?

22. Describe a Sec. 162 bonus (group carve-out) plan.

MULTIPLE-CHOICE PROBLEMS

A sample of multiple choice problems is provided below. Additional multiple choice problems are available at money-education.com by accessing the Student Practice Portal.

1. Betty owns a $150,000 whole life participating insurance policy that she purchased ten years ago. She has paid premiums of $4,000 each year since she bought the policy and the current cash surrender value is $60,000. Betty has received $10,000 in paid dividends since the policy inception. Which of the following statement(s) is/are correct regarding Betty's policy?
    1. If Betty surrenders the policy now, she will have a taxable gain of $30,000 taxed as ordinary income.
    2. The dividends that were paid on Betty's policy were subject to ordinary income tax treatment.
        a. 1 only.
        b. 2 only.
        c. Both 1 and 2.
        d. Neither 1 nor 2.

2. Watson, Inc. has four equal partners. All four partners are interested in entering into a buy-sell arrangement. How many life insurance policies would be purchased to properly fund using a cross-purchase agreement?
    a. 4 policies.
    b. 6 policies.
    c. 8 policies.
    d. 12 policies.

3. All of the following are reasons that an employer might favor a nonqualified plan over a qualified retirement plan except:
    a. There is more design flexibility with a nonqualified plan.
    b. A nonqualified plan typically has lower administrative costs.
    c. Nonqualified plans typically allow the employer an immediate income tax deduction.
    d. Employers can generally exclude rank-and-file employees from a nonqualified plan.

4. Which of the following is false regarding a deferred compensation plan that is funded utilizing a rabbi trust?
    1. Participants have security against the employer's unwillingness to pay.
    2. Rabbi trust provide the participant with security against employer bankruptcy.
    3. Rabbi trusts provide tax deferral for participants.
    4. Rabbi trusts provide the employer with a current tax deduction.
        a. None, they are all true.
        b. 2 and 4.
        c. 1, 2, and 4.
        d. 1, 2, 3, and 4.

5. A viatical settlement company purchased a $250,000 policy for $160,000. It paid additional premiums of $7,000 (in total) over the next three years before the insured died. What income must the viatical company report from the policy proceeds in the year of the insured's death?

    a. $0.
    b. $83,000 ordinary income.
    c. $83,000 capital gain.
    d. $90,000 ordinary income.

QUICK QUIZ EXPLANATIONS

Quick Quiz 5.1

1. True.
2. False. If the insured dies owning a policy on his or her own life, the death benefit is income tax free but will be included in the gross estate for estate tax purposes.
3. False. Dividend distributions are a tax-free return of premium unless the total amount of dividends distributed to the policy owner exceeds the total premiums paid.
4. True.

Quick Quiz 5.2

1. True.
2. False. There is no income tax due, and the basis carries over, but additional premiums increase basis.
3. False. When a policy is transferred in exchange for value (as when it is sold to someone else), the acquiring owner is purchasing the policy an investment and will be taxed (at ordinary income rates) on the amount of death benefit received in excess of their cost basis.
4. True.

Quick Quiz 5.3

1. False. If the insured was terminally ill at the time of the sale, no gain on the sale of the policy is realized, regardless of what the money is actually used for.
2. True.
3. True.
4. False. When a policy is sold to a viatical settlement company, the viatical company becomes the policy owner and the beneficiary of the full death benefit amount.

Quick Quiz 5.4

1. True.
2. False. An entity approach requires that the entity purchase one policy per owner, therefore, 5 policies are required.
3. True.
4. False. Premiums paid for life insurance to fund any type of buy-sell agreement are not tax deductible.

Quick Quiz 5.5

1. False. With a nonqualified deferred compensation plan, the employer may take a compensation deduction in the same year the deferred compensation is taxed to the employee.
2. True.
3. False. A rabbi trust can protect the employee in the event of a change in ownership or management of the business, but assets must remain available to the employer's creditors.
4. True.

QUICK QUIZ EXPLANATIONS

Quick Quiz 5.6
1. True.
2. False. A substantial risk of forfeiture exists when rights in property that are transferred are conditioned, directly or indirectly, upon a future performance or occurrence.
3. True.
4. True.

Quick Quiz 5.7
1. True.
2. False. Key person insurance premiums are not deductible by the employer, however, provided that the rules of IRC Sec. 101(j) have been followed, the death benefit is tax free.
3. True.
4. True.

Additional multiple choice problems
are available at
money-education.com
by accessing the
Student Practice Portal.
Access requires registration of the title using
the unique code at the front of the book.

6

DISABILITY INSURANCE

LEARNING OBJECTIVES

1. Understand the need for disability insurance.
2. Describe the provisions of an appropriate disability insurance policy including coverage, definition, benefits, taxation, elimination period, residual benefits, and renewability.
3. Describe differences between short-term and long-term disability plans and identify the policy provisions that should be included in privately-purchased disability policies.*
4. Create a plan for meeting individual disability income needs, in consideration of household financial resources, and existing coverage under employer plans, Social Security, and disability income insurance options.*
5. Calculate the tax implications of paying for and receiving disability benefits.*

*CFP Board Resource Document - Student-Centered Learning Objectives based upon CFP Board Principal Topics.

INTRODUCTION

Disabilities are part of life. Approximately 15 percent of the world's population lives with a disability.[1] Approximately 57 million Americans, or 1-in-5, live with disabilities, which represents about 19 percent of the population. Thirty-eight million disabled Americans, or 1-in-10, live with severe disabilities.[2] As people age, the likelihood of a disability increases significantly.

Exhibit 6.1 | Prevalence of Disabilities by Age (in America for 2016)

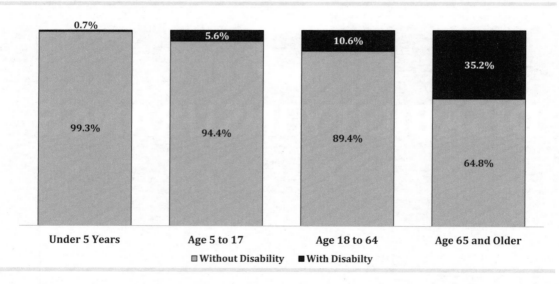

One of the greatest risks faced by people is the possibility of not being able to work during their earning years – the prospect of becoming disabled. While life insurance acts as a hedge against the possibility of early death, **disability insurance** acts as a hedge against being unable to work. The risk of being unable to work (referred to by actuaries as morbidity risk) at any age is greater than the risk of untimely death (mortality risk). According to statistical data derived from the Society of Actuaries, the National Safety Council, and the Disability Fact Book, the likelihood of disability over death at various ages is:

1. https://www.who.int/disabilities/world_report/2011/report/en/
2. Census.gov and Americans With Disabilities: 2010.

Age	Likelihood of Disability vs Death
30	4.0 to 1
35	3.5 to 1
40	2.7 to 1
45	2.1 to 1
50	1.8 to 1
55	1.5 to 1

Disability is a two-edged sword. One edge cuts into the family's income when the wage earner is unable to work. The second edge of the disability sword may cut into both the family income and the family's accumulated savings because of increased medical expenses.

In spite of the catastrophic potential, disability income protection is one of the most overlooked personal risks and is likely to be a weakness in the client's financial plan. People have a tendency to protect all of their other assets – houses, cars, boats, jewelry, etc. – but often forget to protect (or make a conscious decision not to protect) their most valuable asset – their future earnings. Some planning clients will recognize the risk of disability but assume that Social Security Disability Income (SSDI) or employer-provided disability benefits will be enough to maintain their lifestyle without really understanding how these programs work or the amount of monthly benefits they could expect to receive.

Key Concepts

1. Differentiate between the likelihood of becoming disabled compared to dying prematurely.

2. Describe the moral hazard that is associated with disability insurance.

3. Contrast the importance of short versus long-term disability risk.

While medical science has improved treatments and substantially reduced the risk of death from heart disease and cancer, the risk of disability from these diseases has remained the same or increased. Individuals who rely on employment-related income to meet their current and future financial planning needs should consider hedging their risk of disability with disability insurance policies.

There are three primary sources of disability insurance benefits. These sources include:
1. the government
2. employers
3. individual or personal policies

Governmental benefits can be provided through the Social Security system or through worker's compensation.

Social Security disability benefits are available to anyone insured under the system who meets the strict definition of disability. However, Social Security disability benefits will not likely provide adequate income replacement, except for those with fairy low incomes, and the Social Security Administration (SSA) has a very strict definition for being classified as disabled. SSA "defines disability as the inability to engage in any substantial gainful activity (SGA) by reason of any medically determinable physical or mental impairment(s) which can be expected to result in death or which has lasted or can be expected to last for a continuous period of not less than 12 months." In addition, there is a five-month waiting period before benefits can begin.

This definition of disability is difficult to meet. In fact, less than 25 percent of initial applications get approved. There is an appeal process, but the overall approval rate for Social Security disability claims is less than 35 percent and, depending on the area of the country, it can take anywhere from six months to two years to get a hearing.[3] Meanwhile, the disabled worker still needs to make the house payment, car payment, and eat. There are some attorneys who specialize in Social Security Disability claims who may help clients draft "dire need" letters (e.g., "If I don't get my hearing soon, they are going to foreclose on my house, or I will no longer be able to afford my medication.") that may help to expedite the hearing, and an inquiry from the client's Congressman might also help, but for planning purposes, it is best to prepare for a potentially lengthy wait. Even if the client could eventually qualify, it is best to be prepared to provide income from another source for a minimum of two years just in case the application gets denied and must be appealed.

If the client does qualify for SSDI payments, other members of the family such as a spouse (who is age 62 or older or who is caring for a child under age 16) of the disabled worker, and children under age 18 (19 if still in high school) may also qualify for benefits. These benefits are discussed in detail in Chapter 11.

> ### ✏ Quick Quiz 6.1
>
> 1. Americans are far more likely to die prematurely than to suffer a disability.
>   a. True
>   b. False
>
> 2. If a person is covered by a private disability insurance policy, then he or she could also receive benefits from Social Security.
>   a. True
>   b. False
>
> 3. Adequate disability insurance coverage is generally defined as 40 percent to 50 percent of a person's income.
>   a. True
>   b. False
>
> False, True, False.

Worker's compensation is designed to provide benefits to workers who are injured while working. Worker's compensation laws eliminate the need for litigation by providing fixed monetary awards to injured workers. It is important to note that this protection applies to injuries sustained while working. Worker's compensation will not provide protection for an employee who cannot work due to an injury outside of work, whereas a private disability policy may provide protection. According to the SSA, 95 percent of all disabling illnesses and accidents happen outside of the workplace.

Employers may provide employees with sick leave, short-term disability benefits, and long-term disability benefits. These benefits are generally provided to all employees in the form of a group benefit. Finally, private disability insurance policies may be acquired directly from an insurance company. This chapter discusses non-governmental disability insurance.[4]

---

3. Annual Statistical Report on the Social Security Disability Insurance Program, 2018.
4. Disability benefits under the Social Security system are discussed in the Social Security chapter.

Amount of Coverage

As a rule of thumb, individuals should have a minimum of 60 to 70 percent of their gross income protected with a disability insurance policy. In some cases, the replacement percentage may be greater, particularly for younger individuals with few assets who have families with young children. One reason that 100 percent of pre-disability gross income is not necessary is the tax treatment of disability insurance benefits. Premiums for individual disability policies are not tax deductible, but benefits received are tax-free.

Example 6.1

Andre's pre-disability gross income is $4,000 per month and he has an effective tax rate of 25%. The net amount Andre has available to spend each month after paying taxes is $3,000 ($4,000 x (1 - 0.025) = $3,000). Since disability income insurance benefits are received tax-free, he can maintain his pre-disability standard of living with a policy that provides benefits equal to 75% of gross income (or less).

Due to the moral hazards that can present themselves with this type of coverage, insurance companies will not issue disability insurance policies that will cover more than 100 percent of the insured's income (alone or in combination with other policies) and often will limit coverage to a fraction of the insured's income. The reasoning behind this limitation is that, if the insured has no incentive to work, that may increase disability insurance claims for the insurer, particularly when own-occupation policies (covered below) are issued.

Group long-term disability insurance offered by employers will generally provide for approximately 60 percent coverage of pre-tax compensation. However, in some cases the amount may be lower or higher. It is important to know that additional coverage can be obtained from other disability insurance companies to increase the coverage to closer to 100 percent. Additional coverage may be important for those who cannot tolerate the risk of a 40 percent reduction in income due to a disability.

Example 6.2

Mick worked as a foreman for Acme, Inc., a manufacturing company. Acme provides group benefits for employees, including disability coverage. Mick signed up for the disability protection, which provides for 60 percent coverage in the event of disability due to sickness or accident. Unfortunately, Mick was involved in a motorcycle accident that left him paralyzed. His disability policy will only pay him 60 percent of his pre-tax income. Mick could have purchased an additional policy that would have increased the coverage from an outside insurance company.

Given the facts in the above example, Mick is likely to also qualify for disability benefits under Social Security. As of April 2020, the average Social Security monthly disability benefit was $1,258 for disabled workers.[5] For many, if not most disabled workers, the benefits from Social Security are not sufficient to provide for their required financial needs. Therefore, it is critically important that the right amount of coverage is obtained.

---

5. SSA.gov: Monthly Statistical Snapshot, April 2020.

Term of Coverage

Coverage under disability insurance policies is typically split between short-term coverage and long-term coverage. Short-term disability insurance policies often provide benefits for a period of one to two years, while long-term disability insurance policies can provide coverage until normal retirement age or death. When an individual is covered under both short-term and long-term disability insurance policies, the benefit periods should be coordinated so that there is no gap in coverage. For example, if a short-term disability insurance policy covers benefits for two years, the insured's long-term disability policy should provide benefits beginning two years after the disability began (when the short-term disability benefits terminate) to normal retirement age or death. Once the individual reaches normal retirement age, disability coverage is generally no longer needed, since retirement income will commence.

Exhibit 6.2 | Disability Term

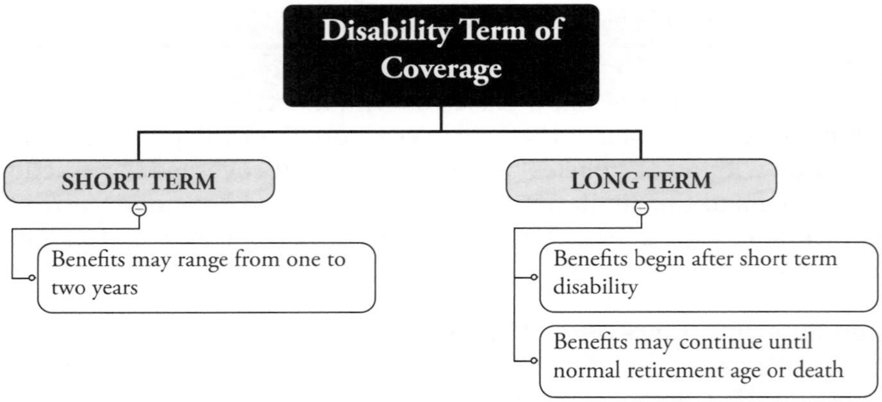

It should be noted that while it is helpful to have short-term disability coverage, it is far more important from a risk perspective to have long-term disability coverage.

Analyzing Disability Income Policies and Client Need

Disability income insurance is important to both the single person and the family breadwinner because the insurance replaces income the person would have earned if he or she had remained healthy.

Sticker shock is one of the biggest reasons many clients do not purchase individual disability income (DI) policies. Premiums tend to seem expensive in comparison to other types of insurance. Keep in mind that the premium directly reflects the risk. DI policies are priced this way due to the high probability of benefits being paid for a disability. The financial planner will need to work with clients to structure the policy to fit the budget while still providing adequate protection.

In order to analyze disability income policies, planners need to have a good understanding of the various components of a DI policy and of how provisions in these policies affect coverage and premiums. Premiums for disability protection are based on age, health, occupation, and avocation, as well as the features and provisions of the policy. As we discuss the features and provisions of DI policies, be sure to pay close attention to the effect on premiums, and ways to maintain adequate coverage while keeping the cost affordable.

Disability Income Insurance Underwriting

Careful underwriting is of critical importance for insurers in disability income insurance, particularly because of the high degree of moral and morale hazard that is potentially present (insureds may prefer to not work and receive policy benefits than to go to work every day).

In addition to the applicant's age and gender (females have a higher morbidity rate than males, so females will pay higher premiums, all else being equal), the occupational classification into which the insured falls is important in the underwriting process. Applicants are assigned to an underwriting class based on job title and description of job duties performed. For example, a job title of "construction project manager" might have different underwriting classes and premiums, depending on whether the primary duties involve work on construction sites (wearing a hardhat), or coordinating subcontractors by calling them from the office. Underwriting standards are also sometimes more liberal for professionals than for blue-collar workers, it being assumed (not always correctly) that professionals are more motivated and stable in their work. Each insurer will have their own classification system and clients applying for disability insurance should expect to be asked questions about not only their job title but also about the types of activities they engage in and the amount time spent with each activity.

Exhibit 6.3 | Example of Disability Underwriting Occupation Classification System

Occupation Class	Descriptions	Example of Occupations this Insurer Includes in the Class
Class 5A	Certain professionals and select white-collar occupations	Architects, Attorneys, Nursing Home Administrator (office only)
Class 4P	Medical professionals who do not perform any type of surgery or interventional procedures with some exceptions	General Practitioners, Internists
Class 4A	Certain professionals and select white-collar occupations	School Principals, Large Animal Veterinarians, Investment/Financial Consultant (not floor trader or commodity broker; documented income $75,000+ with minimum 3 continuous years in the business)
Class 3P Surgeon	A sub-class of 3P for certain surgeons	Plastic Surgeons, Neurosurgeons
Class 3P	Emergency room physicians and physicians who perform interventional procedures, with some exceptions	Obstetricians, Non-specialty Dentists
Class 3A	Most professionals, and technical and managerial occupations	Surgical Assistant, Market Research Analyst (office only), Pastor, X-Ray Technician (4 year degree), Investment/Financial Consultant (not floor trader or commodity broker)
Class 2P	Medical professionals with high risk practices, and other health care providers with strenuous manual duties	Anesthesiologists, Registered Nurses, Acupuncturists
Class 2A	Supervisors of various occupations who do not perform manual labor	Court Reporter, Surveyors, Floral Arrangers, X-Ray Technician (2 year degree)
Class A	Manual workers who have no unusual occupational hazard	Hair Stylists, Electricians, Gem/Diamond Cutter, EMT
Class B	This class covers the most hazardous work that the company will insure	Carpenters, Chiropractors, Underground Mine Manager (underground no more than 6 hours per week), Cocktail Waitresses/Waiters, Game Warden (with field duties, does not carry a gun), Firefighter (private industry)
Will Not Insure		Military, Foreign Correspondent, Explosives Handler, Game Warden (with field duties, carrying a gun), Sports Referee/Umpire, Singer, Hedge Fund Manager, Law Enforcement, Firefighter (municipal, state, federal), Day Trader, Floor Trader

Underwriting requires an earnings history, typically for the past two years, and it will require medical history. Underwriting for medical history is more complicated for disability policies than for life insurance policies. For life insurance, the concern is only with medical conditions that are likely to result in death, but for disability policies underwriters look at a much larger list of potential illnesses and injuries. Underwriters will also consider factors about personal habits and lifestyle; for example, they may ask whether you travel outside of the country, whether you are a pilot, whether you scuba dive, whether you engage in parachuting, or whether you have ever been arrested.

By the time the underwriting process is completed it is quite possible that the client will not be offered the most desirable choices of policy provisions. For example, even though they may have a condition that would require a short elimination period, the insurer may offer only a longer elimination period; or perhaps the insurer may offer only a limited benefit period for the particular occupation. In factoring the maximum benefit that will be offered, the underwriters may also consider other available coverage (for example, group disability and Social Security) in order to ensure that the total combined benefit amount remains below the pre-disability earnings. Different insurance companies may have different underwriting requirements, so applying for benefits with multiple companies, or using an insurance broker, may allow the client to compare the coverage and benefits actually available to them. For example, some insurance companies prefer to underwrite white-collar occupations and will place numerous restrictions on policies for blue-collar workers, while another insurance company might be much more liberal in their offerings for blue-collar workers.

CHARACTERISTICS OF DISABILITY INSURANCE POLICIES

As with other types of insurance, disability insurance is a contract, or agreement between the owner and the insurance company. It is important to understand the various aspects of disability contracts, including:

- the definition of disability
- the benefit period
- other policy provisions

These aspects of the disability policy are discussed below.

Definition of Disability

Policies specify the conditions under which the insured will be considered "disabled" and therefore entitled to benefits under the contract. Disability policies will generally provide coverage if a person is disabled due to accident or sickness. However, there are disability policies that may only cover accidents and not sickness. Sickness accounts for approximately two thirds of the disabilities and accidents account for the other third.Policies that cover accidents only are rather inexpensive, but, since the majority of disability claims arise from illness, a policy that covers only accidents will leave the client with a major planning weakness.

Key Concepts

1. Describe how any occupation disability insurance works in regard to highly skilled professionals.

2. Describe what is meant by a split definition of disability.

3. Identify conditions under which a disability policy will make payments without a total disability.

4. Select the correct elimination period based on other relevant factors.

5. Choose other riders that may enhance a disability policy.

Exhibit 6.4 | Proportion of Disability Claims

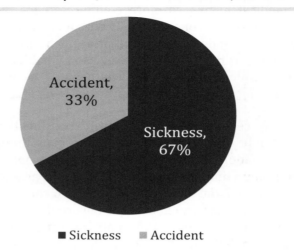

Accident, 33%

Sickness, 67%

■ Sickness   ■ Accident

In addition to accident and sickness coverage, policies will define a disability in terms of total or partial disability and will define disability in terms of the types of job duties, or occupation, that the insured can no longer perform due to the disability. The three standard definitions in terms of occupation are:

1. own-occupation policies
2. any-occupation policies
3. split (hybrid) definition policies

Exhibit 6.5 | Definition of Disability

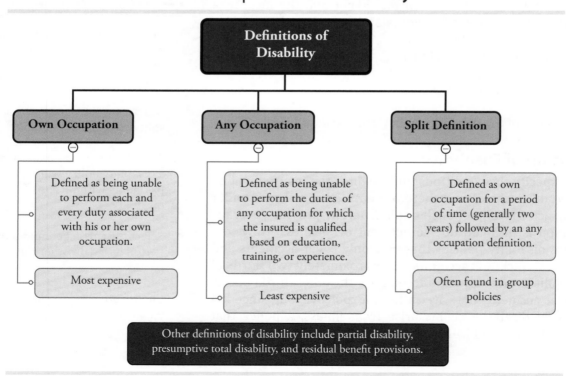

Definitions of Disability

Own Occupation

Defined as being unable to perform each and every duty associated with his or her own occupation.

Most expensive

Any Occupation

Defined as being unable to perform the duties of any occupation for which the insured is qualified based on education, training, or experience.

Least expensive

Split Definition

Defined as own occupation for a period of time (generally two years) followed by an any occupation definition.

Often found in group policies

Other definitions of disability include partial disability, presumptive total disability, and residual benefit provisions.

Own-occupation policies state that if the insured is unable to perform each and every duty associated with his or her own occupation, the insured is deemed to be disabled and the policy will provide benefits.

Example 6.3

Zuri is a concert pianist and has spent her lifetime practicing and performing piano concertos around the world. She recently contracted a disease that affected the dexterity of her hands, which has prevented her from being able to perform at concerts. She purchased an own-occupation disability insurance policy 25 years ago. The insurance policy will pay disability benefits to Zuri since she can no longer perform the duties of her occupation as a pianist.

Own-occupation policies were popular tools in the late 1980s and early 1990s, particularly with physicians, musicians, and other professionals whose income was dependent on their ability to perform specific tasks. Over time, insurance companies recognized that there was a large adverse selection risk associated with these policies, which are now less available. When an own-occupation policy is issued, the premium is high due to the risks being undertaken by the insurance company.

An **any-occupation** disability insurance policy provides benefits to a policyowner if he or she is unable to perform the duties of any occupation. In the past, this type of policy followed a very strict definition that literally meant "any" occupation, making it much less attractive to individuals in high-skill professions. A surgeon, for example, would probably not want a policy that will not pay benefits unless he/she could not perform telemarketing services. The courts have limited the interpretation of this definition of disability to mean that the insured can collect benefits if he/she is unable to perform any occupation for which he/she is suited based on training, experience, and educational degrees.[6] Continuing our example, if the surgeon is unable to perform surgery due to an injury to his hands, but could teach medical school to new physicians, he would be expected to earn income in that fashion and would not be considered disabled under the policy contract. The surgeon would not, however, be required to perform telemarketing services as a means of minimizing benefits received under the policy Since the insurance company is much less likely to pay long-term claims under this definition, premiums will be lower than for an own occupation policy. The "educated, trained, or experienced" definition is a good trade-off between adequate coverage and the cost of premiums for most clients.

Many disability insurance policies, especially group policies, use a **split definition** (hybrid) of disability. Under a split definition policy, an insured will be covered against the risk of not being able to perform his or her own occupation for a period of time and, after that period expires, an any-occupation definition of disability would be used. This type of policy gives the insured a period to adjust to his or her new reality and perhaps obtain the training necessary to perform other occupations that will allow him/her to replace some or all of the lost income from the old occupation. Some disability policies will provide coverage for retraining.

One of the advantages of an own-occupation definition policy is that if the insured is disabled in terms of their occupation, then they can receive benefits and still pursue another career. However, insurance policies are contracts and thus, the exact language of the contract is critical. It turns out that some insurance carriers market policies as "own occupation" that pay benefits as long as the insured is not

---

6. See Bacon v. Government of Saskatchewan (1990) 88 Sask. R. 182 (Q.B.)

engaged in another occupation. The term, "modified own occupation" is often used to describe this type of coverage. In addition, there are other definitions that are used that are variations of the true own occupation definition. For example, there is a specialty own occupation definition that is even more restrictive to the insured. This type of definition would protect a surgeon that had a specific medical specialty, such as a gastroenterologist. With all of the variations in the types of coverage being marketed, it is critical to read the definition in the contract that deals with disability.

Example 6.4

Randy went to the LSU School of Dentistry, graduated and has been working as a dentist in Metairie, Louisiana. However, he was diagnosed with a tumor at the top of his spine and is unable to work as a dentist since he cannot bend over. Fortunately, Randy purchased an own occupation policy that now provides him with 60 percent of his prior earnings. In addition, he has been able to obtain an new job as a disability insurance sales person selling disability insurance to dentists. He is the top performing rep in the country and this new occupation does not interfere with his disability benefits.

Presumptive Total Disability Coverage

Many disability policies have a provision, known as **presumptive total disability coverage**, which automatically considers certain conditions to be totally disabling. These conditions generally include:
- loss of sight in both eyes
- loss of hearing in both ears
- loss of the use of both hands
- loss of the use of both feet
- loss of the use of one foot and one hand

If any of these conditions arise, the policy automatically presumes total disability and will begin payments according to the contract. This type of provision expedites income to those who need it without having to go through the normal steps to be considered disabled buy the insurance company.

Partial Disability

Many policies include coverage for **partial disability**, either as a policy provision or a rider that can be added for an additional premium. Partial disability is defined as the inability to perform at least one important duty of the insured's normal occupation. The partial disability provision provides payments that are less than those paid for total disability (usually 50%) but these benefits usually last for only a short period of time (such as six months), and may only be available following a period of total disability (some policies do not have this requirement). By covering partial disability in this manner, the insurer gives the insured an incentive to return to work, with reduced duties or time, sooner than he or she otherwise might if required to be fully recovered prior to returning to work.

Example 6.5

Hap is a construction worker. He is a supervisor, but also performs some of the work, which requires heavy lifting. Hap suffered a back injury sled riding with his kids and was fully disabled for a period of 18 months while going through multiple surgeries and recoveries. Fortunately, Hap had disability insurance to replace 65% of his income during this period. Hap is on the road to full recovery, but is still unable to lift more than

---

30 pounds. Hap's DI insurance policy includes a provision for partial disability so he can return to work as a supervisor, but not work requiring heavy lifting, part-time and still collect 50% of the full disability benefit for a period of six months.

Residual Benefit Provision

Experiencing a condition that prevents an insured from working for a period of time may lead to a permanent loss of income. This may be particularly true when an insured is covered by an any-occupation disability policy or an own-occupation disability policy that morphs into an any-occupation policy after a specified period of time. While the insured may be able to work, it is possible that the conditions causing the disability will prevent him/her from being able to perform all of the requirements of the prior job, resulting in a loss of income. A **residual benefit provision** will provide continuing benefits for an insured who returns to work but suffers a loss of income due to the disability. Residual disability benefits may be included as a policy provision or may require purchase of a rider that can be added for an additional premium.

Insurance companies typically use two approaches to determine eligibility for residual benefits: (1) the loss of earnings method or (2) the loss of time or duties method. Under the loss of earnings method, residual benefits are usually payable if the insured's earnings loss exceeds 20 percent. Under the loss of time or duties method, if, as a result of the insured's disability, compensation is adjusted for time away from the job, or the income is adjusted because the insured cannot perform the same duties, a residual benefit may also be available. To qualify for benefits, the insured is required to prove an earnings loss (usually by submitting earnings statements before and after the period of disability). Disability insurance policies often compare income before and after on an average basis, such as the average monthly earnings for the 12-month period immediately preceding disability.

Residual disability is typically measured by the ratio of a person's reduction in earnings after recovery from total disability to his or her earnings before disability. Therefore, the residual disability coverage will provide a benefit that is the same percentage of the maximum policy benefit as the percentage reduction in the insured's earnings. Residual disability is often permanent; therefore, benefits may continue for the maximum benefit period of the basic coverage – perhaps for the insured's lifetime.

Example 6.6

Antoinette is a CPA who earned $100,000 during the 12 months prior to becoming disabled. She has partially recovered but has permanent ongoing issues related to the disability that will prevent her from being able to put in the long arduous hours that she normally worked during tax season. For this reason, she had to reduce the number of clients she works with and is now only able to earn $70,000 per year, a 30% reduction in income. Fortunately, her disability income insurance contains a residual disability benefit. The benefit paid to her when she was fully disabled was $5,000 per month, so she will receive 30% x $5,000 = $1,500 per month as a residual disability benefit.

Some residual benefit provisions also index benefits for inflation, usually based on the Consumer Price Index. While this increase may not match future increases in income that would have been attained had no disability been suffered, at least it attempts to preserve the purchasing power of the benefit.

Elimination Period

Most disability policies only provide benefits after an elimination period has been satisfied. The **elimination period** is the period of time, beginning upon injury or sickness, that an insured is disabled but is not yet eligible to collect benefits from the insurer. The elimination period ensures that benefits are not paid unless the insured experiences a disability that could deprive the insured of income for a long period of time, and also helps the insurance company manage the moral hazard associated with fraudulent disability insurance claims.

The elimination period can be as short as one month and can be extended depending on the needs of the insured. If, for example, the insured's employer will continue to pay the employee's salary to the insured for up to three months in the event of a disability, the elimination period on the disability insurance policy can be set to three months. This selection would ensure continuous income for the insured while lowering the cost of the insurance protection. As the elimination period increases up to a point (usually 180 days), the premium for the policy will decrease.

Individuals who do not have short-term disability coverage need to make sure that their emergency fund is sufficient to sustain them throughout the disability elimination period. If the emergency fund and the elimination period are not properly coordinated, then the person may be without income for a period of time until disability benefits begin.

Example 6.7

Darius works as a graphic designer and earns $4,000 per month. He has a disability policy that will pay him 60 percent of his benefits, which will cover most of his basic needs. When he bought the policy, he chose an 18-month elimination period to reduce the policy premium. Although he does not have a short-term disability policy, he has a sufficient emergency fund to cover his needs during the 18-month period before any disability benefits would begin.

Benefit Period

Disability insurance distinguishes between short-term and long-term coverage. **Short-term disability** provides coverage for up to two years, and typically has a short elimination period (typically 5-30 days). Many employers offer group short-term disability insurance that provides employees with a percentage of their salary while disabled.

Long-term disability typically has a longer elimination period (30-180 days) and provides coverage until normal retirement age, until death, or for a specified term. The most common benefit period is to age 65, but policies may have benefit periods of two years, five years, or even lifetime benefits. Some insurers impose limitations on the maximum length of the benefit period for insureds working in certain occupations, often those that are dangerous or require difficult physical labor. Some employers offer group long-term disability insurance with premiums generally paid by the employee. Employer-sponsored plans are usually not portable and terminate when the employee leaves the employer unless the reason for leaving employment is directly related to the disability.

Other Disability Policy Provisions and Riders

There are many other provisions that might be included in a disability insurance policy. Waiver of premium, recurrent disability, change of occupation, COLA, future increase, automatic increase riders, and Social Security riders are discussed below.

Waiver of Premium Provision or Rider

Benefits awarded under a disability income policy are provided because the insured no longer has income, or has reduced income, from employment. Most disability insurance policies waive future premium payments under the policy once the elimination period has been met and the insured is receiving disability benefits under the policy. The insured must continue to pay the premiums during the elimination period, but once the elimination period has passed the waiver is often retroactive to the start of disability and premiums paid during the elimination are refunded. If the insured regains his or her health and returns to work, the premiums on the policy must be paid in order to keep the policy in force.

This rider is standard in most disability policies and may not increase the cost of the policy.

Recurrent Disability Provision

The purpose of a recurrent disability clause is to differentiate between two separate disabilities and a continuation of the same disability. The distinction is important in that, if the two losses constitute two separate disabilities, two elimination periods and two benefit maximums are applicable, whereas if the two losses are deemed to be one disability, only one waiting period and one benefit maximum apply. The typical recurrent disability clause specifies that if, within six months of a total disability, the insured sustains a subsequent period of disability from the same or a related cause, the second disability will be deemed a continuation of the first one. Otherwise, it will be deemed a new disability, regardless of the cause.

Change of Occupation Provision

The change of occupation provision permits the insurer to reduce the benefit payable in the event the insured changes to a more hazardous occupation. The benefit is reduced to the amount the premium paid would have purchased at the more hazardous employment classification. If the insured changes to a less hazardous occupation, the premium is reduced, but the benefit typically remains the same.

COLA Rider

Some disability insurance policies also provide a cost of living adjustment (**COLA**) to the benefit payments. Since the cost of products and services used by the insured increases as inflation increases, a COLA adjustment helps the insured maintain his or her purchasing power during a long period of disability. Typically, COLA adjustments are tied to the consumer price index (CPI). All else being equal, a disability insurance policy with a COLA provision will have a higher premium than one without a COLA provision.

Future Increase Rider and Automatic Increase Rider

In addition to protecting current income, some insureds would like assurance that, as their income increases, they are able to get additional disability income insurance. The following two riders are commonly used to achieve this objective:

- **Future increase option rider** - permits the insured to increase the monthly benefit as the insured gets older. This rider effectively guarantees insurability for a certain period of time (such as to age 55) so that as the insured's income increases, they can acquire additional coverage to maintain the same level or percentage of income replacement. Proof of increased income will be required, but proof of insurability is not required.
- **Automatic increase rider** - automatically increases the monthly benefits by a stated percentage every year. The advantage of this rider is that the increase is automatic. It does not require the insured to purchase additional coverage. However, the premiums may increase.

If either of these two options is chosen, the premium on the policy, all else equal, will be greater than a policy that does not provide these protections.

Social Insurance Substitute Benefit, Social Security Rider, or Social Insurance Rider

This type of rider, sometimes referred to as an SIS benefit, effectively integrates the maximum disability benefit with Social Security. There are two main reasons that insurers offer the Social Security rider. First, the rider can provide benefits to a disabled individual while an application for Social Security benefits is pending. Approximately 75 percent of applications are denied initially, and the hearing and appeal process can take more than a year. Even if the initial application is accepted, there is a five-month waiting period. The rider can provide benefits during this interim period. Second, the rider can replace benefits that are not paid when a Social Security claim is denied.

The SIS rider provides for higher benefits during the first year of a disability while the insured is waiting for benefits from Social Security. The rider, which increases the cost of the policy, can be structured as an "all or nothing" benefit or as "an offset" benefit. With an all or nothing rider, the benefit will be paid if Social Security does not pay and will not pay if Social Security does pay. With an offset rider, the benefits are reduced to the extent of benefits received from Social Security. When an insurer's underwriting limit for a disability policy is set at, for example, 60 percent of the insured's earnings, this limit is based in part on the likelihood that some earnings will be replaced by Social Security. If the Social Security benefits are not paid, then the insured will want additional benefits. The rider can act as a supplement to provide these benefits.

Example 6.8

Jackson buys a disability policy with a base benefit of $8,000 and an SIS offset benefit of $1,500. Jackson becomes disabled and eventually receives $1,000 in Social Security disability benefits. Jackson will initially receive $9,500 in benefits. However, once Social Security begins paying benefits, Jackson will only receive $8,500 from the insurance company.

Incontestability Clause

Similar to life insurance policies, most disability policies contain an incontestability clause that prevents the insurer from voiding the contract after the specified period of time (generally two years). This type of clause protects the insured from several potential issues, including preexisting conditions, misstatements or misrepresentations, and unknown conditions. Therefore, after two years, the issuing company cannot claim that the insured misrepresented some aspect of the application. After the two years, the claim must be paid. However, there is one caveat in this type of clause. The clause is not valid if the insured fraudulently or intentionally misrepresented material or substantial information.

Example 6.9

Drake applies for a disability policy with Secure Insurance Company (SIC). During the process of filing out the forms, Drake put an incorrect birth date. His birthday is August 1, 1980 or 8/1/80. Instead of filling out his correct birthday, he wrote 1/8/80. Five years later he had an accident with his lawn mower in which he became disabled. Because of the incontestability clause, the company cannot void the contract because of a misstatement or error, as long as it was not intentional.

Renewability

Insured individuals who have disability policies that are renewed each year are potentially subject to a risk of policy cancellation. In fact, it would be in the best interest of the insurance company to cancel policies held by individuals who are likely to become disabled as a means of avoiding benefit payments. To prevent this from happening, and to provide policy holders some protection against policy cancellation, different renewability rights are provided for in disability insurance contracts. These rights include: (1) non-cancelable policies, and (2) guaranteed renewable policies.

Non-Cancelable

Non-cancelable policies prevent the insurance company from canceling the policy for any reason provided the policy premium is paid. Usually, the policy will specify that it is non-cancelable for a specific period of time or until the insured reaches a stated age. Some policies also specify that, during the non-cancelable period, no changes to the policy may be made, including changes to the premium. Non-cancelable policies provide the greatest degree of protection to the insured since the insured can force the insurance company to provide continued coverage simply by paying the premium on the policy.

Guaranteed Renewable

Guaranteed renewable disability insurance policies require the insurance company to renew the policy for a specified period of time or until the insured attains a certain age. Provided the insured pays the premium, the insurance company must renew the policy during the period stated in the contract. Unlike the case with non-cancelable policies, which do not permit increases in premium, the premium on a guaranteed renewable policy may be increased on a class basis (i.e., increased across the board for all similarly situated insureds), but may not be increased for one participant simply because he or she has been exposed to a disease or health condition that increases the likelihood of suffering a period of disability.

While a non-cancelable policy is preferable to guaranteed renewable, it will also have a higher premium. For most insureds, a guaranteed renewable policy will provide adequate coverage at a more palatable price, although there is a risk that the premiums will increase in the future.

Exclusions

There are generally only a few exclusions in individual disability income policies. Common exclusions include war, self-inflicted injuries, work-related injuries, criminal activities, driving a vehicle while intoxicated, and preexisting conditions.

A preexisting condition is a disabling physical condition for which the insured sought treatment before the disability income policy was issued. Such preexisting conditions are usually excluded from coverage under individual disability income policies.

Some states allow policies to exclude injuries or sickness that results from alcoholism or drug addiction, while other states do not allow such exclusions.

Some disability income policies, particularly short-term policies covering blue-collar industrial workers, exclude illnesses or accidents resulting from occupational exposures. In most cases, the workers with occupational disabilities will receive benefits under workers' compensation laws. Double payment would only encourage the feigning of disabilities, and insurers do not want to encourage dishonesty. Policies excluding occupational disabilities are known as nonoccupational policies. Policies which are written and issued or professional and other white-collar insureds often provide benefits for both occupational and nonoccupational disabilities.

Probationary Period

Some disability policies include a probationary period. The probationary period is the period of time after issuance of a disability insurance policy, usually fifteen to thirty days, during which there is no coverage for disabilities due to sickness. Thus, the provision will deny coverage for a sickness that was in the incubation stage when the policy was issued. The probation period helps to protect the insurance company from paying for preexisting conditions. Note that coverage still applies during the first few days for any bodily injuries arising out of accidents.

GROUP DISABILITY INSURANCE

Disability insurance is also available on a group basis, and is a benefit that is commonly available to employees of larger companies.

≡ Key Concepts

1. Describe the possible tax consequences of disability benefits.

Group disability insurance can be provided on a short-term or long-term basis, and in many cases, both short-term and long-term policies are offered or provided. The elimination periods for these policies are typically coordinated so that there is continuous income coverage for the insured. Often, the short-term group coverage will begin after employer coverage for sick time ends, and the long-term group coverage will begin when the short-term coverage terminates. Long-term group disability coverage usually terminates when the insured reaches normal retirement age or dies.

The advantage of group disability coverage is that premiums are typically lower than premiums on individual coverage. Employers may pay the premiums on behalf of the employees or may permit the employees to pay the coverage directly through payroll deduction.

While group policies provide coverage to employees at a reasonable cost, they are generally not portable, unlike personal policies. Consequently, employees who anticipate frequent changes in employment may wish to consider the purchase of individual private coverage. For these clients, the individual DI policy should be the base of the disability protection plan, and the employer-sponsored group disability should serve as a supplement. Group rates on DI insurance are also often available through professional organizations and can offer significant cost-savings over an individual policy. As long as the client remains in good standing with the professional organization, the client can continue the policy, even when changing employers.

A common planning mistake for clients is the belief that group disability coverage at work is all that they need, without really understanding how the policy works. It is important for planners to be able to evaluate the group coverage and identify weaknesses that may exist. Disability income benefits are one of the few employee benefits that allow employers to discriminate and offer a higher level of benefits to executives while still being allowed a tax deduction, so it is very common to find several different levels of benefits within the group plan. If a planner works with several employees of the same company, the planner will likely find that these employees have different disability benefits, so a planner should try not to make assumptions without verifying the coverage, length of employment, number of years the employee was an officer, etc. For example, a company may offer benefits at 50 percent of salary for full-time salaried employees (while hourly employees are not covered), but 60 percent of salary for officers, and anyone VP or above gets 90 percent of salary for the number of months equal to the number of years they have been a VP or above followed by 75 percent of salary through age 65.

Planners and clients will need to consult the Summary Plan Description (SPD) for disability benefits to determine precisely what type of coverage is offered, as well as the amount. Generally, individual policies are not issued, the sponsoring employer will have a master contract, and employees are given a certificate of coverage and an SPD that outlines the details of the coverage.

Some group policies will also have a dollar cap on the amount that can be received. For example, the group policy might pay a maximum monthly benefit of $5,000. This maximum is to avoid making it likely that executives who earn high salaries will simply adjust their lifestyles to live on 60 percent or 75 percent of their former high salaries; there should always be incentive to go back to work. For those not subject to the dollar cap, benefits of 50 to 70 percent of the employee's pre-disability income are typical.

Social Security Offset

To avoid providing employees with benefits that exceed their usual earnings, employers usually integrate long-term disability income benefits with benefits and income from other sources. The employee's benefits under a group disability plan will be reduced when benefits are received from Social Security, workers' compensation, retirement plans, other insurance paid for by the employer, and any earnings from employment. Most state laws do not permit reduction in benefits due to individual disability policies purchased by the employee.

With some plans, integration with Social Security is determined only from what the disabled employee receives from Social Security (primary insurance amount). Under other plans, if there are dependents, integration may be based on the total benefit received by the employee's family (as discussed in Chapter 11).

Disability benefits may be reduced in part or in full by Social Security benefits. Under a full-integration approach (also known as substitution), the group long-term disability benefits are reduced to the full extent of the Social Security benefits. In this situation, the group benefits are a substitute for Social Security unless or until Social Security becomes available.

Under a dual-percentage approach, the group disability benefits are based on different percentages of the employee's earnings, depending upon whether other sources are available or not. For example, when no other sources are available, the employee might receive 50 percent of earnings; but when other sources are available, the employee can receive benefits until the combined total reaches 70 percent of earnings. Employers can adopt plans with different integration formulas, depending upon their budgets and objectives. It is also common for group benefits to be offset by other types of social insurance and by workers' compensation.

Social Security Backpay

As discussed previously, Social Security disability applications are rarely approved with the initial application. The appeals and hearing process often takes one to two years to complete, but for those who eventually do get approved, the benefits are paid retroactively to the 6th month of disability. This creates a lump sum payment for past-due benefits, commonly referred to as "backpay."

If Social Security disability benefits are delayed, a long-term disability plan pays full benefits up until the point where the Social Security Administration approves the application. When the insured finally receives the Social Security payments, some of the insurance benefits may need to be repaid to reflect the offset that should have occurred. It will be important for the planner and client to check the terms of the long-term disability policy (both individual and group) to determine whether it includes a clause requiring excess payments made by the insurance company to be repaid. Most companies will require full payment immediately when the lump-sum amount is received from Social Security, although some insurance companies will be willing to reduce future payment amounts until the debt is paid off. Some policies also factor in lump-sum SSDI payments made to other family members (such as a spouse or child) when calculating the amount to be repaid.

The insurance company issuing the long-term disability policy will typically require the insured to sign a Social Security Reimbursement Agreement, and it will require that the insured apply for Social Security disability when the insurance company payments begin.

If an attorney is hired to assist with the SSDI application and appeals process, it is typical for the attorney to charge up to 25 percent of the backpay amount as a fee. The backpay amount is normally reduced by this fee in determining the actual dollar amount owed to the insurance company.

TAXATION OF DISABILITY INSURANCE BENEFITS

The taxation of benefits received under a disability insurance policy depends on who paid the policy premiums. If the insured paid the premiums with after-tax dollars (as is the case when individual disability insurance is purchased, or when group insurance is purchased with after-tax dollars), the benefits received under the policy are not subject to income tax. Benefits provided under a policy paid for with pre-tax dollars (such as when the employer provides disability benefits at no cost to the employees as an employee benefit) are subject to income tax.

If the employer pays all premiums under the plan, benefit payments are not only subject to income tax but are also subject to Social Security and Medicare taxes (FICA taxes, discussed in Chapter 11), but only during the first six full months of disability.[7] Benefits offered under cafeteria plans, however, are generally not subject to FICA taxes, even during the first six months.

Quick Quiz 6.4

1. Generally, it is more effective to pay disability insurance premiums with after-tax dollars, to avoid paying income tax on disability benefits.
   a. True
   b. False

2. If the employer pays 60% of the disability insurance premium and the employee pays 40% of the premium with after-tax dollars, the full amount of the monthly benefit will be subject to tax.
   a. True
   b. False

True, False.

Example 6.10

Ronaldo's last day of work before he became entitled to disability income from a group plan paid for by his employer was December 11, 2019. He was paid disability income for nine months before returning to work on September 16, 2020. The income he received from January 1 - June 30 (the first 6 full months of disability income) is subject to both income tax and FICA taxes because his employer paid the full premium amount. However, the benefits he receives after June 30, 2020 are subject only to income taxes, not FICA taxes.

If given a choice, an employee with access to employer group disability insurance should pay for the coverage with after-tax dollars to ensure that benefit payments are received on a tax-free basis. If the employee receives benefits under the policy, that implies he or she is unable to work, and that would probably not be the best time to have to worry about an additional cash outflow – in the form of income tax. Many employers who offer group disability policies to their employees permit them to pay for the policies with after-tax dollars to achieve this benefit.

7. See IRS Pub. 15-A for additional details.

Some employer-sponsored group disability policies require the employee to pay a portion of the premium, while the employer pays the remainder of the premium. In these type of plans, any income from the policy will be partially taxable and partially tax free. The portion of the income that is subject to tax is equal to the percentage portion of the premium paid by the employer. The portion of the income that is not subject to tax is equal to the percentage portion of the premium paid by the employee with after-tax dollars.

Generally, partnerships and S corporations cannot deduct premiums paid for disability policies for partners or owners. In some cases, the company may deduct the premium and report the payment as income to the partner or owner. In either case, the partner or owner is effectively paying for the premium with after-tax dollars. Therefore, any disability benefits received will not be taxable.

Example 6.11

Lindy works for Alpha Company, which pays the entire premium for disability insurance for its employees. If Lindy is disabled, her benefits are fully taxable.

Example 6.12

Cindy works for Bravo Company, which permits employees to purchase disability insurance as part of a group plan with pre-tax dollars. If Cindy is disabled, her benefits are fully taxable.

Example 6.13

Mindy works for Charlie Company, which permits employees to purchase disability insurance as part of a group plan with after-tax dollars. If Mindy is disabled, her benefits are not taxable.

Example 6.14

Vindy works for Delta Company, which provides disability insurance for its employees, but only pays 75 percent of the premium. The other 25 percent of the premium is paid by the employee with after-tax dollars. If Vindy is disabled, 75 percent of her benefits are taxable.

Example 6.15

Finley is a >2% owner/employee of The Flower Shop (TFS), an S corporation. TFS offers group disability insurance to all employees. The cost of the protection for Finley, paid for entirely by TFS, is $2,000 per year. The cost of the premium is reported as taxable compensation on Finley's W-2. If Finley is disabled, her benefits are not taxable.

It should be noted that the Internal Revenue Code (IRC) provides some relief for those who are disabled. Taxpayers who are blind are permitted to have an additional standard deduction. In addition, IRC §22 provides for a credit for disabled persons that can provide some tax relief.

DISABILITY INSURANCE - EMPLOYEE BENEFIT ANALYSIS

There may be times when the financial planner is working with a business owner to determine which, if any, employee benefits should be offered to employees and how those benefits should be structured. In deciding whether to offer a disability income plan to employees, an employer must consider the trade-off between paying the premiums and paying employees a bonus that can be used for the premiums on individual coverage (similar to the Sec. 162 group carve-out life insurance plans discussed in Chapter 5). This evaluation is especially important when the employer chooses to offer disability insurance only to a select group of executives.

While the employee pays no income tax on group disability insurance premiums paid by the employer, the disability benefits from an employer-paid group plan are taxable to the employee. If no disability occurs, the employee avoids taxes with the employer paying the premiums; but if a disability occurs, the employee will have income tax on the benefits received.

On the other hand, if the bonus plan is used instead, the employee must pay income taxes each year on any bonus and receives no deduction for paying the premiums on a disability policy. The disability benefits, however, will be received tax-free. If an executive expects tax rates to rise in the future, the option of receiving disability income tax-free may be attractive. Moreover, the additional taxes from the bonus might be alleviated by providing a double bonus plan (as described in Chapter 5) that pays the income taxes. Thus, if a disability occurs, the bonus approach may be more beneficial. The double bonus amount can be calculated by dividing the premium by (1- tax bracket).

Example 6.16

The premium on an individual disability income insurance policy for Simone is $3,000 and she in the 35% tax bracket. Simone's employer pays her a "double bonus" to cover both the cost of the premiums and the taxes generated by the salary bonus paid to her to cover the cost of the premiums. Simone's total salary bonus is 3,000/(1 - 0.35) = $4,615. By providing a bonus of $4,615 to Simone, the company has provided her with enough additional net income to purchase the insurance policy and pay the additional taxes due on the bonus. The company can deduct the full $4,615 as compensation expense (provided that Simone's total compensation is reasonable).

For a business structured as a pass-through entity (partner in a partnership, >2% owner in an S-corp, or LLC member), the business can take a tax deduction for the premiums paid, but it is income for the owner. This tax treatment also applies to health insurance premiums, but health insurance premiums can be deducted above-the-line on the owner's tax return. DI premiums are not deductible by the individual taxpayer. Double bonuses generally do not help owners of pass-through entities (sole proprietorships, partnerships, LLCs, and S corporations) due to the flow-through of taxation (it is beneficial for their non-owner employees, just not for the owners). Owners of C-corporations are treated the same as other employees, so the double bonus will work well for them.

Remember that insurers will usually set a limit on the amount of disability insurance they will issue for a given person, and that limit includes disability insurance purchased for uses such as nonqualified deferred compensation, keyperson disability insurance, group disability insurance plans, and individual disability policies. However, timing is important. When underwriting an individual policy, insurers usually look at how much group coverage there is, but when they underwrite group policies, insurers generally do not have individual underwriting considerations or the ability to ask about existing individual policies. Therefore, a small business owner who is also an employee of the business can typically obtain more coverage by purchasing the individual policy first and then adopting the group policy for the business. By following this timing, the owner could end up with more coverage than the insurer would ordinarily issue for an individual.

CREATING A PLAN FOR DISABILITY INCOME NEEDS

In creating a plan to address disability income needs, the planner should consider household financial resources, existing coverage under employer plans, the likelihood of qualifying for Social Security disability benefits, and individual disability income insurance options.

Household Financial Resources

In determining the amounts and types of coverage for disability income insurance, the planner will want to ask the following questions concerning financial resources:

- **Income significance:** How strongly does the family rely on this income? Is it the income of a single parent supporting three kids, or is it the part-time wages earned by a spouse used to provide extra spending and vacation money?
- **Emergency funds:** With current emergency funds, how long could the family continue to pay expenses before a hardship is incurred?
- **Fixed and variable expenses:** Which of the current expenses are fixed and essential and which may be delayed or reduced during a period of disability?
- **Higher expenses:** What additional expenses might be incurred as a result of the disability (e.g., will the client continue to be covered under the employer group health plan, or will the client eventually need to convert to an individual policy; will the client need to pay someone else to mow the lawn)?
- **Lower expenses:** What expenses might be reduced as a result of the disability (e.g., the expense of parking in the parking garage at the office)?
- **Other income:** What other sources of income may be available in the event of disability (e.g, investment portfolio earnings)?
- **Asset sales:** If assets will need to be liquidated to replace income, which assets are most advantageous to liquidate?
- **Tax issues:** What are the investment and tax consequences of selling assets or withdrawing funds from accounts, including CDs, life insurance, annuities, retirement accounts, brokerage accounts, and real estate?
- **Collateral:** What collateral may be used for loans if needed and what is the availability of credit?

Existing Coverage Under Employer Plans

The planner will want to ask the following questions about employer disability income plans:

- What is the elimination period for short-term and long-term disability?
- How long is the benefit period?
- What percentage of salary is covered, and is it integrated with Social Security?
- What is the definition of disability?
- If I leave this employer, is the coverage portable?
- Will benefits received be taxable or tax-free?

Social Security Disability

The following points are important to review with the client when considering disability income protection:

- The rules for qualifying for Social Security disability benefits are strict.
- There is a five month waiting period before benefits start.
- Projections are available at SSa.gov to evaluate potential disability income.

Individual DI Policy Options

When making individual policy decisions that coordinate with the other planning considerations discussed above, the planner and client must consider the following:

- Individual DI allows the client and planner the flexibility to design the policy to meet the client's needs (employer DI requires the employee to accept what is offered).
- Premiums for individual DI can be high for certain types of occupations, short elimination periods, long benefit periods, and high income replacements.
- Policies should be guaranteed renewable or non-cancelable (a cancelable policy can be canceled by the insurance company and is a weakness in the plan).
- Benefit periods should extend to retirement age, or as long as the client can afford to purchase.
- Elimination periods should be no longer than the period of time emergency funds will cover.
- The definition of disability should be more liberal than the Social Security definition.
- Clients close to or in retirement should not buy additional disability income insurance and should terminate existing policies.

Despite the danger of losing coverage when the client moves from one employer to another, many clients and planners like to use the group coverage as the "base" of the plan because of the lower premiums for group versus individual policies. If the group benefits are adequate to cover current expenses, but additional income is needed for COBRA health insurance premiums or funding retirement contributions to stay on track, or to pay for additional medical expenses, etc., there will still be a need for additional coverage. This additional insurance should be provided through an individual policy. Some insurers offer a rider so a retirement contribution is made in addition to the stated disability income amount, to ensure that a period of disability does not derail the client's plans for saving for retirement.

Selecting an Insurance Company

Once the planner and client have determined that an individual disability policy is needed, they should evaluate the policy features and provisions available through different insurance companies. As with life insurance, an insurance broker can assist by obtaining quotes from multiple insurers simultaneously, allowing for the financial advisor and client to compare policy features and underwriting standards across several companies.

When recommending a particular insurer for the client, the planner should evaluate its:

- Financial safety
- Occupational classification system
- Specific products offered
- Attitude toward writing disability income coverage generally
- Underwriting philosophy and standards
- Claims-paying reputation
- Efficiency in processing applications

CONCLUSION

In many ways, disability insurance can be more important than life insurance since the incidence of disability is significantly greater than untimely death. It is important to address and cover the risk of not being able to work. This risk is precisely what disability insurance covers. As with other insurance, there are many choices and many alternatives that one must consider when purchasing disability insurance.

KEY TERMS

Any Occupation - Type of disability insurance policy that provides benefits to a policyowner if he or she is unable to perform the duties of any occupation for which he or she is suited by education, training, or experience.

Automatic Increase Rider - A provision that automatically increases the monthly benefit by a stated percentage each year.

COLA Rider - Provides a cost of living adjustment to benefit payments based on increases in inflation.

Disability Insurance - A type of insurance that provides supplementary income in the event of an illness or accident resulting in a disability that prevents the insured from working at his or her regular employment.

Elimination Period - The period of time, beginning upon injury or sickness, that an insured is disabled but is not collecting benefits from the insurer.

Future Increase Option Rider - A provision that permits the insured to increase benefit coverage as they get older.

Guaranteed Renewable - A provision that requires the insurance company to renew the policy for a specified period of time or until the insured attains a certain age.

Long-Term Disability - Provides coverage for specified term, until specified age, or until death.

Non-Cancelable - A provision that prevents the insurance company from canceling the policy for any reason provided the policy premium is paid.

Own Occupation - Type of disability insurance policy that provides benefits to a policyholder if he is unable to perform the duties of their occupation. This type of policy is more expensive than an any occupation policy.

Partial Disability - A provision that provides payments that are less than those paid for a total disability.

Presumptive Total Disability Coverage - A provision that automatically considers certain conditions to be totally disabling, such as loss of sight in both eyes, hearing in both ears, the use of both hands, the use of both feet, or the use of one foot and one hand.

Residual Benefits Provision - A provision that will provide continuing benefits for an insured who returns to work but suffers a reduction of income due to a disability.

Short-Term Disability - Provides coverage for up to two years, and typically has a five to 30 day elimination period (the period an insured must wait before receiving benefits).

Social Security Disability Benefits - Available to anyone insured under the system who meets the strict definition of disability.

Split Definition - Type of disability policy where an insured is covered against the risk of not performing his or her own occupation for a period of time, and after that period expires, an any-occupation definition of disability is used.

Worker's Compensation - Designed to provide benefits to workers who are injured while working.

DISCUSSION QUESTIONS

SOLUTIONS to the discussion questions can be found exclusively within the chapter. Once you have completed an initial reading of the chapter, go back and highlight the answers to these questions.

1. List and define the three common definitions used in disability insurance policies.

2. List and describe provisions commonly found in disability insurance policies.

3. Explain the relative importance of short- versus long-term disability coverage.

4. Explain why it is important to not just accept an own occupation definition as described by a representative or by marketing literature.

5. Describe the impact to disability policy premiums of increasing the elimination period.

6. Compare and contrast the future increase option rider and the automatic increase riders.

7. Identify the primary issue in determining whether disability benefits are taxable or tax-free.

8. What is the purpose of disability income insurance, and what are some of the various definitions of disability?

MULTIPLE-CHOICE PROBLEMS

A sample of multiple choice problems is provided below. Additional multiple choice problems are available at money-education.com by accessing the Student Practice Portal.

1. Which one of the following statements regarding disability insurance is false?
   a. The longer the elimination period, the less expensive the policy.
   b. An own-occupation policy will provide disability benefits if the insured is unable to perform the duties of his or her own occupation.
   c. An any-occupation policy is less expensive than an own-occupation policy.
   d. A residual benefit clause provides the insured with benefits that extend beyond the disability period.

2. Gunther has a disability income policy that pays a monthly benefit of $2,400. Gunther has been disabled for 60 days, but he only received $1,200 from his disability insurance. Which of the following is the probable reason that he only received $1,200?
   a. The policy has a deductible of $1,200.
   b. The elimination period is 45 days.
   c. The policy has a 50% coinsurance clause.
   d. Gunther is considered to be only 50% disabled.

3. Andrea owns and runs a printing company that is organized as an S corporation. Unfortunately, she has an accident with a printing press and is rendered disabled. She receives $4,000 per month in disability payments. The S corporation had paid the premiums on the policy, but reported the payments on her W-2. How much of the benefit is subject to income tax?
   a. $0.
   b. $2,000.
   c. $3,000.
   d. $4,000.

4. How long would someone have to wait to receive Social Security disability benefits if they qualify?
   a. 5 months.
   b. 6 months.
   c. 12 months.
   d. Benefits are paid immediately if eligible.

5. Caden has a disability policy with a 12-month elimination period. He was in a bizarre accident involving a crane falling on a building causing part of the building's exterior wall to fall on his van. He lost the use of both of his legs in the accident. If his policy has a presumptive total disability coverage provision, when will he begin receiving benefits?
   a. Immediately.
   b. After six months as the provision accelerates the waiting period.
   c. After a one month statutory administrative time period.
   d. He will have to wait the 12 months.

QUICK QUIZ EXPLANATIONS

Quick Quiz 6.1
1. False. It is far more likely for people to suffer a disability than to die early.
2. True.
3. False. Generally, people should have between 60 and 70 percent of their income protected by disability coverage.

Quick Quiz 6.2
1. True.
2. False. Generally, once an insured becomes disabled and the elimination period has passed, future premiums are waived.
3. False. Own occupation disability insurance is the least sold type of disability insurance.

Quick Quiz 6.3
1. False. A COLA rider will increase the benefit payments once payments have begun based on increases in inflation. There are other riders that will increase coverage based on increases in income.
2. False. An own occupation policy will be more expensive than an any occupation policy because it is more defined in terms of the duties the insured cannot perform.
3. True.
4. False. Incontestability clauses protect the insured from unintentional misrepresentations or errors, generally after two years.

Quick Quiz 6.4
1. True.
2. False. The proportionate amount of benefit purchased by the employee's after-tax premiums, 40% of the benefit in this case, will be tax free.

> **Additional multiple choice problems
> are available at
> money-education.com
> by accessing the
> Student Practice Portal.
> Access requires registration of the title using
> the unique code at the front of the book.**

7

LONG-TERM CARE INSURANCE

LEARNING OBJECTIVES

1. Discuss the aging characteristics of the population of the United States.
2. Explain why there is a need for long-term care services.
3. Identify those persons who need long-term care services.
4. Summarize long-term care services.
5. Compare and contrast long-term care services with traditional medical services.
6. Assess the costs of long-term care services.
7. Discuss alternative ways to pay for long-term care services.
8. Evaluate Medicaid as an alternative to long-term care insurance.
9. Differentiate between mandatory and optional Medicaid benefits that may apply depending on the state.*
10. Explain common Medicaid eligibility requirements, how assets are treated in determining eligibility, and how asset transfers may be subject to a look back period.*
11. Identify planning strategies, in accordance with Medicaid regulations, to maximize client benefits and available resources.*
12. Explain estate recovery implications for Medicaid recipients.*
13. Identify personal risk factors when considering long-term care.
14. Justify the financial considerations and trade-offs relative to purchasing long-term care insurance.
15. Identify the basic factors in establishing premiums for long-term care insurance.
16. Describe common policy features in long-term care insurance policies.
17. Identify services that are excludable in long-term care policies.
18. Discuss the merits of inflation protection in a long-term care policy.
19. Identify and describe the optional benefits in a long-term care policy.
20. Discuss the decision of how long a term of benefits to select for a long-term care policy.
21. Explain the income tax benefits of a long-term care policy.
22. Explain the benefits and limitations of tax-qualified long-term care contracts.
23. Identify activities of daily living that can trigger the need for long-term care.*
24. Develop an appropriate long-term care insurance plan based on needs, financial resources, policy coverage, and cost.*
25. Describe the three methods used by an insurer to pay long-term care benefits.

* CFP Board Resource Document - Student-Centered Learning Objectives based upon CFP Board Principal Topics.

INTRODUCTION

The United States has an aging population. The total population was approximately 309 million as of 2010. Of those, 49,572,181 were age 62 or older (2010) and 40,267,984 were age 65 or older.[1] The U.S. Census Bureau estimates that there were 52 million people in the U.S. who are age 65 or older, about 16 percent of the population in 2018.[2]

The following chart provides a comparison of the aging population from 2001 to 2010 for the total population as well as by gender. The chart reflects a sizable increase in Americans over the age of 60 for both men and women. However, the increase in men over the age of 60 is significantly higher than for women.

1. The United States Census Bureau "Profile of General Population" 2010. Estimate of boomers turning 65 and new births is based on census data.
2. https://www.census.gov/library/stories/2019/12/by-2030-all-baby-boomers-will-be-age-65-or-older.html

Exhibit 7.1 | U.S. Population Totals by Age Group and Sex in the 2010 and 2000 Censuses

	Total Population		Male Population		Female Population	
	2010 Census	2000 Census	2010 Census	2000 Census	2010 Census	2000 Census
Total US Population	308,745,538	281,421,906	151,781,326	138,053,563	156,964,212	143,368,343
60 to 64 years	16,817,924	10,805,447	8,077,500	5,136,627	8,740,424	5,668,820
65 to 69 years	12,435,263	9,533,545	5,852,547	4,400,362	6,582,716	5,133,183
70 to 74 years	9,278,166	8,857,441	4,243,972	3,902,912	5,034,194	4,954,529
75 to 79 years	7,317,795	7,415,813	3,182,388	3,044,456	4,135,407	4,371,357
80 to 84 years	5,743,327	4,945,367	2,294,374	1,834,897	3,448,953	3,110,470
85 years and over	5,493,433	4,239,587	1,789,679	1,226,998	3,703,754	3,012,589
60 and over	57,085,908	45,797,200	25,440,460	19,546,252	31,645,448	26,250,948
65 and over	40,267,984	34,991,753	17,362,960	14,409,625	22,905,024	20,582,128
70 and over	27,832,721	25,458,208	11,510,413	10,009,263	16,322,308	15,448,945
85 and over	5,493,433	4,239,587	1,789,679	1,226,998	3,703,754	3,012,589

2000 to 2010	Increase	Increase %	Increase	Increase %	Increase	Increase %
60 and over	11,288,708	25%	5,894,208	30%	5,394,500	21%
65 and over	5,276,231	15%	2,953,335	20%	2,322,896	11%
70 and over	2,374,513	9%	1,501,150	15%	873,363	6%
85 and over	1,253,846	30%	562,681	46%	691,165	23%

Source: For 2010 Data: U.S. Census Bureau, 2010 Census.

As medical advances increase average life expectancy, advanced age presents additional medical problems for individuals. Prolonged illness or mental impairments, such as senile dementia and Alzheimer's disease, often require an affected individual to receive assistance for both medical and custodial care. Experts suggest that someone turning age 65 today has a 70 percent chance of needing some type of long-term care services (care provided at home or in a facility) at some point during their lives, with 42 percent receiving paid care at home and 37 percent receiving care in a facility.[3] Sometimes, nursing home care is required for rehabilitation after surgery, usually for a relatively short duration. Cognitive impairments, however, may prevent a person from engaging in normal **activities of daily living (ADLs)** without assistance, and in these circumstances nursing home stays may last for several years or longer. Activities of daily living include eating, bathing, dressing, transferring, toileting, and continence.

The cost of receiving nursing home care is expensive. Depending on the area of the country where services are provided, costs can range from $60,000 to over $160,000 per year. While medical insurance plans may cover a short stay in a skilled nursing home for rehabilitation purposes after surgery or a hospital stay, medical insurance does not cover the costs of extended nursing home stays. Long-term care insurance is one product that can be used to cover the cost of nursing home care that exceeds the coverage provided by medical insurance and Medicare, and cover the cost of custodial care (assistance with activities of daily living) provided at home. Neither medical insurance nor Medicare covers the cost of custodial care (personal assistance services, including assistance with activities of daily living, taking medicine and similar personal needs, that does not require skilled care from a licensed medical professional.

> ## ≔ *Key Concepts*
>
> 1. Explain how the aging population in the United States impacts the need for long-term care.
>
> 2. Understand how the needs for long-term care services increase with age.

3. https://longtermcare.acl.gov/the-basics/how-much-care-will-you-need.html

Exhibit 7.2 | The Risk of Adverse Events Impacting Those Age 65 and Older

Adverse Events That Occur	Lifetime Possibility Beyond Age 65	
	Men	Women
Major House Fire Fact: There are 363,000 major house fires annually (2018 statistic)*	2.2%	2.6%
Severe Car Accident Fact: Approx. 2.55 million accidents result in death or injury (2017 statistic)**	15.5%	18.0%
Becoming ADL Disabled or Cognitively Impaired (Dept. of Health and Human Services)	64.0%	75.0%

Source: The 2014 Sourcebook for Long-Term Care Insurance Information / LTC Facts and Figures /
Summarization of data compiled by Dawn Helwig, Miliman.
* National Fire Protection Association
** U.S. Department of Transportation

This chapter discusses the need for long-term care services, long-term care insurance, the coverages and benefits under these policies, and alternatives to long-term care insurance.

Long-Term Care Services

Long-term care services are a range of personal care and supportive services that a person might need if they were unable to care for themselves because of illness, disability, or cognitive impairment. Long-term care services meet the needs of frail, older people and other adults who lack the capacity to care for themselves.

Long-term care services differ from traditional medical services in that **traditional medical care** services attempt to treat or cure illnesses. Long-term care services usually do not attempt to improve the medical condition of the recipient but, rather, help to maintain lifestyle. Long-term care services help the recipient to manage routine activities of daily living (ADLs). Long-term care services can also assist a person who needs supervision, protection, or reminders to take medicine or perform other activities. Thus, long-term care services include ADLs and instrumental activities of daily living (IADLs) such as medication management, housework, health maintenance tasks, and other activities that allow an individual to live independently in the community.

Exhibit 7.3 | ADLs vs IADLs

Activities of Daily Living (ADLs)	Instrumental Activities of Daily Living (IADLs)
• Eating • Bathing • Dressing • Transferring • Toileting • Continence	• Medicine Management • Shopping • Preparing Meals • Housekeeping • Doing Laundry • Using Transportation • Handling Finances • Communicating via telephone

Long-term care services are provided in a variety of settings. Long-term care services may be provided at home, in the community, in a residential setting, or in an institutional setting (nursing home). Services can be provided at home either by a home health agency or by family or friends. In the community, long-term care services can be provided at an adult day care center. In a residential setting, long-term care services are provided by assisted living communities. Nursing homes provide institutional care.

:≡ *Key Concepts*

1. Describe long-term care services.

2. Explain the costs of long-term care services.

3. Identify the activities of daily living and the instrumental activities of daily living.

As mentioned above, the average stay for LTC patients may be relatively short or it may extend for years. According to the National Care Planning Council, the average stay in a nursing home is 835 days. The next section discusses the cost of long-term care services. However, it is important to keep in mind that many stays in these facilities are relatively short and often long-term care services are provided at home by family members. Therefore, while the cost of long-term care can be enormous for some patients, it is fairly minimal for many others.

The Cost of Long-Term Care Services

Long-term care services can be expensive. The cost depends on the amount of care and the type of care that one receives. It also depends on where the care is received (both the type of setting and the geographical location) and what type of medical professional provides the service.

Exhibit 7.4 | Long-Term Care Room Rates (2019)

Type of Facility	Monthly	Median Annual Rates
Nursing Home - Private	$8,517	$102,204
Nursing Home - Semi-Private	$7,513	$90,156
Assisted Living	$4,051	$48,612

Source: Genworth 2019 Cost of Care Survey

Exhibit 7.5 | Long-Term Care Assistance Rates (2019)

	Median Rate
Home Health Aides	$4,385/month
Homemaker / Companion	$4,290/month
Adult Day Services	$1,625/month

Source: Genworth 2019 Cost of Care Survey

Paying for Long-Term Care Services

Given the pervasive need for long-term care for our elderly, the question arises as to how this service is to be provided. Often, an unpaid caregiver, such as a family member or friend, provides long-term care services. In many other cases, people must pay for the service. There are four common methods for paying for long-term care services.[4] These are:

1. Medicare
2. Medicaid
3. Personal assets and savings
4. Long-term care insurance

Medicare

Medicare is a federal program that pays for healthcare for persons age 65 and over and for people under age 65 with disabilities. Medicare generally does not cover long-term care services. However, Medicare will help pay for a short stay in a skilled nursing facility, for hospice care, or for home health care if the recipient meets the following conditions:

- Has had a recent prior hospital stay of at least three days
- Is admitted to a Medicare-certified nursing facility within 30 days of the prior hospital stay
- Needs skilled care, such as skilled nursing services, physical therapy, or other types of therapy, as a result of some medical condition that caused the hospital stay

If all of these conditions are met, Medicare will pay for some of the costs up to 100 days. However, Medicare payments are limited and, thus, are inadequate to provide for extended care needs as illustrated in the following exhibit.

Exhibit 7.6 | Skilled Nursing Facility Time Line (2020)

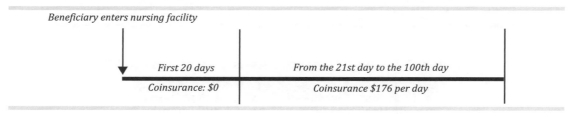

Beneficiary enters nursing facility

First 20 days — Coinsurance: $0

From the 21st day to the 100th day — Coinsurance $176 per day

Medicaid

Title XIX of the Social Security Act is a Federal/State entitlement program that pays for medical assistance for certain individuals and families with low incomes and resources. This program, known as **Medicaid**, became law in 1965 as a cooperative venture jointly funded by the Federal and State governments (including the District of Columbia and the Territories) to assist States in furnishing medical assistance to eligible needy persons. Medicaid is the largest source of funding for medical and

:≡ *Key Concepts*

1. Identify the four common methods for paying for long-term care services.

2. Explain why Medicare is not an appropriate option to pay for long-term care services.

3. Describe what options are available to those persons who do not have long-term care insurance and who find themselves in need of long-term care.

4. Understand the limitations of Medicare and Medicaid for long-term care services.

---

4. Another source of funding for long-term care services is through veteran's benefits. Veterans' benefits are not discussed in this text, but planners should be aware that government funds may be available to help disabled veterans and their spouses pay for personal care services provided at home or in a VA nursing home. Additional information can be found at www.va.gov.

health-related services for impoverished Americans. Additional details regarding Medicaid are discussed later in this chapter.

Personal Assets and Savings

Paying for long-term care out of personal savings can be an option for some. However, it depends on how long the services are needed and the amount of liquid wealth (assets that are easily turned into cash) the client has available to pay for services. In many cases, long-term care services may only be needed for a short period of time. In other cases, individuals may need the service for an extended period of time. In these cases, paying for the service can be financially devastating. However, once a person's assets are depleted, they may become eligible for Medicaid.

It is important to keep in mind that while paying for long-term care services out of savings is devastating to the person who needs the care, it can also be devastating to the person's spouse. Couples accumulate assets together over many years to pay for their needs (and wants) during retirement. If long-term care is needed for one spouse for an extended period of time, it can be a financial disaster for the other spouse, who will still need financial resources for years or decades.

Long-Term Care Insurance

Long-term care insurance is an option that can mitigate the risks of needing and having to pay for long-term care services for an extended period of time. Unlike traditional health insurance, long-term care insurance is designed to cover long-term services and supports, including personal and custodial care in a variety of settings. While health insurance may pay the entire bill for a week at a hospital, it will not pay for an indefinite stay at a nursing home. Long-term care insurance pays for home health care, nursing home stays, and hospice care. Long-term care insurance policies have many choices, limitations, and costs that need to be considered. Additional details regarding long-term care insurance are discussed later in this chapter.

MEDICAID

Medicaid is by far the largest source of funding for long-term care services, providing 42.2 percent of funding for long term services and support in 2106.

Medicaid is the nationwide program (administered by the individual states) that provides medical assistance to those without resources to pay. The federal government oversees the Medicaid program through the Centers for Medicare and Medicaid Services (CMS). The states administer their Medicaid programs through agencies at the state and local level. The federal government establishes broad national guidelines, however, each State establishes its own eligibility standards; determines the type, amount, duration, and scope of services; sets the rate of payment for services; and administers its own program. Some states combine their Medicaid program with other programs, such as the Children's Health Insurance Program (CHIP) which provides medical insurance for children under age 19 in families whose income is too high to qualify for Medicaid.

Medicaid policies for eligibility, services, and payment are complex and vary considerably, even among states of similar size or geographic proximity. Thus, a person who is eligible for Medicaid in one state may not be eligible in another state, and the services provided by one state may differ considerably in amount, duration, or scope from services provided in a similar or neighboring state. In addition, state legislatures may change Medicaid eligibility, services, and/or reimbursement at any time.

Exhibit 7.7 | Who Pays for Long-Term Care Service

Congressional Research Service
Informing the legislative debate since 1914

IN FOCUS

August 22, 2018

Who Pays for Long-Term Services and Supports?

Long-term services and supports (LTSS) refers to a broad range of health and health-related services and other types of assistance that are needed by individuals over an extended period of time. The need for LTSS affects persons of all ages and is generally measured by limitations in an individual's ability to perform daily personal care activities such as eating, bathing, dressing, or walking, and activities that allow individuals to live independently in the community, including shopping, housework, and meal preparation. The probability of needing LTSS increases with age. As the nation's population aged 65 and older continues to increase in size, and individuals continue to live longer post-retirement, the demand for LTSS is also expected to increase. In addition, advances in medical and supportive care may allow younger persons with disabilities to live longer.

Total U.S. spending on LTSS is a significant component of all personal health care spending. In 2016, an estimated $366.0 billion was spent on LTSS, representing 12.9% of the $2.8 trillion spent on personal health expenditures. LTSS payments include those made for services in nursing facilities and in residential care facilities for individuals with intellectual and developmental disabilities, mental health conditions, and substance abuse issues. LTSS spending also includes payments for services provided in an individual's own home, such as personal care and homemaker/chore services (e.g., housework or meal preparation), as well as a wide range of other community-based services (e.g., adult day health care services). A substantial amount of LTSS is also provided by family members, friends, and other uncompensated caregivers. Thus, formally reported spending on LTSS underestimates total expenditures, as spending data do not include uncompensated care provided by these caregivers. This report provides information on who the primary LTSS payers are and how much they spend.

Who Pays for Long-Term Services and Supports?

LTSS are financed by a variety of public and private sources. **Figure 1** shows LTSS spending by payer for 2016. Public sources paid for the majority of LTSS spending (70.3%). Medicaid and Medicare are, respectively, the first- and second-largest public payers, and in 2016 accounted for nearly two-thirds (64.0%) of all LTSS spending nationwide. Other public programs that finance LTSS for specific populations are a much smaller share of total LTSS funding (6.3%). These public sources include the Veterans Health Administration (VHA) and Children's Health Insurance Program (CHIP), among others. It is important to note that the eligibility requirements and benefits provided by these public programs vary widely. Moreover, among the various public sources of LTSS financing, none are designed to

cover the full range of services and supports that may be desired by individuals with long-term care needs.

There is some disagreement over the classification of Medicare benefits in LTSS or post-acute (i.e., skilled care provided over a short-term, typically after a hospitalization) categories. This is likely due to the fact that both Medicare and Medicaid cover stays in nursing homes as well as visits by home health agencies, although the service type and scope of coverage generally differ. Excluding Medicare spending on home health and skilled nursing facilities, total LTSS spending in 2016 was $286.1 billion, or 10.1% of U.S. personal health expenditures, with Medicaid spending paying for more than half (54.0%) of all LTSS spending (as redefined).

In the absence of public funding for LTSS, individuals must rely upon private sources of funding. In 2016, private sources accounted for 29.7% of LTSS expenditures. Within the category of funding, out-of-pocket spending was the largest component (over one-half of private sources), comprising 15.6% of total LTSS expenditures. Second was private insurance (7.5%), which includes both health and long-term care insurance. Other private funding, which largely includes philanthropic contributions, comprised 6.5% of total LTSS. The following provides a brief discussion of the various public and private sources of LTSS funding.

Figure 1. Long-Term Services and Supports (LTSS) Spending, by Payer, 2016

(in billions)

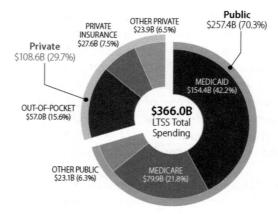

Source: CRS analysis of National Health Expenditure Account data obtained from the Centers for Medicare & Medicaid Services, Office of the Actuary, prepared November 2017.

Who Pays for Long-Term Care Service Continued

Medicaid

Medicaid is a means-tested health and LTSS program funded jointly by federal and state governments. Medicaid funds are used to pay for a variety of health care services and LTSS, including nursing facility care, home health, personal care, and other home and community-based services. Each state designs and administers its own program within broad federal guidelines. Medicaid is the largest single payer of LTSS in the United States; in 2016, total Medicaid LTSS spending (combined federal and state) was $154.4 billion, which comprised 42.2% of all LTSS expenditures. In 2016, Medicaid LTSS accounted for 30.6% of all Medicaid spending, which represented about 5.9% (4.2 million) of the enrolled population receiving LTSS in FY2013 (the most recent year for which data are available).

Medicare

Medicare is a federal program that pays for covered health services for the elderly and for certain non-elderly individuals with disabilities. Medicare covers primarily acute and post-acute care, including skilled nursing and home health services. Medicare-certified nursing homes are referred to as skilled nursing facilities (SNFs). Unlike Medicaid, Medicare is not intended to be a primary funding source for LTSS. These post-acute Medicare benefits provide limited access to personal care services both in the home care setting and in SNFs for certain beneficiaries. While Medicaid nursing and home health benefits are available to eligible beneficiaries for as long as they qualify, Medicare benefits are generally limited in duration. In addition, Medicare SNF and home health benefits include coverage of rehabilitation services that will, presumably, prevent a decline in the beneficiary's physical condition or functional status. In 2016, Medicare spent $79.9 billion on SNF and home health services combined, which was over one-fifth (21.8%) of all LTSS spending. These expenditures include Medicare Parts A and B (also referred to as "Original Medicare") and estimated Medicare Part C (Medicare Advantage) payments attributable to SNF care and home health care. Of total Medicare LTSS spending, 49.2%, or $39.3 billion, was paid to home health agencies, and 50.8%, or $40.6 billion, was paid to SNFs.

Other Public Payers

Of all LTSS expenditures in the United States, a relatively small portion of the costs are paid for with public funds other than Medicare or Medicaid. Collectively, these payers covered 6.3% of all LTSS expenditures in 2016, totaling $23.1 billion. Among these public payers, over half of spending ($12.8 billion, or 55.5%) was for LTSS provided in residential care facilities for individuals with intellectual and developmental disabilities, mental health conditions, and substance abuse issues. Spending in this category also includes LTSS paid for or operated by VHA ($5.7 billion, or 24.6%). Another $3.8 billion, or 16.4%, includes state and local subsidies to providers and temporary disability insurance. A smaller percentage was spent on general assistance, which includes expenditures for state programs modeled after Medicaid, as well as federal and state funding for nursing facilities and home health under CHIP. In addition, some public LTSS spending includes two types of programs that capture federal health care funds and grants to various federal agencies and Pre-existing Conditions Insurance Plans. Collectively public spending from these sources totaled $800 million, or 3.5%.

Out-of-Pocket Spending

Out-of-pocket spending was 15.6% of total LTSS spending, or $57.0 billion, in 2016. Expenditures in this category include deductibles and copayments for services that are primarily paid for by another payment source as well as direct payments for LTSS. While there are daily copayments for skilled nursing services after a specified number of days under Medicare, there are no copayments for Medicare's home health services. In addition, some private health insurance plans provide limited skilled nursing and home health coverage, which may require copayments. Moreover, private long-term care insurance (LTCI) often has an elimination or waiting period for policyholders that requires out-of-pocket payments for services for a specified period of time before benefit payments begin. Once individuals have exhausted their Medicare and/or private insurance benefits, they must pay the full cost of care directly out-of-pocket. With respect to Medicaid LTSS, individuals must meet both financial and functional eligibility requirements. Individuals not initially eligible for Medicaid, and not covered under a private LTCI policy, must pay for LTSS directly out-of-pocket. Eventually, these individuals may spend down their income and assets and thus meet the financial requirements for Medicaid eligibility.

Private Insurance

Private health and long-term care insurance plays a much smaller role in financing LTSS; 7.5% of total LTSS spending, or $27.6 billion, was funded through these sources. Private insurance expenditures for LTSS include both health and LTCI. Similar to Medicare LTSS funding, private health insurance funding for LTSS includes payments for some limited home health and skilled nursing services for the purposes of rehabilitation. Private LTCI, on the other hand, is purchased specifically for financial protection against the risk of the potentially high costs associated with LTSS. In addition, a number of hybrid products that combine LTCI with either an annuity or a life insurance policy have emerged. The Medicaid Long-Term Care Insurance Partnership Program offers a LTCI policy that is linked to Medicaid eligibility.

Other Private Funds

Other private funds generally include philanthropic support, which may be directly from individuals or obtained through philanthropic fund-raising organizations such as the United Way. Support may also be obtained from foundations or corporations. In 2016, other private funding accounted for 6.5% of total LTSS spending, or $23.9 billion.

Kirsten J. Colello, kcolello@crs.loc.gov, 7-7839

IF10343

Source: www.crs.gov

Funding

The federal and state governments jointly fund the Medicaid program. The federal contribution to Medicaid expenditures in each state is determined by a formula that is set by federal statute. The portion that the federal government must pay is called the Federal Medical Assistance Percentage (FMAP). The formula used to calculate FMAP has resulted in the federal government paying a larger percentage to states with lower per capita income and a smaller percentage to states with higher per capita income. The minimum percentage that states can be required to pay is 50 percent of the Medicaid expenses, but states with lower per capita incomes may receive up to 75 percent of their Medicaid expenditures from the federal government. There is no limit on the amount that the federal government will pay when a state pays its share. Medicaid is a substantial part of the budget for each state and is larger than any other item in most state budgets. The state and federal payments account on average for approximately 29 percent of state budgets. Under federal law, states may obtain up to 60 percent of their share of Medicaid funding from local governments.

Mandatory and Optional Benefits

The federal government has set broad guidelines for the benefits that states must provide under a Medicaid program. In addition to the mandatory benefits, states may provide additional optional benefits. Each state establishes and administers its own Medicaid program and can determine, within the federal guidelines, the amount and type of services it will provide.

Exhibit 7.8 | Medicaid Mandatory and Optional Benefits

Mandatory Benefits	Optional Benefits*
• Inpatient and outpatient hospital services	• Prescription drugs
• Physician services	• Dental services
• Nursing facility services	• Hospice
• Home health services	• Preventive and rehabilitative services
• Early and periodic screening, diagnostic, and treatment services	• Physical therapy
• Laboratory and x-ray services	• Chiropractic services
• Rural health clinic services	• Personal care
• Federally qualified health center services	• Clinic services
• Family planning services	• Occupational therapy
• Nurse midwife services	• Speech, hearing, and language disorder services
• Certified pediatric and family nurse practitioner services	• Respiratory care services
• Freestanding birth center services	• Podiatry services
• Transportation to medical care	• Optometry services
• Tobacco cessation counseling for pregnant women	• Dentures
	• Prosthetics
	• Eyeglasses

Other optional benefits may also be available.

It is important to distinguish home care from home health services. Home health services consist of medical care provided in the home by trained professionals such as doctors and nurses. Home care is personal care provided by family members or paid caregivers. Home health services are mandatory while home care is optional. Not all states pay for the expenses of home care, but more states are offering it due to its lower cost compared to care in nursing homes.

Nursing facility services are mandatory, and must be provided at Medicaid certified nursing homes. Medicaid will not pay for expenses at a nursing home that has not been certified. Nursing homes will often obtain certification even though most of their residents are not eligible for Medicaid. By becoming certified, these nursing homes can continue to receive payment for nursing facility services in the event their residents exhaust their resources and become Medicaid eligible.

Nursing homes, assisted living facilities, and other services are not required to accept Medicaid reimbursement, and some do not. Nursing facilities often care for individuals who are Medicaid recipients as well as those who are not. Consequently, the quality of care received may often not be much different between Medicaid recipients and others. Since some nursing homes do not accept Medicaid, however, the choices of nursing homes may be more limited for those receiving Medicaid assistance. In some states, Medicaid will not help with paying for assisted living care, so individuals may not have that option with Medicaid. A person who has his or her own resources, or who has long-term care insurance, to pay for nursing home care when first applying will have more options.

States can apply to the Centers for Medicare and Medicaid Services (CMS) for a waiver of federal law to expand health coverage beyond the mandatory eligibility groups. Many states have expanded coverage above the federal minimums, especially for children.

State and federal officials have been seeking to shift more care from nursing homes to home and community services. The cost of long-term care in nursing homes and similar institutions averaged $82,128 per person in 2016. In contrast, community-based services for long-term care beneficiaries averaged only $45,800.

Eligibility

While Medicaid will pay for most long-term care expenses for eligible low-income persons, it is often difficult to qualify for the government service. To be eligible, a person must meet both the general requirements as well as meet the financial requirements. In most cases, a person must be one of the following to meet the general requirements:
- Be age 65 or older
- Have a permanent disability as that term is defined by the Social Security Administration
- Be blind
- Be a pregnant woman
- Be a child, or the parent or caretaker of a child

A person must have limited income and limited assets to meet the financial requirements for Medicaid.

Income

The amount of income a person can have varies by state, and also varies depending on which eligibility groups each state covers. Each state's Medical Assistance Office is usually the best resource to determine the eligibility requirements within that state. In the state determination of a person's financial eligibility for Medicaid, the state will only count certain types of income. A person's income includes these sources:

- Regular benefit payments such as Social Security retirement or disability payments
- Veterans benefits
- Pensions
- Salaries
- Wages
- Interest from bank accounts and certificates of deposit
- Dividends from stocks and bonds

However, Medicaid generally does not count such things as:

- Nutritional assistance (food stamps)
- Housing assistance provided by the federal government
- Home energy assistance

The states set varying income eligibility requirements, but for applicants who live in the community (i.e., not in a nursing home, hospital, or other institution), the limit is generally a percentage of the federal poverty level. A common income standard is 133 percent of the federal poverty level. In 2019, 133 percent of the federal poverty level for an individual is $1,414.23 monthly or $16,970 annually. The amount increases for a family with two, three, four or more persons.

There is another option for those individuals whose income exceeds the state limits, called the special income level group. The special income level group is an optional group for states, meaning that states can choose to cover or not cover this group. Over 40 states have chosen to cover this group though, so it is widely available as a pathway to receiving long-term care services under Medicaid. This group is aimed specifically at people who need long-term care services. The income requirement is significantly higher for this group (typically 300% of the Supplemental Security Income (SSI) limit of $783 in 2020, which is $2,349 per month in 2020), but receiving benefits under this category may require the person to "share in the cost" of the service provided.[5] The group has the same general requirements and similar asset requirements. Before Medicaid will pay nursing home expenses, residents must pay all of their income toward the cost of care. Residents are permitted to retain a personal allowance of $30 to $40 per month. A married couple's income is generally counted separately, so that the income of the non-applicant spouse is not used to determine eligibility of the applicant spouse. This helps to protect the spouse of a nursing home resident from impoverishment.

Assets

In the process of a state determining a person's financial eligibility for Medicaid, certain types of assets are counted, while others are excluded. During the Medicaid application process, applicants must provide documentation of the assets they own.

The amount of countable assets a person can have and still qualify for Medicaid varies from state to state. In most states a person can retain about $2,000 in countable assets, and married couples that are still living in the same household can retain about $3,000 in countable assets. This may not sound like much, but it is important to understand that many assets are not counted at all when determining Medicaid eligibility.

---

5. https://www.medicaidplanningassistance.org/medicaid-eligibility/

Assets that are usually counted for Medicaid eligibility include:
- Checking and savings accounts
- Stocks and bonds
- Certificates of deposit
- Real property other than your primary residence
- Additional motor vehicles if you have more than one
- Retirement plan assets that can be withdrawn in a lump sum (such as IRAs and 401(k)s)

Assets that do not usually get counted for Medicaid eligibility include the following:
- Primary residence
- Personal property and household belongings
- One motor vehicle
- Life insurance with a face value under $1,500
- Up to $1,500 in funds set aside for burial
- Certain burial arrangements such as pre-need burial agreements
- Assets held in specific kinds of trusts
- Retirement plan assets that cannot be withdrawn in a lump sum (such as defined benefit pension plans in which a lump sum distribution is not available)

The personal residence is often a person's largest and most valuable asset and is not considered for Medicaid eligibility purposes. However, there are limits to the amount of equity that a person can maintain and still qualify for Medicaid. In 2020, the equity limit is in excess of $595,000. Medicaid must deny benefits above this limit.[6]

Community Spouse Resource Allowance

When both spouses are in a nursing home, the couple is limited to $3,000 of assets, but the law is different for married couples when only one spouse is in a nursing home. The Medicaid law provides special protection to prevent spousal impoverishment. When one spouse enters a nursing home, the law wants to make it possible for the other spouse to continue living in the community. The spouse who does not need long-term care is permitted to retain certain assets, which are called the "community spouse resource allowance." The couple's assets are counted as of the day the applicant enters the nursing home, and the community spouse is entitled to retain one-half of the couple's countable assets up to a maximum of $128,640 (2020).

Example 7.1

On the day Danny Fontaine enters a nursing home, he and his wife Sandy have a home valued at $240,000, a car worth $28,000, and a stock portfolio with a market value of $140,000. The house and car are not countable assets, so the Fontaines have countable assets of $140,000. They divide the $140,000 equally so Sandy gets $70,000 for her community spouse resource allowance. Danny can retain $2,000, so the Fontaines must spend down $68,000 before Danny will qualify for Medicaid.

---

6. Source: CMCS Informational Bulletin for 2020: States have the option of using a higher limit, which can be as high as $893,000 in 2020. Most states have chosen to use the lower limit, but some states, especially in parts of the country where housing is expensive, use the higher amount. These limits are adjusted each year to account for inflation. (source: http://longtermcare.gov/Medicare-Medicaid-more/Medicaid/Medicaid-eligibility/financial-requirements-assets/)(latest available at time of printing).

When an applicant needs to spend down assets to qualify for Medicaid, the money can be spent on more than just nursing home care. The following expenditures are permitted:
- Paying off debts, including credit cards, mortgages, auto loans, taxes, and other legitimate debts
- Purchase of a new exempt asset such as a car or home
- Payments for home improvements and repairs to a home and car
- Pre-payment of funeral and burial expenses
- Payments for services under caregiver agreements, even when a child or sibling is the caregiver
- Purchase of certain annuities (Medicaid-compliant annuities are discussed below)

Partnership Programs

Middle-income individuals generally cannot qualify for Medicaid, and generally do not have enough resources to adequately self-insure. The Deficit Reduction Act of 2005 (DRA) created the Qualified State Long Term Care Partnership program to encourage more people to purchase long-term care insurance. Residents of some states may be able to find long-term care coverage through a State Partnership Program that links special Partnership-qualified (PQ) long-term care policies provided by private insurance companies with Medicaid. These Partnership-qualified policies:
- Help people purchase shorter term, more complete long-term care insurance
- Include inflation protection, so the dollar amount of benefits received can be higher than the amount of insurance coverage originally purchased
- Allow people to apply for Medicaid under modified eligibility rules if there is continued need for long-term care after the policy maximum is reached
- Include a special "asset disregard" feature that allows individuals to keep assets like personal savings above the usual $2,000 Medicaid limit

The following example shows how a Partnership-qualified policy works:

Example 7.2

Axel, a single man, purchases a Partnership policy with a value of $100,000. Some years later he receives benefits under that policy up to the policy's lifetime maximum coverage (adjusted for inflation) equaling $150,000.

Axel eventually requires more long-term care services, and applies for Medicaid. If Axel's policy was not a Partnership-qualified policy, in order to qualify for Medicaid, he would be entitled to keep only $2,000 in assets. He would have to spend down any assets over and above this amount.

However, because Axel bought a Partnership-qualified policy, he can keep $152,000 in assets and the state will not recover those funds after his death. Axel would only have to spend down his assets over and above the $152,000 in order to be eligible for Medicaid.

States must certify that partnership policies meet the specific requirements for their partnership program, including that those who sell partnership policies are trained and understand how these policies relate to public and private coverage options.

Only traditional long-term care insurance policies qualify; life insurance and annuity policies with LTC riders (discussed later in this chapter) do not qualify. Not all long-term care insurance (LTCI) policies are partnership-qualified, so it is important to understand the rules of the partnership program within the client's state. Partnership-qualified policies must be tax-qualified, contain certain consumer protections, and must include an inflation adjustment for applicants under age 75 in most states. Since Partnership-qualified policies must include inflation protection, the amount of the benefits received can be higher than the original amount of insurance protection purchased. The insurance company will provide notice in writing, either in a separate letter or in the policy declarations, that the policy is a partnership-qualified policy. If a separate letter is sent, it should be kept in a safe place along with the policy. The state's insurance commission websites may be consulted for state-specific requirements. Individuals who may wish to receive care in a different state, for example, to be closer to children who have moved to another area, should inquire in advance of the purchase whether the states offer reciprocity if the insured moves.

Medicaid Planning and the Look Back Period

The Medicaid program provides coverage for long-term care services for individuals who are unable to afford it. Some individuals, with assistance from financial planners and attorneys, have found ways of arranging assets so that the assets are preserved for the individual and/or family members, but are not countable when Medicaid eligibility is determined. The Deficit Reduction Act of 2005 (DRA) addresses key areas related to transfers of assets for less than fair market value and makes it more difficult for individuals with the resources to pay for their own long-term care services to inappropriately transfer assets in order to qualify for Medicaid.

When an individual applies for Medicaid coverage for long-term care, States conduct a review, or "look-back," to determine whether the individual (or his or her spouse) transferred assets (e.g., cash gifts to children, transferring home ownership) to another person or party for less than fair market value (FMV). When individuals transfer assets at less than the FMV they are subject to a penalty that delays the date they can qualify to receive Medicaid long-term care services. The DRA lengthened the "look-back period" to the 60 months (five years) prior to the date the individual applied for Medicaid.

Previously the penalty period began with the month the assets were transferred. However, under the DRA, the penalty period, for transfers made on or after February 8, 2006, begins on the later of:
1. the date of the asset transfer, or
2. the date the individual enters a nursing home and is found eligible for coverage of institutional level services that Medicaid would pay for were it not for the imposition of a transfer penalty.

The illustration below provides a time line for Medicaid eligibility. A "look-back" period applies to the 60 months prior to applying for Medicaid, while the penalty period begins after the applicant has:
1. filed for Medicaid and moved into the nursing home, and
2. spent down assets to an amount to become eligible for Medicaid.

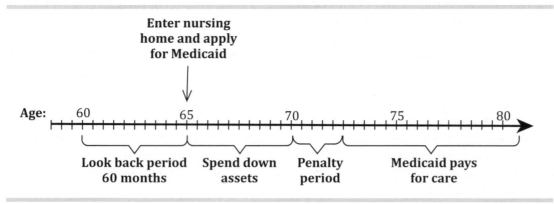

Exhibit 7.9 | Medicaid Eligibility Timeline

The penalty period is calculated by dividing the value of the property transferred by the average monthly cost of a nursing home in the state. If the value of the property transferred was $50,000 and the average monthly cost of nursing home care is $5,000, the penalty period is 10 months ($50,000/$5,000).

Example 7.3

Chenglei gave his two sons gifts of $15,000 each 12 months ago. This year, Chenglei will enter a nursing home that costs $6,000 per month and will apply for Medicaid benefits. He is a widower and has countable assets of $122,000. The average monthly cost of nursing home care in his state is $6,000. The look back period is 60 months, so Chenglei will have a penalty period of five months ($30,000/$6,000 = 5 months) due to the gifts to his two sons.

Medicaid eligibility will not begin until after Chenglei has spent down his countable assets to $2,000. The countable assets will be spent on the nursing home care and will be depleted down to $2,000 after 20 months. The penalty period will apply after his assets have been spent down, resulting in a total of 25 months before Medicaid will begin paying for his care.

Some transfers are permitted even after an individual enters a nursing home. The following transfers can be made without causing a period of Medicaid ineligibility:

- Transfer to a spouse
- Transfer to a child who is blind or disabled
- Transfer in trust for the benefit of a person under age 65 and disabled
- Transfer of a home to a child under the age of 21 or a child who has lived in the home for at least two years before the applicant moved to a nursing home and provided care that enabled the applicant to stay in the home during that time
- Transfer of a home to a sibling who has an equity interest in it and who lived in it at least a year before the applicant moved to a nursing home

Medicaid planning is often undertaken to preserve assets for children or relatives, or to preserve assets for a spouse. It is also done to preserve assets that could be used to enhance care above what is provided for under Medicaid. There is a valid question as to whether Medicaid planning is ethical and/or moral. There are many advisors and attorneys who assist people in transferring assets to qualify for Medicaid benefits. There are also many advisors and attorneys who believe it is unethical and will not engage in this type of planning. Consider the following two examples:

Example 7.4

Barry worked as a plumber since he was 18 years old. He worked hard his entire life and has saved a fair amount of money by not going on vacations, eating at home, and living modestly. He just turned age 65 and has been diagnosed with Alzheimer's disease. He had hoped that he would be able to leave some of his money to his daughter for his grandson's college education. However, he is concerned that he will spend his life's savings on long-term care. He is also concerned that his wife will be without the necessary funds to care for her needs.

Example 7.5

Larry worked as a plumber since he was 18 years old. He worked hard his entire life, but also enjoyed his life by buying expensive cars, vacationing every change he had, and always buying the latest in fashion trends. While he has earned a significant amount of money over his career, he has almost nothing saved and lives in an apartment. He just turned age 65 and has been diagnosed with Alzheimer's disease. He is very concerned about the progressiveness of the disease and the prospect of needing long-term care and not being able to afford it.

Despite the fact that Larry has been at least somewhat irresponsible in terms of spending, he is entitled to Medicaid. From an ethical perspective, the case can be made that Medicaid is designed for the poor and therefore Larry should receive it and Barry should not. This outcome may or may not be palatable. Barry, on the other hand, is left with the choice of spending down his assets (using them for long-term care needs) and then applying for Medicaid or engaging in Medicaid planning.

In Helvering v. Gregory, Judge Learned Hand famously wrote about tax planning: "Any one may so arrange his affairs that his taxes shall be as low as possible; he is not bound to choose that pattern which will best pay the Treasury; there is not even a patriotic duty to increase one's taxes." Considering this quote and the idea of preserving assets for a spouse, one might conclude that Medicaid planning is not unethical. Some might even conclude that Medicaid planning is not only ethical, but also prudent. However, what is certain is that there is an ethical question that must be answered before undertaking this type of planning.

Special Needs Trust
The assets of certain kinds of trusts are not considered for purposes of determining eligibility for Medicaid. These trusts are generally classified as special needs trusts. A **special needs trust** is a specific type of trust that is used to provide benefits to persons or beneficiaries with special needs. Typically, these trusts are established to ensure that benefits available from federal and state agencies are preserved and maintained. The more common special needs trusts are the Third Party Special Needs

Trust, the self settled type trust that is established and exempt under 42 U.S.C. Sec. 1396p(d)(4)(A), and what is referred to as a pooled trust, which is exempt under 42 U.S.C. Sec. 1396p(d)(4)(C).

A third party special needs trust is sometimes referred to as a family trust as the trust is a receptacle for funds from a parent, guardian or other family member. The assets of these trusts, if properly structured, are not counted or considered for purposes of available federal or state benefits for the beneficiary.

These trusts can be funded by a parent or guardian during life or at death and are sometimes funded through the proceeds from a life insurance policy. The funds are contributed to a trust by the grantor or settlor for the benefit of the person with the special needs (beneficiary). The assets were never the property of the beneficiary and are therefore not counted as assets for purposes of federal or state benefits.

The trust must be established so as to not provide food, shelter or any asset that could be converted into food or shelter, such as cash. It may provide for other benefits, such as medical treatment, therapy, education, travel, computer equipment, or other opportunities allowing the individual with special needs to pursue new and enjoyable experiences. These types of benefits can improve the lifestyle of the beneficiary and not interfere with governmental benefits.

The assets of a pooled trust are also ignored for Medicaid purposes. However, these two trusts require that assets remaining in the trust be available for state recovery to the extent that state funds were used to care for the beneficiary.

Medicaid-Compliant Annuities

A "spend down" strategy that can be useful to the spouse of a nursing home resident is the purchase of a Medicaid-compliant (or Medicaid-qualified) annuity. An annuity is a financial product that allows a lump-sum amount to be converted to a guaranteed income stream over a set period of time or based on someone's lifetime, with no access to the principal amount once the income stream is started. The purchase of a Medicaid-compliant annuity is not available in all states and should only be undertaken with an adviser knowledgeable in the use of these annuities. It is not a very useful strategy for unmarried individuals.

✎ Quick Quiz 7.1

1. Long-term care insurance does not cover hospice care.
   a. True
   b. False

2. Because everyone qualifies for Medicaid, long-term care insurance is only for those who want more choices in long-term care than Medicaid offers.
   a. True
   b. False

3. If Bob had a home worth $300,000, it is possible he could qualify for Medicaid.
   a. True
   b. False

4. Paying for long-term care services out of pocket is not a wise choice for anyone.
   a. True
   b. False

5. Activities of daily living include eating, bathing, dressing, transferring, toileting, continence and exercising.
   a. True
   b. False

False, False, True, False, False.

In many states, the purchase of an immediate annuity that pays income to the community spouse is not a gratuitous transfer for purposes of Medicaid eligibility. The payments from the annuity must be made to the community spouse to avoid affecting the Medicaid eligibility of the nursing home resident. It is important that the annuity be immediate (with the income stream beginning immediately) because the purchase of a deferred annuity (one in which the receipt of income is delayed) is not a permitted transfer,

and the deferred annuity will be a countable asset. In addition, for an annuity to avoid being treated as an impermissible transfer it must meet the following requirements:
- It must be irrevocable and non-assignable.
- It must be actuarially sound so the payments over the community spouse's life expectancy will at least equal what was paid for the annuity. If there is a term certain it must be shorter than the community spouse's life expectancy.
- Payments must be in equal amounts with no deferral or balloon payments.
- The state must be named the remainder beneficiary up to the amount of Medicaid payments made for the resident spouse.

The purchase of an immediate annuity will change a countable asset into an income stream for the community spouse. Since the spouse's income is not considered in the determination of Medicaid eligibility, the annuity will not result in any period of ineligibility.

Example 7.6

Karl and Rita Djocavich live in a state where the maximum community spouse resource allowance is $128,640 (2020). Karl is in a nursing home, and has transferred his assets to Rita so she has countable assets of $218,640. Rita can take the excess of $90,000 over her allowance and purchase an annuity. Karl will immediately be eligible for Medicaid, and Rita will receive monthly payments for life from the annuity.

The use of these annuities has been opposed by several states on the grounds that they involve impermissible transfers, but courts have recognized the annuities as part of the overall federal legislative design to assure that the healthy spouse will have sufficient income to remain in the community.

The community spouse can spend the income from the annuity as he or she wishes and can even make gifts or transfers of this income to children or relatives.

Exhibit 7.10 Strategies for Medicaid Eligibility

- Spending down of assets and income
- Transfer of assets to spouse
- Special needs trust
- Medicaid qualified annuity

Estate Recovery

The federal government requires states to try to recover Medicaid costs for long-term care. States generally pursue two approaches to cost recovery: (1) from the deceased individual's estate, and (2) from liens on the individual's property.

The extent to which a state can recover the repayment of Medicare costs from a deceased individual's estate will depend to some extent on the way state law defines an "estate." The definition will determine the type of property the state can recover, and states define the term differently. Some states will limit the property that can be recovered to the deceased person's probate estate. The probate estate includes only the property solely owned by the individual at death. Joint property, life estates, contracts with a named beneficiary, and payable on death accounts are not assets belonging to the probate estate. Other states will define the "estate" to include life insurance and assets in which the individual held an interest at death and which are not included in the probate estate, such as joint tenancy interests or life estates.

States cannot recover Medicaid costs paid for the deceased spouse while the surviving spouse is still living. Assets of surviving spouses are exempt from recovery; however, recovery may be made after the death of the surviving spouse.

Liens can be used to recover Medicaid costs by allowing the state to collect repayment when property is sold. Liens can be placed on real property during the lifetime of the individual receiving Medicaid benefits. The state collects its payment for the Medicaid costs when the property is sold. Liens may be placed on the individual's home, even though it is exempt property for purposes of eligibility. A state may waive recovery and not try to collect repayment where it would cause undue hardship to the deceased's heirs.

Estate recovery for Medicaid benefits can mean that the individual ends up paying for Medicaid expenses after death, even though the individual avoided payment during lifetime. Assets that were exempt during the individual's lifetime, such as a home or a car, are subject to the estate recovery.

THE NEED FOR LONG-TERM CARE INSURANCE

Not everyone will need long-term care services or long-term care insurance. However, as the average age of the United States population is increasing, and as the life expectancy is increasing, the need for both long-term care services and long-term care insurance is also increasing.

Population Statistics for the United States

There are more than 52 million (2018) persons over age 65 in the United States today. This number is expected to increase to over 98 million by 2060. Approximately 70 percent or 36 million will need long-term care services. As of 2020, there were 7.2 million persons receiving Medicaid for the aged.[7]

There are 10.23 million people (2018) who have a net worth (excluding housing) equal to or greater than $1 million.[8] These higher net-worth persons can be presumed to be able to self-insure against the risk of long-term care needs, as long as the wealth is liquid or able to be liquidated to cover long-term care expenses. A large portion of the remainder will not qualify for Medicaid and are not sufficiently wealthy to self-insure against the risk of needing long-term care services.

> ### ⋮☰ *Key Concepts*
>
> 1. Understand the U.S. population long-term care statistics.
>
> 2. Explain the various factors that influence the need for long-term care.
>
> 3. Identify the primary issues involved in choosing to purchase long-term care insurance.

---

7. www.medicaid.gov
8. https://spectrem.com/Content_Press/press-release-spectrem-groups-2019-market-insights-report.aspx.

Example 7.7

Apollo and Adrian met while living in a retirement community in Florida. Apollo, who is 6'2" and over 200 pounds, was a ship captain on the great lakes. Adrian, who is 5'2", was a welder. They were married 20 years ago when Adrian was 75 years old and Apollo was 70. Today, they live in a retirement complex in South Florida that offers independent living, assisted living, as well as skilled care and rehab services. Apollo, who can see partially but is legally blind, has recently developed dementia and has urinary incontinence. At 95, Adrian is incapable of caring for Apollo. He needs help getting in and out of bed, getting dressed, and is unaware of his circumstances. However, Apollo is perfectly healthy otherwise and is expected to live for another five years or more. Apollo needs long-term care but does not have long-term care insurance. They have approximately $400,000 in savings. Based on their assets, he is unlikely to qualify for Medicaid and will have to spend his assets for care. Given the cost of care and his life expectancy, he may outlive their resources. In addition, he is likely to spend the money that would have been used to provide for Adrian.

While many people spend down their assets to meet Medicaid thresholds, many others should consider purchasing long-term care insurance. Their alternative is to self-insure and risk financial disaster. The risk of financial disaster is not only applicable to the spouse who is in need of long-term care services, but also the other spouse who may live for many years and be in desperate need of financial resources. It is important to consider the needs of both spouses when making the decision to purchase LTC insurance.

Factors that Influence the Need for Long-Term Care Insurance

Long-term care insurance helps protect accumulated assets against the risk of the high cost of extended long-term care. Long-term care insurance makes economic sense if the person has assets to protect. Otherwise, the individual would qualify for Medicaid. Those who have assets that they intend to bequeath to heirs or preserve for a spouse should consider long-term care insurance.

If long-term care insurance is not affordable, a person might be better off simply spending down his or her assets to qualify for Medicaid. To decide whether long-term care insurance is appropriate, one should consider personal risk factors as well as financial considerations.

Personal Risk Factors

Personal risk factors include life expectancy, gender, family situation, and family health history.

Life Expectancy

The longer a person lives, the more likely he is to need long-term care services. An evaluation of the immediate and surrounding family for a tendency for long life expectancy will help to clarify this factor.

If a person is expected to have a long life expectancy (perhaps due to family history or current health status), long-term care insurance should be considered. In fact, the longer the person's life expectancy, the greater the need for long-term care insurance. Recall that 37 percent of adults over the age of 65 will need nursing home care at some point during their lifetimes. The general health of the family should also be considered. If older family members suffer from health ailments that are likely to require nursing home care, such as Alzheimer's disease or senile dementia, the person's risk of developing one of these conditions might be greater than average, suggesting a greater need for long-term care insurance.

Gender

Women are much more likely to need long-term care insurance than are men, because women have longer life expectancies.

Family Situation

If a person has a spouse, adult children, or other family members who can and will care for them at home, he or she may not need a long-term care insurance policy that pays for home health services. Instead, such a person may want to consider a long-term care policy that pays only for facility-based services such as assisted living and skilled nursing care. In addition to the policy, however, significant funds may need to be set aside to provide for costs incurred to outfit the home for the level of care that may be needed. Adding features such hand rails in the bathrooms are not overly expensive, but other adjustments such as wheel chair ramps or stair lifts, widening hallways to fit a wheelchair, and moving bedrooms and bathrooms to the first floor can be substantial. Some long-term care insurance policies provide limited benefits for home modification.

Assuming that a family member will be able to provide care at the time it is needed should be approached with caution. In a perfect world, we might plan for a spouse or child to provide any care that is needed; unfortunately, many events and circumstances can undermine such plans. Most long-term care needs arise later in life, when the spouse and adult children are retired and may be dealing with health issues of their own. Family members may be prevented from providing the care that is needed on a daily basis. Children who are healthy enough to provide the care may be in a different geographic region or may be in the peak earning years of their careers. Asking those children to become full-time caregivers may require asking them to give up their careers and their own retirement security, and they may even need to sell their homes and move, or make room for the parents in the child's home. Moreover, providing care on a full-time basis is both physically and emotionally strenuous, and can have a negative impact on the relationships among family members. When family-provided care is the plan of choice it is wise for the financial planner to host a family meeting with all of those involved to discuss putting a plan in place and ensure that every member of the family understands what is expected of them and can choose to commit to the plan as outlined or suggest that an alternative plan be discussed. Documentation of the meeting, those in attendance, the alternatives discussed, and agreement or disagreement to the suggested plan is a good business practice. Unfortunately, even if everyone is in agreement at the time the plan is discussed, outside events such as the onset of diseases or ailments that prevent the intended caregiver from having the ability to provide the agreed-upon care are possible, so having a back-up plan is also recommended. Long-term care insurance can overcome many of the potential problems associated with reliance on family to provide care.

Family Health History

A person may have a probability of greater need for long-term care if chronic or debilitating health conditions historically run in the family.

Financial Considerations

Long-term care premiums are typically less expensive if a policy is purchased when the insured is younger. The premiums are usually paid until death or until benefits have begun. However, some policies have paid up provisions (e.g., paid up in 20 years). When considering the payment of long-term care insurance premiums, one should consider how current and retirement income will be affected by the payments. It is beneficial to forecast the likely increase in premium costs caused by waiting until a later age to purchase a long-term care insurance policy. Many financial and insurance professionals suggest that the optimal time to purchase a long-term care policy is between the ages of 55 and 65.

The person's financial status is also an important factor when considering long-term care insurance. If long-term care services are needed, and the person does not have sufficient insurance to cover the costs, the person's assets may have to be liquidated

Persons with relatively low net worth and low income may not be able to afford long-term care insurance premiums. Long-term care insurance premiums can be expensive, particularly at older ages, and if the premium represents a significant portion of the person's net worth or income, it may not be an appropriate risk management tool. People with lower amounts of assets have less to lose by self-insuring. Once their assets are depleted, they may be able to qualify for long-term care coverage through Medicaid. One thing to keep in mind, though, is that many middle-class senior citizens have sacrificed some retirement savings to pay for children to attend college. Those children who are now prospering in their careers may be more than willing to fund the cost of long-term care insurance for their parents. The child may want the peace of mind from knowing that a parent can be cared for in a high-quality care facility or at home, whichever is most desirable, and alleviate the difficult position the child might otherwise have to face in choosing between caring for parents or continuing a career.

Quick Quiz 7.2

1. More than 50 million people in the United States are over the age of 65.
   a. True
   b. False

2. Medicaid pays for approximately 80 percent of the nation's nursing home expenditures.
   a. True
   b. False

3. Men are more likely to need long-term care insurance than women.
   a. True
   b. False

4. Important factors in determining a need for long-term care insurance include the health of the person, the life expectancy of the person and the person's financial situation.
   a. True
   b. False

True, False, False, True.

Persons with moderate and above levels of net worth may wish to protect those assets for the benefit of family members (spouse and descendants), and therefore may not want to spend down assets to pay for long-term care needs. Long-term care insurance may be an appropriate solution for these persons, since the risk of paying for long-term care needs is transferred to an insurance company in return for premium payments. Moderate to high net worth clients with significant bequest motives should also consider long-term care insurance as a risk transfer tool.

Some planners believe that wealthy individuals do not need long-term care insurance because they can afford to self-insure and still transfer some of their assets to their heirs. Because long-term care insurance premiums, particularly at older ages, are perceived to be expensive, risk retention is viewed as one alternative choice. However, it may be prudent for high net worth individuals to purchase and maintain long-term care insurance, particularly when bequest motives are strong. In order to self-insure, the person would have to retain sufficient assets to pay for care over an extended period of time, and those assets would have to be retained until death since many long-term care expenses are often incurred shortly before death. By retaining assets to self-insure against long-term care risk, the person cannot transfer those assets to family members as part of a lifetime gifting strategy. This approach could result in higher gift and estate tax consequences for the family upon the person's death.

Exhibit 7.11 | Who Should Buy Long-Term Care Insurance - Financial Considerations

Low Net Worth	Long-term care insurance premiums may be unaffordable; likely to qualify for Medicaid. However, children with higher income or net worth may desire to pay long-term care insurance premiums to provide protection for the parents.
Moderate Net Worth	Good candidates for long-term care insurance, especially if they have wealth transfer goals or want to ensure the ability to choose the care provider or facility.
High Net Worth	Likely able to self-insure but may desire to purchase long-term care insurance to protect assets for wealth transfer goals.

Paying long-term care premiums so that the insurance company will cover those costs will free-up assets that can be used for transfer tax planning purposes and may result in significant savings of gift and estate taxes. Instead of considering the long-term care premiums solely in dollar terms, it may be practical for higher net worth individuals to consider the premiums as a percentage of their asset portfolio being protected with the long-term care insurance premiums. If the dollar amount of the premium is high, but that dollar amount only represents a small amount of assets when compared to the size of the person's asset base, incurring the premium to protect the entire asset base may be reasonable, and doing so may also create an opportunity for gift and estate planning. In addition, premium payments reduce a person's estate, which may be beneficial from a transfer tax perspective.

Exhibit 7.12 | Strategies to Manage the Cost of Long-Term Care Insurance Premium

Shop extensively
Apply while young
Reduce benefits
Manage daily limits
Manage lifetime benefits
Manage COLA 3% flat vs 5% compound

One final consideration when determining whether or not to purchase long-term care insurance is whether the person wishes to retain the ability to choose care providers. If a person decides not to purchase long-term care insurance and self-insures, he or she can go on public assistance (Medicaid) once his or her assets are spent down. However, the person will receive care at the facility where the first bed becomes available. There is great disparity in the quality of care at various locations, particularly when considering long-term care services. If the person relies on public assistance to pay for these costs, he or she loses the ability to choose the facility where care will be provided. Individuals who purchase long-term care insurance, however, have a choice in the care provider, and can ensure that they will receive a higher quality of care. For some people, having the ability to choose the care provider is a more important consideration than preserving assets for family members or avoiding taxes and should be considered when developing a comprehensive financial plan.

While many nursing homes are adequate, many others have serious deficiencies. The Centers for Medicare & Medicaid Services (CMS) contracts with state survey agencies to conduct inspections, known as standard surveys, and complaint investigations to determine whether nursing homes are complying with federal quality standards. Nursing homes must meet those standards to participate in Medicare and Medicaid. GAO (Government Accountability Office) reports have found that some nursing homes are chronically noncompliant; that is, they have been cited repeatedly by state survey agencies for serious deficiencies such as residents having preventable pressure sores that harmed them or put them at risk of death or serious injury. It is important to research facilities before choosing one for a loved one.

While there is a strong case for long-term care insurance, only about seven million Americans have currently own long-term care insurance policies. Long-term care insurance, like any other financial services product, is not right for everyone. The general rule of thumb is that LTCI premiums should be no more than seven percent of income, although this rule will vary from client-to-client depending on other expenses, such as medical insurance, housing expenses, and other out-of-pocket expenses. The effect of potential increases in premium must also be factored in to the decision-making process.

Exhibit 7.13 | Long-Term Care Insurance Claims 2018

Percentage of new claims started at age 81 or older	69.7%
Total claims paid (in 2018)	$10.3 billion
Most expensive claim (still ongoing)	$2.6 million
Number of claimants (in 2018)	303,000
Percentage of claims that ended as a result of exhausting benefits	13.5%
Percentage of claims that ended as a result of death	72.5%
Claim started with home care	51.5%
Claim started with assisted living facility	24.5%
Claim started with nursing home care	23.0%

Source: https://www.aaltci.org/long-term-care-insurance/learning-center/ltcfacts-2019.php#2019buyers

LONG-TERM CARE INSURANCE

As with other financial services products, long-term care insurance has many aspects that must be considered before choosing to purchase a long-term care policy. The various aspects of long-term care insurance policies are discussed below.

When designing a long-term care plan which includes LTC insurance for a client, the planner should discuss with the client all of the following details:
- Factors that affect LTC policy premiums (discussed in detail later in this chapter)
- Partnership program coordination
- Liquid assets available to pay for care
- Desirability of asset protection for heirs
- Family history
- Client risk tolerance/aversion

HIPAA Rules and NAIC Model Legislation

Long-term care insurance is a relatively new insurance product in that it has only been available for about 40 years (versus life insurance, which has been around for hundreds of years). When reviewing existing policies, it is important to understand that some significant changes have come about in the way policies are structured, and policies issued prior to 1997 are likely to have coverage gaps. Some of the early private LTCI policies provided benefits only if the insured person required skilled nursing care. If the physician would not certify that the insured needed skilled nursing care, the insured person would not be eligible for benefits to cover the cost of a long-term care facility. Most people prefer to receive care at home for as long as possible.

In the late 1980's, the National Association of Insurance Commissioners (NAIC) created a Long-Term Care Insurance Model Act to establish standards for long-term care insurance policies, to protect applicants from unfair or deceptive sales practices, and to facilitate public understanding and comparison among LTCI policies. The model legislation has been updated frequently throughout the years, and most states have adopted it in some form.

The Health Insurance Portability and Accountability Act (HIPAA) of 1996 led the way to much more comprehensive policies and added a number of requirements that are a great benefit to insureds and policy owners. Most policies issued today will be HIPAA-qualified policies and will, therefore, qualify for certain tax advantages (discussed later in this chapter). HIPAA contains the following requirements for long-term care insurance policies (details of these requirements will be discussed later):

1. A requirement that policies be either noncancellable or, at least, guaranteed renewable.
2. A maximum limit of six months on the time during which preexisting conditions may be excluded, together with a maximum look-back period of six months, relating to pre-existing conditions.
3. Limitations on exclusions in long-term care insurance policies.
4. Requirements for continuation or conversion for those who are covered under group policies.
5. A requirement that someone other than the policyholder receive a notice of policy termination due to nonpayment of premium, as well as a requirement that a lapsed policy be reinstated if proof of cognitive impairment or loss of functional capacity is provided to the insurer as the reason for the lapse.
6. Prohibition of post-claims underwriting.
7. Minimum standards applicable to benefits for home health care and community health care.
8. A requirement that specified inflation protection benefits be offered.
9. Prohibition of policies requiring prior hospitalization or prior institutionalization in order to qualify for nursing home care, as well as prohibition of requiring prior nursing home care in order to qualify for home health care benefits.
10. A requirement that a nonforfeiture benefit be made available.

The Health Insurance Portability and Accountability Act of 1996 also provides the following consumer protection standards relating to long-term care insurance companies:

1. A requirement that insurers establish a process to ensure against inappropriate replacement of existing long-term care insurance policies.
2. A requirement that insurers report lapse rates, replacement sales, and denied claims each year.
3. A requirement that advertising materials used by insurance companies be filed with the state regulatory authority.
4. A requirement that insurers establish marketing standards to prevent twisting, high-pressure sales tactics, and "cold lead" advertising.
5. A requirement that agents make reasonable efforts to determine the appropriateness of a recommended policy for the individual insured.
6. A requirement that prospective purchasers be given an outline of coverage, as well as an approved shopper's guide.

7. A requirement that group certificates include a description of the policy's principal benefits and exclusions.
8. A requirement that a full refund of premium be paid up to 30 days after the policy is purchased, if requested.
9. A requirement concerning disclosure and reporting for accelerated death benefits that are subject to the NAIC's Long-Term Care Insurance Model Act and Regulation.
10. A requirement of a defined incontestability period, as well as a requirement that conditions be spelled out for rescission of the policy by the insurance company.

Eligibility and Underwriting

Some insurance companies have a minimum age of 40 for writing LTCI policies, but many will write policies beginning at age 18 or at any age. Most companies have a maximum age of approximately 84 to 89 years for issuing a policy.

While the health of the insured is important for underwriting long-term care policies, planners will find that underwriting considerations for LTCI are unique in comparison to underwriting for other types of insurance, such as life or disability. Insurers may make use of cognitive questionnaires in addition to physical exams since cognitive impairment is one of the most important issues for LTCI. Depending on a client's age and history, this may be as simple as a telephone interview, or may require an in-person interview.

Underwriters are also likely to be more concerned with an applicant's physiological age (age as measured by health and function) than chronological age (number of years since birth). Musculoskeletal issues (such as osteoporosis) and recent physical therapy can throw up red flags, as can combinations of medical histories, such as diabetes combined with heart disease. Even something as simple as taking multiple medications may cause the underwriter to seek additional information because of the potential for drug interactions that may adversely affect intellectual capacity or physical ability. Some insurance companies may be more liberal than others in underwriting certain conditions, so it may be beneficial to review policies from several different insurers. Some insurance companies will also offer preferred health discounts.

Most policies specify that benefits will not be paid for a preexisting condition for which treatment was recommended or received within six months of the purchase of the coverage, or for alcohol or drug addictions within two years of the purchase of coverage.

The best age at which to purchase a policy is often in the 50's to early 60's when the client is likely to be healthy enough to qualify, premiums will be low, and preferred health discounts may be available. In 2019, 44 percent of applications of those age 70-74 were declined, but only 21 percent of applications for those age 50-59 were declined.[9]

Some companies will also offer premium discounts if both spouses purchase policies, and some companies allow spouses to use "shared benefits." For example, if each spouse purchased a policy providing benefits for two years, and spouse 1 needed care and used up all of his or her two years of benefits, he or she could then draw against the benefits from spouse 2's policy (assuming he or she was

9. https://www.aaltci.org/long-term-care-insurance/learning-center/ltcfacts-2019.php#2019buyers

not yet using his or her benefits). When working with married clients, it is important to ask the insurer whether discounts for shared benefits are available.

Long-Term Care Premium Factors

Long-term care premiums are initially based on several factors including the amount and duration of coverage selected, age, gender, the health of the person insured, the area in which he or she lives, and the elimination period.[10] Married applicants may be offered lower premium rates due to the potentially shorter duration of claims, because the spouse is able to provide care for a period of time. Premium pricing is further affected by inflation and other riders added to the policy.

Exhibit 7.14 | Long-Term Care Premium Variable

Age and Gender
Benefits (amount and duration)
Health Characteristics
Geographical Location
Elimination Periods
Inflation Protection
Additional Riders

Exhibit 7.15 | Common Features of Long-Term Care Insurance Policies

Renewability - Guaranteed renewability
Nonforfeitures Benefits - Return of Premium or Shortened Benefit Period
Waiver of premium while receiving benefits

The policy premium is directly related to the age and gender of the insured, the benefits provided and inflation protection. As the age of the insured increases, so does the premium. Since 2013, LTC insurance companies are charging higher premiums for women, since more benefits are historically paid to women than to men. As the benefits increase, so does the premium. Inflation protection also increases the premium. The elimination period, however, is inversely related. As the elimination period (the period between being eligible medically and when benefits begin) increases, the premium will decrease.

Long-Term Care Insurance Features and Benefits

Long-term care insurance has a variety of features and benefits that are important to understand. Some of these features and benefits are mandatory, while others are optional. Below is a discussion of these characteristics.

Renewals and Cancellations

Long-term care policies are **guaranteed renewable**. This means the insurance company must renew the policy each year as long as premiums are paid. Policies can be canceled by the policy owner at any

---

10. LTC insurance companies began charging higher premiums for women in 2013 due to the higher likelihood of needing the benefits. Genworth Financial, the first company to begin charging women higher premiums, states that women receive approximately 67 percent of LTC benefits.

time by notifying the insurance company. Unearned premium payments are returned if the policy is canceled. Premiums are paid on a monthly, quarterly, or annual basis. In some states, unearned premium return does not apply to a single premium policy or to policies that are paid in full in one to four years. Even policies that are paid in full from five to 10 years are subject to a return of premium provision.

After a long-term care policy has been in force for a period of two years, the insurer cannot cancel and cannot refuse to pay claims because there was incorrect information provided in the application unless that information is fraudulent. If the policy has been in force for less than two years, the insurer can deny a valid claim or cancel the policy if it can prove fraud or intentional misrepresentation of a material fact.

The insurance company is permitted to increase premiums for a guaranteed renewable policy, as long as it is an increase for the entire class of insureds and is approved by the state's Insurance Commission. Clients and planners should be aware of the possibility of a rate increase. In 2012 many insurers applied for and received permission to increase rates on LTCI policies by as much as 40 percent. These increases were necessary at the time due to the limited claims history available when the policies were first sold and priced many years before. Insurance companies found that they had underestimated the size of the claims and overestimated lapse rates (the expected number of policies that insureds would allow to lapse due to a change of mind about retaining the coverage). New policies purchased today are priced higher based on the new information that has become available over these past 40 years. While such large increases are not expected to be typical going forward, it is worth doing some research in advance of the purchase of a policy. Some state insurance departments provide historical information regarding rate increases for the various insurance companies permitted to sell LTCI policies within the state, and some states require the rate increase history for the past 10 years to be provided to the applicant prior to issuing the policy. The insurance company can also provide its historical premium increase information upon request or may make it available online.

> ## ⋮☰ *Key Concepts*
>
> 1. Identify the factors that affect premiums for long-term care insurance.
>
> 2. Explain the type of benefits provided under long-term care policies.
>
> 3. Contrast tax-qualified contracts from those that are not qualified.
>
> 4. Recognize required and optional features of long-term care policies.
>
> 5. Provide examples of the ways benefit limits may be specified in a long-term care policy.

Types of Care

While long-term care insurance policies are often viewed as policies that cover skilled nursing home costs, the benefits provided under the policy are generally much more extensive, including custodial care, home health care, hospice care, adult day care, assisted living facilities, and other long-term care services.

Skilled Nursing Care

Skilled nursing care refers to a level of care that includes services that can only be performed safely and correctly by a licensed nurse (either a registered nurse or a licensed practical nurse), doctor or therapist. Inpatient care refers to healthcare for those admitted to a hospital or skilled nursing facility.

Custodial Care

Custodial care refers to non-skilled, personal care, such as help with activities of daily living (eating, bathing, transferring, dressing, toileting, and continence). A healthy individual with a cognitive impairment, for example, may not need constant medical attention, but may need assistance so that he or she does not pose a risk to himself, herself, or others.

Home Heath Care

If given the choice, most individuals prefer to live at home rather than move into a nursing home. Most long-term care policies will pay for the cost of care provided at home (referred to as a **home health care benefit**). Home heath care may encompass limited part-time or intermittent skilled nursing care and home health aide services, physical therapy, occupational therapy, speech-language pathology services, medical social services, durable medical equipment (such as wheelchairs, hospital beds, oxygen, and walkers), medical supplies, and other services provided in the patient's home.

Hospice Care

For individuals with incurable illnesses who are in the terminal stages of life, long-term care insurance policies typically pay for the cost of hospice care. **Hospice care** typically utilizes a team-oriented approach to address medical, physical, social, emotional, and spiritual needs of the terminally ill. Hospice also provides support to the patient's family or caregiver. Hospice care is generally short-term, supportive care for individuals who have a life expectancy of six months or less. Hospice care does not provide therapeutic treatment (treatment designed to cure the individual of their condition), but rather provides pain management treatment and psychological and spiritual support services for patients to permit them to die with dignity and comfort. Hospice services, under most policies, can be provided in a dedicated hospice facility, in a hospital, or at the recipient's home.

Adult Day Care Services

A policy may pay for **adult day-care** services. Individuals needing supervision who live with other family members may not need assistance 24 hours a day. Adult day care facilities provide supervision during the day at a community-based center while caretaker family members are at work. Programs address the individual needs of functionally or cognitively impaired adults. These structured, comprehensive programs provide social and support services in a protective setting during any part of a day, but not 24-hour care. Many adult day service programs include health-related services. Given the opportunity, insurance companies prefer to pay for lower-cost alternatives rather than pay for skilled nursing or custodial care.

Assisted Living Facility

A policy may pay for all or part of the costs of an **assisted living facility**. An assisted living facility is a residential living arrangement that provides individualized personal care, assistance with activities of daily living, help with medications, and services such as laundry and housekeeping. Facilities may also provide health and medical care, but care is not as intensive as care offered at a nursing home. Types and sizes of facilities vary, ranging from small homes to large apartment-style complexes. Levels of care and services also vary. Assisted living facilities allow people to remain relatively independent.

Long-Term Care Services

Long-term care services include medical and non-medical care for people with chronic illnesses or disabilities. Most long-term care services assist people with activities of daily living. Long-term care services can be provided at home, in the community, or in a facility. For purposes of Medicaid eligibility and payment, long-term care services are those provided to an individual who requires a level of care equivalent to that received in a nursing facility.

Skilled Care and Immediate Care Facilities

A **skilled care facility** provides the highest level of service combining both daily medical and custodial care. An **intermediate-care nursing facility** typically provides custodial care along with intermittent, as opposed to daily, medical care. Services in either a skilled-care or intermediate-care facility are ordered by a physician, and medical treatments are provided under the supervision of a physician.

Coverage

A long-term care policy may pay different dollar amounts for different types of long-term care services. Policies usually pay benefits by the day, week, or month. For example, a policy that pays with the **expense - incurred method** might pay a daily nursing home benefit of up to $200, a weekly benefit of up to $1,400, or a monthly benefit of up to $6,000. The advantage of a monthly benefit period is that the policyholder may receive higher benefits. Consider the following example.

Example 7.8

Mike, who recently had surgery, has a long-term care policy and uses his home healthcare benefit to have a licensed aide assist him at home three times each week. Each visit costs $400. If Mike has a daily benefit of $150, he would have to pay $250 out of pocket for each visit. This cost is approximately $3,000 for an entire 30 day month. However, with a monthly benefit of $4,500, his out of pocket cost would only be $300 (12 x $400 = $4,800 - $4,500 = $300). As a result, daily benefit policies are generally cheaper.

If a policy covers home healthcare, the benefit is usually a percentage of the benefit for skilled nursing home care. For example, a policy with a $200 per day benefit for skilled nursing home care may only pay $100 per day for home healthcare. However, many policies pay the same benefit amount for home care as for skilled nursing home care.

An insured can usually choose the benefit amounts. It is important that the insured knows the cost of skilled nursing care, assisted living homes, and home healthcare in the local market before choosing benefit amounts.

Most long-term care policies limit the total amount of benefits that can be paid over the life of the policy. Some policies state the maximum benefit limit in terms of years. Other policies state the maximum benefit limit in terms of dollars. The maximum benefit limit is referred to as the **maximum lifetime benefit** or the **total plan benefit**.

While most skilled nursing home stays are relatively short, there are some illnesses (Alzheimer's) that can last several years or longer. Therefore, selecting the appropriate total amount of coverage or the appropriate term of coverage is important. In general, policies with longer maximum benefit periods provide higher policy limits and are more expensive.

Services Not Covered by Long-Term Care Insurance

Long-term care insurance policies may exclude coverage for some conditions, either completely or for a limited period. Policies typically exclude:

- **Pre-existing conditions.** A pre-existing condition is an illness or disability for which an insured has received previous medical advice or treatment usually within six months prior to the application for long-term care coverage. A long-term care policy may delay coverage on a pre-existing condition for up to six months after the policy's effective date for coverage.
- **Mental and nervous disorders.** Long-term care insurance policies can exclude coverage of some mental and nervous disorders but the policy must cover serious biologically-based mental illnesses and other diseases, such as schizophrenia, major depression disorders, Alzheimer's disease, and other age-related disorders. However, a long-term care insurer may refuse to sell a policy to someone already suffering from these otherwise covered exclusions.
- **Care provided by family members or loved ones.** Many long-term care policies will not pay members of the family of the insured to provide care to the insured. However, some policies will pay to train family members to be caregivers or may provide "respite care" to give the caregiver a "break."

State-Specific Exclusions

Various states permit long-term care insurance policies to exclude coverage for conditions resulting from:

- alcoholism and drug addiction
- suicide, attempted suicide, or self-inflicted injuries
- participation in a riot, felony, or insurrection
- war or an act of war whether declared or undeclared
- service in the Armed Forces
- aviation activities, if the insured was not a fare paying passenger on a commercial airline

Long-term care policies will not pay for care that is covered under a government program. The exceptions are Medicaid and expenses that Medicare pays as a secondary payor.

Optional Features of Long-Term Care Insurance (Required to be Offered)

Issuers of long-term care policies must offer inflation protection and a nonforfeiture benefit, but probably will charge extra for those features.

Inflation Protection

It is likely to be years after purchasing the policy before the insured needs long-term care services. During that time, long-term care costs could increase significantly. **Inflation protection** helps the insured to maintain the purchasing power of the original contract benefit. The younger the insured, the more important inflation protection. Long-term care policies must offer inflation protection in at least one of the following ways:

1. benefits automatically increasing by five percent or more each year compounded annually,
2. the policy limits increase three percent compound annually, or
3. the policy limits increase at five percent level per year.

In lieu of automatic inflation protection, some companies offer a **Guaranteed Purchase Option** or a Guaranteed Future Purchase Option which allows the insured to increase the benefits by a stated percentage periodically. The down side to this approach is that the premium increases as the benefit is increased and the right to purchase future increases may be lost if one or more purchase options are not taken.

An insured must be provided with a graphical comparison of benefits for a policy with and without inflation protection for a 20-year period. If the insured does not want inflation protection, it must be rejected in writing. The exhibit below illustrates inflation over the period from 2009 to 2019.

Exhibit 7.16 | Consumer Price Index

Consumer Price Index (CPI) All Urban Consumers (All Items)	
Year	Annual
2009	2.7%
2010	1.5%
2011	3.0%
2012	1.7%
2013	1.5%
2014	0.8%
2015	0.7%
2016	2.1%
2017	2.1%
2018	2.4%
2019	1.8%
CPI Increase	
1.85% average 2009-2019	

Source: Bureau of Labor Statistics

Non-forfeiture Benefit

The insurer must offer to guarantee that the insured will receive some of the benefits for which the premium was paid, even upon cancellation or lapse of the policy. This guarantee, which can be rejected, is called a **non-forfeiture benefit**. The longer premiums are paid, the larger the non-forfeiture benefit will be. A non-forfeiture benefit will generally be the greater of the total amount of premiums paid or 30 times the daily skilled nursing home benefit at the time the policy lapsed.

Policies with non-forfeiture benefits are more expensive than policies without them. To reject the non-forfeiture benefit the rejection must be made in writing, and the insurer will explain its contingent non-forfeiture benefit. The contingent non-forfeiture benefit comes into being when an insurance company increases premiums to a certain level. At that point, the insured can either choose a reduced benefit amount to prevent premium increases or convert the policy to a paid-up policy. If the insured fails to make an election, the insurance company can change the policy to a paid-up status if that period is longer than 120 days. The paid-up benefit will be the greater of the total sum of premiums paid for the policy or 30 times the daily skilled nursing home benefit at the time the policy lapsed.

Optional Benefits (May or May Not Be Offered)

Several optional benefits may be offered with the purchase of a long-term care insurance policy. Some of these are waiver of premium, refund of premium, restoration of benefits, and bed reservation.

Waiver of Premium

Many policies include a waiver of premium provision. This provision allows the insured to stop paying premiums during the period in which they are receiving policy benefits. However, this provision may only apply to certain benefits, for example, nursing home or home healthcare.

Refund of Premium

The company will refund some or all of the insured's premiums minus any claims paid under the policy if the policy is canceled. The insured's beneficiary will receive such refund if the insured dies.

Restoration of Benefits

Long-term care policies have a maximum benefit amount. Often, policies will restore the maximum benefit amount in the event that the insured receives benefits, then recovers and does not receive benefits again for a specific period of time, often 180 days.

Example 7.9

Sallie has a policy with a maximum benefit of $100,000. She has already received $30,000 in benefits. Her remaining benefit maximum would be $70,000. If she does not receive additional benefits for a specified period of time, her maximum benefit can be restored to the original $100,000 if she has a restoration of benefits rider.

Bed Reservation

Some policies will pay to reserve a bed in the nursing home when the insured leaves the facility for a period of time, such as to go into a hospital. This reservation can last a specified number of days or until the insured returns from the hospital. The reason for a bed reservation benefit is that the cost of an empty bed at a facility is high, and many high-quality skilled and intermediate care facilities have waiting lists of individuals who would like to move into the facility when a bed opens up. This demand means that if a resident leaves the facility for a period of time, perhaps to spend a couple of weeks at home with family over the holidays or due to hospitalization, there is a risk that the facility will place another patient in the open bed, or the family will be required to continue to pay out-of-pocket to reserve the bed. The bed reservation benefit allows for the institutionalized individual to have a short-term absence without fear of losing his or her place in the institution. Bed reservation benefits are typically limited to 15 or 30 days.

Respite Care

Serving as a caregiver can be very mentally, emotionally, and physically challenging. Caregivers often experience depression and a decline in physical health. It is important for the caregiver to have a respite from providing care on a regular basis. Most modern long-term care policies provide respite care as a covered service.

Shared Benefits

Policies that have this benefit permit a person who has fully exhausted the benefits under his or her own policy to make use of the benefits available under his or her spouse's policy.

The optional benefits above are examples of benefits that may or may not be offered by a specific carrier. There are certainly other optional benefits that may be offered in addition to the ones listed above.

Exhibit 7.17 | Important Coverages in Long-Term Care Policies

Coverage for Alzheimer's Disease
At least one year of nursing home and/or home health care coverage, not limited primarily to skilled care
Inflation protection
No requirement to first be hospitalized to receive benefits

Long-Term Care Benefit Periods (Benefit Multiplier)

Long-term care insurance policies provide coverage for long-term care costs in one of two ways:
- benefits are provided for a fixed period of time, or
- a fixed dollar amount is available for the payment of long-term care benefits.

Policies that provide coverage for a defined benefit period may specify the maximum number of months or years for which coverage will be provided, or may provide coverage for the life of the insured once the need for long-term care services is established and the elimination period has been met.

Persons who are relatively conservative, or who have family histories indicating that they may be prone to non-life threatening diseases requiring long-term care services (such as Alzheimer's disease and senile dementia), may wish to choose policies that provide lifetime coverage although lifetime benefits are becoming increasingly rare.

Persons who are willing to retain more risk to themselves and whose family histories indicate that they are not prone to long-term debilitating diseases may wish to choose a shorter coverage period, such as three or five years. The average stay in a nursing home is approximately 2.4 years, but there is no guarantee that the persons will fall into the average category.

Long-term care policies that specify a maximum benefit payment amount may also be appropriate, depending on the client circumstances. Once the maximum benefit amount has been distributed, the long-term care policy will not pay for additional care. The dollar limit should be chosen carefully by the planner and client after considering the client's health, family history, and preferences.

Tax-Qualified Long-Term Care Contracts

Most traditional long-term care policies issued today are tax-qualified contracts, however, combination life insurance/long-term care and annuity/long-term care policies (discussed later in this chapter) are not tax qualified. Tax-qualified implies that the long-term care insurance policy is treated as health insurance for federal income tax purposes and is therefore deductible on income tax returns either as self-employed health insurance (an above-the-line, or adjustment to income deduction), or as a medical expense itemized deduction subject to the adjusted gross income hurdle (below-the-line deduction). If long-term care insurance premiums are paid for by an employer, the employer may deduct the premium cost as an employee benefit, and the employees will not be required to report the value received in their incomes for the year. Long-term care contracts cannot, however, be provided as a benefit under cafeteria plans.

To meet the definition of a tax-qualified contract, the long-term care insurance policy:[11]
1. must provide benefits that are limited to long-term care services (exception for per diem policies)
2. does not provide a cash surrender value or access to funds that can be paid, assigned, borrowed, or pledged as collateral for a loan
3. provides that refunds may be used only to reduce future premium payments or increase future policy benefits
4. must meet consumer protection standards defined in the Health Insurance Portability and Accountability Act of 1997 (HIPPA)
5. must coordinate benefits with Medicare
6. must offer a nonforfeiture benefit
7. must be guaranteed renewable

Policies issued after January 1, 1997 that are tax qualified will typically have a statement on the declarations page of the policy identifying it as a tax-qualified policy.

Long-term care contracts that do not meet the above requirements are not considered to be tax qualified, and will not permit the policy owner to take a tax deduction for premium payments made on the policy. The maximum deductible long-term care premium (under IRC § 213(d)(10)), which is a deduction for medical expenses, depends on the age of the insured. The same dollar limits apply to self-insured individuals (sole proprietors, partners in a partnership, S corporation owners, and LLC members), although self-employed individuals get the advantage of deducting premiums above-the line. These limits are reflected for 2020 in **Exhibit 7.18 | Maximum Long-Term Care Premium Tax Deduction (2020)**.

In addition to the tax advantage of deductible premiums, benefits received from LTCI policies are generally tax-free. Benefits from reimbursement policies will be tax-free because they reimburse for actual expenses. Per diem benefits from indemnity policies are tax-free up to $380 per day (2020). Reimbursement and indemnity policies are discussed later in this chapter.

Exhibit 7.18 | Maximum Long-Term Care Premium Tax Deduction (2020)

Age 40 and younger	$430
Age 41 - 50	$810
Age 51 - 60	$1,630
Age 61 - 70	$4,350
71 and older	$5,430

---

11. IRC Section 7702B(b).

Conditions that Trigger Long-Term Care Benefits

To receive benefits under a long-term care insurance policy, an insured individual must generally be classified as chronically ill.

Chronic illness must be determined by a health care practitioner and consists of either a physical impairment or a cognitive impairment.

- Physical impairment - defined as being unable to perform, without substantial assistance from another individual, at least two activities of daily living (ADLs) due to a loss of functional capacity. The loss of functional capacity must be expected to exist for a period of at least 90 days, or

- Cognitive impairment - requiring substantial supervision to prevent the insured from posing a danger to himself, herself, or others due to a severe cognitive impairment. A severe cognitive impairment is a loss or deterioration of intellectual capacity that is similar to and includes Alzheimer's disease or similar forms of dementia. Short and long-term memory, orientation as to people, time, and places, deductive or abstract reasoning, and judgment as to safety awareness are often evaluated in the determination of whether a person is cognitively impaired.

To be considered chronically ill, the insured individual must be certified as such by a qualified health professional within the previous 12 months.

The six ADLs are generally defined in a contract as follows:
1. Bathing - washing oneself by sponge bath; or in either a tub or shower, including the task of getting into or out of the tub or shower.
2. Dressing - putting on and taking off clothes and assistive devices, such as prosthetic devices or hearing aids.
3. Eating - taking nourishment by getting food into the body by way of a plate or cup, or by a feeding tube. It does not mean cooking or preparing meals.
4. Continence - the ability to maintain control of bowel and bladder functions or when unable to control bowel or bladder functions, the ability to perform associated personal hygiene, such as caring for catheter or colostomy bag.
5. Toileting - the ability to get on and off the toilet and perform associated personal hygiene tasks.
6. Transferring - moving in and out of a bed, chair, or wheelchair.

These six ADLs are the most common trigger found in modern LTCI policies because they are specifically identified in HIPAA. For a policy to be tax qualified, it must list at least five of these six ADLs, and must define physical impairment as inability to perform at least two of the ADLs without substantial assistance from another person. Since elderly people typically require assistance with bathing before they need help with other ADLs, a policy that does not list bathing as an ADL may be slower to pay benefits. Some older policies also include ambulating (walking) as an ADL to trigger benefits; however, ambulating is not an ADL identified by HIPAA for tax-qualified policies.

> ## ∷≡ *Key Concepts*
>
> 1. Provide examples of the conditions necessary for benefits to be paid under a long-term care policy.
>
> 2. Recall the six activities of daily living.

Example 7.10

Roger has been having trouble lately getting dressed and bathing. If, after 90 days, he could be certified as chronically ill, then he would be entitled to benefits under a long-term care policy.

Example 7.11

Oliver's mom has Alzheimer's disease and is therefore deemed chronically ill and eligible for long-term care benefits.

Example 7.12

Kobe is able to eat and has full control over his bowels and bladder. However, he is not able to dress himself or move from his bed to his wheelchair. Because he cannot perform at least two ADLs, he should be classified as chronically ill and thus, eligible for long-term care benefits.

In some long-term care policies, **terminal illness** may trigger benefits in the form of hospice care at home or in a licensed facility if the terminal illness is expected to be six months or less.

Benefit payments cover expenses actually paid (reimbursement plan) or pay a flat daily or monthly amount, regardless of expenses paid, depending on the contract.

Selection of Long-Term Care Policy

Long-term care insurance is sold directly to individuals as individual policies. It is also sold through employer group plans or other organizations. With group policies, there may be limited choices in the amount of coverage and options as well as no choice as to the insurance company. With individual policies, there is a wider range of companies and optional coverages.

The cost of a LTCI policy varies considerably from insurance company to insurance company. It also depends on the level of benefits, the elimination period, the length of the benefit period, and the age of the insured when the coverage takes effect.

The policy's outline of coverage is a good place to look to compare the features of various policies before making a decision. Decisions should not be made purely based on cost due to the vast differences in the ways in which policies can work.

Two of the most important factors in policy selection are actually qualifying for coverage (underwriting, as discussed previously in this chapter) and the financial strength/claims-paying ability of the insurer (as discussed in Chapter 2). The number of insurers offering traditional stand-alone LTC insurance has dropped considerably, from over 100 in 2004 to about a dozen in 2018, greatly narrowing the field in terms of insurer selection.[12]

---

12. https://content.naic.org/cipr_topics/topic_long_term_care_insurance.htm

When deciding on a policy, one should consider the following:
- the premium
- the period of coverage or total benefits
- any inflation adjustment
- the elimination (deductible) period
- services covered
- services excluded
- who is the gatekeeper to determine qualification for benefits
- how are benefits paid
- what triggers benefits

The Period of Coverage (Benefit Period)

The insured can select terms of coverage of 1, 2, 3, 5, 7, 10 years, or lifetime benefits. Obviously, the longer the term of benefits, the higher the amount of lifetime benefits and the more costly the premiums. The historical average stay in a facility is 18-36 months, but the range is quite wide - one day to over 50 years. In addition, most people who eventually need care in a facility initially receive care at home. Some clients will choose two or three years as the benefit period based on these statistics. Some will choose five years based on the idea that if they transfer all of their assets to family members on the day they begin receiving care, they can overcome the Medicaid 5-year look-back rules. If the goal is to eventually qualify for Medicaid, the planner and client should look at a Long-Term Care Partnership policy, as discussed previously in this chapter. In 2019, 52.4 percent of new long-term care insurance buyers purchased coverage of three years or less.[13]

Another way to determine the appropriate length of the benefit period is to consider family history, personal health history, and risk tolerance (or aversion). Clients with a history of longevity in the family are more likely to need care for longer periods of time. If that longevity is combined with an aversion to Medicaid, the client is likely to desire a longer benefit period. Other clients may already have health issues or come from a family that generally does not live long and may not have an aversion to Medicaid. These clients would be willing to accept a shorter benefit period.

13.https://www.aaltci.org/long-term-care-insurance/learning-center/ltcfacts-2019.php#2019buyers

Exhibit 7.19 | Long-Term Care Insurance Claims - How Long Do They Last?

Length of Claim by Policy Benefit Period (claim duration in months)					Claims Closed Due to Exhaustion of Policy Benefits	
Benefit Period of Policy	24+	36+	48+	60+	Benefit Period of Policy	Closed %
2 Years	14.0%	1.4%	0.4%	0.1%	2 Year Benefit Period	9.7%
3 Years	25.0%	10.9%	1.4%	0.3%	3 Year Benefit Period	8.0%
4 Years	23.9%	12.1%	6.0%	1.0%	4 Year Benefit Period	5.1%
5 Years	15.9%	10.2%	6.1%	2.9%	5 Year Benefit Period	1.5%
Lifetime	23.3%	13.9%	7.6%	4.5%		
For the 3-year benefit period, only 8 in 100 claimants exhausted their policies.						

Source: The 2014 Sourcebook for Long-Term Care Insurance Information / A revealing look at the duration of policy claims by individuals with long-term care insurance conducted by Miliman, Inc.

The Benefit Amount

Another important decision in structuring the LTCI policy is the selection of the benefit amount, which is the daily maximum that will be paid from the policy. The amount may range from as low as $150 to above $500 per day. Of course, the higher the daily benefit, the higher the premium. Some policies will also allow the applicant to select a home health benefit of 50 percent, 75 percent, or 100 percent of the institutionalized daily benefit amount.

The planner should do some research to determine the average daily cost for home health aides, custodial care, and skilled care in the client's geographic area to ensure adequate coverage is purchased at a reasonable premium.

Exhibit 7.20 | Median Daily Cost of Care in Select Geographic Regions (2019)*

Location	In-Home Care (Home Health Aide)	Assisted Living Facility	Nursing Home Facility (Semi-Private Room)
National	$144	$133	$247
New York, NY	$157	$228	$400
Bismark, ND	$88	$112	$428
Oklahoma City, OK	$138	$109	$170
Los Angeles, CA	$172	$148	$260
Anchorage, AK	$188	$197	$1,011

* The median cost is the cost that is in the middle of the range. Source: https://www.genworth.com/aging-and-you/finances/cost-of-care.html.

The Inflation Adjustment

Recall that planners will most often recommend purchase of a policy when clients are in their 50's to early 60's, but the need for care will likely arise 20 or 30 years later. In order to be tax-qualified, HIPAA requires that LTCI policies offer the option of purchasing an inflation protection rider (also called an inflation protection endorsement). The inflation protection rider will allow the daily benefit amount to increase over time, and the increase can be based on simple or compound inflation with varying percentage increases available.

The cost of an inflation adjustment is an additional premium from 47 percent to 82 percent (for 66-year-old male, seven-year benefits). The younger a person buys a long-term care policy, the more important inflation protection is as a policy feature. Inflation of long-term care services costs is expected to outpace general inflation over the next several years as demand increases due to the aging of baby boomers and as the industry faces a shortage of skilled workers.

With an automatic inflation adjustment the monthly or daily benefit and the lifetime benefit increases. The inflation adjustment options vary widely with policies but generally include zero, three percent compound, five percent equal, and five percent compound.

A simple (equal) inflation protection rider at five percent would increase the benefit by five percent of the initial daily benefit every year. For a policy with a $100 initial daily benefit amount, the benefit would increase by $5 each year so that after 10 years, the benefit amount is $150 per day.

A compound inflation protection rider at five percent would increase the benefit by five percent using compounding interest (each year the increase is five percent of the previous year's daily benefit amount). With an initial daily benefit of $100, after 10 years the new daily benefit would be $163.

When added as an endorsement to the LTCI policy, the premium for compound inflation protection will be higher than the premium for a simple inflation protection rider. The age of the insured at the time of purchase will likely dictate which is appropriate, simple or compound. For older applicants (approximately age 70-75 or older), simple inflation protection may be adequate; however, for younger applicants, compound inflation will be necessary to ensure that the daily benefit keeps up with increases in costs over the long period of time before benefits are needed.

Exhibit 7.21 | Annual Cost of a Long-Term Care Insurance Policy with Various Inflation Adjustments Including None ($3,000/month for 60 months)

Year	Inflation Benefit with No Adjustment		Benefit with 3% Compound		Benefit with 5% Equal		Benefit with 5% Compound	
	Per Month	Total	Per Month	Total	Per Month	Total	Per Month	Total
1	$3,000	$180,000	$3,000	$180,000	$3,000	$180,000	$3,000	$180,000
6	$3,000	$180,000	$3,484	$209,040	$3,750	$225,000	$3,850	$231,005
11	$3,000	$180,000	$4,048	$242,880	$4,500	$270,000	$4,941	$296,460
16	$3,000	$180,000	$4,702	$282,120	$5,250	$315,000	$6,341	$380,460
21	$3,000	$180,000	$5,462	$327,736	$6,000	$360,000	$8,138	$488,280
Expected Annual Premium (age 66 male)	$1,755		$2,588		$2,622		$3,195	
% Increase	N/A		+ 47%		+ 49%		+ 82%	

Elimination (Deductible) Period

The period between being eligible medically and when benefits begin is called the elimination period. The elimination period is similar to a deductible. The elimination period may be 0, 30, 60, 90, or 180 days. In some policies, the elimination period for skilled nursing care may be different from home health care. In general, the longer the elimination period, the lower the premium.

Selecting the appropriate elimination period requires some planning. The client should have enough liquid assets available to cover long-term care costs during the entire elimination period. If the current cost of care in the client's geographic region is $250 per day, and a 90-day elimination period is selected, the client will need a minimum of $22,500 of liquid assets designated to cover the elimination period. Since the client is usually purchasing the policy many years before the need for care will arise, and the cost of care will be increasing, the client will also need to gradually allocate additional liquid assets to the reserves set aside to cover the elimination period so that the appropriate amount of funds are available at the time of a claim.

When evaluating policies, the planner and client must take care to review how care received at home will be counted toward the elimination period. Some policies may use actual days (3 days of care = 3 days), while other policies may count any care received during a week as a full week. Another important question to ask is whether care received by family members counts toward the elimination period if a doctor certifies that care is needed. Some policies may not count days where care is provided by an unlicensed family member.

Services Included and Excluded

Long-term care services may include help with personal care, activities of daily living (ADLs), home health care, respite care, hospice care, and/or adult day care. The care may be provided in the insured's home, at a day care facility, in an assisted living facility, or in a skilled nursing home. Care services can also include the cost of a case manager to determine need and recommend and monitor services. The cost of such a case manager is usually provided as part of the policy and for no additional premium. This cost will not reduce monthly or lifetime benefits.

For home health care, some policies only cover the cost of licensed caregivers or agencies. Some cover non-licensed caregivers, and some may cover related party caregivers who are licensed or not.

Most long-term care insurance policies do not cover:
- mental or nervous disorders other than Alzheimer's or dementia
- alcohol or drug addiction
- illness or injury caused by acts of war
- treatment in a government facility or paid for by the government
- self-inflicted injuries

The Gatekeeper

When selecting a policy, it is important to know who the gatekeeper to benefits is. The policy may require that a case worker for the insurance company evaluate and certify that the insured is eligible for benefits.

How Benefits are Paid

Benefits are generally paid in one of three ways. The first is the expense incurred method (reimbursement). The expense incurred method pays for the actual expense up to the dollar limit whichever is less, which is paid to the providers or the insured. The second way is the indemnity method. The indemnity (per diem) method is a set dollar amount paid to the insured for each period he or she qualifies. The third method is the disability method in which the insured only needs to meet the eligibility criteria once. Once the eligibility criteria is met, the insured receives the full daily benefit until death or until the benefits are exhausted. The most common policy benefit paid method is the expense incurred method (reimbursement).

Another important consideration regarding how benefits are paid is how the insurance company calculates the amount it will pay. The following two examples highlight the different methods. Both examples assume a $100 per day benefit.

Example 7.13

Company A uses a daily limit. On one day, $50 in home health care cost is incurred. The next day, nothing is spent. On the third day, $150 is incurred. In this case, $150 would be paid ($50 + $0 + $100).

Example 7.14

Company B uses a monthly limit. $100 x 30 days = $3,000 monthly limit. Assuming the same daily expenses, and assuming the total expenditures for the month do not exceed $3,000, the $200 incurred during the period above would be reimbursed.

Reimbursement policies, in effect, create a pool of money to be used for long-term care expenses.

Example 7.15

Deshaun purchased a long-term care insurance policy with a daily benefit of $250 and a benefit period of 3 years. The policy uses the reimbursement approach to pay for expenses. Deshaun has a pool of money of $250 x 365 days x 3 years = $273,750 available to pay for LTC services. Some days his expenses may be more than the daily benefit amount of $250 (in which case the payment will usually be limited to the daily maximum of $250 to ensure that the benefits last at least as long as the benefit period), and some days his actual expenses may be less. If his expenses are less than $250 per day for a period of time, then the benefits may actually last longer than 3 years (his selected benefit period).

A policy using the indemnity (per diem) approach will pay the selected daily benefit for each day care is received, regardless of the amount of actual expenses incurred. An indemnity policy will never last longer than the benefit period selected.

Some insurers issue policies that permit pooled (shared) benefits, for example, between spouses (as discussed previously).

ALTERNATIVES TO LONG-TERM CARE INSURANCE

As discussed earlier in the chapter, certain individuals may be better off not purchasing a long-term care insurance policy. While these policies are appropriate for many individuals, there are risks that need to be considered. Four risks to a standalone long-term care policy include:
- they can be expensive
- they accumulate no cash value
- the premiums may increase
- the underwriting process can be time-consuming

A major problem with long-term care policies arises when they lapse due to the policy owner's inability to continue to pay premiums. Affordability can be a major issue in purchasing long-term care, especially if premiums increase. As a result, hybrid solutions have been created to meet the needs of long-term care. These include life insurance with accelerated benefits, annuity contracts permitting cash withdrawals without penalty, viatical or life settlement contracts, and reverse mortgages.

Life Insurance with Long-Term Care Rider

Life insurance policies can be used to cover the costs of long-term care via accelerated death benefits, life settlements, and viatical settlements, as discussed in Chapter 5. Policy owners can also access cash to pay long-term care costs by borrowing from their life insurance policy cash value. A disadvantage of accelerated death benefits, life settlements, viatical agreements, and loans is that the death proceeds will be reduced or eliminated when the insured dies. Consequently, the original need that gave rise to the life insurance will not be met.

Rather than relying on accelerated death benefits (terminally ill), life settlement, or viatical settlements, a long-term care rider can be added to some life insurance policies. These hybrid policies are often viewed as a middle ground for those who are concerned about long-term care, but who don't like the fact that a traditional long-term care policy works like a homeowner policy in that if you have a claim you get reimbursed, but if you never have a claim you don't get anything back at the end. By purchasing a life insurance policy with a long-term care rider, either the insured will receive a payout for long-term care (which may reduce the death benefit) or the beneficiary will receive the full death benefit if LTC services are not needed.

> ### ≔ *Key Concepts*
>
> 1. Compare the costs and benefits of long-term care insurance to the alternatives to long-term care insurance.
>
> 2. Understand how long-term care riders can be purchased.
>
> 3. Explain how reverse mortgages could be used in lieu of long-term care insurance.
>
> 4. Discuss how annuities might be favorable over long-term care insurance.

Some people are attracted to this flexibility and like the fact that they will get some money back no matter what happens. The market for hybrid life insurance/LTC products is growing rapidly. In 2018, 85 percent of LTC product sales were hybrid sales.[14]

In the past, combination policies typically required a large up-front payment. For example, a healthy 60-year-old male non-smoker might pay $100,000 in premiums in three annual installments of $33,333. The insured could receive a maximum monthly benefit of $5,787 for a maximum of six years, and if it is not used, his beneficiaries would receive $138,896. In more recent years, hybrid life/LTC policies with recurring premiums have become more popular due to the increased affordability of recurring premiums versus single premium policies. In most policies, the benefit paid under the long-term care rider is a monthly benefit of two to four percent of the face value, up to a maximum of two- to three-times the face value amount.

Life insurance policies with long-term care riders can pay the long-term care benefits under a reimbursement method or an indemnity method. A rider using the reimbursement method provides reimbursement for long-term costs actually incurred; whereas, a rider using the indemnity method will pay out a set dollar amount per week or month once benefits are triggered (for example, two percent of the death benefit per month). One advantage to the indemnity rider is the flexibility of receiving the set dollar amount, which can be used to pay any expenses rather than being limited to just a reimbursement for qualified expenses. Indemnity benefits are tax-free up to $380 per day (2020).

---

14. https://www.naic.org/meetings1908/cmte_b_senior_issues_2019_summer_nm_schoonveld.pdf

The triggers to receive benefits under the long-term care rider are typically similar to the triggers in traditional long-term care policies (unable to perform two or three from a list of five or six activities of daily living). The benefits received from the policy will generally be income tax-free, but the premiums are not tax deductible. Planners and clients should keep in mind that the premium will reflect a cost for both long-term care and the death benefit, so the purchase of these policies will make more sense for a client who needs or has a desire for both elements. A client who only needs one of these elements will be overpaying for the policy. Other important planning considerations are that the hybrid policies do not qualify as long-term care insurance under the Partnership plans in many states, and most will not offer inflation protection since the amount of long-term care benefits is based on the fixed death benefit amount, although a few insurers do offer inflation protection.

One advantage to purchasing the hybrid life insurance policy with long-term care rider is that the life insurance premiums are generally fixed (or are a single-premium amount), whereas most traditional long-term care policies are guaranteed renewable, meaning that the premiums can, and often do, increase if the insurer increases the premium for the entire class of insureds. This factor may make it difficult to plan for the premium expense of a traditional LTC policy during retirement.

Annuity Contracts with Long-Term Care Provisions

Annuities (discussed in Chapter 8) are an insurance product that allows for tax-deferred growth on a cash accumulation account and the ability to convert the cash account to a periodic income stream for a fixed period of time or for the life of the annuitant. The Pension Protection Act of 2006 paved the way for a tax-qualified hybrid annuity/long-term care product where a qualified long term care (LTC) rider is attached to an annuity from which distributions used to pay for long-term care expenses are tax-free.

Clients who do not wish to pay for traditional LTC insurance might have a particular sum of money they plan to save toward potential long-term care expenses. That lump sum can be placed in an annuity with a qualified LTC rider that will provide a higher long-term care benefit if needed, or, if long-term care expenses are not needed, will pay the value of the cash account to the owner's named beneficiaries upon the death of the owner. For example, the annuity product might offer a long-term care benefit of double or triple the cash accumulation account. If long-term care services are needed, they are paid first from the cash account and, when it is exhausted, from the additional rider benefits. If LTC services are not needed, the annuity can be used to provide income similar to a traditional annuity product or the cash account will be paid to beneficiaries upon the death of the owner.

One of the biggest advantages of the annuity/LTC hybrid is that underwriting is much less rigid than for traditional stand-alone LTC insurance or Life/LTC hybrid policies, allowing many clients who may not qualify for other types of coverage an opportunity to acquire it via the annuity hybrid. Most insurers will have a minimum, such as $50,000, that must be contributed to the contract, so clients will need to have a substantial amount of savings to be able to afford to set aside this amount outside from their regular income-producing portfolio in retirement. In addition, hybrid policies typically do not qualify for state Medicaid LTC partnership programs.

Clients who already have an existing traditional annuity and wish to change to a hybrid policy may be able to do so under a Section 1035 tax-deferred exchange if the rules of the 1035 exchange are followed. These rules are discussed in Chapters 5 and 8.

When comparing hybrid products to traditional LTC insurance, the traditional LTC policy will typically offer higher benefits for each premium dollar; however, the traditional LTC policy pays nothing if there is never a need for long-term care. Whether the traditional or hybrid policy is better for the client will depend on each client's unique circumstances, goals, perceptions, and risk tolerance level.

Another factor to evaluate is the alternative of investing the lump sum elsewhere. Could the investment returns be used to purchase a traditional LTC policy that will pay a higher benefit amount, without tapping into the principal amount invested? If so, the LTC benefit is higher and may qualify for the partnership program, plus the principal sum is still available to pass to heirs. Of course, with a traditional policy you also have to be prepared for potential premium increases. Again, it comes down to client preferences and risk tolerance, and in some cases to a desire for simplicity.

Longevity Annuities (Also known as Deferred Income Annuities)

Longevity annuities are contracts between individuals and insurance companies. A contract will often be purchased as a single investment (single premium) in exchange for a guaranteed income stream for life beginning at a later age, such as 80 or 85. The income is based on the premium or investment, the age of the contract owner, his life expectancy and the period over which the income will be paid. The annuity payments can be used to supplement income needs during the later parts of retirement or supplement long-term care needs. The primary advantage of this approach is that the funds can be used for more than just long-term care. Longevity annuities are discussed more thoroughly in the Annuities chapter.

Reverse Mortgages

A reverse mortgage is a specific type of home equity loan that permits the borrower to receive cash against the value of his or her home without selling the home. In general the money can be received in a lump sum payment, a monthly payment, or as a line of credit. There are no restrictions on the use of the remainder of the money after paying off any initial first and second mortgage. The borrower will continue to live in the home and retain title and ownership of the home and will continue to be responsible for taxes, homeowners insurance, and home repairs. The borrower does not have to make monthly payments to repay the loan, instead, the amount that is owed based on the loan payout and interest and expenses on the loan become due when the last borrower (usually the last remaining spouse) dies, sells, or permanently moves out of the home. There are a number of disadvantages to reverse mortgages including the costs and the fact that there may be little or no equity left in the home to go to beneficiaries since the homeowner has a bequest interest.

✎ Quick Quiz 7.5

1. An alternative to long-term care insurance is a viatical settlement contract.
   a. True
   b. False

2. An alternative to long-term care insurance is a reverse mortgage.
   a. True
   b. False

3. Longevity annuities can be used to supplement income needs or to provide for long-term care.
   a. True
   b. False

4. Distributions from a hybrid life/LTC contract to pay for long-term care services are taxable.
   a. True
   b. False

True, True, True, False.

Exhibit 7.22 | Medicaid Eligibility Timeline

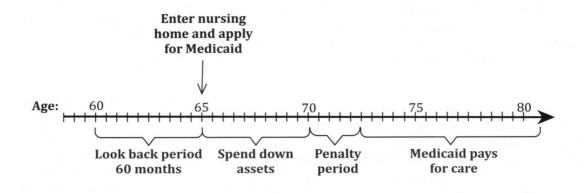

A COMPREHENSIVE INDIVIDUAL ILLUSTRATION OF A LONG-TERM CARE POLICY

One of the earlier sections in this chapter discussed numerous long-term care policy features, each of which impacts the cost of the policy depending on what is selected. This section is included to illustrate the impact to the cost of a long-term care policy of various changes in the features of the policy. To illustrate the impact on the price of a policy for various policy changes, a 66-year-old male was chosen to initially price a policy and then to compare the price based on policy feature changes.

This illustration is for a 66-year-old man, in good health, with an initial monthly benefit of $3,500, with a five percent equal inflation adjustment for a term of six years (72 months), with 180-day elimination period and an annual premium of $3,059.71 having no return of premium option nor a non-forfeiture option.

It is important to note that policy premiums will be different from what is illustrated in this section depending on the age and health of the insured, as well as other factors. It should also be noted that premium adjustments may occur over time. Below is the policy detail used for these illustrations.

Exhibit 7.23 | Long-Term Care Policy Description

Long-Term Policy Description	
Age	66 (male)
Monthly Benefit	$3,500
Period of Coverage	72 Months
Total Initial Benefit	$252,000
Elimination Period	180
Inflation	5% Equal
Restoration of Benefits	Included
Premium Payment	Lifetime
Payment Mode	Annual
Annual Premium	$3,059.71
Non-Forfeiture Option	None
Return of Premium Option	None

The initial policy choices were as follows:

Item	Range
Monthly Benefit	$2,500 - $4,500
Benefit Multiplies (term)	24 - 120 months
The Elimination Period	0 - 180 days
Benefit Increase Options (inflation)	0 - 5% compounded
Restoration of Benefits	no / yes
Non-Forfeiture Benefit Options	include / exclude
Enhanced Survivorship Option	include / exclude
Return of Premium after 10 Years	include / exclude

Exhibit 7.24 | Benefit Option Comparison (the current policy features are in bold)

Benefit Option	Change Benefit To	New Annual Premium	Amount of Change
Monthly Benefit Maximum	$2,500 per month	$2,185.51	($874.20)
	$3,000 per month	$2,622.61	($437.10)
	$3,500 per month	**$3,059.71**	**0**
	$4,000 per month	$3,496.82	$437.11
	$4,500 per month	$3,933.91	$874.20
Benefit Multiplier	24 months	$1,799.95	($1,259.76)
	36 months	$2,311.24	($748.47)
	48 months	$2,568.50	($491.21)
	60 months	$2,855.81	($203.90)
	72 months	**$3,059.71**	**0**
	96 months	$3,395.69	$335.98
	120 months	$3,635.50	$575.79
Elimination Period	30-Day	$3,558.04	$498.33
	90-Day	$3,227.70	$167.99
	180-Day	**$3,059.71**	**0**
Benefit Increase Option	None	$2,047.92	($1,011.79)
	3% Compound	$3,019.94	$39.77
	5% Equal	**$3,059.71**	**0**
	5% Compound	$3,728.40	$668.69
Restoration of Benefits Option*	None	$2,886.52	($173.19)
Non-Forfeiture Benefit Option**	Include	$3,896.80	$837.09
Enhanced Survivorship 7-Year Option***	Include	$3,204.04	$144.33
Return of Premium Option - After 10 Years****	Include	$4,467.17	$1,407.46

Restoration of benefits - the benefits in the policy will be restored if the insured gets better. Benefits can be reinstated if there is a six month or longer benefit free period as long as benefits have not been exhausted.

*** A non-forfeiture option provides some coverage after making premium payments for a specific time period. The option offers protection from cancellation or stopping paying premiums.*

****Enhanced survivorship rider is a spousal survivorship benefit. The surviving spouse no longer has to pay long-term care insurance premiums. The forgiveness of premiums after the death of the first spouse.*

***** Return of premium pays back all premiums paid if policy is canceled after a selected term.*

Comparisons of various combinations of policy options, as illustrated in **Exhibit 7.24** above, are extremely valuable in assisting the client to design a policy that best meets their needs. In most cases, as with other insurances, the allocated dollars in the budget to support the purchase of long-term care insurance will be limited. Clients will need to understand the trade-offs between coverage options and premiums based on what is most important to them. A client who places the most value on having the choice of how to receive care and where (in the home or in their choice of skilled nursing facilities, for example, may prefer a higher daily benefit amount (allowing them to choose the very best nursing home) and be willing to accept a shorter benefit period in order to meet that preference.

Exhibit 7.25 | Benefit Increase Comparison for Various Inflation Adjustments

Policy Year	No Increases		5% Equal		3% Compounded		5% Compounded	
	Monthly Maximum	Total Personal Benefit Account	Monthly Maximum	Total Personal Benefit Account	Monthly Maximum	Total Personal Benefit Account	Monthly Maximum	Total Personal Benefit Account
1	$3,500	$252,000	$3,500	$252,000	$3,500	$252,000	$3,500	$252,000
5	$3,500	$252,000	$4,200	$302,400	$3,939	$283,628	$4,254	$306,308
10	$3,500	$252,000	$5,075	$365,400	$4,567	$328,803	$5,430	$390,935
15	$3,500	$252,000	$5,950	$428,400	$5,294	$381,173	$6,930	$498,943
20	$3,500	$252,000	$6,825	$491,400	$6,137	$441,884	$8,844	$636,791
25	$3,500	$252,000	$7,700	$554,400	$7,115	$512,264	$11,288	$812,725

Inflation Adjustments

Notice that three percent compounded (the approximate long-term historical increase in the CPI) is very close to five percent equal as are the monthly premiums (See Benefit Option Comparison).

Exhibit 7.26 | Plan Options Comparison

No Benefit Increases Option						
Elimination Period	**Benefit Multiplier**					
	36 Months (3 Years)	48 Months (4 Years)	60 Months (5 Years)	72 Months (6 Years)	96 Months (8 Years)	120 Months (10 Years)
30 Days	$1,753.92	$1,899.52	$2,196.32	$2,374.40	$2,611.84	$2,789.92
90 Days	$1,602.72	$1,751.12	$1,988.56	$2,136.96	$2,374.40	$2,552.48
180 Days	$1,512.00	$1,662.08	$1,899.52	$2,047.92	$2,255.68	$2,433.76

5% Equal Benefit Increases Option						
Elimination Period	**Benefit Multiplier**					
	36 Months (3 Years)	48 Months (4 Years)	60 Months (5 Years)	72 Months (6 Years)	96 Months (8 Years)	120 Months (10 Years)
30 Days	$2,678.36	$2,970.67	$3,323.86	$3,558.04	$3,935.57	$4,205.66
90 Days	$2,440.06	$2,706.52	$3,018.16	$3,227.70	$3,593.95	$3,833.77
180 Days	$2,311.24	$2,568.50	$2,855.81	**$3,059.71**	$3,395.69	$3,635.50

3% Compound Benefit Increases Option						
Elimination Period	**Benefit Multiplier**					
	36 Months (3 Years)	48 Months (4 Years)	60 Months (5 Years)	72 Months (6 Years)	96 Months (8 Years)	120 Months (10 Years)
30 Days	$2,502.36	$2,790.81	$3,233.94	$3,501.35	$3,880.36	$4,148.08
90 Days	$2,284.33	$2,523.69	$2,942.18	$3,180.22	$3,530.44	$3,773.51
180 Days	$2,175.46	$2,411.80	$2,781.61	$3,019.94	$3,345.53	$3,583.86

5% Compound Benefit Increases Option						
Elimination Period	**Benefit Multiplier**					
	36 Months (3 Years)	48 Months (4 Years)	60 Months (5 Years)	72 Months (6 Years)	96 Months (8 Years)	120 Months (10 Years)
30 Days	$3,089.32	$3,445.55	$3,992.55	$4,322.59	$4,790.65	$5,120.98
90 Days	$2,820.18	$3,115.51	$3,632.24	$3,926.37	$4,358.51	$4,658.58
180 Days	$2,685.62	$2,977.50	$3,433.98	$3,728.40	$4,130.27	$4,424.70

Exhibit 7.27 | Cost of Waiting (One and Five Years)

When Purchased	Age	Monthly Benefit Amount	Annualized Premiums (Rounded)	Total Premiums Paid to Age 85 of Proposed Insured	Cost of Waiting
Today	66	$3,500	$3,060	$58,140	$0
In 1 Year*	67	$3,675	$3,524	$63,432	$5,292
In 5 Years*	71	$4,467	$6,172	$86,408	$28,268

Assuming the insured is still insurable.

Exhibit 7.28 | Break Even Analysis in Days of Use

Number of Years Premiums are Paid	Total Premium Paid	Monthly Benefit	Break Even Days
2	$6,119	$3,675	50
5	$15,299	$4,200	109
10	$30,597	$5,075	181
15	$45,896	$5,950	231

Exhibit 7.29 | Payment Options Comparison

Policy Period	Age	Lifetime Total Premiums Paid	Lifetime Policy Paid Up	10-Pay Total Premiums Paid	10-Pay Policy Paid Up	Pay-to-65 Total Premiums Paid	Pay-to-65 Policy Paid Up
First Year	66	$3,059.71	No	$5,721.71	No	N/A	N/A
After 10 Years	76	$30,597.10	No	$57,217.10	Yes	N/A	N/A
After 20 Years	86	$61,194.20	No	$57,217.10	Yes	N/A	N/A

As illustrated in the exhibits above, there are many variations of long-term care policies. Each of these variations impacts the cost of the policy.

CONCLUSION

Health insurance and long-term care insurance permit clients to purchase a hedge against the risk of incurring large out-of-pocket medical and/or nursing home and long-term care expenses. All U.S. citizens are required, under current law, to maintain adequate health insurance. Long-term care insurance should be considered by any client who wishes to retain the ability to choose service providers or who has bequest motives that could be thwarted (or, possibly, be subject to higher gift and/or estate taxes) if long-term care coverage is not purchased. Planners and clients should carefully consider the most appropriate forms of insurance to purchase so that the appropriate amount of client risk exposure is transferred to insurance companies while protecting the client's asset base to achieve the client's other financial goals.

KEY TERMS

Activities of Daily Living (ADL) - Physical functions that an independent person performs each day, including bathing, dressing, eating, transferring, toileting, and maintaining continence.

Adult Day Care - Services provided during the day at a community-based center. Programs address the individual needs of functionally or cognitively impaired adults.

Assisted Living - Senior housing that provides individual apartments, which may or may not have a kitchenette. Facilities offer 24-hour on site staff, congregate dining, and activity programs. Limited nursing services may be provided for an additional fee.

Bed Reservation - Some policies will pay to reserve a bed in the nursing home when the insured leaves to go into a hospital. This reservation can last a specified number of days or until the insured returns from the hospital.

Chronic Illness - Having a physical or cognitive impairment that prevents the insured individual from performing at least two of the six activities of daily living for at least a 90-day period, or requiring substantial supervision to prevent the insured from posing a danger to himself, herself, or others.

Custodial Care - Board, room and other personal assistance services (including assistance with activities of daily living, taking medicine and similar personal needs) that may not include a skilled nursing care component.

Expense Incurred Method – This method provides for reimbursement of expense once bills are submitted to the insurance company. The reimbursable amount cannot exceed the benefit amount.

Guaranteed Purchase Option - Allows the insured to increase the benefits by a stated percentage periodically.

Guaranteed Renewable - The company must renew the policy each year as long as premiums are paid.

Home Health Care - Limited part-time or intermittent skilled nursing care and home health aide services, physical therapy, occupational therapy, speech-language pathology services, medical social services, durable medical equipment (such as wheelchairs, hospital beds, oxygen, and walkers), medical supplies, and other services provided in the patient's home.

Hospice Care - Offers a special way of caring for people who are terminally ill, typically utilizing a team-oriented approach to address medical, physical, social, emotional, and spiritual needs.

Inflation Protection - Helps the insured to maintain the purchasing power of the original contract benefit.

Intermediate-Care Nursing Facility - A licensed facility with the primary purpose of providing health or rehabilitative services. Typically provides custodial care along with intermittent, as opposed to daily, medical care.

Long-Term Care Insurance - Coverage that pays for all or part of the cost of home health care services or care in a nursing home or assisted living facility.

Long-Term Care Services - Medical and non-medical care for people with chronic illnesses or disabilities that assists people with Activities of Daily Living, such as dressing, bathing, and using the bathroom. Long-term care can be provided at home, in the community, or in a facility.

Maximum Lifetime Benefit - The total amount of money that could be paid under the LTC policy for charges incurred for covered services.

Medicaid - A state and federal assistance program that pays for medical care and most long-term care expenses for eligible persons with low incomes and limited assets.

Medicare - A federal program that pays for healthcare for persons age 65 and over and for people under age 65 with disabilities.

Mental and Nervous Disorders - Long-term care insurance policies can exclude coverage of some mental and nervous disorders, but the policy must cover serious biologically-based mental illnesses and other diseases, such as schizophrenia, major depression disorders, Alzheimer's disease, and other age-related disorders. However, a long-term care insurer may refuse to sell a policy to someone already suffering from these otherwise covered conditions.

Non-Forfeiture Benefit - The insurer must guarantee that the insured will receive some of the benefits paid for even upon cancellation or lapse of coverage.

Pre-Existing Conditions - A pre-existing condition is an illness or disability for which an insured has received previous medical advice or treatment usually within six months prior to the application for long-term care coverage.

Refund of Premium - The company will refund some or all of the insured's premiums minus any claims paid under the policy if the policy is canceled. The insured's beneficiary will receive such refund if the insured dies.

Restoration of Benefits - Some policies restore benefits to the original maximum amounts if the insured no longer needs long-term care services, usually after 180 days.

Shared Benefits - Policies that have this benefit permit a person who has fully exhausted the benefits under his or her own policy to make use of the benefits available under his or her spouse's policy.

Skilled Care Facility - 24-hour nursing care for chronically-ill or short-term rehabilitative residents of all ages. It provides the highest level of service, and combines daily medical and custodial care.

Special Needs Trust - A specific type of trust that is used to provide benefits to persons or beneficiaries with special needs. They are designed to protect eligibility for government assistance programs while improving the life of the beneficiary.

Terminal Illness - Having a life expectancy of less than 24 months, which must be certified by a qualified health professional.

Total Plan Benefit – The total amount of money that could be paid under the LTC policy for charges incurred for covered services.

Traditional Medical Care - Attempts to treat or cure illnesses.

Waiver of Premium - Allows the insured to stop paying premiums during the period in which he or she is receiving policy benefits. However, this provision may only apply to certain benefits, for example, nursing home or home healthcare.

DISCUSSION QUESTIONS

SOLUTIONS to the discussion questions can be found exclusively within the chapter. Once you have completed an initial reading of the chapter, go back and highlight the answers to these questions.

1.   What is the trend of the average age in the United States?

2.   What is an ADL?

3.   What are the six ADLs?

4.   What is the estimated percent of people over age 65 who will need some form of long-term care?

5.   What needs do long-term care services meet?

6.   What are IADLs?

7.   Where are long-term services provided?

8.   What are the common methods for paying for long-term care services?

9.   What programs pay for most long-term care services?

10.   What factors influence the need for long-term care insurance?

11.   What variables influence long-term care insurance premiums?

12.   What are some common features of long-term care insurance policies?

13.   What are the typical coverages for long-term care insurance policies?

14.   What are typical exclusions from long-term care insurance policies?

15.   Describe the purpose of long-term care insurance.

16.   What are the two primary issues a planner should consider when advising regarding the purchase of long-term care insurance?

17.   What conditions will trigger long-term care benefits to be paid?

18.   What are some of the alternatives to long-term care insurance?

19.   What is the advantage of life insurance with a long-term care rider versus traditional stand-alone LTC insurance?

MULTIPLE-CHOICE PROBLEMS

A sample of multiple choice problems is provided below. Additional multiple choice problems are available at money-education.com by accessing the Student Practice Portal.

1. Medicare is primarily for those people who meet the following eligibility requirements:
   a. Disabled.
   b. Children.
   c. Low Income.
   d. Elderly.

2. Medicaid is primarily for those people who meet the following eligibility requirements:
   a. Disabled.
   b. Children.
   c. Low Income.
   d. Elderly.

3. All of the following are activities of daily living (ADLs) as provided under the Health Insurance Portability and Accountability Act (qualified plans), except:
   a. Eating.
   b. Bathing.
   c. Maintaining continence.
   d. Cognitive thinking.

4. There is more than one way to obtain benefits for nursing home coverage. All of the following sources provide some benefits, except:
   a. LTC insurance.
   b. Heath insurance.
   c. Medicare.
   d. Medicaid.

5. Which of the following is the highest level of care under the category of long-term care?
   a. Custodial care.
   b. Intensive care.
   c. Skilled nursing care.
   d. Advanced nursing care.

QUICK QUIZ EXPLANATIONS

Quick Quiz 7.1
1. False. Long-term care insurance coverage includes: nursing homes, home health, and hospice.
2. False. One must qualify financially for Medicaid.
3. True.
4. False. For those individuals with significant assets or few assets, it may make sense to pay for the services in lieu of paying for the insurance.
5. False. All are correct except exercising.

Quick Quiz 7.2
1. True.
2. False. Medicaid pays approximately 40 percent of the cost, not 80 percent.
3. False. Women tend to need it more due to longer life expectancies.
4. True.

Quick Quiz 7.3
1. False. The six activities of daily living are eating, bathing, dressing, transferring, toileting, and continence.
2. True.
3. True.
4. False. One way to qualify as chronically ill is the inability to perform two of the six activities of daily living.
5. False. It is at least two, not five of the six activities of daily living.

Quick Quiz 7.4
1. True.
2. True.
3. True.
4. False. The most common method is the expense incurred method (reimbursement).

Quick Quiz 7.5
1. True.
2. True.
3. True.
4. False. Distributions from a hybrid life/LTC contract to pay for long-term care services are tax-free.

**Additional multiple choice problems
are available at
money-education.com
by accessing the Student Practice Portal.
Access requires registration of the title using
the unique code at the front of the book.**

8
ANNUITIES

LEARNING OBJECTIVES

1. Understand how life expectancies have increased and the impact of that increase on retirement planning, including superannuation.
2. Discuss the retirement life expectancy concept and the impact inflation has on purchasing power.
3. Understand the impact of the change from employer sponsored defined benefit plans to employer sponsored defined contribution plans.
4. Explain the characteristics of an annuity including contribution and distribution options and differentiate between immediate and deferred annuities.*
5. Identify the use of annuities in retirement planning.
6. List the parties to an annuity.
7. Differentiate between single and joint life annuities.
8. Explain term certain annuities.
9. Identify the unique characteristics of variable annuities.
10. Discuss equity-indexed annuities.
11. Distinguish between deferred and immediate annuities.
12. List the advantages and disadvantages of annuity contracts.
13. Illustrate the income taxation of annuities.
14. Recognize the estate taxation issues regarding annuities.
15. Define longevity insurance.
16. Describe and discuss the secondary market for annuities.
17. Outline the regulation of annuities.
18. Describe what happens if an annuity issuer fails.
19. Compare and contrast annuities (fixed and variable) with other investment alternatives, including an analysis of costs, contract terms, and taxation.*

* CFP Board Resource Document - Student-Centered Learning Objectives based upon CFP Board Principal Topics.

INTRODUCTION

One of the common goals for most Americans is to live comfortably in retirement. This objective requires either a substantial accumulation of assets, a reliable source of income during retirement or a combination of the two. Even when individuals have accumulated assets or have reliable income, there can be risks to financial security during retirement. Two important risks to the security of retirement income are **superannuation** (outliving one's money) and **inflation** (loss of purchasing power). Superannuation or longevity risk is the risk of running out of money before death due to long life and can be mitigated by using annuities. However, commercial annuities are generally not adjusted for inflation, and therefore do not mitigate the risk of loss of purchasing power. Social Security retirement benefits generally mitigate both of these risks because the benefits last for life and are adjusted for inflation. The increase in benefits due to inflation helps maintain the purchasing power of the benefits. Annuities are not only used to provide income streams for retirees. Annuities are frequently used as a method of accumulating assets on a tax-deferred basis. This chapter discusses the various features and characteristics of annuities, including types, options, advantages, disadvantages, costs, taxation, as well as the primary uses for annuities.

As medical technology has improved and individuals have led healthier lifestyles over the past century, life expectancy has increased.[1] For example, there is an 80 percent probability that a 65-year-old will live to be age 80 and a 22 percent probability that the same 65-year-old will live to age 95 or longer. A longer retirement period increases the chance that an individual will run out of money (superannuation).

One way to mitigate against superannuation is through the use of annuities. Annuities are contracts that can provide income for the life of a person or the lives of more than one person. Annuities are more important in retirement planning today due to increased life expectancies and a decline in the number of retirement plans that pay pensions for life.

Exhibit 8.1 | Life Expectancy for All Individuals and 65-Year-Olds

	2017	2012	1960	1940	1930
Average Life Expectancy	78.6	78.8	69.7	62.9	59.7
Males Only	76.1	76.4	66.6	60.8	58.1
Females Only	81.1	81.1	73.1	65.2	61.6
All 65-Year-Olds	19.4	19.3	14.3	13.8	Not Reported
Males Only (Age 65)	18.0	17.9	13.2	12.7	Not Reported
Females Only (Age 65)	20.6	20.5	17.4	14.7	Not Reported

www.ssa.gov and National Vital Statistics System www.cdc.gov/nchs

The period between retirement and death, sometimes referred to as **retirement life expectancy** is uncertain, but the longer the period, the greater the risk that a retiree will exhaust his or her retirement assets or capital. Exhaustion of retirement capital can result from an increase in the number of years in retirement, thereby increasing consumption needs during retirement, or from the loss of purchasing power due to inflation during retirement.

Inflation is the increase in the general price level and is generally measured by the Consumer Price Index (CPI). When annual inflation is low (in the 1-3% range), it is hardly noticeable, especially for those persons who are employed because wages tend to rise with price increases. However, for a retiree on a fixed income, inflation can have a devastating effect on purchasing power over a long period of time. For example, if a retiree purchases a market basket of goods priced at $1,000 per month, and the annual rate of inflation is 3.5 percent during the retirement period, the cost to purchase the same market basket of goods will increase ratably over the retirement period. The following chart illustrates the cost of that $1,000 basket of goods in future years and the corresponding decline in purchasing power for a person retiring at age 65 (all numbers in the chart are rounded except for age).

⁝☰ *Key Concepts*

1. Understand inflation and its impact on retirement and purchasing power.

2. Discuss the retirement life expectancy concept.

3. Discuss risk of running out of money for those with longer life expectancies.

4. Understand the risk of defined contribution plans in long-term planning.

---

1. For a person aged 65 today, there is a life expectancy of about 18 years for males and 20 years for females.

Exhibit 8.2 | The Effect of Inflation on Cost and Purchasing Power

Time Period	Future Value Cost	Purchasing Power of $1,000	Decline in Purchasing Power of $1,000
Now (Age 65)	$1,000	100%	0
In 5 Years (Age 70)	$1,188	84%	16%
In 10 Years (Age 75)	$1,411	71%	29%
In 15 Years (Age 80)	$1,675	60%	40%
In 20 Years (Age 85)	**$1,990**	**50%**	**50%**
In 25 Years (Age 90)	$2,363	42%	58%
In 30 Years (Age 95)	$2,807	36%	64%
In 35 Years (Age 100)	**$3,334**	**30%**	**70%**

As the chart above illustrates, a retiree living to average life expectancy (in this case assume age 85) has a decline in purchasing power of 50 percent assuming inflation is 3.5 percent annually. Instead of needing $1,000 to purchase the market basket of goods at age 65, the same market basket of goods would cost approximately $2,000. If the retiree lives to age 100, which is becoming more common today, the decline in purchasing power is 70 percent. The retiree would need $3,334 per month at age 100 to purchase the same goods that cost $1,000 at age 65.

While there has always been inflation, 50 or so years ago life expectancy was much shorter than it is today. Therefore, depletion of retirement assets was less likely. Shorter retirement periods meant less consumption needs (fewer years in retirement) and fewer years of purchasing power erosion (caused by inflation).

Historically, individuals received Social Security retirement benefits and a fixed pension during retirement. Pension payments are generally made from retirement plans known as defined benefit plans. These plans pay fixed pensions to retired workers, typically for life. While Social Security remains, there has been a significant decline in the number of defined benefit plans over the last thirty years. In fact, in 1985, there were about 170,000 defined benefit plans. In 2017, there were fewer than 47,000 defined benefit plans.

When defined benefit plans were prevalent, the risk of superannuation was pooled together for most people. The defined benefit plan was responsible for paying a fixed pension for as long as the retired participants lived. Naturally, some retirees would live longer than others and some would die prematurely. Actuaries could mathematically estimate the average life expectancy of the pool of employees and determine the funding necessary to meet those requirements. However, the pooling of risk ceased as defined benefit plans were replaced with defined contribution plans.

No longer is the risk of outliving resources mitigated with shared risk. Now, retirees are responsible for the funds they have accumulated and must determine how to make those funds last throughout their lives. While self-reliance is generally a great attribute, the reality is that many, if not most, retirees are ill-equipped to manage their investment portfolios themselves and will need the assistance of financial advisors.

Exhibit 8.3 | Defined Contribution vs. Defined Benefit Plans

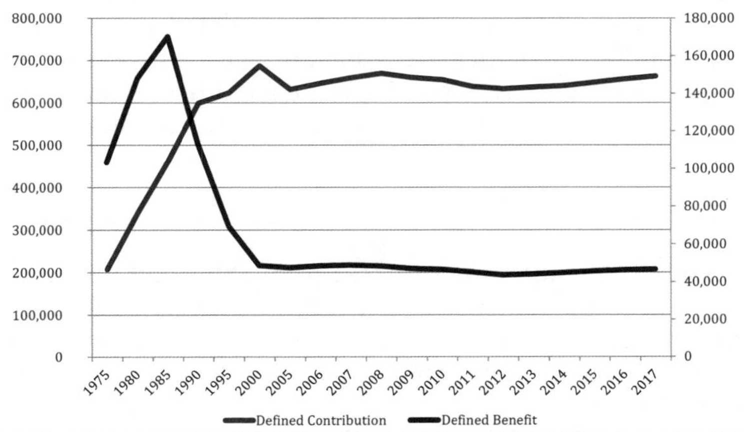

With longer life expectancies and less income from defined benefit plans, it is important for many individuals to mitigate the risk of superannuation. Annuities help individuals mitigate this risk in two ways. First, annuities are often used to accumulate wealth while preserving capital. Secondly, annuities, if annuitized, can provide for lifetime income. Often, annuities are not annuitized and owners simply take withdrawals or surrender the policies. There are numerous features and choices regarding annuities that are discussed throughout the chapter.

CHARACTERISTICS OF ANNUITIES

What is an Annuity?

An **annuity** is a contract that is designed to provide a specified income that is payable at stated intervals for a specified period of time. Traditionally, individuals received fixed annuities from employer defined benefit plans, from government retirement plans or from insurance companies. However, individuals can purchase commercial annuities from insurance companies and other financial services firms. These annuities are not uniform in any respect. There are many choices a consumer must make when purchasing an annuity. Annuities can be characterized based on several factors, such as the type of payout (fixed or variable), frequency and flexibility of premium (single premium or flexible premium), the timing of when income is payable (immediate or deferred), tax considerations and funding vehicles.

In general, commercial annuities have two distinct phases. The first phase is the **accumulation phase**, which is the period over which funds are contributed and accumulated. With deferred annuities, this accumulation takes place over time within the annuity. With immediate annuities, this accumulation of funds comes from some other source, such as life insurance, retirement savings, or an inheritance. The second phase is referred to as the **annuitization** phase, which occurs when the funds are exchanged by contract for a stream of income guaranteed for a period of time.

Once there is an exchange of funds for the annuity stream, then the owner no longer has access to that sum of funds. It is also important to understand that there are many choices regarding the annuity stream that is chosen. These choices are discussed later in this chapter.

Annuity contracts may protect people from outliving their assets by providing a series of periodic payments to the annuitant, typically lasting as long as the annuitant lives. An annuity is not life insurance, even though it is sold by life insurance companies. Like life insurance, annuities are based on mortality risk, but for annuities the focus is on living "too long" whereas life insurance is based on a life that is "too short." Insurance companies use mortality tables to determine benefits paid under annuities, but these tables are slightly different (anticipate a slightly longer life expectancy) than the mortality tables used for life insurance since those who purchase and annuitize an annuity are likely to be healthy and have a family history of longevity. Generally, annuities are commonly used to fund retirement benefits.

Example 8.1

Diamond retires with $2 million in her 401(k) plan. She could attempt to manage the funds herself and budget the money over her retirement years. Alternatively, she could purchase an annuity with all or part of her $2 million that would guarantee her a steady stream of income for life. The annuity could be paid over her life or could be paid over the joint lives of she and her spouse.

Annuity payouts are calculated based on the life expectancy of a group (or pool) of annuity contract owners. Some annuitants live to be age 90 or 100, while others die at much younger ages. Consequently, some annuitants will be paid more money than others and the risk of living "too long" is thus shared among the group. The remaining principal contributed by those who die at younger ages (before their actuarial life expectancy) is used to pay benefits to those who survive (beyond their actuarial life expectancy). This concept is known as **pooling of risk**.

Exhibit 8.4 | Pooling of Risk

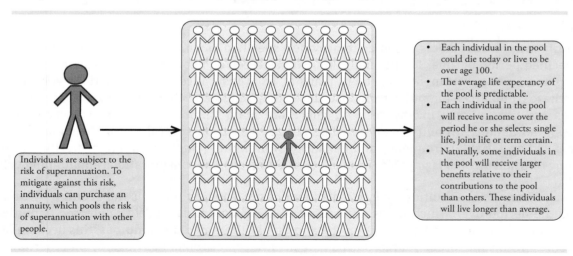

Individuals are subject to the risk of superannuation. To mitigate against this risk, individuals can purchase an annuity, which pools the risk of superannuation with other people.

- Each individual in the pool could die today or live to be over age 100.
- The average life expectancy of the pool is predictable.
- Each individual in the pool will receive income over the period he or she selects: single life, joint life or term certain.
- Naturally, some individuals in the pool will receive larger benefits relative to their contributions to the pool than others. These individuals will live longer than average.

Exhibit 8.5 | Annuities Summary

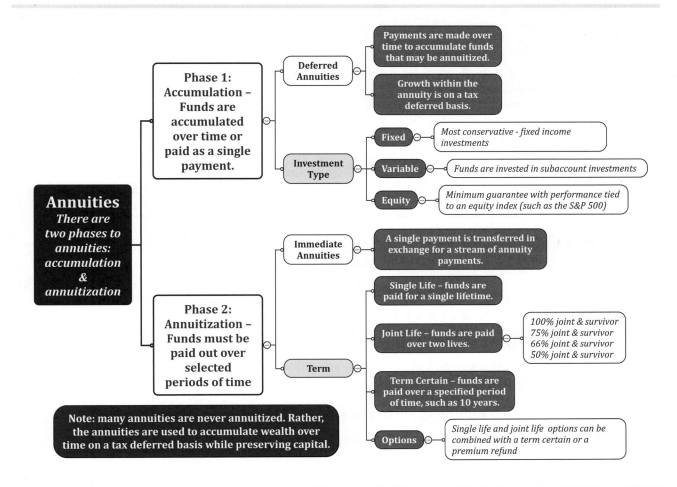

Annuity contracts are not appropriate for all investors. An annuity is designed to provide guaranteed lifetime income and protect against running out of money during retirement. Buyers need to weigh the value of this guarantee against the costs and risks from fees, taxes, and the illiquid nature of annuity contracts. For persons who have bequest motives, it is important to remember that once the premium payments are transferred to the insurance company under an annuity contract and the contract has entered the annuitization phase, the funds are no longer available to bequeath to the person's heirs and are not directly available for any other expenditures. Deferred annuity contracts that are in the accumulation phase (have not yet been annuitized) do allow limited access to the funds during the annuitant's lifetime and can be transferred to heirs upon death.

Exhibit 8.6 | Advantages and Disadvantages of Annuities

Advantages	Disadvantages
• Provides lifetime income • Structure of income can be based on a single life or multiple lives • Eliminates superannuation risk • May provide protection from creditors • Earnings are tax-deferred • Investment options allow for fixed or variable earnings	• Complexity, so many choices make it difficult for investors to understand • Costs and fees reduce returns within the annuity • Once funds are exchanged for the annuitized income stream, they are no longer available for bequests or other needs • Taxable benefits consist entirely of ordinary income, as opposed to capital gains and/or qualifying dividends

Parties to an Annuity Contract

Generally, there are four parties to an annuity contract:
- The **annuitant** is the individual upon whose life the contract is dependent. It is generally the life expectancy of the annuitant that affects the timing and amount of payout under the contract.
- The **beneficiary** is entitled to the death benefit, if such a benefit exists.
- The **owner** owns the annuity contract and names the annuitant and beneficiaries. The owner could also be the annuitant and/or the beneficiary. It is also possible that the owner not necessarily be an individual, but could also be a trust or a company.
- The **insurance company** issues the contract.

Exhibit 8.7 | Parties to an Annuity Contract

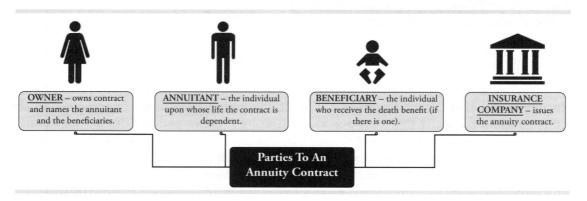

Annuity Payout Period

An annuity may provide payments for a fixed term such as 20 years (term certain) or for an indefinite term such as the lifetime of the annuitant (life annuity). Payments may also be based on the life expectancy of two people, such as married couples. The payout periods are discussed further in the following section.

Immediate vs. Deferred

The payout method used by an annuity contract can be either immediate or deferred.

An **immediate annuity** is an instrument created when the contract owner trades a sum of money in return for a stream of income that begins immediately. Immediate annuities are purchased with one, single, lump sum payment (a Single Premium Immediate Annuity, or SPIA). Immediate annuities are commonly used by individuals upon retiring to fund recurring, basic expenses that a retiree faces, such as the costs of shelter, clothing, food, and other necessities of life. Immediate annuities can also be the result of a government obligation, such as Social Security, or a corporate obligation, as in a defined benefit plan.

The benefit of an immediate annuity comes from the certainty it provides. Immediate annuities provide a guaranteed income while stocks and the value of other investment securities may fluctuate up or down. This type of fluctuation results in uncertain and potentially risky retirement cash flows. A steady stream of income is particularly important for retirees, at least with respect to their ongoing, basic consumption needs. Most retirees prefer a steady stream of income to cover all of their basic needs and expenses. In practice, however, many retirees are unwilling to give up ownership of their assets in exchange for a guaranteed steady stream of income. Many retirees take a balanced approach by having a portion of their assets annuitized (including Social Security and other retirement annuities) to cover basic consumption needs while preserving other assets for additional consumption and bequest motives.

> ### Key Concepts
> 1. Define an annuity.
> 2. Identify the use of annuities in retirement planning.
> 3. List the parties to an annuity.
> 4. Define the different payout methods for annuities.

Immediate annuities require a sum of money to be exchanged for the annuity payments. However, annuities can be used to accumulate a sum of money over time prior to the funds being paid out (annuitized) in the form of an annuity. These types of annuities are referred to as deferred annuities. A **deferred annuity** is an annuity contract that does not begin distributions immediately, but rather defers distributions into the future. The premium payments used to fund a deferred annuity can be either a single lump sum payment (a Single Premium Deferred Annuity, or SPDA), or a series of payments made over time (generally years; a Flexible Premium Deferred Annuity, or FPDA). Deferred annuity contracts permit a client to invest the premium payments in various underlying investments inside of the annuity contract for a period of time with the goal of accumulating assets that can then be paid out in the form of a series of periodic payments.

Deferred annuity contracts may be attractive options for both young and old. Young individuals with a long work life expectancy (the work period that remains at a given point in time before retirement) may use deferred annuities to accumulate a pool of funds that can be annuitized later. This approach allows them to capture investment growth between the time the premium payments are made and the date of annuitization. It should be noted, however, that there are other investment vehicles that provide the same tax deferral with lower fees and less complexity (such as IRAs and 401(k) plans). Therefore, annuities are typically used for additional retirement savings when these other options have been maximized. Older individuals closer to retirement may use deferred annuities for "longevity insurance," which is a strategy that permits retirees to consume their retirement funds over their normal life expectancy without the fear of living beyond their assets and thus, running out of money. Longevity insurance is discussed later in this chapter.

One of the advantages of annuities is their favorable income tax treatment. Income earned within the annuity is not subject to income tax until such time as it is distributed or paid out. This feature allows the annuity to accumulate earnings on a tax-deferred basis. Deferred annuities take advantage of this feature by accumulating assets over a period of years. The taxation of annuities is further discussed later in this chapter.

Flexible Premium vs. Single Premium

As mentioned earlier, annuities can be purchased with flexible premiums or with a single premium. A **flexible premium annuity** allows the owner the option to vary premium deposits over time. Under a flexible premium plan, the owner spreads payments out over a designated period of time by paying periodic premiums. These payments can be made in equal installments or can vary in terms of amount and timing. Earnings on the deposits are tax-deferred until the annuity is annuitized and begins making payments. The size of the annuity payments are dependent on the premiums that are paid and the earnings accumulated prior to annuitization.

An annuity purchased with a single lump sum is known as a **single premium annuity**. The funds used for purchasing a single premium annuity can come from a variety of sources, such as life insurance, retirement funds or savings. Proceeds of life insurance policies can be used to purchase single premium annuities at special rates under life income settlement options. Retiring individuals often purchase single premium annuities upon retirement using some or all of their qualified retirement plan money.

Earnings

The value of an annuity account increases as a result of premiums and earnings. Annuities will either be fixed or variable. Fixed annuities invest in less risky investments and guarantee returns for a period of time. Variable annuities have a wider array of investment choices, including equity investments. These options are more thoroughly discussed later in the chapter.

ANNUITY BENEFIT OPTIONS

An annuity is an agreement whereby a person exchanges a sum of money for a series of periodic payments. These payments can be structured in many different ways, which are referred to as benefit options. The standard benefit options are to have the annuity paid over a single life, a specific period of years (term certain), or over the lives of two individuals. There are variations in these standard options, which are discussed below.

Exhibit 8.8 | Annuity Benefit Options

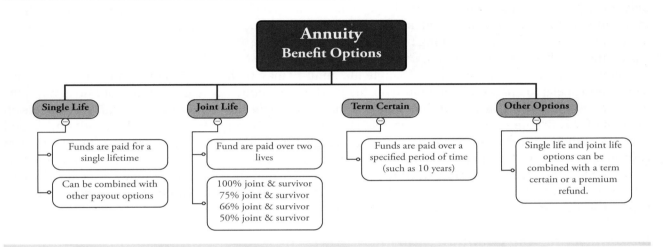

Single Life Annuities

A **single life annuity** is an annuity that only provides payments to one person. Although a single life annuity has many payout options available, a straight single life annuity will cease paying benefits when the annuitant dies. Single life annuities include:

- Straight or pure life annuities
- Installment refund annuities
- Cash refund annuities
- Term certain annuities

Straight or Pure Life Annuities

A **straight or pure life annuity**, provides a stream of income to the annuitant for life. When the annuitant dies, the annuity payments end. Compared to other types of annuity contracts, a pure life annuity provides a greater cash-flow benefit for a given premium payment since only one measuring life is used for determining the annuity payment term.

Many individuals will not purchase single life annuities because the mortality risk is retained by the annuitant. Recall that annuity contracts offer an opportunity for individuals to hedge against the risk of running out of money by transferring that risk to an insurance company. The insurance company pools the risks represented by many annuitants, and uses the premiums paid by those who die early (before actuarial life expectancy) to fund the annuity payments of those who live longer than their actuarial life expectancy. It is possible, therefore, that someone could purchase a life annuity contract and die after receiving only one, or a few payments. Since there is no guaranteed minimum number of payments on a single life annuity, the annuitant's heirs will receive nothing from the contract once the annuitant has died. For this reason, using all of an individual's retirement savings to purchase a pure single life annuity may be ideal for the person who is very risk averse and seeks to spread income out over his lifetime to smooth his consumption but does not have any bequest motives. If a person has bequest motives, single life annuities may still be valuable in planning for retirement income when used in combination with other strategies. Many individuals will use part of their retirement savings to purchase a single life annuity that covers basic cash flow needs in retirement, such as housing, food, clothing, and medical costs. They retain control of their other retirement assets for use during retirement and for possible distribution to heirs after death. This bifurcated approach allows individuals to transfer part of the risk of running out of money to the insurance company without completely having to disinherit heirs.

Installment Refund Annuities

An **installment refund annuity option** provides for the insurer to continue periodic annuity payments after the annuitant has died until the sum of all annuity payments made equals the original purchase price of the annuity. This option reduces the risk that an unexpected early death will result in a large sum of money being exchanged for only a few annuity payments.

Cash Refund Annuities

A **cash refund annuity option** also guarantees that the annuitant or the annuitant's family will receive the premium payments made to purchase the annuity, but instead of continuing to make periodic payments until there is a full recovery of the premium, the remaining balance is paid in cash (lump sum) at the annuitant's death. All else equal, a cash refund annuity will pay a lower monthly income than an installment refund annuity providing the same level of payment since the insurance company's obligation to refund the premium payment may be accelerated at the death of the annuitant.

Both installment and cash refund annuities provide lifetime income for the annuitant. These refunds are only considered if the annuitant dies before the total amount of premiums have been paid out. In addition, these options result in a smaller annuity amount as compared to the straight life annuity option because these options have less risk for the annuitant.

Term Certain (Guaranteed Minimum Payment)

A **term certain annuity** (also known as period certain) pays annuity benefits for a specified period of time, regardless of whether the original annuitant lives or dies. This term could be for ten or twenty years. With a term certain annuity, it will pay benefits for only that period of time. Once the final payment is made, the annuity payments are complete. Based on this type of structure, a term certain annuity continues to subject the annuitant to the risk of superannuation.

Two common guarantee options for term certain annuities are the ten-year period certain and the twenty-year period certain. If the annuitant dies before the end of the guarantee period, the named beneficiary receives the remaining guaranteed payments. If the annuitant outlives the term certain period, payments continue to the annuitant until the annuitant's death, if combined with a life annuity (called a life with period certain option).

While a term certain will only make payments for the specified period of time, a term certain option can be combined with a life annuity. Unlike a straight life annuity, which does not guarantee a minimum number of payments, a life annuity with a term certain provision ensures that the annuitant or his heirs receives a minimum number of payments or, alternatively, if the annuitant lives for a long time, the annuitant will receive a lifetime of income. A life with period certain annuity acts as a hedge against the mortality risk retained when an individual purchases a single life annuity. In the case that the annuitant dies before his or her life expectancy, it preserves some of the capital for distribution to the annuitant's heirs. However, this hedge comes at a cost. For a given level of premium payment, the monthly payment received by the annuitant of a single life annuity with a term certain provision will be less than the payment received by the purchaser of a straight life annuity. In the unusual case of a single life annuity with a term certain equal to the life expectancy of the annuitant, the insurance company is retaining both the risk that the insured will die before life expectancy, and the risk that the insured will die after life expectancy. With a straight life annuity, the insurance company retains the risk that the annuitant will die after their actuarial life expectancy.

Example 8.2

Scott is retiring and is concerned about the risk of running out of money during retirement. He will receive Social Security benefits, but they are not large enough to cover his basic financial needs. He was advised to consider an annuity, which appears to have many advantages. However, he does not want to run the risk of exchanging a large sum of money and then only receiving a few payments if he were to unexpectedly die shortly after purchasing the annuity. Given his fear, he might consider an installment refund annuity, a cash refund annuity or a term certain annuity. Either of these options will "guarantee" a minimum amount of income from the annuity, but they will all have lower monthly payments than a straight or pure life annuity.

Joint and Survivor Life Annuities

A **joint and survivor annuity** promises to make payments over the lives of two or more annuitants, and annuity payments are made until the last annuitant dies. Joint and survivor annuities are commonly used to fund the retirement cash-flow of married couples. Without a joint and survivor option, a surviving spouse could be subject to a significant decrease in income if the annuity payments stopped at the death of the first spouse.

A **100 percent joint and survivor annuity** pays the specified monthly payment to the annuitants while both are alive and continues to make the same payment to the survivor after the first annuitant's death.

Some individuals may determine that, after the first death, the survivor would not need 100 percent of the original annuity payment since the deceased spouse will no longer have consumption expenses. They may choose a joint and survivor annuity that pays the survivor only a portion of the payment that was paid on both lives. For example, a married couple may purchase an annuity that pays $2,000 per month while both spouses are alive, but upon the death of the first spouse, the payment is reduced to $1,500 (75% of the original payment). This form of annuity contract is referred to as a **75 percent joint and survivor annuity**.

When a married person is a participant in a qualified defined-benefit retirement plan, the Retirement Equity Act (REA) requires that the pension benefit be paid in the form of a **50 percent joint and survivor annuity**. Retirement plan participants can elect to increase the payment made to a survivor to a higher percentage, but they cannot reduce the percentage below 50 percent or elect to receive a straight life annuity without the written consent of the nonparticipant spouse. For a given level of annuity benefit, the higher the percentage of the initial payment paid to the survivor of a joint and survivor annuity, the lower the amount of periodic income. The premiums for joint and survivor annuities are typically greater than the premiums charged for single life annuities because the insurer promises to make payments over a longer period of time.

Example 8.3

Gavin and Claire are 65 years old, have been married for forty years, and are getting ready to retire. They have accumulated $1 million that they would like to convert into an annuity. The annuity company might provide for the following annual options:
- Single life annuity over Gavin's life of $76,000 per year
- Single life annuity over Claire's life of $65,000 per year
- 100% joint life annuity of $57,000 per year
- 75% joint life annuity of $62,000 per year

They need to decide if they prefer one of these options over the other. They might also decide to consider one of the other options, such as an installment refund annuity option or a cash refund annuity option.

TYPES OF ANNUITY CONTRACTS

Several different forms of annuity contracts are offered for sale to consumers, including fixed annuities, variable annuities, and equity-indexed annuities. Investors will often choose an annuity for potential growth, tax deferred savings and/or principal protection. The annuity may or may not ever be annuitized by the investor.

- A **fixed annuity** provides payments of a fixed dollar amount that is typically determined when the annuity payments begin. The income is fixed based on the guaranteed returns provided by the insurer in the account.
- **Variable annuities** offer a variable rate of return based on the overall return of the investment options that are chosen. Variable annuities offer potentially higher returns than fixed annuities, but they also carry a greater risk of loss. Variable annuities offer an opportunity to mitigate the risk of inflation by investing in equities (stocks). Variable annuities also mitigate against investment risk since they have some minimum guarantees built into the contracts.
- An **equity indexed annuity** has characteristics of both fixed and variable annuities. It offers a minimum guaranteed interest rate combined with an investment return linked to the performance of a specific equity-based market index, such as the S&P 500. Equity indexed annuities also mitigate investment risk, longevity risk and inflation risk.

Exhibit 8.9 | Types of Annuity Contracts by Underlying Investments

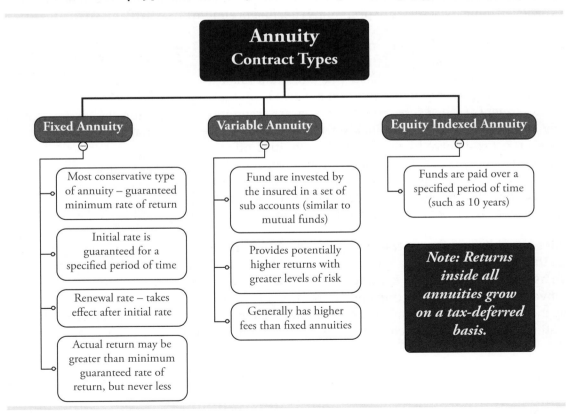

Fixed Annuity

A fixed annuity is the most conservative type of annuity. A fixed annuity is a contract that provides full principal protection combined with a guaranteed rate of return that is stated in the annuity contract.

Typically, the premiums paid for the annuity contract will begin earning an interest rate, which is dependent on current fixed income interest rates and known as the **initial rate**. This initial interest rate is guaranteed for a period of time. Once the initial interest-rate-guarantee period expires, a **renewal rate** for the policy will go into effect, and will typically change based on current rates each year. This rate will never be less than the **minimum interest rate** stated in the annuity policy. As a result, the actual rate of return on the contract may be higher than the stated guaranteed rate of return in the contract, depending on prevailing interest rates. However, it will never be less than the guarantee.

Withdrawals from deferred fixed annuities during the accumulation period will generally be limited to 10 percent of contract value per year without a fee. Withdrawals in excess of this amount will be subject to a surrender charge for a period of time, usually five to seven years. Surrender charges and free withdrawal provisions are discussed in greater detail later in this chapter.

Variable Annuity

A variable annuity is a contract between an annuitant and an insurance company whereby the insurance company agrees to make periodic payments to the annuitant in an amount to be determined in the future that is based on the accumulated value of the contract. Variable annuities can be purchased with either a single premium or a series of premiums (flexible premium).

A variable annuity, like all other annuity contracts, has two phases: the accumulation phase and the annuitization, or payout phase. During the accumulation phase the annuitant makes payments into the contract that are invested in various mutual-fund-like investments (called subaccounts or separate accounts) chosen by the annuitant. The earnings on these investments accumulate on a tax-deferred basis. Variable annuities offer a variable rate of return based on the overall return of the investment options chosen by the contract owner. The payout phase begins when the annuitant elects to annuitize the contract and receive regular payments from the insurance company.

> ### :≡ Key Concepts
>
> 1. Define fixed annuity payments.
> 2. Identify the characteristics of variable annuities.
> 3. Identify advantages and disadvantages of variable annuities.
> 4. Describe equity-indexed annuities.
> 5. Discuss common indexing methods.

Some older variable annuity contracts require the annuitant to annuitize the contract no later than the attainment of a specified age, such as age 85-90. Once the contract is annuitized, control of the investment account is transferred to the insurance company in exchange for the promise to make annuity payments. Annuitization typically terminates any accumulation-phase benefits, such as living or death benefits (discussed below), provided for in the contract.

Some people view variable annuities as an investment option that offers features not typically found in other types of non-qualified investments, including: tax-deferred earnings, the ability to avoid income tax when one investment in the annuity contract is sold and replaced with another investment (sometimes referred to as a tax-free transfer among subaccounts), death benefit protection options, living benefit protection options, and lifetime income options (discussed below).

Since control of the underlying investments in the variable annuity contract rests with the contract holder, variable annuities offer potentially higher returns than fixed annuities but also involve investment risk. The **prospectus** provided to purchasers of variable annuities contains important information about the annuity contract, including fees and charges, investment options and objectives, risks, death benefits, living benefits, and annuity income options. All of these factors should be carefully considered by purchasers of variable annuities. Variable annuities typically have a trial period of 10 or more days from the receipt of the contract, known as a free-look period. During this time the purchaser can terminate the contract and recover the premium paid without being subject to any surrender charges (discussed below).

Variable Annuity Fees

Variable annuity products have unique fees and charges designed to cover the cost of contract administration, portfolio management, and insurance benefits (for example, death benefits before annuitization and lifetime income benefits). Fees and charges may be assessed on the original investment, the current account value, or on the benefit's base value (benefit base). Variable annuities may impose a variety of fees and expenses. Variable annuity fees are typically described in terms of basis points (abbreviated bps, and pronounced as "bips" by those in the industry). A basis point is 1/100th of one percent. So, a fee of 40 basis points is equal to 0.40 percent, while a fee of 100 basis points is equal to one percent. The most common fees and charges associated with a variable annuity are discussed below:

Mortality and expense risk charges - These charges compensate the insurance company for insurance risks and are deducted from the value of the contract. These expenses are intended to cover the risk of annuitants living too long. The fees for guaranteed death benefits are included in mortality and expense risk charges. The typical mortality and expense risk charge ranges from 1.15 percent to 1.85 percent (115 to 185 bps) annually.

Administrative and distribution fees - These are the fees that cover the costs associated with servicing and distributing the annuity. These fees typically range from zero percent to 0.35 percent (0 to 35 bps) annually.

Annual fee - An annual fee is a flat fee charged for record keeping and administration. The fee typically ranges from $30 to $50 and is charged on the contract anniversary date. This fee is regularly waived for contract values of $50,000 or more.

Subaccount fees and expenses - These fees and expenses are charged to the investment subaccounts inside the annuity, and include investment management fees. Additional expenses include the transaction cost of buying and selling securities within the subaccounts. These are asset-based expenses that will vary by subaccount but typically range from 0.7 percent to 2.5 percent annually (70 to 250 bps).

Surrender charges - Many variable annuities have sales charges or surrender charges, known as contingent deferred sales charges (CDSC). Most variable annuities do not have an initial sales charge. However, insurance companies often assess surrender charges to annuitants who liquidate their contract during the surrender period. Surrender charges do not apply, however, if the annuity is annuitized.

The surrender charge is typically a percentage of the amount withdrawn in excess of a 10 percent free withdrawal amount (discussed below) and declines gradually over time. The surrender charge is effectively a way for the insurance company to recoup the broker's commission. A typical surrender charge ranges from seven percent to nine percent, decreasing over the surrender period to zero percent.

Exhibit 8.10 | Example of 7-Year Surrender Period Schedule

Withdrawal or Surrender Within:	Year 1	Year 2	Year 3	Year 4	Year 5	Year 6	Year 7	Year 8
Surrender Charge:*	8%	7%	6%	5%	4%	3%	2%	0%

*At no time will the aggregate surrender charge applied under the policy exceed nine percent (9%) of the total premium payments

Variable annuities are offered by share class with B shares typically having a six to eight-year period of surrender charges for each contribution (this is called a rolling surrender charge; some annuities apply the surrender charge only for a period of years following the initial contribution), L shares having a three to four-year surrender charge period for each contribution, and C shares having no surrender charge period making them fully liquid. The B shares typically have slightly lower fees. It is important to read the variable annuity prospectus (disclosure document) to understand exactly how the surrender charge is applied and under what circumstances it may be waived. Surrender charges are often waived for required minimum distributions from IRA-annuities, upon the death of the annuitant or owner, when the annuitant is admitted to a nursing home, or when the annuity is annuitized. Additional waivers may also be available.

There is generally a direct link between the CDSC and the commission the broker receives as part of the sale. Often, a seven year CDSC implies a seven percent commission. While this is not always the case, it is important to keep this in mind when selecting annuities.

Not all annuities have sales charges or a CDSC. Annuities that do not have sales charges can be purchased directly from companies such as Fidelity and Vanguard. In addition, fee-only advisors also sell annuities that do not charge a sales charge.

Example 8.4

Elmer purchases a variable annuity contract with a $100,000 purchase payment. The contract has a schedule of surrender charges, beginning with a 7% charge in the first year, and declining by 1% each year. In addition, he is allowed to withdraw 10% of the contract value each year free of surrender charges. In the first year, Elmer decides to withdraw $50,000, or one-half of his contract value of $100,000 (assuming the contract value has not increased or decreased because of investment performance). In this case, Elmer could withdraw $10,000 (10% of contract value) free of surrender charges, but he would pay a surrender charge of 7%, or $2,800, on the other $40,000 withdrawn.

During the accumulation phase, a variable annuity offers a wide range of both fixed and variable subaccounts with different investment objectives and strategies. The value of the variable annuity at any point in time will be a function of the performance of the investment options chosen by the contract holder. Variable subaccounts include actively managed portfolios, exchange traded funds, indexed or index-linked portfolios, alternative investments, and other quantitative-driven strategies. The subaccounts invest in various asset classes that include stocks, bonds, real estate, derivatives, commodities, and money market instruments.

Within the variable annuity during the accumulation period, the annuitant can transfer money from one subaccount to another without paying current income taxes on any earnings. The number of transfers per year may be limited by the annuity contract. Variable annuity issuers typically limit the number of transfers to discourage day trading-type activity within the contract.

During the accumulation period the earnings grow on a tax-deferred basis. During the surrender period, both fixed and variable annuity contracts generally offer a **free withdrawal provision** which allows the contract holder the right to withdraw up to 10 percent of the contract value annually without incurring a surrender charge. Withdrawal of money from a fixed or variable annuity will subject earnings to income tax at ordinary income tax rates, and if a withdrawal is taken prior to the attainment of age 59½, the annuitant may be subject to an additional 10 percent early withdrawal penalty on the amount that is subject to income tax.

Premiums paid during the accumulation phase of a variable annuity are used to purchase accumulation units in the investment account. The valuation of each unit is determined by dividing the total market value of all assets in the account by the number of accumulation units outstanding. Since the value of each unit is constantly changing, the number of units purchased with each additional deposit will vary. Reinvested dividend distributions from the selected investments are used to purchase additional units.

When entering the annuitization (liquidation) period, the accumulation units are exchanged for annuity units. The annuitant usually may elect either a fixed monthly payout or a variable monthly amount. When the variable payout is selected, the insurance company determines the number of benefit payment units the annuitant is to receive each month. This number of units is determined from the dollar amount in the annuitant's account at the start of the liquidation period, the life expectancy of the annuitant, and the payout arrangement selected by the annuitant.

The value of the benefit payment unit is determined by dividing the value of the total assets supporting the benefit payment units by the total number of benefit payment units outstanding. The monthly payment is the current value of the benefit payment unit multiplied by the number of benefit payment units to be paid to the annuitant each month. This payment will vary as the value of each unit fluctuates based on the investment performance of the underlying subaccounts. The calculation of the variable monthly payment amount can be summarized as:

Monthly Payment = # of Units x Current Value of 1 Unit

Variable annuity contracts, similar to other annuity contracts, allow for the contract value to be paid to a named beneficiary upon the death of the annuitant if the annuitant dies prior to annuitizing the contract. Variable annuity contracts also frequently provide a standard death benefit that is calculated as the greater of the return of premiums paid on the annuity less withdrawals, or the contract value at the death of the annuitant. Some contracts offer additional enhanced death benefits such as the ability to lock in a death benefit equal to the highest value of the contract. Optional death benefits typically cost from 0.25 percent to 1.5 percent annually and may terminate once an income option is elected and the annuitization period or payout period begins. Unlike life insurance, annuity death benefits are subject to income tax on the earnings portion of the contract when distributed to the named beneficiary (distribution options for beneficiaries are discussed later in this chapter).

Guaranteed Living Benefit Riders

The equity markets provide investors with an opportunity to generate investment returns that outperform inflation and taxes and increase wealth significantly over longer compounding periods. The primary concern with equity markets is the significant risk or at least the perceived risk that goes along with the "stock market." For example, in 1987 (Black Monday), the equity market dropped close to 30 percent in one day. In 2008, the market dropped over 30 percent for the year. In the first quarter of 2020, the market fell 35 percent from the market high in response to forced temporary business closures put in place to slow the spread of the Coronavirus. The exhibit below illustrates the volatility on an annual basis for the S&P 500 Index. Guaranteed living benefit riders are sold and marketed with the notion of combining the upside potential available in the equity markets with a guaranteed rate of return and principal protection.

Exhibit 8.11 | S&P 500 Index Annual Returns

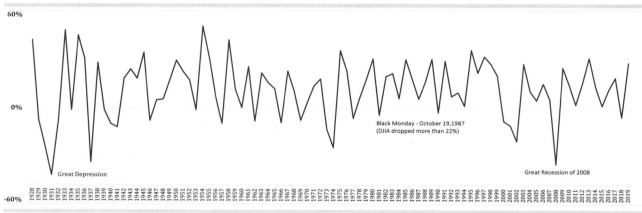

Many annuities offer living benefits that provide principal and or income guarantees to help protect retirement income from declining markets during the accumulation phase. Living benefit riders provide income protection while allowing for investment growth opportunities. There are three basic types of living benefits:

1. the guaranteed minimum accumulation benefit (GMAB)
2. the guaranteed minimum income benefit (GMIB)
3. the guaranteed minimum withdrawal benefit (GMWB)

The cost of additional optional living benefits typically ranges from 0.3 percent to two percent annually, and may be either fixed or variable, depending on the contract provisions. Purchasers should be aware that the costs on these riders, in combination with the other fees outlined above, can greatly decrease the upside growth potential within the annuity.

The general concepts of the GMAB, GMIB and GMWB living benefit riders are discussed below, in addition to the Guaranteed Lifetime Income Benefit (GLIB). However, it is important to understand that the contract from each insurance company may have differences in terms of guarantees, minimums, costs and other variables. Therefore, it is critical to carefully read and understand these types of riders before considering the appropriateness of the annuity or rider.

Guaranteed Minimum Accumulation Benefit

A guaranteed minimum accumulation benefit (GMAB) rider guarantees that for a specified period of time (typically 7-10 years), an investor's contract value will be at least equal to a certain minimum percentage (usually 100%) of the amount invested regardless of investment performance. The rider combines principal protection with upside potential. Many GMABs require the funds to be invested in a specified set of subaccounts or in a specified asset allocation.

Guaranteed Minimum Income Benefit

A guaranteed minimum income benefit (GMIB) rider is designed to provide the investor with a minimum amount of lifetime income during retirement, regardless of investment performance. The contract guarantees an income stream based on a minimum benefit base. The benefit base initially equals the initial investment, but will increase over time, usually at a pre-specified interest rate. Generally, investors must wait for a period of time (often ten years) before annuitizing and cannot withdraw the value as a lump sum. The rider guarantees the income even if the benefit base goes to zero.

Some GMIBs allow the benefit base to be "stepped up" to the account balance if the latter is higher at certain policy anniversaries. When the GMIB is utilized, the payment amount, in most cases, will be fixed, so the ability to keep up with inflation is lost, and there may be restrictions on the underlying investment options that may be selected. The cost for this benefit is typically 0.6 percent to 0.8 percent (60 to 80 basis points) per year. Some insurance companies guarantee that this cost will not increase, but with other companies the charges may be increased, so it is important to review the prospectus to determine both how the feature works and how the costs may change.

Guaranteed Minimum Withdrawal Benefit

A guaranteed minimum withdrawal benefit (GMWB) rider guarantees that a certain percentage (usually 5-7%) of the amount invested can be withdrawn annually until the entire amount is completely recovered, regardless of investment performance of the underlying asset base. A GMWB rider does not require annuitization to receive benefits. Like the GMIB, it does not guarantee a lump sum value, instead, withdrawals are made over a period of time. Unlike the GMIB, there is usually no waiting period before the withdrawals can begin.

If the underlying investments perform well, then there are additional funds in the policy at the end of the withdrawal period. If the underlying investments perform poorly or if the account value drops to zero, the investor can still continue to take withdrawals until the full amount of the original investment is recovered.

There is often a step-up feature that permits the investor to lock in a higher benefit base if the underlying investments perform well. The cost of the GMWB rider is typically 0.7 percent to 0.95 percent (70 – 95 basis points), with prospectus maximums of up to about 1.2 percent (120 basis points), meaning that the cost may be increased in the future, but not above the stated maximum.

Guaranteed Lifetime Income Benefit

The Guaranteed Lifetime Income Benefit (GLIB) guarantees that a certain percentage (typically 2-8%, often based on age) of the amount invested can be withdrawn each year for as long as the contract holder lives. The percentage will be lower for younger investors and higher for older investors when withdrawals begin.

These riders have been extremely popular and often misunderstood given the volatility in the equity markets and the low interest rates available on fixed income securities. The living benefit riders are continuously being enhanced, modified, and changed, and they are becoming increasingly complex. Marketing materials tend to provide very limited information, so it is imperative for planners to read and understand the prospectus for each variable annuity before making a recommendation on the purchase of the contract or the addition of a rider. Most of these riders are available on fixed annuities as well as variable annuities.

Exhibit 8.12 | Comparison of Fixed and Variable Annuities

Characteristics	Fixed	Variable
Benefit Payments	Fixed amount is paid monthly, quarterly, or annually.	Amount paid each period varies with the investment results of separate accounts.
Investment of Premiums	Premiums are invested in the insurer's general account.	Premiums are invested in separate accounts.
Assets	General account assets are mostly fixed-income.	Owner selects among investment options, similar to stock or bond mutual funds.
Investment Returns	A fixed return is guaranteed during accumulation and payout years.	Returns depend on the success of separate accounts; there is no guarantee (unless purchased via rider for an additional fee).
Investment	Insurer assumes the investment risk.	Owner assumes the investment risk.
Voting Rights	Owner has no voting rights for investment policies or adviser.	Owner has voting rights for investment policies and adviser.

Equity-Indexed Annuities

Equity-indexed annuities are fixed annuities, either immediate or deferred, that earn interest or provide benefits that are linked to an external equity reference or an equity index. The value of the index might be tied to an equity index or some other index. One of the most commonly used indices for annuity products is the Standard & Poors 500 composite stock price index (S&P 500), which is an equity-based index. The value of any index varies from day to day and is not predictable or guaranteed.

An equity indexed annuity differs from other fixed annuities because of the way it credits interest to the contract value. Some fixed annuities only credit interest at a rate set in the contract. Other fixed annuity contracts credit interest at rates that are set from time to time by the insurance company. In contrast, equity-indexed annuities credit interest using a formula based on changes in the index to which the annuity is linked. The formula determines how the additional interest is calculated and credited to the contract. An equity indexed annuity is a compromise between a variable annuity and a straight fixed annuity having little downside risk and modest upside potential. An equity-indexed annuity will have more risk and greater potential return than a fixed annuity, but will have less risk and less potential return than a variable annuity.

An equity indexed annuity, like other fixed annuities also promises to pay a minimum (guaranteed but low) interest rate. This minimum rate guarantee is paid regardless of whether the index-linked interest rate is lower than the guaranteed rate. The value of the annuity will also not decline below a guaranteed minimum value because it is guaranteed by the issuer. For example, many single premium annuity contracts guarantee that the minimum value will never be less than 90 percent of the premiums paid plus at least three percent plus annual interest less withdrawals.

The two features of an equity indexed annuity contract that have the greatest effect on the amount of additional interest that may be credited to the contract are:
- The indexing methods specified in the contract
- The participation rate

It is important for contract owners to understand the features of the contract and how those features work together.

The **indexing method** is the approach used to measure the amount of change, if any, in the index. Some common indexing methods include:
- The annual reset (ratcheting) method
- The high watermark method
- The point-to-point method

When the **annual reset method** is used, the index-linked interest crediting rate is determined each year by comparing the index value at the end of the contract year with the index value at the beginning of the contract year. Interest is then added to the annuity each year during the term. The advantage of the annual reset method is that the interest earned is locked in and the index value is reset at the end of each year. Future decreases in the index will not affect the interest already earned and credited to the contract. The trade-off for this indexing method is that the participation rate may change each year and will generally be lower than other indexing methods. Furthermore, an annual reset design may use averaging to limit the total amount of interest earned each year.

The **high watermark approach** to determining index-linked interest is accomplished by comparing the value of the index at various points during the term (usually on anniversary dates). The interest credited is based on the difference between the highest index values and the index value at the start of the term. Interest is added to the annuity at the end of the term. Since interest is calculated using the highest value of the index, this design may credit higher interest to the contract than some other interest crediting designs if the index reaches a high point early or in the middle of the term and then drops off later. The trade-off is that interest is not credited until the end of the term. Equity-indexed annuities taking this approach may cause the loss of interest for the last accumulation period prior to annuitization or surrender of the contract, since surrendering an annuity before the end of the term will result in forfeiting the indexed-linked interest for that term. Contracts with this design may have a lower participation rate than annuities using other designs, or they may use a cap to limit the total amount of interest that can be earned.

The **point-to-point index-linked crediting method** is based on the difference between an index value at the end of the term compared with the index value at the start of the term. Interest is then added to the annuity at the end of the term. Since interest cannot be calculated before the end of the term this design permits a higher participation rate than annuities using other indexing methods. The term over which the index value is compared could be one year or as long as six or seven years, and the annuitant will usually not be able to receive the index-linked interest until the end of the term.

Exhibit 8.13 | Common Indexing Methods

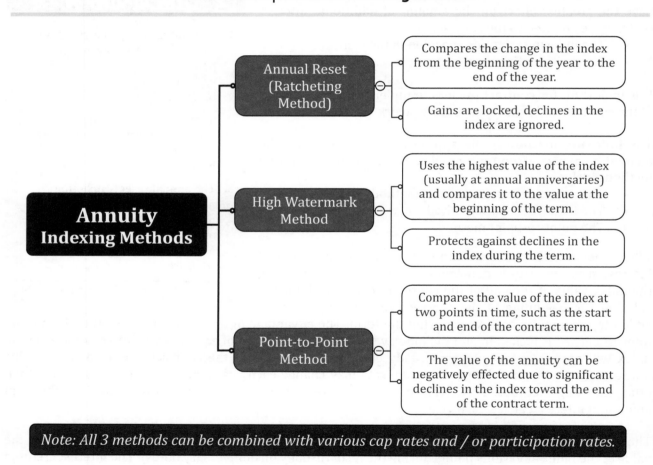

The **index term** is the period over which index-linked interest is calculated. For most equity-indexed annuities, interest is credited at the end of a time period ranging from one to ten years, with six or seven years being the most common. Surrender of the contract in the middle of the term will typically result in loss of interest crediting. Due to this interest forfeiture and the surrender fees involved, equity-indexed annuities should be viewed as long-term investments that will be held at least through the end of each interest crediting term. Some indexed annuities offer single terms while others offer multiple, consecutive terms. If an annuity has multiple terms, there will usually be a window at the end of each term (typically 30 days) during which the annuitant may withdraw money without penalty.

The **participation rate** determines how much of the increase in the index will be used to calculate the index-linked interest. For example, if the calculated change in the index is 10 percent, and the participation rate is 70 percent, the index-linked interest will be seven percent. A company may set a different participation rate for newly issued annuities as often as each day. Therefore, the initial participation rate in the annuity will depend on when it was issued. The company usually guarantees the participation rate for a specific period (from one year to the entire term of the contract). When that period is over the company sets a new participation rate for the next period. Some annuities guarantee that the participation rate will never be lower than a specified minimum amount and will never be higher than a specified maximum amount.

Some indexed annuities impose an upper limit on the index-linked interest rate, referred to as the **cap rate**. This rate is the maximum rate of interest that the annuity will earn. For example, if an indexed annuity contract has a 6.5 percent cap rate, only 6.5 percent would be credited to the contract even if the index had a higher return. Not all indexed annuities have cap rates.

> **✓ Quick Quiz 8.5**
>
> 1. Mortality and expense charges for a variable annuity may exceed one percent.
>   a. True
>   b. False
>
> 2. Variable annuities permit the owner to invest in traditional closed-end mutual funds.
>   a. True
>   b. False
>
> 3. The annual reset (ratcheting) method is a common indexing method for equity-indexed annuities.
>   a. True
>   b. False
>
> True, False, True.

The **floor crediting rate** for an indexed annuity is the minimum index-linked interest rate that will be credited to the contract in a given period. The most common floor used in indexed annuities is zero percent. A zero percent floor assures the contract holder that even if the index decreases in value, the index-linked interest credited to the account will be zero (no losses will be allocated to the contract). Purchasers of indexed annuities should be aware, however, that not all annuities have a stated floor on the index-linked interest rates. Those contracts with a floor, however, will retain a minimum guaranteed value.

As an alternative to a cap and floor, some indexed annuities use the average of an index value as the crediting rate rather than the actual value of the index on a specified date. When the averaging approach is employed, the index averaging may occur at the beginning, at the end, or throughout the entire term of the indexed annuity contract.

Example 8.5

Homer buys an equity-indexed annuity that has a guaranteed minimum rate of 2% and a participation rate of 75% of the increase in the S&P 500 index over a 1-year period. The interest crediting is capped at 9%. On the day Homer purchases his annuity, the S&P 500 index is at 1800, and one year later the index is at 2050, an increase of 13.88%. With a 75% participation rate, Homer may be expecting to be credited with 10.42% interest (0.75 x 13.88 = 10.42); however, the contract caps his interest at 9% so he will be credited with a 9% rate. If the S&P 500 return is instead -7.3%, Homer will be credited with the minimum rate of 2%.

Some indexed annuities pay simple interest during an index term, while others pay compound interest during the term. In either case, the interest earned in one term is usually compounded in the next term.

In some indexed annuity contracts, the index-linked interest rate is computed by subtracting the margin (spread), or administrative fee. For example, if the calculated change in the index is 10 percent, the annuity might specify that 2.5 percent will be subtracted from the rate to determine the interest rate credited to the contract. In this example, the crediting rate for the contract would be 7.5 percent. The insurance company would only subtract the administrative fee if it would not produce a negative interest crediting rate for the contract.

Equity-indexed annuities provide a variety of death benefits. The most common death benefit is either the guaranteed minimum value of the annuity or the value as determined by the index-linked formula.

ADVANTAGES AND DISADVANTAGES

Advantages of Annuity Contracts

Annuities provide several benefits that make them particularly attractive for some individuals, including reducing the risk of outliving retirement savings, tax deferral, and creditor protection.

Individuals concerned with the possibility of outliving their retirement savings may transfer that longevity risk to an insurance company by purchasing an annuity. From a planning perspective, the problem is predicting how long a person will live. With no further advances in medical technology, a male who has attained the age of 66 now has a 50 percent chance to live to age 84 and almost a 20 percent chance to live to age 90. It is prudent, in many situations, to purchase an annuity contract to cover basic consumption needs during retirement so that the annuitant does not have to worry about running out of money at an advanced age.

Annuities also provide an opportunity to defer income taxation on the investment earnings in the contract beyond the contribution limitations imposed on ordinary qualified plans and IRAs. Most non-qualified annuities (annuities funded with after-tax contributions) require the account holder to annuitize by a certain age, but many of these contracts impose an age requirement significantly above age 70½ (age 72, as amended by the SECURE Act of 2019), the age at which required minimum distributions (RMDs) from qualified retirement plans and IRAs must begin. Generally, income tax deferral benefits an individual who expects to have a long accumulation period or who expects to be in a lower tax bracket in retirement than when the annuity is funded.

Key Concepts

1. Discuss the advantages and disadvantages of annuities.

2. Understand the tax consequences of annuities.

An ancillary benefit to tax deferral is the ability to rebalance the portfolio inside of variable annuity contracts without incurring any immediate income taxation on asset sales. If investment rebalancing is completed in a non-qualified portfolio outside of an annuity contract, the assets sold in the rebalancing will trigger taxable gain or loss that must be reported on the investor's current income tax return.

Annuities also provide another advantage when unexpected creditor issues arise. Federal law exempts all qualified retirement plans and IRAs from a bankruptcy estate. This exemption means that qualified plan assets and IRA assets are protected from creditors. Annuities are protected from creditors in some states. For example, Louisiana protects most life insurance and annuity contracts.

Disadvantages of Annuity Contracts

While there are many advantages, annuities also have several disadvantages, including complexity, costs, and tax consequences.

Complexity

Annuity contracts are often difficult for investors to understand. The purchase of an annuity contract involves a risk trade-off whereby the risk of living too long is transferred to an insurance company that will pool the funds of many annuitants, using some of the capital paid by those who die before their actuarial life expectancies to pay benefits to those who live beyond their actuarial life expectancies. For many, the possibility of losing capital if they die too young overshadows the benefits of transferring longevity risk to an insurance company. Annuity contracts also have several features such as guaranteed death benefits, guaranteed life income, and guaranteed terms. Each of these features has a cost associated with it, and it is not uncommon for annuity costs to range between 2.5 percent to 3.5 percent of invested capital. While these costs are similar to those associated with permanent life insurance, they are expensive when compared with other investment alternatives. One of the reasons for these high costs is that the insurance company cannot predict future medical advances and other items that could dramatically increase life expectancy and therefore significantly increase their costs of providing lifetime income streams for annuitants.

Costs and Fees

One of the major disadvantages of annuity contracts is the costs and fees charged by the insurance company to issue a contract and undertake the longevity risk obligation.

A fixed annuity typically does not impose any direct expense charges on the contract owner other than a surrender charge. Variable annuities, on the other hand, have several types of expenses, including investment management fees for the underlying investment portfolios and annual insurance charges in addition to the surrender charges. These fees and charges were discussed in detail previously in the review of variable annuity contracts.

Surrender charges are commonly used by insurers to recoup the costs of issuing the annuity when the annuitant surrenders the contract within a few years of issuance. These charges typically range from five percent to nine percent of the annuity value and usually decline to zero over a period of time, such as from three to nine years. Each state regulates the maximum term for which a surrender charge may be applied, so the length of the surrender charge period may differ for individuals residing in different jurisdictions.

Insurance charges generally include administrative and distribution charges and mortality and expense risk charges. The administrative and distribution charges pay for all the services involved in the maintenance of variable annuity contracts such as the preparation of the contract statement, mailings, and customer service. Recall that some variable annuity contracts also impose an annual contract fee.

Tax Consequences

While one of the benefits of using an annuity contract is the ability to achieve deferral of income taxation on investment gains until amounts are distributed from the contract to the annuitant or a beneficiary, all distributions of income in excess of basis are considered ordinary income, and are subject to tax at the taxpayer's highest ordinary income tax rate. In contrast, investments held outside of annuity contracts do not achieve tax deferral, but they may qualify for favorable capital gains and qualified dividend tax rates that are significantly lower than the tax rates imposed on ordinary income. A more comprehensive discussion of the tax consequences of annuity contracts follows, but it is important to recognize that the purchase of an annuity contract involves a trade-off between the benefits of tax deferral and the benefits of generating investment income taxable at more favorable rates.

Since 2013, distributions from annuity contracts made to high income taxpayers are also subject to the Medicare surtax on investment income of 3.8 percent. A high income taxpayer is an individual with more than $200,000 of adjusted gross income, or a married couple filing jointly with more than $250,000 in adjusted gross income. Currently, the law does not index these thresholds for inflation. Therefore, in addition to all distributions being subject to ordinary income tax (currently, the highest rate is 37%), high income individuals may have to pay an additional 3.8 percent tax (raising the income tax rates on annuities to 40.8%). Interestingly, distributions from qualified retirement plans and IRAs are not subject to the 3.8 percent Medicare surtax, so one way to avoid this additional tax is to purchase an annuity contract inside of a qualified retirement plan or IRA.

> ### ✍ Quick Quiz 8.7
>
> 1. Annuities provide an opportunity to defer income taxation on investment earnings.
>   a. True
>   b. False
>
> 2. Advantages of annuities include simplicity, low costs, tax advantages.
>   a. True
>   b. False
>
> 3. All deferred annuity contracts are subject to the Medicare surtax of 3.8 percent.
>   a. True
>   b. False
>
> True, False, False.

TAXATION OF ANNUITIES

Income Taxation

Typically, distributions are not made to the annuitant until the contract is **annuitized**. An annuity contract is annuitized when regular, periodic (such as monthly or annual) payments begin for life or for a specified period of time in excess of one year. In some instances, however, the owner may surrender the contract or decide to take a one-time distribution without annuitizing the contract.

The extent to which distributions from an annuity contract are subject to income tax is determined by reference to the annuitant's basis in the contract. Basis represents after-tax dollars that were invested in the contract. An annuitant who has basis in an annuity contract will receive their basis back income-tax free over their actuarial life expectancy if the contract is annuitized. Distributions from annuity contracts in excess of basis are subject to income tax at ordinary tax rates.

If an annuity owner surrenders the contract prior to annuitization, the distribution is taxable to the extent that the distribution exceeds the owner's basis in the contract.

> ### ⋮☰ *Key Concepts*
>
> 1. Explain the income taxation of annuity benefits.
> 2. Define a non-qualified annuity.
> 3. Understand the estate tax implications of any remaining value in an annuity at the annuitant's death.

Example 8.6

Jasper purchased an annuity contract 10 years ago for $100,000. He feels his retirement funds from other sources are adequate, and needs money now to cover a pressing financial need. Jasper surrendered the annuity contract when the value of the contract was $175,000. Jasper will receive his basis in the contract ($100,000) free of income tax, but will have to pay ordinary income tax on the additional $75,000 he receives when surrendering the contract.

Sometimes, the owner of an annuity does not need to access the full value of the contract, but does need to withdraw some money. When distributions (withdrawals) are taken from an annuity before annuitizing, the entire distribution must be included in the taxpayer's gross income until all of the gain in the contract has been distributed. Once all of the gain in the contract is distributed, further distributions are treated as tax-free returns of invested dollars. Annuity contracts follow a LIFO (last-in, first-out) approach to income reporting in which the gain in the contract (generated from the investment made in the contract) must be fully distributed before a tax-free return of basis may be received. However, annuities issued prior to August 14, 1982 receive FIFO (first-in, first-out) treatment. Distributions of earnings may also be subject to a 10 percent early withdrawal penalty if the account holder is under age 59½ (discussed below).

Example 8.7

Hope purchased an annuity contract 10 years ago for $100,000. The current value of the annuity is $175,000. Hope decides to withdraw $100,000 from the contract to pay for her daughter's graduate education since Hope believes she has enough money saved for retirement. The gain in the contract ($75,000) will be fully subject to income tax when Hope makes the withdrawal, and the additional $25,000 will be treated as a return of Hope's basis. After the withdrawal, Hope will have an annuity contract with a value of $75,000 and a basis of $75,000 ($100,000 original basis less the $25,000 of basis withdrawn from the contract).

Annuities purchased with pre-tax dollars typically do not have any basis (after-tax dollars invested in the contract) for income tax purposes. Examples of annuity contracts that are purchased with pre-tax dollars include annuities purchased with funds from a 401(k) plan or a deductible traditional IRA plan. In addition, some annuities received as settlements from court cases (to the extent that the payments are not made as compensation for a physical injury) will have a zero basis. Consequently, each payment received by the owner will be fully subject to tax at the owner's ordinary marginal income tax rate.

When an annuitant purchases an annuity contract with after-tax dollars, also known as a **non-qualified annuity**, the after-tax dollars invested in the contract create basis for income tax purposes. Examples of annuity contracts purchased with after-tax dollars include contracts purchased individually by taxpayers outside of retirement plans, annuity contracts received as life insurance settlement options from the death benefits on life insurance policies, and annuities received as settlements from lawsuits to the extent that the damages were for physical injuries sustained by the plaintiffs.

Each annuity payment received from a non-qualified annuity is split into two pieces:
- A tax-free return of basis
- Taxable income

This split is determined by using an inclusion/exclusion ratio similar to that used for the installment method settlement option associated with life insurance death benefits.

The exclusion ratio equals the owner's investment in the annuity contract divided by the expected return on the annuity. The resulting percentage is multiplied by the distribution, or payment, received to calculate the portion of the payment that is not subject to income tax. When performing this calculation, the investment in the contract is the total amount of after-tax dollars invested in the contract, and the expected return is the total amount of dollar distributions expected to be received under the contract. The remaining portion of the payment received by the annuitant is subject to income tax.

Example 8.8

Kevin invested $100,000 in an annuity contract. Many years later, he annuitized the contract. The insurance company agreed to pay him $1,388.89 per month for 15 years. His expected return, therefore, is $250,000.02 (15 years x 12 months x $1,388.89 per month). The exclusion ratio is 40%, calculated by taking Kevin's investment in the contract of $100,000 and dividing it by his expected return of $250,000.20. The amount of each payment excluded from tax is $555.56 (calculated by multiplying the exclusion ratio of 40% by the payment of $1,388.89). The difference between the payment of $1,388.89 and the portion excluded from income ($555.56) is $833.34 (60%), which is subject to income tax.

The amount excluded from gross income in a twelve-month period would be $6,666.68 (12 x $1,388.89 x 0.40) and the amount excluded over the entire 15 years would be $100,000 (15 x 12 x $1,388.89 x 0.40). Note that the total amount excluded from income tax in this example equals Kevin's taxable basis in the contract.

The amount included in gross income is the inclusion ratio (60% times each payment received).

Application of the exclusion ratio may be perceived as more difficult if a life annuity payment is chosen instead of a period certain, as illustrated in the preceding example. A simple adjustment, however, is all that is necessary for the exclusion ratio to work. Instead of calculating the return on the contract using the term certain, for tax purposes, it is assumed that the owner will die at actuarial life expectancy. This life expectancy is used as the measuring period for calculating the return on the contract.

Example 8.9

Kasey invested $100,000 in an annuity contract. Many years later, he annuitized the contract. The insurance company agreed to pay him $1,388.89 per month for the rest of his life. Using mortality tables provided by the Internal Revenue Service, Kasey's life expectancy was determined to be 15 years. As in the preceding example, the expected return is $250,000.20 (15 x 12 x $1,388.89) and the amounts excluded from and included in gross income are the same.

For a variable annuity, because the expected distribution amount is not known, the investment in the contract is divided by the number of years of expected payout (either life expectancy or a period of years) to determine an excludible dollar amount for each payment received. If one of the variable payments happens to fall below the exclusion amount, a new exclusion amount is recalculated based on the remaining life expectancy or remaining period of years of payout. Like fixed annuities, once the investment in the contract has been fully recovered, all payments will be fully taxable as ordinary income.

Exhibit 8.14 | Calculating the Exclusion Amount for a Non-Qualified Annuity

Type of Annuity	Formula	Comments
Term Certain (Fixed Period Payout)	$$\text{Exclusion Amount} = \frac{\text{Basis}}{\text{\# of Payments}}$$	The number of payments is known, so basis is spread equally among the payments.
Life Annuity	$$\text{Exclusion Percent} = \frac{\text{Basis}}{\text{Expected Return}}$$	The number of payments is not known. Expected return = annual payout x life expectancy. Payments beyond life expectancy are fully taxable.
Variable Annuity	$$\text{Exclusion Amount} = \frac{\text{Basis}}{\text{\# of Expected Payments}}$$	The exclusion amount is recalculated if, during the annuitization period, one of the variable payments falls below the initial exclusion amount.

Note: Basis = Investment in the contract

If an annuitant is receiving a life annuity and dies prior to his or her actuarial life expectancy, the full amount of his or her basis in the contract will not be recovered by the date of death using the exclusion ratio approach to annuity taxation. When this occurs, the annuitant may claim a miscellaneous itemized deduction (not subject to the two percent of adjusted gross income limitation), for the unrecovered basis on his or her final federal income tax return.

If an annuitant is receiving a life annuity and lives beyond his or her actuarial life expectancy, he or she would have recovered the full basis in the contract upon attainment of life expectancy. All payments received by the annuitant after attaining life expectancy, therefore, will be fully subject to tax, and the exclusion ratio will no longer apply.

In addition to the regular income tax that applies to distributions from annuity contracts, two situations will impose additional taxes on the annuitant. If the account holder takes a distribution of income from an annuity contract before age 59½, a 10 percent penalty tax applies to the earnings portion of the distribution, and if the account holder is a high income taxpayer and the annuity distribution is not made through an IRA or qualified plan, a 3.8 percent Medicare surtax will apply.

When taxable income is received from an annuity before the recipient (account holder) reaches the age of 59½, a 10 percent penalty tax (10% of the taxable income) is imposed on the taxable income unless certain exceptions apply, such as distributions made in the form of substantially equal periodic payments to the owner under the provisions of IRC Sections 72(t) or 72(q). This penalty is also waived if the distribution is made due to the disability or death of the account holder (or annuitant if the account owner is a non-natural person). Prior to annuitization, the last-in, first-out (LIFO) method is used to determine the character of the distribution. This means all of the income of the contract is distributed prior to any distribution of principal. If an annuity owner takes a distribution before reaching age 59½ and the distribution is greater than the income on the contract, the distribution in excess of income is treated as a return of capital and is not subject to income tax or the ten percent penalty.

Exhibit 8.15 | Taxation Summary Chart

	Qualified Annuity	Non-qualified Annuity
Source of funds	Qualified Plans, IRAs, 403(b) Plans	After-Tax Funds
Tax-deferred earnings	Yes	Yes
Taxation of distributions	Fully Taxable (generally)	Partially Taxable and Partially Return of Basis
10% early withdrawal penalty applies to distributions prior to age 59½	Yes	Yes
Required minimum distributions at age 70½ (or at age 72)	Yes	No
Distributions subject to 3.8% Medicare surtax for high income owner	No	Yes

Aggregation Rules

To prevent the manipulation of tax rules, the IRS will treat all annuities purchased from the same insurer in the same year by the same policyholder as a single contract. The IRS views the purchase of multiple similar small contracts as an abusive strategy and, to prevent its use, treats all annuity contracts purchased in the same year from the same insurer as a single contract for tax purposes.

Example 8.10

Ken purchases an annuity for $5,000, and it grows to $6,000. Ken wants to take a withdrawal (partial surrender) of $500, which will be treated by the IRS as a distribution of earnings and taxed as ordinary income.

Ken's brother Len, anticipating that he may need to take a few partial withdrawals later on, purchased five different policies for $1,000 each, at the same rate of earnings as Ken. Each policy grows to $1,200 (the total of all policies being $6,000, the same as Ken's). If there were no aggregation rules, Len could withdraw his $500 from just one contract and only pay tax on $200, with the other $300 treated as a return of principal. Due to aggregations rules, Len will be in the same tax situation as his brother Ken.

Annuities Surrendered for a Loss

One of the advantages of variable annuities is that the funds can be invested in subaccounts that invest in stocks, bonds, real estate or other types of investments which can provide for sizable growth. However, there are times when the value of an investment in an annuity declines due to changes in the market. In these cases, the owner can surrender the annuity and claim a tax-deductible loss. The annuity must be surrendered and not exchanged. Annuities exchanged for other annuities fall under IRC Section 1035.

The value of the loss on the surrender of an annuity is equal to the investment in the annuity less the value upon surrender. The loss does not include the amount of any surrender charges.

The character of the loss is somewhat unsettled at this point. Annuities are not capital assets. Therefore, the loss is not reported as a capital loss. Annuities produce ordinary income. Thus, there is a case to be made that a loss on a surrendered annuity is an ordinary loss. This approach is more aggressive than the other option, which is to report the loss as a miscellaneous itemized deduction subject to two percent of AGI (adjusted gross income).[2] For years 2018 through 2025, the Tax Cuts Jobs Act of 2017 (TCJA) suspends the deduction for miscellaneous itemized deductions subject to the two percent floor.

Example 8.11

Jack purchased a variable annuity and invested $150,000. He made a few poor investment decisions, and the market dropped. Like many investors, he decided to sell when the value was low. He decided to surrender the annuity, which cost him a $4,000 surrender fee. He only received $96,000 back. He can take a loss of $50,000. This loss can be taken as an ordinary loss or as an itemized deduction subject to two percent of AGI (prior to 2018 and after 2025). However, if he takes the loss as an ordinary loss, it could be reversed upon audit.

Section 1035 Exchanges

As discussed in Chapter 5, there are certain tax-free exchanges of life insurance policies and annuities that are permitted under IRC §1035. Section 1035 of the Code states that if a policy is exchanged for another similar policy (for example, life insurance for life insurance, MEC for MEC, or annuity for annuity), or for an insurance product that increases the potential for assessment of income tax, the exchange of the policies is a tax-deferred exchange. No income tax will be due at the time of the exchange. If a tax-deferred exchange is desired, therefore, life insurance policies can be exchanged for other life insurance policies, MECs, or annuity contracts. MECs can be exchanged for other MECs or annuity contracts, and annuity contracts can be exchanged only for annuity contracts.

To qualify under Section 1035, the annuitant must remain the same under the old and new annuity contracts, and the transfer must be completed as a trustee-to-trustee transfer between the insurance companies. If any amount is distributed to the owner of the contract, it will be irrevocably treated as a taxable distribution. A Section 1035 exchange should not be done without appropriate cost-benefit analysis, keeping in mind factors such as the implications of starting a new surrender charge period under the new annuity contract.

Exhibit 8.16 | Tax Treatment of Exchange for Life Insurance and Annuities

Exchange To	Exchange From	
	Life Insurance	Annuity
Life Insurance	Tax Free	Taxable
Annuity	Tax Free	Tax Free

In the case of a tax-free exchange, the basis of the original contract will carry over to the new contract and will increase if additional premium payments are made to the insurance company.

---

2. See Rev. Rul. 61-201, which provides some support for the more aggressive position of deducting the loss as an ordinary loss. However, losses on IRAs are claimed as miscellaneous itemized deductions subject to the two percent limit.

Example 8.12

Brendan purchased an annuity 15 years ago. He has exchanged the annuity for another annuity. This exchange is not a taxable transaction under Section 1035. If Brendan wanted to exchange the annuity for a life insurance policy, then it would be a taxable transaction.

Under a provision of the Pension Protection Act of 2006, beginning in 2010 nonqualified annuity distributions used to pay for qualified long-term care insurance (LTCI) premiums are income tax-free.

For deferred annuities, the tax-fee treatment is accomplished through a partial Section 1035 exchange from the nonqualified annuity to the LTCI issuer. Each partial exchange will reduce the earnings and basis of the annuity pro rata.

Income from a nonqualified SPIA paid to the LTCI carrier is treated as a partial assignment of income in a 1035 exchange and is also tax-free.

In both cases the funds must be paid directly from one insurance company to the other, and other 1035 exchange rules, such as the requirement that the contracts be for the same insured, must also be followed.

While the annuity-to-LTCI transfer is tax-free, planners should remain aware of any surrender charges that may be due if the amount of the LTCI premium is greater than any free withdrawal amount (typically 10% can be withdrawn each year without a surrender charge, but that amount can vary from contract-to-contract).

> **📝 Quick Quiz 8.8**
>
> 1. A non-qualified annuity is an annuity purchased with pre-tax dollars.
>   a. True
>   b. False
>
> 2. The exclusion ratio equals the portion of the payment that is subject to income tax.
>   a. True
>   b. False
>
> 3. A single premium deferred annuity purchased with after-tax funds will be subject to the minimum distribution rules.
>   a. True
>   b. False
>
> 4. Annuities are considered IRD assets.
>   a. True
>   b. False
>
> False, False, False, True.

It should also be noted that not all LTCI carriers accept 1035 exchanges, so a little research may be needed before policies are selected. Also note that the Section 1035 exchange to LTCI is only available for nonqualified annuities. Qualified annuities are not permitted to be used.

Estate Taxation

One estate planning advantage of annuities is that they transfer directly to the named beneficiary upon the death of the owner, avoiding the probate process (the legal process of validating the will and transferring assets upon death). However, the remaining value of an annuity contract held by an individual at death is included in the individual's gross estate for estate tax purposes.

If the owner annuitizes the annuity under a life income option prior to his death, there is no residual value at the date of the owner's death, and therefore nothing is included in the gross estate for estate tax purposes. Only annuities owned by an individual that had not yet been annuitized, and annuities making term-certain payments extending beyond the date of the original annuitant's death, will be included in the estate of the annuitant at its date of death value.

Annuities are considered **IRD (income in respect of a decedent) assets**. IRD assets represent assets that have a deferred income tax liability that was not paid prior to the date of the owner's death. To preserve the right to subject the deferred income to income tax, the tax law does not permit IRD assets to receive a basis adjustment (equal to the fair market value of the asset at the date of the owner's death) at the death of the owner. Therefore, a beneficiary of an annuity contract will inherit the remaining basis of the original owner, and will pay income taxes on any distributions in excess of basis. To the extent that the inclusion of an IRD asset, such as an annuity contract, in the estate of a decedent increases the decedent's estate tax liability, the increase in estate tax liability becomes an income tax deduction (a miscellaneous itemized deduction not subject to the two percent of AGI limit) in the hands of the beneficiary.[3] This income tax deduction offsets some of the income included in the beneficiary's income tax return as a result of receiving the annuity payments.

Example 8.13

Pursuant to a retirement plan, ABC Company (ABC) was paying Chuck an annuity for life. Chuck died at age 92, at which time the annuity payments stopped. No part of the annuity is included in Chuck's gross estate.

Example 8.14

Tianna, who is unmarried, retired at age 62 and purchased an immediate annuity for $1 million. She was concerned that if she died prematurely she would have wasted her savings. As a result, she decided to purchase a single life annuity with a ten-year term certain option. She named her friend, Richie, as the beneficiary. Unfortunately for Tianna, she was hit by a baseball and died four months after purchasing the annuity. Since the annuity will continue to make payments for the remainder of the ten years, that value is included in Tianna's gross estate.

Example 8.15

Sergio, who just died, purchased an annuity contract under the terms of which the issuing company agreed to pay an annuity to the decedent for his life and, upon his death, to pay a specified lump sum to his designated beneficiary. Sergio was drawing his annuity at the time of his death. The amount of the lump sum payment to the beneficiary is includible in the Sergio's gross estate

Example 8.16

Pursuant to a retirement plan, ABC Company (ABC) was paying Chuck an annuity for life, and was to provide Ronda, Chuck's wife, upon his death after retirement, with a similar annuity for life. Assume that Chuck died at age 67, after the annuity began, when he fell of a treadmill while working out. The value of the wife's annuity is includible in the Chuck's gross estate.

---

3. IRC §691(c). The TCJA did not impact the deductibility of the IRD deduction.

Example 8.17

Ira has always been a planner and very methodical about his finances. Twenty years ago, he purchased a deferred variable annuity that is now worth $1 million. Unfortunately for Ira, he stepped on a piece of glass and the wound got infected. The infection went untreated, and he died. The value of the annuity, which was not annuitized, is included in his estate.

As the examples above illustrate, if annuity payments continue beyond death, then the value of those payments will generally be included in the owner's gross estate. Depending on the size of the estate, the decedent's estate may or may not be required to pay estate tax. The lifetime exclusion is well over $10 million per person and effectively over $20 million for a married couple. From an income tax perspective, the beneficiary will have to recognize some or all of the payments as income, depending on the basis in the contract.

Rules for Distributions to Beneficiaries

When the owner of a deferred annuity dies before benefit payments begin, the beneficiary will generally be paid a death benefit that is the account balance or the amount of premiums paid.[4] To the extent that there is gain in the contract, the beneficiary will have to report this gain as ordinary income. If there is substantial gain in the contract, a designated beneficiary can extend the income-tax-paying period by choosing a life annuity, a distribution over life expectancy, or an annuity with a specified number of installments shorter than life expectancy, but to qualify the first distribution must be taken by the first anniversary of the owner's death.[5]

The following is a summary:
1. If annuity payments have begun, the remaining amount in the contract must be distributed at least as rapidly as under the method of distribution in effect at the time of the owner's death. (Note that the person receiving the annuity payments has not necessarily died since the owner and annuitant can be two different people, so the insurer remains obligated to make payments to the annuitant, but the annuity owner has died.)
2. If the annuity has not begun payments, then the entire interest must be distributed within five years after the owner's death. Alternatively, a named beneficiary can distribute over her life expectancy (or any shorter period) as long as the first payment is received within one year of the owner's death.
3. When the beneficiary is the surviving spouse of the owner, then the spouse can treat the annuity as his or her own, and the spouse can delay distributions as could the owner. In other words, the surviving spouse steps into the deceased owner's shoes and continues the contract as if he or she were the original owner.
4. When the beneficiary is not an individual (for example, an estate, a trust, a partnership, or a corporation), the five year rule must be followed and the entire interest must be distributed within five years after the owner's death. For example, if Joe is the owner of an annuity and he names a testamentary trust created in his will as the beneficiary of the annuity contract, then the entire value of the annuity must be distributed within five years of Joe's death.

4. These examples assume an owner-driven annuity, which means that the death of the owner triggers the death benefit. Some annuities are annuitant-driven, meaning that it is the death of the annuitant, not the owner, that triggers the payment of the death benefit.
5. IRC Section 72(s).

It is good practice to also name successor or contingent beneficiaries in case the primary beneficiary predeceases the owner.

Tax Treatment for Non-Natural Owners

Non-natural owners, such as corporations, once had the same tax-deferral as individuals during the accumulation phase of an annuity. Now, any non-natural owner must report any earnings or accruals in an annuity as ordinary income in the year in which it is credited to the contract. This rule applies to any non-natural owner, except trusts acting as agents for natural persons.

Example 8.18

The Anderson Plastics Corporation purchased an annuity to fund a supplemental executive retirement plan for its officers. The purchase price was $80,000, and the gain that accumulated during the current year was $10,000. The plan will not pay benefits until the officers retire. The Anderson Plastics Corporation is a non-natural person, so it must report the internal buildup in the annuity as ordinary income in the current year. The same rule applies to variable and fixed annuities.

USES AND APPLICATIONS

Use of Annuity Contracts

There are two primary sources of funding for annuity contracts. Annuity contracts purchased with funds in a qualified retirement plan or IRA are referred to as **qualified annuities**, since the annuity is funded with pre-tax dollars.[6] Annuity contracts purchased with funds outside of qualified retirement plans or IRAs (for example, from investment accounts or private savings) are referred to as non-qualified annuities. Both qualified and non-qualified annuity contracts can be used to supplement an individual's cash-flow during retirement.

Annuities may also be used as structured settlements to fund damages awarded in lawsuits. It is common when the plaintiff in the lawsuit has ongoing needs for cash to pay medical and personal expenses over a long period of time. If there is concern that a lump-sum payment awarded to the plaintiff might be mismanaged, the court may order the defendant to provide a life annuity instead of a single payment.

Lottery winners are frequently given the choice of taking a lump-sum payment for their winnings or receiving a series of payments in the form of an annuity. Usually, the lottery winnings are stated in the amount that a person would receive if the annuity option were selected. The lump-sum payment is always less than the annuity option. With a lottery annuity, the entire payment will be subject to ordinary income tax.

> ### ⋮≡ *Key Concepts*
>
> 1. Discuss uses of annuities in retirement planning.
>
> 2. Define longevity insurance.
>
> 3. List the sources of annuities in the secondary market.
>
> 4. Identify the risks associated with the purchase of annuities in the secondary market.

---

6. The term "qualified annuity" refers to the annuity being tax qualified (funded with pre-tax contributions), rather than inferring that it is within or rolled over from a qualified defined benefit or defined contribution plan under ERISA.

Life insurance policies typically permit beneficiaries of the policy to receive an annuity payout instead of a lump-sum payment. These life insurance settlements consist of the basis from the life insurance proceeds and ordinary income from the earnings.

The tax consequences of receiving annuity payments depends partly on the source of funds used for the purchase of the annuity contract, as discussed previously.

Use of Annuities in Retirement Planning

Annuity contracts are often used to provide a stable cash-flow stream so that retirees insure that they have enough money during retirement to cover basic consumption needs.

The benefit of an immediate annuity from the perspective of the client is certainty. Immediate annuities are often purchased when an individual retires, since this type of annuity offers a guaranteed income, insulating the owner from the ups and downs of the stock market. In retirement planning, a steady stream of income to cover basic and recurring expenses during retirement is important. In theory, many retirees would prefer a steady stream of income; but, in practice, those same retirees may be unwilling to give up ownership of their assets in exchange for a guaranteed steady stream of income. Retirees may look upon annuities as a gamble on life expectancy with those who live longer winning the bet, and those who die younger losing the bet. Retirees with single life annuities may be concerned that they will die early (losing the annuity life expectancy bet) and, as a consequence, will have squandered their assets.

When an individual approaches retirement, he or she should make a detailed budget for retirement expenses taking into consideration monthly expenses and those expenses that are only paid on an annual basis. In addition, a potential retiree should project the budget forward three or four years to see if these expenditures might change or if major purchases, such as a new vehicle or other durable goods, may be necessary. Once the retirement needs budget has been established, the pre-retiree, or his or her advisor, should determine the sources of retirement income, such as Social Security retirement benefits, government or private pensions, and private savings. Many retirees prefer to have recurring expenses during retirement covered by guaranteed income sources, such as Social Security, defined benefit pension plans, and annuity distributions.

There has been significant academic research published in recent years evaluating sustainable withdrawal rates for retirement portfolios. Traditionally, practitioners have felt comfortable using a four percent withdrawal rate to prevent a retiree from running out of money during retirement. While the four percent withdrawal rate has been criticized by some as being too high, it is still a useful starting place to ascertain how much of a retiree's retirement savings should be annuitized. If Social Security benefits plus pension benefits plus four percent of the retiree's retirement savings equals or exceeds 100 percent of the retiree's projected retirement needs, there is a reduced need for the purchase of annuities to fund the retirement.

Example 8.19

Jay, who is single and age 70, has determined after a detailed budget analysis that his retirement needs are $100,000 per year on a pre-tax basis. His Social Security retirement benefits, which he plans to claim this year, will be $36,000 per year. In addition Jay has $2 million of investment assets. Four percent of $2 million is $80,000, which, when added to the Social Security benefit of $36,000 equals $116,000. In this case, Jay has 36% of his retirement needs in Social Security and the balance is made up of withdrawals from his capital accounts. Upon further analysis, Jay decides that he will prepare a bare-bones budget. This kind of budget takes all discretionary expenditures away from the budget to determine the minimum amount that Jay would need to live on. Jay has determined that his bare-bones budget is $48,000 per year and thus 75% of his bare-bones budget is met by Social Security retirement benefits. After conducting this analysis Jay concludes that he has no need for an individually-owned annuity contract.

Example 8.20

Ross and Rachel are both age 62. Both of Rachel's parents are still living and are in their 90s. Ross's mother is also living in her 90s. Both family histories suggest that almost everyone lives into their mid 90s with some family members living beyond 100. Ross and Rachel's Social Security retirement benefits are as follows: Ross: $20,000 at age 62, $28,571 at age 67, and $35,429 at age 70. Rachel has been a stay-at-home mom and has never worked outside of the home. They have estimated that at their retirement age of 66 they will need $100,000 of pretax income to meet their retirement budget, two-thirds of which will need to be inflation adjusted. They have calculated that their combined Social Security benefits will be roughly $40,000 at age 66. In addition to their Social Security benefits they expect to have $1 million in retirement savings at age 66. Using the 4% withdrawal rate plus the $40,000 of Social Security retirement benefits would only give them $80,000 of income. Presuming they have a bare-bones budget of $75,000 per year they may want to use some of their capital to purchase a joint and survivor annuity policy to reduce the risk of running out of money.

Longevity Insurance

Medical science has made significant progress in extending life expectancy over the past century. As life expectancies increase, the possibility of running out of money in retirement increases. One of the most difficult assumptions to make when calculating and funding retirement needs is the number of years an individual will be living in retirement. If retirement funding was based on the assumption of too short a life expectancy, an individual may run out of money during retirement, reducing the enjoyment of later retirement years.

As a hedge against running out of money in retirement, some individuals purchase life annuity contracts. **Life annuity contracts** guarantee payments for as long as an individual lives. Using all of one's retirement savings to purchase annuity contracts, however, may not be prudent. Individuals who purchase immediate life annuities at retirement and die before life expectancy will have reduced their potential consumption during retirement years, and have nothing left for transfer to their heirs. In addition, annuitizing the full amount of savings leaves nothing available for large lump sum purchases or emergencies. On the other hand, those who live beyond actuarial life expectancy benefit from the purchase of an annuity contract. Recall that annuity contracts are expensive as there are numerous fees and charges associated with them. Therefore, placing all of one's retirement funds in an annuity contract may still reduce lifetime consumption due to the transfer to the insurance company in the form of annuity contract expenses.

An intermediate approach to dealing with this problem is **longevity insurance**. Longevity insurance is a sophisticated name for a deferred annuity purchased by an individual at or before retirement that will not begin to make payments until that person reaches an advanced age. The size of the payment on the longevity insurance contract is often designed to cover non-discretionary expenses during retirement after taking into consideration other fixed lifetime income sources available to the retiree, such as Social Security and pension payments. Typically, longevity insurance contracts begin making payments (are annuitized) at age 85. Delaying annuitization to older ages results in higher monthly income payments, all else being equal, due to the shorter life expectancy. If a longevity insurance contract is purchased, the retiree does not have to worry about running out of money if he or she lives to an advanced age, and his or her remaining retirement funds can be consumed from the date of retirement to age 85, potentially increasing the total amount of consumption that can be enjoyed by the retiree.

The cost of longevity annuity contracts is very reasonable compared to the promised payments on the contract for two reasons. First, the contract is purchased at or before retirement, and payments do not generally begin until age 85. This allows a 20+ year accumulation period for the typical longevity insurance annuity. The longer the accumulation period, the more benefit the owner will receive from compound growth of the investments backing up the annuity contract. Second, since payments on the contract do not begin until age 85, and average life expectancy is about 81 years, more than half of those purchasing longevity annuities will not receive any annuitized payments (although their may be a return of premium feature allowing the deceased owner's beneficiary to receive back the amount of premium paid to purchase the contract), preserving that capital for those who do live beyond average life expectancy. While those who die before life expectancy do not receive payments on the annuity contract, the overall cost of longevity insurance contracts is reduced due to this actuarial adjustment, and those dying early can preserve the rest of their retirement assets for transfer to heirs without having to worry about running out of money.

Example 8.21

Travis, who is 50 years old, has developed a thoughtful retirement plan. He expects that as long as the rate of return on his portfolio yields approximately 300 basis points in excess of inflation, he will be fine. That conclusion assumes he does not live beyond about age 90. However, two of Travis's grandparents lived to age 90 and one is approaching age 100. Given his family longevity and his propensity to be active and health conscious, he is concerned about outliving his retirement assets. He realizes that the return on his assets may or may not exceed his expected return. In addition, he thinks he might very well live beyond age 100. Given these facts, he is considering using 10 percent of his investment portfolio to purchase a longevity annuity that would begin at age 85, assuming he lives to that age.

On July 1, 2014, the IRS issued final regulations governing the tax treatment of qualified longevity insurance contracts (QLACs). As our discussion on the taxation of annuity contracts highlighted, high income taxpayers should purchase retirement annuity contracts inside qualified retirement plans and IRAs to avoid the 3.8 percent Medicare surtax. If a deferred annuity contract is purchased inside a qualified plan or IRA, however, it can pose a problem since its value must be included when determining required minimum distributions, but the money inside of the annuity will not be available for distribution until the retiree attains age 85. The longevity insurance regulations address this problem by specifying that if a qualified longevity insurance contract is purchased inside of a qualified retirement plan or IRA, the value of the contract will not be considered when calculating required minimum distributions. To be considered a qualified longevity insurance contract, the premium for the deferred annuity purchased must not exceed the lesser of 25 percent of the account balance or $135,000 (as indexed in 2020), and the contract must be specified to be a longevity annuity contract at issuance.

A QLAC is a deferred annuity set to begin at an advanced age, but no later than age 85. Contracts are permitted to offer a return of premium (ROP) feature both before and after the annuity start date such that a lump sum death benefit may be paid to a beneficiary to the extent that the premium payments made with respect to the QLAC exceed the payments made to the employee under the QLAC. When a QLAC is providing a life annuity to a surviving spouse, it may also provide a similar ROP benefit after the death of both the employee and the spouse. When a beneficiary receives payment from the QLAC it will follow the same tax and distribution rules as other qualified plan inheritances.

Variable and indexed annuities are not permitted to be QLACs. In addition, QLACs are not permitted to offer a cash surrender value.

Social Security

While many retirees do not view Social Security payments as annuities, Social Security payments have all the characteristics of annuity contracts, and under current law are indexed for inflation. As the examples earlier in the chapter illustrate, since Social Security payments are received on an inflation adjusted basis for the life of the taxpayer, Social Security reduces the need to purchase annuity contracts to cover basic necessities of living during retirement.

Structured Settlements

A structured settlement is an agreement under which someone who is entitled to receive a large, lump-sum payment of money decides, instead, to accept periodic sums of money. Frequently, structured settlements arise as ways of compensating a party who has been injured, such as in an auto accident or a medical malpractice claim. Often, an annuity is purchased by an insurance company that has insured the defendant to provide a benefit that is a long-term solution for the claimant in lieu of a lump-sum settlement. The annuity contracts are specifically tailored to meet the needs of the injured or wronged party.

Advantages of structured settlement annuities:
- Financial security for the injured or aggrieved person
- Benefit payments that match cash needs in amount and timing
- Professional management of the funds
- If payments are a result of physical injury, the payments, both principal and interest, are tax-free. In contrast, if the claimant received the lump sum and invested the entire amount, the earnings would be taxable.

Disadvantages:
- The insurer issuing the annuity might become insolvent, causing payments to the injured or aggrieved party to be delayed and subject to limits imposed by the state guaranty fund (discussed later in this chapter).
- The actual cash needs, in amount or timing, might exceed those anticipated when the structured settlement agreement was finalized.

Damages

Damages are a monetary amount paid in settlement or awarded to a party for an injury or harm. Damages may be compensatory (to pay for actual financial losses sustained and perhaps to compensate for pain and suffering, disfigurement, etc.) or punitive (to punish the tortfeasor for an especially malicious or callous act of wrongdoing).

Compensatory damages for personal physical injuries or physical sickness are generally not subject to income taxes, but punitive damages are taxable. Damages in a wrongful death action are deemed compensatory and not taxable.

Employment discrimination claims and damage to reputation do not involve physical injuries, so the damages are taxable. Emotional distress by itself does not involve physical injuries, so these damages are taxable. When emotional distress requires medical care, however, the amounts paid for medical care can be excluded from income.

Structured Settlements and the Secondary Market

Sometimes, a person may be entitled to a pension or may be awarded a series of payments over time (an annuity) as the result of a lawsuit or from winning a state lottery (instead of a lump sum payment). After receiving the annuity, some individuals decide they want their cash now and that they do not want to wait to receive the periodic payments over time. An annuity contract can be sold to someone else in exchange for a lump-sum payment today, discounted for the time value of money. The purchase and resale of these annuities form the secondary market for annuity contracts.

These **secondary market annuities** are often called pre-owned annuities or in-force annuities. These annuities can be purchased from the original owner at a discount or from a third party, and the stream of income is assigned to the purchaser. Secondary market annuities typically offer a rate of return or yield that is well above the yield available on standard fixed annuities, immediate annuities, or even bonds of a similar credit quality. The increased yield is created when the original owners sell the annuity payments at a discount. It is not the result of the insurer paying a higher rate of return. The insurance company that originally issued the annuity is obligated to make the annuity payments regardless of whether the original owner, or the new owner, is entitled to the payment. When the original payment streams on the annuity were calculated, current market rates were used to determine the payment.

Example 8.22

Wilma is injured by Betty in an automobile accident. The claim is not settled and ultimately goes to court. Wilma wins the case and settlement money is offered to pay Wilma either a lump-sum payment or a structured settlement making payments over Wilma's lifetime. Wilma, who is now unable to work, accepts the structured settlement annuity. The court order specifies that Wilma shall receive $2,000 per month for life, with a 20-year guaranteed payment period. Neither Wilma, nor the court, want Betty or Betty's auto insurance company to pay the annuity. Therefore, Betty's insurance company purchases an annuity from a major life insurance carrier to pay the annuity of $2,000 per month with a 20-year guarantee. Betty's auto insurance company is the owner of the policy, the life insurance company is the issuer, and Wilma is the payee. If, by chance, the life insurance company goes out of business and the state-guarantee funds that guarantees insurance also go out of business (not likely), then Wilma can go back to

---

the original automobile insurance company and demand that they make the required payments as specified in the court settlement.

Five years into the annuity, Wilma needs money, and because she does not work, she decides to sell some or all of her annuity payments in return for a lump-sum payment. Wilma sells the annuity at an 8.5% discount rate and receives $203,000 from the structured settlement company. The structured settlement company then re-offers the annuity for $253,000 (equating to a yield of approximately 5%) over the term of the annuity. The yield is substantially higher than the yield on CDs or treasuries. A similar 15-year guaranteed annuity of $2,000 per month might cost $300,000 and yield 2.5%.

There are, however, risks when purchasing structured settlement annuities.

The SEC has issued an investor bulletin on pension or settlement income streams to advise annuitants of what they need to know before buying or selling annuities. The person or structured settlement companies purchasing annuities are sometimes called factoring companies. Factoring companies offer a lump sum which is less than the total of the periodic payments that the seller would otherwise receive. They then sell these income streams to retail investors through financial advisors, brokers, or insurance agents. These investments from a purchaser's point of view can be risky and complex.

In a typical transaction, the recipient of the pension or structured settlement will sign over his or her rights to some or all of his or her monthly payments to the factoring company in return for a lump sum amount. Many states require factoring companies that purchase structured settlements to disclose the difference between the lump sum payment that they are offering and the present value of the future income stream discounted at an appropriate interest-rate (for example, the federal AFR (applicable federal rate, published monthly by the IRS) for the appropriate time period).

There are several factors to consider before selling rights to a pension or structured settlement annuity. Transactions costs including brokerage commissions, legal and notary fees, and administrative charges may all be deducted from the lump sum proceeds. The SEC suggests asking the following questions:

1. Is the transaction legal? Federal or state law may restrict or prohibit retirees from assigning their pensions to others. The secondary sale of a structured settlement frequently must be approved by a court in keeping with the Uniform Periodic Payment of Judgments Act.
2. Is the transaction worth the cost? This is a simple comparison of the present value of the annuity stream discounted at the federal AFR and compared to the lump sum payment net of all fees and costs charged by the factoring company.
3. What is the reputation of the factoring company?
4. Will the factoring company require life insurance? Should the annuitant die before all payments that were assigned to the factoring company have been received, funds will be paid by the life insurance policy to cover any remaining balance. Purchasing life insurance will add to the annuitant's transaction expenses and reduce the lump sum payout.
5. What are the income tax consequences? The lump sum payments received may be subject to federal and state income tax.
6. Does the sale fit the annuitant's long-term financial goals? There may be better alternatives than selling a structured annuity.

From the buyer's perspective, the recent stock market volatility and low interest rate environment have encouraged investors to look for more attractive returns. Buying the rights to someone else's pension or structured settlement income stream may look like a good alternative to other options because advertised yields from 5.75 percent to 7.75 percent are common. However, these pensions and structured settlement income streams are generally not registered with the SEC. As such, reliable information about these products may be difficult to find, and resolving disputes may be difficult. These products are illiquid, which means they may be difficult to sell later. Purchased rights to an income stream could face legal challenges later, and it could be difficult to legally force the original owner to forward or assign their income to the factoring company or the investor.

It is clear that both sellers and buyers of annuities should conduct substantial due diligence prior to entering into this type of transaction. The following exhibit includes a sample of annuities that might be sold on a secondary market.

Exhibit 8.17 | Sample of Secondary Market Annuities

Company	Cost	Payout	Rate	Income Amount	Frequency	Start Date	End Date
Pacific Life	$124,876	$133,680	2.75%	$2,156	62 monthly	07-04-20	08-04-25
Pacific Life	$102,274	$134,988	3.21%	$605	223 monthly	07-15-20	01-15-39
Farmers New World	$174,599	$234,000	3.23%	$1,000	234 monthly	07-20-20	12-20-39
AXA Equitable	$80,883	$98,677	3.75%	$450	269 monthly	03-20-21	07-20-43
John Hancock	$36,328	$50,623	3.40%	$50,623	1 lump sum	07-07-30	07-07-30
Prudential Life	$44,480	$63,000	3.42%	$63,000	1 lump sum	12-11-30	12-11-30
Allstate	$112,074	$217,424	4.50%	$2,283	86 monthly	12-15-31	1-15-39
Prudential Life	$22,210	$28,352	3.24%	$3,544	8 semi-annual	07-01-26	01-01-30
Transamerica	$64,708	$125,534	4.00%	$313	192 monthly	11-01-27	10-01-43
AIG	$33,741	$48,500	3.43%	$48,500	1 lump sum	05-01-31	05-01-31

https://www.immediateannuities.com/secondary-market-annuities/; June 9, 2020

Regulation of Annuity Contracts

Most annuity contracts are regulated by the state insurance commissioner in the state in which the contract is sold. The state insurance commissioner approves the annuity contract forms to be issued by insurance companies in that state, and requires that insurance companies keep specified reserves to ensure that they will be able to make promised payments to annuitants. The state insurance commissioner also requires insurers to provide detailed reports on the investments backing up annuity contracts, including an assessment of the investment risk undertaken by the insurance company in investing the money of the annuity pool. The investment risk assessment is sometimes referred to as **risk-based capital**.

Variable annuities provide consumers with an opportunity to tailor the investments backing up the annuity contract to their unique needs, and equity-indexed annuities provide investment returns linked to market-based indexes. Consequently, individuals selling variable annuities are required to obtain state insurance licenses from the State Insurance Commission, as well as securities licenses from FINRA in order to sell these products. These licensing requirements are designed to ensure that individuals offering annuity products for sale to the public have a specified level of knowledge about the product, and about the suitability of the product for consumer needs.[7] Beginning June 30, 2020, the SEC's new Regulation Best Interest (Reg. BI) will require that investment recommendations, including variable annuities, not only be suitable for the client, but that they be in the in the client's best interest based on the client's investment profile and the potential risks, rewards, and costs associated with the recommendation.

A variable annuity must be sold with a prospectus, which will describe how the annuity works as well as the fees and risks. Effective July 1, 2020, agents selling VUL policies and variable annuities are required to either deliver a summary prospectus (a disclosure document outlining key information relating to the contract's terms, benefits, and risks; including web addresses to obtain more detailed information) to the policy owner or make the statutory prospectus available online. The initial summary prospectus must be delivered "no later than the time of the carrying or delivery of the contract security."[8] Before recommending a variable annuity to a client, the planner should read the full prospectus and ensure that he or she fully understands all of the information provided within it.

In recent years FINRA has been viewing many variable annuity sales, especially those to seniors, with scrutiny.[9] While variable annuities can be a good match for the right client, they also present a temptation to a few unscrupulous financial advisors due to their high commission payout rates. FINRA has also shown recent concern for potential abuses involving a Section 1035 exchange from variable annuities into equity-indexed annuities. Again, there are valid reasons for making these changes, but the potential for abuse is high.

---

7. FINRA Rule 2111 requires, in part, that a broker-dealer or associated person "have a reasonable basis to believe that a recommended transaction or investment strategy involving a security or securities is suitable for the customer, based on the information obtained through the reasonable diligence of the [firm] or associated person to ascertain the customer's investment profile." In general, a customer's investment profile includes the customer's age, other investments, financial situation and needs, tax status, investment objectives, investment experience, investment time horizon, liquidity needs and risk tolerance. The rule also explicitly covers recommended investment strategies involving securities, including recommendations to "hold" securities. The rule, moreover, identifies the three main suitability obligations: reasonable-basis, customer-specific, and quantitative suitability. As of the time of printing, FINRA had proposed amendments to this rule in response to the SEC's Regulation BI, but no final amendment had yet been adopted. Source FINRA.
8. https://www.sec.gov/rules/final/2020/33-10765.pdf; effective July 1, 2020.
9. https://www.finra.org/sites/default/files/InvestorDocument/p125846.pdf

The Importance of Company Credit Rating

Annuity contracts require the payment of an up-front premium by the contract holder in return for the insurance company's promise to make payments under the contract for years into the future. The financial stability of the company issuing the annuity contract is of major concern to contract holders, and should be a consideration in determining which annuity contract to purchase. The insurance company offering the smallest premium for a given annuity payment may not be the most appropriate choice if its financial stability is in question.

Several rating agencies assess the financial strength of insurance companies issuing annuity contracts. These include A.M. Best (with a rating scale from A++ to S), S&P (with a rating scale of AAA to R), and Moody's (with a rating scale from Aaa to C).

While a full review of the rating scales of these various companies is beyond the scope of this textbook, financial advisors should take into consideration company rating agency scales when making recommendations to clients, and clients should also take this information into account when making their purchasing decisions.

What Happens if an Insurance Company Fails?

Insurance company ratings are important, and consumers should attempt to purchase annuities from companies with a strong likelihood of survival. What happens when a company that issues an annuity contract fails? All states have **guarantee funds** run by the state insurance commission that act as the payor of last resort in the case of an insurance company failure. Each year, insurance companies that issue annuities pay a premium to the state guarantee fund. If a company fails with outstanding annuity obligations, the guarantee fund makes the promised annuity payments to contract holders. In the event that the guarantee fund does not have sufficient funds to make those payments, the guarantee fund will assess the surviving annuity contract issuers to obtain the money to make payments, or will arrange to have existing insurance companies take over the payment of the obligations. While a few insurance companies have failed, no annuity contract holder in the United States has been deprived of promised payments to date. In many ways, the state guarantee fund acts as an insurer of insurers to make certain that consumer interests are protected.

Other Factors to Consider When Evaluating Annuity Decisions

Other factors to consider when evaluating annuities include bonus rates, guaranteed minimum withdrawal benefits, the timing of annuitization, and decisions to annuitize or take withdrawals.

Bonus Rates

Some fixed annuities will offer a "bonus" interest rate for a short period of time, followed by interest being credited at a current rate in later years. When evaluating these bonus features, a planner should consider how long the bonus rate will apply, the renewal rate after it expires, how withdrawals may affect the rate (in some cases withdrawals will reduce the bonus rate either prospectively or retroactively), and whether the contract can be terminated without a surrender charge after the bonus rate expires. For example, the contract may state that if the renewal rate is two percent lower or more, the contract can be terminated without a surrender charge. If the contract is surrendered, however, the owner will pay taxes on the earnings (plus a 10% penalty if under age 59½).

A planner should always ask to see the company's renewal rate history, which may provide a better idea of whether the rates typically drop to the guaranteed minimum rate (usually 1.5% or 2%) after the bonus period expires, or whether they renew at rates above the minimum. For many fixed annuities, the bonus rate will be offset by increased expenses, so the long term rate is no different.

Guaranteed Minimum Withdrawal Benefits (GMWBs)

GMWBs can be a beneficial feature for the right client, but can also be very difficult to understand. Planners should read the prospectus and ensure that they understand and can communicate to the client all of the rules and features. If the rider is too complicated for the planner to understand and articulate clearly to the client, it will also be too complicated for the client to fully understand, and should be avoided.

Timing of Annuitization

Since payments increase from annuitization beginning at later ages, higher payment amounts can be made available by delaying the decision to annuitize. Delaying also allows an opportunity to evaluate ongoing health issues that may affect life expectancy or lump sum needs. Clients who are particularly risk averse, however, may choose to annuitize sooner rather than later.

Since current interest rates impact the amount of the annuity payments, clients will typically be offered higher payouts during higher interest rate environments. In low rate environments, if clients can hold off on annuitizing for a few years until interest rates rise, they will have both the advantage of higher age and higher rates.

The Decision to Annuitize or Take Withdrawals

The owner of an annuity will have the option of taking withdrawals from an annuity instead of annuitizing. The owner can take withdrawals as the money is needed rather than accepting the periodic payments.

The pros and cons of annuitization versus withdrawals from a variable annuity depend on many factors, such as the amount of money invested, the length of time the money is invested, the growth of the annuity, the owner's risk tolerance, the annuitant's need for annuity payments, and the income tax bracket of the annuitant-owner. The age and health of the annuitant and his or her life expectancy will also be important in making the decision. The owner should also consider what assets are held outside the variable annuity.

For purposes of simplicity, assume that the owner-annuitant has invested $100,000 in the variable annuity at least 10 years ago and is past the surrender charge period, the annuity has doubled in value, and the annuitant is over age 59½ so there is no 10 percent early withdrawal penalty.

First, the owner-annuitant should consider the tax implications. With a withdrawal, the LIFO rule of taxation applies. If the owner withdraws $25,000, it will all be taxable as ordinary income due to the earnings in the annuity. If the annuitant is in a high tax bracket, this withdrawal could give rise to substantial additional tax. With annuitization, a portion of the distribution will be tax free return of investment, so the tax consequences are lower.

Second, if the annuitant needs to withdraw a significant amount from the annuity, then a withdrawal may be necessary regardless of income tax consequences, and is available. Annuitization, however, will generally set payments at an amount that is based on life expectancy with no availability for lump sum withdrawals. It will be important to determine whether the owner/annuitant needs or wants a life income or has immediate need for cash, or a combination of both (annuitizing is not an all-or-nothing decision since a portion of the account can be 1035 exchanged to another annuity.

Third, with annuitization, the payments will continue to the annuitant for life whereas withdrawals are likely to deplete the amount in the annuity and could mean the annuitant runs out of money prematurely.

Fourth, if the annuitant lives beyond his or her life expectancy, the total amount that will be paid to the annuitant after annuitization is likely to be higher than the amount that can be withdrawn. A portion of the annuitized payments are funded from the early deaths of other annuitants. Thus, the annuitants who are the survivors will benefit by receiving amounts that are not paid to the deceased annuitants.

Fifth, there are costs associated with the additional risks taken by the insurance company, but the annuitant will likely find that the benefit of an assured life income is worth these costs. Nevertheless, an owner may believe that the costs are not worthwhile because he or she does not need the guaranteed life income and will want to take withdrawals only as needed.

Sixth, with annuitization, the owner will be giving up the flexibility of making withdrawals of varying amounts. The owner's ability to give up this flexibility by annuitizing may depend on whether other resources are available to fund sporadic needs.

Seventh, annuitization will affect the owner's ability to leave the assets in the annuity to heirs if the owner dies prematurely.

Eighth, a planner may need to consider the possibility that the annuitant will want to preserve Medicaid eligibility. Withdrawals might be taken from the annuity and given to a spouse who does not need nursing home care. The community spouse can buy a SPIA and receive income without the income being counted for Medicaid eligibility.

Other General Information to Consider
- Fee-based planners can offer no-load annuities that do not pay a commission and often do not have a surrender charge.
- Due to the lack of liquidity in annuities, clients should always maintain sufficient liquidity outside of an annuity.
- While annuities do avoid probate, they do not avoid estate taxes. Many clients get confused on this issue and mistakenly believe that probate and estate taxes are one and the same.

CONCLUSION

Annuities may be suitable for several types of clients. A client who has already accumulated a significant amount of money may wish to liquidate that sum in a scientific manner. The client can buy an annuity that will produce income as long as the client is alive and the income stream will not be disrupted by business reversals or unwise investments. A client who has not yet accumulated a significant sum of money may find an annuity an attractive vehicle for periodically saving money in a tax-preferenced manner. Annuities are frequently used as a vehicle to accumulate additional funds for retirement after a person has made the maximum contributions permitted to qualified retirement plans and IRAs. Annuities are also frequently used for structured settlements, such as from a lawsuit. Annuities can be fixed, variable, or equity-indexed and each of these has a multitude of options available for the owner/annuitant to select from based on their needs; however, annuities also have numerous disadvantages that must be considered before determining whether it is the right investment for the client.

KEY TERMS

Accumulation Phase - The period over which annuity funds are accumulated.

Annual Reset Method - The index-linked interest crediting rate is determined each year by comparing the index value at the end of the contract year with the index value at the beginning of the contract year. Interest is then added to the annuity each year during the term.

Annuitant - The individual upon whose life the contract is dependent. It is generally the life expectancy of the annuitant that affects the timing and amount of payout under the contract.

Annuitization - The time when annuity funds are exchanged for a stream of income guaranteed for a period of time.

Annuitized - The time when regular, periodic (such as monthly or annual) payments begin for life or for a specified period of time in excess of one year.

Annuity - A contract between an individual (annuitant) and an insurance company which promises to pay an income on a regular basis for a specified period of time.

Beneficiary - Those persons entitled to the death benefit of the annuity.

Cap Rate - Some indexed annuities impose an upper limit on the index-linked interest rate.

Cash Refund Annuity - Guarantees that the annuitant or the annuitant's family will receive the premium payments made to purchase the annuity, but instead of continuing to make periodic payments until there is a full recovery of the premium, the balance is paid in cash at the annuitant's death.

Deferred Annuity - An annuity contract that does not begin payments immediately, but waits until some future time to start payments.

Equity-Indexed Annuities - Have characteristics of both fixed and variable annuities, either immediate or deferred, that earn interest or provide benefits that are linked to an external equity reference or an equity index.

50% Joint and Survivor Annuity - Pays the survivor 50% of the annuity payment after the death of the first annuitant. The initial annuity payment will be larger than with a 100% or 75% joint and survivor annuity.

Fixed Annuity - The most conservative type of annuity that earns a minimum guaranteed rate of return.

Flexible Premium Annuity - Allows the insured the option to vary premium deposits.

Floor Crediting Rate - An indexed annuity is the minimum index-linked interest rate that will be credited to the contract in a given period.

Free Withdrawal Provision - Allows the contract holder the right to withdraw up to a stated percentage (usually 10 percent) of the contract value annually without incurring a surrender charge.

Guarantee Funds - Run by the state insurance commission, they act as the payor of last resort in the case of an insurance company failure.

High Watermark Approach - Determining index-linked interest is accomplished by comparing the value of the index at various points during the term (usually on anniversary dates).

Immediate Annuity - An instrument created when the contract owner trades a sum of money in return for a stream of income that begins immediately.

Index Term - The period over which index-linked interest is calculated for equity-indexed annuities.

Indexing Method - The approach used to measure the amount of change, if any, in the index. Some common indexing methods include: (1) the annual reset (ratcheting) approach, (2) the high watermark approach, and (3) the point-to-point approach.

Inflation - The increase in the general price level and is often measured by the Consumer Price Index (CPI).

Initial Rate - The first rate of interest that is earned under a fixed annuities contract and is guaranteed for a specified period of time.

Installment Refund Annuity - A special type of term certain annuity whereby the insurer promises to continue periodic annuity payments after the annuitant has died until the sum of all annuity payments made equals the purchase price of the annuity.

IRD Assets - Assets that have a deferred income tax liability that was not paid prior to the date of the owner's death.

Joint and Survivor Annuity - Promises to make payments over the lives of two or more annuitants. Annuity payments are made until the last annuitant dies. This is commonly used to fund the retirement cash-flow needs of married couples. A 100 percent joint and survivor annuity pays the specified monthly payment to the annuitants while both are alive and continues to make the same payment to the survivor after the first annuitant's death. A 75 percent joint and survivor annuity pays the specified monthly payment to the annuitants while both are alive and continues to make a payment equal to 75 percent of the original payment to the survivor after the first annuitant's death. A 50 percent joint and survivor annuity pays the specified monthly payment to the annuitants while both are alive and continues to make a payment equal to 50 percent of the original payment to the survivor after the first annuitant's death.

Life Annuity Contracts - Protect clients from outliving their assets by providing a series of periodic payments to the annuitant, typically for as long as the annuitant lives.

Longevity Insurance - A sophisticated name for a deferred annuity purchased by an individual at or before retirement that will not begin to make payments until that person reaches an advanced age.

Minimum Interest Rate - The minimum rate to be paid on a fixed annuity's principal balance for the duration of the annuity contract.

Non-Qualified Annuities - Annuity contracts purchased with funds outside of qualified retirement plans or IRAs (for example, from investment accounts or private savings).

100% Joint and Survivor Annuity - Pays the survivor 100% of the annuity payment after the death of the first annuitant.

Owner - Person, trust, or company that owns the annuity contract and names the annuitant and beneficiaries. The owner could also be the annuitant and/or the beneficiary.

Participation Rate - Determines how much of the increase in the index will be used to calculate the index-linked interest.

Parties to Annuity Contract - The annuitant, the beneficiary, the owner, and the insurance company.

Point-to-Point Index-Linked Crediting Method - Based on the difference between an index value at the end of the term compared with the index value at the start of the term.

Pooling of Risk - The spreading of risk among a large number of similar contributors to the pool. Protection is provided to the entire pool of contributors. With annuities, the risk that is being spread is the risk of outliving retirement funds, or superannuation.

Prospectus - A disclosure document provided to purchasers of variable annuities and variable life insurance products that contains important information about the contract, including fees and charges, investment options and objectives, risks, death benefits, living benefits, and other important information.

Qualified Annuities - Annuity contracts purchased with funds in a qualified retirement plan or IRA.

Renewal Rate - The interest rate offered on a fixed annuity after the expiration of the initial rate.

Retirement Life Expectancy - The period between retirement and death.

Risk-Based Capital - The investment risk assessment undertaken by the insurance company in investing the money backing up the annuity pool.

Secondary Market Annuities - Called pre-owned annuities or in-force annuities. These annuities can be purchased from the original owner at a discount or from a third party, in which the stream of income is assigned to the purchaser. These typically offer a rate of return or yield that is well above the yield available on standard fixed annuities, immediate annuities, or even bonds of a similar credit quality.

75% Joint and Survivor Annuity - Pays the survivor 75% of the annuity payment after the death of the first annuitant. The initial annuity payment will be larger than with a 100% joint and survivor annuity.

Single Life Annuity - Also known as a straight life annuity, provides a stream of income to the annuitant for life.

Single Premium Annuity - An annuity purchased with a single lump sum.

Straight or Pure Life Annuity - An annuity that provides a stream of income to the annuitant for life.

Superannuation - The risk of running out of money before death due to long life and can be mitigated by using annuities.

Term Certain Annuity - Acts as a hedge against the mortality risk retained when an individual purchases a single life annuity by preserving some or all of the capital for distribution to the annuitant's heirs, but this hedge comes at a cost.

Variable Annuities - Provide consumers with an opportunity to individually tailor the types of investments backing up the annuity contract to their unique needs.

DISCUSSION QUESTIONS

SOLUTIONS to the discussion questions can be found exclusively within the chapter. Once you have completed an initial reading of the chapter, go back and highlight the answers to these questions.

1. What major risk to retirement income do annuities mitigate?

2. Discuss the impact of Social Security retirement benefits on superannuation.

3. What is the impact of inflation on retirement income?

4. What role did defined benefit plans play in retirement income when they were prevalent?

5. Discuss the impact of the shift from defined benefit plans to defined contribution plans for retirees.

6. Define an annuity.

7. List the parties to an annuity.

8. What is the annuity payout period?

9. What is the difference between an immediate annuity and a deferred annuity?

10. What is the difference between a flexible premium annuity and a single premium annuity?

11. Identify the different types of annuity benefit options.

12. Define the types of single-life annuity options.

13. What is a benefit of a term certain (or period certain) annuity?

14. Define joint and survivor life annuities.

15. Explain the difference between a fixed annuity, a variable annuity, and an equity indexed annuity.

16. What are the common fees and charges associated with variable annuities?

17. List the advantages of an annuity contract.

18. List three disadvantages of annuities.

19. How are annuities subject to income tax?

20. Define longevity insurance.

21. What are the estate planning issues regarding holding a single-life annuity versus a joint and survivor annuity?

22. What are the distribution options for the beneficiary of a non-qualified annuity?

23. List the advantages and disadvantages of annuities issued as a result of a structured settlement.

24. What are the risk factors to consider when selling an annuity in the secondary market?

MULTIPLE-CHOICE PROBLEMS

A sample of multiple choice problems is provided below. Additional multiple choice problems are available at money-education.com by accessing the Student Practice Portal.

1. Which of the following is true?
    a. A fixed annuity mitigates the risk of superannuation.
    b. A fixed annuity mitigates the risk of superannuation and inflation.
    c. A fixed annuity is always a deferred annuity.
    d. A fixed annuity is always for a single life expectancy.

2. Which of the following risks can an annuity mitigate?
    a. Superannuation.
    b. Mortality.
    c. Superannuation and purchasing power.
    d. Mortality and purchasing power.

3. Harry, age 63 purchased an immediate annuity. The annuity will provide monthly payments to Harry for as long as he lives. If he dies before receiving payments for 20 years, the remaining payments will go to his beneficiary. What type of annuity did Harry purchase?
    a. A life annuity with a term-certain guarantee.
    b. An installment refund annuity.
    c. A straight-life annuity.
    d. A joint and survivor annuity.

4. Kareem is a drug rep and planning on retiring next month. He is using his accumulated $200,000 to purchase an annuity. Which of the following options will give him the largest monthly annuity payment assuming his life expectancy is 20 years and his spouse's life expectancy is 22 years.
    a. 10 year term certain.
    b. Single life annuity over Kareem's life.
    c. 100% joint life annuity over Kareem and his spouse's lives.
    d. 75% joint life annuity over Kareem and his spouse's lives.

5. Perry, who is 50 years old, was building a new home for his family. However, he was running out of money and could not afford the pool they fell in love with. Since his family was upset, he decided to take a withdrawal from his annuity. He had contributed $100,000 to the annuity, and the value of the annuity today is $300,000. He decided to take a withdrawal of $60,000 from the annuity. Which of the following is correct?
    a. $40,000 is taxable as ordinary income.
    b. $40,000 is taxable as ordinary income and subject to the early withdrawal penalty.
    c. $60,000 is taxable as ordinary income.
    d. $60,000 is taxable as ordinary income and subject to the early withdrawal penalty.

QUICK QUIZ EXPLANATIONS

Quick Quiz 8.1
1. True.
2. True.
3. False. Defined benefit plans paid out a fixed annuity for the life of the annuitant, and in many cases a joint and survivor annuity for the benefit of a surviving spouse. Today, defined contribution plans are used.

Quick Quiz 8.2
1. True.
2. False. Immediate annuities are purchased with one, single, lump sum payment. However, the premium payments used to fund a deferred annuity can be either a single lump sum payment, or a series of payments into the future.
3. False. The income earned from a deferred annuity is treated as ordinary income for federal income tax purposes only upon receipt of distributions.

Quick Quiz 8.3
1. False. The term may be for a specific number of years or over the life of a person or persons.
2. False. A joint and survivor annuity will pay the survivor the contracted percentage.
3. True.
4. True.

Quick Quiz 8.4
1. True.
2. False. Surrender charges are prevalent in variable annuities prior to annuitization.
3. True.

Quick Quiz 8.5
1. True.
2. False. Variable annuities permit the owner to invest in subaccounts of the fund manager.
3. True.

Quick Quiz 8.6
1. True.
2. False. Fixed annuities typically do not impose any direct expense charges on the contract owner other than a surrender charge. Variable annuities have several types of expenses, including investment management fees, annual insurance charges, and surrender charges.
3. True.

Quick Quiz 8.7
1. True.
2. False. Disadvantages of annuities include complexity, costs, and tax consequences. While tax-deferred growth is an advantage, the disadvantage is that distributions are taxed on a LIFO basis at ordinary income rates and may be subject to a 10% penalty for early distributions.
3. False. Since 2013, distributions from annuity contracts made to high income taxpayers (more than $200,000 AGI) are subject to the Medicare surtax of 3.8 percent.

QUICK QUIZ EXPLANATIONS

Quick Quiz 8.8

1. False. A non-qualified annuity is an annuity contract purchased with after-tax dollars. The after-tax dollars invested in the contract create basis for income tax purposes.
2. False. The exclusion ratio equals the owner's investment in the annuity contract divided by the expected return on the annuity. The resulting percentage is multiplied by the distribution or payment received to calculate the portion of the payment that is not subject to income tax.
3. False. Qualified annuities are subject to the minimum distribution rules, but not non-qualified annuities.
4. True.

Quick Quiz 8.9

1. True.
2. False. Longevity insurance is a deferred annuity purchased by an individual at or before retirement that will not begin to make payments until that person reaches an advanced age.
3. False. An annuity contract can be sold to someone else in exchange for a lump-sum payment today, discounted for the time value of money.

> **Additional multiple choice problems**
> **are available at**
> **money-education.com**
> **by accessing the**
> **Student Practice Portal.**
> **Access requires registration of the title using**
> **the unique code at the front of the book.**

9

PROPERTY AND LIABILITY INSURANCE

LEARNING OBJECTIVES

1. Identify personal property and liability insurance risks for individuals.
2. Identify the primary components of property and casualty insurance and how each component fits into a client's comprehensive financial plan.*
3. Differentiate among the basic homeowners insurance (HO) forms and features and explain how to evaluate and compare policies.*
4. List the general exclusions to homeowners policies.
5. List the common provisions in homeowners insurance policies.
6. Describe the automobile insurance legal environment.
7. Identify the primary components of automobile insurance and assess any potential property damage or liability exposures.*
8. Understand personal automobile policy limits.
9. Explain the role personal and business liability insurance plays in comprehensive financial planning and how a personal liability umbrella policy (PLUP) and business liability insurance interact with other property and liability insurance products.*
10. Describe the defenses to liability.
11. Identify the various business and professional property and liability insurance policies and compare them to individual policies.

*CFP Board Resource Document - Student-Centered Learning Objectives based upon CFP Board Principal Topics.

INTRODUCTION

Risk management is a fundamental component of a comprehensive financial plan. Major risk exposures should be addressed prior to engaging in longer-term saving and investing objectives because exposure to a large loss that has not been appropriately hedged may result in a loss of an important asset and the loss of savings and investments. Advisors should be knowledgeable about general and liability risks associated with property as well as the financial risks that can be addressed with the use of life, health, disability, long-term care and liability insurance.

Property insurance provides financial protection for losses on houses, condominiums, automobiles, boats and other property assets. Liability insurance protects individuals against the financial loss associated with legal action, generally due to property damage, personal injury, or loss of income. When constructing a risk management plan, both property and liability coverages should be addressed.

⫶☰ *Key Concepts*

1. Identify the three types of insurance that are most commonly purchased to protect against liability and risks to personal property.

2. Identify and describe the four areas of coverage in Section I of a homeowners insurance contract.

3. Describe the coinsurance clause in property insurance contracts.

4. Identify and describe the two areas of coverage in Section II of a homeowners insurance contract.

Property insurance coverages that are frequently used in constructing a risk management plan include homeowners insurance, renters insurance, automobile insurance, and insurance on other high-value assets (such as boats). Business owners and self-employed professionals can purchase similar coverages through commercial package policies, business owners policies, professional liability insurance, and business automobile insurance policies.

This chapter introduces the three insurance policies most commonly used to protect against personal property and liability risks. These three insurance policies are:

1. the homeowners insurance policy
2. the automobile insurance policy
3. the personal liability umbrella insurance policy

Homeowners and automobile insurance are package policies that include both property and liability coverage in one contract. The **personal liability umbrella** policy is an excess liability policy that provides a layer of personal liability protection above the liability coverages provided in the underlying homeowners, automobile and other policies when the liability coverage provided in those policies is insufficient to cover a claim.

Understanding the protections afforded by each of these policies assists an advisor to adequately evaluate a person's property and liability exposures and to recommend appropriate levels of coverage.

RISK MANAGEMENT PRINCIPLES & PERSONAL PROPERTY AND LIABILITY INSURANCE

One characteristic that is common across the risks covered by homeowners insurance, automobile insurance, and personal liability umbrella policies (PLUPs) is a low frequency of loss. For example, most houses will not burn down this year, and most drivers (good ones, at least) will not be involved in an automobile accident on a regular basis. The low frequency of loss may entice some consumers to retain that risk even though risk transfer devices (such as homeowners insurance, automobile insurance, and PLUPs) are readily available and relatively efficiently priced. While exposure to the perils that could cause a loss is small, the severity of the loss, when experienced, is often high. Due to the high severity of loss (for example, the loss of most of the value of a home that burns down), transferring that risk to an insurance company that spreads the risk out over the pool of insureds is often the most effective method of managing that risk.

Exhibit 9.1 | Fire Statistics in the United States (2018)

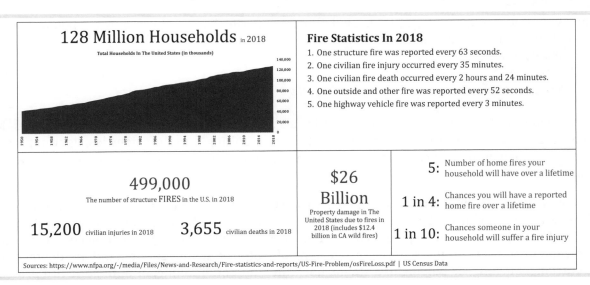

128 Million Households in 2018

Total Households In The United States (in thousands)

Fire Statistics In 2018

1. One structure fire was reported every 63 seconds.
2. One civilian fire injury occurred every 35 minutes.
3. One civilian fire death occurred every 2 hours and 24 minutes.
4. One outside and other fire was reported every 52 seconds.
5. One highway vehicle fire was reported every 3 minutes.

499,000
The number of structure FIRES in the U.S. in 2018

15,200 civilian injuries in 2018   **3,655** civilian deaths in 2018

$26 Billion
Property damage in The United States due to fires in 2018 (includes $12.4 billion in CA wild fires)

5: Number of home fires your household will have over a lifetime

1 in 4: Chances you will have a reported home fire over a lifetime

1 in 10: Chances someone in your household will suffer a fire injury

Sources: https://www.nfpa.org/-/media/Files/News-and-Research/Fire-statistics-and-reports/US-Fire-Problem/osFireLoss.pdf | US Census Data

Furthermore, over time, insurance companies have collected loss data that can be used to predict the occurrence of perils that will cause a loss very precisely. This precision permits the insurance company to have very reliable estimates of claims, with the result that the premiums for homeowners, automobile, and personal liability umbrella policies are very efficient.

HOMEOWNERS (HO) INSURANCE

For most people in the United States, the largest single purchase made during their lifetime is their home, and it is often one of the largest component's of their net worth. Most people would suffer a severe financial setback if their home was destroyed, and would have difficulty replacing the home without assistance that could be provided through the use of insurance. Protecting the value of the home against loss is certainly a major concern for most people, and is required by lenders when a mortgage is used to finance the purchase of the home. **Homeowners insurance** is available to protect against the loss of the value of the home (property insurance), and to provide liability protection for events that may occur at the home (liability insurance) for which the homeowner is determined to be responsible.

Exhibit 9.2 | Homeowners Insurance Policy - Property and Liability Coverage

Section I	Coverage A - Dwelling
	Coverage B - Other Structures
	Coverage C - Personal Property
	Coverage D - Loss of Use
Section II	Coverage E - Personal Liability
	Coverage F - Medical Payments

As with other types of insurance coverage, the homeowner must select a policy that provides adequate coverage at a reasonable price. One of the most important elements of the homeowner policy to evaluate is the definition of covered perils.

Covered Perils

A homeowner policy will contain a provision defining the perils that are covered by the policy. There are three categories of perils that may be covered:
- basic coverage
- broad coverage
- open coverage

Basic coverage protects the homeowner from losses associated with specifically named perils. Most basic coverage policies protect homeowners from losses resulting from fire, vehicles, lightning, smoke, windstorm, vandalism or malicious mischief, hail, explosions, riots or civil commotion, theft, aircraft, and volcanic eruptions.

Broad coverage, as its name implies, provides protection for all of the named perils covered in basic coverage, plus additional protection for named perils not covered under basic coverage. Additional protection found in broad coverage policies include losses resulting from falling objects; the weight of ice, snow, or sleet; accidental discharge or overflow of water or steam; sudden and accidental tearing apart, cracking, burning, or bulging of a steam, hot water, air conditioning, or automatic fire protective sprinkler system, or from within a household appliance; freezing of plumbing, heating, air conditioning, or automatic fire sprinkler system, or of a household appliance; and sudden and accidental damage from artificially generated electrical currents.

Both basic and broad coverage policies only protect homeowners against losses arising from perils that are specifically listed in the policy, and, as a result, are sometimes referred to as "named peril" policies. Losses resulting from perils not listed in the policy are therefore not covered. While the list of covered perils in a broad coverage policy may appear on the surface to be fairly comprehensive, it is actually very limited and leaves the homeowner exposed to a long list of uncovered perils. For that reason, most homeowners will not be adequately covered through the purchase of a basic or broad perils policy.

Example 9.1

Shania has several cats that love to go in and out of the house so she installed a cat door to allow them to come and go as they please. Much to her dismay, she returned home from a weekend out of town to discover that a family of raccoons had entered through the cat door and made themselves at home. Never before did she realize that raccoon claws are sharp enough to tear through the linoleum floors in the kitchen and the carpeting in the bedrooms, shred the couch, mar the kitchen cabinets (the poor critters needed food, after all) and destroy the bed mattresses. Even more troubling, Shania discovered that her homeowner policy only provided broad perils coverage, and that damages caused by wild animals was not on the list of covered perils.

Unlike basic and broad coverage policies, **open perils policies** cover any risk to the home that is not specifically excluded in the policy. Open perils policies, therefore, provide the homeowner with additional protections from perils causing loss that are not among those in the broad form and may not be known or anticipated. While each homeowners policy is unique, and may include additional coverage exclusions, the general exclusions that apply to most homeowner's policies include losses from:
- Movement of the ground (earthquake, volcanic eruption, mud/landslide, and sink hole)
- Ordinance or law regulating the construction, repair or demolition of a building or structure
- Damage from rising water (including floods; surface and tidal water; waves; water below the surface that exerts pressure on buildings, structures, and improvements; and water backing up through drains and sewers)
- War
- Nuclear hazards (including radiation or radioactive contamination)
- Power failure caused by an uninsured peril (such as spoilage due to a freezer thawing out)
- Intentional acts
- Neglect

The last two exclusions are necessary to protect the integrity of the insurance markets. If an insured could obtain coverage for losses resulting from his or her own intentional acts, this would create a moral hazard and would jeopardize the insurance company's ability to properly price the policy based solely on the risk posed by the random occurrence of a peril. If, for example, an individual could obtain insurance, burn his or her house down, and receive an insurance payout, the insured would be able to profit from his or her own bad act at the expense of the insurance company, and this would result in an inability to efficiently price the policy and spread the risk among the pool of insureds. Likewise, if an insured does not take reasonable and necessary means to protect the property during or after the loss, or when the property is endangered by an insured peril, the loss would not be covered.

Exhibit 9.3 | List of Covered Perils

Basic-Named Perils (1-12)	
1. Fire	7. Theft
2. Smoke	8. Vandalism
3. Explosions	9. Damage from vehicles
4. Lighting	10. Damage from aircraft
5. Hail	11. Riots and civil commotion
6. Windstorm	12. Volcanic eruption

Broad-Named Perils Includes Coverage for Basic-Named Perils (1-12) plus Perils 13-18
13. Falling objects
14. Weight of ice, snow, or sleet
15. Sudden and accidental tearing apart, cracking, burning, or bulging of a steam, hot water, air conditioning, or automatic fire protective sprinkler system, or from within a household appliance
16. Freezing of a household system, such as plumbing, heating, air conditioning, or automatic fire sprinkler system, or of a household appliance
17. Accidental discharge or overflow of water or steam
18. Sudden and accidental damage from artificially-generated electrical current

Open Perils (Includes Coverage for Basic and Broad Perils)
Open perils means the insurance covers any risk that is not specifically excluded in the policy.

Some of the perils excluded from the standard homeowners insurance policy form can, however, be covered by purchase of an endorsement. An **endorsement** is a supplement to a policy that provides additional coverage. This additional coverage comes at an additional price or additional premium (similar to a rider added to a life or disability policy). Excluded perils that may be covered by purchase of an endorsement include, in most jurisdictions:
- sink hole collapse
- earthquake
- sewage backup
- refrigerated property coverage

Example 9.2

Hutch just purchased a new house in San Francisco, which is very near the San Andreas Fault. He is concerned about earthquakes, and while many people believe that earthquake damage is covered under a homeowners policy, Hutch knows that it is not. However, he must decide whether the cost of the premium is worth it to him. It turns out that many people who live along or near the San Andreas Fault do not carry earthquake insurance due to the high cost of the insurance.

Protection from loss associated with floods is also available by purchasing a separate insurance policy from the National Flood Insurance Program. Clients with homes near the ocean or near lakes, ponds, rivers, streams, and other waterways may wish to purchase this additional protection. Mortgage companies commonly require flood insurance as a condition of obtaining financing if the property is located in a known flood zone. Flood insurance is relatively inexpensive and floods occur all over the U.S.

Exhibit 9.4 | Facts about Floods in The United States and Flood Insurance

FACT: Floods are the nation's most common and costly natural disaster and cause millions of dollars in damage every year.
FACT: Homeowners and renters insurance does not typically cover flood damage.
FACT: Floods can happen anywhere. More than 20 percent of flood claims come from properties outside the high risk flood zone.
FACT: Flood insurance can pay regardless of whether or not there is a Presidential Disaster Declaration.
FACT: Most federal disaster assistance comes in the form of low-interest disaster loans from the U.S. Small Business Administration (SBA), and you have to pay them back. FEMA offers disaster grants that do not need to be paid back, but this amount is often much less than what is needed to recover. A claim against your flood insurance policy could, and often does, provide more funds for recovery than those you could qualify for from FEMA or the SBA -and you do not have to pay it back.
FACT: You may be required to have flood insurance. Congress has mandated federally regulated or insured lenders to require flood insurance on mortgaged properties that are located in areas at high risk of flooding. But even if your property is not in a high-risk flood area, your mortgage lender may still require you to have flood insurance.

98%
The percent of U.S. counties
impacted by a flooding event

$43,000
The average flood claim payout from the
National Flood Insurance Program

$700
The cost of an average annual flood
insurance policy premium

Source: https://www.fema.gov/national-flood-insurance-program

Property Insurance Coverages

Property insurance coverage is provided in Section I of most homeowners insurance contracts. In addition to providing property insurance coverage of the homeowner's dwelling, homeowners insurance policies also provide coverage for **other structures**, **personal property**, and loss of use of the property. Additional coverage is often provided for debris removal, such as damage to trees, credit card loss, and other incidental losses. Business property and rental property is not covered under standard homeowners insurance policies, but separate coverage may be obtained to hedge against these risks.

Dwelling Coverage (Coverage A)

Typically, a homeowner purchases insurance coverage equal to the replacement cost of his or her **dwelling**, which is referred to as "Coverage A" in Section I in homeowners insurance contracts. This coverage pays for repair and replacement of damage to the house, any attached structures, and building materials on the premises. If the residence is mortgaged, the bank or financing company typically requires the home to be insured at a higher value (at least equal to the outstanding mortgage balance on the property) to protect the mortgagor in the event of a loss. When residential property is subject to a mortgage, the bank or financing company is generally listed as the beneficiary (loss payee) of the policy to the extent of the outstanding mortgage.

> ### ⽤ *Key Concepts*
>
> 1. Describe the difference between replacement value and actual cash value.
>
> 2. Describe the difference between open perils coverage and broad coverage or named perils coverage.
>
> 3. Describe an "endorsement."

Losses associated with the dwelling and other structures are paid on a replacement cost basis. No deduction to the value of the loss is taken for depreciation. **Replacement cost** is the amount necessary to repair or replace the dwelling with materials of the same or similar quality at current material prices.

Some policies require the insured to carry homeowners insurance of at least 80 percent of the replacement cost of the home at the time of the loss to be fully covered for partial losses (this requirement is a coinsurance provision). **Coinsurance** is the percentage of financial responsibility the insured and the insurer must uphold in order to achieve equity in rating. Coinsurance in property insurance encourages insureds to cover their property to at least a stated percentage of the property's value, or else suffer a financial penalty. If less than 80 percent of the replacement cost is covered, the insured receives payments for partial losses calculated as follows:

$$\frac{\text{Amount of Insurance Carried}}{\text{Coinsurance Requirement}} \times \text{Amount of Loss}$$

Example 9.3

Terrell owns a home with a replacement cost of $400,000. He purchases $200,000 of property insurance with a coinsurance requirement of 80%. If Terrell experiences a $50,000 loss, the insurance company will pay:

$$\frac{\text{Insurance Purchased}}{\text{Coinsurance Requirement}} \times \text{Amount of Loss}$$

$$\frac{\$200,000}{80\% \times \$400,000} \times \$50,000 = \$31,250$$

The insurer will pay Terrell $31,250 less his deductible. Note, he will not receive the full loss of $50,000 even though his total coverage is $200,000. The reason he did not receive the full amount of the loss is that he did not have the minimum coinsurance coverage. If he had at least $320,000 of coverage, he would have received the entire $50,000 from the insurance company less his deductible.

Example 9.4

Assume the same facts as the previous example. However, assume that Terrell has $320,000 of coverage and that he has a house fire that results in a loss of $350,000. In this case, Terrell is not in a coinsurance situation. However, the insurance company will only pay $320,000 because that is the policy limit.

Other Structures Coverage (Coverage B)

Small, detached structures on the property are also covered by homeowners insurance. Examples include detached garages, small greenhouses, and storage buildings. Often referred to as "Coverage B" in insurance policies, the limit of insurance is typically 10 percent of the "Coverage A" (dwelling) limit. These structures, like the dwelling, are insured on a replacement cost basis. Detached structures, other than private garage spaces, that are used for business purposes, or structures rented to a person who is not a tenant of the dwelling are not covered under a homeowners insurance policy. Separate business coverage must be obtained for these structures.

Certain items attached to the dwelling, or considered an integral part of the dwelling, and personal property inside the dwelling are generally insured on an actual cash value basis. **Actual cash value** is the depreciated cost of the item. These items include awnings, household appliances, outdoor antennas, outdoor appliances, and non-building structures. Building glass is replaced with safety-glazing materials, if required by local building codes.

Personal Property Coverage (Coverage C)

Personal property includes any tangible, movable property owned by the homeowner, such as furniture, entertainment equipment, music collections, videos, paintings, lamps and books. Homeowners insurance policies refer to personal property insurance as "Coverage C" and the limit is typically 50 percent of the Coverage A (dwelling) limit. Personal property does not have to be at the dwelling at the time of loss to be covered by the policy.[1]

Personal property coverage is generally at actual cash value, which is typically far lower than the cost to replace the lost items. Since the value of personal property depreciates rapidly, an insured may find that he or she cannot afford to replace all of the items after a loss, since the policy only pays for the actual cash value instead of the replacement cost of the items. A homeowner can pay an additional premium to purchase an endorsement to change the property insurance "Coverage C" standard of value from actual cash value to replacement cost. Due to the significant loss that most individuals would face if they lost most of their personal property, a replacement cost endorsement is recommended for most homeowners. Some insurance companies automatically include replacement cost coverage in their standard policy forms, so it is always important to read and understand the terms of the policy.

---

1. Note that the term "personal property" does not mean "non-business" or "personal use" property. Rather, it refers property that is not real estate or attached to real estate. Business policies (discussed later in this chapter) cover both real and personal property used for business purposes.

Example 9.5

Lisa bought a new 80" television for $2,800. Three years later the television was stolen. The television depreciated by 60% in the three years. Today, the same television costs $1,500. Lisa will receive $600 ($1,500 - $900 depreciation, $1,500 x 60% = $900) in actual cash value. However, she would receive the full $1,500 if she has replacement cost coverage instead of actual cash value coverage. Note that the amount she paid for the property is irrelevant. Only the current cost is considered.

Insurance policies typically limit the amount an insurer will pay for the loss of specified personal property. Although policies are contracts and may contain variations, most homeowners insurance policies contain the following limits on personal property items:

$200	-	money, bullion, coin collections, and bank notes
$1,500	-	securities, bills, evidence of debt, airline tickets, and manuscripts
$1,500	-	theft of jewelry, watches, gems, precious metals, and real furs
$1,500	-	watercraft, including trailers (not boat affiliated) and equipment
$2,500	-	theft of firearms
$2,500	-	theft of silverware, goldware, pewterware, and similar property
$500	-	loss of business use property not on premises
$2,500	-	loss of business use property on premises
$1,500	-	loss of electronic apparatus

Additional insurance protection for these items is available by purchasing a **scheduled personal property endorsement** to the homeowners insurance policy, or, in the case of particularly valuable items, the purchase of a separate insurance policy. When an endorsement is purchased, the additional amounts of insurance are listed in a **schedule** that specifies the dollar limits of insurance for specified personal items attached to the homeowner's policy. Scheduled items have no deductible and are valued at agreed-upon values, which may require an appraisal.

Example 9.6

Chet has a significant collection of guns, ranging from historic guns to unique low production guns. His valuable collection is not fully protected under his homeowners policy. He would have to separately insure his gun collection.

Example 9.7

Robin is a competitive boat racer, and she just purchased a new boat made of carbon fiber for $12,500. Her boat would not be covered under her homeowners insurance policy if it was stolen from her house without additional coverage.

Example 9.8

Seth is an avid coin collector. He has been collecting coins since he was 10 years old and his nanny introduced him to it. He now has a collection worth over $50,000. His coin collection is not fully protected without a separate rider.

In most homeowner policies, Coverage C provides protection only for broad perils (as described previously). However, an endorsement can be added to provide protection on an open perils basis if the insured desires more comprehensive coverage. Many clients will find the cost of this endorsement to be reasonable considering the increased protection afforded.

Some types of personal property are excluded from coverage under a homeowners insurance policy because they are either uninsurable, or are outside the "normal" range of properties owned by a typical homeowner. Most homeowners insurance policies exclude the following items from coverage:

- Animals, birds, and fish
- Articles separately described and specifically insured
- Motorized land vehicles used off premises
- Property of roomers or boarders not related to the insured
- Aircraft and parts
- Furnishings on property rented out to others
- Property held as samples, held for sale, or sold but not delivered
- Business data, credit cards, and fund transfer cards
- Business property held away from the residence premises

Homeowners with these types of personal risk exposures should request special coverage in addition to the coverage provided by their homeowners insurance policies.

Loss of Use Coverage (Coverage D)

Homeowners who experience a loss associated with their property also experience an indirect loss - the **loss of use** of the property - which can cause the insured to incur significant expenses until the home is repaired and able to be used again. For example, a family that has been displaced by a home fire may have to live in a hotel or apartment for days, weeks, or months while the home is being repaired, and the costs incurred in these temporary arrangements are greater than the normal costs they would have incurred had no loss been experienced. Homeowners insurance policies provide "Loss of Use" coverage, referred to as "Coverage D," which will pay for additional living expenses incurred for part of the premises occupied by the insured, and for any loss of rental income by the insured. When lost rental income is covered, the lessor may recover the loss of fair rental value of the property held for rental purposes by the insured, less charges and expenses that are avoided during the period in which the property is uninhabitable.

Example 9.9

George (lessor) owns a house in which he rents a room to a student (lessee) for $400 per month. If the house is deemed uninhabitable for two months following a fire, George can recover $800 for loss of rent if he is covered under loss of use.

While standard policies limit the "Coverage D" (loss of use) amount to 30 percent of the Coverage A (dwelling) limit, policies covering condominiums typically have a limit of 50 percent of Coverage C (personal property), and modified homeowners insurance policies (HO 8 policies, described later in this chapter) provide for a limit of 10 percent of Coverage A (dwelling).

Example 9.10

Alejandro, his wife, and his three teenage boys live in Baton Rouge. Unfortunately, Baton Rouge was subjected to a hurricane last year, which caused a huge oak tree to fall on Alejandro's house, splitting it in half. As a result, he had to move out for nine months while his home was being repaired. The cost of the home he rented was covered under Coverage D of his homeowners policy. Note that if he had been a renter, the loss of use would only pay him the differential cost.

Example 9.11

Kokoro rents a first floor apartment for $1,000 per month. Recently a vehicle ran off the road and through the wall of her apartment unit. She was forced to temporarily stay at a hotel for two months at a cost of $1,500 per month. Coverage D of her renters policy will pay the additional $500 above the normal cost of rent.

If a civil authority prevents an insured from using his or her premises due to damage by a covered peril to a neighborhood or neighbor property, loss of use coverage is provided for up to two weeks. Under this provision, the insured does not need to suffer a loss him/herself to collect benefits from the policy. This policy provision can be very valuable to homeowners. For example, if a civil authority orders a homeowner to vacate the property due to encroaching forest fires or oncoming hurricane, the cost of putting a family of four in a hotel room, plus the costs of eating at restaurants, obtaining laundry service, pet boarding, and other extraordinary expenses can add up to several thousand dollars in a very short period of time.

In addition to the standard coverages found in homeowners insurance policies (Coverages A through D), most homeowners policies also provide several supplementary coverages, including:

- All-risk coverage for property while it is being moved from one place to another, and for an additional thirty days thereafter.
- The cost of removing debris of covered property damaged by an insured peril.
- A fire department service charge up to $500 for loss by an insured peril (a special exclusion is a charge for a fire department call for rescuing a cat from a tree or rescuing people in a home being threatened by a flood).
- The cost of reasonable repairs to protect the property from further damage after a covered loss.

> ### ☑ Quick Quiz 9.1
>
> 1. Replacement cost is generally higher than actual cash value.
>   a. True
>   b. False
>
> 2. In an open perils coverage policy the burden lies with the insured to prove that the damages were caused by an insured-against event.
>   a. True
>   b. False
>
> 3. It is possible to obtain an endorsement for liability insurance against unintentional damage to another's reputation.
>   a. True
>   b. False
>
> 4. While you could insure a small sailboat (under 26 feet long) under a homeowners policy, it is wiser to purchase a separate boat owners policy.
>   a. True
>   b. False
>
> True, False, True, True.

- Damages to trees, shrubs, plants, and lawns from all covered perils except wind, limited to five percent of the dwelling coverage, but not more than $1,000 ($500 in some policies) for any one tree or plant.
- Up to $1,000 per loss for assessments against an insured by a group of property owners arising from loss or damage to property jointly owned by all of the members collectively.
- Damage to property from the collapse of a building caused by an insured peril.
- Damage caused by breaking of glass or safety glazing material that is part of the building, storm doors, or storm windows.
- Up to $2,500 for damage to landlord's furnishings in an apartment on the insured's dwelling premises.
- Up to $500 for loss due to unauthorized use of credit cards, fund transfer cards, forgery of checks, acceptance of counterfeit money.
- Any incurred court costs or attorneys fees related to a claim.

Liability Insurance Coverage in Homeowners Policies

In addition to covering damages to property, homeowners insurance policies also provide coverage for losses associated with use of the property, or liability insurance (sometimes referred to as Section II coverage). Two types of liability insurance are provided in Section II: personal liability insurance ("Coverage E"), and medical payments to others ("Coverage F").

Personal Liability Coverage (Coverage E)

Personal liability coverage (Coverage E) protects the named insured and all resident family members in the case of bodily injuries and property damages to others caused by them or their resident premises (caused by the negligence of the insured or insured resident family members or pets). Minimum coverage is typically $100,000 per occurrence, but many homeowners carry $200,000 to $300,000 of liability coverage. The insurer also pays all legal defense and settlement costs associated with a claim for damages made by an injured party if the insurer is not willing to pay the limit of the policy.

Example 9.12

Latoya lives in a neighborhood where houses are fairly close together and have small yards. During a severe storm, a large healthy tree on Latoya's property is hit by lightening and falls onto the roof of her neighbor's house. Since the tree fell due to an act of nature, and not due to Latoya's negligence, the neighbor's homeowners policy will cover the damages to the neighbor's house (under Coverage A).

Example 9.13

Arty lives in a neighborhood where the houses are fairly close together and have small yards. Arty is aware that one of the large trees on his property is diseased and unstable, but has not yet gotten around to having it removed. As a result, a mild storm blows the tree over onto the neighbor's roof. The storm was not heavy enough to blow over other, healthy, trees. Since the damage was a result of Arty's negligence, his homeowners policy will cover the damage to the neighbor's house (under Coverage E).

Insurance policies have broad language indicating that the policy protects against claims or suits for bodily injury or property damage, but then exclude most non-personal liability situations and other uninsurable exposures. Liability for business activities is not covered under a homeowners insurance policy. The following exhibit lists the exclusions that apply to personal liability coverage (Coverage E) and medical payments (Coverage F).

Example 9.14

Darin's wife, Lulu, bought him a dog for his birthday. The dog was raised in a loving home from eight weeks old and is unusually sweet. However, when John and Patty come over, the dog turns aggressive. It rips off John's arm, takes it outside and buries it. Darin, Lulu and Patty are all in shock at what happened. Naturally, John needs medical attention and ends up suing Darin and Lulu successfully for $500,000. If Darin and Lulu's policy provides for $300,000 of liability, then Darin and Lulu will have to pay the excess of the award to John personally. The medical expenses for reattaching John's arm will likely also exceed the policy limits. These costs will likely be covered under John's medical policy, but Darin and Lulu may also be responsible for some of these costs. Millions of people are bitten by dogs each year. Dog bites are one of the most common causes of liability claims on a homeowners policy.

Medical Payments to Others (Coverage F)

Coverage F pays all necessary medical expenses, without regard to liability, for others arising out of the insured's activities, premises, or animals. To be covered, medical expenses must be incurred within 3 years of the accident. Insurance policies limit the amount of medical expenses that are paid, typically to $1,000 per person per occurrence. Coverage F does not pay for medical expenses incurred by the insured or a member of the insured's household unless the member of the household is a residence employee (such as a butler, valet, housekeeper, or cook).

While Coverage E requires the insured to be legally liable for the payments for coverage to apply, Coverage F (**medical payments**) is provided on a no-fault basis.

Example 9.15

Jordan is celebrating her 6th birthday with a party at her house. One of her guests, Dylan, age six, falls and hits his head causing a gash on his forehead. Donna, Jordan's mother, rushes Dylan to the emergency room where he receives six stitches and returns to the party as a hero. Coverage F of Donna's homeowners policy will pay for the emergency room expenses for Dylan. If Dylan's mother later sues, any judgment for the fault will be paid under Coverage E.

Example 9.16

If guests at Luke's dinner party get sick from eating bad oysters, each one of them may receive up to $1,000 to reimburse them or pay for necessary medical expenses that result.

Section II of the policy also provides coverage for Damages to Property of Others as an additional coverage, separate from Coverage E, that will pay up to $1,000 when an insured damages property of others, regardless of negligence. This coverage covers intentional acts by insureds under age 13, but excludes intentional acts by an insured who is age 13 or over.

Example 9.17

While visiting at a friend's house, Sunny's daughter got a hold of some permanent markers and drew all over the neighbor's hallway walls. Under the Damages to Property of Others section, Sunny's homeowners insurance will cover up to $1,000 to have the walls repainted, even though the damage was intentional. Had Sunny's daughter been age 13 or older, the damage would not be covered under this coverage, and also would not be covered under Coverage E because Coverage E excludes intentional damages (as described below).

Example 9.18

Priyanka borrowed her neighbor's chainsaw to cut down a tree in her yard. Unfortunately, the chainsaw broke when she was attempting to cut a large limb from the tree. The Damages to Property of Others section of the homeowners policy will cover the repairs, up to $1,000, even though there is no evidence that Priyanka's negligence caused the damages.

The standard homeowners policy contains three different types of exclusions: those that apply to both Coverages E and F, those that apply only to Coverage E, and those that apply only to Coverage F.

Exhibit 9.5 | Liability Exclusions Applicable to Homeowners Policy Coverages E and F

Exclusion	Coverage E: Personal Liability	Coverage F: Medical Payments
Intentional injury	✓	✓
Business and professional activities	✓	✓
Rental of property	✓	✓
Professional liability	✓	✓
Uninsured premises	✓	✓
Motor vehicles (ATV or golf cart)	✓	✓
Watercraft	✓	✓
Aircraft or hovercraft	✓	✓
War (directly or indirectly)	✓	✓
Communicable disease	✓	✓
Sexual molestation, physical or mental abuse	✓	✓
Nuclear reaction, radiation or radioactive contamination	✓	✓
Workers compensation	✓	✓
Controlled substance	✓	✓
Contractual liability	✓	–
Property owned by or in the custody of the insured	✓	–
Residence employee away from premises	–	✓
Persons residing on premises	–	✓

Homeowners Liability Insurance Exclusions

Personal liability coverage (Coverage E) and medical payments coverage (Coverage F) do not pay for injuries or damages:

- That are expected or intended by the insured.
- Resulting from the insured's business or professional activities.
- Resulting from the rental of the premises, except when part of an insured location is rented
  - either on an occasional basis, or solely as a residence to no more than two roomers or boarders; and
  - as an office, school, studio, or private garage.
- Arising out of premises the insured owns, rents, or leases to others that have not been declared an insured location.
- Arising out of ownership or use of watercraft, motorized vehicles, and aircraft. However, certain vehicles and watercraft are covered for liability exposures, including:
  - Trailers that are not connected to a motorized land conveyance.
  - A vehicle designed primarily for use off of public roads that the insured does not own or that the insured does own but that is on an insured location.
  - Motorized golf carts while being used on a golf course or on the insured premises.

- Vehicles not subject to motor vehicle registration (lawn mowers, motorized wheelchairs, and vehicles in dead storage on the insured location).
- Non-motorized watercraft (canoes, rowboats, paddle boats).
- Low-powered boats the insured owns or rents, or small sailboats (under 26 feet long).
- Model or hobby aircraft that are not designed to carry people or cargo.
- Caused by war or nuclear weapons of any kind.
- Caused by the transmission of a communicable disease.
- Arising out of sexual molestation, corporal punishment, or physical or mental abuse.
- Arising out of the use, sale, manufacture, delivery, transfer, or possession of a controlled substance other than legally-obtained prescription drugs.

Exclusions of watercraft liability are very detailed. Any time an insured plans to purchase, rent, or use a watercraft, the homeowners insurance policy should be consulted to determine whether coverage exists, and whether supplemental coverage should be obtained.

Likewise, the homeowner policy should be consulted to determine whether coverage exists for golf carts when used for anything other than basic usage on a golf course or on the insured premises. Some homeowners policies cover use of golf carts in private residential communities that allow the use of golf carts, but many policies will require that a golf cart endorsement be added to the policy. Carts with speed modification or that are used on public roads usually require a separate golf cart policy or an endorsement to the auto policy.

An exception to these exclusions includes liability coverage for injuries to a residence employee (butler, valet, housekeeper, nanny, cook, etc.). The homeowners insurance policy provides coverage for residence employees to protect homeowners against injuries to domestic servants when the homeowner is not required to purchase workers compensation coverage for those workers.

In addition to the exclusions that apply to all of the liability coverages in a homeowners insurance policy, personal liability coverage (Coverage E) also excludes:
- Damage to property of any insured (this loss is covered by property insurance in Section 1 of the policy).
- Damage to the premises the insured is renting or has control of, unless those damages are caused by fire, smoke, or explosion.
- Contractual liability other than:
  - The insured has entered into a contract that directly relates to the ownership, maintenance, or use of an insured location, or
  - When the liability of others is assumed by the insured in a contract prior to an occurrence.
- Liability for loss assessments charged against the insured as a member of an association or organization of property owners (such as a condominium association).
- Liability for injuries to employees that fall under a workers compensation or other disability law.
- Liability for bodily injury or property damage for which the insured is also covered by a nuclear energy liability policy.

Likewise, some specific exclusions apply only to medical insurance payments (Coverage F), including bodily injuries sustained:

- by the insured or a family member
- by a regular resident of an insured location
- by a residence employee of the insured that occur outside of the scope of employment
- by anyone eligible to receive benefits for their injuries under a workers compensation or similar disability law
- from nuclear reaction or radiation, regardless of how the injuries were caused

Exhibit 9.6 | Homeowners Coverage

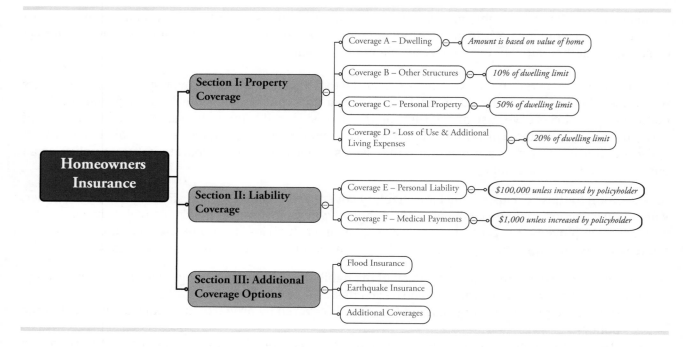

Homeowners (HO) Insurance Policy Forms

Homeowners insurance policies are available under standard policy forms to make it easier for insureds to purchase desired coverage.

HO-2: The broad form of homeowners insurance, HO-2, provides for basic perils plus the additional perils associated with falling objects, the weight of ice, snow, sleet, accidental discharge or overflow of water, bursting of steam appliances or hot water systems, freezing, and accidental damage caused by artificially-generated electrical current.

HO-3: The special form of homeowners insurance, HO-3, provides greater protection for the dwelling by using an "open perils", or "all-risks" definition instead of specifically listing the perils that are covered. If a specific peril is not excluded from coverage in the policy, the policy covers losses associated with that peril. Personal property coverage under a HO-3 policy is still provided on a named perils broad form basis.

HO-4: Renters and tenants have a need for homeowners insurance, but do not have to insure the dwelling, since that is a responsibility of the landlord. A contents broad form homeowners policy, HO-4, provides personal liability coverage plus coverage for personal contents on a broad perils basis and loss of use of the premises. Since a tenant or renter does not own the dwelling, Coverage A (dwelling) and Coverage B (additional structures) are not included in the policy. The minimum amount of personal property coverage (Coverage C) sold is $6,000, and the loss of use coverage (Coverage D) is equal to 30 percent of the Coverage C limit.

HO-5: Comprehensive homeowners insurance (HO-5) is very similar to the special form of homeowners insurance (HO-3), with one major change. An HO-5 policy provides personal property protection on an open perils, instead of a broad perils basis.

HO-6: Condominium owners also need a special form of coverage, since they own the inside structure of their unit and all of its contents, but the outside structure is maintained and owned by the association. A unit owners form of homeowners insurance (HO-6) covers the same perils provided in the HO-2 and HO4 forms, but does not provide building coverage other than for additions and alterations. Like renters insurance (HO-4), the minimum amount of personal property coverage (Coverage C) that can be purchased is $6,000, and loss of use (Coverage D) is limited to 40 percent of the Coverage C limit.

HO-8: The last form of homeowners insurance is referred to as a modified form policy (HO-8). Instead of providing replacement cost coverage (using materials of like kind and quality) for damage to property by a covered peril, an HO-8 policy provides repair cost (materials that are functionally equivalent to those used prior to the loss) coverage. HO-8 policies are typically used by individuals who live in older homes that can be quite expensive to repair if the insurance is required to use original construction materials and workmanship. In many of these situations, providing coverage of replacement cost with like kind and quality materials could create a moral hazard. Since the cost to rebuild with functionally equivalent materials is much lower, the insured could receive a monetary windfall by collecting the higher insurance proceeds and rebuilding with functionally equivalent materials. Therefore, HO-8 policies provide coverage for basic perils, but provide "functional replacement cost" coverage. The insured's damaged dwelling and other structures will be repaired or replaced in the event of a covered loss, but the insurer pays only for currently accepted building materials and workmanship.

Quick Quiz 9.2

1. The three types of insurance most commonly purchased to protect against liability and risks to personal property are: homeowners insurance, automobile insurance, and personal liability umbrella insurance.
   a. True
   b. False

2. Section I of a homeowners insurance contract covers: the dwelling, other structures, personal property, and loss of use.
   a. True
   b. False

3. Both Coverage E (personal liability) and Coverage F (medical payments to others) pay claims regardless of fault.
   a. True
   b. False

True, True, False.

Exhibit 9.7 | HO Policy Summary

Coverage for Different Forms of Homeowners Insurance - Section 1						
	Broad Form HO-2	Special HO-3	Renters Policy HO-4	Comprehensive Form HO-5	Condominium Owners Form HO-6	Modified Coverage Form HO-8
Coverage A Dwelling	Broad	Open	N/A	Open	Broad	Basic
Coverage B Other Structures	Broad	Open	N/A	Open	N/A	Basic
Coverage C Personal Property	Broad	Broad	Broad	Open	Broad	Basic
Coverage D Loss of Use	Broad	Open	Broad	Open	Broad	Basic

Financial Planning Applications and Homeowners Insurance

Homeowners insurance policies have many limitations that need to be addressed when completing a comprehensive financial plan. Many of the gaps in policy coverage can be filled by purchasing policy endorsements to protect the insured in the event of a loss.

A major gap in basic homeowners coverage arises due to the standard for personal property loss coverage (Coverage C), which is actual cash value (or depreciated value). The actual cash value of household contents is typically about 25 percent of the replacement cost value, which, in the event of a loss, could exact a hardship on the insured. For many people, it is appropriate to recommend the purchase of a replacement cost endorsement for personal property, if available in the state where the home is located.

Some people may also wish to add an endorsement that covers personal property on an open perils, or all-risk basis. This endorsement provides coverage that is much broader than named-perils coverage. Under an all-risk policy, an insurance company must provide evidence that the loss is not covered under the policy before it can deny payment, and the burden of proof lies with the insurer. In some homeowners insurance policies, some amount of all-risk coverage may be included on certain types of property. If it is not included, however, purchase of an open-perils or all-risk endorsement is recommended for Coverage A (dwelling) and Coverage C (personal property).

For an insured to be fully covered for partial losses under a homeowners insurance policy, he or she typically must have purchased insurance equal to at least 80 percent of the value of the property. To be fully covered for a total loss, the property must be covered for the full replacement cost of the dwelling. As property values increase over time, the insurance amount may slip below 80 percent, resulting in only a partial recovery when exposed to a loss. An inflation protection endorsement can be used to protect against this risk. The inflation protection endorsement increases the face value of the insurance for Coverage A (dwelling) and other coverages by a specified percentage at specified intervals (for example, every three months, or every year). While the inflation protection endorsement provides some degree of protection for the homeowner, it is important to review the coverage limits in comparison to the replacement cost of the home on a regular basis, since the specified inflation rate in the endorsement may be lower than the actual increase in the replacement cost of the home.

Homeowners living in areas of the country that are susceptible to earthquakes and sink hole collapses should also consider purchasing an endorsement to cover these risks. If the endorsement is purchased, a minimum deductible of $250 applies to any one loss, and there is a two to five percent deductible of the total amount of the applicable insurance that applies to the loss.

A refrigerated property coverage endorsement can be purchased to cover damage to property stored in refrigerators or freezers caused by the interruption of electrical service. These endorsements typically include a $500 limit and a $100 deductible.

Costs associated with sewage backup can be mitigated by purchasing a sewer backup endorsement.

Homeowners insurance policies can be endorsed to provide limited personal injury protection to the insured. The standard homeowners policy protects against liability for bodily injury and property damage, but an endorsement may be available to cover unintentional personal injury or damage to someone's reputation as well. Personal injury endorsements typically provide coverage for false arrest, detention and imprisonment, or malicious prosecution; libel, slander, defamation of character or violation of the right of privacy; and invasion of the right of private occupation, wrongful eviction, or wrongful entry.

While homeowners insurance policies do not cover business activities, and no endorsement can be purchased to add that coverage to the homeowners policy (separate business insurance is necessary), an endorsement providing the insured with liability protection for business activities in which he or she does not have an ownership interest may be purchased. This endorsement is designed to protect the insured as an employee of someone else who may or may not provide liability protection for the insured.

> ### ✍ *Quick Quiz 9.3*
>
> 1. In a partial loss scenario, an insured could be paid less than the full loss amount due to coinsurance requirements.
>   a. True
>   b. False
>
> 2. Coverage F of a homeowners policy pays medical expenses relating to a bodily injury suffered by someone who lives in the home.
>   a. True
>   b. False
>
> ---
> True, False.

Some other miscellaneous endorsements that may be appropriate for a given client include:
- An "other members of your household" endorsement to extend the definition of the insured to include non-relatives over age 21. This endorsement is in response to our changing society and the increase in non-traditional households.
- An "assisted living endorsement" extends the definition of the insured to provide coverage for personal property of relatives, not necessarily a household member, in a care facility. The endorsement includes loss of use and liability coverages.
- An "open-perils endorsement" for computers used in the home.
- An "endorsement available for golf carts" can be added to the homeowners policy and is generally owned to cover property damage. This endorsement is usually subject to a $500 deductible and can also include collision liability coverage.

Exhibit 9.8 | Homeowners Checklist for Preferred Provisions

Part A - Dwelling	• Replacement cost • Open perils
Part B - Other Structures	• Replacement cost • Open perils
Part C - Personal Property	• Replacement cost (by endorsement) • Open perils (by endorsement)
Additional Endorsements and Rider	• Extra coverage for valuable personal property • Aircraft • Watercraft • Furnishings on property rented out to others • Business property • Earthquake insurance • Sewer backup coverage

The Duties of an Insured after a Loss and Contractual Limitations

Upon the occurrence of a loss to the insured's property, the insured is contractually required to fulfill a number of obligations before the loss can be settled. Immediately after the loss, the insured must:

1. Give notice immediately (some policies state a time deadline, such as within 10, 20, or 30 days) to the insurance company or agent as to the time, place and circumstances of the occurrence, as well as the names and addresses of any claimants and witnesses.

2. Protect the property from any further damage. This might include, for example, attaching a tarp to a roof so that water does not enter the home and cause further damage.

3. Prepare an inventory of loss to the building and personal property. An itemized report must contain the quantity, description, actual cash value, and the amount of the loss to the damaged property. Receipts, bills, and related information that verify the valuations should be attached. It is recommended that a video inventory, along with receipts, bills, etc., be kept in a location outside of the covered property (such as in a safe deposit box at the bank).

4. File written proof of the loss with the insurance company, given the company's time constraints set forth in the policy. The insurer must provide a state-mandated form for the proof of loss.

> ### ≔ *Key Concepts*
>
> 1. Highlight the obligations of the insured.
>
> 2. Highlight the obligations of the insurer.
>
> 3. Describe how a claim is paid when the loss is insured by more than one insurer.
>
> 4. Highlight the differences between the different standard HO forms 2 – 6.

Example 9.19

Marleen and Billy live in Louisiana and their house was flooded during hurricane Katrina. The water rose 18 inches in the house. As a result, Marleen and Billy need to remove carpets and remove about two feet of sheetrock throughout the house. These steps prevented further damage to the property, such as mold and mildew.

In some cases, an insured may suffer a loss to a pair or set of personal property, such as a partial loss of a set of china, or the theft or loss of one earring. At the insurer's option, the insurer can repair or replace the damaged/lost items, or pay the difference between the value of the property as a set before the loss and the value of the remaining items after the loss.

If an insured believes that the loss suffered is greater than the insurance company's proposed settlement, either the insured or the insurer may demand an appraisal. Both parties would hire their own appraisers, and if the two appraisers cannot reach an agreement on the amount of the loss, a third appraiser, sometimes called an umpire, would be chosen to mediate their differences. Each party would bear the cost of hiring their own appraiser, and the parties would share the cost of hiring the umpire, if necessary.

Most policies also include an other insurance clause that states that when another policy also covers a specified loss, the insurer only pays a proportion of the loss based on the limits of coverage provided by each policy. This clause protects the insurance company, and the integrity of the insurance system, since permitting an insured to profit from a loss (by collecting two times the value of the loss from two insurance companies) violates the principle of indemnity.

Example 9.20

Suppose Phyllis has two HO policies. One provides a limit of $100,000 and one provides a limit of $200,000. Her house is worth $100,000, and after a fire destroys it, she collects a proportion of the loss from each insurer. Because the first insurer provides 1/3 of all coverage provided ($100,000/$300,000), it pays 1/3 of the loss, or $33,333. The second insurer pays 2/3 of the loss, or $66,667.

If a dwelling is subject to a mortgage, the mortgagee (lender) has the right to receive payment for valid claims on the property, and be notified of denied claims to protect the mortgagee's interest in the home. A lender also has the right to receive notice of policy cancellation or nonrenewable at least 10 days before coverage on the property ends. In return for these protections, the lender must notify the insurer if there is a change in ownership or occupancy of the mortgaged property, and must pay any unpaid homeowner premiums that are due and file proof of loss statements if the insured fails to do so.

Once an agreement is reached concerning the amount of the loss, an insurer has 60 days to make the payment to the insured. Policies also permit the insurer to repair or replace any part of a damaged property with similar property as long as the insurer notifies the insured of this right within 30 days after receiving the insured's sworn proof of loss.

In an effort to limit remote claims for damage, homeowners insurance policies state that insureds have the right to sue the insurer only after the insured has complied with all of the policy provisions, and suits must be brought within one year of the date of the loss.

Insurers are not required to accept property abandoned by the insured, and are not required to cover damage to property left with a bailee (such as a moving company or dry cleaner) since the business policy should cover those losses.

Contractual provisions relating to Liability Insurance Coverages (Section II)

An insurer will not pay more than the policy's coverage limit for each occurrence, regardless of the number of suits or claims filed against the insured for any one event. If the insured would like protection in excess of homeowner's policy coverages, a personal liability umbrella policy (PLUP) should be purchased.

In the event an insured is sued for a loss covered under the homeowners policy, the insured must give notice of the accident or occurrence to the insurer or the insurer's agent, and must promptly forward all summons and demand letters received from the injured party. The insured has a duty to cooperate and assist the insurer in the investigation and settlement of any claims, and must not voluntarily make payments for anything other than first aid at the time a bodily injury is sustained, since those payments could be construed an admission of fault.

If an injured party is seeking medical expense coverage (Coverage F), he or she must give the insurer written proof of the claim as soon as possible after the loss, give the insurer permission to obtain medical records of the injured person, and submit to a physical exam by the insurer's doctor if instructed to do so by the insurer. Any payments made by the insurer under Coverage F for medical expenses is not considered an admission of liability by the insurer or the insured.

General Duties of the Insured

Policy holders have specific general duties that are a condition of receiving property and liability coverage. These duties are discussed below.

If an insured wishes to receive benefits under the policy, he or she must deal honestly with the insurance company. Dishonesty (such as intentionally concealing or misrepresenting material facts or intentionally causing losses to receive insurance payouts) either before or after a loss may void the policy.

Insureds may not assign their rights under the policy to another party without the insurer's written consent, and insureds must generally assign their right of recovery for payments made by the insurer to the insurer (referred to as a right of subrogation). The right of subrogation permits the insurer to take over the insured's rights against negligent third parties if the insurer chooses to do so. Subrogation is not available for medical expense payments under Coverage F of homeowners insurance policies.

☑ Quick Quiz 9.4

1. If a homeowner has two HO policies on the home and suffers a loss, the formula for determining the payout by each insurer is to put the total amount of all insurance as the denominator and each insurer's policy's limits in the numerator.
   a. True
   b. False

2. The insurer may owe a duty to the mortgagee of the home.
   a. True
   b. False

3. Generally, the insurer has one year to pay the insured for a loss suffered.
   a. True
   b. False

4. Generally, the insurer may cancel the policy at any time by notifying the insured.
   a. True
   b. False

True, True, False, False.

Generally, an insured may cancel a policy at any time by notifying the insurer, while the insurer may cancel the policy only for certain reasons, such as nonpayment of premium, material misrepresentation of fact, or a substantial change in the risk undertaken by the company. In most cases, the insurance company must provide a 10-day notice of cancellation when it is canceling a newly issued policy or when it is canceling for nonpayment of premium, while cancellations for other purposes require a 30-day notice. When a policy is canceled by either the insured or insurer, a pro-rata refund of the unused premium is returned to the insured.

Example 9.21

Bill and Beth live in a wonderful part of New Orleans called River Ridge. They have a two-story home with five bedrooms and six bathrooms. Their house was damaged in Hurricane Belinda. Because the storm was a Category 4, they evacuated to Texas. When they returned, they found part of the second-floor roof missing. Bill and Beth have the duty to report the loss to the insurance company and to cover the hole in the roof to prevent further damage.

Exhibit 9.9 | Summary of Homeowners Insurance Policies

	HO-2 (Broad Form)	HO-3 (Special Form)	HO-5 (Comprehensive Form)	HO-8 (For Older Homes)	HO-4 (Renter's Contents Broad Form)	HO-6 (For Condominium Owners)
Perils covered	Perils 1 - 18	All perils except those specifically excluded on buildings; perils 1 - 18 for personal property	All perils except those specifically excluded	Perils 1 - 12	Perils 1 – 18	Perils 1 – 18
Section 1: Property coverages/limits						
House and any other attached buildings	Amount based on replacement cost, minimum $15,000	Amount based on replacement cost, minimum $20,000	Amount based on replacement cost, minimum $20,000	Amount based on actual cash value of the home	10% of personal property insurance on additions and alterations to the apartment	$1,000 on owner's additions and alterations to the unit
Detached buildings	10% of insurance on the home	10% of insurance on the home	10% of insurance on the home	10% of insurance on the home	Not covered	Not covered
Trees, shrubs, plants, etc.	5% of insurance on the home, $1,000 maximum per item	5% of insurance on the home, $1,000 maximum per item	5% of insurance on the home, $1,000 maximum per item	5% of insurance on the home, $1,000 maximum per item	10% of personal property insurance, $1,000 maximum per item	10% of personal property insurance, $1,000 maximum per item
Personal property (contents)	50% of insurance on the home	50% of insurance on the home	50% of insurance on the home	50% of insurance on the home	Chosen by the tenant to reflect the value of the items, minimum $6,000	Chosen by the home-owner to reflect the value of the items, minimum $6,000
Loss of use and/or add'l living expenses	30% of insurance on the home	30% of insurance on the home	30% of insurance on the home	10% of insurance on the home	30% of personal property insurance	50% of personal property insurance
Credit card, forgery, counterfeit money	$500	$500	$500	$500	$500	$500
Section 2: Liability						
Comprehensive personal liability	$100,000	$100,000	$100,000	$100,000	$100,000	$100,000
Damage to property of others	$1,000	$1,000	$1,000	$1,000	$1,000	$1,000
Medical payments	$1,000	$1,000	$1,000	$1,000	$1,000	$1,000
Special limits of liability	Special limits apply on a per-occurrence basis (e.g. per fire or theft): money, coins, bank notes, precious metals (gold, silver, etc.), $200; securities, deeds, stocks, bonds, tickets, stamps, $1,500; watercraft and trailers, including furnishings, equipment, and outboard motors, jewelry, watches, furs, $1,500; silverware, goldware, etc., $2,500; guns, $2,500.					

AUTOMOBILE INSURANCE

Automobiles are basic necessities for most people in the Unties States, except maybe for those who live in large cities with accessible and reliable public transportation, such as New York City or Washington, D.C. With more than 330 million people and more than 250 million automobiles, it is easy to make the case that most adults in this country own and operate an automobile. Automobiles are necessary to get to and from work, school, grocery stores, children's activities, relatives, vacations, and many other destinations.

Because automobiles weigh on average 4,000 pounds and travel at speeds of 70 or 80 miles per hour (or more), they have the potential to kill or injure other people, as well as inflict a tremendous amount of damage on personal property. Automobile insurance is designed to provide financial protection for damages that result from automobile accidents.

Key Concepts

1. Describe the three major risks that should concern an automobile owner/operator.

2. Highlight what could be defined as "your covered auto" in a standard PAP.

3. Highlight the six parts/ categories of a standard PAP.

4. Describe several exclusions that are regularly found in standard PAPs.

Introduction to Liability Coverage

Automobile insurance is designed to protect automobile owners from financial loss, either when their property is lost or damaged, or when they are liable for damage or personal injury to others in the case of an automobile accident or collision. Most states require automobile owners to purchase and maintain a minimum amount of liability insurance for the protection of other people and property. States do not require owners to maintain insurance for the protection of property of the insured. That risk can be insured or not based on the owner's aversion to risk. In lieu of maintaining automobile liability insurance, some states permit automobile owners to purchase a bond up to a state mandated limit. The bond covers expenses up to the limit of the bond.

Automobile owners are often protected by different levels of liability coverage depending on the policy they purchase. Coverage is frequently presented as 100/300/100. The first two numbers are for liability coverage for bodily injury for persons. In the 100/300 example, the policy pays $100,000 per person up to $300,000 in total for all persons injured in an accident. The last number is the liability coverage limit for property damage. Property damage covers the other driver's vehicle or property damage resulting from an accident, but does not cover the driver's own vehicle, which is covered under a different section of the policy. Some states require personal injury protection that covers medical bills, work time lost, and many other costs. An automobile owner can also purchase uninsured or under-insured motorists for coverage of loss resulting from another driver injuring the auto owner's person or property. Most states require drivers to carry mandatory liability insurance to ensure that their drivers can cover the cost of damage to other people or property in the event of an accident.

Example 9.22

Assume that A, who is the insured, carried 100/300/50 limits and had a serious accident that was deemed to be his fault. Imagine the following claims filed by injured parties in the other vehicle:

- V sustains $20,000 in bodily injuries.
- X sustains $110,000 in bodily injuries.
- Y sustains $120,000 in bodily injuries.
- Z sustains $170,000 in bodily injuries.
- X, the other driver, also incurs $35,000 in automobile repair and rental car costs.
- W, a nearby homeowner, sustained $21,000 in property damage.

Assume that all claims are settled in the order in which they are mentioned above. First, address the bodily injury claims. V can collect the full $20,000 since it is below the per-person limit. X is allowed to collect $100,000, because that is the per person liability limit. Note that X may sue for the $10,000 deficiency. Y collects $100,000, and may sue for the additional $20,000. Z collects only $80,000 because at that point, the $300,000 per occurrence limit has been reached. In most areas of the country, claims are paid in the order in which they are settled, although some areas settle on a pro rata basis, so it is important that claimants begin the settlement process as soon as possible. Z will likely sue the insured for the remaining $90,000 of damage.

Next, consider the property damage claims. The policy provides a total of $50,000 of coverage, yet there is a total of $56,000 in property damage claims. Thus, the insurer pays all of X's damages, and W receives only $15,000 and may sue for the additional $6,000.

The driver of an insured automobile is protected from liability to the extent of the minimum of state liability coverage or policy coverage, whichever is more, when traveling to another state by virtue of the privileges and immunities clause of Article 4 of the U.S. Constitution.

Example 9.23

Hiral is a resident of Louisiana and maintains the minimum liability limits required for Louisiana drivers, which are 10/25/10. Hiral drives through Texas, where the liability limits are 20/40/15. The personal auto policy automatically provides the increased limits required by the state law in which the driver has the accident. Therefore, Hiral's Louisiana driver's insurance policy would pay up to 20/40/15 if an accident occurred while he was driving in Texas.

PERSONAL AUTO POLICY (PAP) COVERAGES

Automobile insurance coverages are usually sold in a package insurance policy. The most common package is the personal automobile policy (PAP). Personal automobile policies include liability coverage, medical payments coverage or personal injury protection, collision coverage, other than collision coverage, **uninsured motorist** coverage, and under-insured motorist coverage in one policy.

The ISO **personal automobile policy** is the policy that is sold in most states.[2] However, it is important to note that various states may have different requirements that result in different policy provisions and that it is important for consumers to read all insurance policies. The PAP covers liability, property damage, the covered automobile and medical payments and is organized into the following parts:

- Part A - liability coverage
- Part B - medical payments coverage
- Part C - uninsured and under-insured motorist coverage
- Part D - coverage for damage to the insured's automobile
- Part E - duties after an accident or loss
- Part F - general provisions

Part A: Liability Coverage (Bodily Injury and Property Damage)

Liability coverage (casualty insurance) covers bodily injury or property damage to others for which the insured driver is deemed to be responsible. The amount of minimum coverage required to be carried by the insured varies from state to state. While the state requires a minimum liability coverage, the owner/insured can and generally should increase the coverage for an additional premium charge.

Bodily injury occurs when an insured driver causes bodily harm to a third party and the insured driver is deemed responsible for the injuries. Property damage occurs when an insured driver drives his or her automobile into the property of another person, which results in damage and a financial loss. The liability coverage for property pays for such damage. While most states have split limit policies, some states have combined single limits that cover both bodily injury and property damage.

A split limit policy is one in which the liability for bodily injury per person, bodily injury per accident, and property damage are all separately stated. For example, Louisiana requires:

- $15,000 of bodily injury coverage per person
- $30,000 of bodily injury coverage per accident
- $25,000 of property damage coverage

A combined single limit policy has a fixed amount of coverage that the insurance company pays, whether the loss is attributable to bodily injury or property damage. For example, a policy might be issued with a $300,000 limit, which is the max coverage for a single accident, regardless of whether the liability was due to bodily injury or property damage.

---

2. ISO stands for Insurance Services Office, Inc. ISO has been a leading source of information about property/casualty insurance risk since 1971.

Part B: Medical Payments Coverage

Medical payments coverage generally pays for medical costs or funeral service expenses for the insured when they are involved in an auto accident. The coverage is provided without regard to fault of the injury. Medical payments coverage generally covers the insured, who includes the policy owner or family member, as well as any other person occupying a vehicle covered by the insurance policy. Below are examples of categories of covered medical costs:

- Injuries sustained while occupying a motor vehicle
- Injuries sustained as a pedestrian when struck by a motor vehicle
- Funeral expenses
- Dental expenses resulting from an auto accident

Examples of types of medical expenses covered include medications, orthopedic devices, eyeglasses, physical therapy, vocational rehabilitation, as well as surgery. Typically, medical coverage does not include experimental treatments, thermography, or acupuncture. In addition, coverage will not apply if the injury arises when the insured is engaged in racing, committing a crime, or when engaged in a business involving transportation (livery).

Part C: Coverage for Uninsured or Under-Insured Motorists

Coverage for uninsured or under-insured motorist is referred to as UM or UIM coverage. If a party is uninsured or under-insured and is at fault, this coverage purchased by the insured pays the property damage or bodily injury of the insured carrying this type of coverage. This coverage provides compensation to insureds who have suffered bodily injury in an auto accident with an at-fault motorist who had no insurance or who had insurance below the amounts required by the state's financial responsibility law. This coverage will also pay benefits to the insured who is a victim of a hit-and-run accident, and it will pay benefits when the at-fault driver's insurer denies coverage, or when the other driver's insurer becomes insolvent. While the coverage ordinarily matches the liability coverage carried by the insured, UM coverage is not always mandatory and can be carried in a variety of amounts for either bodily injury or property damage or both. In some states, UM coverage is mandatory although, even in some of those states, it may be waived. According to the Insurance Information Institute (III), the estimated percentage of uninsured motorists for 2015 (latest data available) was 13 percent.

Example 9.24

J.J. is driving his new Mercedes to a wedding reception. Suddenly, Deion changes lanes without looking and rams his 1971 Ford Pinto into J.J.'s Mercedes and causes $23,000 of damage to J.J.'s car. In addition, J.J. suffers a grade III acromioclavicular joint separation, which requires J.J. to undergo surgery to repair the shoulder. The surgery entails cutting off part of the clavicle and J.J. has six months of physical therapy. Deion's car has $7 of damage and he is perfectly fine after the accident. He has the state minimum coverage of 15/30/25. Based on this coverage, the $23,000 of property damage is covered but the bodily injury is limited to $15,000 for J.J. Fortunately, J.J. has uninsured motorist coverage. As a result, J.J.'s insurance company pays J.J. $75,000 for the injury to his shoulder. If he did not have this coverage, he would have only received $15,000 for his shoulder damage. J.J.'s insurance company may then sue Deion for the damages paid under the subrogation clause of the policy.

Exhibit 9.10 | The Top 10 Highest and Lowest States by Estimated Percentage of Uninsured Motorists (2015)

Highest			Lowest		
Rank	State	Uninsured	Rank	State	Uninsured
1	Florida	26.7%	1	Maine	4.5%
2	Mississippi	23.7%	2	New York	6.1%
3	New Mexico	20.8%	3	Massachusetts	6.2%
4	Michigan	20.3%	4	North Carolina	6.5%
5	Tennessee	20.0%	5	Vermont	6.8%
6	Alabama	18.4%	6	Nebraska	6.8%
7	Washington	17.4%	7	North Dakota	6.8%
8	Indiana	16.7%	8	Kansas	7.2%
9	Arkansas	16.6%	9	Pennsylvania	7.6%
10	Washington, D.C.	15.6%	10	South Dakota	7.7%

https://www.iii.org/fact-statistic/facts-statistics-uninsured-motorists

Part D: Damage to Insured's Automobile

Comprehensive and **collision** coverages are designed to repair or replace the insured's automobile when it is damaged. Collision coverage pays if the automobile is damaged in an accident with another vehicle or an object such as a fence, tree, or garage door. It also covers damage resulting from a single-car accident that involves the automobile rolling over, which might be due to ice on the road or happen in heavy rain.

Comprehensive coverage helps pay to repair or replace a vehicle that is stolen or is damaged in an incident that is not a collision. Comprehensive insurance is defined as "other than collision coverage" and provides coverage for insured automobiles damaged by perils that are not considered collisions including:
- fire
- theft
- vandalism
- weather-related (falling tree, flood, earthquake, hail, hurricane, sinkhole)
- running into animals
- riots
- falling objects

Typically, vehicles that are financed are required to have coverage for both comprehensive and collision in order to protect the interest of the financial institution that granted the credit. Liability limits and minimum coverages and deductibles may be determined in the lending contract. Failure to maintain required coverages may result in the lien holder purchasing the required insurance and simply adding the cost to the monthly payment of the vehicle.

Exhibit 9.11 | Comprehensive and Collision Coverage

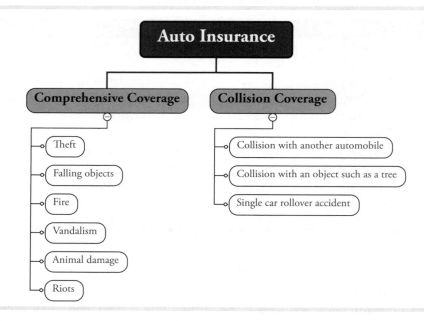

Example 9.25

Dennis was headed back from the gym at 6:00 a.m. He was driving at about 65 miles per hour in his BMW M3 when out of the woods jumped a deer headed across the road. It collided with the BMW and caused about $18,000 worth of damage to the right side of the car. The deer hit the front right side of the car and then bounced against the door and the back of the car. Fortunately, neither Dennis nor anyone else was injured in the accident. In addition, Dennis' damage to his M3 was covered under his comprehensive coverage since the damage was due to an animal.

Rental Cars

Generally, liability coverage purchased for an owned automobile extends to rental cars. Comprehensive and collision coverages may or may not apply to rental vehicles because the limits on collision are limited to the value of the owned automobile, which may be substantially less than the value of the rental vehicle. Thus, rental companies offer insurance for a premium to cover the rental automobile. They also offer liability insurance. Customers of credit card companies using credit cards to charge rental automobiles may be covered for collision by the credit card company as a credit card benefit. Keep in mind that not all types of rental vehicles (i.e. exotic cars and vans) are covered by a credit card company.

Coverage for Loss of Use

Loss of use coverage is also known as rental coverage and provides reimbursement for rental expenses associated with having to rent an automobile while an insured automobile is being repaired due to a covered loss.

Coverage for Towing

Automobile towing coverage is also sold as roadside assistance coverage and covers towing related to accidents covered under the policy but also may cover towing related to mechanical breakdowns, flat tires, and non-accident related tows.

Coverage for Personal Property

Personal property items in an automobile that are damaged due to an accident typically are not covered under the automobile insurance policy. Rather, property that is not attached to the vehicle is ordinarily covered under a homeowners insurance or renters insurance policy.

Part E: Duties After An Accident Or Loss

As part of the automobile insurance policy, the insured has specific duties outlined in the agreement. These duties include providing information to the insurance company, cooperating with any accident investigation, and submit to medical or physical exams as necessary. Specific duties generally include the following:

- Notify the insurance company of how, when and where an accident or loss occurred, including all facts, names, phone numbers, and addresses of those involved, license plate information, as well as driver's license information.
- Report within 24 hours or as soon as practicable of any loss to the police or other local law enforcement.
- Cooperate with the insurance company in any investigation, settlement or defense of any claim or lawsuit. This cooperation may include making settlements, giving evidence, or testifying in court. It may also include providing lawsuit information to the insurance company or submitting to a medical exam.
- Take all reasonable steps after a loss to protect all property insured from further loss.

Coverage for GAP Insurance

Gap coverage or gap insurance provides protection to consumers due to the sharp decline in value immediately following the purchase or lease of an automobile, especially a new one. For cars that are financed, especially those that are financed for one hundred percent of the value of the automobile, the value at the time of loss may be less than the loan balance. If the automobile is damaged to such an extent that it is considered a total loss, the borrower may owe more than they receive from the insurance company. The Insurance Information Institute recommends gap insurance for those who:[3]

- made less than a 20 percent down payment,
- financed for 60 months or longer,
- leased the vehicle,
- purchased a vehicle that depreciates faster than average, or
- rolled over negative equity from an old car loan to a new one.

Thus, gap insurance is available to provide protection between the actual value and the balance of the loan. Gap insurance does not always pay off the full loan balance in cases in which there are unpaid delinquent payments, payment deferrals or extensions, refinancing or late fees or other administrative fees that have been assessed after the commencement of the loan.

---

3. https://www.iii.org/article/what-gap-insurance

Public Policy Issues

Liability insurance for bodily injury and property damage is compulsory in most states. Penalties for failure to carry liability insurance vary by state but often include fines, license suspension, or revocation and, for repeat offenders, jail time.

Compulsory automobile liability insurance presumes that the person at fault may not be able to pay for the damages for the other person's bodily injury and/or property damage. The only way to ensure that at-fault drivers pay for the damages they cause is to require mandatory automobile liability insurance.

There are states that do not require automobile liability insurance. Two of these states are New Hampshire and Virginia. Vehicle owners must satisfy a personal financial responsibility requirement in New Hampshire. In Virginia, automobile owners may pay an Uninsured Motor Vehicle (UMV) fee.

The minimum liability insurance coverage in mandatory states ranges from 10/20/10 in Florida to 50/100/25 in Maine and Alaska.

Is the minimum coverage sufficient for liability for bodily injury? The answer is no. Most casualty insurance professionals recommend liability coverage limits to be at least 100/300/50.

Coverage for Personal Injury Protection (PIP)

In no-fault states each driver files a claim with their own insurance after an accident, regardless of who was at-fault. In these states there is a requirement for personal injury protection (PIP) coverage. PIP coverage covers injuries to the insured and his or her passengers as well as some other costs (medical, funeral, lost income, child care, survivors loss, household services). Since PIP is a no-fault claim, payments can be made quickly by the insured's own carrier.

There are 12 no-fault states. Under the provisions of a "pure" no-fault law, there would be no tort claims for automobile injuries. All accident victims would be indemnified by their own insurer. No state has a "pure" no-fault law; instead, the use a "modified" no-fault plan. A modified no-fault plan leaves tort liability in place for injuries meeting specified conditions, notably, for more serious injuries as determined by the nature of the injury or the total amount of medical expense. A monetary or verbal threshold is frequently used, and the threshold must be exceeded before a tort claim may be pursued.

Covered Autos

The covered auto is the vehicle described in the declarations page. A private passenger auto, pickup, or van acquired during the policy period as an additional vehicle is covered. Notice of such additional vehicle must be given to the insurer within 14 days since an additional vehicle clearly affects the premium.

Replacement vehicles automatically receive the same coverage as the vehicle being replaced. Notice of the replacement must be made within 30 days. Vehicles being used as temporary substitutes for an insured vehicle are also covered. Such substitute vehicles must not be owned by the insured, but only driven while an insured vehicle is unusable because it has been destroyed or is being repaired or serviced. A utility trailer is also automatically covered under the policy.

Insured Individuals

The policy covers the named insured, his or her spouse, and family members living with the named insured or spouse (a family member is any person related to the named insured or spouse by blood, marriage, or adoption). Other persons are covered only while using a covered auto with permission. Also insured is any person or organization legally responsible for one who is using a covered auto. For example an employer or charity organization would be an insured while a family member provides a service by driving the covered auto. A spouse who is not a named insured and who ceases to live with the named insured has coverage continued for 90 days.

Exclusions to the Auto Policy

As with all insurance contracts, there are limitations or exclusions for automobile insurance policies. The common limitations or exclusions to an automobile insurance policy are:

1. Named driver. Some policies only cover household residents specifically named in the policy.
2. Excluded driver. Excludes persons specifically named in an endorsement attached to the policy.
3. Intentional acts. Excludes coverage for losses caused by intentional acts.
4. Racing. Coverage is excluded if the auto is used in a racing event.
5. Vehicles with fewer than four wheels are not covered.

Exclusions can be related to a person, property, location, peril, or specific situation. Exclusions reduce the scope of coverage provided by the insurer. Insurers utilize exclusions to eliminate coverage for risks they are unwilling to insure. Exclusions include intentional acts, normal wear and tear, losses resulting from violations of the law, losses that are catastrophic to the insurer (nuclear war), and some exposures that require an additional premium. The purpose of clearly listing the exclusions from coverage in the automobile policy is to avoid the adhesion issue since the insurer is the drafter of the insurance policy without any input from the insured.

Coverage in Other States, Canada, and Mexico

An automobile insurance policy covers the insured driving in any U.S. state and Canada. However, the same policy does not cover the insured in Mexico as Mexico does not recognize U.S. automobile liability policies.

U.S. citizens who plan on driving in Mexico need to purchase car insurance from an authorized Mexican auto insurance company. Acquiring this type of insurance may not be too difficult. Often, U.S. citizens can work through their U.S.-based insurance companies to obtain the right type of policy. The consequences for not obtaining insurance and driving in Mexico or any other foreign country could include being arrested. There are other requirements to consider before driving in any foreign country.

> ### ☑ Quick Quiz 9.5
>
> 1. An automobile owner/operator should only insure against risks to persons inside the vehicle.
>   a. True
>   b. False
>
> 2. In a standard PAP, "your covered vehicle" includes a new automobile for no more than the first thirty days of ownership or until the insurer is notified.
>   a. True
>   b. False
>
> 3. There may be three separate liability coverage limits.
>   a. True
>   b. False
>
> 4. If you drive "your covered vehicle" into Mexico, your PAP coverage is effective.
>   a. True
>   b. False
>
> False, True, True, False.

Driving in Canada for U.S. citizens is a lot easier to navigate as Canada and the U.S. have reciprocal agreements to recognize each other's insurance policies. However, as with Mexico and other countries, it is wise to consider the requirements and other issues before driving in another country. The consequences may be far worse than one could imagine being used to U.S. law.

Premiums

Auto insurance companies are in the business of pooling and assessing risk, predicting the frequency and severity of claims, and competing against other auto insurance companies in an attempt to earn a profit. As a result, these companies must assess the risk of each person. Fortunately for the insurance companies, there is a tremendous amount of data relating to claims history that can be used to create models and assess the risk of a particular driver. For example, young drivers have higher incidents of car crashes and auto insurance claims than more experienced drivers. Regardless of why the data reflect that younger drivers are more risky, insurance companies have to pay more claims associated with younger drivers and are therefore going to charge higher premiums for younger drivers. The following factors affect auto insurance premiums:

1. Age for younger drivers
2. Marital status
3. Driving record and claims history
4. Location where the car is kept
5. Type of car
6. Use of the car and mileage
7. Possibly the credit score of the insured
8. Policy coverages and deductibles

The more precise an insurance company can be in assessing risk for a group of drivers, the better it will be in determining a premium that will be competitive and will allow the company to both attract customers and make a profit. As a result, insurance companies offer discounts for factors that reduce the company's risk. The following discounts are available from most automobile insurance companies:

1. Defensive driving courses
2. Driver education courses for young drivers
3. Students with good grades
4. Multiple cars on the same policy
5. Policy renewal with good claims history
6. Multiple lines of insurance with the same insurer
7. Airbags and automatic seatbelts
8. Automatic daytime running lights
9. Anti-lock brakes
10. Anti-theft passive devices

As mentioned, there is an enormous amount of data available to insurance companies in assessing risk and in determining appropriate levels of premiums for drivers. The following charts help provide some insight to the data behind the premium amounts. Some of the themes that are evident from the data are:

- Young drivers have higher claim rates than other age groups.
- Cars have more safety features and more anti-theft features today than in years past. These factors have resulted in fewer fatalities and fewer auto thefts over the last several decades, despite the increase in the number of cars and the number of miles driven.
- Drunk driving is no longer acceptable or tolerated and as a result, there are fewer drunk driving fatalities both in total and as a percentage of total auto related fatalities.

Exhibit 9.12 | Automobile Insurance Rates by Age

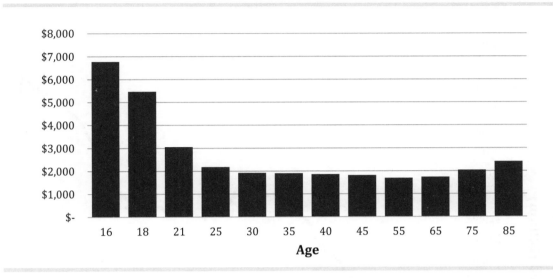

Source: https://www.valuepenguin.com/how-age-affects-auto-insurance-costs

Exhibit 9.13 | Passenger Vehicle Drivers Involved in Fatal Crashes by Age Group, 1975-2018

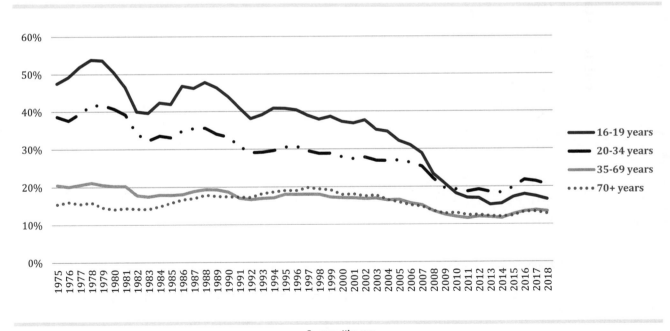

Source: iihs.org

Exhibit 9.14 | 12-Month Average Total Miles Driven in the United States

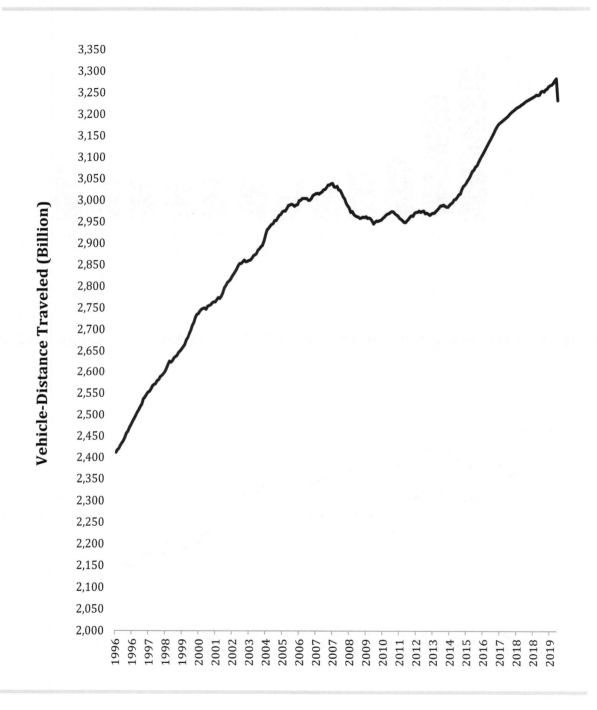

Source: Federal Highway Administration, 2020

Exhibit 9.15 | Fatal Crash Statistics (2017)

Behavior	Number	Percent
Driving too fast for conditions or excess of posted speed limit or racing	8,856	16.9
Driving under the influence of alcohol, drugs or medication	5,507	10.5
Failure to keep in proper lane or running off road	3,826	7.3
Failure to yield right of way	3,711	7.1
Driving distracted (phone, talking, eating, etc.)	2,994	5.7
Operating vehicle in a careless manner	2,961	5.7
Failure to obey traffic signs, signals or officer	2,095	4.0
Operating vehicle in an erratic, reckless or negligent manner	1,996	3.8
Over-correcting / Over-steering	1,837	3.5
Driving with vision obscured (rain, snow, glare, lights, buildings, trees, etc.)	1,581	3.0
Drowsy, asleep, fatigued, ill or blacked out	1,306	2.5
Driving the wrong way in one-way traffic or on the wrong side of road	1,187	2.3
Swerving or avoiding due to wind, slippery surface, other vehicle, object, non-motorist in roadway, etc.	1,103	2.1
Making improper turn	498	1.0
Other factors	6,225	11.9
None reported	13,421	25.7
Unknown	11,710	22.4
Total Drivers	**52,274**	**100.0**

Source: U.S. Department of Transportation, National Highway Traffic Safety Administration, Traffic Safety Facts 2017

Exhibit 9.16 | Auto Theft Statistics (2009 - 2018)

Year	Vehicles Stolen	Percent Change
2009	795,652	- 17.0
2010	739,565	- 7.0
2011	716,508	- 3.1
2012	723,186	0.9
2013	700,288	- 3.2
2014	686,803	- 1.9
2015	713,063	3.8
2016	767,290	7.6
2017	772,943	0.7
2018	748,841	-3.1

Source: U.S. Department of Justice, Federal Bureau of Investigation, Uniform Crime Reports

Exhibit 9.17 | Deer / Vehicle Collisions

Rank	State	2019 Odds
1	West Virginia	1 in 38
2	Montana	1 in 48
3	Pennsylvania	1 in 52
4	South Dakota	1 in 54
5	Iowa	1 in 55

Source: State Farm

Exhibit 9.18 | Distracted Driving 2017

	Crashes	Drivers	Fatalities
Total Fatal Crashes:	34,247	52,274	37,133
Distracted-affected fatal crashes			
Number of distracted-affected fatal crashes	2,935	2,994	3,166
Percent of total fatal crashes	9%	6%	9%
Cellphone in use in distracted-affected fatal crashes:			
Number of cellphone distracted-affected fatal crashes	401	404	434
Percent of fatal distracted-affected crashes	14%	13%	14%

Source: U.S. Department of Transportation, National Highway Traffic Safety Administration

Exhibit 9.19 | Drunk Driving

Alcohol Impaired Crash Fatalities*			
Year	Total Traffic Fatalities	Number	As a Percent of All Crash Deaths
1985	43,825	18,125	41
1990	44,599	17,705	40
1995	41,817	13,478	32
2000	41,945	13,324	32
2005	43,510	13,582	31
2010	32,999	10,136	31
2011	32,479	9,865	30
2012	33,782	10,336	31
2013	32,894	10,110	31
2014	32,744	9,943	30
2015	35,485	10,320	30
2016	37,806	10,996	29
2017	37,473	10,908	29
2018	36,560	10,511	29

*Source: U.S. Department of Transportation, National Highway Traffic Safety Administration
and https://www.iii.org/fact-statistic/facts-statistics-alcohol-impaired-driving*

Exhibit 9.20 | Drivers in Motor Vehicle Crashes by Age

Age Group	Number of Licensed Drivers	Percent of Total	Drivers in Fatal Crashes	Involvement Rate*
16 - 20	12,019,891	5.3%	4,278	35.6
21 - 24	14,358,274	6.4%	5,007	34.9
25 - 34	39,831,017	17.7%	10,876	27.3
35 - 44	37,090,912	16.5%	8,217	22.2
45 - 54	39,175,690	17.4%	8,118	20.7
55 - 64	39,178,953	17.4%	7,271	18.6
65 - 74	27,330,881	12.1%	4,107	15.0
Over 74	16,284,040	7.2%	3,120	19.2
Total	225,346,257	100.0%	52,274**	23.2

Per 100,000 licensed drivers (rounded).

*** Includes drivers under the age of 16 and of unknown age.*

Source: U.S. Department of Transportation, National Highway Traffic Safety Administration, Federal Highway Administration and https://www.iii.org/table-archive/20671

Exhibit 9.21 | Percent of Alcohol-Impaired Drivers Involved in Fatal Crashes by Age (2009 and 2018)*

Alcohol Impaired Crash Fatalities*			
Age	2009	2018	Percent Change
16 - 20	19%	15%	- 4 points
21 - 24	34%	27%	- 7 points
25 - 34	31%	25%	- 6 points
35 - 44	26%	21%	- 5 points
45 - 54	22%	19%	- 3 points
55 - 64	13%	15%	2 points
65 - 74	7%	10%	3 points
Over 74	3%	7%	4 points

Alcohol-impaired driving crashes are crashes that involve at least one driver or a motorcycle operator with a blood alcohol concentration of 0.08% or above, the legal definition of drunk driving.

Source: U.S. Department of Transportation, National Highway Traffic Safety Administration and https://www.iii.org/fact-statistic/facts-statistics-alcohol-impaired-driving

LEGAL LIABILITY

The categories of legal liability to which individuals are exposed are:
- torts (civil wrongs)
- breach of contract
- criminal offenses

Liability insurance covers certain classes of torts, but it does not cover breaches of contract or criminal offenses. If an individual is liable for a civil wrong that caused injury to another, the individual is required to make restitution. Restitution may take more than one form, but it generally involves paying money to the injured party.

There are three general types of torts related to liability: intentional interference, strict and absolute liability, and negligence. **Intentional interference** is an intentional act committed against another that causes injury. Many of the actions that fall under intentional interference are also criminal acts and would not be covered under a liability insurance policy. Slander and libel, however, while intentional acts, are usually covered under personal liability insurance policies. **Slander** is defamation or harm caused by a verbal statement, and **libel** is defamation caused by a written statement.

> ### ☷ *Key Concepts*
>
> 1. Identify the three types of standards of care.
>
> 2. Differentiate between contributory negligence, comparative negligence, and the last clear chance rule.

Strict and absolute liability occurs as a result of legislation in which one party is held legally liable regardless of who is responsible for the injury. Workers compensation laws are examples of strict liability. The employer is liable for any injury to an employee while the employee is engaged in business activities. Under a strict liability definition, responsible parties have few defenses. Under absolute liability, the responsible party has no defense.

If an individual causes harm to another by acting or failing to act with appropriate care, he or she can be subject to liability due to **negligence**. In determining whether an individual has acted with appropriate care, the courts use the "prudent man" standard. The standard is met if a reasonable person confronted with the same circumstances would have performed the same acts. Direct negligence refers to acts or omissions directly attributable to an individual. An individual may also be liable for indirect or vicarious acts, which are negligent acts performed by someone else but for which the individual is held at least partially responsible. For example, parents may be held liable for the acts of their children. **Vicarious liability** extends to employers liable for the acts of the employees. Liability insurance generally covers both types of negligence.

Standards of Care
Negligence is defined as an act or failure to act in a way that is reasonably prudent. In short, negligence is imprudent behavior. The types of liability that may be created from negligent behavior include:
- **Strict (Absolute) Liability** - The two terms are used interchangeably and mean liability without regard to negligence or fault. It applies to damage resulting from some extraordinarily dangerous activity or other statutorily defined activity (e.g., product liability, hazardous materials, blasting operations). Negligence does not have to be proven; however, defenses may be allowed to refute or lessen liability. Workers are indemnified for employment-connected injuries regardless of

who was at fault (e.g., workers compensation). Negligence does not have to be proven on the part of the employer nor are defenses permitted by the employer to refute or lessen liability.

- **Negligence per se** - The act itself constitutes negligence, thereby relieving the burden to prove negligence (e.g., drunk driving). Burden of proof is initially borne by the injured party. Standard of proof in most civil cases is the preponderance of the evidence (more than 50%). Other concepts to consider include *res ispa loquitur* ("the act speaks for itself"). **Res ispa loquitur** is a doctrine of the law of negligence that permits the use of reasonable evidence when a specific explanation of negligence is not available. For example, if a plane crashes, there is negligence. It does not have to be proven. There mere fact that a plane crashes implies negligence. Planes do not just fall out of the sky.

Damages

Damage from a tort can take two forms - bodily injury and property damage. Bodily injury may lead to medical expenses, loss of income, pain and suffering, mental anguish, and/or loss of consortium. The damages for bodily injury can be:

- Special damages compensate for measurable losses (loss of limbs).
- General damages compensate for intangible losses (pain and suffering).
- Punitive damages are amounts assessed against the negligent party as punishment for the act.

Property damage is usually measured by the actual monetary loss caused by the act.

The **collateral source rule** holds that damages assessed against a negligent party should not be reduced simply because the injured party has other sources of recovery available such as insurance or employee benefits (health or disability insurance).

Vicarious Liability

One person may become legally liable for the torts of another (e.g., parent / child, employer whose employee is acting in the scope of employment).

Example 9.26

Joan is the president of Meal Deal Delivery, which delivers homemade meals to customers. Joan hires Red to drive the meals and Red hits a customer's car. Joan, and/or her business may be responsible for the damage.

Defense to Negligence

There are various defenses available to alleged negligent parties that can relieve them of legal liability in spite of their negligent behavior. These defenses include assumption of the risk, contributory negligence, comparative negligence, and the last clear chance rule.

Assumption of the risk - The injured party fully understood and recognized the dangers that were involved in an activity and voluntarily chose to proceed. This defense is not available in all states.

Example 9.27

Nick decided it would be a good idea to go skydiving and jumped out of a perfectly safe airplane. Unfortunately, his parachute and backup parachute malfunctioned and Nick broke both legs upon landing. Clearly, Nick assumed the risk of this risky endeavor.

Negligence on the part of the injured party can be either **contributory negligence**, in which there is evidence that the injured party did not look out for his own safety, or **comparative negligence**, in which the amount of damage is adjusted to reflect the injured party's proportion of contribution to the cause of the injury (same with multiple defendants). Contributory negligence theories often result in the entire action failing. Many states allow recovery for that portion of damages not caused by the injured party (comparative negligence). The "**last clear chance**" **rule** may apply. This rule states that a claimant who is endangered by his own negligence may recover if the defendant has a "last clear chance" to avoid the accident and failed to do so.

PERSONAL LIABILITY INSURANCE

Most individuals have liability insurance as part of their personal auto package (PAP) and homeowners policy (HO). In most cases, the state minimum required liability insurance for the PAP is inadequate to cover liability for anything other than minor claims for bodily injury or property damage. Liability coverage for auto policies can be increased to limits of 100/300/50 or even 300/500/100 and may still be inadequate in certain circumstances. Homeowners policies typically provide $100,000 or $300,000 of liability protection, which, once again, may be inadequate.

Two important factors should be considered when deciding on liability insurance for an individual:
1. Earning power
2. Net worth

Because judgments from liability can be perfected by levy and seizure, both assets and earning power are at risk.

It is not uncommon for bodily injuries from an automobile accident to far exceed normal liability coverages of 100/300. A slip and fall or drowning in a backyard pool can create liability claims far in excess of the normal homeowners liability insurance for such accidents of $100,000.

A personal liability policy (PLP) or personal liability umbrella policy (PLUP) is used to provide protection for these higher types of claims. The PLUP is an excess liability policy that covers liability in excess of the underlying liability coverage for auto and home policies. While it may be a stand alone insurance policy, more commonly it is issued by the underlying auto or homeowners insurance carrier. A PLUP will not be issued without the PLUP carrier insisting on certain levels of underlying liability coverages for both auto (typically 100/300) and home (300), as well as any other policies such as boat or ATV insurance. An insured who fails to maintain the minimums on the underlying coverage required by the umbrella policy will need to pay the difference out-of-pocket if a claim arises.

> ### ⫶☰ *Key Concepts*
>
> 1. Describe the categories of liability to which one may be exposed.
>
> 2. Describe the purpose of PLUP.
>
> 3. Describe some insurance needs faced by businesses.

Example 9.28

Geraldo purchased an umbrella policy providing $1 million of coverage. The policy requires that Geraldo maintain homeowners liability coverage (Coverage E) of $250,000. Geraldo got tired of paying the higher HO insurance premium and reduced the liability coverage to $100,000. The following month a neighbor was seriously injured when she was standing on Geraldo's second story deck and the floorboards gave way, causing her to fall on the concrete below. The liability claim was for $550,000. Geraldo's homeowners policy will pay $100,000 and Geraldo must pay the next $150,000 out of his pocket to bring the total up to the $250,000 underlying coverage limit required by the umbrella policy. The umbrella policy will then pay the remaining $300,00.

The PLUP policy supplements the underlying liability coverages of auto and home (or renters) and usually provides coverage of $1 million or more. The primary purpose of this type of policy is to protect assets and earning power from levy and seizure in which the insured is held liable for damages to property or to persons.

Umbrella policies generally provide some coverages for the entire family or household that auto and home policies do not. For example, some policies provide legal fees outside of the policy limits, and some provide coverages for false arrest (unlawful detainment), libel and slander. Where these additional coverages are provided, the insured is usually required to pay a self-insured retention (SIR) for each loss. This SIR is similar to a deductible.

While most umbrella policies provide for legal defense (this does not affect the policy limits), that is not always the case and, once again, there is no substitute for reading the policy. Also, in a situation in which the PLUP insurance is willing to pay the face of the policy, there is no additional requirement to legally defend the insured.

PLUP policies are very inexpensive, often $100 to $300 per $1,000,000 of coverage. However, the premium is determined by an assessment of the risks by the PLUP insurer, and the premiums for the underlying homeowners and auto policies may be higher due to the increase in liability limits required by the PLUP insurer. For example, the following situations have significantly higher risk exposures than typical policy holders. As a result, premiums will be higher to accommodate the increased risk.

- A person with two or three homes (primary residence and two vacation homes)
- A person with three cars and teenage drivers
- A person with a boat, two ATVs, and a large dog
- A person with a swimming pool that has a diving board and a slide
- A person with young kids and a trampoline

✍ Quick Quiz 9.6

1. Courts generally use the "prudent man" standard to determine whether one acted with the appropriate amount of care in a given situation.
   a. True
   b. False

2. PLUP forms are considered standard forms, and thus it is easy to generalize about PLUP coverage.
   a. True
   b. False

3. Only doctors need malpractice insurance.
   a. True
   b. False

4. The commercial package policy (CPP) is business property and business liability coverage combined in one policy.
   a. True
   b. False

True, False, False, True.

The list above includes examples of situations that statistically result in higher payouts from insurance companies. As a result, insurance companies will charge policy holders higher premiums. The list above is not intended to be all inclusive. Rather, it is intended to illustrate the relationship between the level of risk and the policy premium.

It should be noted that umbrella policies do not cover all liabilities. Criminal acts and intentional acts are not covered. Slander and libel are the exceptions. Generally, PLUP policies cover swimming pools, trampolines, outdoor play equipment and some but not all dogs. Umbrella policies typically exclude domestic workers, workers on personal property and losses resulting from driving while intoxicated (DUI). In addition to excluding intentional acts and crimes, liability resulting from rental activities and business activities is excluded unless specifically covered under the contract.

BUSINESS AND PROFESSIONAL PROPERTY AND LIABILITY INSURANCE

Business owners and professionals face similar risks to those of individuals, mainly losses from property damage and losses from liability.

Risk of Loss of Assets and Liability Insurance

A business owner can purchase a commercial package policy (CPP) that covers loss of assets from various perils and some liability. The coverages, similar to homeowners policies, include basic, broad, or open perils, and typically include a coinsurance provision similar to those found in homeowners policies. A CPP does not cover losses from flood or other exclusions (earth movement). A business owner can add an endorsement for business interruption (lost profits). Businesses also have automobile package policies (BAP) covering physical damage to autos and liability.

Like individuals, businesses often find the need to buy excess liability coverage. Commercial liability umbrella policies (CLUP), which provides coverage beyond (and in addition to) what is covered in Commercial General Liability (CGL) and BAP policies, are available. Manufacturers of products may need products liability insurance.

Professionals

Professionals are also businesses and therefore need both asset and general liability protection. In addition, they need to consider adding malpractice and error and omission insurance.

Professional liability insurance provides coverage for legal liability arising from the failure of a person to use the care and the degree of skill expected of a practitioner in a particular profession. The liability coverage available to professionals is twofold:
1. malpractice insurance to cover exposures to bodily injury liability (designed for doctors, dentists, and hospitals), and
2. errors and omissions insurance to cover exposures to property damage liability, including intangible property (designed primarily for insurance agents, attorneys, accountants, architects, and real estate agents).

Professional liability policies may be written on an occurrence basis or on a claims-made basis.
- The occurrence basis of coverage protects against liability only for events that occur within the term of the policy, regardless of when the claim for damages is made.
- The claims-made basis of coverage protects against liability only for claims that are made within the term of the policy or during a specified extended reporting period thereafter, regardless of when the event creating the liability occurred.

Occurrence coverage in liability insurance means the "trigger" to make the insurance effective is that the incident causing the damage happens during the policy period, even though the claim may not be made until after the policy has been canceled.

Claims-made coverage in liability insurance means that the "trigger" to make the insurance effective is the making of a claim for damages during the policy period even though the injury or damage may have occurred prior to the policy's inception.

Extended Reporting Periods (ERPs, sometimes called tails) extend the time within which the insured may report a claim and be eligible for coverage. On a claims-made policy, the extended reporting period extends coverage to claims that are first reported after the expiration of the policy, but the claims are for bodily injury or property damage that occurred prior to cancellation of the policy. For example, if a surgeon retires she may cancel her claims made policy, but will need ERP coverage for any claims that arise from prior surgeries performed. If the surgeon had occurrence basis coverage, an ERP would not be needed.

Products Liability Insurance

Businesses that manufacture products are subject to liability with respect to those products. Acts that can expose a company to product liability include:
- Manufacturing a harmful product
- Selling a defective product
- Packaging the product inappropriately
- Providing insufficient directions or warnings for use

Exhibit 9.22 | Insurance Needs Summary for Businesses and Professionals

Insurance Needs	Businesses	Professionals
Property Insurance	Yes	Yes
General Liability Insurance	Yes	Yes
Business Interruption Coverage	Maybe	Maybe
Workers Compensation	If employees	If employees
Business Automobile Policy	If autos/BAP yes	If autos/BAP yes
Commercial Liability Umbrella Policy	Excess liability coverage / yes	Excess liability coverage / yes
Malpractice Insurance	No	Yes
Errors and Omissions Insurance	No	Yes
Products Liability Insurance	If a manufacturer	No

KEY TERMS

Actual Cash Value - The depreciated value of personal property.

Assumption of Risk - The injured party fully understood and recognized the dangers that were involved in an activity and voluntarily chose to proceed.

Basic Perils Coverage - Protects the homeowner from losses associated with specifically named perils.

Bodily Injury - Occurs when an insured driver causes bodily harm to a third party and the insured driver is deemed responsible for the injuries.

Broad Perils Coverage - Provides protection for the perils covered in basic coverage, plus additional protection for named perils not covered under basic coverage.

Coinsurance - The percentage of financial responsibility the insured and the insurer must uphold in order to achieve equity in rating. Coinsurance in property insurance encourages insureds to cover their property to at least a stated percentage of the property's value, or else suffer a financial penalty.

Collateral Source Rule - Holds that damages assessed against a negligent party should not be reduced simply because the injured party has other sources of recovery available, such as insurance or employee benefits (health or disability insurance).

Collision - Auto insurance coverage that protects the insured against upset and collision damages, such as those sustained in an accident involving other vehicles, or those sustained when an auto runs off the road and into a lake.

Combined Single Limit Policy - An auto insurance policy that has a fixed amount of coverage that the insurance company pays, whether the loss is attributable to bodily injury or property damage.

Comparative Negligence - The amount of damage is adjusted to reflect the injured party's proportion of contribution to the cause of the injury.

Comprehensive (or Other than Collision) - Auto insurance coverage that protects the insured's auto against perils out of the insured's control, such as missiles or falling objects, fire, theft, earthquake, hail, flood, and vandalism.

Contributory Negligence - Negligence on the part of the injured party that contributes to the harm and, therefore, requires the injured to bear some responsibility for the injury.

Dwelling - Residential structure covered under a homeowners insurance policy.

Endorsement - Attachment or addition to an existing insurance policy that changes the original terms.

Homeowners Insurance - A package insurance policy that provides both property and liability coverage for the insured's dwelling, other structures, personal property, and loss of use.

Intentional Interference - Intentional act committed against another that causes injury.

Last Clear Chance Rule - This rule states that a claimant who is endangered by his own negligence may recover if the defendant has a "last clear chance" to avoid the accident and failed to do so.

Liability Coverage - Covers bodily injury or property damage to others for which the insured driver is deemed to be responsible.

Libel - A written statement that causes harm to another.

Loss of Use - Under homeowners insurance coverage, loss of use is a combination of additional living expenses and loss of rental income.

Medical Payments - A no-fault, first-party insurance coverage designed to pay for bodily injuries sustained in an auto accident.

Negligence - Harm caused by failure to use reasonable care.

Open Perils Policy - All-risk coverage for personal property that provides for a much broader and more comprehensive protection program than named-perils coverage.

Other Structures - Small detached structures on the insured's property not attached to the main house, such as detached garages, greenhouses, or storage buildings.

Personal Automobile Policy - Insurance policy that covers liability for injuries and damages to persons inside and outside the vehicle and covers the cost to repair/replace a damaged or stolen vehicle.

Personal Liability Umbrella Policy (PLUP) - Coverage designed to provide a catastrophic layer of liability coverage on top of the individual's homeowners and automobile insurance policies.

Personal Property - Valuable items owned by the insured that are covered under homeowners insurance.

Replacement Cost - The amount necessary to purchase, repair, or replace the dwelling with materials of the same or similar quality at current prices.

Res ispa loquitur - A doctrine of the law of negligence that is concerned with the circumstances and the types of accidents, which affords reasonable evidence if a specific explanation of negligence is not available.

Schedule - Attachment or addition to an existing insurance policy that lists individual items.

Scheduled Personal Property Endorsement - An endorsement to a homeowner policy that covers specified items of personal property at an agreed-upon value in excess of the standard coverage limits for the type of property.

Slander - Verbal statement that causes harm to another.

Split Limit Policy - An auto insurance policy with three separate liability coverage limits covering bodily injury (per person and per occurrence) and property damage.

Strict and Absolute Liability - Liability resulting from law. Strict liability allows for defense, absolute liability does not.

Uninsured / Underinsured Motorist - A motorist without liability coverage or whose insurer can/will not pay claim, such as a hit-and-run driver, or motorist with insufficient liability coverage according to state law.

Vicarious Liability - One person may become legally liable for the torts of another (e.g., parent/child, employer whose employee is acting in the scope of employment).

DISCUSSION QUESTIONS

SOLUTIONS to the discussion questions can be found exclusively within the chapter. Once you have completed an initial reading of the chapter, go back and highlight the answers to these questions.

1. Explain the need for property insurance.

2. What are the basic, broad, and open-perils coverages provided by a homeowners policy?

3. Identify the various homeowners forms that are available.

4. What do Sections I and II of a homeowners policy provide?

5. What is a named-perils policy?

6. Identify and explain the various contractual options and provisions in homeowners insurance.

7. Explain why intentional acts are not usually covered by insurance.

8. If an insured could obtain coverage for losses resulting from his or her own intentional acts, this would create a moral hazard and would jeopardize the insurance company's ability to properly price the policy based solely on the risk posed by the random occurrence of a peril. What legal principle implies that property insurance policies only pay for the policy owner's insurable interest in a loss?

9. What are the ways in which property insurance policies determine how losses are valued?

10. List two major general exclusions in almost all homeowners insurance policies that cover real property.

11. What are the coverages provided by a personal automobile insurance policy (PAP)?

12. Identify and explain the various contractual options and provisions in a PAP.

13. What is the need for a personal umbrella policy, and what are the umbrella's distinguishing characteristics?

14. What are three types of property and liability loss exposures facing families and businesses?

A sample of multiple choice problems is provided below. Additional multiple choice problems are available at money-education.com by accessing the Student Practice Portal.

1. Otto rents an apartment for $500 per month and has $50,000 content coverage. If he is unable to occupy his apartment due to a negligent fire caused by a neighbor, for up to how many months could he rent another apartment if the cost of the new apartment is $750 per month?
    a. 60 months.
    b. 6 months.
    c. None because negligent acts are not covered.
    d. None because content coverage does not cover reimbursement for rent.

2. Mary lives in Idaho where she carries the state-mandated minimum liability insurance on her car (15/30/10) through her personal automobile policy (PAP). She is driving through Oklahoma and has a wreck with Gerri. Oklahoma requires minimum liability insurance of 30/50/20. Gerri suffers bodily injury in an amount of $40,000 and Gerri's vehicle is damaged in an amount of $22,000. How much will Gerri collect from Mary's PAP policy?
    a. Bodily injury $40,000 and property $22,000.
    b. Bodily injury $15,000 and property $10,000.
    c. Bodily injury $30,000 and property $20,000.
    d. Bodily injury $30,000 and property $22,000.

3. Which of the following would not be considered an insured person for the purposes of Part A (Liability Coverage) for a Personal Auto Policy?
    a. You.
    b. Any family member.
    c. Any person using "your covered auto" with permission.
    d. Any person using "your covered auto" without permission.

4. Mike has the following split limits of coverage on his Personal Auto Policy of 100/300/50. Which of the following best describes Mike's coverage?
    a. $100,000 per person for bodily injury, $300,000 per occurrence for bodily injury and $50,000 for property damage.
    b. $100,000 per covered auto, $300,000 per occurrence for covered auto and $50,000 for uninsured motorist.
    c. $100,000 per person for bodily injury, $300,000 per occurrence for property damage and $50,000 for uninsured motorist.
    d. $100,000 for property damage, $300,000 per person for bodily injury and $50,000 for property damage.

5. All of the following statements are correct regarding a personal liability umbrella policy except:
    a. The PLUP provides protection above and beyond the liability limits of your homeowners and automobile insurance policies.
    b. The PLUP requires the insured to carry certain underlying minimum amounts of liability for homeowners and PAP.
    c. The PLUP insurer provides legal defense to the insured.
    d. The PLUP is only appropriate for individuals with a high net worth.

**Additional multiple choice problems
are available at
money-education.com
by accessing the
Student Practice Portal.
Access requires registration of the title using
the unique code at the front of the book.**

QUICK QUIZ EXPLANATIONS

Quick Quiz 9.1
1. True.
2. False. In an open-perils policy, the insurance company must prove that a loss is not covered under the policy before it can deny payment.
3. True.
4. True.

Quick Quiz 9.2
1. True.
2. True.
3. False. Liability is only paid when there is legal liability, whereas medical payments to others pays claims if someone is injured, regardless of fault.

Quick Quiz 9.3
1. True.
2. False. Coverage F pays necessary medical expenses suffered by someone other than the insured or any regular resident of the household, except a domestic employee.

Quick Quiz 9.4
1. True.
2. True.
3. False. Generally, the insurer has sixty (60) days after an agreement is reached regarding the amount of loss.
4. False. Generally, the insured may cancel the policy at any time by notifying the insurer (not the other way around, as stated in the question).

Quick Quiz 9.5
1. False. The three major risks to insure against are for liability and injury to those inside and outside the vehicle, as well as to the vehicle itself.
2. True.
3. True.
4. False. PAP coverage is only within the U.S. and its territories and possessions.

Quick Quiz 9.6
1. True.
2. False. PLUP forms are nonstandard. It is difficult to generalize about the coverage provided and excluded.
3. False. All professional service providers face liability risks; malpractice insurance is a necessity.
4. True.

10

CREDIT PROTECTION

LEARNING OBJECTIVES

1. Understand the importance of consumer spending in the economy.
2. Identify the types of loans and credit that make up consumer lending.
3. Contrast secured and unsecured loans.
4. Identify the three major credit reporting agencies.
5. Summarize the most important information in a credit report.
6. Explain how frequently and under what conditions a consumer has free access to his or her credit reports.
7. Discuss the likelihood of errors in credit reports and how to fix those errors.
8. Understand credit scores, especially FICO and Vantage, and the factors that influence the scores.
9. Justify the purpose of credit scores.
10. Describe factors that positively and negatively impact FICO scores.
11. Review a consumer's credit report and identify how different debt management approaches will impact the consumer's credit score and develop a plan to maximize the credit score over the short and long run.*
12. Understand how to establish good credit.
13. Know what actions damage an otherwise good credit score.
14. Differentiate among credit cards, debit cards, and charge cards.
15. Recall how identity theft is committed.
16. Understand identity theft, its sources and consequences.
17. Explain what to do if a person is a victim of identity theft.

*CFP Board Resource Document - Student-Centered Learning Objectives based upon CFP Board Principal Topics.

INTRODUCTION

As Ben Franklin said, "glass, china, and reputation are easily cracked, and never well mended." Reputation is an important element of credit because they both involve trust. The willingness to grant credit to someone is a decision that is based on the borrower's reputation. The creditor is seeking certainty of desired behavior. This certainty includes repayment of debt, payment on time, and payment under the terms of the agreement. Any negative deviation from the terms of the agreement, no matter how small, could change the expectations of the creditor from certainty to uncertainty. This uncertainty is known as risk. Future creditors decide whether or not to extend credit to a potential debtor based on the reported experiences of previous creditors.

History of Consumer Lending

Individuals have entered into debt obligations for thousands of years, but consumer credit is a relatively modern concept. Debt was a part of American colonial life, but failing to repay obligations was met with harsh punishment, including imprisonment.

Beginning in the nineteenth century, installment payment plans were made available by sellers for purchases of furniture, sewing machines, and other durable domestic goods. However, before the 1920s, there was little demand for credit for automobiles, college tuition, home modernization and repairs, and durable goods, which make up the bulk of consumer credit today. Financial institutions in the nineteenth and early twentieth centuries were less willing to extend consumers credit as lenders did not have sufficient information to assess the creditworthiness of individual borrowers.

Today, the credit reporting system is extremely efficient and almost everyone in the U.S. uses debt for some or all of their purchases. Consumers use debt for everything from gas and groceries to mortgages. The chart below depicts the increase in consumer debt over the last six decades as compared to the U.S. population. Consumer debt exceeded $4 trillion at the end of 2019, with consumer debt service payments making up an average of 5.61 percent of disposable personal income.

Exhibit 10.1 | Consumer Debt & U.S. Population

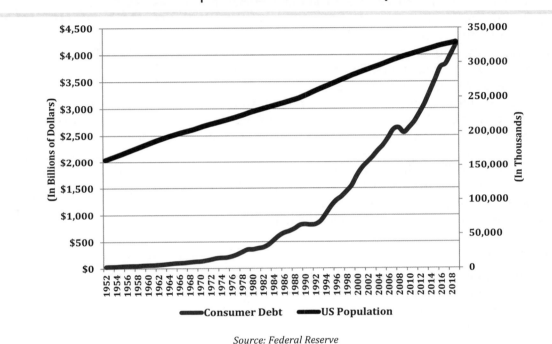

Source: Federal Reserve

CONSUMER LENDING

Consumer lending is a broad field that has a significant economic impact on the economy. Sixty to seventy percent of GDP growth in the United States is a result of consumer spending. Credit cards, home equity loans, home equity lines of credit, auto loans, other recreational vehicle loans, and appliance loans are all included in consumer lending.[1]

Consumer confidence plays a significant role in the overall lending industry. When consumer confidence is high, consumers are more willing to borrow and spend. Lenders are also more confident of being repaid and are, therefore, more willing to lend. This positive scenario generally occurs when the economy is expanding and jobs are plentiful. The reverse is also true. When the economy is contracting, it is generally more difficult for businesses and consumers to obtain credit.

---

1. The Federal Reserve excludes debt secured by real estate from the definition of consumer credit.

Secured vs. Unsecured Loans

Consumer lending may either be secured or unsecured. **Secured loans** are secured by collateral that may be repossessed if the loan is not repaid as agreed. Examples of secured loans are mortgages and automobile loans, where the house or car is considered collateral towards the debt. If the consumer defaults on the loan, the lender may seize the collateral. An **unsecured loan** has no such collateral and is only backed by the borrower's promise to pay. Examples of unsecured loans are personal loans and non-secured credit cards. Secured loans are considered higher quality loans by lenders because of the collateral.

There are numerous risks associated with lending money or extending credit. Specifically, not being repaid or not being repaid within the terms of the lending agreement. Banks, mortgage companies, and other creditors accept these risks when they make loans to consumers. The approval of and terms for consumer loans are highly dependent on a borrower's credit rating. If the potential borrower has a poor credit history as determined by the potential lender, the lender has choices. One choice is simply to not extend the credit. Other choices include charging a higher interest rate, requiring a larger down payment or more collateral, or a co-borrower. This is particularly true for unsecured loans or general credit loans. These loans are a bigger risk for lenders and, therefore, generally have higher interest rates than secured loans.

Credit Reports

Today, credit reports are available on almost everyone. Creditors and lenders report their customers' borrowing activity and history to credit agencies. There are three major credit reporting bureaus or agencies that collect credit information.
- Experian: www.Experian.com
- Equifax: www.Equifax.com
- TransUnion: www.Transunion.com

> ### ≡ *Key Concepts*
>
> 1. What percentage of GDP growth in the United States is a result of consumer spending?
>
> 2. Recognize how consumers spend and borrow when confidence is high versus low.
>
> 3. Identify the three major private credit reporting agencies.
>
> 4. Identify the relationship between credit and personal reputation.
>
> 5. Identify the information (data) included in a credit report.

These **credit agencies** are for-profit companies and are not government agencies. They compile and maintain credit information from credit card companies, banks, mortgage companies, and other creditors for the purpose of creating a personal in-depth credit report on individuals. Lending institutions and other creditors electronically send updated consumer credit information to one or more of the three major credit reporting agencies on a monthly basis.[2] This information includes how much an individual consumer owes and whether payments are made on a timely basis. In addition, when a consumer submits an application for credit, all of the information contained in the application is sent to the credit reporting agencies. The credit reporting agencies also review public records for financial information, such as court records of liens, judgments, foreclosures, and bankruptcies. In other words, a consumer's credit report is a record of credit history and serves as a credit reference for creditworthiness.

---

2. According to the Consumer Financial Protection Bureau, banks, credit unions, retail credit card issuers, auto lenders, mortgage lenders, debt collectors and others voluntarily send information to credit reporting companies.

The information within the credit report is used by the credit reporting agency to calculate a credit score. A credit score estimates a consumer's creditworthiness with a single numerical value, while a credit report shows how well the consumer repays debt obligations in a detailed manner over time.

Credit agencies share an individual's credit information with their members when there is an inquiry. There are two types of inquiries: hard and soft. **Hard inquiries** are made by creditors or potential creditors when making a lending decision. **Soft inquiries** are made by the consumer or by a prospective or current employer, typically as part of a background check. When a consumer applies for credit, the bank or credit card company contacts one or more of the credit reporting agencies to review the credit report and credit score. Based on the information provided and any other criteria the lender chooses, the lender decides whether to extend a loan and at what interest rate.

Exhibit 10.2 | Hard vs. Soft Inquiries

Hard Inquires	Soft Inquires
• Occur when a consumer is applying for an auto loan, mortgage, student loan, personal line of credit, or credit card. • May occur when renting an apartment or opening a checking or brokerage account.	• Occur when a consumer is checking his or her own credit score or when a potential employer is conducting a background check. • May occur when renting an apartment or opening a checking or brokerage account.

The three credit reporting agencies are independent companies that each collect information in different ways. Therefore, a credit report from one agency may contain slightly different information than a credit report from another agency. Not every creditor or lending institution reports to all three credit agencies, leading to the potential for differences between and among the different agencies reports.

A credit report generally includes the following information:
- Personal information, such as name, address, Social Security number, date of birth, and employment information. These factors are not included in the calculation of a credit score.
- Credit account information, such as the type of account (credit card, auto loan, mortgage, etc.), the date the account was opened, the credit limit or loan amount, the account balance, and the payment history.
- Any inquiries, such as creditors who accessed the credit information within the last two years.
- Delinquency information and other negative items such as late payments.
- Any information from collection agencies.
- Any public record information from state and other courts, including liens, garnishments, legal suits and judgments, foreclosures, and bankruptcies.

Exhibit 10.3 | Sample Credit Report

:::: Experian™
A world of insight

Online Personal Credit Report from Experian for

Experian credit report prepared for
JOHN Q CONSUMER
Your report number is
1562064065
Report date:
04/24/2012

1

Index:
- Potentially negative items
- Accounts in good standing
- Requests for your credit history
- Personal information
- Important message from Experian
- Contact us

2

Experian collects and organizes information about you and your credit history from public records, your creditors and other reliable sources. Experian makes your credit history available to your current and prospective creditors, employers and others as allowed by law, which can expedite your ability to obtain credit and can make offers of credit available to you. We do not grant or deny credit; each credit grantor makes that decision based on its own guidelines.

To return to your report in the near future, log on to www..experian.com/consumer and select "View your report again" or "Dispute" and then enter your report number.

If you disagree with information in this report, return to the Report Summary page and follow the instructions for disputing.

Potentially Negative Items   **3**

Public Records

Credit grantors may carefully review the items listed below when they check your credit history. Please note that the account information connected with some public records, such as bankruptcy, also may appear with your credit items listed later in this report.

MAIN COUNTY CLERK

Address:	Identification Number:	Plaintiff:
123 MAINTOWN S	1	ANY COMMISSIONER O.
BUFFALO , NY 10000		

Status:	Status Details:
Civil claim paid.	This item was verified and updated in Apr 2012.

Date Filed:	Claim Amount:
10/15/2012	$200
Date Resolved:	Liability
03/04/2012	Amount:
	NA
Responsibility:	
INDIVIDUAL	

Credit Items

For your protection, the last few digits of your account numbers do not display.

ABCD BANKS

Address:	Account Number:
100 CENTER RD	1000000....
BUFFALO, NY 10000	
(555) 555-5555	

Status: Paid/Past due 60 days.   **4**

Date Opened:	Type:	Credit Limit/Original Amount:
10/2012	Installment	$523
Reported Since:	Terms:	High Balance:
11/2012	12 Months	NA
Date of Status:	Monthly	Recent Balance:
04/2012	Payment:	$0 as of 04/2012
	$0	Recent Payment:
Last Reported:	Responsibility:	$0
04/2012	Individual	

Account History:
60 days as of 12-2012
30 days as of 11-2012

Report number:

You will need your report number to contact Experian online, by phone or by mail.

Index:

Navigate through the sections of your credit report using these links.

Potentially negative items:

Items that creditors may view less favorably. It includes the creditor's name and address, your account number (shortened for security), account status, type and terms of the account and any other information reported to Experian by the creditor. Also includes any bankruptcy, lien and judgment information obtained directly from the courts.

Status:

Indicates the current status of the account.

If you believe information in your report is inaccurate, you can dispute that item quickly, effectively and cost free by using Experian's online dispute service located at:

www.experian.com/disputes

Disputing online is the fastest way to address any concern you may have about the information in your credit report.

Sample Credit Report Continued

MAIN COLL AGENCIES

Address: PO BOX 123 ANYTOWN, PA 10000 (555) 555-5555	Account Number: 0123456789	Original Creditor: TELEVISE CABLE COMM.

Status: Collection account. $95 past due as of 4-2012.

Date Opened: 01/2005	Type: Installment	Credit Limit/Original Amount: $95
Reported Since: 04/2012	Terms: NA	High Balance: NA
Date of Status: 04/2012	Monthly Payment: $0	Recent Balance: $95 as of 04/2012 Recent Payment: $0
Last Reported: 04/2012	Responsibility: Individual	

Your statement: ITEM DISPUTED BY CONSUMER

Account History:
Collection as of 4-2012

Accounts in Good Standing   **5**

Accounts in good standing:

Lists accounts that have a positive status and may be viewed favorably by creditors. Some creditors do not report to us, so some of your accounts may not be listed.

AUTOMOBILE AUTO FINANCE

Address: 100 MAIN ST E SMALLTOWN, MD 90001 (555) 555-5555	Account Number: 12345678998....	

Status: Open/Never late.

Date Opened: 01/2006	Type: Installment **6**	Credit Limit/Original Amount: $10,355
Reported Since: 01/2012	Terms: 65 Months	High Balance: NA
Date of Status: 04/2012	Monthly Payment: $210	Recent Balance: $7,984 as of 04/2012 Recent Payment: $0
Last Reported: 04/2012	Responsibility: Individual	

Type:

Account type indicates whether your account is a revolving or an installment account.

MAIN

Address: PO BOX 1234 FORT LAUDERDALE, FL 10009	Account Number: 1234567899876	

Status: Closed/Never late.

Date Opened: 03/1997	Type: Revolving	Credit Limit/Original Amount: NA
Reported Since: 03/2012	Terms: 1 Months	High Balance: $3,228
Date of Status: 08/2012	Monthly Payment: $0	Recent Balance: $0 /paid as of 08/2012 Recent Payment: $0
Last Reported: 08/2012	Responsibility: Individual	

Your statement:
Account closed at consumer's request

Sample Credit Report Continued

Requests for Your Credit History

Requests Viewed By Others

We make your credit history available to your current and prospective creditors and employers as allowed by law. Personal data about you may be made available to companies whose products and services may interest you.

The section below lists all who have requested in the recent past to review your credit history as a result of actions involving you, such as the completion of a credit application or the transfer of an account to a collection agency, application for insurance, mortgage or loan application, etc. Creditors may view these requests when evaluating your creditworthiness.

HOMESALE REALTY CO

Address:	Date of Request:
2000 S MAINROAD BLVD STE	07/16/2012
ANYTOWN CA 11111	
(555) 555-5555	

Comments:
Real estate loan on behalf of 3903 MERCHANTS EXPRESS M. This inquiry is scheduled to continue on record until 8-2014.

M & T BANK

Address:	Date of Request:
PO BOX 100	02/23/2006
BUFFALO NY 10000	
(555) 555-5555	

Comments:
Permissible purpose. This inquiry is scheduled to continue on record until 3-2008.

WESTERN FUNDING INC

Address:	Date of Request:
191 W MAIN AVE STE 100	01/25/2006
INTOWN CA 10000	
(559) 555-5555	

Comments:
Permissible purpose. This inquiry is scheduled to continue on record until 2-2008.

Requests Viewed Only By You

The section below lists all who have a permissible purpose by law and have requested in the recent past to review your information. You may not have initiated these requests, so you may not recognize each source. We offer information about you to those with a permissible purpose, for example, to:

- other creditors who want to offer you preapproved credit;
- an employer who wishes to extend an offer of employment;
- a potential investor in assessing the risk of a current obligation;
- Experian or other credit reporting agencies to process a report for you;
- your existing creditors to monitor your credit activity (date listed may reflect only the most recent request).

We report these requests **only to you** as a record of activities. We **do not** provide this information to other creditors who evaluate your creditworthiness.

MAIN BANK USA

Address:	Date of Request:
1 MAIN CTR AA 11	08/10/2012
BUFFALO NY 14203	

MYTOWN BANK

Address:	Date of Request:
PO BOX 825	08/05/2006
MYTOWN DE 10000	
(555) 555-5555	

INTOWN DATA CORPS

Address:	Date of Request:
2000 S MAINTOWN BLVD STE	07/16/2006
INTOWN CO 11111	
(555) 555-5555	

Requests for your credit history:

Also called "inquiries," requests for your credit history are logged on your report whenever anyone reviews your credit information. There are two types of inquiries.

i.
Inquiries resulting from a transaction initiated by you. These include inquiries from your applications for credit, insurance, housing or other loans. They also include transfer of an account to a collection agency. Creditors may view these items when evaluating your creditworthiness.

ii.
Inquiries resulting from transactions you may not have initiated but that are allowed under the FCRA. These include preapproved offers, as well as for employment, investment review, account monitoring by existing creditors, and requests by you for your own report. These items are shown only to you and have no impact on your creditworthiness or risk scores.

Sample Credit Report Continued

Personal Information **8**

The following information is reported to us by you, your creditors and other sources. Each source may report your personal information differently, which may result in variations of your name, address, Social Security number, etc. As part of our fraud prevention efforts, a notice with additional information may appear. As a security precaution, the Social Security number that you used to obtain this report is not displayed. The Name identification number and Address identification number are how our system identifies variations of your name and address that may appear on your report. The Geographical Code shown with each address identifies the state, county, census tract, block group and Metropolitan Statistical Area associated with each address.

Names:
JOHN Q CONSUMER
Name identification number: 15621

JONATHON Q CONSUMER
Name identification number: 15622

J Q CONSUMER
Name identification number: 15623

Social Security number variations:
999999999

Year of birth:
1959

Spouse or co-applicant:
JANE

Employers:
ABCDE ENGINEERING CORP

Telephone numbers:
(555) 555 5555 Residential

Address: 123 MAIN STREET
ANYTOWN, MD 90001-9999
Address identification number:
0277741504
Type of Residence: Multifamily
Geographical Code: 0-156510-31-8840 **9**

Address: 555 SIMPLE PLACE
ANYTOWN, MD 90002-7777
Address identification number:
0170086050
Type of Residence: Single family
Geographical Code: 0-176510-33-8840

Address: 999 HIGH DRIVE APT 15B
ANYTOWN, MD 90003-5555
Address identification number:
0170129301
Type of Residence: Apartment complex
Geographical Code: 0-156510-31-8840

Your Personal Statement **10**

No general personal statements appear on your report.

Important Message From Experian

By law, we cannot disclose certain medical information (relating to physical, mental, or behavioral health or condition). Although we do not generally collect such information, it could appear in the name of a data furnisher (i.e., "Cancer Center") that reports your payment history to us. If so, those names display in your report, but in reports to others they display only as MEDICAL PAYMENT DATA. Consumer statements included on your report at your request that contain medical information are disclosed to others.

Contacting Us

Contact address and phone number for your area will display here.

Personal information:
Personal information associated with your history that has been reported to Experian by you, your creditors and other sources.

May include name and Social Security number variations, employers, telephone numbers, etc. Experian lists all variations so you know what is being reported to us as belonging to you.

Address information:
Your current address and previous address(es)

Personal statement:
Any personal statement that you added to your report appears here.

Note - statements remain as part of the report for two years and display to anyone who has permission to review your report.

The Fair Credit Reporting Act of 1971 provides that U.S. citizens have free access to their credit reports and credit scores from the three national credit reporting agencies. In the case of a denial of credit based on such a report, citizens also have the right to know exactly why their credit request was denied.

Consumers should examine their credit report regularly because they frequently contain errors. According to a Federal Trade Commission study, one in five people have an error on at least one of their credit reports that could lead to them paying more for products such as auto loans and insurance.[3] Some of the most common errors in credit reports are:

- a report containing information on someone else with the same name
- errors in identity data, such as wrong name or address
- incorrect accounts resulting from identity theft
- information reported twice (either positive or negative)
- closed accounts reported as open
- accounts incorrectly reported as late or delinquent
- incorrect public information such as court records and bankruptcy reports
- the failure of credit card companies to report credit limits, or incorrect limits reported, thus distorting the credit utilization ratio of the debtor

> ### ≔ *Key Concepts*
>
> 1. From the creditor's point of view, why is a credit score superior to a full credit report?
>
> 2. Explain why credit scores are used.
>
> 3. Explain how a FICO score is determined.
>
> 4. Understand what is not included in a credit score.

Every person should regularly review and monitor each of his or her credit reports for accuracy and completeness. Free credit reports from all three major reporting agencies are available from annualcreditreport.com.[4] One free credit report from each of the three major credit reporting agencies is available every 12 months, allowing for the ability to check one report every four months to ensure accuracy and identify fraudulent new accounts quickly. Consumers need to be careful when checking their credit score as there are many phishing and imposter sites offering free access to credit reports. These sites are scams and sell consumer information. See further discussion of identity theft later in this chapter.

Consumer Financial Protection Bureau (CFPB)

The Consumer Financial Protection Bureau (CFPB) was established in 2010 to identify dangerous and unfair financial practices. The CFPB has made its complaint database available to the public.

The Consumer Financial Protection Bureau began collecting complaints about credit reporting in July 2011. They received more than 140,000 complaints about credit reporting by April 2017. The three national credit reporting agencies (Equifax, TransUnion, and Experian) represented about 95 percent of all consumer complaints. The types of complaints and frequency are identified below.[5]

---

3. https://www.ftc.gov/news-events/press-releases/2013/02/ftc-study-five-percent-consumers-had-errors-their-credit-reports
4. This site is maintained by Central Source LLC, which is sponsored by Equifax, Experian and TransUnion.
5. consumerfinance.gov (2012-April 2017 data).

Exhibit 10.4 | Types of Complaints about Credit Reporting

Type of Complaint	2012	2013	2014	2015	2016	April 2017	Percentage
Incorrect information on credit report	1,259	9,499	21,592	25,461	32,570	12,306	73.1%
Credit reporting company's investigation	312	1,989	2,966	3,837	5,446	2,333	12.0%
Unable to get credit report/credit score	162	1,701	2,819	2,582	2,744	851	7.7%
Improper use of my credit report	77	695	819	1,390	1,931	668	4.0%
Credit monitoring or identity protection	63	496	1,043	1,003	1,390	429	3.2%
Grand Total	1,873	14,380	29,239	34,273	44,081	16,587	100.0%

The credit reporting complaint data from the CFPB show that credit reporting continues to be a significant problem for consumers. Credit reporting accuracy is an even larger issue than depicted by CFPB data as most consumers are unaware of the role of the CFPB. In a national survey, 81 percent of respondents said they did not know enough about CFPB to have an opinion about the agency.[6] Based on these studies, it is clear that consumers have to be diligent about checking the accuracy of the information on their credit reports.

Repairing a Credit Report

Repairing a credit report requires planning, due diligence, and persistence. Any negative information in the report that is incorrect should be addressed immediately and in writing (limited to 100 words) to the credit reporting agency. It is helpful to include any documentation to support and clarify that the negative information reported is incorrect. The credit reporting agency has 30 days to investigate and reply in writing to the consumer with its findings. If the reporting agency's findings do not support a correction, the consumer can still request that his or her letter be appended to the credit report. Such an addendum helps to notify third parties as to the nature and details of the disagreement.

If a person's credit report identifies negative, but not incorrect items, it is a good idea for the consumer to negotiate directly with the creditor and attempt to have such things as late payments, charge-offs, or collections removed from being reported and then removed from the credit report. The creditor is not obligated to remove negative items, but may do so if there is a compelling reason.

Credit Scores

A **credit score** is a number that summarizes a person's credit risk based on an evaluation of his or her credit report at a particular point in time. Credit scores are calculated using a formula with four or more variables with various weightings. Credit scores are often referred to as FICO scores because most credit agencies' scores are produced from software developed by FICO (formerly named Fair Isaac Corporation). However, there are various credit scoring companies and many different credit scores. The most important credit score for a consumer is the one the lender is using to grant credit.

---

6. Source: creditcards.com: Poll: Few aware of embattled consumer watchdog, March 1, 2017.

The two most well-known credit scores are FICO and Vantage. However, even these two credit agencies provide a large number of different scores for the same person depending on the particular credit granting user. A particular user (creditor) simply changes the weights or the variables in the formula for different uses. All of the scores are based on payment history, debt utilization, age of credit accounts, credit type mix, and credit inquiries. All scores are designed to predict the likelihood of debt repayment.

The credit score actually used by a particular lender is unlikely to be the exact credit score either provided by one of the credit reporting agencies or the particular credit company, and the lender/creditor is unlikely to reveal the actual scoring method it is using.

TransUnion conducted a survey in 2015 to determine how well the public understood what was included in a credit score. Some of the results are reported in **Exhibit 10.5**.

Exhibit 10.5 | What is Not in a Credit Score

- **Pay raises:** 48 percent of those surveyed erroneously believed that an increase in income improves their credit scores.

- **Credit inquires:** 40 percent surveyed were unsure of the impact of checking a credit score. 20 percent surveyed erroneously believed checking a credit report causes it to go down.

- **Paying down debts:** 61 percent erroneously believed paying off debts from late payments automatically increases their score. Generally, negative records, such as late payments, remain on credit reports for up to seven years.

- **Trended information:** 70 percent of those who have checked their reports in the last year incorrectly assumed that they reflected recent changes or trends in their finances over time.

Source: TransUnion Survey (released March 12, 2015).

FICO Score

The **FICO score** is calculated using a formula that evaluates many types of information in the credit report at that credit reporting agency and base FICO scores ranges from 300 to 850.[7] The FICO score estimates the level of future credit risk. FICO scores can be delivered electronically, almost instantaneously, helping lenders speed up the time for the loan approval process to minutes rather than hours or weeks.

The FICO scoring system dramatically lowers the cost of borrowing and the cost of capital in the United States. Quick, easy access to credit is a major source of economic strength and stability for consumers and businesses alike. It also differentiates the Untied States from other emerging economies many of which have little credit granting.

Factors such as gender, race, religion, nationality and marital status are not included in FICO scores. Below is a chart with the interpretation of the various ranges in FICO scores.

---

7. FICO industry-specific (auto and credit card) scores range from 250-900. Source: myfico.com.

Exhibit 10.6 | FICO Score Range

FICO Score	Description of Credit	Chance for Delinquency
800 - 850	Exceptional	1%
740 - 799	Very Good	2%
670 - 739	Good	8%
580 - 669	Fair	28%
300 - 579	Poor	61%

FICO8 credit scores

A report of any negative item can lower a FICO score quickly and negatively affect the score for a long period of time. For example, a single 30-day late payment could remain on the credit report for up to seven years. However, while destroying a FICO score can happen quickly, improving a FICO score takes a long time. As mentioned at the beginning of this section, credit and reputation are similar in terms of being fragile and needing protection.

How a FICO Score is Determined

Five primary factors determine a person's FICO credit score. These factors include payment history, the amount of credit and the credit utilization, the length of credit history, the mix of credit types, and new credit or new accounts. All of the factors are considered in the determination of the FICO score. According to FICO, the percentages in the chart below are averages for the general population. However, the percentages may vary for particular groups, such as people who have limited credit history. The percentages may also be changed to provide custom credit scores for a particular user, such as a bank offering a loan to the consumer or an insurance company underwriting an auto policy for the consumer.

Exhibit 10.7 | How a FICO Score Breaks Down

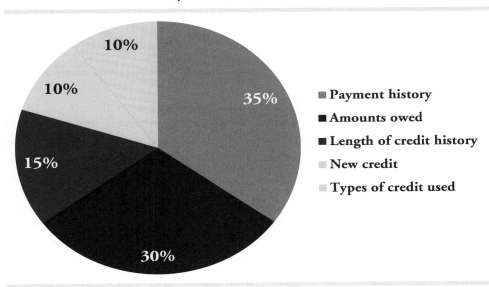

- ■ Payment history
- ■ Amounts owed
- ■ Length of credit history
- ■ New credit
- ■ Types of credit used

Payment History (35%)

Payment history is the most important factor in the determination of a FICO score and accounts for 35 percent of the score. Up to seven years of payment history is included in this category, as well as the presence or absence of derogatory payment information.[8] A few late payments will not destroy a person's credit score. The FICO score also takes into consideration the details of late payments, such as how late they were and how much was owed.

Amounts Owed (30%)

Debt burden and credit utilization is the second most important factor in determining a FICO score and accounts for 30 percent of the score. Included in this category are such items as credit utilization, the number of accounts with balances, the amounts owed over various types of accounts, and the down payments made on installment loans. Borrowers who are close to maximizing their currently available credit are considered a higher risk than those who have a substantial amount of available credit.

The optimal credit utilization percentage is between one and 30 percent of total credit available.

Example 10.1

Yolanda has five credit cards with a $5,000 limit on each for a total credit available of $25,000. If she owes $2,500, she has a 10% utilization.

Exhibit 10.8 | Impact of Credit Utilization Percents on Credit Score*

Utilization	Negative / Positive	Impact of Score
0%	Negative	<20 Points>
1% - 20%	Positive	0 Points
21% - 30%	Positive	0 Points
31% - 40%	Negative	<30 Points>
51% - 75%	Negative	<75 Points>
76% - 100%	Negative	<100 Points>

Author Estimates (note that 0% utilization is negative)

Simply closing accounts can have a negative impact on credit score because credit utilization may be affected. In addition, the age of any account that is closed may negatively impact a credit score. If the oldest account is closed, the average age of credit history declines, which is a negative factor in determining credit score.

Length of Credit History (15%)

The length of credit history is the third factor and accounts for 15 percent of the FICO score. This factor includes the average age of credit accounts and the age of the oldest account, as well as the age of the newest account. It is generally more favorable to have older accounts that have a longer history of favorable credit activity. However, newer accounts may show a requisite amount of activity from which to determine a credit score.

---

8. Derogatory marks are long-lasting negative records on a credit report. Examples include bankruptcy, civil judgments, foreclosures, etc.

Credit Mix (10%)

The mix of credit is the fourth factor and accounts for approximately 10 percent of the total FICO score. Consumers might have credit from a home loan, auto loan, credit cards, school loans, bank, or other lenders. Lenders are generally more impressed if the consumer can manage a mix of credit including credit cards, installment payments, and mortgage payments, rather than simply one type of credit (e.g., credit cards). FICO scores increase as the consumer demonstrates a history of managing different types of credit (i.e., credit cards, bank loans, installment loans). This factor may be more important for consumers with otherwise limited information on their credit report.

New Credit (10%)

According to FICO, opening several new lines of credit in a short period of time represents an increase in risk for potential creditors. Recent hard inquiries and new credit represent the fifth factor and account for approximately 10 percent of the FICO score. Hard inquiries that are made by potential creditors for granting of credit remain on the report for two years. However, they only count negatively for 12 months. The impact of one hard inquiry is generally less than negative five points on the overall score. However, it is best not to open new accounts too quickly. Otherwise, there may be a negative impact on the FICO score. When a consumer is shopping for rates for a particular type of loan, such as a mortgage or auto loan, the credit bureaus recognize that there may be multiple hard inquiries in a short period of time and will typically count all hard inquiries of the same type within a 14-to-45 day period as a single inquiry. Hard inquiries of different types, such as an auto loan and a credit card, in a short period of time, however, are not counted as a single inquiry. Requesting a credit report from a credit reporting agency does not impact the credit score. Below is a distribution of various FICO scores for the period 2007-2018.

✍ Quick Quiz 10.1

1. A credit report includes information about a person's income.
   a. True
   b. False

2. A credit report includes moving vehicle citations.
   a. True
   b. False

3. A credit report can be used to determine the risk of a person filing an automobile insurance claim.
   a. True
   b. False

4. A credit report can be used to determine the risk of a person filing a homeowner's insurance claim.
   a. True
   b. False

False, False, True, True.

Exhibit 10.9 | Distributions of FICO Scores by Percentages for 2007 - 2018

FICO Score	Percent of Population											
	October 2007	October 2008	October 2009	October 2010	October 2011	October 2012	October 2013	October 2014	October 2015	October 2016	April 2017	April 2018
300-499	7.1	7.2	7.3	6.9	6.3	6.0	5.8	5.2	5.0	4.6	4.7	4.2
500-549	8.0	8.2	8.7	9.0	8.7	8.5	8.4	7.9	7.4	7.1	6.8	6.8
550-599	8.7	8.7	9.1	9.6	9.9	9.9	9.8	9.5	9.2	9.0	8.5	8.1
600-649	9.7	9.6	9.5	9.5	9.8	10.1	10.2	10.3	10.3	10.3	10.0	9.6
650-699	12.1	12.0	11.9	11.9	12.1	12.2	12.7	12.8	13.0	13.3	13.2	13.0
700-749	16.2	16.0	15.9	15.7	15.5	16.2	16.3	16.6	16.8	16.9	17.1	16.2
750-799	19.8	19.6	19.4	19.5	19.6	18.8	18.4	18.1	18.3	18.5	19.0	20.2
800-850	18.4	18.7	18.2	17.9	18.1	18.4	18.6	19.6	20.0	20.4	20.7	21.8
Total	100%	100%	100%	100%	100%	100%	100%	100%	100%	100%	100%	100%

Source: http://www.fico.com

It should be noted that the percentages in each category of the above exhibit remained relatively constant across the time year period 2007-2018. This stability is especially interesting given the economic crisis that occurred during this period. The mean or average FICO score was 686 in 2009 and has been trending upward over the last seven years. The average score in 2019 was 706.

Exhibit 10.10 | Average FICO

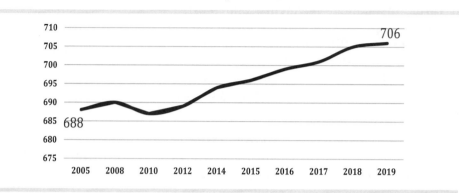

In April 2015, FICO announced a piloted alternative scoring system to make millions of Americans who currently do not have a FICO score credit worthy. FICO joined with Equifax to use data from cable, cell phone, electric and gas bills to produce a score of credit worthiness for persons who would not have scores otherwise. In 2019, FICO announced a new UltraFICO™ score which allows consumers the option to link their checking, savings, or money market accounts in order to provide additional indicators (such as consistent positive balances and cash on hand) to enhance their credit score.

The newest versions of the FICO score, FICO Score 10 and 10T, will be available beginning in 2020. These models treat late payments and debt more severely than prior models, but also consider historical information about credit card balances (reducing, maintaining, or increasing) and payment amounts (both minimum payment and amount paid). The FICO Score 10T will be the first FICO score to use trended data (time-series data) showing how the consumer managed their accounts over the previous 24 months. Consumers who pay their balances in full each month are considered lower risk than those who revolve balances from month-to-month.

Understanding the elements of the credit score and actively managing one's own credit score is important because credit scores can determine whether a consumer is likely to obtain credit and if so, at what rate of interest. Borrowers with higher credit scores are considered less risky and are generally able to obtain credit at a lower cost, which is reflected in a lower rate of interest. Higher interest rates increase the total cost of ownership, whether that is a home, a car, or other items. This concept is demonstrated in the following exhibit.

Exhibit 10.11 | Cost of Poor FICO Scores (760-850 vs 620-639)

Impact of Credit Score (FICO)*			
	30-Year Mortgage	**15-Year Home Equity Loan**	**36-Month Auto Loan**
Loan Amount	$250,000	$100,000	$30,000
FICO Score	**Interest Rates**	**Interest Rates**	**Interest Rates**
760-850	3.564%	6.037%	4.119%
620-639	5.153%	10.362%	10.545%
Differential Cost / %	<1.588%>	<4.325%>	<6.426%>
FICO Score	**Monthly Payment**	**Monthly Payment**	**Monthly Payment**
760-850	$1,131.56	$845.86	$887.32
620-639	$1,365.53	$1,096.86	$975.71
Differential Cost/Month ($)	<$233.97>	<$251.00>	<$88.40>
Additional Interest Cost with Poor FICO Score over Term of Loan			
Additional Interest ($)	$84,227.61	$45,180.35	$3,182.45
Additional Interest (%)	21%	30%	10%

https://www.myfico.com/credit-education/calculators/loan-savings-calculator/

As the exhibit above illustrates, consumers with poor FICO scores or credit scores pay more for the same good or service than consumers with higher credit scores if they need to obtain credit for the purchase. This same concept is also illustrated in the exhibit below. The exhibit below illustrates the total interest cost for a mortgage, an auto loan, and a credit card over a lifetime, based on various credit ratings.

Exhibit 10.12 | Interest Impact of Less-Than-Excellent Credit Score on Overall Debt Over a Lifetime (Dollars and Percent)

Cost of Debt (37 Year Old)**		
Assumptions	**Balances and Payments**	
Mortgage	$350,000	
Auto Loan	$30,000 (every 4 years)	
Credit Card	$10,000 (paying $200 month)	
Credit Rating	**Interest over Lifetime (dollars)***	**% Increase from Excellent**
Excellent Credit	$261,495	0%
Good Credit	$293,475	+12.23%
Fair Credit	$353,953	+35.36%
Poor Credit	$470,585	+79.96%
Bad Credit	$580,630	+122.04%

* Calculated using Credit.com calculator.

** Assume the 37-year-old has a $350,000 mortgage, purchases an automobile for $30,000 every four years and finances 80%, and has credit cards with a balance of $10,000 paying $200 a month.

As illustrated above, a lower credit score will cost a consumer more in terms of interest on borrowings. Below are exhibits that depict factors that positively and negatively impact credit scores, the numerical impacts to credit scores for certain negative events, and the time it takes for a credit score to recover from negative information. Websites such as Credit Karma and numerous others offering free credit scores also provide credit score simulators, allowing consumers to view how particular actions will impact their individual score (be sure to note the guidance later in this chapter to avoid identity theft by ensuring that any personal identifying information provided is to a legitimate and secure website).

Exhibit 10.13 | FACTORS THAT MAY AFFECT CREDIT SCORES

Positively Affects Credit Score	Negatively Affects Credit Score
Consistent, Timely Payments over Time	Late Payments
More History Accounts	Significant Change in Utilization Rate
No 30/60/90 Days Late	Closing Accounts
No Late Charges	Opening New Accounts
Credit Utilization	Liens
No New Hard Inquiries	Judgments
No Recently Closed Accounts	Foreclosures
No Charge-Offs	New Hard Inquiries
No Liens	Bankruptcy
No Judgments	Child Support in Arrearage
No Foreclosures	Wage Garnishments
No Bankruptcy	

Exhibit 10.14 | Impact to FICO Score*

	Consumer A	Consumer B	Consumer C
Starting FICO Score	680	720	780
FICO score after these independent events:			
30 days late on mortgage	600 - 620	630 - 650	670 - 690
90 days late on mortgage	600 - 620	610 - 630	650 - 670
Short sale / deed-in-lieu / settlement (no deficiency balance)	610 - 630	605 - 625	655 - 675
Short sale (with deficiency balance)	575 - 595	570 - 590	620 - 640
Foreclosure	575 - 595	570 - 590	620 - 640
Bankruptcy	530 - 550	525 - 545	540 - 560

Source: FICO Banking Analytics Blog. 2011 Fair Isaac Corporation.
* These are approximations.

Exhibit 10.15 | Estimated Time for a FICO Score to Fully Recover*

	Consumer A	Consumer B	Consumer C
Starting FICO Score	680	720	780
Time for a FICO Score to recover after these independent events:			
30 days late on mortgage	9 months	2.5 years	3 years
90 days late on mortgage	9 months	3 years	7 years
Short sale / deed-in-lieu / settlement (no deficiency balance)	3 years	7 years	7 years
Short sale (with deficiency balance)	3 years	7 years	7 years
Foreclosure	3 years	7 years	7 years
Bankruptcy	5 years	7 - 10 years	7 -10 years

Source: FICO Banking Analytics Blog. 2011 Fair Isaac Corporation.
* These are approximations.

Note: Estimates assume all else held constant over time (e.g., no new account openings, no new delinquency, similar outstanding debt).

VantageScore

The three major credit bureaus (Equifax, Experian, and TransUnion) joined together to create the **VantageScore**, which was launched in March of 2006. The VantageScore weighs payment history more than FICO and now ranges from 300 to 850.[9] The credit agencies' objective in creating VantageScore was to make credit scoring more consistent and accurate across all of the bureaus. VantageScore attempts to remedy this issue by putting more weight on the past 24 months of credit history. Although relatively new, VantageScore is widely used by financial institutions, credit card issuers, and auto lenders.

Exhibit 10.16 | Factors that Influence VantageScore

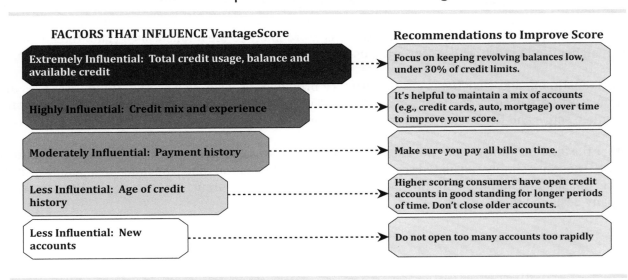

9. Earlier VantageScores ranged from 501 to 990. However, VantageScore 3.0 and 4.0 now range from 300 to 850.

VantageScore 4.0 (VS4) is the next generation credit score from the company that became available in the fall 2017. VS4 builds upon the National Consumer Assistance Plan (NCAP), which is an initiative of Equifax, Experian, and TransUnion that attempts to improve the accuracy of credit reports and increase the ease with which consumers can correct errors on their credit reports.

The NCAP is a result of a settlement between a group of state attorneys general and the three national credit reporting agencies, which was announced on March 9th, 2015. The purpose of the settlement, and the National Consumer Assistance Plan, is to improve accuracy of credit reports and make it easier for consumers to be aware of their credit history and credit information.

> ### ☷ *Key Concepts*
>
> 1. Explain a VantageScore.
>
> 2. Identify how a VantageScore is different from a FICO score.
>
> 3. Recognize if a secured credit card is a good way to establish credit.
>
> 4. Identify one of the easiest loans to obtain.

VantageScore 4.0 incorporates trended data and distinguishes medical collections from other types of collection accounts. By providing insight about the changes in a consumer's credit behaviors over time, trended data provides benefits to those with low credit scores who are diligently paying off debt. Medical collections less than six months old are ignored to permit insurance payment processing to occur. VantageScore 4.0 also weighs medical collections less than other collections.

Other Scores

There are many credit scores other than FICO and Vantage, including credit scores for the automobile insurance industry and the homeowners insurance industry. FICO first introduced insurance scores in 1993. Today, many property and casualty insurers use some form of credit score. According to FICO, there is a direct relationship between the likelihood of an insurance claim and a person's credit score. In other words, a person with a lower credit score is more likely to file an insurance claim than a person with a higher credit score. These scores are used in part to determine a person's insurance premium.

FICO, TransUnion, and LexisNexis are the primary providers of insurance scores. Standard scores and custom scores are used by the insurance industry. Two of the more common credit scores are the **auto insurance score** and the home owner insurance score.

Neither the auto insurance score nor the **home insurance score** require that a person own a car or own a home. These are simply calculated scores based on the information that is included in a person's credit report. Consumers may or may not be able to obtain their insurance scores, depending on which company designed them.

Establishing Credit

If a person has no credit, the easiest way to establish credit is with a secured credit card, a co-signer, a single purpose card (e.g. gas card), or an automobile loan with a substantial down payment.[10] A secured credit card requires the consumer to place a security deposit with the issuer. The issuer then provides a credit card usually with a dollar limit equal to the security deposit. These cards are available to many of those who have little or no credit.

When first establishing credit, the borrower (debtor) should clearly understand the terms of any loan or credit agreement. For example, the fee structure of a credit card. Understanding the agreement will help prevent borrower mistakes that can be costly, such as not knowing about the annual fee, late fees, penalties, interest rates, rewards, and interest-free financing.

The best kind of credit card to initially establish credit is one that is simple to understand: no annual fee, no penalty interest, no international transactions fees, and waives the first late payment fee or no late fees. It is important to know the statement date, the minimum payment due, and the due date of the payment. It is advisable to set up electronic transfer payments from a bank account to be received by the creditor four to five days before the actual due date of the payment. By making the payment a few days early, a debtor is able to monitor the credit card balance online to make sure that the payment was received on time and posted by the credit card company. If a consumer is carrying credit card debt from month to month, it is considerably advantageous to make payments as soon as possible, well in advance of the due date. The reason for this timing is that most credit cards use the average daily balance method to calculate interest charges, which effectively takes advantage of the fact that most consumers wait until the end of the month to pay.

Another way to establish credit is to buy a car using a car loan. Most people do not know that the credit score used to determine a car loan is called the FICO auto industry option score (auto credit score). This score is different from the auto insurance score and from the regular FICO score. The **auto credit score** is usually calculated by FICO for use by auto lenders to determine loan qualifications, down payments, and interest-rates. About 90 percent of auto lenders base their lending decisions on auto credit scores. The auto credit score is calculated principally on previous auto loan history. Many auto lenders are willing to make auto loans even to those with less desirable auto credit scores. The reason for this is that persons who borrow money on automobiles generally make their payments. Even those with other credit problems tend to make their auto loan payments in order to keep their automobiles. Automobile dealers regularly install GPS systems in cars sold to those with marginal credit. The borrower approves such installation in the financing agreement. The GPS is used to locate the car for purposes of repossession in the event of missed or late payments.

> ### ☑ *Quick Quiz 10.2*
>
> 1. Payment history is the most heavily weighted variable in a FICO score.
>   a. True
>   b. False
> 2. Opening new lines of credit in a short period of time can have a negative impact on a credit score.
>   a. True
>   b. False
> 3. Credit from a mix of lenders is considered superior to a single source of credit (e.g., credit card) for credit score purposes.
>   a. True
>   b. False
>
> True, True, True.

10. In *Fundamentals of Financial Planning*, good debt versus bad debt is discussed. Automobile loans that extend beyond three to five years and/or have a high rate of interest are generally considered bad debt. Remember that automobiles are depreciating assets and borrowing money for a depreciating asset is not the best use of credit.

It is generally easier to obtain an auto loan than any other type of loan, and is a great way to begin to build good credit. Once an automobile loan has been made, it is a good idea to pay the loan automatically from a bank on a recurring basis to assure that all payments are made on time.

FICO Score 9 allows rental payments to be added to the credit report and treats medical collections more favorably (they have a less negative impact on the score) than other types of debt. Reporting housing rental payments is sometimes a good idea for those with no credit histories (a "thin" credit file) or insufficient data to have credit scores. Often adding rental history payments to an otherwise incomplete credit report can make the report scoreable. While those with mortgage payments are regularly reported to credit agencies, those who rent have not been reported. All of the major reporting agencies now include rental payments (if reported). However, consumers cannot directly report their own rental payments. The property manager or landlord can report the rental history directly to reporting agency or the lesser (tenant) can sign up with a third-party rent reporter (for example, Rent Reporters).

Exhibit 10.17 | Credit Card Statement

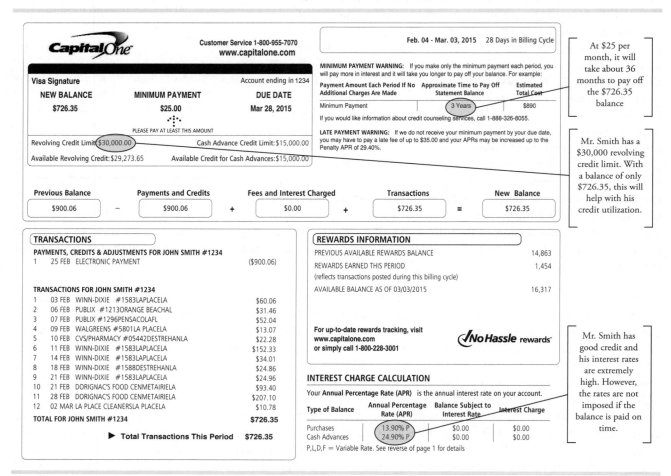

What is a Good Credit Score

A good credit score is one that permits the borrower to get the very best terms, such as down payment, term of loan, any points, and interest rate for the credit or loan desired.[11] The best score will vary with the type of debt and the lending environment. However, auto loans and credit cards generally require lower minimum FICO scores than mortgages. FICO public relations personnel suggest that a score of 760 will provide for the best credit rates and terms. For a mortgage, a score of around 700 is needed for conventional loans, and 620 for FHA loans. An automobile loan will require a lower score.

Even a good credit score may not be approved for credit by a particular lender. Often, a lender will use income, employment, and other criteria in addition to the credit score for purposes of credit approval. The lender obtains such information not from the credit score or credit report but rather from the credit application filled out by the potential borrower.

Exhibit 10.18 | Managing the Basics of Credit

Suggestion	Factor
Keep credit balances low but not $0*	Credit utilization
Do not close accounts	Credit history
Pay accounts on time	Payment history
Only apply for credit as needed	Hard inquiries
Have a mix of credit (cards, installments, mortgages)	Credit mix
Get free credit reports annually	Monitor

* This statement does not mean maintain balances on credit cards. Having a balance as of the end of the payment cycle is counted toward utilization. It simply means that having zero debt (that is, not using the credit line at all) does not help a person's credit score, which is an indication of how well the person handles debt.

A wise user of credit, in addition to the suggestions above, will establish and frequently monitor all transactions on ATMs, debit cards, credit cards, bank accounts, and mortgages. It is always a good idea to obtain and read credit reports and obtain credit scores prior to seeking additional credit. Everyone is entitled to receive a free credit report from annualcreditreport.com. In addition, there are other providers of free credit reports.

Consumer credit scores are usually updated monthly. However, in cases of frequent creditor reporting, a credit score could be updated almost daily. Some credit agencies will provide a "rescore" for a fee. The usual turnaround time for a rescore is three days.

11. In mortgage loans, a point is equal to one percent of the loan amount and is paid up-front as prepaid interest to reduce the interest rate of the loan.

Avoid Damaging a Credit Score

Once credit is established, it is important to avoid activities that are perceived as negative by the credit reporting agencies. Below are a few examples of activities that are perceived negatively by credit reporting agencies.

Even if paid off every month, accumulating large credit card balances and thus increasing credit utilization can have a negative effect on credit scores. Credit utilization of less than one percent is negative and credit utilization in excess of 30 percent is negative. The best percentage for credit utilization is between one percent and 30 percent utilization. For example, if the total credit available is $10,000 on all cards then utilization per month should not exceed a total of $3,000.

Closing and opening several credit card accounts at once will have a negative impact on credit scores even if the closed accounts have zero balances. This is because closing accounts changes credit utilization percentages and may affect credit history.

Example 10.2

Rose has the following credit card accounts on her credit report:

Account	Age of Account	Credit Limit	Balance
Credit Card A	10 years	$10,000	$0
Credit Card B	5 years	$5,000	$2,000
Credit Card C	3 years	$4,000	$1,000
Credit Card D	2 years	$3,000	$500
		$22,000 Total Available	$3,500 Outstanding

The average age of Rose's accounts is five years and her utilization is $3,500/$22,000 = 15.91%.*

Rose has not used Credit Card A for several years, so she decided to cancel it. On a recent shopping trip, Rose opened two new store card accounts to take advantage of special promotions. Her credit card accounts now appear as follows:

Account	Age of Account	Credit Limit	Balance
Credit Card B	5 years	$5,000	$2,000
Credit Card C	3 years	$4,000	$1,000
Credit Card D	2 years	$3,000	$500
Credit Card E	0 years	$750	$350
Credit Card F	0 years	$1,000	$525
		$13,750 Total Available	$4,375 Outstanding

The average age of Rose's accounts is reduced to 2 years and her utilization is $4,375/ $13,750 = 31.82% (above the recommended maximum of 30%). Both of these changes will negatively impact her credit score.**

Had Rose not canceled Credit Card A, her credit card accounts would be reported as:

Account	Age of Account	Credit Limit	Balance
Credit Card A	10 years	$10,000	$0
Credit Card B	5 years	$5,000	$2,000
Credit Card C	3 years	$4,000	$1,000
Credit Card D	2 years	$3,000	$500
Credit Card E	0 years	$750	$350
Credit Card F	0 years	$1,000	$525
		$23,750 Total Available	$4,375 Outstanding

The average age of Rose's accounts would be reduced to 3.33 years and her utilization would be $4,375/$23,750 = 18.42% (well below the recommended maximum of 30%).

*Average age of accounts is calculated based on the number of months on all accounts from open date to present. It was calculated in the example using years for simplicity of illustration.

**Some of the various credit scoring methods do include closed accounts in the calculation of average age of credit for a period of time. In this example, the closed account was not included.

Hard credit inquiries remain on the credit report for 24 months and negatively affect the calculation of the credit score for approximately 12 months. Soft credit inquiries do not negatively affect credit scores.

Other Users of Credit Information
This chapter has described and illustrated the impact in terms of the cost of maintaining a low credit score. However, there are other users of credit information that make decisions based on a consumer's credit scores. Potential employers, life insurance providers, potential landlords, and cell phone companies are examples of other users of credit information.

Employers routinely check the credit of applicants who are seeking employment with their organization. Those employers in the financial services industry, such as banks, brokerage houses, and insurance companies, are in the business of helping customers with their financial situation. They cannot afford to employ someone who is not responsible with money. Accounting and money management positions also require employees who are financially responsible. Certainly, credit is not the only criteria in these employment decisions. However, it is a fact today that many jobs require the candidate to permit the employer to review their credit history.

Life insurance providers check credit as part of the process of evaluating the risk of an applicant for life insurance. Life insurance companies want to verify that the applicant can afford the amount of life insurance they are requesting. A lower credit score may or may not impact life insurance premiums.

Landlords often check the credit history of those renting or leasing an apartment or condominium. Landlords want tenants who do not create problems and who pay their rent on time, every month. An applicant with a history of credit problems may be required to pay a higher security deposit than an applicant who has better credit.

Cell phone carriers routinely check credit history for those applying for cellular phone service. This credit history may impact the type of plan a person is eligible for and whether or not a security deposit may be required.

Many people do not realize how important their credit history is in many facets of daily life. Like a person's reputation, credit is hard to build and easy to damage.

DEBIT, CREDIT, AND CHARGE CARDS

Debit Cards vs. Credit Cards

Debit cards and credit cards each have individual benefits and risks. Debit cards are linked directly to a consumer's bank account. Charges are debited from the bank account very rapidly. Many people think that the funds are immediately debited from an account when using a debit card. In actuality, a transaction may clear within 24 hours, but it could take as long as 72 hours or longer. Regardless of the exact time, debit card transactions result in funds being taken from a person's account significantly faster than the required payment for a credit card. Credit cards allow consumers to borrow money from the card issuer, which is essentially a line of credit or loan from the card issuer.

Exhibit 10.19 | Comparison of Debit and Credit Cards

	Credit Card	Debit Card
Usage	A line of credit loan	A direct deduction from a bank account
Connected to an account	No	Yes, directly linked to a consumer's bank account
Receive monthly bills	Yes	No
Statements available	Yes	Yes
Credit score required	Yes	No
Spending limit	Card limit	Account limit
Interest	Yes. Generally on any late and/or outstanding balances and usually very high	No
Security	Poor	PIN increases security
Fraud	Relatively low since consumers are generally not held liable for fraudulent activities. Credit card charges are relatively easy to contest. The liability is limited to $50 for fraudulent purchases.	Potentially very high. If someone steals a debit card the money is removed directly from the consumer's bank account. The liability limit depends on timeliness of reporting.
Other fees	Late payment	Overdraft fees
Credit reporting	Usually monthly to each of three reporting agencies	No reporting

Card skimmers (magnetic strip type readers) are probably the greatest risk to debit and credit cards. Criminals can easily install card skimmers at stores such as gas stations. Restaurants can also be a source of trouble for both credit and debit cards as unscrupulous waiters may bring hand-held card skimmers to work and swipe a patron's card information.

It is always a wise idea to use credit cards rather than debit cards for significant purchases because of the leverage that the customer has with the credit card provider. In addition, credit cards have warranties that go beyond the manufacturer warranties. This feature is one of the benefits of credit cards. Credit cards also have better limited liability exposure ($50) than debit cards. For online purchases it is always a better idea to use credit cards than debit cards. The fraud protection of credit cards is better than that of debit cards, and hackers cannot overdraft a bank account using a credit card.

Under the Fair Credit Billing Act (FCBA), the maximum liability for unauthorized use of a credit card is $50. However, individuals are not responsible for charges that arise from a stolen credit card number. Unfortunately, worldwide credit card fraud is nearing $30 billion, according to The Nilson Report.[12]

The Electronic Fund Transfer Act (EFTA) provides limitation for losses due to unauthorized transactions for ATM cards and debit cards. However, liability is dependent upon how quickly the fraudulent activity is reported.

If a consumer reports an ATM or debit card missing to the institution that issued the card before someone uses the card without permission, the consumer is not responsible for any unauthorized withdrawals. However, if unauthorized use occurs before it is reported, the amount the consumer can be responsible for depends on how quickly the loss is reported to the card issuer.

- Consumers who report losses within two business days after they realize their card is missing will not be responsible for more than $50 of unauthorized use.
- Losses reported within 60 days after a statement is mailed to a consumer could result in responsibility of $500 due to an unauthorized transfer.
- Unlimited loss may result if an unauthorized use of a card is not reported within 60 days after the card issuer mails a statement.

12. Issue 1164 / November 2019

Exhibit 10.20 | Liability Limits for Lost or Stolen Credit and Debit Cards

Situation	Time-Frame for Reporting	Liability Limit
Lost or stolen credit card	• Card company notified before unauthorized charges are made	$0
	• Card company notified after unauthorized charges made, within 60 days after the creditor transmitted the first statement that reflects the unauthorized charges	$50
Credit card not lost, but account number stolen	• Card company notified within 60 days after the creditor transmitted the first statement that reflects the unauthorized charges	$0
Lost or stolen ATM or debit card	• Bank notified before unauthorized charges made	$0
	• Bank notified within 2 business days of learning of the loss or theft	$50
	• Bank notified more than 2 business days after learning of the loss or theft, but less than 60 calendar days after the statement is sent	$500
	• Bank notified more than 60 calendar days after the statement is sent	Unlimited*
ATM or debit card not lost, but account number stolen	• Bank notified within 60 days of statement being sent	$0

Some states cap liability to $50.

Credit card companies charge merchants for processing their customer transactions. When a customer uses a credit card to make a purchase, the credit card company pays the merchant, but charges the merchant a fee. These merchant fees generally range between two percent and five percent of the sales price. As a result, credit card companies offer consumers incentives to use their card over cards from other companies. These incentives often include airline miles, cash back bonuses, as well as other benefits. Consumers can take advantage of these benefits with cards that have a low annual fee or no annual fee.

The credit CARD Act, often referred to as the Credit Cardholders Bill of Rights, was signed into law in May of 2009. The law's two primary purposes are to improve fairness with credit card customers and improve transparency. The law does this by prohibiting certain practices that are unfair or abusive such as hiking up the rate on an existing balance or allowing a consumer to go over their credit limit and then imposing an over limit fee. The law also makes the rates and fees on credit cards more transparent so consumers can understand how much they are paying for their credit card and can better compare different cards. Finally, the CARD Act requires that any payment above the minimum required payment amount be applied first to the balance with the highest interest rate. For example, if the cardholder carries balances on purchases at 14 percent, cash advances at 24 percent, and a balance transfer offer at zero percent, any payment remitted in excess of the minimum payment must be applied toward the cash advance balance because it has the highest interest rate.

Charge Cards

Charge cards are different from credit cards because charge card issuers expect payment of the full balance within 30 days. Secondly, charge cards generally charge annual fees. The balance that may be accumulated is not generally limited like a traditional credit card as individual purchases are approved electronically as they are made. American Express is the most well-known charge card issuer at this time.[13] American Express also has credit cards in addition to charge cards. Charge cards are useful for business transactions, but credit cards can be used equally well and with no annual fee.

IDENTITY THEFT AND FRAUD

Identity theft is a crime where a thief steals personal information, such as full name or Social Security number, to commit fraud. The identity thief can use the information to fraudulently apply for credit, file taxes, or get medical services. These acts can damage credit status and cost time and money to restore a good name. A person may not know that they are the victim of identity theft until they experience a financial consequence, such as mystery bills, credit collections, or denied loans. These consequences result from actions that a thief has taken with the stolen identity.

Criminals have incurred credit card debt, depleted debit cards, obtained home loans, and have purchased weapons in victims' names. Identity theft is a big business, estimated to be $16.9 billion (2019), up from $14.7 billion (2018). Identity theft affected 5.1 percent of consumers in 2019.[14]

📝 *Key Concepts*

1. Understand the steps that should be taken by a victim of identity theft.

2. Identify the sources of identity theft.

3. Explain the acronym SCAM.

4. Differentiate an extended fraud alert from an account freeze.

Exhibit 10.21 | How Victims' Information is Misused (2019)*

Type of Identity Theft Fraud	Percent
Employment or Wage-Related Fraud	3.0
Tax Fraud	4.2
Credit Card Fraud - Existing Accounts	4.8
Credit Card Fraud - New Accounts	37.9
Other Identity Theft	0.8
Medical Services	4.3
Phone or Utilities Fraud	14.4
Bank Fraud**	9.7
Loan or Lease Fraud	19.1
Government Documents or Benefits Fraud	3.9

Percentages are based on the total number of identity theft complaints in the Federal Trade Commission's Consumer Sentinel Network (650,572 in 2019). Percentages total to more than 100 because some victims reported experiencing more than one type of identity theft.

*** Includes fraud involving checking, savings, and other deposit accounts and debit cards and electronic fund transfers.*

Source: https://www.ftc.gov/system/files/documents/reports/consumer-sentinel-network-data-book-2019/consumer_sentinel_network_data_book_2019.pdf

---

13. American Express does permit certain charges to be paid over time. These charges will incur interest until fully paid.
14. 2020 Identity Fraud Study by Javelin Strategy Research.

Example 10.3

On April 11, 2015, the U.S. Attorney for the Southern District of Florida announced the arrest of 42 defendants who used tens of thousands of stolen IDs to try to collect $22 million in tax refunds and other government benefits.

There are several common types of identity theft:

- **Child ID Theft:** Children's IDs are vulnerable because they may go undetected for many years. By the time they are adults, the damage has already been done to their identities.
- **Tax ID Theft:** A thief steals and uses a Social Security number to falsely file tax returns with the IRS or state government.
- **Medical ID Theft:** This form of ID theft happens when someone steals personal information, such as a Medicare ID or health insurance member number to get medical services or to issue fraudulent billing to a health insurance provider.
- **Senior ID Theft:** ID theft that targets seniors. Seniors are vulnerable to ID theft because they are in more frequent contact with medical professionals who get their medical insurance information, or caregivers and staff at long-term care facilities that have access to personal information or financial documents.
- **Social ID Theft:** A thief uses your name, photos, and other personal information to create a phony account on a social media platform.
- **New Account Takeover ID Theft:** A thief creates a new account under your name using personal information they received from stealing your data (directly or via a data breach).

Consumers who suspect that they have been a victim of identity theft should take action immediately. According to the Federal Trade Commission, identity theft made up 20 percent of consumer complaints, with nearly half involving credit card information. A person affected should contact the credit card issuer to report suspicious activity or a misplaced credit card. Early reporting improves the chances that fraudulent charges will be refunded. The person affected should contact the credit agencies and report the situation. Credit card information may be used to compromise other types of accounts. Therefore it is essential for consumers to closely monitor all credit and bank accounts.

When businesses ask for Social Security numbers, some consumers simply provide it to them. In fact, physician offices generally ask new patients to fill out many forms and a patient's Social Security number is almost always one of the requested items. The best advice is to leave it blank. They do not need it and patients should not give it to them. Another tactic is to ask why someone needs a person's Social Security number. Most of the time, they do not need it.

Many consumers click on random links in emails that ultimately lead to malware, which infects their computers and captures private information. To avoid identity theft consumers should check their credit and bank accounts for a few minutes each day to make sure that all the transactions and accounts are correct. Consumers should take the time to shred sensitive documents such as bills, tax returns, property tax notices, and insurance papers. It is imperative to ensure that all devices, including computers, tablets, and smart phones, are secure. Often times these devices store user names and passwords that allow thieves access to banking and financial accounts. Consumers must take the time to also guard sensitive data from those who would contact them through phone, text, social media, or email. Consumers simply have to jealously guard their privacy and be highly suspicious of any phone, text, social media, or email contact not initiated by the consumer or risk becoming the victim of identity theft.

Exhibit 10.22 | Steps to Protect Yourself from Identity Theft

1. Secure your Social Security number (SSN). Do not carry your Social Security card in your wallet or write your number on your checks. Only give out your SSN when absolutely necessary.

2. Do not respond to unsolicited requests for personal information (your name, birth date, Social Security number, or bank account number) by phone, mail, or online.

3. Contact the three credit reporting agencies to request a freeze of your credit reports (discussed later in this chapter).

4. Collect mail promptly. Place a hold on your mail when you are away from home for several days.

5. Pay attention to your billing cycles. If bills or financial statements are late, contact the sender.

6. Enable the security features on mobile devices, especially if you have contacts, banking websites and applications saved.

7. Update sharing and firewall settings when using a public wifi network. Consider using a virtual private network, which can give privacy of secured private network.

8. Review your credit card and bank account statements. Promptly compare receipts with account statements. Watch for unauthorized transactions.

9. Shred receipts, credit offers, account statements, and expired credit cards, to prevent "dumpster divers" from getting your personal information.

10. Store personal information in a safe place.

11. Install firewalls and virus-detection software on your home computer.

12. Create complex passwords that identity thieves cannot guess easily. Change your passwords if a company that you do business with has a breach of its databases.

13. Review your credit report at least once a year to be certain that it doesn't include accounts that you have not opened. You can order it for free from Annualcreditreport.com.

Exhibit 10.23 | Steps that Victims of Identity Theft Should Take

Steps That Victims of Identity Theft Should Take	
1.	File a report with law enforcement.
2.	File a complaint with the Federal Trade Commission at www.identitytheft.gov or the FTC Identity Theft Hotline at 1-877-438-4338 or TTY 1-866-653-4261.
3.	Place a 'fraud alert' on the all credit records by contacting one of the three major credit bureaus: • Equifax, www.Equifax.com, 1-800-525-6285 • Experian, www.Experian.com, 1-888-397-3742 • TransUnion, www.TransUnion.com, 1-800-680-7289
4.	Contact the victim's financial institutions and close any accounts opened without permission or that have been tampered with.
5.	Check the Social Security Administration earnings statement annually. Accounts can be accessed online at www.ssa.gov.

Consumers with compromised Social Security numbers and victims of tax-related identity theft should also complete IRS Form 14039, Identity Theft Affidavit, continue to pay their taxes and file their tax returns, even if they must do so by paper.

An often overlooked item in identity protection is the mailbox, which presents an opportunity for a thief to steal sensitive documents. A consumer should either secure the mailbox or alternatively set up a mailbox at the post office to receive mail. Consider what arrives in the mailbox: W-2 forms, 1099 forms, and other important documents such as Social Security information, earnings information, account information, banking, and insurance information.

Identity theft and identity fraud are federal crimes. Many people have reported that criminals have taken funds from credit cards, bank accounts, or other financial institutions. In the worst cases, these criminals have taken over entire identities, incurring large debts and committing crimes while using the victim's identity and name. The cost in many cases is not only the direct financial loss, but the cost of restoring the victim's reputation.

Sources of Identity Theft

The identity theft assistance center (ITAC) reports that 72 percent of victims do not know the source of the crime.

Exhibit 10.24 | Sources Reported by Identity Theft Assistance Center (ITAC)

Sources of Fraud or Identity Theft	
Knew source	28.0%
Computer-related identity crime	21.6%
Lost/stolen wallet, purse, checkbook, credit/debit card	15.1%
Corrupt business or employees	11.6%
Breaches of computer data	4.7%
Total accounted for	91.0%
Other	9.0%
Grand Total	**100.0%**

Almost one in four consumers who received a data breach letter became a victim of identity fraud. Those with Social Security numbers compromised were five times more likely to become fraud victims than those whose Social Security numbers were not compromised.[15] Personal information lost in data breaches is frequently used to commit identity fraud.

In addition to online fraud or data breaches, 1.5 million consumers were victims of familiar fraud, which means the victim knew the criminal.[16]

---

15. 2013 Identity Fraud Report by Javelin Strategy Research.
16. 2013 Identity Fraud Report by Javelin Strategy Research.

Exhibit 10.25 | Number of Data Breaches and Records Exposed 2017 - 2018

Industry	2017		2018	
	Number of Breaches	Number of Records Exposed	Number of Breaches	Number of Records Exposed
Banking/Credit/Financial	134	3,230,308	135	1,709,013
Business	907	181,630,520	571	415,233,143
Education	128	1,418,455	76	1,408,670
Government / Military	79	6,030,619	99	18,236,710
Medical / Healthcare	384	5,302,846	363	9,927,798
Total	1,632	197,612,748	1,244	446,515,334

Source: https://www.idtheftcenter.org/2018-end-of-year-data-breach-report/

Ways Identity Theft or Fraud is Committed

Most people do not realize how easily criminals can obtain personal data. Direct stealing of information, shoulder surfing, dumpster diving, mailbox searching, discarded credit offers, SPAM, phone scams, and card readers are all ways that criminals can obtain personal information.

Shoulder surfing is essentially eavesdropping on those who punch in numbers or verbally give numbers over the phone. **Dumpster diving** is going through the trash while looking for identity information from canceled checks, bank statements, credit card statements, federal or state tax documents, discarded credit card offers, and phone numbers.

There are scams to get the consumer to voluntarily disclose personal information. As previously mentioned, criminals install electronic card readers in gas pumps and on other devices to record credit or debit card numbers. Employees in the food service industry may also use small hand-held card readers to record a person's credit card information. Sometimes the crime is as unsophisticated as the thief simply writing down credit card and other numbers.

More sophisticated methods include intercepting information between two parties, such when a victim performs a web search for a particular company and the link redirects them to a different site that mirrors that of the company entered in the search. When account login information or credit card information is entered, the criminal records the personal information and transactions as he or she relays them between the real site and the victim. Another popular method is through the installation of malware on electronic devices by sending an authentic-looking text or email message from a financial services firm or credit card company with whom the victim might have an account, stating that urgent attention is needed and to click the link to resolve the situation. Clicking the link allows the malware to be installed and the criminal to track keystrokes and gather personal and login information from the device.

More recently, a larger number of identify thefts are the result of a data breach. According to a 2017 FTC study, it took only nine minutes for criminals to begin using information obtained through a fake data breach, with attempts to use the fake consumer's credit card information to purchase everything from clothing to online dating memberships to pizza.[17]

17.https://www.consumer.ftc.gov/blog/2017/05/how-fast-will-identity-thieves-use-stolen-info

Exhibit 10.26 | Time it Takes for Criminals to Begin using Information from a Data Breach

Nine minutes after a data breach, criminals are able to use private information to (illegally) purchase goods and services.

Signs of Identity Theft

There are telltale signs of identity theft. The graphic below identifies some of the more frequent signs of identity theft.

Exhibit 10.27 Signs of Identity Theft

Unexplainable bank withdrawals
Failure to receive bills or mail
Merchants refuse checks
Debt collectors call about unknown debt
Unknown accounts appear on credit reports
Receipt of unknown medical bills
IRS notices of multiple tax returns or unknown income reported
Notice of data breach from business with which there is a legitimate account

Avoid Becoming a Victim of Identity Theft

SCAM is an acronym from the Justice Department to help avoid identity theft. The S is for stingy about giving out any personal information unless the person or institution is known, identified, and trusted. S could also be for skeptical. Be skeptical of any and all inquiries. Hold mail when traveling. C is for check financial information, such as accounts, balances, and transactions, regularly. Pay particular attention to what should be there and what should not be there, such as addresses, number of accounts, recent transactions, etc. A is for ask for credit reports and review them carefully. M is for maintain careful records. Keep records for at least one year and documents, such as tax returns, for at least three years.

SCAM	
S	Be Stingy and skeptical about giving out personal data and information.
C	Check financial information often (alerts, accounts, etc.).
A	Ask for credit reports and review them regularly.
M	Maintain careful records.

CASE STUDY 10.1

Former Bank Employee and Co-Defendant Sentenced in Identity Theft Tax Fraud Scheme

On Sept. 11, 2014, in Miami, Florida, Tenisha Nkesha Francis, of Lake Worth, was sentenced to 42 months in prison, three years of supervised release and ordered to pay $117,002 in restitution. Ryan Michael Francis, of Riviera Beach, was sentenced to 57 months in prison, three years of supervised release and ordered to pay $202,720 in restitution. The defendants each previously pled guilty to one count of aggravated identity theft and one count of theft of government funds. According to court documents, Tenisha Francis worked as a Financial Services Representative at a bank. Tenisha Francis opened seven fraudulent accounts at the bank with stolen identification information obtained from co-defendant Ryan Francis. She was paid between $200 and $500 to open each fraudulent account. After opening the accounts, Tenisha Francis performed maintenance on these accounts and changed certain identifiers associated with the accounts, such as customers' dates of birth, addresses and telephone numbers. Stolen U.S. Treasury checks were deposited into the accounts, and funds were withdrawn via check card purchases, ATM withdrawals and checks payable to third parties including Ryan Francis, his wife, Vanessa Brown, and Ryan Francis' company, J.A. Kingz Automotive, LLC.

New types of scams and frauds arise on a frequent basis, especially during times when consumers may be under distress, such as when charities appear in the aftermath of natural disasters. The 2020 Coronavirus epidemic is no exception to the rule. Shortly after the U.S. government announced that Americans would receive stimulus checks as a result of the pandemic, fraudsters began initiatives to take advantage of the situation through scams such as making phone calls posing as IRS agents or other government representatives asking for personal information allegedly needed to ensure the stimulus check would be received. From January 1, 2020 to April 15, 2020 the FTC (Federal Trade Commission) received 18,235 Coronavirus-related claims, with fraud losses of $13.44 million. It is always wise for consumers to remain diligently aware of the newest scams and methods used to gain access to personal information. The FTC Recent Scam Alerts website includes scams involving everything from mortgages to funerals.

Sources of Information Regarding Recent Scams and Frauds
http://www.usa.gov/scams-and-frauds
https://www.consumer.ftc.gov/scam-alerts
http://www.consumerfraudreporting.org/

CASE STUDY 10.2

Return Preparer Sentenced for Tax Fraud and Identity Theft Schemes

On Sept. 12, 2014, in Miami, Florida, Stevens Nore, of Port Saint Lucie, was sentenced to 84 months in prison, three years of supervised release and ordered to pay $2,761,397 in restitution. Nore was previously convicted by a jury of 30 counts, including 21 counts of preparing false tax returns, four counts of filing false individual tax returns, three counts of theft of public money, and two counts of aggravated identity theft. According to court records, from June 11, 2009 through April 2012, Nore owned and operated Fraternity Tax and Services, a tax return preparation business. Nore prepared and submitted Individual Tax Returns (Forms 1040), with accompanying schedules, to the IRS on behalf of taxpayers claiming false deductions and credits for tax years 2009 to 2011. Nore also filed false personal tax returns for 2010 through 2013 by falsely stating the amount of gross receipts and sales on Schedule C forms. Nore stole three tax refunds totaling $26,349 to which he was not entitled, and used the identity of two individuals without their permission.

What to do if You are a Victim of Identity Theft

Victims of identity theft should immediately attempt to minimize the damage by taking actions such as notifying agencies:

- Contact Federal Trade Commissions (FTC) online, by mail, or by phone.
- Contact any other relevant federal agency such as Post Office Inspection Service, Social Security Administration, or Internal Revenue Service.
- Call the fraud units of each of the principal credit reporting agencies and place a fraud alert.
- Contact all creditors and financial institutions.
- Contact police to file a report.

Placing a fraud alert with the credit reporting agencies stays on the credit report for 90 days but can be renewed. A fraud alert provides the victim with a right to one free copy of each credit report. The victim should then order all credit reports, review them carefully, and then monitor progress.

The next step for a victim is to consider placing an extended fraud alert or a credit freeze on the credit file. Such an alert requires that potential creditors verify the identity of the person seeking credit. A freeze stops all access to the credit report. A fraud alert is free and is a federal right. A freeze is dependent on state law and may or may not be free. An extended fraud alert entitles the person to two free credit reports from each credit reporting agency within 12 months. The extended fraud alert lasts for seven years.

Following a credit freeze, the victim will have to request it to be lifted to allow a creditor or potential creditor to review the file. The request can be specific to the creditor, or it can be lifted temporarily or permanently for all inquiries.

Once credit reports have been obtained and examined, the victim of identity theft should dispute the errors on the report resulting from the thief with the credit bureaus and the specific creditor involved.

The victim should request that the credit reporting agencies block the disputed information from appearing on his or her credit report.

Radio Frequency Identification Cards (RFID)

There are many **radio frequency identification (RFID) cards** in use today including passports, debit, and credit cards. These cards can be identified by looking for the symbol with four curved lines (waves) or by inquiring of the card service representative. The RFID debit and credit cards permit payment by tapping the card or waving the card near a payment terminal. These cards are susceptible to theft by scanning equipment and thus need protection. These cards may be protected by using an RFID protected wallet or purse. Aluminum foil has been touted as providing protection for RFID cards. However, there is much dispute about aluminum foil's efficacy.

Chip and Pin Technology (EMV)

Magnetic stripe credit cards were used for years in the United States. However, these magnetic stripes presented a serious security flaw. This flaw is the same flaw that was exploited at Target and Neiman Marcus in 2014 to steal millions of credit card numbers. Due to the massive security breaches, credit card companies have moved to a new security technology known as EMV smart card payment system, often referred to as **Chip and Pin.**[18]

Quick Quiz 10.4

1. Victims of identify theft should act immediately to protect themselves.
   a. True
   b. False

2. When a doctor or another "official" asks for your Social Security number, you should generally give it to them.
   a. True
   b. False

3. The Justice Department's acronym, SCAM stands for Sensitive, Careful, Alert, Monitor.
   a. True
   b. False

True, False, False.

This technology, which was created in the mid-1980s, inserts an embedded computer chip in the card, creates a unique number for each transaction, and requires a pin to approve any charge. The microchip in the credit card is referred to as an EMV smart chip. The C and P card is more expensive but far superior to the stripe and sign card. It is used in most of the world outside of the United States. U.S. banks had previously resisted this technology because of its costs, but it has been adopted in the United States to reduce fraud

Digital Wallets

The latest development in the evolution of payment methods are digital wallets, such as Apple Pay. A digital wallet allows the user to make payments in person, via phone apps, or on the web without the need for a physical credit card by storing the card information, using encrypted software, in an app on the user's phone. The device is then tapped or waved in front of an NFC (near-field-communication) enabled payment device which uses tokenization to hide the credit card information in a randomly generated numeric code know as a token (similar to the technology used by an EMV smart chip card). Digital wallets can provide additional security by requiring a biometric login, but digital wallets, like credit cards, are not entirely foolproof against fraud.

18. EMV stands for Europay, MasterCard, and Visa. Chip and PIN is actually a brand name for the EMV smart card payment system.

CASE STUDY 10.3

Former New York City Police Department Officer Sentenced in Manhattan Federal Court to 28 Months in Prison for Fraud and Identity Theft (source: FBI)

JOHN L. MONTANEZ, a former police officer with the New York City Police Department ("NYPD"), was sentenced February 18, 2015 in Manhattan federal court to 28 months in prison for credit card fraud and identity theft. The sentence was imposed by U.S. District Judge Katherine Polk Failla.

Law enforcement executed a search of his apartment and of his locker at his precinct. The search of the apartment yielded, among other things, identification documents in other names and a device allowing for the swiping of a credit/debit card. The search of the locker yielded 16 identification documents in other names, including driver's licenses, benefits cards, and Social Security cards. The identification documents obtained from the search of the locker appeared to come from arrests that MONTANEZ affected or participated in throughout the course of his career as a police officer.

CASE STUDY 10.4

Maryland Man Sentenced to Prison for Scheme that Used Stolen Identifying Information to Fraudulently Seek More Than $20 Million in Tax Refunds

According to the U.S. Justice Department, Kevin Brown, from Maryland, was sentenced December 20, 2016 to 135 months in prison on federal charges stemming from his role as a key organizer and leader of an identity theft and tax fraud scheme involving the filing of fraudulent returns falsely seeking more than $20 million in refunds.

"Kevin Brown led a sprawling identity theft scheme that cost the government millions in fraudulently claimed income tax refunds, and caused substantial harm to those whose identities were stolen," said Principal Deputy Assistant Attorney General Ciraolo. "Today's significant prison sentence punishes Brown for his conduct and serves as a clear warning to those engaged in or considering similar conduct that the government will prosecute these crimes and will seek incarceration and restitution."

"Although Kevin Brown owned a neighborhood barbershop, he was making most of his money through illegal means, as a key organizer and leader of a massive tax fraud scheme," said U.S. Attorney Phillips. "He and his many co-conspirators falsified tax returns in the names of some of the most vulnerable members of our society, including individuals who were elderly, infirm, disabled, incarcerated, and deceased, and then pocketed millions of dollars in tax refunds at a cost to hard-working taxpaying citizens. Thanks to a concerted effort by law enforcement, this defendant and the others in the scheme will be held accountable with prison terms and orders for restitution."...

CASE STUDY 10.4 CONTINUED

According to the government's evidence, Brown, formerly of Capitol Heights, Maryland, and others participated in a massive and sophisticated stolen identity refund fraud scheme that involved an extensive network of more than 130 people, many of whom were receiving public assistance. Brown and his co-conspirators fraudulently claimed refunds for tax years 2005 through 2012, often in the names of people whose identities had been stolen, including the elderly, people in assisted living facilities, drug addicts and incarcerated prisoners. Returns were also filed in the names of, and refunds were issued to, willing participants in the scheme. The returns filed listed more than 400 "taxpayer" addresses located in the District of Columbia, Maryland and Virginia.

The participants played various roles in the scheme: stealing identifying information; allowing their personal identifying information to be used; creating and mailing fraudulent federal tax returns; allowing their addresses to be used for receipt of the refund checks; cashing the refund checks; providing bank accounts into which the refund checks were deposited; and forging endorsements of identity theft victims on the refund checks. The false returns typically reported inflated or fictitious income from a sole proprietorship and claimed phony dependents to generate an Earned Income Tax Credit, a refundable federal income tax credit for working families with low to moderate incomes.

KEY TERMS

Auto Credit Score - Score calculated principally based on previous auto loan history.

Auto Insurance Score - Using data from the TransUnion credit report, it helps auto insurance companies to assess the risk of insuring a consumer by measuring the probability that an auto insurance claim might be filed.

Chip and Pin (EMV Technology) - An embedded computer chip in the card (card is more expensive), creates a unique number for each transaction and requires a pin to approve any charge.

Consumer Lending - Credit cards, home equity loans, home equity lines of credit, auto loans, other recreational vehicle loans, and appliance loans.

Credit Agencies - Companies that compile and maintain credit information from credit card companies, banks, mortgage companies, and other creditors for the purpose of creating personal in-depth credit reports on individuals. The major credit reporting agencies are Experian, Equifax, and TransUnion.

Credit Score - A number that summarizes a person's credit risk based on an evaluation of his or her credit report at a particular point in time.

Digital Wallet - Allows the consumer to make payments in person, via phone apps, or on the web without the need for a physical credit card by storing the card information, using encrypted software, in an app on the user's phone.

Dumpster Diving - A means of identity theft, that involves going through someone's trash while looking for identity information from canceled checks, bank statements, credit card statements, federal or state tax documents, discarded credit card offers, and phone numbers.

FICO Score - A credit score developed by FICO (formerly know as Fair Isaac Corporation) that estimates the level of future credit risk for an individual. It is calculated using a formula that evaluates many types of information in the credit report at that credit reporting agency and ranges from 300 to 850.

Hard Inquiries - Inquiries made by creditors or potential creditors.

Home Insurance Score - Ranges from 150 to 850 and is once again calculated using the TransUnion credit report. It is primarily used by home insurance companies to assess the probability that a homeowner will file a homeowner's insurance claim.

Radio Frequency Identification (RFID) Cards - The wireless use of electromagnetic fields to transfer consumer information. This is being adopted by debit and credit card companies to deter identity theft.

SCAM - An acronym from the Justice Department to help avoid identity theft.

Secured Loans - Loans secured by collateral that may be repossessed if the loan is not repaid as agreed.

Shoulder Surfing - A means of identity theft by the eavesdropping on those who punch in numbers or verbally give numbers over the phone.

Soft Inquiries - Inquiries made by the consumer or by a prospective or current employer.

The Fair Credit Reporting Act of 1971 - Provides that U.S. citizens have free access to their credit reports and credit scores from each of the three national credit reporting agencies.

Unsecured Loans - Loans with no collateral and only backed by the borrower's promise to pay.

VantageScore 4.0 - Ranges from 300-850 and was developed by the three major credit bureau agencies.

DISCUSSION QUESTIONS

SOLUTIONS to the discussion questions can be found exclusively within the chapter. Once you have completed an initial reading of the chapter, go back and highlight the answers to these questions.

1. Why is a credit rating like a reputation?

2. What is the history of consumer lending?

3. What portion of GDP is consumer spending?

4. What are the three credit reporting agencies?

5. What information is included in a credit report?

6. What information is not included in a credit report?

7. Do credit reports ever contain errors?

8. What is a credit score, and why would a lender use a credit score?

9. What is a FICO score?

10. What is a VantageScore?

11. What is the difference between a FICO score and a VantageScore?

12. What impact does a low credit score have on a the terms of a borrower's loan?

13. It is said that "to destroy or seriously negatively impact a credit score only takes a few events but to positively impact a credit score takes a long time." Explain.

14. What are some of the easier ways to obtain initial credit for a person with little or no credit history?

15. Why is an automobile loan a relatively easy loan to obtain?

16. What is a good credit score?

17. Can a person with a good credit score be denied credit? Explain.

18. Explain the differences between credit, debit, and charge cards.

19. How widespread is identity theft and credit fraud?

20. What steps should consumers take if they are a victim of identity theft?

21. What are the sources of fraud or identity theft?

22. What are the signs of identity theft?

23. What is SCAM?

24. Explain the chip and pin credit card security available today.

MULTIPLE-CHOICE PROBLEMS

A sample of multiple choice problems is provided below. Additional multiple choice problems are available at money-education.com by accessing the Student Practice Portal.

1. Why are auto loans generally the easiest loans to get?
   a. Due to consumer protection.
   b. There is usually a down payment, and an auto loan is secured.
   c. An auto loan only requires a minimum credit score.
   d. Automobiles are easy to repossess due to GPS being placed in all cars with loans.

2. Which of the following likely has the highest credit score?
   a. Forrest has five credit cards, credit utilization of 40%, and a perfect payment history for five years.
   b. George has three credit cards, credit utilization of 29%, an installment loan, a mortgage, and a perfect payment history for three years.
   c. Connor has two credit cards totaling a $50,000 limit.
   d. Floyd has a 30-year mortgage in the 10th year with a perfect payment history and the mortgage is his only debt.

3. The two most well-known credit scores are?
   a. FICO and Auto.
   b. Auto and Vantage.
   c. Vantage and FICO.
   d. FICO and Rico.

4. Which of the following is the acronym recommended by the U.S. Justice Department to avoid identity theft?
   a. SCRAM.
   b. SNAG.
   c. SHAKE.
   d. SCAM.

5. Which of the following is incorrect about credit freezes and extended fraud alerts?
   a. A credit freeze stops all access to the credit report.
   b. An extended fraud alert allows the consumer two free credit reports within 12 months from each of the reporting agencies.
   c. The extended alert lasts 24 continuous months.
   d. Some states charge a fee for placing a credit freeze.

QUICK QUIZ EXPLANATIONS

Quick Quiz 10.1

1. False. It does not include information on a person's income. A credit report includes a consumer's debt and history of debt payments.
2. False. It does not include information regarding moving violations. A credit report includes a consumer's debt and history of debt payments.
3. True.
4. True.

Quick Quiz 10.2

1. True.
2. True.
3. True.

Quick Quiz 10.3

1. False. A secured credit card requires that funds are deposited before using the card. If a person puts up $500, then he can charge $500. Thus, the card requires 100%, not 50%.
2. True.
3. False. A consumer may be turned down for credit for other reasons than a credit score. Therefore, a good credit score does not assure credit approval.

Quick Quiz 10.4

1. True.
2. False. In most cases, people asking for your Social Security number do not need it and you should not give it to them.
3. False. SCAM stands for Stingy (regarding personal data), Check (financial information often), Ask (for credit reports often), Maintain (careful records).

**Additional multiple choice problems
are available at
money-education.com
by accessing the
Student Practice Portal.
Access requires registration of the title using
the unique code at the front of the book.**

11
SOCIAL SECURITY

LEARNING OBJECTIVES

1. Understand the history and purpose of the Social Security program and the conditions under which it was enacted.
2. Provide an overview of the Social Security system, including payroll taxes, benefits, and qualifications.
3. Explain how a client may qualify for Social Security benefits, given their payroll taxes and available benefits structure.*
4. Identify possible beneficiaries under the Social Security system and the types of benefits they may be entitled to receive.
5. Explain the computation of the Average Indexed Monthly Earnings (AIME) and the Primary Insurance Amount (PIA) and the impact on benefits relative to historical earnings.*
6. Explain disability benefits, survivor benefits, and maximum family benefits under the Social Security system.*
7. Advise clients in choosing the optimal date to begin receiving Social Security benefits, considering the impact of taxation, benefit reductions and credits, reductions under the earnings test, as well as life expectancy.
8. Understand proposed or possible changes to the Social Security system and the possible impact on retirement and other financial planning.
9. Describe the taxation of Social Security benefits.*
10. Explain the windfall elimination and government pension offset on retirement benefits.*
11. Provide an overview of the Medicare program, including the payroll taxes and eligibility structure.*
12. Identify the four Parts of Medicare coverage, the benefits provided by each, common out-of-pocket costs required for insured individuals, and alternative insurance options to cover the gaps associated with Medicare.*
13. Assist a client in selecting proper Medicare coverage and any supplemental coverage with careful attention to appropriate deadlines.*
14. Understand the enrollment requirements and timing deadlines for Medicare enrollment.

*CFP Board Resource Document - Student-Centered Learning Objectives based upon CFP Board Principal Topics.

Social Security and other forms of social insurance were born out of changes in economies and in families. For centuries, farming and agriculture provided families with the foundation of their economic security. Farms provided food, shelter, and resources for families to survive. As family members aged, they were cared for on the farms. However, as economies changed as part of the industrial revolution, more and more people became employees working for someone else. This demographic shift continued such that a higher percentage of people began moving from the farms to the cities. As a result, people were less capable of providing for their own welfare as they aged, especially in difficult economic times.

These demographic shifts and the Great Depression set the stage for the Social Security system, which was signed into law by Franklin D. Roosevelt on August 14, 1935. At the signing of the law, President Roosevelt made the following statement:

> "Today a hope of many years' standing is in large part fulfilled. The civilization of the past hundred years, with its startling industrial changes, has tended more and more to make life

insecure. Young people have come to wonder what would be their lot when they came to old age. The man with a job has wondered how long the job would last.

This Social Security measure gives at least some protection to thirty millions of our citizens who will reap direct benefits through unemployment compensation, through old-age pensions and through increased services for the protection of children and the prevention of ill health.

We can never insure one hundred percent of the population against one hundred percent of the hazards and vicissitudes of life, but we have tried to frame a law which will give some measure of protection to the average citizen and to his family against the loss of a job and against poverty-ridden old age."

Today, the Social Security system is significantly different than what it was envisioned more than 80 years ago in terms of the programs offered and the size of the program. The system provides tremendous benefits to millions of Americans, as indicated in **Exhibit 11.1 | Social Security Basic Facts**. However, the system also has significant fiscal problems that must be addressed and resolved if there is any chance that it continues for generations to come. Two of the primary issues with the program are the number of workers paying into the system relative to the number of retirees and other beneficiaries and the significant increase in the life expectancy of our current and future population.

Exhibit 11.1 | Social Security Basic Facts[1]

1.	In 2020, over 67 million Americans will receive approximately one trillion dollars ($1,000,000,000,000.00) in Social Security benefits.
2.	An estimated 173 million workers are covered under Social Security. • 50% of the workforce has no private pension coverage. • 36% of workers report that they and/or their spouse have no savings set aside specifically for retirement.
3.	Social Security is the major source of income for most of the elderly. • Nine out of ten individuals age 65 and older receive Social Security benefits. • Social Security benefits represent about 33% of the income of the elderly. • Among elderly Social Security beneficiaries, 48% of married couples and 69% of unmarried persons receive 50% or more of their income from Social Security. • Among elderly Social Security beneficiaries, 21% of married couples and about 44% of unmarried persons rely on Social Security for 90% or more of their income.
4.	In 1940, the life expectancy of a 65-year-old was almost 14 years; today it is just over 20 years.
5.	By 2035, there will be almost twice as many older Americans as today - from 49 million today to 79 million.
6.	There are currently 2.8 workers for each Social Security beneficiary. By 2035, there will be 2.2 workers for each beneficiary.

---

1. Social Security Basic Facts, March 2019.

KNOW THE NUMBERS (2020)

Social Security Wage Base	$137,700
Social Security Quarter of Coverage	$1,410
Social Security Bottom Bend Point	$960
Social Security Top Bend Point	$5,785
Social Security Maximum Monthly Benefit	$3,011
Social Security Medicare Part A Deductible Days 1-60	$1,408 per benefit period
Social Security Medicare Part A Deductible Days 61-90	$352 per day
Social Security Medicare Part A Deductible Days 91 and Over	$704 per day
Social Security Medicare Part B Deductible	$198
Social Security Skilled Nursing Care Deductible Days 21-100	$176.00 per day
Social Security Disability Monthly Earnings Limit	$1,260
Social Security Disability Monthly Earnings Limit if Blind	$2,110
Social Security Death Benefit	$255
Social Security Earnings Limitation (under full retirement age)	$18,240
Social Security Earnings Limitation (full retirement age)	$48,600

INTRODUCTION

Social Security benefits were never intended to provide total pre-retirement wage replacement upon retirement. Social Security was created to supplement a covered worker's pension, savings, investments, and other earnings from assets to make up an appropriate wage replacement ratio (e.g., 70 percent). Individuals who retire may need 70 to 80 percent of their pre-retirement income during their retirement to maintain their pre-retirement standard of living.

Low wage earners receive Social Security retirement benefits averaging 60 percent of pre-retirement income. Average wage earners receive an average of 42 percent of pre-retirement income from Social Security benefits, whereas high wage earners receive an average of 26 percent of pre-retirement income (see **Exhibit 11.2 | Social Security Benefits as a Percentage of Pre-Retirement Income**).

From a financial planning standpoint, it is important to understand Social Security law and the various benefits that are available from Social Security. This chapter provides an overview of the Social Security system and its benefits. The six major categories of benefits administered by the Social Security Administration are:

1. Retirement benefits
2. Disability benefits
3. Family benefits
4. Survivors' benefits
5. Medicare
6. Supplemental Security Income (SSI) benefits. SSI benefits are not funded by Social Security taxes but are funded by general funds from the Treasury.

The **retirement benefit** is the most well-known benefit from Social Security. Full retirement benefits are payable at "full retirement age" (reduced benefits are available as early as age 62) to anyone who has obtained a minimum amount (40 quarters) of Social Security credits. Based on the Social Security law in 1983, the age when full retirement benefits are paid began to rise from age 65 in the year 2000, and increases to age 67 by the year 2027. Workers who delay retirement beyond the full retirement age receive a special scheduled increase (**Exhibit 11.13 | Percentage Increases for Delayed Retirement**) in benefits for each delayed year extending until age 70.[2]

Exhibit 11.2 | Social Security Benefits as a Percentage of Pre-Retirement Income

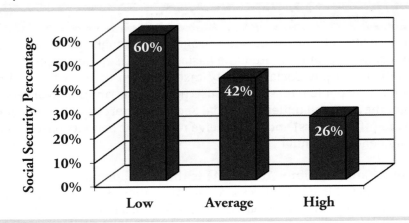

The **disability benefit** is payable at any age to workers who have sufficient credits under the Social Security system to qualify for disability benefits. Recipients must have a severe physical or mental impairment that is expected to prevent them from performing "substantial" work for at least a year or to result in their death. Monthly earnings of $1,260 for 2020 (if the individual is blind, then the amount is increased to $2,110 per month for 2020) or more is considered substantial. The disability insurance program has built-in incentives to smooth the transition back to the workforce including continuation of benefits and health care coverage.

⁝☰ *Key Concepts*

1. What are the six major categories of benefits administered by the Social Security Administration?

2. How are funds collected for Social Security?

The **family benefit** is provided to certain family members of workers eligible for retirement or disability benefits. Such family members include spouses age 62 or older, spouses under age 62 but caring for a child under age 16, unmarried children under 18, unmarried children under age 19 and full-time students, and unmarried children of any age who were disabled before age 22.

Survivors' benefits apply to certain members of the deceased worker's family if the worker earned sufficient Social Security credits. Family members entitled to survivors' benefits include those listed for family benefits and may also include the worker's dependent parents if the worker was their primary means of support. A special one-time payment of $255 may be made to the spouse or minor children upon the death of a Social Security covered worker.

---

2. The increases are not compounded, and there are no increases for delay beyond age 70.

Medicare provides hospital and medical insurance. Those who have attained age 65 or those who receive disability benefits for at least two years automatically qualify for Medicare. Others must file an application to become qualified.

Finally, **Supplemental Security Income (SSI)** (funded by general tax revenues and not by Social Security taxes) is another benefit that provides monthly payments to those disabled or at full retirement age who have a low income and few assets. Generally, those who receive SSI also qualify for **Medicaid**, food stamps, and other governmental assistance.

SOCIAL SECURITY TAXES AND CONTRIBUTIONS

Although the Social Security retirement benefits program is thought by many to be one of the most complicated and confusing programs created, the basic concept is quite simple. Employees, employers, and self-employed individuals pay Social Security taxes, known as FICA taxes, during their working years. These payments are pooled in special trust funds. Contributing workers become "covered" workers, meaning that they will fall under the Social Security umbrella of benefits after contributing for approximately 10 years (40 quarters) and will receive retirement benefits based on those contributions and the Social Security benefits formula.

The **Federal Insurance Contributions Act (FICA)** is the law allowing Social Security taxes, including Medicare taxes, to be deducted from paychecks. A portion of these FICA taxes pays part of the Medicare coverage. Both employers and employees pay the taxes for Social Security and Medicare. For the year 2020, an employer and employee each pay 6.2 percent of the employee's gross salary up to a limit of $137,700 for **OASDI (Old Age, Survivor, and Disability Insurance)**. The salary limit rises annually based on annual increases in average wages. Self-employed workers pay 12.4 percent (6.2 percent x 2) of their taxable income up to the same salary limit. The Medicare portion of the Social Security tax is 1.45 percent for both employers and employees and is 2.9 percent for self-employed workers with no limit on the amount of compensation taxed.

Example 11.1

If an employee earns a salary of $150,000 in 2020, the first $137,700 of the employee's salary will be subject to a tax of 7.65 (6.2 + 1.45) percent while the remaining $12,300 will be subject to a tax of only 1.45 percent. The employer pays the same amount as the employee.

	Taxable Amount	x	Tax Rate	Total Tax
Employee - Social Security	$137,700		6.20%	$8,537.40
Employee - Medicare	$150,000		1.45%	$2,175.00
Total Tax				$10,712.40

Additional Medicare Taxes Beginning in 2013

The Affordable Care Act created two additional Medicare taxes that impact wealthier taxpayers. The first is an additional Medicare tax of 0.9 percent on wages or self-employment income. The second is a 3.8 percent tax on certain amounts of net investment income.

The additional Medicare tax equal to 0.9 percent applies to wages or self-employment income that is above the following threshold amounts:

Married Filing Jointly	$250,000
Married Filing Separately	$125,000
Single	$200,000
Head of Household	$200,000

Only employees pay this Medicare tax. Employers do not pay this tax, but must withhold the tax from wages if the taxpayer has income in excess of $200,000.

Example 11.2

Carlos, a single filer, has $130,000 in wages and $145,000 in self-employment income. His wages are not in excess of the $200,000 threshold for single filers, so Carlos is not responsible for Additional Medicare Tax on these wages.

Before calculating the Additional Medicare Tax on self-employment income, the $200,000 threshold for single filers is reduced by his $130,000 in wages, resulting in a reduced self-employment income threshold of $70,000. Carlos is required to pay Additional Medicare Tax on $75,000 of self-employment income ($145,000 in self-employment income minus the reduced threshold of $70,000). Carlos has total earnings of $275,000, which is $75,000 over the $200,000 threshold.

Example 11.3

Dave and Dana are married and file jointly. Dave has $150,000 in wages and Dana has $175,000 in self-employment income. Dave's wages are not in excess of the $250,000 threshold for joint filers, so Dave and Dana are not responsible for Additional Medicare Tax on Dave's wages.

Before calculating the Additional Medicare Tax on Dana's self-employment income, the $250,000 threshold for joint filers is reduced by Dave's $150,000 in wages resulting in a reduced self-employment income threshold of $100,000. Dave and Dana are required to pay Additional Medicare Tax on $75,000 of self-employment income ($175,000 in self-employment income minus the reduced threshold of $100,000). Dave and Dana have total earnings of $325,000, which is $75,000 over the $250,000 threshold.

The 3.8 percent Medicare tax is imposed on the lesser of net investment income or modified AGI over the following threshold amounts:

Married Filing Jointly	$250,000
Married Filing Separately	$125,000
Single	$200,000
Head of Household	$200,000

Net investment income is a broadly defined term that includes gross income from interest, dividends, annuities, royalties, and rents other than such income derived from the ordinary course of a trade or business, **plus** other trade or business income, for which the entity is a passive activity (or if the entity is trading financial instruments or commodities), **plus** net gain attributable to the disposition of property other than property held in a trade or business. It should be noted that net investment income does not include any distribution from a 401(k), 403(b), 457(b) plan or an IRA or Roth IRA. However, such distributions may cause a taxpayer to exceed the threshold amounts.

Example 11.4

In 2020, Dan and Mary (MFJ) have $250,000 of dividend income. In this case, they are not subject to the 3.8% surtax.

Example 11.5

Same as **Example 11.4** but Dan and Mary convert a traditional IRA to a Roth IRA. The taxable amount of the conversion is $100,000. Thus, they will have AGI of $350,000, and $100,000 will hence be subject to the 3.8% surtax.

Example 11.6

Same as **Example 11.4** but Dan and Mary also take minimum distributions of $50,000. They will be subject to the 3.8% tax on $50,000, which is the lesser of Net Investment Income and the AGI above $250,000.

Exhibit 11.3 | 3.8% Medicare Tax

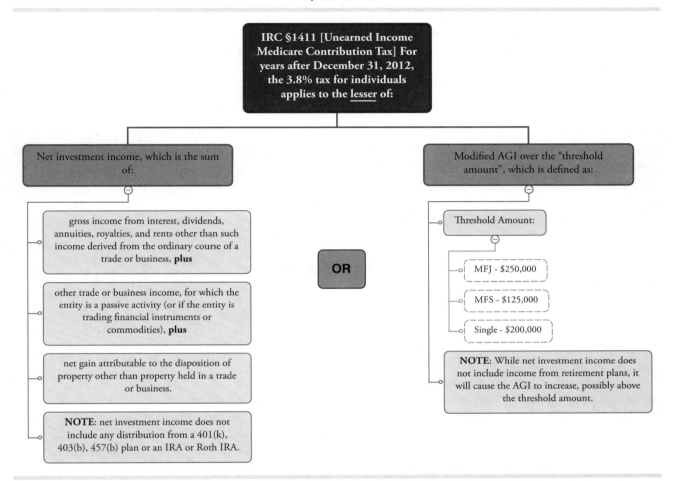

Example 11.7

In 2020, Steve and Ashley (MFJ) have $100,000 of dividend income and $100,000 of wages. In this case, they are not subject to the 3.8% surtax because they are not over the $250,000 limit.

Example 11.8

Same as **Example 11.7** but Steve and Ashley convert a traditional IRA to a Roth IRA. The taxable amount of the conversion is $100,000. Thus, they will have AGI of $300,000. The lesser of $50,000 (the AGI in excess of the $250,000 threshold) or $100,000 (the dividend income) will be subject to the 3.8% surtax.

Example 11.9

Jack and Jill (MFJ) each earn $250,000 and have interest income of $1,000. The $1,000 would be subject to the 3.8% tax. The answer would not change if they each made $125,000, $500,000, or $1 million. In each case, there would be $1,000 subject to the 3.8% tax.

Trust Funds

The United States Social Security system operates on a "pay-as-you-go" basis. Social Security taxes are collected and divided among several trust funds. The federal **Old Age and Survivors Insurance ("OASI") Trust Fund** pays retirement and survivors' benefits. The OASI Trust Fund receives 5.30 percent of the FICA tax. The federal **Disability Insurance ("DI") Trust Fund** pays benefits to workers with disabilities and their families. The DI Trust Fund receives 0.90 percent of the FICA tax. OASI and DI are the two trust funds used for payment of Social Security benefits (total 6.2 percent).

The two Medicare trust funds are the federal **Hospital Insurance ("HI") Trust Fund**, which pays for services covered under the hospital insurance provisions of Medicare (Part A), and the federal **Supplementary Medical Insurance ("SMI") Trust Fund**, which pays for services covered under the medical insurance provisions of Medicare, known as Part B and the prescription drug provisions known as Part D.[3] The SMI Trust Fund is partially funded by the general fund of the Treasury with the remaining funding coming from monthly premiums paid by the individuals enrolled in Part B.

Exhibit 11.4 | Sources Of Funding To Social Security Trust Funds

OASI Trust Fund	5.30 percent (limited to the maximum taxable earnings)
DI Trust Fund	0.90 percent (limited to the maximum taxable earnings)
HI Trust Fund	1.45 percent (all earnings are taxed) (In 1993, the Omnibus Budget Reconciliation Act of 1993 abolished the ceiling on taxable earnings for Medicare.)
SMI Trust Fund	-0- (no FICA taxes used; funded by general federal tax revenues and monthly premiums paid by enrollees)

---

3. Medicare Prescription Drug. Improvement and Modernization Act of 2003 (PL 108-173).

CASE STUDY 11.1

The case of ***Veterinary Surgical Consultants, P.C. v. C.I.R.***, involved an owner of an S corporation who attempted to avoid FICA and FUTA taxes by declaring his remuneration as a K-1 distribution of corporate net income and not W-2 wages.[1] Dr. Sadanaga performed substantial services for the S corporation, Veterinary Surgical Consultants, P.C. ("VSC"). Dr. Sadanaga worked approximately 33 hours per week for VSC. He was the only individual working for VSC. Tellingly, all of VSC's income was generated from the consulting and surgical services provided by Dr. Sadanaga. As officer and sole shareholder, Dr. Sadanaga declared all remuneration he received on a K-1 form, not on a W-2 form, thus avoiding FICA and FUTA taxes.

VSC claimed that the amounts paid to Dr. Sadanaga were distributions of its corporate net income, rather than wages, and that as an S corporation it passed its net income to Dr. Sadanaga as its sole shareholder. Not surprisingly, the Court disagreed with VSC, i.e., Dr. Sadanaga, and concluded that an S corporation cannot avoid federal FICA and FUTA employment taxes by characterizing compensation paid to its sole director and shareholder as distributions of the S corporation's net income rather than wages. The Court's analysis focused on whether payments represented remuneration for services rendered. To characterize the payments to Dr. Sadanaga as distributions of VSC's net income was "but a subterfuge for reality." The payments constituted remuneration for services performed by Dr. Sadanaga on behalf of VSC. Regardless of how an employer may choose to characterize payments made to its employees, the true analysis is whether the payments represent remuneration for services rendered.[2] Dr. Sadanaga's reporting of the distributions as nonpassive income from an S corporation had no bearing on the Federal employment tax treatment of those wages. He was VSC's sole source of income, thereby requiring treatment as an employee. In short, while an S corporation is permitted to pass through items of income in calculating its income tax liability, it may not pass through its tax liability for federal employment taxes.

1. *Veterinary Surgical Consultants, P.C. v. C.I.R.*, 117 T.C. No. 14, 117 T.C. 141, 2001 WL 1242120 (U.S.Tax Ct.), Tax Ct. Rep. (CCH) 54,527, Tax Ct. Rep. Dec. (RIA) 117.14 (U.S.Tax Ct. 2001).
2. See also *Spicer Accounting, Inc. v. United States,* 918 F.2d 90 (9th Cir. 1990); *Joseph Radtke, S.C. v. United States*, 895 F.2d 1196 (7th Cir. 1990).

SOCIAL SECURITY BENEFITS – ELIGIBILITY AND CALCULATIONS

Covered Workers and Insured Status

To qualify for retirement benefits, a worker must be "**fully insured,**" which means that a worker has earned a certain number of quarters (credits) of coverage under the Social Security system. Since 1978, quarters of coverage have been determined based on annual earnings. In other words, earning a designated amount of money, regardless of when it was earned during the year, will credit the worker with a quarter of coverage for that year. In 2020, the designated amount for a quarter of coverage is $1,410. Thus, workers who earn at least $5,640 are credited with four quarters of coverage for 2020. No worker may earn more than four quarters in one year, regardless of earnings. The following is a list of the designated amounts for a quarter of coverage dating back to 1989:

⠿ *Key Concepts*

1. Who are covered workers with regard to Social Security?

2. Who are beneficiaries of Social Security benefits?

Exhibit 11.5 | Designated Amounts for a Quarter of Social Security Coverage

Year	Amount Needed to Receive a Credit for One Quarter	Year	Amount Needed to Receive a Credit for One Quarter
1989	$500	2005	$920
1990	$520	2006	$970
1991	$540	2007	$1,000
1992	$570	2008	$1,050
1993	$590	2009	$1,090
1994	$620	2010	$1,120
1995	$630	2011	$1,120
1996	$640	2012	$1,130
1997	$670	2013	$1,160
1998	$700	2014	$1,200
1999	$740	2015	$1,220
2000	$780	2016	$1,260
2001	$830	2017	$1,300
2002	$870	2018	$1,320
2003	$890	2019	$1,360
2004	$900	2020	$1,410

For most persons, 40 quarters of coverage (10 years of work in employment covered by Social Security) or one quarter per year from age 21 to age 62 will fully insure a worker for life. Fully insured workers are entitled to the benefits under the Social Security system. Some benefits, like survivors' benefits, are available to "currently" (although not necessarily fully) insured individuals. **"Currently" insured workers** are those individuals who have at least six quarters of coverage out of the previous 13 quarters.

Example 11.10

In 2020, William earned $10,000 from employment subject to Social Security between January 1 and March 31. He was then unemployed for the remainder of the year. How many quarters of coverage did he earn for Social Security 2020?

For 2020, a worker receives one quarter credit for each $1,410 in annual earnings on which Social Security taxes are withheld up to a maximum of four quarters. It is irrelevant that William earned the $10,000 all in the first quarter. William has earned four quarters for the year.

Example 11.11

How is a worker's insured status determined under Social Security?

It is determined by the number of quarters of coverage received. To achieve currently insured status under Social Security, a worker must have at least six quarters of coverage out of 13 calendar quarters prior to retirement, disability, or death. Any worker with 40 covered quarters is fully insured.

Social Security Beneficiaries

Social Security benefits are paid upon retirement, disability, or death if the eligibility requirements are satisfied. The worker's spouse and children may also be eligible to receive benefits when the worker satisfies eligibility requirements. Generally, monthly Social Security benefits can be paid to:

- A disabled insured worker under age 65.
- A retired insured worker at age 62 or older.
- The spouse of a retired or disabled worker who:
  - is at least 62 years old, or
  - is caring for a child who is under age 16 or disabled.
- The divorced spouse of a retired or disabled worker entitled to benefits if the divorced spouse is age 62 or older and was married to the worker for at least 10 years.
- The divorced spouse of a fully insured worker who has not yet filed a claim for benefits if both are at least age 62, were married for at least 10 years, and have been finally divorced for at least two continuous years.
- The dependent, unmarried child of a retired or disabled worker or of a deceased insured worker if the child is:
  - under age 18;
  - under age 19 and a full-time elementary or secondary school student; or
  - age 18 or over but disabled (if the disability began before age 22).
- The surviving spouse (including a surviving divorced spouse) of a deceased insured worker if the widow(er) is age 60 or older.
- The disabled surviving spouse (including a surviving divorced spouse in some cases) of a deceased insured worker if the widow(er) is age 50 or older.
- The surviving spouse (including a surviving divorced spouse) of a deceased insured worker, regardless of age, if caring for an entitled child of the deceased who is either under age 16 or disabled before age 22.
- The dependent parents of a deceased insured worker at age 62 or older.

> ### ✎ *Quick Quiz 11.2*
>
> 1. "Fully insured" means that a worker has earned a certain number of quarters (generally 40) of coverage under the Social Security system.
>   a. True
>   b. False
>
> 2. Social Security benefits can be paid to the dependent parents of a deceased insured worker at age 62.
>   a. True
>   b. False
>
> True, True.

In addition to monthly survivors' benefits, a lump-sum death payment of $255 is payable upon the death of an insured worker. **Exhibit 11.6 | Summary of Social Security OASDI Benefits (As a Percentage of PIA)** provides a summary of those eligible for OASDI benefits and the percentages of the worker's primary insurance amount ("PIA") that each beneficiary will receive. The PIA is the retirement benefit that the worker would receive if the worker retires at full retirement age.

Example 11.12

Steve, age 38, has just died. He has been credited with the last 35 consecutive quarters of Social Security coverage since he left college. He did not work before leaving college. Which of the following persons are eligible to receive Social Security survivor benefits as a result of Steve's death?

1. Tim, Steve's 16-year-old son
2. Grace, Steve's 18-year-old daughter
3. Olivia, Steve's 38-year-old widow
4. Arline, Steve's 60-year-old dependent mother

Answer: Grace is too old; Olivia does not have a child under 16 and she is too young; and Arline is not eligible because she is too young. Thus, only Tim is eligible.

Example 11.13

Under Social Security (OASDI), what benefits are available to the survivors of a deceased but only currently insured worker?

A $255 lump-sum death benefit, which is generally payable to the insured's spouse, and 75 percent of the worker's PIA is available to a child under 18 or to a surviving spouse with a dependent child under the age of 16.

Exhibit 11.6 | Summary of Social Security OASDI Benefits (As a Percentage of PIA)

	Assuming Full Retirement Age of the Worker			
	Retirement	Survivorship		Disability
	Fully Insured[2]	Fully Insured[2]	Currently Insured[3]	Disability Insured[4]
Participant	100%	Deceased	Deceased	100%
Child Under 18[6]	50%	75%	75%	50%
Spouse with child under 16[7]	50%	75%	75%	50%
Spouse - Full Age Retirement[1]	50%	100%	0%	50%
Spouse - Age 62[1, 8]	32.5% to 35%	80% to 81%[9]	0%	32.5% to 35%
Spouse - Age 60[1]	N/A	71.5%	0%	N/A
Dependent Parent (age 62)	0%	75/82.5%[5]	0%	0%

1. Includes divorced spouse if married at least 10 years (unless they have remarried). Survivorship benefits are also available to divorced spouse if remarried after age 60.
2. Fully insured is 40 quarters of coverage or one quarter for each year after age 21 but before age 62 (with at least six quarters of coverage).*
3. Currently insured is at least six quarters of coverage in the last 13 quarters.
4. Disability insured is based on age as follows:
   - Before age 24 - Must have 6 quarters of coverage in the last 12 quarters.
   - Age 24 through 30 - Must be covered for half of the available quarters after age 21.
   - Age 31 or older - Must be fully insured and have 20 quarters of coverage in the last 40 quarters.
5. Parent benefit is 82.5 percent for one parent and 75 percent for each parent if two parents.
6. Child under age 19 and a full-time student or of any age and disabled before age 22 also qualifies.
7. Spouse with child disabled before age 22 also qualifies.
8. A spouse can choose to retire as early as age 62, but doing so may result in a benefit as little as 32.5 percent of the worker's primary insurance amount. A spousal benefit is reduced 25/36 of one percent for each month before normal retirement age, up to 36 months. If the number of months exceeds 36, then the benefit is further reduced 5/12 of one percent per month.
9. The reduction for a widow(er) is 28.5 percent at age 60. It is prorated for months between full retirement age and age 60.

Note: Notice that when the participant worker is alive (retirement and disability), beneficiaries who qualify for a benefit, qualify for 50% of PIA. When the participant dies, all qualified beneficiaries generally receive 75% of PIA with the exceptions being the spouse who replaces the participant at 100% (benefit reduced below PIA if deceased worker retired before FRA, and benefit above PIA due to delayed retirement credits (DRCs) if worker delayed retirement beyond FRA) and any qualified dependent parents. See note 5.

* 42 U.S.C. 414.

Social Security Retirement Benefits – A Closer Look

The most well known Social Security benefit is the Retirement Benefit. Until 2000, normal age retirement, the age where full retirement benefits are available to the retiree, was 65 years. The age at which full benefits are paid began to rise in the year 2000. **Exhibit 11.7 | Age Full Retirement Benefits Begin (Normal Age Retirement)** illustrates the new law, which eventually raises normal age retirement with full benefits to age 67.

Exhibit 11.7 | Age Full Retirement Benefits Begin (Normal Age Retirement)

Full Retirement Age With Full Benefits	Year Born
65 years	Before 1938
65 years, 2 months	1938
65 years, 4 months	1939
65 years, 6 months	1940
65 years, 8 months	1941
65 years, 10 months	1942
66 years	1943-1954
66 years, 2 months	1955
66 years, 4 months	1956
66 years, 6 months	1957
66 years, 8 months	1958
66 years, 10 months	1959
67 years	1960-present

People who delay receiving Social Security retirement benefits beyond full retirement age receive an increase in their benefit when they do retire. People who take early retirement, currently as early as age 62, receive an actuarially reduced monthly benefit. (Early and late retirement options are discussed later in this chapter.)

When planning for an individual, it may be appropriate to calculate the individual's expected Social Security retirement benefit or to ask the client to request a Social Security statement and consider the benefit in that individual's retirement plan. Some advisors, however, choose not to consider the estimated retirement benefit in order to be conservative in developing a retirement plan. Others justify the exclusion of Social Security retirement benefits from retirement planning based on the belief that there will be drastic changes to the Social Security system through legislative action or through economically-driven forces.

≔ *Key Concepts*

1. How is a person's Social Security retirement benefit calculated?

2. How does retiring early or retiring late affect Social Security retirement benefits?

The Retirement Benefit Calculation

Determining a worker's Social Security retirement benefit requires specific, detailed information pertaining to the person's age, actual earnings history that was subject to Social Security taxes, and the worker's retirement date. Social Security benefits are based on earnings averaged over most of a worker's lifetime. Actual earnings, in historical dollars, are first adjusted or "indexed" to current dollars to account for changes in average wages and inflation since the year the earnings were received. Then, the Social Security Administration calculates **average indexed monthly earnings ("AIME")** during the 35 years in which the applicant earned the most. The Social Security Administration applies a formula to these earnings and arrives at a basic benefit, which is referred to as the **primary insurance amount (PIA)**. The Social Security retirement benefit is based on the worker's PIA. The PIA determines the amount the applicant will receive at his full retirement age, but the dollar amount of the benefit depends on the year in which the worker retires. The PIA is indexed to the consumer price index (CPI) annually.

Figuring the Worker's Average Indexed Monthly Earnings (AIME)

To determine a worker's AIME, the worker's actual annual earnings from age 22 to 62 must be converted into current dollars by multiplying the worker's total annual earnings for each year by an indexing factor. The indexing factor is the result of dividing the national average wage for the year in which the worker attains age 60 by the national average wage for the actual year being indexed. The following exhibit provides national average wages from 1951 to 2018.

Exhibit 11.8 | National Average Wage Indexing Series, 1951- 2018

Year	Amount	Year	Amount	Year	Amount
1951	$2,799.16	1974	$8,030.76	1997	$27,426.00
1952	$2,973.32	1975	$8,630.92	1998	$28,861.44
1953	$3,139.44	1976	$9,226.48	1999	$30,469.84
1954	$3,155.64	1977	$9,779.44	2000	$32,154.82
1955	$3,301.44	1978	$10,556.03	2001	$32,921.92
1956	$3,532.36	1979	$11,479.46	2002	$33,252.09
1957	$3,641.72	1980	$12,513.46	2003	$34,064.95
1958	$3,673.80	1981	$13,773.10	2004	$35,648.55
1959	$3,855.80	1982	$14,531.34	2005	$36,952.94
1960	$4,007.12	1983	$15,239.24	2006	$38,651.41
1961	$4,086.76	1984	$16,135.07	2007	$40,405.48
1962	$4,291.40	1985	$16,822.51	2008	$41,334.97
1963	$4,396.64	1986	$17,321.82	2009	$40,711.61
1964	$4,576.32	1987	$18,426.51	2010	$41,673.83
1965	$4,658.72	1988	$19,334.04	2011	$42,979.61
1966	$4,938.36	1989	$20,099.55	2012	$44,321.67
1967	$5,213.44	1990	$21,027.98	2013	$44,888.16
1968	$5,571.76	1991	$21,811.60	2014	$46,481.52
1969	$5,893.76	1992	$22,935.42	2015	$48,098.63
1970	$6,186.24	1993	$23,132.67	2016	$48,642.15
1971	$6,497.08	1994	$23,753.53	2017	$50,321.89
1972	$7,133.80	1995	$24,705.66	2018	$52,145.80
1973	$7,580.16	1996	$25,913.90		

Source: Social Security Administration (www.ssa.gov)

Example 11.14

For a worker age 62 in 2020, the indexing factor for the year 1980 is determined by dividing the national average wage for 2018 (when the worker attained age 60), which was $52,145.80, by the national average wage for 1980 (the year being indexed), which was $12,513.46, yielding a factor of 4.1672.

Year	AWI	Age 62 in 2020		Age 66 in 2020	
		Age	Factor	Age	Factor
1954	3,155.64		16.5246	0	14.7297
1955	3,301.44		15.7949	1	14.0792
1956	3,532.36		14.7623	2	13.1588
1957	3,641.72		14.3190	3	12.7636
1958	3,673.80	0	14.1940	4	12.6522
1959	3,855.80	1	13.5240	5	12.0550
1960	4,007.12	2	13.0133	6	11.5997
1961	4,086.76	3	12.7597	7	11.3737
1962	4,291.40	4	12.1512	8	10.8313
1963	4,396.64	5	11.8604	9	10.5721
1964	4,576.32	6	11.3947	10	10.1570
1965	4,658.72	7	11.1932	11	9.9773
1966	4,938.36	8	10.5593	12	9.4123
1967	5,213.44	9	10.0022	13	8.9157
1968	5,571.76	10	9.3589	14	8.3423
1969	5,893.76	11	8.8476	15	7.8866
1970	6,186.24	12	8.4293	16	7.5137
1971	6,497.08	13	8.0260	17	7.1542
1972	7,133.80	14	7.3097	18	6.5157
1973	7,580.16	15	6.8792	19	6.1320
1974	8,030.76	16	6.4933	20	5.7879
1975	8,630.92	17	6.0417	21	5.3855
1976	9,226.48	18	5.6518	22	5.0378
1977	9,779.44	19	5.3322	23	4.7530
1978	10,556.03	20	4.9399	24	4.4033
1979	11,479.46	21	4.5425	25	4.0491
1980	12,513.46	22	4.1672	26	3.7145
1981	13,773.10	23	3.7861	27	3.3748
1982	14,531.34	24	3.5885	28	3.1987
1983	15,239.24	25	3.4218	29	3.0501
1984	16,135.07	26	3.2318	30	2.8808
1985	16,822.51	27	3.0998	31	2.7631
1986	17,321.82	28	3.0104	32	2.6834
1987	18,426.51	29	2.8299	33	2.5225
1988	19,334.04	30	2.6971	34	2.4041
1989	20,099.55	31	2.5944	35	2.3126
1990	21,027.98	32	2.4798	36	2.2105
1991	21,811.60	33	2.3907	37	2.1310
1992	22,935.42	34	2.2736	38	2.0266
1993	23,132.67	35	2.2542	39	2.0093
1994	23,753.53	36	2.1953	40	1.9568
1995	24,705.66	37	2.1107	41	1.8814
1996	25,913.90	38	2.0123	42	1.7937
1997	27,426.00	39	1.9013	43	1.6948
1998	28,861.44	40	1.8068	44	1.6105
1999	30,469.84	41	1.7114	45	1.5255
2000	32,154.82	42	1.6217	46	1.4456
2001	32,921.92	43	1.5839	47	1.4119
2002	33,252.09	44	1.5682	48	1.3979
2003	34,064.95	45	1.5308	49	1.3645
2004	35,648.55	46	1.4628	50	1.3039
2005	36,952.94	47	1.4111	51	1.2579
2006	38,651.41	48	1.3491	52	1.2026
2007	40,405.48	49	1.2906	53	1.1504
2008	41,334.97	50	1.2615	54	1.1245
2009	40,711.61	51	1.2809	55	1.1417
2010	41,673.83	52	1.2513	56	1.1154
2011	42,979.61	53	1.2133	57	1.0815
2012	44,321.67	54	1.1765	58	1.0487
2013	44,888.16	55	1.1617	59	1.0355
2014	46,481.52	56	1.1219	60	1.0000
2015	48,098.63	57	1.0841	61	1.0000
2016	48,642.15	58	1.0720	62	1.0000
2017	50,321.89	59	1.0362	63	1.0000
2018	52,145.80	60	1.0000	64	1.0000
2019		61	1.0000	65	1.0000
2020		62	1.0000	66	1.0000

Next, each year's annual earnings must be multiplied by its indexing factor to arrive at the indexed earnings for the years from age 22 to 60. Note that the indexing factor will always equal one for the years in which the worker is 60 or older. After all annual earnings are indexed, or converted to current dollar amounts, the highest 35 years of indexed earnings are added together for a total. The sum of the highest 35 years is then divided by 420 (which represents 35 years multiplied by 12 months per year). This calculation yields the average amount of monthly earnings for all indexed years, hence the name Average Indexed Monthly Earnings (AIME). Once the worker's AIME is determined, the next step in determining the worker's retirement benefit is to calculate the primary insurance amount (PIA) for the worker.

Example 11.15

Assume Ronnie and Karen both retire in 2020. Ronnie retires at age 62. Karen retires at her normal (or full) retirement age. Assume Karen has covered earnings from 1978 through 2020, as shown in columns labeled "nominal earnings" and Ronnie has covered earnings from 1978 through 2020.

Indexing adjusts nominal earnings to near-current wage levels. For each case, the table shows columns of earnings before and after indexing. Between these columns is a column showing the indexing factors. A factor will always equal one for the year in which the person attains age 60 and all later years. The indexing factor for a prior year Y is the result of dividing the average wage index for the year in which the person attains age 60 by the average wage index for year Y. For example, Ronnie's indexing factor for 1978 (4.9399) is the average wage for 2018 ($52,145.80; as provided in the National Average Wage Indexing Table in Exhibit 11.8) divided by the average wage for 1978 ($10,556.03; as provided in the National Average Wage Indexing Table in Exhibit 11.8).

The highest 35 years of indexed earnings are used in the benefit computation. The selected indexed amounts are bold. Below the indexed earnings are the sums for the highest 35 years of indexed earnings and the corresponding average monthly amounts of such earnings. (The average is the result of dividing the sum of the 35 highest amounts by the number of months in 35 years.) Such an average is called the "Average Indexed Monthly Earnings" (AIME).

As reflected in the following chart, Ronnie's AIME is $2,872 and Karen's AIME is $3,753.

Year		Ronnie					Karen			
	Age	Nominal earnings	Indexing factor	Indexed earnings	Top 35	Age	Nominal earnings	Indexing factor	Indexed earnings	Top 35
1978	20	$5,167	4.9399	$25,524		24	$5,194	4.4033	$22,871	
1979	21	$5,525	4.5425	$25,097		25	$5,747	4.0491	$23,270	
1980	22	$5,847	4.1672	$24,365		26	$6,262	3.7145	$23,260	
1981	23	$6,140	3.7861	$23,246		27	$6,746	3.3748	$22,766	
1982	24	$6,452	3.5885	$23,153		28	$7,253	3.1987	$23,200	
1983	25	$7,088	3.4218	$24,254		29	$8,135	3.0501	$24,813	
1984	26	$7,535	3.2318	$24,352		30	$8,815	2.8808	$25,394	
1985	27	$7,988	3.0998	$24,761		31	$9,511	2.7631	$26,279	
1986	28	$8,589	3.0104	$25,856	✓	32	$10,396	2.6834	$27,897	✓
1987	29	$9,186	2.8299	$25,996	✓	33	$11,293	2.5225	$28,487	✓
1988	30	$9,742	2.6971	$26,275	✓	34	$12,151	2.4041	$29,213	✓
1989	31	$10,521	2.5944	$27,295	✓	35	$13,305	2.3126	$30,769	✓
1990	32	$11,447	2.4798	$28,387	✓	36	$14,667	2.2105	$32,421	✓
1991	33	$12,485	2.3907	$29,848	✓	37	$16,197	2.1310	$34,517	✓
1992	34	$13,748	2.2736	$31,257	✓	38	$18,051	2.0266	$36,583	✓
1993	35	$14,513	2.2542	$32,715	✓	39	$19,273	2.0093	$38,726	✓
1994	36	$15,228	2.1953	$33,430	✓	40	$20,445	1.9568	$40,007	✓
1995	37	$16,131	2.1107	$34,047	✓	41	$21,887	1.8814	$41,178	✓
1996	38	$16,827	2.0123	$33,860	✓	42	$23,063	1.7937	$41,368	✓
1997	39	$17,335	1.9013	$32,960	✓	43	$23,994	1.6948	$40,665	✓
1998	40	$18,450	1.8068	$33,335	✓	44	$25,779	1.6105	$41,517	✓
1999	41	$19,369	1.7114	$33,148	✓	45	$27,311	1.5255	$41,663	✓
2000	42	$20,146	1.6217	$32,671	✓	46	$28,659	1.4456	$41,428	✓
2001	43	$21,087	1.5839	$33,400	✓	47	$30,257	1.4119	$42,719	✓
2002	44	$21,884	1.5682	$34,318	✓	48	$31,663	1.3979	$44,260	✓
2003	45	$23,024	1.5308	$35,245	✓	49	$33,582	1.3645	$45,823	✓
2004	46	$23,234	1.4628	$33,986	✓	50	$34,155	1.3039	$44,534	✓
2005	47	$23,869	1.4111	$33,683	✓	51	$35,360	1.2579	$44,478	✓
2006	48	$24,839	1.3491	$33,511	✓	52	$37,071	1.2026	$44,581	✓
2007	49	$26,067	1.2906	$33,641	✓	53	$39,188	1.1504	$45,081	✓
2008	50	$27,602	1.2615	$34,821	✓	54	$41,790	1.1245	$46,993	✓
2009	51	$29,061	1.2809	$37,223	✓	55	$44,305	1.1417	$50,584	✓
2010	52	$30,696	1.2513	$38,409	✓	56	$47,115	1.1154	$52,550	✓
2011	53	$32,410	1.2133	$39,322	✓	57	$50,076	1.0815	$54,156	✓
2012	54	$33,200	1.1765	$39,061	✓	58	$51,629	1.0487	$54,145	✓
2013	55	$33,551	1.1617	$38,976	✓	59	$52,503	1.0355	$54,367	✓
2014	56	$34,388	1.1219	$38,579	✓	60	$54,148	1.0000	$54,148	✓
2015	57	$36,400	1.0841	$39,463	✓	61	$56,092	1.0000	$56,092	✓
2016	58	$37,900	1.0720	$40,630	✓	62	$56,408	1.0000	$56,408	✓
2017	59	$38,113	1.0362	$39,494	✓	63	$57,103	1.0000	$57,103	✓
2018	60	$39,551	1.0000	$39,551	✓	64	$59,955	1.0000	$59,955	✓
2019	61	$40,000	1.0000	$40,000	✓	65	$60,000	1.0000	$60,000	✓
2020	62	$42,000	1.0000	$42,000	✓	66	$62,000	1.0000	$62,000	✓
		Highest-35 total		$1,206,394			Highest-35 total		$1,576,415	
	Total	420 Months	AIME	$2,872				AIME	$3,753	

Calculating the Worker's Primary Insurance Amount (PIA)

Generally, the PIA is the actual Social Security retirement benefit for the single retiree who retires at full retirement age. For those who retire early or late and for family or surviving beneficiaries, the PIA is not the actual amount of the benefit but the PIA is used to determine their actual benefit.

The PIA is a result of applying the AIME to the PIA formula. This benefit formula changes the dollar amounts (by CPI), but not the percentages, from year to year and depends on the worker's first year of eligibility, that is, when the worker turns 62, becomes disabled, or dies.

The PIA is the sum of three separate percentages of portions of the AIME. These portions are also known as "bend points." For the year 2020, these portions are the first $960 of AIME, the amount of AIME between $960 and $5,785, and the AIME over $5,785. The bend points for 2020 are thus $960 and $5,785. For individuals who first become eligible for retirement benefits or disability insurance benefits in 2020 or who die in 2020 before becoming eligible for benefits, their PIA will be the sum of:

> 90 percent of the first $960 of their AIME, *plus*
> 32 percent of their AIME over $960 up to $5,785, *plus*
> 15 percent of their AIME that exceeds $5,785.
> (Maximum PIA for 2020 is $3,011.)

The sum of these three calculations is rounded down to the next lower multiple of $0.10 (if it is not already a multiple of $0.10). For calculations in subsequent years, it is useful to know how to determine a given year's bend points. **Exhibit 11.9 | Bend Point Table** shows the established bend points from 1982 through 2020.

Exhibit 11.9 | Bend Point Table

Dollar Amounts (bend points) in PIA Formula		
Year	First	Second
1982	$230	$1,388
1983	$254	$1,528
1984	$267	$1,612
1985	$280	$1,691
1986	$297	$1,790
1987	$310	$1,866
1988	$319	$1,922
1989	$339	$2,044
1990	$356	$2,145
1991	$370	$2,230
1992	$387	$2,333
1993	$401	$2,420
1994	$422	$2,545
1995	$426	$2,567
1996	$437	$2,635
1997	$455	$2,741
1998	$477	$2,875
1999	$505	$3,043
2000	$531	$3,202
2001	$561	$3,381
2002	$592	$3,567
2003	$606	$3,653
2004	$612	$3,689
2005	$627	$3,779
2006	$656	$3,955
2007	$680	$4,100
2008	$711	$4,288
2009	$744	$4,483
2010	$761	$4,586
2011	$749	$4,517
2012	$767	$4,624
2013	$791	$4,768
2015	$826	$4,980
2016	$856	$5,157
2017	$885	$5,336
2018	$895	$5,397
2019	$926	$5,583
2020	$960	$5,785

Source: Social Security Administration (www.ssa.gov)

These figures for the PIA rise each year based on a cost-of-living adjustment (**COLA**) that is applied to reflect changes in the cost of living. Recent COLAs, which are based on inflation, are shown in **Exhibit 11.10 | Cost-of-Living Adjustment (COLA) Per Year**.

Exhibit 11.10 | Cost-of-Living Adjustment (COLA) Per Year

Year	COLA	Year	COLA	Year	COLA
1993	2.6%	2002	1.4%	2011	3.6%
1994	2.8%	2003	2.1%	2012	1.7%
1995	2.6%	2004	2.7%	2013	1.5%
1996	2.9%	2005	4.1%	2014	1.7%
1997	2.1%	2006	3.3%	2015	0.0%
1998	1.3%	2007	2.3%	2016	0.3%
1999	2.5%	2008	5.8%	2017	2.0%
2000	3.5%	2009	0.0%	2018	2.8%
2001	2.6%	2010	0.0%	2019	1.6%

* Source: www.ssa.gov/oact/cola/colaseries.html

As mentioned, the calculation of the Social Security retirement benefit skews benefits toward the low-income worker. This design is evident in the PIA calculation with a 90 percent wage replacement for extremely low income and only a 15 percent wage replacement for higher income. The following exhibit illustrates the wage replacement ratio provided by Social Security at full retirement age based on the annualized income, which is AIME multiplied by 12 months.

Exhibit 11.11 | Wage Replacement Ratio from Social Security

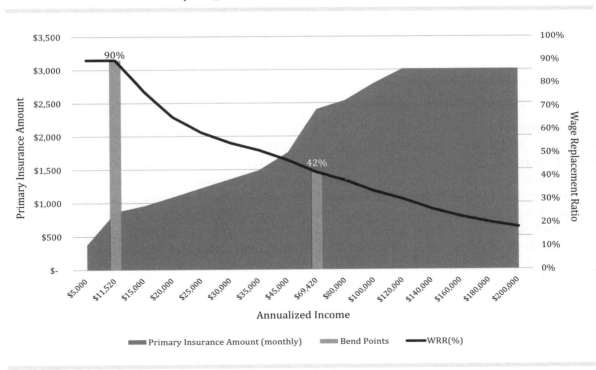

Annual COLA increases are determined by October of each year and go into effect in time so that they first appear on monthly benefit checks received in the following January. In 2020, the maximum monthly retirement benefit for retirees at full retirement age is $3,011, compared to $2,861 in 2019.

Early and Late Retirement Options

Workers entitled to retirement benefits can currently take early retirement benefits as early as age 62. The worker will receive a reduced benefit because he will receive more monthly benefit payments than if the worker had waited and retired at full retirement age. The reduction to one's monthly benefit for early retirement is permanent. Conversely, a delayed or postponed retirement will permanently increase the monthly retirement benefit for a worker.[4]

For each month of early retirement, workers will receive a reduction in their monthly retirement benefit of 5/9 of one percent for up to the first 36 months. For subsequent months of early retirement, the permanent reduction percentage is 5/12 of one percent per month.

Example 11.16

Assume Robin begins receiving benefits at the earliest possible age, which is age 62. Then, the benefit amount for Robin is reduced for 48 months of retirement before Robin's normal retirement age, which is 66 years. Assume Robin's PIA before reduction is $1,421.90. The PIA is thus reduced to a monthly benefit of $1,066.43 (rounded to $1066.40).

PIA	$1,421.90
5/9 x 1% x 36 months	Less 20% reduction
5/12 x 1% x 12 months	Less 5% reduction
Monthly Benefit	$1,066.43

Although the full retirement age will increase to age 67, workers will still have the option of taking early retirement at age 62. However, the reduction percentage that is applied to the monthly retirement benefit will increase until 2027. Before 2000, those who retired at age 62 received 80 percent of their retirement benefit, but the increase in full retirement age has increased the number of months from 62 until full retirement age. For instance, in the year 2009, covered workers who retired at age 62 received 75 percent of their monthly retirement benefit, or 25 percent less than their full retirement benefit. By 2027, covered workers retiring at age 62 (full retirement age would be 67) will receive only 70 percent of their monthly retirement benefit. **Exhibit 11.12 | Social Security Full Retirement and Reductions by Age***, which was compiled by the Social Security Administration, shows the phase-in of the Social Security full retirement age and accompanying reductions for early retirement at age 62.

---

4. A spouse can choose to retire as early as age 62, but doing so may result in a benefit as little as 32.5 percent of the worker's primary insurance amount. A spousal benefit is reduced 25/36 of one percent for each month before normal retirement age, up to 36 months. If the number of months exceeds 36, then the benefit is further reduced 5/12 of one percent per month. Source: SSA.gov.

Exhibit 11.12 | Social Security Full Retirement and Reductions by Age*

Year of Birth	Full Retirement Age	Age 62 Reduction Months	Monthly Percent Reduction	Total Percent Reduction
1937 or earlier	65	36	0.555	20.00
1938	65 & 2 months	38	0.548	20.83
1939	65 & 4 months	40	0.541	21.67
1940	65 & 6 months	42	0.535	22.50
1941	65 & 8 months	44	0.530	23.33
1942	65 & 10 months	46	0.525	24.17
1943-1954	66	48	0.520	25.00
1955	66 & 2 months	50	0.516	25.84
1956	66 & 4 months	52	0.512	26.66
1957	66 & 6 months	54	0.509	27.50
1958	66 & 8 months	56	0.505	28.33
1959	66 & 10 months	58	0.502	29.17
1960 and later	67	60	0.500	30.00

*Percentage monthly and total reductions are approximate due to rounding. The actual reductions are 0.555 or 5/9 of one percent per month for the first 36 months and 0.416 or 5/12 of one percent for subsequent months.
Source: Social Security Administration (www.ssa.gov)

No matter what the full retirement age is, a worker may start receiving benefits as early as age 62 and can also retire at any time between age 62 and full retirement age. However, if a worker starts benefits at one of these early ages, the benefits are reduced a fraction of a percent for each month before the full retirement age.

Example 11.17

Assume that Josephine, a worker born in 1939, decided to retire on her 62nd birthday. Assume that her full retirement benefit would have been $1,429.20 at age 65 and four months, her full retirement age. If she retires at age 62, what is her monthly retirement benefit?

The answer is $1,119. Josephine retired 40 months early. The monthly retirement benefit reduction percentage is 1/180 (5/9 x 1% = 1/180 = 0.0056) for the first 36 months (1/180 x 36 = 20 percent) and 1/240 (5/12 x 1% = 1/240 = 0.0042) for the 4 subsequent months of early retirement (1/240 x 4 = 1.6668 percent), yielding a total permanent reduction to Josephine's monthly retirement benefit of 21.6667 percent. 21.6667 percent x $1,429.20 = $309.66. $1,429.20 - $309.66 = $1,119.50 (rounded).

Example 11.18

What if Josephine retired at age 64 and six months? What is her permanent monthly retirement benefit (subject to COLA increases)? Note she retired 10 months early from normal retirement age.

The answer is $1,349. 1/180 x 10 = 5.5556 percent. 5.5556 percent x $1,429.20 = $79.40. $1,429.20 - $79.40 = $1,349.80 (rounded).

For those covered individuals who take late retirement, or when benefits are lost due to the earnings limitation, the monthly retirement benefit and the benefit paid to the surviving spouse will increase each year (until age 70) as follows:

Exhibit 11.13 | Percentage Increases for Delayed Retirement

Increase For Year Born	Annual Percentage Increase Each Year Of Late Retirement	After Age
1917-1924	3.0%	65
1925-1926	3.5%	65
1927-1928	4.0%	65
1929-1930	4.5%	65
1931-1932	5.0%	65
1933-1934	5.5%	65
1935-1936	6.0%	65
1937	6.5%	65
1938	6.5%	65 and 2 months
1939	7.0%	65 and 4 months
1940	7.0%	65 and 6 months
1941	7.5%	65 and 8 months
1942	7.5%	65 and 10 months
1943 or later	8.0%	66

Example 11.19

Jeanette will turn 66 in 2020 (thus she was born in 1954 and her full retirement age is 66). She is considering taking Social Security retirement benefits at age 62, 66, or 70. Assume her monthly expected benefit is $1,000 at full retirement age, expected inflation is 4%, and her life expectancy is 90. Calculate the present value of her benefits at ages 62, 66, and 70 (A, B, or C).

Choice A – Begin Benefits at age 62.

PMT	$750	($1,000 less 25% reduction)
N	336	(90-62) x 12
i	0.3333	4/12
FV	0	
PV$_{@62}$	**$151,450.19**	

Choice B – Begin Benefits at age 66.

PMT	$1,000	Full benefit at full retirement age
N	288	(90-66) x 12
i	0.3333	4/12
FV	0	
PV$_{@66}$	$184,948.61	

Discount to age 62 for comparison.

PMT	$0	
N	4	(66-62)
i	4	
FV	$184,948.61	
PV$_{@62}$	**$158,094.84**	

Choice C – Begin Benefits at age 70.

PMT	$1,320	($1,000 plus 8% x 4 years increase)
N	240	(90-70) x 12
i	0.3333	4/12
FV	0	
PV$_{@70}$	$217,828.85	

Discount to age 62 for comparison.

PMT	$0	
N	8	(70-62)
i	4	
FV	$217,828.85	
PV$_{@62}$	**$159,165.41**	

As you can see, even though the benefit is reduced if Jeanette begins her benefit early, the PV of the total benefit at age 62 is not much less than if she took the benefit at age 66. Similarly, if she begins her payments later, her yearly payments will be higher but the PV of the benefit at age 62 is not much more than if she had taken benefits at age 66. The significance here is that all things being equal, the acceleration or delay of benefit generally has little impact on the PV of the benefit at age 62. However, the choice of retirement age is significant when considering the annual income needed to maintain one's standard of living.

Another critical factor in this analysis is the life expectancy of the worker. If the life expectancy is significantly less than what was assumed it might not make sense to delay benefits. Another factor that was not considered is the tax impact of benefits, which is discussed later in this chapter.

Although the calculations explained above can provide estimates of the Social Security benefits a retiring worker may receive, an advisor should have the client obtain his entire Social Security earnings history up to the moment of retirement from the Social Security Administration to get the most accurate benefit estimate.

Exhibit 11.14 | Social Security Benefits at Different Ages depicts the percent of PIA that a participant will receive based on the age benefits begin. The increase in the monthly benefit over time compensates for the decrease in life expectancy, such that an individual living to average life expectancy will be expected to receive the same dollar amount of benefits over their lifetime. To the extent an individual expects to live beyond the average life expectancy, delaying benefits is beneficial. To the extent an individual does not expect to reach average life expectancy, beginning benefits at an early age is beneficial.

Exhibit 11.14 | Social Security Benefits at Different Ages

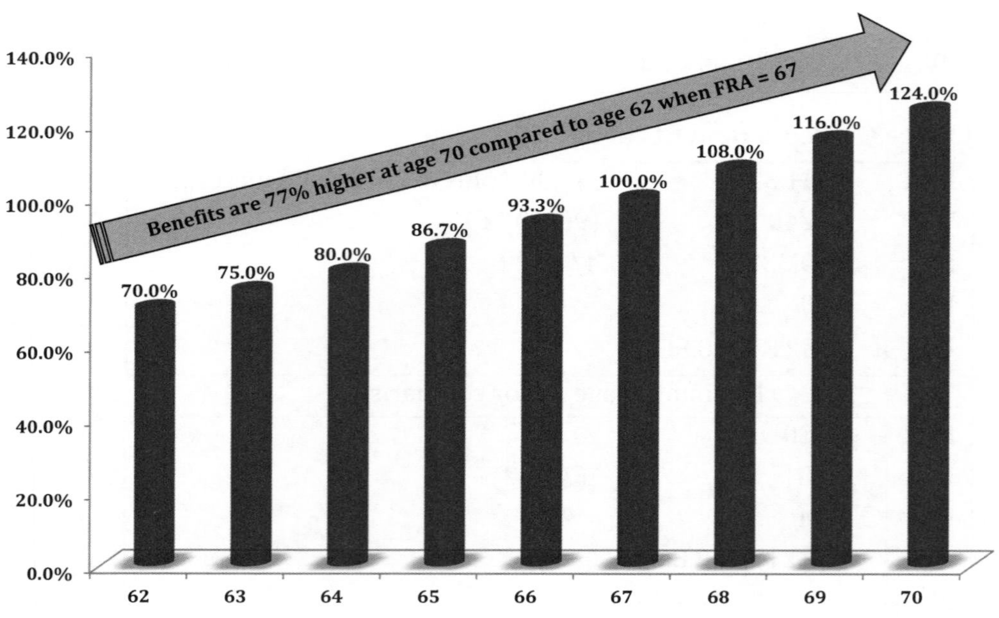

Reduction of Social Security Benefits

Besides early retirement, there are two other situations in which beneficiaries can have benefits reduced. The first instance is a reduction of benefits based on earnings, referred to as the **retirement earnings limitations test**. The other instance is through taxation of Social Security benefits. Both of these measures reduce one's net benefits.

A person may continue to work even though he is considered "retired" under Social Security. For a retiree who receives Social Security retirement benefits before normal retirement age, the earnings received by the beneficiary cannot exceed certain limitations without triggering a reduction in Social Security benefits. Beneficiaries can earn up to the limitation amount and receive all of their benefits, but if their earnings exceed the designated limit for the calendar year, then benefits will be reduced or eliminated. The law provides for earnings limitations of $18,240 for those under the full retirement age for 2020. The Social Security Administration reduces $1 in benefits for each $2 earned by those beneficiaries above $18,240. In the year that the retiree reaches full retirement age, $1 in benefits will be deducted for each $3 earned above the given year's limit but only for earnings before the month the retiree reaches full retirement age. For 2020, the limit for earnings in the year the retiree reaches full retirement age is $48,600. The earnings limitation increases every year as median earnings nationwide increase. Once the retiree reaches normal retirement age, benefits will not be reduced regardless of the earnings limitations.

In the event that a beneficiary, who is younger than normal retirement age, has earnings that exceed the limitation, that beneficiary's benefits will be reduced depending on his or her age. The beneficiary must file an annual report of his earnings to the Social Security Administration by April 15 of the year following the year worked and must provide the exact earnings for that year and an estimate for the current year. The filing of a federal tax return with the IRS does not satisfy the filing requirement with the Social Security Administration. Also, the wages count toward the earnings limitation when they are earned, not when paid, whereas income for the self-employed normally counts when paid, not earned. If other family members receive benefits based on the beneficiary's Social Security record, then the total family benefits may be affected by the beneficiary's earnings that exceed the earnings limitation. In such a case, the Social Security Administration will withhold not only the worker's benefits but will withhold those benefits payable to family members as well. However, if a family member's benefits are reduced based on their own earnings, only that family member's benefits are reduced.

Generally, only wages and net self-employment income count towards the retirement earnings limitation, whereas income from savings, investments, and insurance does not. The following is a nonexclusive list of sources of income that DO NOT count toward the earnings limitation:
- Pension or retirement income
- 401(k) plan and IRA withdrawals
- Dividends and interest from investments
- Capital gains
- Rental income

- Workers' compensation benefits (generally not payable after a worker has retired)
- Unemployment benefits
- Court-awarded judgments, less components of award that include lost wages
- Contest winnings

Example 11.20

Matthew is 64 years old and despite being retired from his occupation as an attorney, earned $20,000 in 2020 while working as a golf instructor at a local golf course. Matthew's monthly retirement benefit from Social Security is normally $1,200, which totals $14,400 for the entire year. Because Matthew exceeded the retirement earnings limitation, how much money will be reduced from Matthew's Social Security retirement benefit for 2020?

Matthew's total earnings in 2020	$20,000
Earnings limitation	($18,240)
Remainder excess	$1,760
One-half deduction	÷ 2
Benefits reduced by:	**$880**

The Social Security Administration will reduce Matthew's benefits for the year by $880. Matthew will receive $13,520 in retirement benefits ($14,400 annual retirement benefit less $880 reduction). Matthew's total income for 2020 will be $33,520, instead of $34,400.

Example 11.21

Gideon is 67 years old. He has a full-time job working as a masseur. This year (2020) he anticipates earning $22,000 from his job. How much, in dollars, will Gideon's Social Security benefits be reduced for the earnings test?

None, because Gideon is over full retirement age.

Special Calculation of Earnings Test in the First Year of Retirement

In the first year of retirement, a special monthly earnings test can be applied so that earnings prior to the month of retirement are not counted. Beginning with the month of retirement, for any month in which earnings are below 1/12 of the annual amount ($1,520 in 2020), the Social Security benefit amount will not be reduced. This special monthly calculation only applies in the first year of retirement; after the first year, the annual test will apply.

Example 11.22

Odell will be turning age 64 on July 31, 2020. Odell's full retirement age is 66. If Odell retires in the month he turns age 64, his Social Security benefit will be $1,200 per month. Odell will earn $25,000 between January and July, but will reduce his hours beginning in August and earn $1,000 per month from August through December. Since Odell's monthly earnings in the months after retiring under Social Security are less than $1,520 ($18,240/12 = $1,520), his Social Security benefits for August - December will not be reduced. For 2021, Odell will be subject to the earnings test based on his annual income.

In 2021, Odell will still be under full retirement age and he reports to Social Security that he expects to earn $23,040 in 2021. If the earnings limit remains unchanged in 2021, he will be over the $18,240 threshold by $4,800. His Social Security benefits will be reduced by $1 for every $2 that he is over the limit, or $2,400 ($4,800/2 = $2,400). Odell will not receive a check in January or February of 2021 (those checks ($1,200 each month x 2 = $2,400) are withheld to cover the earnings test reduction in benefits), and then he will receive the full $1,200 each month from March - December. Odell's Social Security benefit will then increase slightly when he reaches full retirement age to make up for the amount that was withheld due to the earnings test.

TAXATION OF SOCIAL SECURITY BENEFITS

Apart from the earnings limitation, some beneficiaries may be required to pay income tax on their Social Security benefits. For persons with substantial income in addition to Social Security benefits, up to 85 percent of their annual Social Security benefits may be subject to federal income tax. The Social Security Administration is concerned with a beneficiary's **modified adjusted gross income** (MAGI). For purposes of Social Security, MAGI is equal to the taxpayer's adjusted gross income plus tax exempt interest, including:

- interest earned on savings bonds used for higher education;
- amounts excluded from the taxpayer's income for employer-provided adoption assistance;
- amounts deducted for interest paid for educational loans;
- interest earned on tax exempt municipal bonds; and
- income earned in a foreign country, a U.S. possession, or Puerto Rico, that is excluded from income.

> **Key Concepts**
>
> 1. How are Social Security benefits taxed?
>
> 2. What benefits are available from Social Security other than retirement benefits?
>
> 3. What is the maximum family benefit?

Example 11.23

Last year Fred and Velma had adjusted gross income of $40,000. They also had the following items:

- Velma spent three months during the year in Mexico visiting her mother. While she was there, she earned $5,000 that has been excluded from their AGI.

- While in Mexico, Velma fell in love with a little orphan girl. Luckily, Fred's company has an Adoption Assistance Program. The program paid $8,000 towards the adoption and the amount was excluded from Fred's AGI.

- Fred has been attending night school for several years and has several student loans. Last year he paid and deducted $200 in student loan interest.

- Fred and Velma had $900 in interest. $400 was from tax-exempt bonds and the remaining $500 was from corporate bonds.

Fred and Velma's MAGI for last year is:

Adjusted Gross Income (AGI)	$40,000
+ Foreign Income Excluded	$5,000
+ Adoption Assistance Excluded	$8,000
+ Student Loan Interest Deduction	$200
+ Tax-Exempt Bonds Interest	$400
= **Modified Adjusted Gross Income (MAGI)**	**$53,600**

Note that the $500 of corporate-bond interest has already been included in AGI for Fred and Velma.

A taxpayer's "combined" (or provisional) income is equal to: MAGI + ½ of Social Security benefits. Generally, up to 50 percent of Social Security benefits may be subject to federal income taxes for beneficiaries who file a federal tax return as an "individual" and have a combined income between $25,000 and $34,000. For those with a modified adjusted gross income plus one-half of Social Security greater than $34,000, up to 85 percent of their Social Security benefits may be subject to federal income taxation. For those beneficiaries that file a joint federal tax return and have a combined income with their spouse between $32,000 and $44,000, up to 50 percent of their Social Security benefits will be subject to federal income taxes. Finally, if beneficiaries filing a joint tax return have a modified adjusted gross income plus one-half Social Security benefits that exceeds $44,000, up to 85 percent of their Social Security benefits may be subject to federal income taxation.

In summary, for persons with substantial income in addition to their Social Security benefits, up to 85 percent of their annual benefits may be subject to federal income tax.

Exhibit 11.15 | Social Security Hurdle Amounts

	Married Filing Jointly	All Others Except MFS = 0
1st Hurdle	$32,000	$25,000
2nd Hurdle	$44,000	$34,000

If MAGI plus one half of Social Security benefits exceeds the first hurdle but not the second, the taxable amount of Social Security benefits is the lesser of:
- 50% Social Security Benefits, or
- 50% [MAGI + 0.50 (Social Security Benefits) - Hurdle 1]; which is 50% of the amount by which combined income exceeds Hurdle 1.

Example 11.24

A married couple has interest income of $18,000 and Social Security benefits of $20,000. What amount of their Social Security benefits must be included in their taxable income?

Lesser of:
- 0.50($20,000) = $10,000, or
- 0.50 [$18,000 + 0.50 (20,000) - 32,000] = Negative

They would have $0 inclusion due to a negative result.

Example 11.25

A married couple has income of $30,000 and Social Security benefits of $20,000. What amount of their Social Security benefits must be included in their taxable income?

Lesser of:
- 0.50($20,000) = $10,000, or
- 0.50 [30,000 + 0.50 (20,000) - 32,000] = $4,000

They would have $4,000 of Social Security benefits included in taxable income.

If MAGI plus one-half the Social Security benefits exceeds the second hurdle, the taxable amount of Social Security benefits is the lesser of:
- 85% Social Security Benefits, or
- 85% [MAGI + 0.50 (Social Security Benefits) - Hurdle 2], plus the lesser of:
  - $6,000 for MFJ or $4,500 for all other taxpayers, or
  - The taxable amount calculated under the 50% formula and only considering Hurdle 1.

Example 11.26

A married couple has income of $60,000 and Social Security benefits of $20,000. What amount of their Social Security benefits must be included in their taxable income?

0.85 ($20,000) = **$17,000**

0.85 [$60,000 + 0.50 ($20,000) - $44,000] =	$22,100
Plus the lesser of:	
• $6,000, or	
• 0.50($20,000) = $10,000, or	
• 0.50[$60,000+0.50($20,000)-$32,000] = $19,000	
	$6,000
	$28,100

Therefore, **$17,000** must be included in their taxable income.

Example 11.27

A married couple has income of $45,000 and Social Security benefits of $20,000. What amount of their Social Security benefits must be included in their taxable income?

0.85 ($20,000) = **$17,000**

0.85 [$45,000 + 0.50 ($20,000) - $44,000] =	$9,350
Plus the lesser of:	
• $6,000, or	
• 0.50($20,000) = $10,000, or	
• 0.50[$45,000+0.50($20,000)-$32,000] = $11,500	
	$6,000
	$15,350

Therefore, **$15,350** must be included in their taxable income.

Example 11.28

Last year LaWanda, a single taxpayer, received $10,400 in Social Security benefits. For the entire year, she had an adjusted gross income of $28,000. How much, if any, of her Social Security benefit is taxable?

First, determine LaWanda's modified adjusted gross income. Modified adjusted gross income is the sum of adjusted gross income, nontaxable interest, and foreign-earned income. One-half of LaWanda's Social Security benefits must then be added to her MAGI, to arrive at her combined income. For LaWanda, the equation is as follows: $28,000 + [$10,400 x 0.50] = $33,200. Since LaWanda's combined income is between the two base amounts for a single individual of $25,000 and $34,000, we can use the following formula to determine her taxable amount. The income tax base will be the lesser of 50% of her Social Security benefits _OR_ 50% of the amount by which LaWanda's combined income exceeds the base amount of $25,000. Based on this formula, LaWanda will be subject to income tax on $4,100 of her Social Security benefit.

- 0.50($10,400) = $5,200
- 0.50($33,200 - $25,000) = $4,100 (the LESSER amount)

Example 11.29

A married couple files jointly and has an adjusted gross income of $38,000, no tax-exempt interest, and $11,000 of Social Security benefits. How much, if any, of their Social Security benefits is included in gross income?

The lesser of the following:
- 0.50 ($11,000) = $5,500, or
- 0.50 [$38,000 + 0.50 ($11,000) - $32,000] = 0.50 ($11,500) = $5,750

They will include $5,500 in gross income. If the couple's adjusted gross income was $15,000 and their Social Security benefits totaled $5,000, none of the benefits would be taxable since their combined income is below the $32,000 threshold amount.

Example 11.30

Clark and Lois, married filing jointly, have tax-free municipal bond interest of $2,000. Assuming that Clark and Lois have differing AGI amounts ranging from $20,000 to $50,000, the Social Security amount includible in taxable income is shown below. Thus, if Clark and Lois have $20,000 in AGI, then only $1,000 of the Social Security benefit is included (4% of the benefit is included), but if they have AGI of $50,000 then $20,400 is includible (85% of the benefit is included). Notice that once an individual is substantially over the second hurdle they can expect to include 85% of the Social Security benefit.

	$20,000	$25,000	$30,000	$35,000	$40,000	$45,000	$50,000
Preliminary AGI	$20,000	$25,000	$30,000	$35,000	$40,000	$45,000	$50,000
Tax free bond interest	$2,000	$2,000	$2,000	$2,000	$2,000	$2,000	$2,000
MAGI	$22,000	$27,000	$32,000	$37,000	$42,000	$47,000	$52,000
50% of Social Security	$12,000	$12,000	$12,000	$12,000	$12,000	$12,000	$12,000
MAGI plus 1/2 Social Security	$34,000	$39,000	$44,000	$49,000	$54,000	$59,000	$64,000
First hurdle	$32,000	$32,000	$32,000	$32,000	$32,000	$32,000	$32,000
Second hurdle	$44,000	$44,000	$44,000	$44,000	$44,000	$44,000	$44,000
Excess of income over first hurdle	$2,000	$7,000	$12,000	$17,000	$22,000	$27,000	$32,000
Excess of income over second hurdle	$0	$0	$0	$5,000	$10,000	$15,000	$20,000
1. 50% of SSB	$12,000	$12,000	$12,000				
2. 50% [MAGI + 0.50 (SSB) - Hurdle 1]	$1,000	$3,500	$6,000				
3. 85% of SSB				$20,400	$20,400	$20,400	$20,400
4. [85% [MAGI + 0.5 (SSB)- Hurdle 2]] + 6000				$10,250	$14,500	$18,750	$23,000
5. [85% [MAGI + 0.5 (SSB)- Hurdle 2]] + 50% [MAGI + 0.50 (SSB) - Hurdle 1]				$14,450	$18,700	$22,950	$27,200
6. [85% [MAGI + 0.5 (SSB)- Hurdle 2]] + 50% of SSB				$16,250	$20,500	$24,750	$29,000
Includable portion of Social Security	$1,000	$3,500	$6,000	$10,250	$14,500	$18,750	$20,400
Percent of SS Taxed	4%	15%	25%	43%	60%	78%	85%

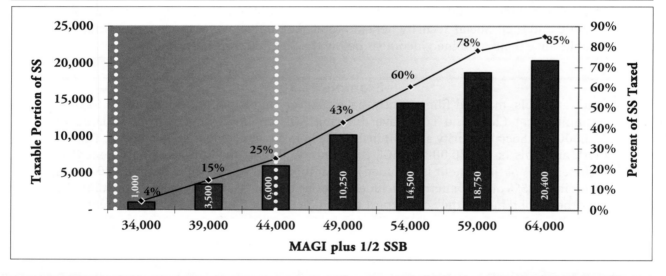

OTHER SOCIAL SECURITY BENEFITS

Disability Benefits and Disability Insured

Benefits are payable at any age to workers who have enough Social Security credits and who have a severe physical or mental impairment that is expected to prevent them from doing "substantial" work for a year or more or who have a condition that is expected to result in death. Workers are insured for disability if they are fully insured and, except for persons who are blind or disabled at age 31 or older, have a total of at least 20 quarters of coverage during the 40-quarter period ending with the quarter in which the worker became disabled. Workers who are disabled before age 31 must have total quarters of coverage equal to one-half the calendar quarters that have elapsed since the worker reached age 21 ending in the quarter in which the worker became disabled. However, a minimum of six quarters is required.

Exhibit 11.16 | Work Credits for Disability Benefits

Born After 1929, Become Disabled at Age:	Number of Credits You Need:
31 through 42	20
44	22
46	24
48	26
50	28
52	30
54	32
56	34
58	36
60	38
62 or older	40

- Before age 24 - The disabled individual may qualify if they have six credits earned in the three-year period ending when the disability starts.
- Age 24 to 31 - The disabled individual may qualify if they have credit for working half the time between age 21 and the time they become disabled. For example, if they become disabled at age 27, they would need credit for three years of work (12 credits) out of the past 6 years (between ages 21 and 27).
- Age 31 or older - In general, the disabled individual needs to have the number of work credits shown in the chart. Unless they are blind, they must have earned at least 20 of the credits in the 10 years immediately before they became disabled.

In 2020, earnings of $1,260 or more per month are considered substantial; therefore, a worker earning more than $1,260 per month would not be eligible for Social Security disability benefits. (If the individual is blind, then the amount is increased to $2,110.) The disability program includes incentives to smooth the disabled individual's transition back into the workforce, including continuation of benefits and healthcare coverage. Disability under the Social Security system is defined as an inability to engage in substantial gainful activity by reason of a physical or mental impairment expected to last at least 12 months or result in death. The impairment must be of such severity that the applicant is not only unable to do his previous work but cannot, considering age, education, and work experience, engage in any other kind of substantial gainful work that exists in the national economy.

There is a five month waiting period for Social Security disability benefits; therefore, benefits will not be paid until the sixth month after the onset of disability.

Family Benefits

If an individual is receiving retirement or disability benefits, other members of the individual's family might receive benefits as well. Family members who may receive retirement or disability benefits include the following:

- A spouse, if the spouse is 62 years old, caring for a child under age 16, or caring for a child who was disabled before age 22.
- A child, if the child is unmarried and under age 18, under age 19 but still in school, or age 18 or older but disabled before age 22.

For those workers who are entitled to retirement or disability benefits, an ex-spouse who was married to the worker for more than 10 years could also be eligible for retirement benefits based on the worker's record. For a divorced spouse to collect spousal retirement benefits, the worker must be at least age 62, but does not have to be receiving benefits him- or her- self, and the divorce must have been final for at least two years. For the current spouse, spousal benefits are available only if the worker is also receiving benefits.

A child's benefit stops the month before the child reaches 18, unless the child is unmarried and is either disabled or is a full-time elementary or secondary school student. Approximately five months before the child's 18th birthday, the person receiving the child's benefits will get a form explaining how benefits can continue. A child whose benefits stop at 18 can have them started again if the child becomes disabled before reaching 22 or becomes a full-time elementary or secondary school student before reaching 19. If the child continues to receive benefits after age 18 due to a disability, the child also may qualify for SSI disability benefits. When a student's 19th birthday occurs during a school term, benefits can be continued up to two months to allow completion of the school term.

Survivors' Benefits

If a worker earned enough Social Security credits during his lifetime, certain members of the worker's family may be eligible for benefits when the worker dies. The family members of the deceased worker who may be entitled to survivors' benefits include:

- A widow or widower age 60 (including a divorced spouse if the marriage lasted at least 10 years and the spouse has not remarried before the age of 60), age 50 if disabled, or any age if caring for a child under age 16 or a disabled child.
- A child of the deceased worker, if the child is unmarried and under age 18, under age 19 but still in school, or age 18 or older but disabled.
- Parents of the deceased worker, if the deceased worker was their primary means of support.

A surviving spouse may elect to receive the widow or widower benefit beginning at age 60, while delaying their own retirement benefit to between full retirement age and age 70, to receive delayed retirement credits. The spouse can elect to switch to their own benefit at any time between age 62 and 70.

A widow or widower who remarries after age 60 is not disqualified from obtaining benefits based on the deceased spouse's earnings. Marriage before age 60, however, will cause such disqualification while the marriage lasts.

A surviving spouse under age 60 will receive Social Security benefits until the youngest child reaches age 16. Spousal benefits will then cease until the spouse turns age 60 (50 if disabled). The years without benefits before age 60 are often referred to as the "blackout period" for the surviving spouse.

A special one-time payment of $255 may be made to a deceased worker's spouse or minor children upon death. If a spouse was living with the beneficiary at the time of death, the spouse will receive a one-time payment of $255. The payment may be made to a spouse who was not living with the beneficiary at the time of death or an ex-spouse if the spouse or ex-spouse was receiving Social Security benefits based on the deceased's earnings record. If there is no surviving spouse, a child (or children) who is eligible for benefits on the deceased's work record in the month of death may claim the payment.

THE MAXIMUM FAMILY BENEFIT

When a person dies, the deceased's survivors receive a percentage of the worker's Social Security benefits ranging from 75 percent to 100 percent each. There is a limit on the amount of monthly Social Security benefits that may be paid to a family. This limit is called the **maximum family benefit** and it is determined through a formula based on the worker's PIA. While the limit varies, it is equal to roughly 150 to 180 percent of the deceased worker's PIA. If the sum of the family members' benefits exceeds the limit, the family members' benefits are proportionately reduced. For old-age and survivor family benefits, the formula computes the sum of four separate percentages of portions of the worker's PIA. For 2020, these portions are the first $1,226 of PIA, the amount between $1,226 and $1,770, the amount between $1,770 and $2,309 and the amount over $2,309. These are the bend points for the maximum family benefit formula for the year 2020, with the following percentage calculations:

150 percent of the first $1,226 of the worker's PIA, *plus*
272 percent of the worker's PIA over $1,226 through $1,770, *plus*
134 percent of the worker's PIA over $1,770 through $2,309, *plus*
175 percent of the worker's PIA over $2,309.
This number is rounded to the next lower $0.10.

Example 11.31

If an individual has the maximum PIA for 2020, $3,011 per month, this would provide a maximum family benefit of $5,269.40 per month as shown by the calculation below:

```
              $1,226  x 1.50 =  $1,839.00
  ($1,770 - $1,226) x 2.72 =  $1,479.68
  ($2,309 - $1,770) x 1.34 =    $722.26
  ($3,011 - $2,309) x 1.75 =  $1,228.50
                              $5,269.44
              Rounded to $5,269.40
```

Example 11.32

Natalie and Brian, both age 50, are married and have two children, Ashley (age 15) and Kayli (age 5). Brian is disabled and has a PIA amount equal to the maximum PIA ($3,011). As calculated in **Example 11.31**, the maximum family benefit is $5,269.40 Because Brian is disabled, Natalie, Ashley, and Kayli are each entitled to receive a benefit equal to 50% of Brian's PIA, subject to the maximum family benefit limit, because the two children are under 18 and Natalie is a spouse/caretaker of a child under 16. Without regard to the maximum family benefit, they would each receive:

Brian	$3,011.00	100% of PIA
Natalie	$1,505.50	50% of Brian's PIA
Ashley	$1,505.50	50% of Brian's PIA
Kayli	$1,505.50	50% of Brian's PIA
Total	$7,527.50	

Because the benefit exceeds the maximum family benefit, the amounts for Natalie, Ashley, and Kayli must be prorated. Therefore, they will each receive $752.80 [($5,269.40 - $3,011) ÷ 3].

Brian	$3,011.00	100% of PIA
Natalie	$752.80	50% of Brian's PIA subject to maximum family benefit
Ashley	$752.80	50% of Brian's PIA subject to maximum family benefit
Kayli	$752.80	50% of Brian's PIA subject to maximum family benefit
Total	$5,269.40	

Assume instead that Ashley is 19 and no longer eligible to receive benefits under Brian. The maximum family benefit would be calculated as follows:

Brian	$3,011.00	100% of PIA
Natalie	$1,129.20	50% of Brian's PIA subject to maximum family benefit
Ashley	$0	Not eligible
Kayli	$1,129.20	50% of Brian's PIA subject to maximum family benefit
Total	$5,269.40	

Now assume Ashley is 19 and Kayli is 17. In this case, Natalie is no longer eligible because she is not caring for a child under 16. The family benefit would be calculated as follows:

Brian	$3,011.00	100% of PIA
Natalie	$0	Not eligible
Ashley	$0	Not eligible
Kayli	$1,505.50	50% of Brian's PIA
Total	$4,516.50	

Notice that Kayli is limited to 50% of Brian's PIA, thus they do not reach the maximum family benefit.

CHOOSING WHEN TO BEGIN SOCIAL SECURITY RETIREMENT BENEFITS

There are many issues in deciding when to begin receiving Social Security retirement benefits. As discussed earlier in this chapter, Social Security retirement benefits may be reduced if other income is earned before full retirement age, benefits may or may not be subject to income tax, and benefits may be increased or decreased depending on the start date of benefits relative to full retirement age. In addition to these issues, there are other considerations that may impact the total benefits collected by the worker and the worker's spouse.

Ideally, the present value of the total lifetime benefits for a person with an average life expectancy would be the same whether the beneficiary takes a smaller benefit at age 62 or a larger benefit at 70, as the calculations are actuarially based. However, that is not the case. Decisions that are made by a worker can greatly impact both the present value of benefits and total lifetime benefits collected. In fact, even if a retiree's life span is cut short, delaying retirement benefits past age 62 may make sense.

As discussed earlier in the chapter, delaying retirement benefits increases the annual benefit when it is received. However, delaying commencement of receipt of retirement benefits should not be confused with a cost-of-living adjustment (COLA). Cost-of-living adjustments have averaged less than two percent over the last ten years, but once retirement benefits are being paid to a retiree, those benefits only increase based on the COLA. Nonetheless, by delaying benefits from age 62 to 63, the yet-to-be-received benefit increases approximately seven percent for that one year. Delaying benefits for anyone born in or after 1943 beyond full retirement age increases benefits by eight percent per year. That return is large for what is considered to be a very secure investment. Once the Social Security benefit is adjusted for inflation through application of the COLA, the rate is even more attractive.

≔ *Key Concepts*

1. How are retirement benefits impacted by cost-of-living adjustments and by delayed credits?

2. What strategies can be used to potentially increase total lifetime benefits under Social Security?

3. How can a divorced spouse born before January 2, 1954 use "file and suspend?"

Is the eight percent increase worth delaying the start of benefits? That question is more complicated than it appears. Some of the important factors in this question are based on an individual's thoughts regarding wealth, cash flow needs, life expectancy, perception of the solvency of the Social Security program, as well as others.

An easy way to estimate a breakeven point for delayed benefits is to consider the benefit that is given up compared to the increase in future benefits. For example, assume a benefit of $1,000 per month or $12,000 per year at full retirement age. If the worker delayed benefits by one year, the benefits would increase by eight percent to $12,960 (without regard to a COLA). Therefore, the benefits that are received are $960 higher, but $12,000 had to be forfeited. Dividing what was given up ($12,000) by the increase ($960) results in a simple breakeven of 12.5 years. This calculation is very simplistic and does not consider the time value of money or other implications, such as taxation of benefits. However, it does provide basic guidance about how long one needs to live to justify giving up current benefits for higher future benefits.

The simplified breakeven analysis can be modified to include a COLA and a discount rate. As the spread between the COLA and the discount rate increases, so does the time it takes for the present value of the delayed benefits to exceed the present value of the benefits commencing immediately. For example, using a discount rate of four percent and a COLA of two percent (a spread of two percent) increases the breakeven point from 12.5 years to approximately 14 years. Thus, for someone to delay benefits until age 70 based solely on payback or breakeven, the person would have to live to at least age 82½, without considering the time value of money. However, there are other reasons that delaying benefits may be beneficial to the worker or their family members.

For non-married, lower wage earners who will not qualify for the maximum retirement benefit, it is important to keep in mind that the retirement benefit formula is based on the highest 35 years of work. If a non-married worker had historically lower earnings compared to earnings today, that worker might consider working longer to not only allow the automatic increase or growth of delaying the retirement benefit, but to also serve to increase the 35 year base, which is the basis for determining the retirement benefit. Delaying is especially helpful to those who do not work all 35 years, as that situation tends to have a more noticeable effect on the retirement benefit.

There has been much written on the topic of maximizing Social Security benefits over the last ten years. Strategies, such as "file-and-suspend," have been used to increase the total dollars that retirees would be receive over their lifetime. However, in 2015 Congress chose to eliminate the benefits of this strategy as they were seen by some as taking advantage of the system. In fairness, the file-and-suspend strategy did provide greater benefits to many seniors. However, the Bipartisan Budget Act (BBA) of 2015 eliminated file and suspend after April 29, 2016.

Married individuals are entitled (1) to a worker-determined retirement benefit based on their own earnings and/or (2) to a spousal benefit equal to one half of their spouse's benefit claimed at normal retirement age. If a married individual files a claim prior to attaining normal retirement age, the laws governing Social Security deem the individual as claiming both types of benefits and the benefits will be permanently reduced.

Example 11.33

Stacy Lynn qualifies for a retirement benefit of $250 and a spouse's benefit of $400. At her full retirement age, she will receive her own $250 retirement benefit, and $150 from her spouse's benefit, for a total of $400. If she takes her retirement benefit before her full retirement age, both amounts will be reduced.

Surviving spouses are entitled to 100 percent of the deceased worker's benefit amount after the worker dies. If the spouse with the higher benefits delays benefits until age 70 and then dies, it will increase the surviving spouse's benefit. This approach was one element of the file-and-suspend strategy. However, it does not appear that the new legislation impacts how this works.

Divorced spouses can also claim benefits based on their ex-spouse's record if they were married ten years or longer. Generally, the divorced spouse can collect based on their ex-spouse's record as long as they are unmarried, they are age 62 or older, and the ex-spouse is entitled to Social Security retirement or disability benefits. If a divorced spouse who was born before Jan. 2, 1954 has reached full retirement age and is eligible for a spouse's benefit, then he or she can choose to receive only the divorced spouse's benefits and delay receiving their own retirement benefits until a later date. If retirement benefits are delayed, a higher benefit may be received at a later date based on the effect of delayed retirement credits. Thus, in effect, the spouse is able to receive a benefit from the ex-spouse's working history and let their own benefit increase until age 70. Divorced spouses born January 2, 1954 or later no longer have the option to file for a divorced spouse's benefit and suspend their own. If these spouses file for one benefit, they are effectively filing for all of the benefits for which they are entitled.

Example 11.34

Joanie and Chachi were happily married and raised four wonderful children, who went on to become contributing members of society: a butcher, a baker, a dancer, and a home maker. However, once the children left the home, Joanie and Chachi grew apart and finally divorced after 25 years of marriage. They both were professionals early in their career and became college professors. As a result, their retirement benefits are comparable. While Chachi has remarried, Joanie remains single. If Joanie was born before January 2, 1954, at full retirement age, Joanie could claim a spouse's benefit and let her retirement benefits increase until she turns age 70.

Deciding when to begin taking Social Security benefits should be planned as it can greatly impact the total benefits received over the life of a a worker and the worker's spouse. The planning should take into consideration the health and longevity of the spouses, as well as the need for income now and into the future.

MEDICARE BENEFITS

Medicare is a federal health insurance plan for people who are 65 and older, whether retired or still working. People who are disabled or have permanent kidney failure are entitled to Medicare at any age. The Health Care Financing Administration, now known as Centers for Medicare and Medicaid Services (or CMS), part of the United States Department of Health and Human Services, administers Medicare. Medicare is the nation's largest health insurance program, covering over 59 million individuals. There are two parts to original (traditional) Medicare: Hospital Insurance (Part A) and Medical Insurance (Part B). In addition, prescription drug coverage can be added by purchasing Part D. As an alternative to traditional Medicare, an individual who is eligible for Medicare may select Medicare Advantage (Part C), with or without prescription drug coverage.

Key Concepts

1. What benefits are provided by Medicare?

2. What benefits are provided by Supplemental Security Income?

3. Explain the major decisions that must be made when an individual becomes eligible for Medicare.

4. How does marriage or divorce affect Social Security benefits?

5. What are the various enrollment periods for Medicare?

Exhibit 11.17 | Social Security Benefits at Different Ages

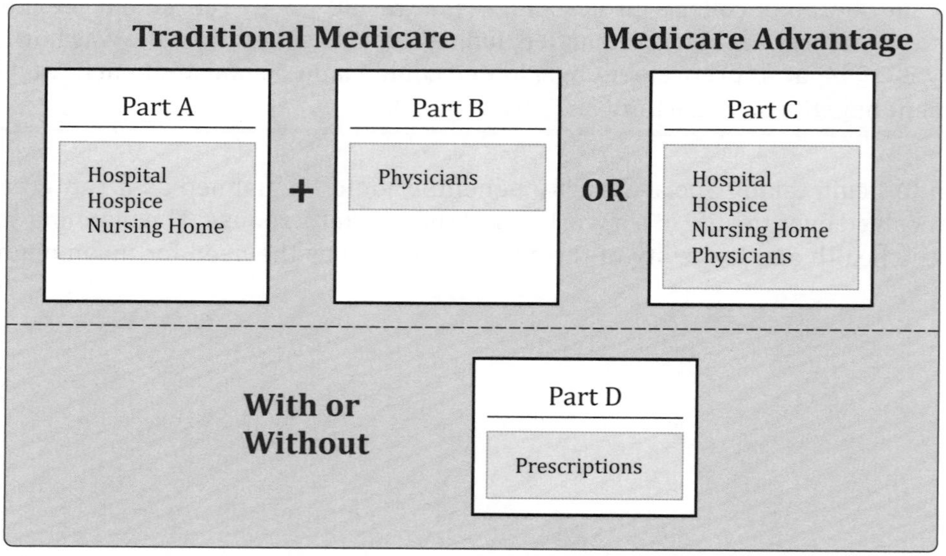

Individuals who are age 65 and over and receive Social Security benefits automatically qualify for Medicare. Also, individuals who have received Social Security disability benefits for at least two years automatically qualify for Medicare. Spouses age 65 or over who are eligible for Social Security benefits based on their spouse's earnings also qualify. All other individuals must file an application for Medicare.

Those who are age 65 or over and not eligible for Social Security Benefits are permitted to enroll in Medicare by paying a fee for Part A along with the Part B premiums discussed below.[5]

Exhibit 11.18 | Medicare Parts

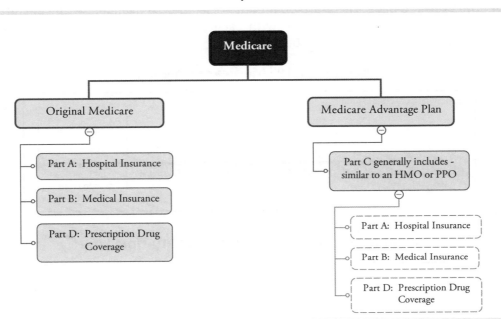

TRADITIONAL MEDICARE

The original Medicare Plan (traditional Medicare, Part A and Part B) is the way most individuals obtain their Medicare benefits. This structure is the traditional payment-per-service arrangement where the individual insured may go to any doctor, specialist, or hospital that accepts Medicare, and Medicare pays its share after approved services are rendered. Medicare Administrative Contractors (MACs) are private insurance organizations that handle claims under the original Medicare Plan. The Social Security Administration does not handle claims for Medicare payments.

Medicare Part A

Part A, Hospital Insurance, is paid for by a portion of the FICA tax (as discussed previously in this chapter). Part A helps pay for necessary medical care furnished by Medicare-certified providers, including inpatient hospital care, skilled nursing care, home health care, hospice care, and other care. The number of days that Medicare covers care in hospitals and skilled nursing facilities is measured in what is termed **benefit periods.** A benefit period begins on the first day a patient receives services in a hospital or skilled nursing facility and ends after 60 consecutive days without further skilled care. There is no limit to the number of benefit periods a beneficiary may have.

---

5. About 99% of Medicare beneficiaries will not pay a premium for Part A because either they or their spouse had 40 quarters of Medicare-covered employment. https://www.cms.gov/newsroom/fact-sheets/2020-medicare-parts-b-premiums-and-deductibles

Benefit periods are identified because deductibles, coinsurance, and premiums relate to a benefit period instead of a calendar year. For instance, coverage under Medicare Part A for 2020 requires a deductible of $1,408 per benefit period. For the 61st through the 90th day of each benefit period, the insured individual must pay $352 per day in the form of coinsurance. Any days over 90 in a benefit period are considered lifetime reserve days. There are 60 lifetime reserve days available with coinsurance of $704 per day. Lifetime reserve days do not renew with each benefit period. It is important, therefore, to determine the number of days used in each benefit period.

Exhibit 11.19 | Medicare Time Line

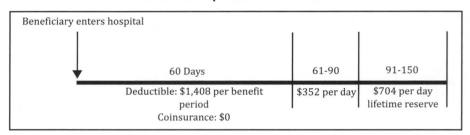

Exhibit 11.20 | Skilled Nursing Facility Time Line

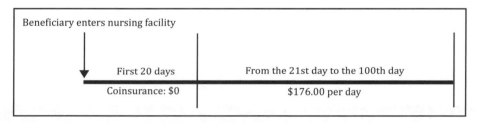

Exhibit 11.21 | Medicare Deductible, Coinsurance, and Premium Amounts (2020)

Hospital Insurance (Part A)
• **Deductible** - $1,408 per benefit period
• **Coinsurance**
• $352 a day for the 61st through the 90th day
• $704 a day for the 91st through the 150th day for each lifetime reserve day (total of 60 lifetime reserve days – nonrenewable)
• **Skilled Nursing Facility Coinsurance** - $176.00 a day for the 21st through the 100th day per Benefit Period
• **Hospital Insurance Premium** - $458 per month (Note: This premium is paid only by individuals who are not otherwise eligible for premium-free hospital insurance and have less than 30 quarters of Medicare covered employment.)
Medical Insurance (Part B)
• **Deductible** - $198 per year
• **Standard Monthly Premium** - $144.60 for new enrollees in 2020. The premium may be higher if income exceeds certain limits.

Source: medicare.gov/pubs/pdf/11579-medicare-costs.pdf

Medicare Part A helps pay for up to 90 days of inpatient hospital care during each benefit period. Covered services for inpatient hospital care include: semiprivate room and meals, operating and recovery room costs, intensive care, drugs, laboratory tests, x-rays, general nursing services, and any other necessary medical services and supplies. Convenience items such as television and telephones provided by hospitals in private rooms (unless medically necessary) are generally not covered. Medicare does not pay for custodial services for daily living activities such as eating, bathing, and getting dressed. Medicare does, however, pay for skilled nursing facility care for rehabilitation, such as recovery time after a hospital discharge. Part A may help pay for up to 100 days in a participating skilled nursing facility in each benefit period. Medicare pays all approved charges for the first 20 days relating to skilled nursing facility care, and the patient pays a coinsurance amount for days 21 through 100. Medicare may also pay the full, approved cost of covered home healthcare services, which includes part-time or intermittent skilled nursing services prescribed by a physician for treatment or rehabilitation of home-bound patients. Normally, the only cost to the insured for home health care is a 20 percent coinsurance charge for medical equipment, such as wheelchairs and walkers.

Medicare Part B

Medicare Part B, Medical Insurance, is optional and is subject to a monthly premium. Part B is financed by the monthly premiums paid by those who are enrolled and out of the general revenues from the U.S. Treasury. Medicare Part B is used to pay for doctors' services; ambulance transportation; diagnostic tests; outpatient therapy services; outpatient hospital services, including emergency room visits; X-rays and laboratory services; some preventative care; home healthcare services not covered by Part A; durable medical equipment and supplies; and a variety of other health services.

Medicare Part B pays for 80 percent of approved charges for most covered services. For those who are already receiving Social Security benefits at the time of enrollment in Medicare, the Part B premium will automatically be deducted from their Social Security benefits. Those not yet receiving Social Security benefits at the time of enrollment can choose to receive a bill from Medicare or can arrange for the premiums to be automatically deducted from a checking or savings account each month. The standard Part B premium amount is $144.60 (or higher depending on your income). The income-related monthly adjustment amount (IRMAA), as illustrated in **Exhibit 11.22 | Medicare Part B Premiums (2020)**, is based on adjusted gross income from two years prior (a two-year look-back). If a Medicare enrollee's income has gone down for any of the following reasons, he or she may appeal the increase in premiums:
- marriage, divorce, or becoming widowed,
- reduction in work hours,
- loss of income-producing property due to disaster or other events beyond the insured's control,
- cessation or termination of an employer's pension plan, or
- settlement from an employer due to the employer's closure, bankruptcy, or reorganization.

The deductible for Part B is $198 per year. The insured is responsible for paying a $198 deductible per calendar year and the remaining 20 percent of the Medicare-approved charges. Medicare Part B usually does not cover charges for prescription drugs, routine physical examinations (it does cover a one-time "Welcome to Medicare" wellness visit and one yearly wellness visit), or services unrelated to treatment of injury or illness. Dental care, dentures, cosmetic surgery, hearing aids, and eye examinations are not covered by Part B.

Exhibit 11.22 | Medicare Part B Premiums (2020)

Premium	Filing Status: Single	Filing Status: MFJ
$144.60	$87,000 or less	$174,000 or less
$202.40	$87,001-$109,000	$174,001-$218,000
$289.20	$109,001-$136,000	$218,001-$272,000
$376.00	136,001-$163,000	$272,001-$326,000
$462.70	$163,001-$500,000	$326,001-$750,000
$491.60	Above $500,000	Above $750,000

Medicare Exclusions

Many retirees will be more interested in what is not covered than what is covered, since they will need a plan to fill in any gaps. Part A does not cover hospital stays beyond 90 days unless lifetime reserve days remain available. Part A also excludes services provided outside the U.S., its territories, and its possessions. It also covers only up to 100 days of skilled nursing care, and only following at least three days of hospitalization. Part A does not cover custodial care.

Medicare Part B excludes prescription drugs not administered by a doctor. It does not cover services provided outside the U.S., its territories, and its possessions. Part B does not cover routine physical exams (except as required by the Affordable Care Act), routine eye exams, dental care, hearing aids, or eyeglasses. It also excludes luxury elective services, custodial care, elective cosmetic surgery, services covered by workers' compensation, and services provided free in a federal facility. Part A and Part B both exclude coverage for the first three pints of blood when a blood transfusion is needed. There is no annual maximum-out-of-pocket limit for original Medicare Parts A and B.

Many private insurance companies sell Medicare supplemental insurance policies, referred to as Medigap policies. These supplemental policies help bridge the coverage gaps in the original Medicare Plan. As outlined in Chapter 3, these supplemental policies can help pay Medicare's coinsurance amounts, as well as other out-of-pocket expenses for health care.

When a worker is first enrolled in Part B at age 65, there is a six-month open enrollment period in Medigap. Enrolling during this time is highly recommended since, during the time of open enrollment, the health status of the applicant cannot be used as a reason to refuse a Medigap policy or to charge more than other open enrollment applicants. If enrollment occurs outside of the initial six-month open enrollment period, the insurer may require a six-month waiting period for coverage of pre-existing conditions and in some cases may deny coverage. The waiting period for pre-existing conditions can be reduced or eliminated if the insured had prior creditable coverage. Each month of prior coverage reduces the waiting period for coverage of preexisting conditions by one month, so if prior coverage lasted at least six months, there will be no wait. However, there cannot be a break in coverage for more than 63 days. If, however, the open enrollment period has expired, the applicant may be denied a policy based on health status or may be charged higher rates.

Medicare Part D Subsidy

Medicare prescription drug plans, known as the Medicare Part D Subsidy (Part D or Medicare Prescription Drug Plan), became available beginning January 1, 2006, to individuals with Medicare. Part D is intended to save participants money on prescription drug costs and help protect against higher drug costs in the future. Insurance companies and other private companies work with Medicare to offer these drug plans by negotiating discounts on drug prices. Both those who enroll in traditional Medicare and those who choose Medicare Advantage have the option to also enroll in Part D.

Medicare prescription drug plans provide insurance coverage for prescription drugs. Part D covers both brand-name and generic prescription drugs at certain pharmacies in a Part D participant's area. If an individual is enrolled in Medicare, then that individual is eligible under Part D regardless of income, assets, health status, or current prescription expenses. Like other insurance, if an individual joins, they pay a monthly premium and pay a share of the cost of their prescriptions. As with Part B, higher income taxpayers will pay higher premiums. In addition, the premiums increase for delayed enrollment into the program by a factor of the "national base beneficiary premium" times the number of full, uncovered months that a senior was eligible but did not join a Medicare drug plan and went without other creditable prescription drug coverage. This premium increase (penalty) will continue to apply for as long as the Medicare drug plan is maintained.

Example 11.35

Mrs. Jones did not join Part D when she was first eligible - by May 15, 2015. She joined a Medicare drug plan with an effective date of January 1, 2020. Since Mrs. Jones did not join when she was first eligible and went without other creditable drug coverage for 55 months (June 2015 to December 2019), she will be charged a monthly penalty of $19.25 in 2020 ($35 x 0.01 = $0.35 x 55 = $19.25) in addition to her plan's monthly premium.[6]

Individuals may enroll in Part D during their Initial Enrollment Period (described below) without any penalty. If Medicare was available due to a disability, the applicant can join from three months before to three months after the 25th month of cash disability payments. There are two ways to obtain Medicare prescription drug coverage. The individual can either join a Medicare prescription drug plan or join a Medicare Advantage Plan or other Medicare Health Plan that offers drug coverage. Whichever plan is chosen, Medicare drug coverage helps the participant by covering brand name and generic drugs at pharmacies.

Drug plans may vary as to what prescription drugs are covered, how much the individual must pay, and which pharmacies they can use. All drug plans will have to provide at least a standard level of coverage, which Medicare will set. The premium, deductible, co-payment/co-insurance, and coverage may vary

6. The "national base beneficiary premium" of $35 is assumed for this example. The 2020 premium is actually $32.74.

from plan to plan. However, some plans might offer more coverage and additional drugs for a higher monthly premium. When an individual joins a drug plan, it is important for them to choose one that meets their prescription drug needs. A list of drugs that a Medicare drug plan covers is called a formulary, which includes generic drugs and brand name drugs. Most prescription drugs used by those with Medicare will be on the given plan formulary, whether it is in brand name or generic form. To insure coverage of an appropriate amount of drugs, a formulary must include at least two drugs in each of the categories and classes of most commonly prescribed drugs. This helps to insure that people with varying medical conditions can get the medication or treatment they need. While a specific drug may not be included, a similar drug should be available. To assist with shopping for plans under Part D, insurance plans offering Part D coverage will typically have a "Drug Calculator" available on their website on which an individual's regular prescriptions may be entered and a cost estimate will be provided. Medicare also provides assistance selecting a plan on their "Find a Medicare Plan" website.[7]

If the insured's needs change, they can change their Part D prescription drug plan each year during the open enrollment period (October 15 - December 7), with new coverage beginning January 1. Since prescription drug plans are based on service areas, a three (or four in some cases) month special enrollment period to change plans is available if the Medicare beneficiary moves.

Even individuals who do not use prescription drugs should consider joining Part D during the initial enrollment period because aging people typically need prescription drugs to stay healthy. For a relatively low premium, Medicare prescription drug coverage can protect the individual from unexpected drug expenses in the future. Enrolling during the initial enrollment period avoids the late enrollment premium penalty, saving potentially thousands of dollars through the duration of the retirement years.

Part D consists of four phases of coverage: the deductible, the copayment/coinsurance phase, the coverage gap, and the catastrophic phase:
1. **Deductible:** The deductible must be satisfied prior to any benefits being provided from the plan. Deductibles can vary between drugs plans, with some plans having no deductible, but the deductible cannot exceed $435 in 2020.
2. **Copayment/Coinsurance:** In the copayment/coinsurance phase, beneficiaries pay a portion of the expenses until the insured and the plan together have paid $4,020 in 2020.
3. **Coverage Gap:** The next phase is the coverage gap, often referred to as "donut hole," because in this phase beneficiaries historically paid all or most of the costs of prescription drugs. The Affordable Care Act has been gradually reducing the size of the donut hole. Within the coverage gap phase for 2020, the Medicare recipient will pay up to 25 percent of the cost of brand name prescription drugs while the manufacturer (via a discount) pays 70 percent and the plan pays five percent of the cost. This phase lasts until the total out-of-pocket costs, including the costs paid by the insured and by the manufacturer for brand name drugs, reach $4,020 in 2020 (for generic drugs, only the costs paid by the insured count as out-of-pocket expenses).
4. **Catastrophic Phase:** The catastrophic phase covers all but a small coinsurance amount for the remainder of the year up to a maximum out-of-pocket cost of $6,350.

---

7. https://www.medicare.gov/plan-compare/#/?lang=en.

Exhibit 11.23 | Four Phases of Coverage Under Part D

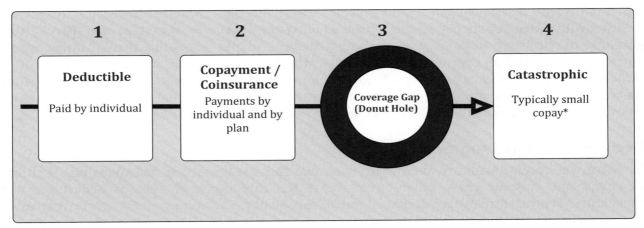

*In 2017, approximately 8% of Part D enrollees reached the catastrophic phase. Those without low-income subsidies spent an average of $3,214 out-of-pocket on prescriptions. Among the top 10 conditions treated for those who reached the catastrophic phase are cancer, hepatitis, and intellectual disabilities.
https://www.kff.org/medicare/issue-brief/how-many-medicare-part-d-enrollees-had-high-out-of-pocket-drug-costs-in-2017/

MEDICARE PART C - MEDICARE ADVANTAGE

Medicare Advantage, Part C, is an option whereby those eligible for the traditional Medicare program can instead elect coverage under Medicare managed care plans such as Health Maintenance Organizations (HMOs), HMOs with a point of service option, Provider Sponsored Organizations (PSOs), and Preferred Provider Organizations (PPOs). These plans provide at least the same benefits as Medicare Parts A and B, and may also include additional benefits for an additional premium charge.

Over the past decade, the percentage of Medicare enrollees choosing Medicare Advantage Plans has nearly doubled, from 16 percent to over 30 percent. One feature that makes Medicare Advantage Plans attractive for retirees who are concerned about the rising cost of health care is that they may have an annual maximum-out-of-pocket amount. Although the maximum amount may increase each year, it eliminates a large portion of the unknown potential costs of medical care for retirees. The Medicare Advantage plans tend to have lower premiums than Medigap policies, and may offer additional benefits, such as dental and vision.

A Medicare Advantage plan eliminates the need for Medigap coverage, therefore, those who enroll in Medicare Part C are not permitted to purchase a Medigap policy. Those enrolling in a Medicare Advantage Plan will still pay the Part B premium, along with a premium for the Part C coverage, which will vary based on the deductibles, coinsurance, co-pay, and maximum out-of-pocket limits of the plan chosen.[8] Medicare Advantage Plans may be limited to only doctors who are in the network, or may allow the covered individual to see doctors outside of the network as well, but with a higher out-of-pocket cost. Medicare Advantage Plans are required to offer at least the same benefits as original Medicare Parts A and B (they will never have less coverage than Parts A and B), although most plans offer greater

---

8. Some Medicare Advantage plans have a $0 premium.

coverage and may also include prescription drug coverage. An additional monthly premium may be charged if Part D prescription drug coverage is included.

One of the biggest decisions upon reaching Medicare eligibility age is whether to enroll in traditional Medicare with a Medigap supplement or to instead purchase a Medicare Advantage plan (Part C). One advantage to selecting traditional Medicare with a Medigap supplement is that there is little ongoing monitoring required since coverages are regulated by the government. Medicare Advantage plans often include additional services beyond what is covered under Parts A and B, but these additional services can be amended by the sponsoring insurance company each year, so an annual review will be necessary to ensure that the plan is still suitable for meeting the Medicare beneficiary's needs.

Medicare Savings Programs

For those who receive Medicare and have low income and few resources, states may pay Medicare premiums and, in some cases, other out-of-pocket Medicare expenses, such as deductibles and coinsurance. The respective state decides if individuals qualify. For more general information about Medicare, Centers for Medicare and Medicare Services' *Medicare & You* Handbook is helpful, as are the websites *www.ssa.gov* and *www.medicare.gov*.

ENROLLING IN MEDICARE

Those receiving Social Security benefits prior to age 65 are automatically enrolled in Medicare Parts A and B at age 65 and will receive a Medicare insurance card in the mail three months before turning age 65. Those not yet receiving Social Security benefits at age 65 will need to enroll for Medicare during the Initial Enrollment Period (IEP) beginning three months before the month of the 65th birthday and ending three months after the month of the 65th birthday (seven months total). Enrollment can be done at www.ssa.gov, by calling the Social Security administration, or visiting the local Social Security office. It is usually best to enroll in the three months prior to the month of the 65th birthday so that coverage will begin on the first day of the month of the 65th birthday (unless the birthday is on the first of the month, then benefits begin the first day of the prior month). For example, if an individual's birthday is on August 15th, coverage will begin August 1st, but if the individual's birthday is August 1st, coverage will begin July 1st. If enrollment is done in the month the client turns age 65 or in the three months following, coverage will be delayed for one to three months after enrollment.

When an individual applies for Part A, they are automatically enrolled in Part B as well unless they opt out of it. Anyone who does not apply for Part B when he or she is initially eligible can apply later, during general enrollment periods, which are the first three months of each year. A person who delays enrollment, however, will pay premiums, increased by 10 percent for each 12-month period that the person was eligible and did not enroll. A person who has continuous group coverage from age 65 until retirement can enroll up to eight months after termination of employment and not be subject to premium increases. The eight month Special Enrollment Period (SEP) applies from the earlier of (1) the month after the employment ends or (2) the month after group health insurance based on current employment ends, regardless of whether COBRA is elected (as discussed in Chapter 3).[9]

---

9. Consolidated Omnibus Budget Reconciliation Act of 1985 (COBRA).

An individual who has group health coverage through an employer or union, may choose to wait to take the action of enrolling in Part B of Medicare and purchasing a Medigap policy. This delay makes sense when the employer plan provides similar coverage. When the employer coverage ends, the individual will have the opportunity to enroll in Part B without a late enrollment penalty during the 8-month Special Enrollment Period (SEP), and the Medigap open enrollment period will begin at that time as well.

Medicare beneficiaries can switch from original Medicare Parts A and B to Medicare Advantage, or switch from Medicare Advantage with a prescription drug plan to Medicare Advantage without a prescription drug plan (or vice versa) during Medicare open enrollment periods each year, which run from October 15th through December 7th. In addition, beneficiaries can switch between Medicare Advantage Plans, or switch from Medicare Advantage to original Medicare (but cannot switch from original Medicare to Medicare Advantage) during the Medicare Advantage Open Enrollment Period (MA OEP), which runs from January 1 - March 31 each year. It is important to note that those who originally selected Medicare Advantage and choose to change to traditional Medicare will be required to go through medical underwriting to obtain Medigap coverage as a supplement to traditional Medicare (Parts A and B).

Exhibit 11.24 | Medicare Enrollment Periods

Enrollment Period	Time Frame	Noteworthy
Initial Enrollment Period (IEP)	Three months before your 65th birthday, the month of your 65th birthday, and three months after your 65th birthday (total seven months)	Two important decisions: 1. Choose between Traditional Medicare or Medicare Advantage. 2. Select your Part D Prescription Drug Plan. *Note*: If you enrolled in Medicare Advantage during your IEP, you can change to another Medicare Advantage Plan or to original Medicare in the first three months you have Medicare
Medigap Open Enrollment Period	Starts the first day of the month in which you are both age 65 or older and enrolled in Medicare Part B, and lasts for six months	No medical underwriting is required during this time, so don't delay.
Part B Special Enrollment Period (SEP)	Starts the earlier of: 1. termination of employment, or 2. termination of group coverage, and lasts for eight months	Requires continuous group coverage from age 65 to retirement or loss of group coverage. The eight months starts at termination of employment or termination of group coverage even if COBRA is elected.
Medicare Advantage and Part D Special Enrollment Period (SEP)	• If you tell the plan before you move, the SEP begins the month before the month you move and lasts for two full months after you move • If you tell the plan after you move, your SEP begins in the month you move and lasts for two full months after you move	These plans are based on service areas, so if you move you probably need to change your Medicare Advantage Plan and/or Part D prescription drug plan.
Medicare Open Enrollment Period (OEP)	October 15 - December 7 (coverage change effective January 1)	During this time you can: • enroll in or change Part D plans • change from original Medicare to Medicare Advantage • change from a Medicare Advantage plan that does not offer prescription drug coverage to one that does (or vice versa)
Medicare Advantage Open Enrollment Period (MA OEP)	January 1 - March 31	During this time, if you have a Medicare Advantage Plan, you can: • change to another Medicare Advantage plan • change from Medicare Advantage to original Medicare
Medicare General Enrollment Period (GEP)	January 1 - March 31	Allows you to enroll if you did not sign up when you were first eligible and you do not qualify for a SEP. Premiums will be higher due to late enrollment. Coverage begins July 1.

SUPPLEMENTAL SECURITY INCOME BENEFITS

Supplemental Security Income (SSI) makes monthly payments to individuals with low incomes and few assets. In order to obtain SSI benefits, an individual must be age 65 or older, disabled, or blind. The definition of disability is satisfied when the individual is unable to engage in any substantial gainful activity due to a physical or mental problem expected to last at least a year or expected to result in death. Children as well as adults qualify for SSI disability payments. As its name implies, Supplemental Security Income supplements the beneficiary's income up to various levels depending on where the beneficiary lives. If an otherwise eligible SSI applicant lives in another's household and receives support from that person, the federal SSI benefit is reduced by one-third.

The federal government pays a basic rate. The basic monthly SSI benefit for 2020 is $783 per month for one person and $1,175 per month for married couples. Some states supply additional funds to qualified individuals. To ascertain the SSI benefit rates in a certain state, the advisor or client can contact a local Social Security office in that state or visit the Social Security Administration's website. Generally, individuals who receive SSI benefits also qualify for Medicaid, food stamps, and other government assistance.

To be eligible for the monthly SSI benefit, the beneficiary must not have assets that exceed $2,000 for one person or $3,000 for married couples. This asset determination does not include the value of the home and some personal belongings, such as one car. If the potential beneficiary does not work, he may be eligible for SSI benefits if monthly income is less than $783 for one person and $1,175 for a couple. If the potential beneficiary works, more monthly income is allowed. SSI benefits are not paid from Social Security trust funds and are not based on past earnings of the beneficiary. Rather, SSI benefits are financed by general tax revenues and assure a minimum monthly income for needy elderly, disabled, or blind persons.

FILING FOR SOCIAL SECURITY CLAIMS

The Social Security Administration reports that many people fail to file claims with the Social Security Administration or fail to do so in a timely fashion. Individuals should file for Social Security or SSI disability benefits as soon they become too disabled to work or for survivors' benefits, when a family breadwinner dies. Social Security benefits do not start automatically. Social Security will not begin payment of benefits until the beneficiary files an application. When filing for benefits, applicants must submit documents that show eligibility, such as a birth certificate for each family member applying for benefits, a marriage certificate if a spouse is applying, and the most recent W-2 forms or tax returns.

To file for benefits, obtain information, or to speak to a Social Security representative, individuals must call the Social Security Administration's toll-free number, 800-772-1213, or visit the Social Security Administration's website. The toll-free number can be used to schedule an appointment at a local Social Security office. The Social Security Administration treats all calls confidentially. Periodically, a second Social Security representative will monitor incoming and outgoing telephone calls to ensure accurate and courteous service.

OTHER ISSUES

Effect of Marriage or Divorce on Benefits

Marriage or divorce may affect one's Social Security benefits, depending on the kind of benefits received. If a worker receives retirement benefits based on his own earnings record, the worker's retirement benefits will continue whether married or divorced. If an individual receives benefits based on his spouse's record, the individual's benefits will cease upon divorce unless the individual is age 62 or older and was married longer than 10 years. Widows and widowers, whether divorced or not, will continue to receive survivors' benefits upon remarriage if the widow or widower is age 60 or older. Disabled widows and widowers, whether divorced or not, will continue to receive survivors' benefits upon remarriage if the disabled widow or widower is age 50 or older.

Example 11.36

Linus was married at the following ages and to the following wives. Linus is now 62 and married to Sally.

	Wife	Current Age	Larry's Age at Marriage	Current Marital Status	Length of Marriage
1	Marcie	62	20	Single	10 years, 1 month
2	Lucy	63	31	Single	10 years, 1 month
3	Patty	64	42	Single	9 years
4	Sally	65	53	Married	9 years

Who, among the wives, may be eligible to receive Social Security retirement benefits based upon Linus's earnings if Linus is retired or not retired?

Any divorced spouse, age 62 and married to Linus for 10 years or longer is eligible to receive benefits. If Linus is retired, then his current wife is also eligible to receive benefits. However, she cannot collect benefits if he is not retired.

If Linus is retired: Marcie, Lucy, and Sally.

If Linus is not retired: Marcie and Lucy.

For all other forms of Social Security benefits, benefits will cease upon remarriage, except in special circumstances. When a person marries, it is presumed that at least one person in the marriage can provide adequate support. Likewise, Social Security benefits may recommence based on the previous spouse's benefits if the marriage ends.

Change of Name

If an individual changes their name due to marriage, divorce, or a court order, that individual must notify the Social Security Administration of the name change so the Social Security Administration will be able to show the new name in their records and properly credit that individual for earnings. This notice will ensure that the individual's work history will be accurately recorded and maintained.

Projected Benefit Statements

The Social Security Administration currently mails projected benefit statements only to those age 60 and older who are not yet receiving benefits and have not set up an online account at SSA.gov. Any individual covered under the Social Security system has the ability to establish an online account in which an individualized statement of projected benefits based on the worker's reported earnings can be viewed.[10] A detailed interactive calculator in which various parameters impacting benefits may be adjusted is also available.[11] A sample Social Security Statement is presented in **Exhibit 11.25 | Sample Social Security Statement**.

Leaving the United States[12]

Beneficiaries who are United States citizens may travel or live in most foreign countries without affecting their eligibility for Social Security benefits. However, there are a few countries where Social Security checks cannot be sent. These countries currently include:

- Cuba
- North Korea

Also, beneficiaries that go to any of the following countries can receive Social Security benefits only if they meet and agree to certain restricted conditions. These countries are:

- Azerbaijan
- Belarus
- Kazakhstan
- Kyrgyzstan
- Moldova
- Tajikistan
- Turkmenistan
- Ukraine
- Uzbekistan

> ### ☑ Quick Quiz 11.7
>
> 1. In order to obtain Supplemental Social Security benefits, the individual must be 62, disabled, or blind.
>   a. True
>   b. False
>
> 2. Social Security beneficiaries who are United States citizens may live in most foreign countries without affecting their eligibility for Social Security benefits.
>   a. True
>   b. False
>
> False, True.

Beneficiaries should inform the Social Security Administration of their plans to go outside the United States for a trip that lasts 30 days or more. By providing the name of the country or countries to be visited and the expected departure and return dates, the Social Security Administration will send special reporting instructions to the beneficiaries and arrange for the delivery of their checks while they are abroad.

---

10. https://www.ssa.gov/myaccount
11. https://www.ssa.gov/oact/anypia/anypia.html
12. ssa.gov (Program Operations Manual (POMS) Effective 2/06/17).

Windfall Elimination Provision (WEP) and Government Pension Offset (GPO) Provision

The Windfall Elimination Provision (WEP) of Social Security applies to those who earned a pension in a job where no Social Security taxes were paid (such as those under the Civil Service Retirement System and some state and local government employees), but who also worked in other jobs long enough to qualify for Social Security retirement or disability benefits. Because Social Security is structured to provide a higher replacement ratio for low-income earners than it does for high-income earners, those who have low earnings from employment for which Social Security taxes are paid, but have a large pension from earnings for which no Social Security taxes are paid, would receive a "windfall" benefit from Social Security (a higher replacement ratio than they would receive if benefits were based on all earnings).

To prevent these workers from receiving a higher than usual replacement ratio from Social Security, the benefit calculation formula is altered to reduce the amount of Social Security benefits paid. The WEP calculation will result in a lower PIA for the worker; therefore, it will also reduce benefits to others who may be eligible to collect based on that worker's PIA as well. However, the reduction in Social Security benefits for the worker will not be more than ½ of the pension that is based on earnings for which no Social Security taxes were paid.

The Windfall Elimination Provision does not apply to federal workers first hired after 1983, or to those with a pension based only on railroad employment. In addition, those who paid Social Security taxes on at least 30 years of substantial earnings ($25,575 in 2020) will have no reduction.

While the Windfall Elimination Provision does not apply to survivor benefits, these benefits may be reduced under the Government Pension Offset Provision (GPO). This provision also affects spousal benefits for retirement and disability. Under the GPO provision, Social Security benefits are reduced by 2/3 of the government pension amount received by the spouse, widow, or widower who earned the government pension. This rule is to ensure that spousal benefits for those working for government employers where earnings are not subject to Social Security get treated in a similar manner to those who have earnings that are subject to Social Security. Government employees who pay Social Security taxes on their government earnings are not subject to the GPO provision.

Example 11.37

August Moone worked for the federal government and has Civil Service Retirement benefits of $800 per month. Since August did not pay into the Social Security system for her earnings from the federal government, she has $0 of Social Security benefits based on her own work record. August's husband, Ron, has worked and paid into the Social Security system and August is entitled to a spousal benefit of $600 based on Ron's PIA. If there were no offset, August would be entitled to both her $800 per month and the spousal benefit of $600 per month. With the GPO offset, August's spousal benefit under Social Security will be reduced by 2/3 of her civil service pension (2/3 x 800 = $533), so her spousal benefit from Social Security will be $67.

Finally, **Exhibit 11.26 | Social Security Fact Sheet** reflects the 2020 Social Security changes for ease of reference.[13]

Exhibit 11.25 | Sample Social Security Statement

Your payment would be about
$1,986 a month
at full retirement age

WANDA WORKER
456 ANYWHERE AVENUE
MAINTOWN, USA 11111-1111

January 2, 2020

Your Social Security Statement

Are you thinking about retirement? Are you ready for retirement?

We have tools that can help you!

- Estimate your future retirement benefits at *socialsecurity.gov/estimator*
- Apply for retirement, spouse's, Medicare, or disability benefits at *socialsecurity.gov/applyforbenefits*
- And once you receive benefits, manage your benefits at *myaccount.socialsecurity.gov*

Your *Social Security Statement* tells you about **how much you or your family would receive** in disability, survivor, or retirement benefits. It also includes our record of your lifetime earnings. Check out your earnings history, and **let us know right away if you find an error**. This is important because we base your benefits on our record of your lifetime earnings.

Social Security benefits are **not intended to be your only source of income when you retire**. On average, Social Security will replace about

To view your *Social Security Statement* online anytime create a **my Social Security** account today!

**my Social Security
myaccount.socialsecurity.gov**

40 percent of your annual pre-retirement earnings. You will need other savings, investments, pensions, or retirement accounts to live comfortably when you retire.

To see your *Statement* online anytime, create a **my Social Security** account at *myaccount.socialsecurity.gov*.

Social Security Administration

Follow the Social Security Administration at these social media sites.

13.ssa.gov and Social Security National Press Office press release.

Your Estimated Benefits

*Retirement
You have earned enough credits to qualify for benefits. At your current earnings rate, if you continue working until…

your full retirement age (67 years), your payment would be about...$ 1,986 a month

age 70, your payment would be about ....$ 2,468 a month

age 62, your payment would be about ....$ 1,376 a month

*Disability
You have earned enough credits to qualify for benefits. If you became disabled right now, your payment would be about...$ 1,956 a month

*Family
If you get retirement or disability benefits, your spouse and children also may qualify for benefits.

*Survivors
You have earned enough credits for your family to receive survivors benefits. If you die this year, certain members of your family may qualify for the following benefits:

Your child..$ 1,467 a month

Your spouse who is caring for your child...$ 1,467 a month

Your spouse, if benefits start at full retirement age..$ 1,956 a month

Total family benefits cannot be more than ....$ 3,568 a month

Your spouse or minor child may be eligible for a special one-time death benefit of $255.

Medicare
You have enough credits to qualify for Medicare at age 65. Even if you do not retire at age 65, be sure to contact Social Security three months before your 65th birthday to enroll in Medicare.

* **Your estimated benefits are based on current law. Congress has made changes to the law in the past and can do so at any time. The law governing benefit amounts may change because, by 2035, the payroll taxes collected will be enough to pay only about 80 percent of scheduled benefits.**

We based your benefit estimates on these facts:

Your date of birth (please verify your name on page 1 and this date of birth) .... April 5, 1960

Your estimated taxable earnings per year after 2018 .... $50,653

Your Social Security number (only the last four digits are shown to help prevent identity theft)......... XXX-XX-1234

How Your Benefits Are Estimated

To qualify for benefits, you earn "credits" through your work — up to four each year. This year, for example, you earn one credit for each $1,410 of wages or self-employment income. When you've earned $5,640, you've earned your four credits for the year. Most people need 40 credits, earned over their working lifetime, to receive retirement benefits. For disability and survivors benefits, young people need fewer credits to be eligible.

We checked your records to see whether you have earned enough credits to qualify for benefits. If you haven't earned enough yet to qualify for any type of benefit, we can't give you a benefit estimate now. If you continue to work, we'll give you an estimate when you do qualify.

What we assumed — If you have enough work credits, we estimated your benefit amounts using your average earnings over your working lifetime. For 2020 and later (up to retirement age), we assumed you'll continue to work and make about the same as you did in 2018 or 2019. We also included credits we assumed you earned last year and this year.

Generally, the older you are and the closer you are to retirement, the more accurate the retirement estimates will be because they are based on a longer work history with fewer uncertainties such as earnings fluctuations and future law changes. We encourage you to use our online Retirement Estimator at *www.socialsecurity.gov/estimator* to obtain immediate and personalized benefit estimates.

We can't provide your actual benefit amount until you apply for benefits. **And that amount may differ from the estimates stated above because:**

(1) Your earnings may increase or decrease in the future.

(2) After you start receiving benefits, they will be adjusted for cost-of-living increases.

(3) Your estimated benefits are based on current law. **The law governing benefit amounts may change.**

(4) Your benefit amount may be affected by **military service, railroad employment or pensions earned through work on which you did not pay Social Security tax.** Visit *www.socialsecurity.gov* to learn more.

Windfall Elimination Provision (WEP) — In the future, if you receive a pension from employment in which you do not pay Social Security taxes, such as some federal, state or local government work, some nonprofit organizations or foreign employment, and you also qualify for your own Social Security retirement or disability benefit, your Social Security benefit may be reduced, but not eliminated, by WEP. The amount of the reduction, if any, depends on your earnings and number of years in jobs in which you paid Social Security taxes, and the year you are age 62 or become disabled. For more information, please see *Windfall Elimination Provision* (Publication No. 05-10045) at *www.socialsecurity.gov/WEP*.

Government Pension Offset (GPO) — If you receive a pension based on federal, state or local government work in which you did not pay Social Security taxes and you qualify, now or in the future, for Social Security benefits as a current or former spouse, widow or widower, you are likely to be affected by GPO. If GPO applies, your Social Security benefit will be reduced by an amount equal to two-thirds of your government pension, and could be reduced to zero. Even if your benefit is reduced to zero, you will be eligible for Medicare at age 65 on your spouse's record. To learn more, please see *Government Pension Offset* (Publication No. 05-10007) at *www.socialsecurity.gov/GPO*.

Sample Social Security Statement Continued

Your Earnings Record

Years You Worked	Your Taxed Social Security Earnings	Your Taxed Medicare Earnings
1976	226	226
1977	592	592
1978	1,144	1,144
1979	2,116	2,116
1980	3,103	3,103
1981	4,125	4,125
1982	5,272	5,272
1983	6,926	6,926
1984	8,692	8,692
1985	10,210	10,210
1986	11,555	11,555
1987	13,305	13,305
1988	14,916	14,916
1989	16,369	16,369
1990	17,925	17,925
1991	19,300	19,300
1992	20,945	20,945
1993	21,695	21,695
1994	22,816	22,816
1995	24,225	24,225
1996	25,858	25,858
1997	27,806	27,806
1998	29,642	29,642
1999	31,658	31,658
2000	33,767	33,767

Years You Worked	Your Taxed Social Security Earnings	Your Taxed Medicare Earnings
2001	34,915	34,915
2002	35,591	35,591
2003	36,717	36,717
2004	38,686	38,686
2005	40,325	40,325
2006	42,315	42,315
2007	44,346	44,346
2008	45,437	45,437
2009	44,784	44,784
2010	45,847	45,847
2011	47,146	47,146
2012	48,349	48,349
2013	48,606	48,606
2014	49,860	49,860
2015	50,850	50,850
2016	50,158	50,158
2017	50,440	50,440
2018	50,653	50,653
2019	Not yet recorded	

Total Social Security and Medicare taxes paid over your working career through the last year reported on the chart above:

Estimated taxes paid for Social Security:		Estimated taxes paid for Medicare:	
You paid:	$70,698	You paid:	$17,020
Your employers paid:	$72,634	Your employers paid:	$17,020

Note: Currently, you and your employer each pay a 6.2 percent Social Security tax on up to $137,700 of your earnings and a 1.45* percent Medicare tax on all your earnings. If you are self-employed, you pay the combined employee and employer amount, which is a 12.4 percent Social Security tax on up to $137,700 of your net earnings and a 2.9* percent Medicare tax on your entire net earnings.

*If you have earned income of more than $200,000 ($250,000 for married couples filing jointly), you must pay 0.9 percent more in Medicare taxes.

Help Us Keep Your Earnings Record Accurate

You, your employer and Social Security share responsibility for the accuracy of your earnings record. Since you began working, we recorded your reported earnings under your name and Social Security number. We have updated your record each time your employer (or you, if you're self-employed) reported your earnings.

Remember, it's your earnings, not the amount of taxes you paid or the number of credits you've earned, that determine your benefit amount. When we figure that amount, we base it on your average earnings over your lifetime. If our records are wrong, you may not receive all the benefits to which you're entitled.

Review this chart carefully using your own records to make sure our information is correct and that we've recorded each year you worked. You're the only person who can look at the earnings chart and know whether it is complete and correct.

Some or all of your earnings from **last year** may not be shown on your *Statement*. It could be that we still were

processing last year's earnings reports when your *Statement* was prepared. Your complete earnings for last year will be shown on next year's *Statement*. **Note:** If you worked for more than one employer during any year, or if you had both earnings and self-employment income, we combined your earnings for the year.

There's a limit on the amount of earnings on which you pay Social Security taxes each year. The limit increases yearly. Earnings above the limit will not appear on your earnings chart as Social Security earnings. (For Medicare taxes, the maximum earnings amount began rising in 1991. Since 1994, **all** of your earnings are taxed for Medicare.)

Call us right away at **1-800-772-1213** (7 a.m.–7 p.m. your local time) if any earnings for years **before last year** are shown incorrectly. Please have your W-2 or tax return for those years available. (If you live outside the U.S., follow the directions at the bottom of page 4.)

3

Some Facts About Social Security

About Social Security and Medicare...

Social Security pays retirement, disability, family and survivors benefits. Medicare, a separate program run by the Centers for Medicare & Medicaid Services, helps pay for inpatient hospital care, nursing care, doctors' fees, drugs, and other medical services and supplies to people age 65 and older, as well as to people who have been receiving Social Security disability benefits for two years or more. Medicare does not pay for long-term care, so you may want to consider options for private insurance. Your Social Security covered earnings qualify you for both programs. For more information about Medicare, visit *www.medicare.gov* or call **1-800-633-4227** (TTY **1-877-486-2048** if you are deaf or hard of hearing).

Retirement — If you were born before 1938, your full retirement age is 65. Because of a 1983 change in the law, the full retirement age will increase gradually to 67 for people born in 1960 and later.

Some people retire before their full retirement age. You can retire as early as 62 and take benefits at a reduced rate. If you work after your full retirement age, you can receive higher benefits because of additional earnings and credits for delayed retirement.

Disability — If you become disabled before full retirement age, you can receive disability benefits after six months if you have:

— enough credits from earnings (depending on your age, you must have earned six to 20 of your credits in the three to 10 years before you became disabled); and

— a physical or mental impairment that's expected to prevent you from doing "substantial" work for a year or more or result in death.

If you are filing for disability benefits, please let us know if you are on active military duty or are a recently discharged veteran, so that we can handle your claim more quickly.

Family — If you're eligible for disability or retirement benefits, your current or divorced spouse, minor children or adult children disabled before age 22 also may receive benefits. Each may qualify for up to about 50 percent of your benefit amount.

Survivors — When you die, certain members of your family may be eligible for benefits:

— your spouse age 60 or older (50 or older if disabled, or any age if caring for your children younger than age 16); and

— your children if unmarried and younger than age 18, still in school and younger than 19 years old, or adult children disabled before age 22.

If you are divorced, your ex-spouse could be eligible for a widow's or widower's benefit on your record when you die.

Extra Help with Medicare — If you know someone who is on Medicare and has limited resources and income, Extra Help is available for prescription drug costs. The Extra Help can help pay the monthly premiums, annual deductibles and prescription co-payments. To learn more or to apply, visit *www.socialsecurity.gov* or call **1-800-772-1213** (TTY **1-800-325-0778**).

Receive benefits and still work...

You can work and still get retirement or survivors benefits. If you're younger than your full retirement age, there are limits on how much you can earn without affecting your benefit amount. When you apply for benefits, we'll tell you what the limits are and whether work would affect your monthly benefits. When you reach full retirement age, the earnings limits no longer apply.

Before you decide to retire...

Carefully consider the advantages and disadvantages of early retirement. If you choose to receive benefits before you reach full retirement age, your monthly benefits will be reduced.

To help you decide the best time to retire, we offer a free publication, *When To Start Receiving Retirement Benefits* (Publication No. 05-10147), that identifies the many factors you should consider before applying. Most people can receive an estimate of their benefit based on their actual Social Security earnings record by going to *www.socialsecurity.gov/estimator*. You also can calculate future retirement benefits by using the Social Security Benefit Calculators at *www.socialsecurity.gov*.

Other helpful free publications include:

— *Retirement Benefits* (No. 05-10035)

— *Understanding The Benefits* (No. 05-10024)

— *Your Retirement Benefit: How It Is Figured* (No. 05-10070)

— *Windfall Elimination Provision* (No. 05-10045)

— *Government Pension Offset* (No. 05-10007)

— *Identity Theft And Your Social Security Number* (No. 05-10064)

We also have other leaflets and fact sheets with information about specific topics such as military service, self-employment or foreign employment. You can request Social Security publications at our website, *www.socialsecurity.gov*, or by calling us at **1-800-772-1213**. Our website has a list of frequently asked questions that may answer questions you have. We have easy-to-use online applications for benefits that can save you a telephone call or a trip to a field office.

You also may qualify for government benefits outside of Social Security. For more information on these benefits, visit *www.benefits.gov*.

If you need more information — Visit *www.socialsecurity.gov* on the Internet, contact any Social Security office, call **1-800-772-1213** or write to Social Security Administration, Office of Earnings Operations, P.O. Box 33026, Baltimore, MD 21290-3026. If you're deaf or hard of hearing, call TTY **1-800-325-0778**. If you have questions about your personal information, you must provide your complete Social Security number. If your address is incorrect on this *Statement*, ask the IRS to send you a Form 8822. We don't keep your address if you're not receiving Social Security benefits.

Form SSA-7005-SM-SI (01/20)

4

Exhibit 11.26 | Social Security Fact Sheet

Fact Sheet

SOCIAL SECURITY

2020 SOCIAL SECURITY CHANGES

Cost-of-Living Adjustment (COLA):

Based on the increase in the Consumer Price Index (CPI-W) from the third quarter of 2018 through the third quarter of 2019, Social Security and Supplemental Security Income (SSI) beneficiaries will receive a 1.6 percent COLA for 2020. Other important 2020 Social Security information is as follows:

Tax Rate	2019	2020
Employee	7.65%	7.65%
Self-Employed	15.30%	15.30%

NOTE: The 7.65% tax rate is the combined rate for Social Security and Medicare. The Social Security portion (OASDI) is 6.20% on earnings up to the applicable taxable maximum amount (see below). The Medicare portion (HI) is 1.45% on all earnings. Also, as of January 2013, individuals with earned income of more than $200,000 ($250,000 for married couples filing jointly) pay an additional 0.9 percent in Medicare taxes. The tax rates shown above do not include the 0.9 percent.

	2019	2020
Maximum Taxable Earnings		
Social Security (OASDI only)	$132,900	$137,700
Medicare (HI only)	No Limit	
Quarter of Coverage		
	$1,360	$1,410
Retirement Earnings Test Exempt Amounts		
Under full retirement age	$17,640/yr. ($1,470/mo.)	$18,240/yr. ($1,520/mo.)
NOTE: One dollar in benefits will be withheld for every $2 in earnings above the limit.		

Social Security Fact Sheet Continued

The year an individual reaches full retirement age	$46,920/yr. ($3,910/mo.)	$48,600/yr. ($4,050/mo.)
NOTE: Applies only to earnings for months prior to attaining full retirement age. One dollar in benefits will be withheld for every $3 in earnings above the limit.		
Beginning the month an individual attains full retirement age	None	

	2019	2020
Social Security Disability Thresholds		
Substantial Gainful Activity (SGA)		
Non-Blind	$1,220/mo.	$1,260/mo.
Blind	$2,040/mo.	$2,110/mo.
Trial Work Period (TWP)	$ 880/mo.	$ 910/mo.
Maximum Social Security Benefit: Worker Retiring at Full Retirement Age		
	$2,861/mo.	$3,011/mo.
SSI Federal Payment Standard		
Individual	$ 771/mo.	$ 783/mo.
Couple	$1,157/mo.	$1,175/mo.
SSI Resource Limits		
Individual	$2,000	$2,000
Couple	$3,000	$3,000
SSI Student Exclusion		
Monthly limit	$1,870	$1,900
Annual limit	$7,550	$7,670
Estimated Average Monthly Social Security Benefits Payable in January 2020		
	Before 1.6% COLA	**After 1.6% COLA**
All Retired Workers	$1,479	$1,503
Aged Couple, Both Receiving Benefits	$2,491	$2,531
Widowed Mother and Two Children	$2,888	$2,934
Aged Widow(er) Alone	$1,400	$1,422
Disabled Worker, Spouse and One or More Children	$2,141	$2,176
All Disabled Workers	$1,238	$1,258

KEY TERMS

AIME (Average Indexed Monthly Earnings) - A worker's highest 35 years of earnings adjusted for inflation and averaged on a monthly basis. AIME is used as the basis for the PIA calculation.

Benefit Periods - Begins on the first day an individual receives services as a patient in a hospital or skilled nursing facility and ends after 60 consecutive days without further skilled care.

Cost-of-Living Adjustment (COLA) - The cost-of-living adjustments applied to Social Security benefits.

Currently Insured Workers - A worker who has earned at least six quarters of coverage out of the previous 13 quarters for Social Security.

Disability Benefit - A Social Security benefit available to recipients who have a severe physical or mental impairment that is expected to prevent them from performing "substantial" work for at least a year or result in death. To qualify for these benefits, the recipient must have the sufficient amount of Social Security credits.

Disability Insurance (DI) Trust Fund - The trust fund that pays benefits to workers with disabilities and their families. It is funded by 0.90 percent of an individual's taxable earnings up to $137,700 (2020).

Family Benefit - A Social Security benefit available to certain family members of workers eligible for retirement or disability benefits.

FICA (Federal Insurance Contributions Act) - A law allowing Social Security taxes, including Medicare taxes, to be deducted from employee's paychecks.

Fully Insured - A worker who has earned 40 quarters of coverage under the Social Security system.

Hospital Insurance (HI) Trust Fund - The trust fund that pays for services covered under the hospital insurance provisions of Medicare (Part A). It is funded by 1.45 percent of an individual's taxable earnings (no limitation).

Maximum Family Benefit - The limit on the amount of monthly Social Security benefits that may be paid to a family.

Medicaid - Provides medical assistance for persons with low incomes and resources.

Medicare - A federal health insurance plan for those who have attained age 65 or have been disabled whether retired or still working.

Modified Adjusted Gross Income (when calculating taxable Social Security) - The sum of an individual's adjusted gross income plus tax exempt interest, including interest earned on savings bonds used for higher education; amounts excluded from the taxpayer's income for employer provided adoption assistance; amounts deducted for interest paid for educational loans; and income earned in a foreign country, a U.S. possession, or Puerto Rico that is excluded from income.

Old Age and Survivors Insurance (OASI) - The trust fund that pays retirement and survivors' benefits funded by 5.30 percent of an individual's taxable earnings up to $137,700 (2020).

Old Age, Survivor, and Disability Insurance (OASDI) - An inclusive title given to the Social Security benefit system.

PIA (Primary Insurance Amount) - The amount on which a worker's retirement benefit is based; the PIA determines the amount the applicant will receive at his full retirement age based on the year in which the retiree turns 62. The PIA is indexed to the Consumer Price Index (CPI) annually.

Retirement Benefit - The most familiar Social Security benefit, full retirement benefits are payable at normal retirement age and reduced benefits as early as age 62 to anyone who has obtained at least a minimum (40 quarters) amount of Social Security credits.

Retirement Earnings Limitations Test - A test that may reduce the Social Security benefit paid to an individual based on their other income.

SSI (Supplemental Security Income) - A program administered by the Social Security Administration and funded by the general Treasury that is available to those age 65 or the disabled who have a low income and few assets.

Supplementary Medical Insurance (SMI) Trust Fund - The trust fund that pays for services covered under the medical insurance provisions of Medicare, known as Part B. The coverage is funded by general federal tax revenues and monthly Medicare premiums paid by enrollees.

Survivors' Benefit - Social Security benefit available to surviving family members of a deceased, eligible worker.

DISCUSSION QUESTIONS

SOLUTIONS to the discussion questions can be found exclusively within the chapter. Once you have completed an initial reading of the chapter, go back and highlight the answers to these questions.

1. List and describe the six major categories of benefits administered by the Social Security Association.

2. How are Social Security funds collected?

3. Which individuals are covered workers under the Social Security system?

4. List the beneficiaries of Social Security benefits.

5. How is a person's Social Security retirement benefit calculated?

6. How does retiring early or retiring late affect the calculation of Social Security benefits?

7. How are Social Security benefits taxed?

8. What other benefits are available from Social Security other than retirement benefits?

9. Discuss the maximum family benefit.

10. What benefits does Medicare provide?

11. Describe the various enrollment periods for Medicare.

12. Describe Supplemental Security Income benefits and when they are available.

13. How does marriage or divorce affect Social Security benefits?

MULTIPLE CHOICE PROBLEMS

A sample of multiple choice problems is provided below. Additional multiple choice problems are available at money-education.com by accessing the Student Practice Portal.

1. Social Security is funded through all of the following except:
    a. Employee payroll tax.
    b. Employer payroll tax.
    c. Sales tax.
    d. Self-employment tax.

2. Brisco, now deceased, was married for 12 years. He had two dependent children, ages 10 and 12, who are cared for by their mother age 48. His mother, age 75, was his dependent and survived him. At the time of his death, he was currently but not fully insured under Social Security. His dependents are entitled to all of the following benefits except:
    a. A lump-sum death benefit of $255.
    b. A children's benefit equal to 75% of Brisco's PIA.
    c. A caretaker's benefit for the children's mother.
    d. A parent's benefit.

3. Medicare Part A provides hospital coverage. Which of the following persons is not covered under Part A?
    a. A person 62 or older and receiving railroad retirement.
    b. Disabled beneficiaries regardless of age that have received Social Security for two years.
    c. Chronic kidney patients who require dialysis or a renal transplant.
    d. A person 65 or older entitled to a monthly Social Security check.

4. A person receiving Social Security benefits under full retirement age can receive earned income up to a maximum threshold without reducing Social Security benefits by the earnings test. Which of the following count against the earnings threshold?
    a. Dividends from stocks.
    b. Rental income.
    c. Pensions and insurance annuities.
    d. Self-employment income.

5. All of the following statements concerning Social Security benefits are correct except:
    a. The maximum family benefit is determined through a formula based on the worker's PIA.
    b. If a worker applies for retirement or survivors' benefits before his 65th birthday, he must also file a separate application for Medicare.
    c. People who are disabled or have permanent kidney failure can get Medicare at any age.
    d. The Social Security Administration is concerned with beneficiaries' combined income, which, on the 1040 federal tax return, includes adjusted gross income and nontaxable interest income

QUICK QUIZ EXPLANATIONS

Quick Quiz 11.1
1. False. Reduced Social Security benefits can be withdrawn as early as age 62.
2. False. Social Security contributions are placed in the following trust funds: OASI, DI, and HI. The SMI Trust Fund is not funded by Social Security contributions.

Quick Quiz 11.2
1. True.
2. True.

Quick Quiz 11.3
1. False. The Social Security retirement benefit is based on the worker's PIA. A worker's PIA is based on the worker's average indexed monthly earnings during the 35 years in which the worker earned the most.
2. False. Full retirement age for Social Security is increasing because of increasing life expectancies.

Quick Quiz 11.4
1. True.
2. False. Once divorced, a non-working ex-spouse who was married to the worker for more than ten years can still receive Social Security benefits based on the worker's record.
3. True.

Quick Quiz 11.5
1. True.
2. False. The increase equals 8 percent per year times three years, which is a 24 percent increase.
3. True.

Quick Quiz 11.6
1. True.
2. False. Medicare Part C (Medicare Advantage) is an alternative to traditional Medicare (Parts A and B). Part D provides prescription drug coverage when purchased with Parts A and B.
3. False. Failure to enroll in Medicare Part B during the initial enrollment period will result in a permanent increase in premium unless the individual maintains creditable health coverage from an employer and enrolls during a special enrollment period following loss of the employer-provided coverage
4. False. Traditional Medicare does not have a maximum out-of-pocket amount, leaving the covered individual at risk for paying large out-of-pocket medical expenses. Some Medigap (Medicare Supplement) policies and some Medicare Advantage plans, however, do offer a maximum out-of-pocket provision.

Quick Quiz 11.7
1. False. In order to obtain SSI benefits, an individual must be 65, disabled, or blind.
2. True.

Additional multiple choice problems
are available at
money-education.com
by accessing the
Student Practice Portal.
Access requires registration of the title using
the unique code at the front of the book.

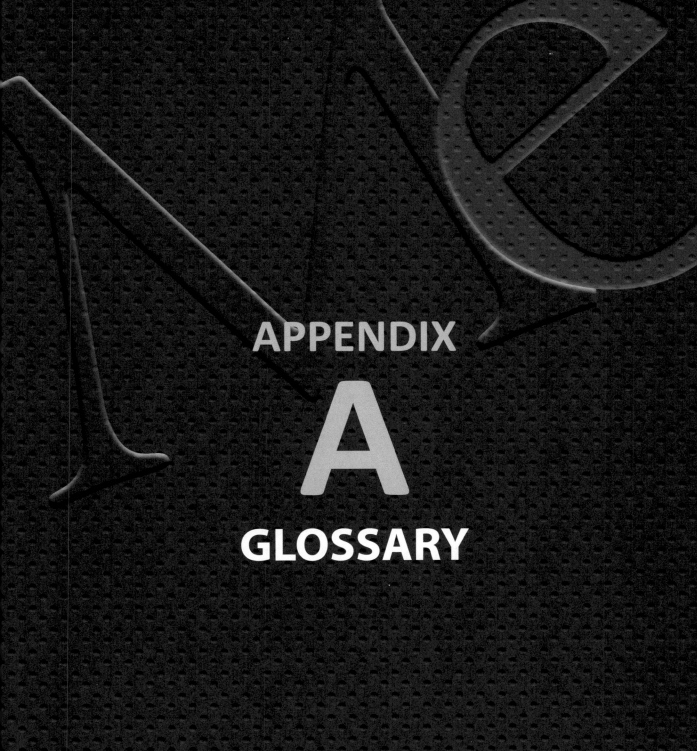

APPENDIX

A

GLOSSARY

A

Accelerated Benefits Provision - Entitles a qualified insured to receive a pre-death benefit deemed nontaxable.

Accumulation Phase - The period over which annuity funds are accumulated.

Activities of Daily Living (ADL) - Physical functions that an independent person performs each day, including bathing, dressing, eating, transferring, toileting, and maintaining continence.

Actual Cash Value - The depreciated value of personal property.

Adhesion - A take it or leave it contract.

Adult Day Care - Services provided during the day at a community-based center. Programs address the individual needs of functionally or cognitively impaired adults.

Adverse Selection - The tendency of those that most need insurance to seek it out.

Agents - Legal representatives of an insurer and act on behalf of an insurer.

AIME (Average Indexed Monthly Earnings) - A worker's highest 35 years of earnings adjusted for inflation and averaged on a monthly basis. AIME is used as the basis for the PIA calculation.

Aleatory - A type of insurance contract in which the dollar amounts exchanged are uneven.

Annual Renewable Term (ART) - Type of term insurance that permits the policyholder to purchase term insurance in subsequent years without evidence of insurability, but premiums on the policy increase each year to reflect the increasing mortality risk being undertaken by the insurer.

Annual Reset Method - The index-linked interest crediting rate is determined each year by comparing the index value at the end of the contract year with the index value at the beginning of the contract year. Interest is then added to the annuity each year during the term.

Annuitant - The individual upon whose life the contract is dependent. It is generally the life expectancy of the annuitant that affects the timing and amount of payout under the contract.

Annuitization - The time when annuity funds are exchanged for a stream of income guaranteed for a period of time.

Annuitized - The time when regular, periodic (such as monthly or annual) payments begin for life or for a specified period of time in excess of one year.

Annuity - A contract between an individual (annuitant) and an insurance company which promises to pay an income on a regular basis for a specified period of time.

Any Occupation - Type of disability insurance policy that provides benefits to a policy owner if he or she is unable to perform the duties of any occupation for which he or she is suited by education, training, or experience.

Apparent Authority - When the third party believes implied or express authority exists, but no authority actually exists.

Appraised or Agreed Upon Value - Used for hard to value items and where the insured may own property that exceeds standard limits of property insurance policy.

Asset Accumulation Phase - This phase is usually from the early 20s to late 50s when additional cash flow for investing is low and debt to net worth is high.

Assignment - The process of transferring all or part of the policy's ownership rights.

Assisted Living - Senior housing that provides individual apartments, which may or may not have a kitchenette. Facilities offer 24-hour on site staff, congregate dining, and activity programs. Limited nursing services may be provided for an additional fee.

Assumption of Risk - The injured party fully understood and recognized the dangers that were involved in an activity and voluntarily chose to proceed.

Auto Credit Score - Score calculated principally based on previous auto loan history.

Auto Insurance Score - Ranges from 150 to 850 and uses data from the Trans Union credit report. It helps auto insurance companies to assess the risk of insuring a consumer by measuring the probability that an auto insurance claim might be filed.

Automatic Increase Rider - A provision that automatically increases the monthly benefit by a stated percentage each year.

B

Basic Coverage - Protects the homeowner from losses associated with specifically named perils.

Bed Reservation - Some policies will pay to reserve a bed in the nursing home when the insured leaves to go into a hospital. This reservation can last a specified number of days or until the insured returns from the hospital.

Beneficiary - Those persons entitled to the death benefit of the annuity.

Benefit Periods - Begins on the first day an individual receives services as a patient in a hospital or skilled nursing facility and ends after 60 consecutive days without further skilled care.

Bodily Injury - Occurs when an insured driver causes bodily harm to a third party and the insured driver is deemed responsible for the injuries.

Broad Perils Coverage - Provides protection for the perils covered in basic coverage, plus additional protection for named perils not covered under basic coverage.

Brokers - Legal representatives of an insured and act in the best interest of the insured.

Buy-Sell Agreements - Arrangements that require the sale and purchase of securities owned by one individual to another following a specified triggering event, such as the death of a business owner.

C

Cap Rate - Some indexed annuities impose an upper limit on the index-linked interest rate.

Capitalized-Earnings Approach - Method to determine life insurance needs that suggests the death benefits of a client's life insurance should equal an income stream sufficient to meet the family's needs without depleting the capital base.

Cash Refund Annuity - Guarantees that the annuitant or the annuitant's family will receive the premium payments made to purchase the annuity, but instead of continuing to make periodic payments until there is a full recovery of the premium, the balance is paid in cash at the annuitant's death.

Chip and Pin (EMV Technology) - An embedded computer chip in the card (card is more expensive), creates a unique number for each transaction and requires a pin to approve any charge.

Chronic Illness - A person is chronically ill if within the past 12 months, a health care practitioner has certified that the individual has been unable to perform, without substantial assistance, at least two activities of daily living (eating, bathing, dressing, transferring, toileting, and continence) for at least 90 days. A person is also chronically ill if substantial supervision is required to protect that person from threats to health and safety due to cognitive disability (such as advanced stages of Alzheimer's disease or senile dementia).

Coinsurance - The percentage of financial responsibility that the insured and the insurer must uphold in order to achieve equity in rating.

COLA Rider - Provides a cost of living adjustment to benefit payments based on increases in inflation.

Collateral Source Rule - Holds that damages assessed against a negligent party should not be reduced simply because the injured party has other sources of recovery available such as insurance or employee benefits (health or disability insurance).

Collision - Auto insurance coverage that protects the insured against upset and collision damages, such as those sustained in an accident involving other vehicles, or those sustained when an auto runs off the road and into a lake.

Combined Single Limit Policy - A policy that has a fixed amount of coverage that the insurance company pays, whether the loss is attributable to bodily injury or property damage.

Comparative Negligence - The amount of damage is adjusted to reflect the injured party's proportion of contribution to the cause of the injury.

Comprehensive (or Other than Collision) - Auto insurance coverage that protects the insured's auto against perils out of the insured's control, such as missiles or falling objects, fire, theft, earthquake, hail, flood, and vandalism.

Concealment - When the insured is intentionally silent regarding a material fact during the application process.

Conditional - The insured must abide by all the terms and conditions of the contract, if the insured intends to collect under the policy.

Conservation (Risk Management) Phase - This phase is from late 20s to early 70s, when cash flow assets and net worth have increased and debt has decreased somewhat. In addition, risk management of events like employment, disability due to illness or accident, and untimely death become a priority.

Constructive Receipt - An income tax concept that establishes when income is includible by a taxpayer and therefore subject to income tax. Income is constructively received in the taxable year during which it is credited to the employee's account, set apart for him, or otherwise made available so that he may draw upon it at any time or so that he could have drawn upon it during the taxable year if notice of intention to withdraw had been given.

Consumer-Directed Health Plan - A combination of a high deductible medical insurance policy and Health Savings Account which is used to accumulate funds on a tax-advantaged basis to pay health care expenses as a result of deductibles and other cost sharing.

Consumer Lending - Credit cards, home equity loans, home equity lines of credit, auto loans, other recreational vehicle loans, and appliance loans.

Contingent Beneficiaries - Person(s) or organization named to receive the death benefit if the primary beneficiary is not available to receive the policy proceeds.

Contributory Negligence - Negligence on the part of the injured party that contributes to the harm and, therefore, the injured has to bear some responsibility for the injury.

Co-Payment - A loss-sharing arrangement whereby the insured pays a percentage of the loss in excess of the deductible.

Corridor Test - One of two Congress-imposed tests to determine whether a life insurance contract meets the definition of an MEC. This test calls for the policy to be tested using actuarial principles and requires the premiums to represent no more than a specified portion of the death benefit.

Cost-of-Living Adjustment (COLA) - The cost-of-living adjustments applied to Social Security benefits.

Credit Agencies - Companies that compile and maintain credit information from credit card companies, banks, mortgage companies, and other creditors for the purpose of creating personal in-depth credit reports on individuals. The major credit reporting agencies are Experian, Equifax, and TransUnion.

Credit Score - A number that summarizes a person's credit risk based on an evaluation of his or her credit report at a particular point in time.

Cross-Purchase Buy-Sell Agreement - An arrangement between individuals who agree to purchase the business interest of a deceased owner.

Currently Insured Workers - A worker who has earned at least six quarters of coverage out of the previous 13 quarters for Social Security.

Custodial Care - Board, room and other personal assistance services (including assistance with activities of daily living, taking medicine and similar personal needs) that may not include a skilled nursing care component.

D

Declarations Section - The section of an insurance policy that describes exactly what property is being covered.

Decreasing-Term Insurance - Type of term insurance that allows the owner to pay the same premium for the insurance protection each year. The death benefit on the policy will, however, decrease each year to offset the increasing mortality cost due to the passage of time.

Deductible - A specified amount of money the insured is required to pay on a loss before the insurer will make any payments under the policy.

Deferred Annuity - An annuity contract that does not begin payments immediately, but waits until some future time to start payments.

Deferred Compensation Arrangements - An arrangement to pay an executive compensation in a future year.

Definition Section - The section of an insurance policy that defines key words, phrases, or terms used throughout the insurance contract.

Description Section - The section of an insurance policy that describes exactly what is being insured.

Digital Wallet - Allows the consumer to make payments in person, via phone apps, or on the web without the need for a physical credit card by storing the card information, using encrypted software, in an app on the user's phone.

Disability Benefit - A Social Security benefit available to recipients who have a severe physical or mental impairment that is expected to prevent them from performing "substantial" work for at least a year or result in death. To qualify for these benefits, the recipient must have the sufficient amount of Social Security credits.

Disability Insurance - A type of insurance that provides supplementary income in the event of an illness or accident resulting in a disability that prevents the insured from working at his or her regular employment.

Disability Insurance (DI) Trust Fund - The trust fund that pays benefits to workers with disabilities and their families. It is funded by 0.90 percent of an individual's taxable earnings up to $137,700 (2020).

Distribution (Gifting) Phase - This phase is from the late 40s to end of life and occurs when the individual has high additional cash flow, low debt, and high net worth.

Dumpster Diving - A means of identity theft, that involves going through someone's trash while looking for identity information from canceled checks, bank statements, credit card statements, federal or state tax documents, discarded credit card offers, and phone numbers.

Dwelling - Residential structure covered under a homeowners insurance policy.

E

Economic Benefit Doctrine - An employee will be taxed on funds or property set aside for the employee if the funds or property are unrestricted and nonforfeitable even if the employee was not given a choice to receive the income currently.

Elimination Period - The period of time, beginning upon injury or sickness, that an insured is disabled but is not collecting benefits from the insurer.

Endorsement - Attachment or addition to an existing insurance policy that changes the original terms.

Entity Purchase (Redemption) Agreement - Type of buy-sell agreement that obligates the business entity to purchase an owner's interest in the entity upon that owner's death.

Equity-Indexed Annuities - Have characteristics of both fixed and variable annuities, either immediate or deferred, that earn interest or provide benefits that are linked to an external equity reference or an equity index.

Estoppel - The legal process of denying a right you might otherwise be entitled to under the law.

Exclusion Section - The section of an insurance policy that will exclude certain perils, losses and property.

Exclusive Provider Organization - A form of managed care in which participants receive all of their care from in-network providers. Unlike an HMO, a referral is not necessary to see a specialist.

Expense Incurred Method – this method provides for reimbursement of expense once bills are submitted to the insurance company. The reimbursable amount cannot exceed the benefit amount.

Express Authority - Authority given to an agent through a formal written document.

F

Family Benefit - A Social Security benefit available to certain family members of workers eligible for retirement or disability benefits.

FICA (Federal Insurance Contributions Act) - A law allowing Social Security taxes, including Medicare taxes, to be deducted from employee's paychecks.

FICO Score - A credit score developed by FICO (formerly know as Fair Isaac Corporation) that estimates the level of future credit risk for an individual. It is calculated using a formula that evaluates many types of information in the credit report at that credit reporting agency and ranges from 300 to 850.

50% Joint and Survivor Annuity - Pays the survivor 50% of the annuity payment after the death of the first annuitant. The initial annuity payment will be larger than with a 100% or 75% joint and survivor annuity.

Financial Risk - A loss of financial value, such as the premature death of a family's primary wage earner.

First-to-Die - Type of joint life insurance policy that covers two individuals, but the death benefit is paid upon the death of the first individual.

Fixed Annuity - The most conservative type of annuity that earns a minimum guaranteed rate of return.

Fixed Deferred Annuity - Accumulates interest at a stated rate that is commonly adjusted on an annual basis, subject to a minimum interest rate guarantee.

Flexible Premium Annuity - Allows the insured the option to vary premium deposits.

Flexible Spending Account (FSA) - Employer-sponsored plan that permits employees to defer pre-tax income into an account to pay for health care expenses. FSAs require the employee to either use the contributed amounts for medical expenses by the end of the year, or forfeit the unused amounts to the company.

Floor Crediting Rate - An indexed annuity is the minimum index-linked interest rate that will be credited to the contract in a given period.

Free Withdrawal Provision - Allows the contract holder the right to withdraw up to a stated percentage (usually 10 percent) of the contract value annually without incurring a surrender charge.

Fully Insured - A worker who has earned 40 quarters of coverage under the Social Security system.

Fundamental Risk - A risk that can impact a large number of individuals at one time (earthquake or flood).

Future Increase Option Rider - A provision that permits the insured to increase benefit coverage as they get older.

G

Grace Period - A provision in most insurance policies which allows payment to be received for a certain period of time after the actual due date without a default or cancellation of the policy.

Group Health Insurance - Health plans offered to a group of individuals by an employer, association, union, or other entity.

Group Term Insurance - A type of life insurance coverage offered to a group of people (often a component of an employee benefit package) that provides benefits to the beneficiaries if the covered individual dies during the defined covered period.

Guarantee Funds - Run by the state insurance commission, they act as the payor of last resort in the case of an insurance company failure.

Guaranteed Purchase Option - Allows the insured to increase the benefits by a stated percentage periodically.

Guaranteed Renewable - A provision that requires the insurance company to renew the policy for a specified period of time or until the insured attains a certain age.

Guideline Premium and Corridor Test - One of two Congress-imposed tests to determine whether a life insurance contract meets the definition of a MEC. This test calls for the policy to be tested using actuarial principles and requires the premiums to represent no more than a specified portion of the death benefit.

H

Hard Inquiries - Inquiries made by creditors or potential creditors.

Hazards - A specific condition that increases the potential or likelihood of a loss occurring.

Health Maintenance Organizations (HMOs) - A form of managed care in which participants receive all of their care from participating providers. Physicians are employed by the HMO directly, or may be physicians in private practice who have chosen to participate in the HMO network. The independent physicians are paid a fixed amount for each HMO member that uses them as a primary care physician.

Health Savings Accounts (HSA) - A plan that permits employees or individuals to save for health care costs on a tax-advantaged basis. Contributions made to the HSA by the plan participant are tax-deductible as an adjustment to gross income (above the line), and distributions from the HSA to pay for medical expenses are excluded from income.

High Deductible Health Insurance Plans - Plans with a deductible of at least $1,400 for individual coverage and $2,800 for family coverage in 2020, with a maximum out-of-pocket amount of $6,900 for single coverage and $13,800 for family coverage in 2020.

High Watermark Approach - Determining index-linked interest is accomplished by comparing the value of the index at various points during the term (usually on anniversary dates).

Home Health Care - Limited part-time or intermittent skilled nursing care and home health aide services, physical therapy, occupational therapy, speech-language pathology services, medical social services, durable medical equipment (such as wheelchairs, hospital beds, oxygen, and walkers), medical supplies, and other services provided in the patient's home.

Home Insurance Score - Ranges from 150 to 850 and is once again calculated using the TransUnion credit report. It is primarily used by home insurance companies to assess the probability that a homeowner will file a homeowner's insurance claim.

Homeowners Insurance - A package insurance policy that provides both property and liability coverage for the insured's dwelling, other structures, personal property, and loss of use.

Hospice Care - Offers a special way of caring for people who are terminally ill, typically utilizing a team-oriented approach to address medical, physical, social, emotional, and spiritual needs.

Hospital Insurance (HI) Trust Fund - The trust fund that pays for services covered under the hospital insurance provisions of Medicare (Part A). It is funded by 1.45 percent of an individual's taxable earnings (no limitation).

Human-Life Value Approach - Method to determine life insurance needs that suggests the death benefit of a client's life insurance should equal to the economic value of the client's future earnings stream.

I

Illustration - A projection of the financial results that can be achieved with a life insurance policy, based on assumptions about premium payments, investment earnings, and dividends.

Immediate Annuity - An instrument created when the contract owner trades a sum of money in return for a stream of income that begins immediately.

Implied Authority - The authority that a third party relies upon when dealing with an agent based upon the position held by the agent.

In-Force Policy Illustration - Allows the planner and client to monitor the performance of the policy versus what was expected, enabling them to correct any potential problems before they occur.

Incontestability Clause - Clause in a health insurance policy that prevents the insurer from challenging the validity of the health insurance contract after it has been in force for a specified period of time unless the insured fraudulently obtained coverage in the beginning of the policy.

Indemnity Health Insurance - Traditional, fee-for-service health insurance that does not limit where a covered individual can get care.

Index Term - The period over which index-linked interest is calculated for equity-indexed annuities.

Indexing Method - The approach used to measure the amount of change, if any, in the index. Some common indexing methods include: (1) the annual reset (ratcheting) approach, (2) the high watermark approach, and (3) the point-to-point approach.

Individual Major Medical Plans - Major medical insurance coverage purchased independently from an insurance company (not as part of a group).

Inflation - The increase in the general price level, and is often measured by the Consumer Price Index (CPI).

Inflation Protection - Helps the insured to maintain the purchasing power of the original contract benefit.

Initial Rate - The first rate of interest that is earned under a fixed annuities contract and is guaranteed for a specified period of time.

Installment Refund Annuity - A special type of term certain annuity whereby the insurer promises to continue periodic annuity payments after the annuitant has died until the sum of all annuity payments made equals the purchase price of the annuity.

Insured - The person whose life is insured by the policy.

Intentional Interference - Intentional act committed against another that causes injury.

Intermediate-Care Nursing Facility - A licensed facility with the primary purpose of providing health or rehabilitative services. Typically provides custodial care along with intermittent, as opposed to daily, medical care.

IRD Assets - Assets that have a deferred income tax liability that was not paid prior to the date of the owner's death.

J

Joint and Survivor Annuity - Promises to make payments over the lives of two or more annuitants, and annuity payments are made until the last annuitant dies. This is, commonly used to fund the retirement cash-flow needs of married couples.

K

Key Person Insurance - A life or disability insurance policy on a key person whose death or disability would cause a substantial hardship to the business. The business is the owner, payer, and beneficiary of the death benefit (or disability income benefit), so that the business is protected against the unexpected loss of the employee due to death or disability.

L

Lacking Sound Mind - The state of not having the capacity to understand the purpose and terms of the contract, therefore the contract lacks a meeting of the minds or mutual consent.

Last Clear Chance Rule - This rule states that a claimant who is endangered by his own negligence may recover if the defendant has a "last clear chance" to avoid the accident and failed to do so.

Law of Large Numbers - A principle that states the more similar events or exposures, the more likely the actual results will equal the probability expected.

Level Premium Term Insurance - Type of term insurance that charges a fixed premium each year over a specified period of years, so the premium does not increase over that period.

Liability Coverage - Covers bodily injury or property damage to others for which the insured driver is deemed to be responsible.

Libel - A written statement that causes harm to another.

Life Annuity Contracts - Protect clients from outliving their assets by providing a series of periodic payments to the annuitant, typically made for as long as the annuitant lives.

Limited-Pay Policies - Type of whole life policy with a payment schedule (typically 10 or 20 years). At the end of the payment period, the policy is considered to be paid-up, at which time no additional premium payments are due.

Long-Term Care Insurance - Coverage that pays for all or part of the cost of home health care services or care in a nursing home or assisted living facility.

Long-Term Care Services - Medical and non-medical care for people with chronic illnesses or disabilities that assists people with Activities of Daily Living, such as dressing, bathing, and using the bathroom. Long-term care can be provided at home, in the community, or in a facility.

Long-Term Disability - Provides coverage for specified term, until specified age, or until death.

Longevity Insurance - A sophisticated name for a deferred annuity purchased by an individual at or before retirement that will not begin to make payments until that person reaches an advanced age.

Loss of Use - Under homeowners insurance coverage, loss of use is a combination of additional living expenses and loss of rental income.

M

Managed Care Insurance - Health-care delivery systems that integrate the financing and delivery of health care. Managed care plans feature a network of physicians, hospitals, and other providers who participate in the plan. Managed care includes HMOs, PPOs, and POS plans.

Maximum Family Benefit - The limit on the amount of monthly Social Security benefits that may be paid to a family.

Maximum Lifetime Benefit - The total amount of money that could be paid under the LTC policy for charges incurred for covered services.

Medicaid - A state and federal assistance program that pays for medical care and most long-term care expenses for eligible persons with low incomes and limited assets.

Medical Payments - A no-fault, first-party insurance coverage designed to pay for bodily injuries sustained in an auto accident.

Medicare - A federal program that pays for healthcare for persons over age 65 and for people under age 65 with disabilities.

Medicare Supplement Insurance (Medigap) - A health insurance policy designed to cover some of the gaps in coverage associated with traditional Medicare.

Mental and Nervous Disorders - Long-term care insurance policies can exclude coverage of some mental and nervous disorders, but the policy must cover serious biologically-based mental illnesses and other diseases, such as schizophrenia, major depression disorders, Alzheimer's disease, and other age-related disorders. However, a long-term care insurer may refuse to sell a policy to someone already suffering from these otherwise covered exclusions.

Minimum Interest Rate - The minimum rate to be paid on a fixed annuity's principal balance for the duration of the annuity contract.

Minors - In most states, a minor is under the age of 18. If a minor enters into a contract, the minor can void the contract at any time.

Modified Adjusted Gross Income (when calculating taxable Social Security) - The sum of an individual's adjusted gross income plus tax exempt interest, including interest earned on savings bonds used for higher education; amounts excluded from the taxpayer's income for employer provided adoption assistance; amounts deducted for interest paid for educational loans; amounts deducted as qualified tuition expense; and income earned in a foreign country, a U.S. possession, or Puerto Rico that is excluded from income.

Modified Endowment Contract (MEC) - A cash value life insurance policy that has been funded too quickly. Under an MEC, the death benefit payable to the beneficiary is not subject to income tax, but policy loans or cash value withdrawals are taxable.

Modified Whole Life Policies - Type of whole life policy with lower premiums than a regular policy for an initial policy period (often 3 to 5 years), which increase to a higher-level premium at the end of the initial period.

Moral Hazard - The potential loss occurring because of the moral character of the insured, and the filing of a false claim with their insurance company.

Morale Hazard - The indifference to a loss created because the insured has insurance.

Mortality Cost - Equals the probability of dying within the year times the face value of the policy.

Mortality Risk - The risk that an individual will die within the year.

Mutual Consent - Common understanding and agreement between parties to a contract regarding what the contract covers and the terms of the contract.

N

Needs Approach - Method to determine life insurance needs that suggests the death benefits of a client's life insurance should equal the cash needs that the family will require at death plus income replacement needs.

Negligence - Harm caused by failure to use reasonable care.

Non-Cancelable - A provision that prevents the insurance company from cancelling the policy for any reason provided the policy premium is paid.

Non-Forfeiture Benefit - The insurer must guarantee that the insured will receive some of the benefits paid for even upon cancellation or lapsed coverage.

Non-Qualified Annuities - Annuity contracts purchased with funds outside of qualified retirement plans or IRAs (for example, from investment accounts or private savings).

Nonfinancial Risk - A risk that would result in a loss, other than a monetary loss.

O

Objective Risk - The variation of actual amount of losses that occur over a period of time compared to the expected amount of losses.

Offer and Acceptance - Consists of one party making an offer to purchase a good or service, and the acceptance is when consideration is received.

Old Age and Survivors Insurance (OASI) - The trust fund that pays retirement and survivors' benefits funded by 5.30 percent of an individual's taxable earnings up to $137,700 (2020).

Old Age, Survivor, and Disability Insurance (OASDI) - An inclusive title given to the Social Security benefit system.

100% Joint and Survivor Annuity - Pays the survivor 100% of the annuity payment after the death of the first annuitant.

Open Perils - All-risk coverage for personal property that provides for a much broader and more comprehensive protection program than named-perils coverage.

Ordinary (or Straight) Life - Type of whole life policy that requires the owner to pay a specified level premium every year until death (or age 100).

Other Structures - Small detached structures on the insured's property in addition to the main house, such as garages, greenhouses, or storage buildings.

Out-of-Pocket-Maximum - The sum of the deductible, the insured's portion of the coinsurance, and generally any copayments by the insured.

Own Occupation - Type of disability insurance policy that provides benefits to a policyholder if he is unable to perform the duties of their occupation. This type of policy is more expensive than an any occupation policy.

Owner - Person, trust, or company that owns the annuity contract and names the annuitant and beneficiaries. The owner could also be the annuitant and/or the beneficiary.

P

Parol Evidence Rule - States that "what is written prevails." Oral agreements that are not reflected in the written contract are not valid.

Partial Disability - A provision that provides payments that are less than those paid for a total disability.

Participation Rate - Determines how much of the increase in the index will be used to calculate the index-linked interest.

Particular Risk - A risk that can impact a particular individual, such as death or the inability to work because of a sickness or accident.

Parties to Annuity Contract - The annuitant, the beneficiary, the owner, and the insurance company.

Perils - The immediate cause and reason for a loss occurring.

Personal Automobile Policy - Insurance policy that covers liability for injuries and damages to persons inside and outside the vehicle and covers the cost to repair/replace a damaged or stolen vehicle.

Personal Liability Umbrella Policy (PLUP) - Coverage designed to provide a catastrophic layer of liability coverage on top of the individual's homeowners and automobile insurance policies.

Personal Property - Valuable items owned by the insured that are covered under homeowners insurance.

Physical Hazard - A physical condition that increases the likelihood of a loss occurring.

PIA (Primary Insurance Amount) - The amount on which a worker's retirement benefit is based; the PIA determines the amount the applicant will receive at his full retirement age based on the year in which the retiree turns 62. The PIA is indexed to the Consumer Price Index (CPI) annually.

Point-to-Point Index-Linked Crediting Method - Based on the difference between an index value at the end of the term compared with the index value at the start of the term.

Point of Service Plan (POS) - A form of managed care that is considered a managed care/indemnity plan hybrid, as it mixes aspects of HMOs, PPOs, and indemnity plans for greater patient choice. A primary care physician coordinates patient care, but there is more flexibility in choosing doctors and hospitals than in an HMO.

Pooling of Risk - The spreading of risk among a large number of similar contributors to the pool. Protection is provided to the entire pool of contributors. With annuities, the risk that is being spread is the risk of outliving retirement funds, or superannuation.

Pre-Existing Conditions - A pre-existing condition is an illness or disability for which an insured has received previous medical advice or treatment usually within six months prior to the application for long-term care coverage.

Preferred Provider Organization (PPO) - A form of managed care in which participants have more flexibility in choosing physicians and other providers than in an HMO. The arrangement between insurance companies and health care providers permits participants to obtain discounted health care services from the preferred providers within the network.

Premium - The amount participants pay to belong to a health plan.

Presumptive Total Disability Coverage - A provision that automatically considers certain conditions to be totally disabling, such as loss of sight in both eyes, hearing in both ears, the use of both hands, the use of both feet, or the use of one foot and one hand.

Primary Beneficiary - Person(s) (may be a group designation) or organization to receive the death benefit upon the death of the insured.

Primary Care Physician - A physician that is designated as a participant's first point of contact with the health care system, particularly in managed care plans.

Principle of Indemnity - Asserts that an insurer will only compensate the insured to the extent the insured has suffered an actual financial loss.

Principle of Insurable Interest - Asserts that an insured must suffer a financial loss if a covered peril occurs, otherwise no insurance can be offered.

Prospectus - A disclosure document provided to purchasers of variable annuities and variable life insurance products that contains important information about the contract, including fees and charges, investment options and objectives, risks, death benefits, living benefits, and other important information.

Pure Risk - The chance of loss or no loss occurring.

Q

Qualified Annuities - Annuity contracts purchased with funds in a qualified retirement plan or IRA.

R

Rabbi Trust - A revocable or irrevocable trust that is designed to hold funds and assets for the purpose of paying benefits under a nonqualified deferred compensation arrangement. The assets in a rabbi trust are for the sole purpose of providing benefits to employees and may not be accessed by the employer, but they may be seized and used for the purpose of paying general creditors in the event of a liquidation of the company. Assets within a rabbi trust are not currently taxable to the employee.

Radio Frequency Identification (RFID) Cards - The wireless use of electromagnetic fields to transfer consumer information. This is being adopted by debit and credit card companies to deter identity theft.

Refund of Premium - The company will refund some or all of the insured's premiums minus any claims paid under the policy if the policy is canceled. The insured's beneficiary will receive such refund if the insured dies.

Reinsurance - A means by which an insurance company transfers some or all of its risk to another insurance company.

Renewal Rate - The interest rate offered on a fixed annuity after the expiration of the initial rate.

Replacement Cost - Represents the amount of money necessary to repair or replace property, without any deduction for depreciation.

Representation - A statement made by the applicant during the insurance application process.

Residual Benefits Provision - A provision that will provide continuing benefits for an insured who returns to work but suffers a reduction of income due to a disability.

Res ispa loquitur - A doctrine of the law of negligence that is concerned with the circumstances and the types of accidents, which affords reasonable evidence if a specific explanation of negligence is not available.

Restoration of Benefits - Some policies restore benefits to the original maximum amounts if the insured no longer needs long-term care services, usually after 180 days.

Retirement Benefit - The most familiar Social Security benefit, full retirement benefits are payable at normal retirement age and reduced benefits as early as age 62 to anyone who has obtained at least a minimum (40 quarters) amount of Social Security credits.

Retirement Earnings Limitations Test - A test that may reduce the Social Security benefit paid to an individual based on their other income.

Retirement Life Expectancy - The period between retirement and death.

Rider - Provisions or endorsements that are added to the life insurance policy in order to increase or decrease benefits, waive a condition, or amend the original contract in some specific manner.

Risk - The chance of loss, uncertainty associated with loss, or the possibility of a loss.

Risk Avoidance - A risk management technique used for any risks that are high in frequency and high in severity.

Risk-Based Capital - The investment risk assessment undertaken by the insurance company in investing the money backing up the annuity pool.

Risk Reduction - The process of reducing the likelihood of a pure risk that is high in frequency and low in severity.

Risk Retention - Accepting some or all of the potential loss exposure for risk that are low in frequency and low in severity.

Risk Transfer - The process of transferring a low frequency and high severity risk to a third party, such as an insurance company.

S

Salary Reduction Plans - A nonqualified plan designed to receive deferral contributions from executives to reduce their current taxable income.

SCAM - An acronym from the Justice Department to help avoid identity theft.

Schedule - Attachment or addition to an existing insurance policy that lists individual items.

Scheduled Personal Property Endorsement - An endorsement to a homeowner policy that covers specified items of personal property at an agreed-upon value in excess of the standard coverage limits for the type of property.

Sec. 162 Bonus Plan (Group Carve Out) - A fringe benefit offered to a select group of executives where the employer pays a salary bonus to the executive for the purpose of paying premiums on a permanent life insurance policy owned by the executive. A double bonus may be paid so that it covers the taxes due on the premium bonus, resulting in a net cost of $0 to the employee.

Second-to-Die - Type of joint life insurance policy that is often used in estate planning to provide liquidity at the death of the second spouse. A second-to-die policy names two insureds and pays the death benefit only when the second insured dies.

Secondary Market Annuities - Called pre-owned annuities or in-force annuities. These annuities can be purchased from the original owner at a discount or from a third party, wherein which the stream of income is assigned to the purchaser. These; typically offer a rate of return or yield that is well above the yield available on standard fixed annuities, immediate annuities, or even bonds of a similar credit quality.

Secular Trusts - Irrevocable trusts designed to hold funds and assets for the purpose of paying benefits under a nonqualified deferred compensation arrangement. A secular trust does not create a substantial fist of forfeiture to the employee. Assets set aside in a secular trust results in immediate inclusion of income to the employee.

Secured Loans - Loans secured by collateral that may be repossessed if the loan is not repaid as agreed.

7-Pay Test - One of two Congress-imposed tests to determine whether a life insurance contract meets the definition of an MEC. This test states that if the cumulative premium payments made on the policy are in excess of the net level premium for the policy during the first seven years (or following a material change to the policy), the life insurance contract will be deemed an MEC.

75% Joint and Survivor Annuity - Pays the survivor 75% of the annuity payment after the death of the first annuitant. The initial annuity payment will be larger than with a 100% joint and survivor annuity.

Shared Benefits - Policies that have this benefit permit a person who has fully exhausted the benefits under his or her own policy to make use of the benefits available under his or her spouse's policy.

Short-Term Disability - Provides coverage for up to two years, and typically has a 5 to 30 day elimination period (the period an insured must wait before receiving benefits).

Shoulder Surfing - A means of identity theft by the eavesdropping on those who punch in numbers or verbally give numbers over the phone.

Simultaneous Death Provision - Provision in a life insurance policy for situations in which the insured and the beneficiary die within a short time of one another and it is not possible to determine who died first, Generally the policy death benefit is distributed as if the beneficiary had predeceased the insured.

Single Life Annuity - Also known as a straight life annuity, provides a stream of income to the annuitant for life.

Single Premium Annuity - An annuity purchased with a single lump sum.

Single Premium Policy - Type of whole life policy that requires the owner to pay a lump sum in return for insurance protection that will extend throughout the insured's lifetime. These policies will always be a MECs.

Sinking Fund - A sinking fund is a fund established by a company to pay for future expenses or to retire debt. It is created by setting aside income over a period of time (generally years).

Skilled Care Facility - 24-hour nursing care for chronically-ill or short-term rehabilitative residents of all ages. It provides the highest level of service, and combines daily medical and custodial care.

Slander - Verbal statement that causes harm to another.

Social Security Disability Benefits - Available to anyone insured under the system who meets the strict definition of disability.

Soft Inquiries - Inquiries made by the consumer or by a prospective or current employer.

Special Needs Trust - A specific type of trust that is used to provide benefits to persons or beneficiaries with special needs. They are designed to protect eligibility for government assistance programs.

Speculative Risk - The chance of loss, no loss, or a profit.

Split Definition - Type of disability policy where an insured is covered against the risk of not performing his or her own occupation for a period of time, and after that period expires, an any-occupation definition of disability is used.

Split-Dollar Arrangement - A discriminatory employee benefit plan using life insurance. The employer and employee share the cost of a life insurance policy on the employee (usually permanent insurance such as whole life insurance or variable universal life insurance). Typically used by businesses to provide low cost insurance to key employees.

Split Limit Policy - Three separate liability coverage limits covering bodily injury (per person and per occurrence) and property damage.

SSI (Supplemental Security Income) - A program administered by the Social Security Administration and funded by the general Treasury that is available to those at full retirement age or the disabled who have a low income and few assets.

Straight or Pure Life Annuity - An annuity that provides a stream of income to the annuitant for life.

Strict and Absolute Liability - Liability resulting from law. Strict liability allows for defense, absolute liability does not.

Subjective Risk - The risk an individual perceives based on their prior experiences and the severity of those experiences.

Subrogation Clause - A clause in an insurance policy that requires that the insured relinquish a claim against a negligent third party, if the insurer has already indemnified the insured.

Substantial Risk of Forfeiture - An income tax concept that relates to when income is subject to income tax. A substantial risk of forfeiture exists when rights in property that are transferred are conditioned, directly or indirectly, upon the future performance (or refraining from performance) of substantial services by any person, or the occurrence of a condition related to a purpose of the transfer and the possibility of forfeiture is substantial if the condition is not satisfied.

Suicide Clause - Provision in a life insurance policy specifying that the insurance company will not pay the benefit if the insured attempts or commits suicide within a specified period from the beginning of the coverage. The clause is designed to hedge against the risk that individuals with suicidal thoughts will purchase life insurance and commit suicide shortly thereafter.

Superannuation - The risk of running out of money before death due to long life and can be mitigated by using annuities.

Supplemental Executive Retirement Plans (Salary Continuation Plan, SERP) - Nonqualified deferred compensation arrangements designed to provide additional benefits to an executive during retirement.

Supplementary Medical Insurance (SMI) Trust Fund - The trust fund that pays for services covered under the medical insurance provisions of Medicare, known as Part B. The coverage is funded by general federal tax revenues and monthly Medicare premiums paid by enrollees.

Surrender Charge - A fee levied on a life insurance policyholder upon cancellation of the policy to cover the up-front costs of issuing the policy.

Survivors' Benefit - Social Security benefit available to surviving family members of a deceased, eligible worker.

Survivorship Clause - Provision in a life insurance policy specifying that the death benefit will only be paid to the beneficiary if the beneficiary survives the insured by a specific number of days.

T

Term Certain Annuity - Acts as a hedge against the mortality risk retained when an individual purchases a single life annuity by preserving some or all of the capital for distribution to the annuitant's heirs, but this hedge comes at a cost.

Term Insurance - Life insurance policy that states that if the premium has been paid and the insured dies during the term of the policy, the insurance company will pay the specified death benefit.

Terminal Illness - Having a life expectancy of less than 24 months, which must be certified by a qualified health professional.

The Fair Credit Reporting Act of 1971 - Provides that U.S. citizens have free access to their credit reports and credit scores from each of the three national credit reporting agencies.

Total Plan Benefit – The total amount of money that could be paid under the LTC policy for charges incurred for covered services.

Traditional Medical Care - Attempts to treat or cure illnesses.

U

Underwriting - The process of classifying applicants into a risk pools, selecting insureds, and assigning a premium.

Unilateral - There is only one promise made; and in the case of an insurance contract, it's made by the insurer to pay in the event of a loss.

Uninsured / Underinsured Motorist - Motorist without liability coverage or whose insurer can/will not pay claim, hit-and-run driver, or motorist with insufficient liability coverage according to state law.

Universal Life Insurance - Type of term insurance with a cash-value accumulation feature allowing individuals to make premium contributions in excess of the term-insurance premium. The excess premiums are deposited into an account with various investment options.

Unsecured Loans - Loans with no collateral and only backed by the borrower's promise to pay.

V

VantageScore 4.0 - Ranges from 300-850 and was developed by the three major credit bureau agencies.

Variable Annuities - Provide consumers with an opportunity to individually tailor the types of investments backing up the annuity contract to their unique needs, and equity-indexed annuities provide returns linked to market-based indexes.

Variable Life Insurance - Type of life insurance policy that permits the owner of the life insurance policy to direct the investment of the policy's cash value. Variable policies typically offer a series of investment options that often include investment funds managed by the insurer and outside investment managers.

Variable Universal Life Insurance Policies (VULs) - Type of life insurance policy that combines variable and universal life insurance and gives the policyholders the option to invest as well as alter insurance coverage.

Variable Whole Life Policies - Type of life insurance that provides for a fixed premium payment and permits the cash value of the policy to be professionally managed by the insurance company or an outside investment manager.

Viatical Settlement - An arrangement in which a policyholder sells their life insurance policy to a third party.

Vicarious Liability - One person may become legally liable for the torts of another (e.g., parent / child, employer where the employee is acting in the scope of employment).

W

Waiver - The relinquishment a known legal right.

Waiver of Premium - Allows the insured to stop paying premiums during the period in which he or she is receiving policy benefits. However, this provision may only apply to certain benefits, for example, nursing home or home healthcare.

Warranty - A promise made by the insured that is part of the insurance contract.

Whole Life Insurance - Type of life insurance that provides guarantees from the insurer that are not found in term insurance and universal life insurance policies.

Worker's Compensation - Designed to provide benefits to workers who are injured while working.

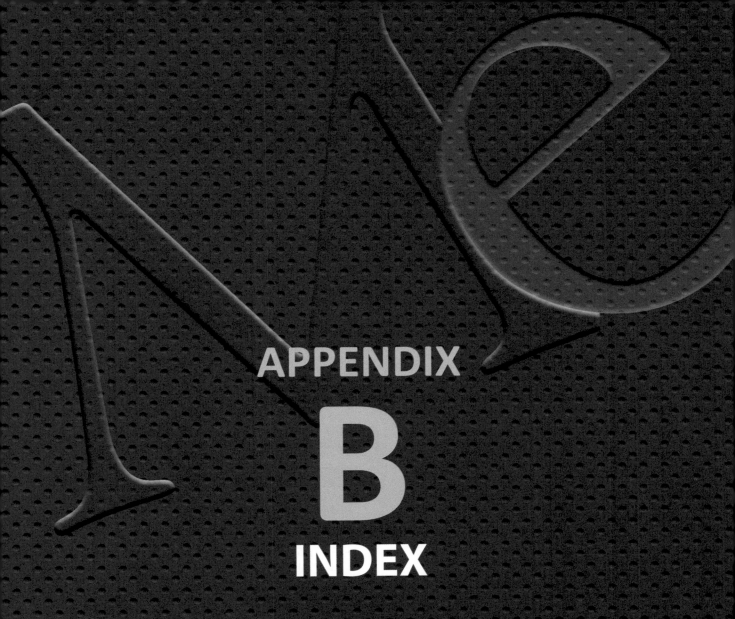

APPENDIX

B

INDEX